T0354041

"Rooted in the author's many years of organic orcharding experience, this book blends ideas from soil science, holistic health, permaculture, and traditional fruit growing into a powerful new approach to orchard design and care. Phillips's firsthand knowledge anchors this innovative and highly readable book in practical wisdom that both beginner and long-time fruit growers will find invaluable."—**Toby Hemenway**, author of *Gaia's Garden: A Guide to Home-Scale Permaculture*

"*The Holistic Orchard* is a stimulating account of fruit production from a biological rather than chemical approach. Phillips's orchard philosophy—learned from keen observation and reflection—will fall and clobber you like a giant Newtonian apple; then, your walk through the orchard will never be the same. Digesting this book is like tasting a delectable new apple variety for the first time."—**Tom Burford**, orchard consultant, author, and apple historian

"A new way of thinking is called for given the failure of chemicals to solve problems and feed the world. Mixing up dozens of organic thoughts, Michael Phillips ushers us into the twenty-first century and virtually creates a new language so we can really understand what is happening in our orchards. Shake off those twentieth-century blues and let's move on with *The Holistic Orchard* as a guiding light."—**Tim Bates**, biodynamic orchardist, The Apple Farm, Philo, California

"Michael Phillips's *Holistic Orchard* is a seminal work, to be compared with Sir Albert Howard's and J.I. Rodale's classic books on soil and organic gardening. This is deep horticulture at its best, showing just how and what we must do to orchard sustainably and ecologically."—**Bill MacKentley**, St. Lawrence Nurseries, Potsdam, New York

"The words 'holistic' and 'comprehensive' barely do honor to Michael Phillips's scope in *The Holistic Orchard*. The author has woven multiple strands of orchard knowledge—based on his expansive vision and a lifetime of experience, together with the wisdom of researchers and fellow fruit growers—into a brilliant web that captures the wonderful complexity of the orchard ecosystem. A sparkling joy to behold!"—**Guy Ames**, orchardist and tree fruit specialist with ATTRA, the National Sustainable Agriculture Information Service

"For decades experts have insisted that organic orcharding is an impossibility. Michael Phillips has led the effort to show that the truly sustainable, organic orchard is something we all can have. His example has been an inspiration. His tireless research has provided a road map to creating our own holistic orchards."—**John Bunker**, apple historian and author, *Not Far from the Tree*

"Michael Phillips does it again! His ability to understand and explain the parts, interactions, and emergent properties of orchard systems is unparalleled. *The Holistic Orchard* integrates fundamental biology with the practical realities of ecologically sound management. The book describes the trek from healthy soil to healthy people, with great fruit all along the way. This is done in a way that can only be achieved by a highly experienced orchardist-practitioner-author-philosopher."—**George W. Bird**, professor of nematology, Michigan State University

The Holistic Orchard

The Holistic Orchard

Tree Fruits and Berries the Biological Way

MICHAEL PHILLIPS

CHELSEA GREEN PUBLISHING
WHITE RIVER JUNCTION, VERMONT

First published by Chelsea Green Publishing | PO Box 4529 | White River Junction, VT 05001 | West Wing, Somerset House, Strand | London, WC2R 1LA, UK | www.chelseagreen.com
A Division of Rizzoli International Publications, Inc. | 49 West 27th Street | New York, NY 10001 | www.rizzoliusa.com

Project Manager: Patricia Stone
Project Editor: Makenna Goodman
Developmental Editor: Ben Watson
Copy Editor: Laura Jorstad
Proofreader: Nancy W. Ringer
Indexer: Linda Hallinger
Designer: Peter Holm, Sterling Hill Productions

ISBN 978-1-933392-13-4 (paperback) | ISBN 978-1-60358-407-4 (ebook)
Library of Congress Control Number: 2011035559 (print)

Our Commitment to Green Publishing
Chelsea Green sees publishing as a tool for cultural change and ecological stewardship. We strive to align our book manufacturing practices with our editorial mission and to reduce the impact of our business enterprise in the environment. We print our books using vegetable-based inks whenever possible. This book may cost slightly more because it was printed on paper from responsibly managed forests, and we hope you'll agree that it's worth it. *The Holistic Orchard* was printed on paper supplied by Versa that is certified by the Forest Stewardship Council.®

Instagram: @ChelseaGreenBooks and @RizzoliBooks | Facebook: @ChelseaGreenPub and @RizzoliNewYork | X: @ChelseaGreen and @Rizzoli_Books | YouTube: @ChelseaGreenPub and @RizzoliNY

Authorized EU representative for product safety and compliance
Mondadori Libri S.p.A. | www.mondadori.it
via Gian Battista Vico 42 | Milan, Italy 20123

Printed in the United States of America.
First printing December 2011
17 16 15 14 13   25 26 27 28 29

FOR DOROTHY and CAROLE,
the hardest-working sisters any farm has ever seen!

Contents

ACKNOWLEDGMENTS

Never did I imagine, when I agreed to write this book, that it would take several years to bring it to fruition! All I was called on to do was to speak some ecosystem truth, right? Well now. It turned out the trees had more to say than even a guy like me imagined. And then there were so many knowledgeable grower friends, offering opinions reflecting a grower diversity equal to that of the plant kingdom, turning regional reality on its head time and time again. Every time I felt near to the *essence of the thing,* a new horizon was revealed. And yet here I was, charged with keeping healthy orcharding simple and understandable. Well now indeed. Let me give thanks to all these wonderful players, in no particular order. My talent has always been to recognize the right bit wherever it happens to spring up. I simply delight that insightful wisdom can be found in so many people!

Nurserymen: John Bunker, Bill MacKentley, Neil Collins, Gordon Tooley, Lee Calhoun, Jim Cummins, Mike McConkey, David Fried, Kevin Bradley, and Todd Parlo. Keep that grafting knife sharp, lads.

Inner circle of organic thought (though by no means certified organic thought!): Brian Caldwell, Alan Surprenant, Hugh Williams, Jim Gallot, John Bemis, Don McLean, Lou Lego, Elizabeth Ryan, Bob Sewall, Chris and Michelle McColl, Linda Hoffman, Tim Bates, Guy Ames, Harry Hoch, Jim Koan, Greg Mund, Tom Rosenfeld, Mark Fulford, Dan Kelly, Don Kretschmann, Nick Cowles, Ted Richardson, Wynne Weinreb and Scott Beaton, Nate Darrow, Dan Bussey, Steve Ela, and, to be honest, many others. You are the true visionaries who opened up the doors.

Soils folk and fungal seers: Paul Sachs, Joe Scrimger, Nicole Masters, Paul Stamets, George Barron, Elaine Ingham, and Mike Amaranthus. May we always be friends connected by our love of the good ol' dirt and the teeming microbe communities found there.

Members of NAFEX/HOS/BYFG/CRFG (some by observations posted in *Pomona* or on discussion groups, some by asking insightful questions, some by standing around in the orchard shooting the breeze): Ben Applegate (VT), Deirdre Birmingham (WI), Scott Bolotin (VT), Tom Brown (NC), Lester Davis (GA), Martha Davis (NM), David Doncaster (BC), Ralph Elwell (ME), Sarah Ewing (ALB), Michael Flynn (CA), Jim Fruth (MN), Dave Griffin (MN), Alan Haigh (NY), Terry and Carolyn Harrison (CA), Chuck Heisinger (IL), Betsy Hillborn (NC), Donna Hudson (TN), Daryl Hunter (NB), Claude Jolicoeur (QUE), Josh Karp (VT), Jack Kertesz (ME), Chris Manning (PA), David Maxwell (NS), Richard Moyer (VA), Ethan Natelson (TX), Stanley Niemiec (OR), Dennis Norton (IL), Lucky Pittman (KY), Lee Reich (NY), Lon Rombough (OR), Emily Brown Rosen (PA), Chuck Shelton (VA), David Sliwa (IA), David Ulmer (CA), Denita Wallace (WA), CJ Walke (ME), and Doug Woodward (ONT).

Mutual respect: George Bird, Art Agnello, Glenn Koehler, Tracy Leskey, Starker Wright, Dave Gadoury, Alan Eaton, Charles Vincent, Turner Sutton, Alan Jones, Mark Longstroth, Alan Biggs, Greg Krawczyk, Jim Travis, David Shapiro, Joel Reich, Elizabeth Beers, Jay Brunner, and Chuck Ingels. Thanks for your open-mindedness and sharing.

Grower connoisseurs who truly know the varieties: Joe Postman (quince), Ted Richardson (Asian pears),

Andrew Mariani and Scott Smith (peaches and nectarines), Bob Purvis (apricots), Ike Kerschner (plums), Ed Fackler and Tom Burford (apples and pears), Doreen Howard (cherries), Pete Tallman and Hector Black (brambles and blueberries), and Terry Durham (elderberries). Researching and writing the varietal part of this book was fun as all get-out! And to all the nurseries from across the continent that shared varietal photos, you are indeed the summer beauts bringing radiance to these pages.

This one's special: A profound thanks to Céline Caron in Québec. This wise woman helped guide the original research on ramial wood chip mulch at Laval University, wrote the words that became the heart of the book *Ecological Fruit Production in the North*, and lives with her jolly husband, Yves, on the most comfrey-dominated homestead I have ever seen. *Bonjour, mon amie.*

A very important circle of fruit-growing friends comes together every March in the Berkshires for a roundtable discussion of the season just past. We've been at it twenty years straight here in the Northeast, asking the right questions and encouraging biological innovation on one another's farms. Other regional groups do similar things, all building the right sort of momentum for deeper understanding. Health-minded growers across the globe are coming together via the Holistic Orchard Network, with big plans afoot to invest far more into grassroots research undertaken within a whole systems (nonreductionist) framework. I'm ever so thankful for the GrowOrganicApples.com website and the impetus provided there to get more communities vested in growing healthy fruit.

This book would not exist without certain fundamental support. Much of my on-farm research down holistic avenues has been made possible by a lady totally committed to local agriculture and healthy living. Wow, Usha, we did it! Another friend literally helped bring this book to the finish line by financing the struggling artist in residence so I could keep at it. If we all had your foresight, Marty, we'd be there by now. Let's lift a glass of cider up high in appreciation to both.

The editing and production team at Chelsea Green Publishing were vital players in creating this book. Ben Watson has been the developmental editor on all my books to date; it could be said we have a rock 'n' roll relationship!—though Ben of course would edit that out as once again stretching the bounds of the English language in a dysfunctional direction. All of you owe this man for his ability to make "me" sound entirely sensible. Makenna, Joni, Susan, and Pati have all worked hard (and patiently!) in making sure all components of the book got signed, sealed, and delivered. Copy editor Laura Jorstad delivered consistency and solid fact checking. Proofreader Nancy Ringer made everything even more perfect. Frank Siteman put up with myriad blackflies in seeking especially good photographs of me in the midst of the trees. Elayne Sears took my rough sketches and created the beautiful and informative artwork throughout the book. Special thanks go to Margo Baldwin for her publishing vision that we humans can indeed do good things by our planet home and each other.

A writer's family especially takes its share of lumps in the process of bringing a book to the light of day. Nancy, the multi-year slog has come to an end. Your support and encouragement every step of the way made this possible. You intuitively knew never to ask the deadline question. Your herbal tea blends soothed this writer's stress and undoubtedly instilled some of the better plant wisdom to be found on these pages. And Gracie—a dad never had a more dependable word adviser. There's a reason a phrase like *get thee to a plummery* is not in this book! May you always be buffered from buffeting breezes, dear one.

Lastly, the trees. My trees. Your trees. Our trees. These friends guide us on our lifelong journey to becoming better fruit growers. How lucky we are to walk in beauty each and every day with such generous green teachers.

Wæs hæil!

Introduction: Getting Started

Growing your own fruit becomes downright fun once you understand organic principles and take them to heart. Soil health and forest-edge ecology are what make good fruit possible, not chemical sprays. Working with Nature using biological methods makes home orcharding a venture that families can enjoy for years to come. Stepping up the size of that planting to grow healthy fruit for your community will be a fun progression for some of you. Now the time has come to plant that very first tree.

Gaining confidence to do this right is key. You simply need to get over that proverbial hump that somehow you're going to screw this up and waste both effort and money. I'm writing *The Holistic Orchard* to give you that shot in the arm, inspiration backed with knowledge that will get you started and provide the sensible guidance you need to succeed in the long haul. More people growing wholesome fruit for family and friends fits right on that shining path to a sustainable tomorrow. Doing this holistically—by stewarding ecosystem connections and overall health—means you'll experience real flavor in a pear or plum for perhaps the first time. That health anxiety many feel when thinking about pesticide residues in food will go out the window. I'm also willing to bet you'll discover a core part of your being, that place where humans find happiness and meaning as we embrace our rootedness on this precious planet. The gift of each day in an ongoing *garden of eden*, wherever you grow and call the land your home, tops any list of blessings.

So let's get cracking, shall we? A book on growing fruit for the family needs to give clear, step-by-step instruction, share which tree fruit and berry varieties it would be wise to consider planting to start, and provide solid insight into horticultural basics like pruning and dealing with pest challenges. Such books have been written before and will be written again. However, this time you and I will go farther. Ours is a journey that won't look only at so-called organic solutions to insects and disease. Far deeper concepts lie in the pages ahead, based upon the advantages that come from fostering biodiversity. Ecosystem dynamics constitute a huge part of what it takes to bring helpful subtleties to the fore. Forget the chemically biased advice that says growing fruit organically can't be done. We have arrived in a new century with eyes open and spirits rarin' to go.

Everyone faces a requisite learning curve when it comes to growing decent-looking fruit. Orcharding, frankly, is more involved than straightforward organic gardening. A first-time gardener plants a certain seed, and chances are fairly good that a red beet gets plucked from the ground sixty days later. A first-time orchardist plants a tree that requires nurturing for two to five years . . . then it blooms and sets fruit . . . which must somehow overcome an onslaught of pests and diseases and four-legged critters throughout all twelve months of the year . . . before that delectable peach finally gets to shout *oh, yes indeed!*

You've been given a generous opportunity right there to come up to speed: Years roll by as you learn what you need to know. Flip to almost any page of this book and chances are you will feel some initial trepidation about the depths of knowledge involved in orcharding. Right? I understand, for, just like you, I too once planted my very first apple tree. This book is not some guide to "instant orcharding," but rather it offers tiers of knowledge meant to be unveiled each time you return to it. We're much alike in this. I do something one way for a while and then comes a day when I'm ready to hear *that next bit* on the way to becoming a better grower. Such moments arrive only when you've come farther along your learning curve and thus have the ability to make sense of the information. Be patient about this. Words on these pages weave back and forth, from friendly explanations of the basics to fascinating nuances that someday you will appreciate knowing. The extensive glossary will be a big help when you're not quite sure what a term means. Zero in on the index as well to find every part of a particular story line. This is an orchard guide to dive back into again and again. Trust that confidence will come from the doing. I'm honored to be one of your teachers, but know that you will encounter many others along the way.

Fruiting plants will tell you where they want to grow, for instance. That makes sense when we start thinking biologically. Plant consciousness is real, but people often get confused by believing that the consciousness part emanates from the human rather than the green guy. This notion that life forces communicate—provided we are receptive to listening—goes back a very long time. Gardeners who possess a *green thumb* are said to be successful growers because they feel what their plants need, whether it be water on a hot sunny afternoon or more root space in the pot. This intuition can be expanded all the more on the orchard front once we probe the science of tree physiology and ecosystem interdependence. Yeah, you're on to me now: We're going deep before we fulfill that step-by-step jazz. Every orchard site is unique. Different challenges wait over the next hill, let alone across this vast continent. You become attuned by fully embracing forest-edge ecology. Healthy trees in turn make for a happy orchardist who can deal with the unexpected.

Human health is a function of plant health, which is a function of soil health, which in turn is a function of fungal health. Now, who ever thought you'd see that kind of a statement in a book on growing fruit? A good apple is about so much more than simply negating insects and disease! A biological approach to orcharding relies first and foremost on supporting system health. Interestingly, the mutually dependent chain that leads to cramming berry after luscious berry into your mouth begins with symbiotic fungi that expand the nutrient reach of feeder roots a hundredfold. We're mistaken if we lump all microorganisms into a *something other than us* category and consider them something to be warded off, sanitized, and otherwise dealt with through toxic means. And yet mainstream agriculture as practiced these past hundred years does precisely this. We've too long forgotten our allies—belowground, aboveground, and on the surface of the plant itself—that can outcompete (for the most part, given nutritional support) other pathogenic organisms that cause disease. Each tree and fruiting shrub is a system within a system dependent on the vitality of all these other life-forms that are invisible to our human eye.

There came a day when I realized that the deep organic principles I wanted to implement in my orchard meshed entirely with the holistic health tenets that my wife, Nancy, was embracing in her herbal studies. But of course! Farming wisely essentially means we are working to heal. *To make things whole.* To foster the connections among the birds and the bees and the trees and ourselves. Everything shifts when looked at in this light. Producing fruit is not about manipulating Nature, but rather about fostering Nature. Acknowledging an element of reverence in the process of growing food for ourselves makes everything we do for the plants and the soil a sacred act.

Orchardists are going to find in these pages an entirely new approach to abating fungal and bacterial disease because of my immersion in these two complementary worlds. Fruit tree culture has been stuck in allopathic mode for far too long, solely seeking out short-term fungicides and antibiotics to destroy disease-causing organisms *from without*. We've failed to understand that the tree's own immune response could be coupled with the stimulation of friendly microbes to defeat disease *from within*. What I am calling the "four holistic sprays of spring" are all about building the health of the system to deal with everyday environmental reality without toxins. Many words are dedicated to helping you understand the whys behind the exceedingly clear recommendations to do just that.

Those of you new to organic orcharding have no idea what it means not to deal with mineral fungicides like copper and sulfur. The caustic days are behind us for the most part . . . noting that unfavorable weather patterns may still make a light touch of organically approved medicine necessary for certain fruits in certain years. But the upshot for home and community orchardists alike is that growing fruit successfully will now be far more fun.

Then there's that often overlooked link between nutrition and our own health. Far too many doctors, and certainly far too many modern farmers, simply don't reckon that the quality of what goes in determines the quality of what becomes. Vitamins and minerals in the foods we eat are the building blocks of healthy bodies. Real food is nutrient-dense in that meat, vegetables, grains, and fruit—nurtured with compost and biologically reared—contain the full and balanced nutrition that our bodies require to maintain healthy function. Humans evolved eating fruits and nuts and green plants and the occasional mastodon. None of these foods was shortchanged nutritionally; every bite had fantastic flavor and substance. Why we accept anything less in modern-day fare is a result of effective advertising coupled with an outright loss of species intelligence. You reclaim your nutritional birthright when you plant that first pie cherry tree. How you grow that fruit in turn determines the nutrient density of your family's own health prospects.

You need to know just enough to get launched into the growing of healthy fruit, but not feel so overwhelmed that you never begin. This book insists that you understand ecosystem health and only then consider the horticultural specifics of what it takes to grow particular fruits. Part of my job has been to deliberately hone the selection of varietal suggestions for different regions. I did this in part by talking with fruit growers across the country about which varieties work best where each lives. Flavor was the biggest underlying consideration, followed by growing insights that should help you understand localized parameters all the better. I expect you to choose from a wider array of varieties than those that are offered here as you discover which fruits are successfully growing nearby. The culture of orcharding is built around sharing grafting wood and berry plants with one another. Seek out a regional fruit explorers group and you will soon have lifelong friends who will share their knowledge as well.

The organic insights and suppositions that other growers shared about their particular pest challenges needed to line up with my own intuitive take on biological science. Some folklore got thrown out along the way, whereas other bits are offered with the greatest esteem for ancestral wisdom. You should find the methods offered here to be simple to employ, cost-effective, and homegrown whenever possible. Any and all feedback is welcome . . . this is a guide I hope to continually update and improve as we discover the nuances of holistic orcharding together. What's needed right now are new fruit growers who are not locked into allopathic thinking (whether through formal training or years' worth of certified habit) and who are thus able to perceive the biological connections that make orchard health possible. Shifting internal perceptions is the first step in bringing subtler methods to the fore.

Now a suggestion: Remain calm. Numerous insect scenarios get discussed in any fruit-growing guide. I often share an especially daunting volume on *moths alone* in my conference presentations. Page after page after page of color plates reveal an array of tortricid fauna of apple known to afflict pome and stone fruits alike. I point out that more moth species have come on the scene since Cornell published that book in the early 1970s. Only then do I turn what seems to be an overwhelming conundrum for the fledgling orchardist into manageable reality by explaining that any one orchard location may have two or three, perhaps four, outstanding concerns for which proactive steps *may be required*—and then only *in some years*—to produce a respectable harvest. The rest add up to a hill of beans, getting dibs on a tenth of the crop at worst.

What counts is learning how to determine what takes place on your home turf and then being able to consider sound advice to proceed accordingly. *The Holistic Orchard* offers friendly guidance throughout to help you understand the ways of fruit trees and berry plants. You may also want to obtain one of the orchard field guides recommended in the appendices, which will help fine-tune the identification of dozens of insects (including beneficial species) and the visual manifestations of disease found in orchards. The color compilations put together by Cooperative Extensions in each region of the country as well as university websites are to be used and appreciated . . . even if the usual accompanying chemical recommendations do not brew the tastiest cup of tea.

Many other wonderful fruits—like grapes, kiwis, and pawpaws—can and should be grown in the home orchard. Not to mention jujubes, mulberries, figs, avocados, citrus, pomegranates, and persimmons. Such selection ultimately depends on the growing zone in which you live. I wrestled with the decision of what to include and decided that "other fruit"

books by people like Lee Reich, Lon Rombough, and Charles Boning address this already. (As always, see those appendices!) Native fruits often enjoy important ecological advantages and lend themselves readily to organic growing methods and permaculture design principles. If you live in the right climate for any of these fruits, I absolutely encourage you to add even more bounty to your orchard planting.

Our biological thinking cap has arrived. The teachings ahead will tell you not only what to do but, more important, how to think from a holistic perspective. Organic orcharding can never be a straightforward recipe where you simply follow steps A, B, and C and then pull a delicious apple strudel hot from the oven. Nature is dynamic . . . climate is changing . . . and every ecosystem is localized. New growing seasons bring shifts in the challenges to be faced. Every variety will not necessarily thrive where you live. A key quality of a good fruit grower is the ability to adapt. What I love about my fruit trees—and all plants— is the *listening* and the *observing*. Seeing the subtleties brought forward by healthy management choices. Knowing I can adjust my understanding in order to help shape a better biological reality. Appreciating the gifts of this special place in the universe. You have that same ability too. You really, really do.

CHAPTER ONE

The Orchard Ecosystem

Forest-edge ecology defines where *fruit trees want to grow*. Berries by their woodsy nature want the very same ecosystem advantages. So we begin here, with the perspective of the plant, not the human.

Orchardists have the choice to honor tree wisdom or not. The means required to produce a reasonable fruit crop will be determined on the basis of this decision: Are numerous spray medicines going to be required to make up for not honoring how Nature works? Tree health is integrally tied to soil health, which in turn flourishes with the health and diversity of biological organisms in the soil. These dynamics lie at the core of an orchard ecosystem, whether we are talking about a multi-acre commercial orchard or the trees and berries you've chosen to grow in your yard. Next we enter the fascinating realm of biodiversity that makes up the potentially seen portion of the place we each call home: the flowers and herbs nearby, the bees and the butterflies, favored root ground, all sorts of beneficial fungi, and even my friends the chickadees. All are players in the growing of fruit. All very much hope that you will choose biological priorities over expedience.

Working with the orchard ecosystem as a whole empowers every fruit grower to succeed. This process of creating a bountiful landscape draws each of us into looking at the big picture of how one life depends upon all the others. The better organic approaches to pest challenges fall into place only once soil and foliar health have been achieved. Good fruit results from emphasizing healthy subtleties in all we do. Things like the relationship between mycorrhizal fungi and a tree's fine root hairs, the way woodsy compost promotes species diversity, and the fact that fermented herbal teas provide deep nutrition to microorganism allies and leaves alike matter very much.

Health across the board provides the flavorful harvests desired by orchardists who choose organic methods. A core paradigm of holistic fruit growing states that we use foliar sprays not so much to destroy problems as to create health, so that the system can take care of itself. This enlightened way of thinking goes beyond product advertising and conventional recommendations, firmly putting biological science in the driver's seat where it belongs. Everything we do in our orchards has meaning and connection to the health of the whole. We are about to take a journey into understanding deeply, which in turn will motivate each of you to perform essential orcharding tasks with a reasonable expectation of success.

FOREST-EDGE ECOLOGY

Few of us have backyards located along the transition zone from field to forest. Yet if we want to grow fruit from woodsy plants, we'd best be aware of where fruit trees and berries claim their ecological niche when given the chance. Observing the conditions that Nature chooses in turn determines the ecosystem guidelines we should strive to emulate in our own orchards.

The progression of plant life on a newly developed house lot—if it were left to time and serendipity

THREE TREES SPEAK

Tree perspective offers insight into our role in the growing of fruit, no matter what your philosophical outlook on orcharding—chemical or organic or somewhere beyond all that. The ecosystem dance taking place speaks observable truth when growers pause to listen.

The Wild Tree speaks

Some years both disease and insect problems seem to be in check in our camp. This happens when weather patterns defeat fungal pathogen plans and a degree of isolation disrupts major pests. A beneficial balance between symbiotic microbes and neighboring plant allies lies at the heart of successful cruise control. And yet all these advantages can fall short in other years . . . and then our fruit can be an ungodly mess. Budwood taken from resilient stock in an untamed setting, then grafted to rootstock, often doesn't prove to be noteworthy once brought to a managed orchard scenario. Hmmm.

The Controlled Tree speaks

More medicine, mon, I need more medicine. Things done in the name of growing a high-yield crop can mess up ecosystem balance through unintended consequences to many species. More and more allopathic sprays are then required to control the situation. We become addicted to the fix, no longer striving to resist disease from within. People have a hard time realizing that trees like us can be found in a certified organic orchard just as surely as on commercial IPM acreage . . . leaving us to wonder about the pace of human observation.

Our job is to provide that occasional nudge toward system health . . . and otherwise listen to tree wisdom every step of the way!

The Holistic Tree speaks

Fruit trees evolved with humankind. You need us just as we need you. Your job is to steward system health rather than disrupt the whole shebang in the name of one-sided control. Pests can be nudged, but eliminating any species outright is beyond your prerogative. Providing health-supporting nutrition to boost immune function and beneficial fungi should be obvious. And when that *scab year from hell* occurs, yes, you might consider harder-hitting spray tools like sulfur to allay pathogen pressure at certain peak moments. Just understand that constantly relying on biological compromise comes at a price to system health. A holistic grower appreciates that the whole often knows more than the human does.

—would go something like this. Annual weeds like shepherd's purse and mustard, appearing hither and thither at first, would eventually grow in profusion. The setting of seed initiates dieback in annuals, which in turn alters the carbon-to-nitrogen (C:N) ratio upward as lush stalks turn brittle and brown. Decay goes slowly at first, but eventually the accumulation of organic matter creates a shift in plant composition. Dandelion and plantain are among the first perennials. Grasses and taprooted volunteers like wild carrot and curly dock get a foothold and never look back. Organic matter continues to build. Goldenrod and raspberries arrive to stay. More carbon is stockpiled as ever-woodier stems decay. Tree seedlings start to appear: species like pin cherry, brought by birds; white birch and willow, carried by the wind; and perhaps apple if deer droppings or a thrown core rolls onto the scene. As woodsy plants grow, shade lessens the grip of perennial weeds. Blackberry canes and short-lived tree species begin to add lignin to the humic crescendo. Hardwoods and softwoods alike find increasingly hospitable ground. Along the very edge, where the bright sunshine can never be denied, those apple trees come into their own.

This is what we humans see . . . but it is far from the whole story.

The soil food web

The soil in the beginning of this plant progression saga could essentially be viewed as an uninhabited medium following that last scrape of the bulldozer. Now begins a biological onslaught of bacteria, fungi, and other soil dwellers that will gradually transition this ground from barren substrate to living earth. Those first weeds produce digestible biomass that becomes organic matter; the microorganism community transforms and releases nutrients from this organic matter so that even more plants can complete the renewal cycle. Bacteria tend to utilize simple organic compounds, such as root secretions and fresh plant residue. Fungi will utilize more complex compounds, such as cellulose, lignins, and soil humus. The ratio of fungi to bacteria begins to shift as succession plant species take over, which in turn provide more fibrous plant residues on which an even greater diversity of fungi thrive. The composition of plants adjusts as the soil becomes increasingly fungus-dominated.

We deem this interaction, which makes life on earth possible, the *soil food web*. Billions of living organisms exist in a single handful of soil. Such mind-boggling numbers serve to remind me that I am but one member of a huge interdependent team striving to "orchard wisely" on my farm. The progression that takes place when microbial feeders restore soil balance—and just where that balance point lies for different plant species—spells out a far more accurate way to grasp plant dynamics than does available mineral fertility as indicated on a typical soil test. All soil organisms work together as a living system to support plant health by decomposing organic matter, cycling nutrients, and improving soil crumb structure. The health of untold organism communities within this living web plays a pivotal role in both enhancing and protecting the physical reality of fruiting trees and berries.

System health springs from the biology in the soil; it's as simple as that. Learning more about the soil food web beyond the basics of fungal dominance won't be necessary for fruit growing per se, but I would encourage it.[1] The humic system performs best when fungi and bacteria are associated with "microvores" such as protozoans and nematodes. All participants in the soil food web play vital roles in the assimilation and mineralization of nutrients for plant growth.[2] The desire to serve this web of life in the soil—for that's what being an enlightened fruit grower really entails—springs from knowing your friends. Choosing to honor and support biological connection will help you avoid the many props required by a sick system. How we travel along this holistic high road begins with understanding what fungi like.

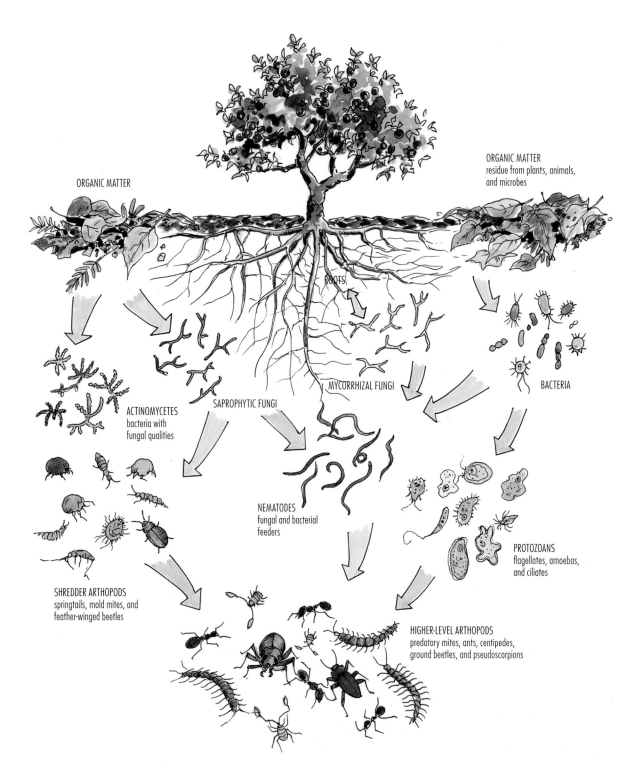

ORGANIC MATTER

ORGANIC MATTER
residue from plants, animals,
and microbes

ROOTS

MYCORRHIZAL FUNGI

BACTERIA

ACTINOMYCETES
bacteria with
fungal qualities

SAPROPHYTIC FUNGI

NEMATODES
fungal and bacterial
feeders

PROTOZOANS
flagellates, amoebas,
and ciliates

SHREDDER ARTHOPODS
springtails, mold mites, and
feather-winged beetles

HIGHER-LEVEL ARTHOPODS
predatory mites, ants, centipedes,
ground beetles, and pseudoscorpions

Interdependent and interconnected networks of organisms interact to make life possible. The soil food web encompasses the microbes and arthropods that ultimately provide balanced mineral nutrition for fruiting plants and thus promote overall tree health. Go, biology, go!

Fungal dominance

The integrated health of any fruit ecosystem correlates directly to the ratio of fungi to bacteria found in the living soil. Orchard soils ideally contain a fungal presence ten times higher than that of bacteria.[3] This ratio defines forest-edge ecology, and it's this ratio that is going to drive all the recommendations about soil nutrition and understory management that lie ahead.

First, though, let's be clear about what we're talking about. *Fungi* are generally multi-cellular organisms with a nucleus and a cell wall made of chitin. They acquire nourishment by absorbing their food, principally carbon. As opposed to plants, which make their own food via chlorophyll, and animals, which eat food in the form of plants or other animals, fungi neither eat nor make food. Instead, they send strand-like parts of their body, called *hyphae*, directly into their food; they secrete chemicals to break the food down into simpler molecules; and then they absorb the food directly into their cells. The body of a fungus is built out of many threads of hyphae, collectively called the *mycelium*. The mycelium grows within the substance of its food—being undigested soil, plant root environs, deadwood, decaying animals—and, in the case of disease-causing fungi, living plant cells. When growing conditions are favorable, the fungus sends up fruiting bodies, which we recognize principally as mushrooms.[4]

Different groups of fungi do different things for plants. **Mycorrhizal fungi** form a symbiotic relationship with feeder roots, extending the nutrient reach of the tree a hundred times over. These microscopic organisms cover the surface of colonized roots, forming a sheath that reaches between the cells of the root for nutrient exchange. Some mycorrhizal species actually penetrate the root cortex itself.[5] Long-threaded hyphae extend outward from these fungal bodies to form a biological *communications network* throughout neighboring ground with other plants. In exchange for their receiving carbon-rich sugars—the product of plant photosynthesis taking place up above in the leaves—these hyphae supply to the tree nutrients like

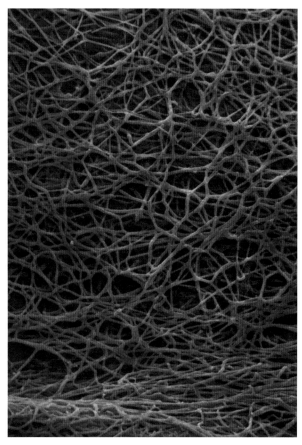

Mycorrhizal outreach through an extensive mycelium network is a major biological asset in the healthy orchard. Balanced mineral nutrition is assured when these fungal allies reach well beyond the rhizosphere (root zone) of fruiting plants. Here's a mind boggler: A handful of woodsy soil contains over twenty miles of these interwoven hyphae! Photo courtesy of Paul Stamets, Fungi Perfecti ©2005.

phosphorus, nitrogen, trace minerals, and even water. The surface area of mycorrhizae belowground far surpasses the surface area of the tree's leaves, making this a very fair trade indeed. The key to tree vitality is this nutrient exchange between the roots—via these fungal helpers—and the soil. Mycorrhizae also secrete growth factors that stimulate root growth and branching, as well as antibiotics that protect the roots from pathogenic organisms.

The decomposers work the top portion of ground. Here in this shallow zone, **saprophytic fungi** convert dead organic matter into fungal biomass and organic acid chains. Complex substrates like cellulose and lignin in wood are their principal food, which makes complete sense on the forest's edge, where fungal dominance paves the way for woodsy species. The so-called sugar fungi in this group like the same simple substrates, as do many bacteria. This breaking-down process ultimately allows nutrients to be retained in the soil in a form readily available for plant uptake. The importance of this humus bank cannot be overstressed: Acid-rich organic matter is resistant to degradation and will remain in the soil for centuries, fueling cycle after cycle of healthy plant growth.

Which brings us to a third group of fungi that has garnered far too much grower attention, relatively speaking: the **problem fungi**. These pathogenic organisms cause what we humans call "disease." Fungal pathogens cause reduced production and/or death when they colonize roots, leaf and fruit surfaces, and other organisms. We will be hearing more about *Venturia* (scab) and *Phytophthora* (root, crown, and collar rot) in the pages ahead. But there are two things I want you to know. Some opportunistic fungi actually help control worse problems; this is the case with *Beauveria bassiana*, which parasitize insect pupae in the soil. More important, a diverse and thus competitive state of affairs in the tree environs reverses problematic potential from the get-go. We have ways of dealing with intransigents in the holistic orchard.

Far less is known about **arboreal fungi**. Frankly, we humans do not come to holistic perception all that readily. The soil food web in a conceptual sense extends upward into the leaf canopy of trees and other fruiting plants. Bacteria and fungi alike coat and interact with every inhabitable surface on the planet.[6] These are allies in the finest sense of the word. I like to use the term *beneficial fungi* here, much as we do when we refer to beneficial insects in discussing biodiversity considerations. Some of the participants in this *arboreal food web* are soil dwellers stretching their legs, so to speak; other canopy organisms are specific to particular plant species and intertwined

with arthropod association.[7] Certain epiphytic fungi are especially intriguing, having mycelia that run along the inner bark and promote overall tree health. Such arboreal relationships will play an integral role when we discuss holistic disease management in the orchard. Leaf colonization provides the desired competitive environment and—perhaps just as telling—phytochemical stimulation by which a plant can stand up to disease pressure all the more. Arboreal fungi are among the subtleties I refer to when stating that the best organic methods depend entirely on orchard health being in place across the board.

WORKING WITH ORCHARD BIOLOGY

We've identified what we want in orchard soil as regards microorganism dynamics. Now the big question is how to achieve such fungal dominance. *Thinking like a tree* again points the way. Nature builds soil from the top down: Leaves fall, tree limbs decay, mulch happens. All of which suggests the right sorts of food sources for fungal allies. We'll add a fertility component when we look at soil amendments in a future chapter, but for now our primary focus centers entirely on the biology. Every orchardist who wants to be successful with organic methods will refer back to this section of the book more than once.

Transition
Fruit plantings happen in one of two ways. The go-getter turns the lawn under and, plop, the trees and assorted berries are in. No real transition toward the fungal state occurs prior to the nursery order being made and delivered. The soil biology can recover from such unbridled enthusiasm—it's not "wrong" to do this—but soil preparation prior to planting offers certain advantages worthy of consideration. People with just a wee bit more foresight understand that a year of cover cropping and woodsy mulching not only offers the grower a chance to build organic matter and correct fertility imbalance but can also hasten fungal

dominance. Here we're talking about transition techniques to jump-start the healthy orchard.

Outside your door lies a lawn, perhaps a pasture area or hay field, maybe an overgrown field with goldenrod and raspberry—situations that can rightly be described biologically as ranging from highly bacterial to lightly fungal at best. First the sod needs to go to clear the way for fruit plantings. Rougher ground with tree saplings may require some lightweight stump pulling within the strips where fruit trees are envisioned.[8] Tilling is a bacterial act in itself, regardless of the mechanics chosen, as the turned-under organic matter creates a "surf's up" call for soil bacteria. Persistent grasses (like quack grass) might require a double sowing of a buckwheat cover crop with more tillage in between to put an end to root runner vigor.[9] Cultivated lawns will generally be ready following initial tillage for the fungal cover crop of choice—red or crimson clover—to be stirred into the top ½ inch of soil.[10] These two nitrogen-fixing legumes have a stronger affinity for mycorrhizal fungi than the white and yellow clover species. Clovers won't make it in arid zones, so growers in the West can use bird's-foot trefoil to fix nitrogen instead. A nurse crop of oats can be seeded with any of these, then the works scythed down in place to decompose once the grain starts to head up, at which point the clover or trefoil will take over in earnest. Let me stress *cutting in place to decompose* that second time in late fall and then *leaving to lie on the soil surface* through the winter. Fungi respond to surface decomposition, whereas bacteria prefer soil disturbance. We are building a fungal duff of organic matter where the biological action desired is going to take place. Compost, deciduous wood chips, seaweed, and raked leaves can be added atop the clover stubble, if available. Yes, the roots of the cover crop are still in the ground and will likely grow anew come spring. Be calm—we have a plan.

The soil will be far more crumbly after this biological massage. You can fork out extant clover root systems in early spring where trees are going to be planted, a 4- to 6-foot diameter being a reasonable goal. Beds for berries (on the order of a 4-foot swath)

can be forked through as well or ever-so-shallowly tilled to break the taproot connection, or they can be mulched with newspaper/cardboard over which wood chips will be spread. The clover beyond the immediate planting zone will share the space with other species in time. Frost seeding of select grasses (lightly, mind) and deliberately introducing taprooted herbs and wildflowers will steer understory diversity further without yet again disturbing the soil life profile.

Ramial wood chips

There are *white rots* and there are *brown rots* related to decomposition. The first support a deciduous environment; the latter deal with high tannin content and thereby define the evergreen forest. Let's talk about *ramial wood chips* as the main course for feeding mycorrhizal and saprophytic fungi in an orchard food web that in turn supports our fruit trees.

Rough, coarse, and lignin-rich is what rocks the biological kasbah. Ramial wood chips are about feeding the biology for the long haul.

This term *ramial* in defining the wood chip mulch of choice is paramount. Québec researchers originally used *bois raméal* to refer to twig wood less than 7 centimeters in diameter.[11] The tops of deciduous trees and woodsy shrubs—not much more than 2½ inches around at the large end of the branch by rough Yankee reckoning—pruned and subsequently run through a chipper into coarse pieces are what rock the biological kasbah. The newest growth of a deciduous tree contains soluble lignins that have not yet polymerized into outright wood. Thus, the proportion of essential twig nutrients in the chips increases as average branch diameter decreases. Nitrogen, phosphorus, potassium, calcium, magnesium, and so forth are found in the green cambium and bud tissues where leaf photosynthesis production and root nutrition come together to make a tree . . . which we in turn can redirect to build ideal soil in our own orchards to make our fruit trees. Soil fungi will incorporate this ramial feast and gradually yield the nutrient profile back to our woodsy plantings through the action of a dynamic soil food web.

The size of the branches being chipped matters yet again when we consider the immediate impact on soil life. Carbon-rich materials used for mulch tie up nitrogen temporarily when soil decomposition forces the use of a limited nitrogen supply entirely for its work. Stunted plant growth can result when this happens. The carbon-to-nitrogen ratios in ramial-diameter wood average on the order of 30:1, going no higher than 170:1 as we consider the larger end of the recommended branch. These C:N ratios rise dramatically in stem wood (which should be used as home heating fuel anyway), running from 400:1 to as much as 750:1, thereby creating that soil dynamic where nitrogen becomes unavailable to the plant world until such log mulch has significantly been broken down.[12] Paying attention to this sort of detail matters.

Soil fungi are adept at creating humus from a lignin source. Again, we are emulating how Nature works with the application of ramial wood chips. Most agricultural soils (other than the prairie grasslands) are of forest origin: Soil that has been built from the top down through fungal action undergoes *humic stabilization*—such soil has staying power and maximized nutrient recycling. Fruit trees belong in such soil. We are dealing with humification enhancement here rather than a mineralization (breakdown) process. Ongoing soil health results from soil structure being managed by soil organisms. Fungal hyphae physically bind soil particles together, creating stable aggregates that help increase water infiltration and the soil's water-holding capacity. This accumulation of acid-rich organic matter as humus is fueled in our orchards through the decomposition of ramial wood chips.

All of which brings us back to that rot business with which we started this discussion of fungal heaven. Rots are decomposing fungi that can be classified into two subgroups.[13] The *white rots* use enzymatic chemistry on decaying hardwood to produce both fulvic and humic acids from lignins. The *brown rots* transform softwood cellulose to produce polyphenols and allopathic compounds specifically relied upon by evergreen species to suppress other plant growth. We've come to the hardwood–softwood divide. Can you tell which is the appropriate rot action for the floor of a deciduous orchard? The source of treetops used to make ramial wood chips must be deciduous species, for the most part. A mixed chipping containing no more than 20 percent softwood still will favor white rots. Don't outright waste the occasional pine sapling in a brush pile offering, but, on the other hand, do steer away from solely softwood wood chips for orchard use.

How to use all this ramial glory comes next . . . provided you first have a source. Having access to several acres of brushy growth along with a decent-sized chipper (though not necessarily a chipper-shredder, as coarser chips are better) makes ongoing ramial wood chip production a homegrown affair. The twig ends will come through such chipping still looking somewhat like a pile of sticks, and that's okay.[14] Knowing a neighbor or two who clears the land in true pioneer fashion means you don't even necessarily have to do the work. Some towns chip landscape brush as part of a compost operation and rarely object to a home orchardist diverting some of that wood chip flow. The ultimate folks to approach work for the power company and clear brush beneath transmission lines. They chip for free, they fill a large truck, and they always need to dump that load. A reasonable spot to deliver is often all it takes for ramial wood chips to come your way.[15]

Haphazard mulching

I'm a guy who likes to take the concept of diversity to extremes. Establishing an orchard intermixed with all sorts of other plants and bugs is a healthy thing to do. We get an especially good start on the diversity highway by being wantonly diverse about how we manage the *understory*, meaning the ground and plantings at the base of our fruit trees. It's time to introduce those of you on the straight and narrow to haphazard mulching . . . or as mom might say, being somewhat less than neat.

I know, I know. You have particular ideas about how often the lawn should be mowed. That all trees shall be in a straight line. That mulch should be applied uniformly and look tidy. That one dandelion uninvited is an abomination. Well, it's time for you to lighten up! The appearance of your orchard isn't about you. *It's about the biology, stupid* (to paraphrase a political inanity). It's about a full smorgasbord of varied tree nutrition to be explored and utilized by tree feeder roots. Life thrives in a diverse environment. Try to let go of cultural notions of a manicured garden, especially with your fruit trees. You can find a way to please the neighbors while accommodating principles of health and diversity. Seek the middle ground, and then, as you see better and better fruit, you can come on board completely. Everything is a process, including the orchardist.

Our goal, plain and simple, is *fungal duff*—that litter layer where mineralization and humification take place. Other plants will grow beneath our trees, certainly tufts of grass, but the density of these other species will be thin, essentially patches of green in between ramial wood chips, piles of shredded leaves,

Feeder roots of healthy fruiting plants seek nutrients in the fungal duff zone. Organism consuming organism in the vicinity of these roots makes available the right sort of nitrogen and other balanced nutrition.

rotting hay, and compost smatterings. The preponderance of all this fungal food is what drives the fungal dominance we want for healthy trees and berries.

Recognizing what makes for acceptable orchard mulch is important. We have defined ramial wood chips, but nevertheless I know landscape notions are going to enter in here and confuse some of you. The arrays of familiar choices at the home and garden center generally do not cut it from a biological perspective. Bark mulch comes from softwood logs, for the most part, and therefore comes rich in tannic compounds that once protected standing evergreen trees from decay. Guess what? Tannins will suppress healthy growth in garden and orchard alike. Dyed bark mulch lifts biological ignorance to a whole new level—mulch that is "pleasingly red" instead of "earth-toned" is that way because of toxic dyes. You would

Your typical haphazard guy delivering ramial wood chip mulch in typical haphazard fashion. Photo by Frank Siteman.

knowingly treat the precious soil this way? Bulk wood chips in a bag, often cedar, sometimes hemlock, are a brown rot phenomenon. Sawdust comes with far too much carbon relative to nitrogen, as does uncomposted horse manure bedding. Let either rot for a few years and it's a whole different story, but applied fresh beneath the trees? No, no, no. And as for some sort of landscape cloth beneath the mulch that keeps volunteer plants at bay? Forget about it. Synthetic fabrics create a bacterial environment beneath that "weed-protected" surface; meanwhile, mulch decomposition above slows to a standstill and no longer replenishes organic matter in the soil. The ground beneath compacts like cement. There's a direct correlation here: Human notions of neatness are rarely biological! Organic growers want ramial wood chips and ramial wood chips alone—applied directly to the living earth—for a woodsy mulch.[16]

Haphazard basically means you don't do everything the same all at the same time. Just like you, feeder roots like an array of nutrient choices and environments. The reception found beneath fresh ramial wood chips is different from that beneath a one-year-old pile or a two-year-old pile or the remnants of a three-year-old pile. All are worthy, just offering slightly different available nutrients and soil food web happenings. The same goes for a rotting hay bale or randomly piled straw. Both of these grassy mulches increase the level of fungal predators—the good nematodes!—which in turn makes available the healthier form of nitrogen (we'll be distinguishing ammonium from nitrate sources ahead) to our fruit plants. Hay provides a good charge of potassium as it breaks down as well—potassium being one of the nutrients taken away when we harvest a full crop. All told, levels of both macronutrients and micronutrients are found to be consistently higher in the leaves of fruit trees that are mulched. The ability to hold moisture in the soil is yet another huge benefit of mulch, especially where the summer months get dry. And often hot: Soil temperatures are moderated considerably by a mulch cover.

Mulch can be thought of as "shade" as well in that it suppresses an excess of competing plant species. This can be especially important during those first five years or so when a young tree needs to grow wood structure.[17] I place a ring of peastone right up against the trunk of my young trees to keep that zone open and drier for many years to come.[18] Small-sized gravel (screened to ⅜ inch) does the trick, about 3–4 inches in depth, placed as a 24- to 30-inch circle with the tree right in the center. Beyond this goes your choice of mulch, replenished as necessary, creating an outer ring within which a young tree can take off (see "Growing productive wood" in chapter 3 for more details). The full-sized tree will eventually shade the ground at its feet more completely, helping to keep a sod cover from filling in this fungal-directed space. We'll be looking at certain herbs and flowers to add here once the trees come into their own.

Ramial wood chips can be put down anywhere from 2–8 inches deep. Perhaps this year I have enough wood chips to dump a wheelbarrow load or even a full tractor bucket on the south side of every tree, keeping it piled thick rather than spreading it out far and wide. Hay bales randomly go on another side of heavy-cropping trees.[19] The next year that ramial dump goes to the north side . . . or the east side . . . or the west side, being rotated so different stages of decomposition can be found beneath every tree throughout the orchard. I watch understory plants shift from season to season, knowing that spiders and predatory ground beetles will find new homes as they move about as well. Spreading woodsy compost in the fall suits this haphazard pattern. The fungal duff stands renewed and healthy, ready and willing to pump out the fruit of our desire.

Let's pause just a moment to consider the conventional alternative.[20] And I'm bringing this up only because I know some well-intentioned souls have asked me in the past if it's okay to use herbicides when growing fruit organically. (We're all learning at our own pace.) These chemicals directed at unwanted species of plants have a number of biological consequences. Decomposing fungi are destroyed and thus are no longer able to sequester atmospheric carbon into humus. The mycorrhizal network that transports nutrients and water to the *rhizosphere* (the zone around the roots) is broken. Now the tree "requires" inorganic fertilization—from chemicals, of course—to make up for this loss. Disease becomes a far bigger problem when nutrition is no longer balanced and scab-infected leaves from the season before lie on top of biologically dead ground. Honestly. Herbicides are part of the mind-set that we are changing here. Choose a diversity of mulches instead.

Pulsing agents

The soil can be a sleepy place, and all the more so when coming out of winter dormancy. Keep in mind that this is the engine that drives our fruit plantings, where soil organisms interact to transform and transport matter and energy to our trees. Nutrition-rich catalyst sprays directed at the ground and the branch structure of the trees are used to activate the ecosystem in early spring and right after harvest for a specific purpose tied to root happenings and the resource needs of the arboreal food web. This "whole new concept" expands what many of you might think orcharding involves, and yet it makes perfect sense once you've come up to biological speed.

Roots start to stir at about the time we observe green tissue springing forth from dormant buds. Mycorrhizae respond, albeit slowly, as the cool earth eventually unveils a late-spring flush of feeder roots and accompanying hyphal growth. The days warm, insects are flying, birds are chirping, leaves are unfolding . . . but still the earth holds back, not quite fully awakened from its winter sleep. What follows sets the stage for managing disease pressures in the orchard by natural means.

Liquid fish and pure neem oil can be used as *pulsing agents* to give soil microbe populations a positive boost just as the trees announce their readiness with a showing of green.[21] We'll be talking more about these spray materials in the chapters ahead. Choose a day warmer than not and spray all your fruit trees and berry patches to the point of extreme runoff . . . wetting the ground thoroughly as well as the trunk and branch structure. This saturation makes nutrients available to both the soil food web and the overwintered species in the arboreal food web. Liquid fish (unlike fish emulsion) has not been pasteurized and thus contains the fatty acids and enzymes that fuel the biology. Cold-pressed neem oil has not been pasteurized and thus contains fatty acids and more than a hundred other compounds that fuel the biology. These fungal foods also help decompose the last of any overwintering leaves laden with potential scab spores from the year before. I add effective microbes to this first spray of the season as well (see "Effective microbes" in chapter 4 for complete instruction) to provide biological reinforcement for the canopy colonization that I'll be wanting in the months ahead.[22]

The pulsing agent part of this biological approach continues with a repeat application one to two weeks later as the bud stage reaches *early pink* to *full pink*. Individual flower buds on fruit trees have spread apart and are right on that brink of popping open to unveil their beauty. Target ground and branch structure once again, but also give full credence to the upper portion of the tree. All sprays from here on out will have foliar uptake purpose, now that receptive green tissue is showing in earnest. A shot of effective microbes comes highly recommended yet again to ensure diverse colonization of leaf and bud surfaces. What seems unusual and new here—introducing *orchard probiotics* to the tree canopy—is absolutely avant garde.

I time a fall application of neem oil and/or liquid fish to when approximately 40–60 percent of the leaves have fallen off the apple trees. Lots of dynamics are going on following harvest. I spray the entire tree and remaining leaves, as it's this stocking of the arboreal pantry that helps our microbial allies buckle down in the bud crevices for the dormant months ahead.[23] I definitely make the ground wet, targeting fallen leaves to increase decomposition with the fatty acids and thinking about the fall root flush, which is now hitting its stride. A brew of non-aerated compost

THE FOUR HOLISTIC SPRAYS OF SPRING (PART ONE)

The heart of a holistic approach to disease comes down to four health-supporting sprays for our fruit trees early in the growing season. We forgo copper, sulfur, and lime sulfur by doing this. These are the long-standing mineral fungicides relied upon in certified organic operations to ward off potential disease . . . but at a cost to mycorrhizal health, fruit finish, yields, and return bloom. An overview of organic allopathy will be coming, along with an understanding of specific challenges when health-minded orchardists might nevertheless feel compelled to call upon traditional spray options. Weather that induces serious disease risk demands focused attention. Yet we can often ride through extenuating circumstances simply by emphasizing orchard health across the board. Which brings us to the *four holistic sprays of spring.* Timing and rates are coming (see part two of this sidebar in chapter 4, on page 142), as now we're about what and why.

These fixings of orchard health consist of pure neem oil, unpasteurized liquid fish, and a diverse complex of microbes. That last component of this holistic recipe can be served up as effective microbes or aerated compost tea. This is primarily a nutritional brew for beneficial fungi that also happens to stimulate tree immune function. A competitive arboreal environment will ward off pathogenic disease, and all the more so when fruit tree phytochemistry is activated. The primary infection period for most tree disease is effectively straddled by these sprays. Yet there's more to this story. The nitrogen boost (from the fish) going into bloom will strengthen pollen viability. Insect pests will be impacted by azadirachtin compounds in the neem, which inhibit the progression from egg to larva to adult. These holistic spray applications serve as a biological replacement for petroleum-based dormant oil as well. Early-season moth cycles get disrupted, setting up "lesser generations" the rest of the season. That should be plenty to wet your whistle for now, methinks.

tea (or effective microbes, if you still have some product remaining from the spring) would be an especially great addition for furthering leaf decomposition and boosting end-of-season diversity yet again.[24]

Arboreal brews

Herbal medicine at its finest is really about deep nutrition. Fermented teas of horsetail, nettle, and comfrey are local brews that offer wide-ranging constituent bioavailability to both foliage and friendly microbes. Kelp can be viewed as an herbal tonic from the sea. Neem oil is most certainly plant-based. A homemade garlic extract works in synthesis with other spray materials. Let's introduce the use of these arboreal brews (full details can be found in the "Herbal teas" section of chapter 4, on page 146) through the heart of the growing season while we're tuned into supporting system biology.

Spring catalyst sprays along with such herbal side dishes provide food resources to canopy allies up until harvesttime. Many of us will likely incorporate specific insect strategies during this time (depending on the pest reality found at each orchard site), but right now we're giving emphasis to sustaining system health. Ours is a forthright approach. We are riding a new wave of thinking, as the time has come to grow nourishing fruit in essentially homegrown ways.[25] The end of peak oil demands that this knowledge be developed and shared widely. We are moving beyond the old organic ways that once seemed necessary to control

Choosing to spray to sustain system health is a far more pleasant option than spraying toxins throughout the orchard ecosystem. Photo by Grace Phillips.

fruit tree disease. We have tuned in to the biological connection, and, by gum, these critters need feeding!

The majority of plant surfaces have been satisfactorily colonized going into bloom with the first two holistic sprays of the season. This despite the vagaries of weather and ultraviolet degradation. The next steps are to support the arboreal food web through the month ahead—just as disease-causing organisms come onto the scene—along with stimulating the immune response of the tree itself. Some may think this sounds dubious, even preposterously risky from a commercial perspective, yet ultimately we can either fight microbe reality with heavy-hitting spray medicines or work from a deeper level of understanding.

Enough rationale has been provided throughout this book for you to make that judgment for yourself. I place my bets for a good fruit harvest on the biological approach.

Those weeks during fruit bloom and early fruit set are when fungal and bacterial pathogens, along with a majority of insect pests, must be reckoned with. We'll examine these dynamics more thoroughly ahead, but the point to be taken now is this: The need to *do something* is far more critical during this phase than it will be throughout the rest of summer. Choosing to spray to sustain system health is different from choosing to spray to kill. If you're in the camp that has always regarded "need to spray" as the ultimate reason not to grow fruit, shift gears, please. Recognizing your inner reluctance around spraying is needed to move ahead.

I use unpasteurized liquid fish two more times in my spray mix at the end of bloom (known as *petal fall*) and about a week to ten days later, absolutely along with pure neem oil and kelp and effective microbes. Fish has a substantial charge of nitrogen as well, and as we will soon learn, such foliar nutrition has high value at this time when our trees are developing seeds (within the fruit) and next year's flower bud cells. The spray schedule is tighter now—more on the order of weekly than biweekly—because the whole of creation takes active interest in this fruition. Growers honoring arboreal allies cannot see the microscopic action going on between good colonization and spore-landing disease organisms during this time . . . but relatively clean fruitlets and leaves as we enter the lazy days of summer eventually tell the story that matters: Health prevails.

Arboreal brews—if you choose to continue spraying for optimum health in the summer months—now go totally herbal. Pure neem oil continues to be at the heart of an ongoing nutritional spray program, along with certain fermented herbal teas. Basically, what's being achieved during these months when the fruit sizes up is ensuring good calcium levels, interrupting the summer moth complex, and upping resistance to rots and other surface diseases by boosting the *cuticle*

This microscopic view of a leaf surface reveals the playing field where beneficial microbes and pathogenic organisms vie for colonization rights. The stem of the leaf stretches above the stomata (respiratory openings), tower-like tricomes (leaf hairs), and chlorophyll-rich cells on the underside of this black walnut leaf. Half again as much resolution would be required to see the microbes that are undoubtedly covering this leaf surface. Photo courtesy of Louisa Howard, Dartmouth Electron Microscope Facility.

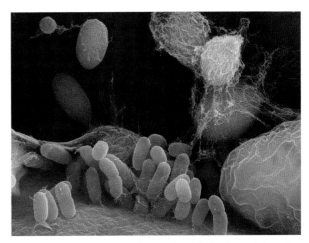

Speak of the devil . . . here stands the arboreal food web revealed in all its complexity. The pill-shaped forms in the front are bacteria. The larger egg-shaped masses are fungi wrapped in their hyphal strands. (Those that seem to be floating in the background are attached to the leaf surface as well, just a visually distorting micron away.) This is the realm of competitive colonization wherein lies a core tenet of holistic understanding. You can almost hear a disease spore yelling out, *Quick, beam me up, Scotty!* Photo courtesy of Louisa Howard, Dartmouth Electron Microscope Facility.

defense of the tree. I maintain a ten-day application schedule through the month following petal fall, then go biweekly up until harvest to achieve a darned good fruit finish for community sales.[26] Commercial fruit growing demands additional attention to be directed at aesthetic fungal diseases like flyspeck and sooty blotch that feed on cuticle exudates . . . which may not matter quite so much in home plantings, thus making the recommendation for summer applications just that—a recommendation. The four holistic spring sprays should make a decent fruit crop achievable, whether you choose to go for the gold or not.

HOLISTIC HEALTH

Anyone looking to grow fruit faces a good hundred years' worth of chemical obstinacy despite this lengthy rundown of biological advantages. We must make

certain our philosophy once and for all to answer that pivotal question with which we began this chapter: Are we going to honor tree wisdom or not?

Our grandparents' generation didn't make the turn toward chemical agriculture so much out of dire necessity as out of uncomprehending enthusiasm. Pest and disease problems are frustrating when you've worked so hard to plant, water, and cultivate, only to see moths gain the upper hand or rot ruin nearly every peach in a particularly wet summer. Blunt chemicals like lead arsenate and Bordeaux copper dealt a blow to mortal pest enemies in the Roaring Twenties. Insidious chemicals like DDT (among the many organochlorine/organophosphate compounds developed as nerve toxins during and after World War II) upped the ante. And what do we really know about the "softer chemicals" like imidacloprid being used today, other than that honeybee populations worldwide have crashed precipitously?[27] Advocates for chemical agriculture make a tantalizing case for labor saved, the certainty that food will come to hand, and the moral imperative that a burgeoning human population must be fed by industrial means. All this can be argued. Health data presented. Refined thinking pursued. I'm not going to engage anyone's beliefs here about what makes for righteous agriculture.[28] I am, however, going to make clear what happens in the orchard ecosystem when chemicals are relied upon as a primary means of growing fruit.

In a sense, pests and disease in the orchard—whatever the scale—should be thought of as symptoms that show up whenever system health is less than optimum. Environmental stress, nutrition imbalance, lack of diversity, input ramifications, and human arrogance all contribute to this broad mandate for trouble. We may want to make big-picture decisions, yet almost invariably we react to a perceived threat in the here and now by seeking a potent medicine to alleviate a crop-threatening situation. Such short-term solutions merely address symptoms and can never be more than a prop for a sick patient . . . although they may seem to *do good* at the time. Eventually stronger medicine is needed as the system gets weaker from not having relied on its own internal fortitude. Mycorrhizal fungal connections are lost as fungicides used to prevent potential disease up high in the tree (a fairly common orchard strategy) change the hospitality of the living soil below. Feeder roots limit their reach in favor of the intravenous-like drip provided by soluble nitrogen. Mites and other foliar pests weaken plant vitality as beneficial allies disappear due to the use of broad-acting toxins. Inherent nutrition in the food we eat becomes a degenerative joke when there's little respect for soil biology. The grower, of course, gets a crop. Some say the fruit even looks grand. Next year it's more of the same. Chemicals again prop up a less-than-optimum situation. The next year the grower gets another crop, just as empty of real nutrition as the one before. The beat goes on.

This is not a basis for a happy home orchard where children walk through the grass to pick berries and birds sing. Nor will any fruit grower find joy in contemplating the "-ide side" of conventional thinking: Insecticides, fungicides, herbicides, and soluble

fertilizer-ides come with complicated instructions and myriad danger warnings. Perpetuating imbalance takes more effort than some people might wish to admit.

Choosing to *go organic* is no reason to be smug, however, if we fail to make the connection to health across the board. Utilizing a substitute arsenal of natural toxins does not change the underlying paradigm of how we view food production. Dealing with symptoms—be it codling moth stings or nutrient deficiency or rust defoliation—is not the same as supporting health and biodiversity throughout the orchard ecosystem. Sometimes growers refer to this broader paradigm as *deep organics*, but I actually have more useful words to set the stage from an earlier book of mine, *The Apple Grower*:

> Two terms from medicine lend far more credence to describing how we as orchardists relate to our trees in the quest to produce healthy, locally grown fruit. I would argue that each of us makes *allopathic* and *holistic* choices within the approach we've chosen to grow fruit. Every organic sulfur spray, for instance, works in an allopathic manner just as does every organophosphate spray. Both are aimed at removing the perceived threat by toxic means. Holistic actions on the other hand undertake to embrace the orchard system as a whole rather than address recurring symptoms. The more toxic a procedure, of course, the further we remove ourselves from integrating soil and tree health into self-sustaining solutions.

Natural defense mechanisms abound in a healthy orchard. Our job as growers is to support the underlying biology and abet biodiversity. Always and in all ways. Plants possess an immune system (of sorts) that can ward off pathogenic fungal disease. We can make herbal brews to help stimulate this internal phytochemistry in our trees. Creating diverse habitat for predators like ladybugs and lacewings keeps pest

The living mulch system provided by comfrey plants creates a self-sustaining tree with all sorts of health connections in its favor.

numbers in check. Mulching with ramial wood chips helps mycorrhizae thrive, and it's this fungal connection that provides the balanced nutrition necessary for a tree to better stand up to disease. Human ingenuity can direct insect traffic—aye, curculio, I'm going to tell my species how to finally outwit your species![29]—and then make a serious dent in returning population numbers. Effective trap-out methods for other major pests, devised by recognizing varietal preferences and behavior patterns, make the beneficial math we'll be talking about a no-brainer in this choice surrounding the use of ecosystem-altering chemistry.

I am not a purist by any means. There may be times when an allopathic touch will seem justified in a community orchard. Remember, I'm referring here not just to chemicals but to approved organic materials like mineral fungicides as well. The pivotal distinction for any orchard input should be *does it build system health?* Or does it cut, slash, and burn to suppress a symptomatic situation instead? Fruit growers with their livelihoods on the line naturally feel extreme angst when conditions for fire blight threaten or borer pressure increases to a crescendo. Weighing the options to deal with devastating fungal disease or a spike in badass bug populations should be a grower's decision based on keeping a community orchard effort viable in the long run.

All these considerations happily shift in the attentive home orchard. You don't need every apple and peach to be perfect to be able to pay the taxman. You can choose varieties with reasonable fortitude and be more hands-on with problematic pests. A portion of the fruit can be sacrificed as long as your share is bountiful and reasonably unmarred. Harvests here in Lost Nation Orchard come in along the lines of 60–80 percent dessert-grade fruit, by which I mean *reasonable to eat* by any appreciative standard. The rest of our apple crop gets squeezed into real cider, truly one of the delights of this good life. Of course, crop appearance varies somewhat by variety, and curveballs are inevitably thrown to us in each new season. Yet what really matters goes on inside every piece of that fruit. Nutrient density and medicinal attributes of the food we eat correlate directly with how we grow our food. More flavorful fruit results when we optimize biological health. No amount of propaganda changes that truth.

You are on the way to becoming that attentive orchardist who observes and emulates Nature's ways. Decades of trial and error make up the path that has led to my recognition of the health connections being shared here. However, you alone will decide which ecosystem recommendations can reasonably be achieved in your own orchard. I can't emphasize enough that everything you do for the biology will come back to you many times over in terms of fruit-growing success. Put your energy into building health rather than battling opportunistic foes and thus often contributing to further problems. Trust that biodiversity has ways of restoring balance when short-term situations flare up. Honor all species, even when you take action to deter the select few. Give thanks every day, as attitude is part of this orchard journey too. Keep celebrating biological connection, knowing the next growing season and the season after that will get better and better.

Holistic health in the orchard absolutely rocks. With that as our guiding light—tree wisdom, if you will—we are ready to consider the scope of what you are about to undertake.

CHAPTER TWO

Orchard Design

Any planting site for fruit trees and berries should be considered from two points of view. Old-time land sense reflects the *green thumb consciousness* of successful gardeners, who take into account what the individual plant requires physically to thrive. Modern notions of permaculture bring deeper principles of ecosystem interconnection into focus. I weave the two together whenever I envision the next aspect of my farm . . . and you can do the very same. Every yard has its advantages as well as limitations. The absolutely ideal site for fruit trees may not exist at your place, but that doesn't mean you can't come up with reasonable accommodation. Families with several acres have more choice in these matters than those with a narrow yard. Still, following a few basic site rules ensures fruiting potential. We'll weave permaculture considerations in around those as best we can. Favoring biological advantage will always be the driving imperative behind every orchard layout.

KEEPING LIFE REASONABLE

My wife, Nancy, would likely tell you that I am not the guy to be giving advice about not overdoing when it comes to planting fruit trees and making gardens. It's ever so easy to get caught up in all the wonderful possibilities! Still, keeping a sense of balance in life requires that we go into any new venture with some idea of what lies ahead.

A good part of the satisfaction of growing your own food in a diverse landscape lies in keeping up with all that needs to be done in a timely manner. Constantly having to look at tasks that should have been done last week, if not a month ago, will bring agonizing joy at best. It might start one spring with never getting the far raspberry bed pruned at all. Or you'll score several truckloads of wood chips from a local landscaper and still be looking at the untouched pile a couple of years later. The grass grows up around young apple trees in the back forty until you forget things even got planted. How many seasons has it been since the currants were actually picked and put up as tasty preserves? *I sure didn't stick those fly-encrusted sticky ball traps in the back closet, honey.* You get the idea. Far better to see half a dozen apple trees with good branch structure, haphazard mulch in place, the peaches thinned to assure good fruit size, and healthy foliage supported by deep nutritional sprays . . . not to mention all those luscious blackberries ripening down yonder.

Ask yourself a few basic questions up front: *How much fruit is enough? How much fruit is too much? Can my family commit to an ongoing list of orchard tasks? What do I need to achieve each week in the orchard? How does all this fit with the rest of my life?*

Starting small is far better than going for the gusto. This has always been true of the better home orchardists I've known. Experience brings understanding as to when things need to be done. Confidence builds when a pruning cut follows the rules or certain bugs obey the plan. Now you can see how adding two apricot trees would be a next bit of fun. Maybe it's training an Asian pear on espalier; maybe it's grafting in heirloom apple varieties from your region. You're starting

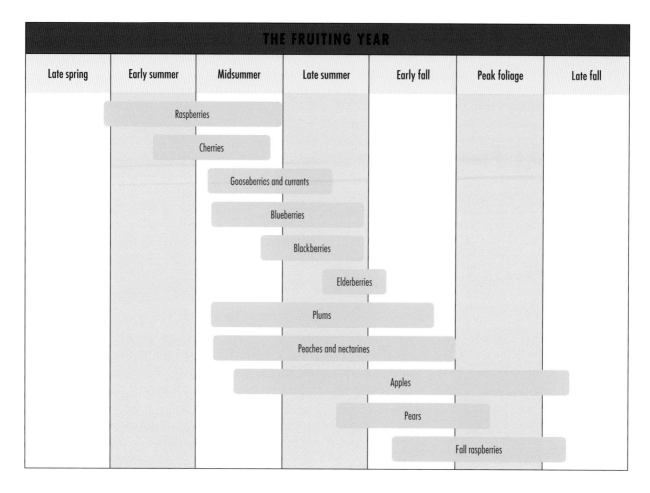

THE FRUITING YEAR						
Late spring	Early summer	Midsummer	Late summer	Early fall	Peak foliage	Late fall

Raspberries

Cherries

Gooseberries and currants

Blueberries

Blackberries

Elderberries

Plums

Peaches and nectarines

Apples

Pears

Fall raspberries

to recognize beneficial species and appreciate the role of all sorts of flowering plants in the landscape. Brewing fermented herbal teas has become as natural as remembering to hang those renewed fly traps in June.

Things start to flow in the home orchard for two reasons. One, you've taken the plunge and planted a few things. Moving beyond intentions requires you to get your hands in the dirt. And that in turn will launch your personal learning curve into the fascinating world of actually growing fruit. Be patient about this. Everything isn't going to go right. Recognize such learning opportunities as a chance to do better next year. In fact, be stubborn about this. Every back-to-the-lander quickly learns that something else does go right in that very same season. Nature gives and Nature takes. Here's a beautiful argument for an even

wider diversity of fruit plantings, to gain the best crop insurance going for your family.

Which brings us back to that point about me not being *the guy* to set the limits on anyone's orcharding horizon. Fruit growing quickly becomes a passion. Keep it reasonable enough so that you never lose sight of the fun.

TREE PRACTICALITIES

Choosing the types of fruit you first wish to grow begins the process of putting in an orchard. Lay of the land insists that certain practicalities be met, and chief among these is well-drained ground. Terrain adjustments prior to planting can improve root prospects considerably where conditions may be less than optimum. Good air movement plays a huge role in abating disease pressure and getting tender blossoms through tenuous times. Orientation to the sun may be helpful if you have a choice in the matter. Direct sunshine throughout the day empowers fruit buds, so sidestepping excessive shade from tall trees and nearby buildings will be integral to productive cropping. The soil structure at your place may seem mostly a matter of destiny. Hold tight, however, for soil biology has the power to turn even a heavy clay soil into receptive earth as well as bind a porous sandy soil back toward fertile promise.

Aerobic ground

The roots of fruit trees need to be able to "breathe" throughout the active growing season. Choose planting locations where groundwater finds its summer equilibrium point a good 3–4 feet beneath the surface. Pear trees will tolerate *wet feet* to some extent, but berries, stone fruits, and apples will develop root rot in constantly anaerobic conditions.[1]

Don't worry about puddles on semi-frozen ground at the height of spring thaw. It's the normal depth of the water table (once it settles) that determines whether tree roots will thrive or wallow. Impermeable ledge relatively close to the surface can create drainage issues, even on sloping ground. Some of you will be able to improve drainage by resurfacing your land to allow a lower-lying swale to drain such pockets. Others may be able to install drainage tile to capture a high water table above the tree site and redirect it via the flow of gravity to lower ground. Flexible black plastic pipe with moisture-collecting slits, placed in a gravel trench, buried at least 24 inches deep, and then covered with landscape cloth before backfilling does the job admirably. Such steps need to be taken before the trees are planted, of course.

Creating planting mounds for individual trees, or more extended berms for group plantings, will work provided you achieve depth enough for roots before they encounter permanent groundwater or that impermeable ledge. Such rising of the earth happens

in one of two ways. Importing structural soil is fine if you can indeed get decent dirt. That means asking precisely where that convenient dump-truck-load of loam might be coming from. Chemically treated soil taken from a non-organic farm field is so biologically impoverished that vast amounts of fertilizer are needed to get a crop. Mixing this abused soil with a significant amount of woodsy compost and soil amendments will be necessary to restore some oomph within the terrain being formed. Cover cropping the resulting berms for a year must be part of the plan as well. A better source (with respect to your orchard needs anyway) is native topsoil being scraped away for yet another development. Creating miniature dales with the soil already on site may gain that slight bit of elevation needed. Sloped terrain lends itself to terracing—the piled edge of the berm now having the greater depth for fruiting plants. Both approaches are absolutely ripe for some biological riffs.

Deeper berms can be made across a mild slope by trenching the uphill side of an envisioned row of fruit trees and placing the removed soil along the downhill side. Filling the resulting trench with ramial wood chips (above where the trees will go) creates a *biological deposit account* for tree roots and mycorrhizae alike. This particular approach will be vital to create a catch basin for moisture in inland regions on the West Coast, where irrigation is a far bigger issue than drainage.

A permaculture technique from Germany takes this idea of burying woodsy debris for long-term fungal fertility to new heights. So-called *Hugelkultur* is nothing more than creating planting mounds filled principally with decomposing wood and other compostable roughage.[2] This makes for raised beds loaded with organic material, nutrients, and air pockets for roots. The deep soil of the bed becomes incredibly rich and loaded with soil life as the years pass. More tiny air pockets form as the wood continues to decompose . . . and this aeration has healthy impact for the various soil fungi we want in an

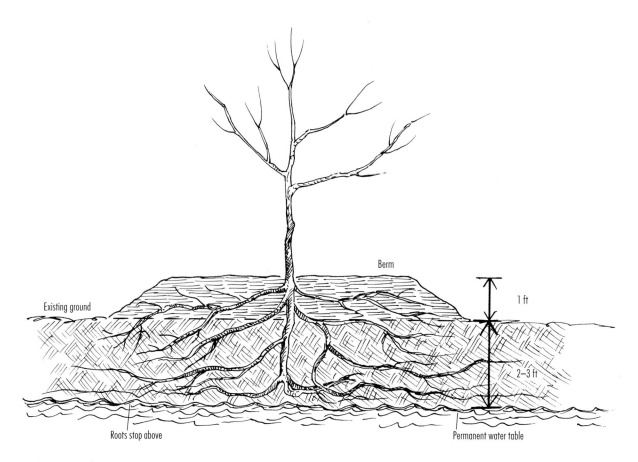

Existing ground

Berm

1 ft

2–3 ft

Roots stop above

Permanent water table

Slightly raising the elevation by creating a planting berm can often make enough of a difference on sites with a higher water table.

orchard setting. The woody debris in turn helps hold nutrients and keep them from passing through to the groundwater below.

A grower named Sepp Holzer in the Austrian Alps has taken this agroforestry notion even farther to create a swale-based microclimate for tender fruit trees.[3] In this case, the woodsy debris forms the core of earthen mounds alongside the tree row, on one side or perhaps even both sides, depending on the terrain and prevailing wind direction. The bottoms of the inward slopes are lined with rocks to collect summer heat and radiate it back into the sheltered tree swale. The tops of the mounds and outward slopes are interplanted with an assortment of small fruits, which benefit from the soil food web activity accentuated by the organic matter below. Poles can be used to

extend mound height to prop up fir boughs, which provide a winter shadow for tender trees.[4] Holzer's use of ecological relationships and cycles to provide sheltered living conditions for tree fruits growing a zone farther north than recommended deserves serious scrutiny.

Let's add one more element to this discussion about planting mounds. Burying burnt woodsy debris beneath the ground provides a nutrient haven for mycorrhizal fungi. Some of you might have heard the buzz around using *biochar* as an ancient means of fostering long-term fertility. The pore structure of blackened carbon (essentially) serves as a physical sanctuary for mycorrhizal hyphae and various symbiotic bacteria, thereby promoting microbe diversity. (I know I appear to be straying beyond mere drainage

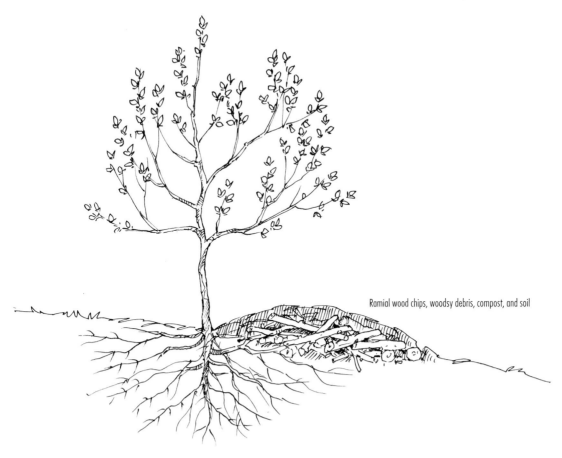

Ramial wood chips, woodsy debris, compost, and soil

The permaculture technique know as *Hugelkultur* involves utilizing woodsy debris to form sheltering berms around fruit trees. This essentially creates a mycorrhizal haven beneath the ground that promotes tree health for many years to come.

issues here, but bear with me. Orchard design based on biological principles sometimes leads to unexpected places.)

An experiment on my part several years back incorporated all these notions. I knew nothing of *Hugelkultur* at the time and in truth was simply being practical about clearing ground.[5] I piled brush and pulled root systems (of hardwood trees located in intended apple tree rows) on a downhill slope and deliberately scorched the branch ends and larger stump surfaces with a dry leaf fire. Notch one up for crude biochar made in place. Uphill soil was then pushed over the works to create a level planting plateau. Since then, much work has gone into mulching with ramial wood chips, all deciduous, all in the guise of building woodsy soil from the top down. The apple trees

planted at the intersection of this altered slope are the healthiest on my farm. Now, that's a biological planting mound!

Air movement

A bit of light wind helps keep disease at bay and can deter frost at blossom time. Planting on a slight slope usually ensures better air movement. Flatter ground will work too so long as nearby impediments can be made less so—a well-placed opening or two in a downhill hedge or solid-board fence may be necessary to allow the wind to stir the air. On the other hand, some sites will require a windward hedge to buffer persistently strong winds. Possibilities for a windbreak can be far more diverse than the short-lived, root-competing poplars people often seem to rely upon

Biological terracing brings deciduous banking into full play. Uphill swales filled in with woodsy matter in dry areas can be used to retain moisture for trees planted on a slope. Conversely, the very ground being cleared to make way for an orchard (where rainfall is not an issue) can provide a similar mycorrhizal resource to build up the planting terrace in the first place.

for this purpose. Dual-purpose plants will feed wildlife or fix nitrogen or provide habitat for bird friends. Consider hybrid hazelnuts, Nanking cherry (also know as sweet bush cherry), beach plums, or Siberian pea shrub (*Caragana arborescens*), as well as ornamentals like dogwoods, lilac, or highbush cranberry. The wind's drying qualities in winter can be a bigger problem in prairie orchards, where fruit buds desiccate in part due to frozen trunks and branches not being able to supply water from the roots. A tart cherry or apricot tree in the Midwest may require the protection of scattered evergreens (to take the brunt of cold winds) in order to successfully fruit.

Sun access

Excessive shade simply won't do. The fruiting process is driven by photosynthesis. That requires access to plenty of sunshine. Morning sun has better value in terms of drying out the orchard after a heavy dew or night rain. Still, the longer those trees can find the light throughout the day—from sunrise to sundown—the better. Fruiting plants require a minimum of six to eight hours of sun per day during the growing season; stone fruits do better with even more. Southern growers will find that gooseberries and currants actually need some overstory shading in order to deal with excessive heat, whereas farther north a location in full sun for the *Ribes* family will probably be fine.

Aspect to the sun has some relevance but will not doom any effort outright. Stone fruits bloom before apples and many of the berries by two weeks or more. Tender blossoms touched by an early-spring frost will be lost as far as fruit set goes that season. Planting such earlier-blooming fruits on a north-facing slope can help delay bloom and thus may save the day in

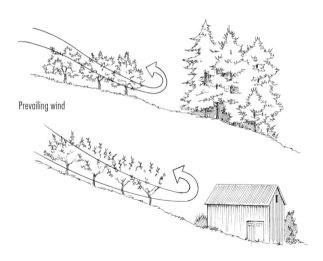

Prevailing wind

Slope alone does not guarantee frost will pass you by. Openings in a frost barrier that allow cold air to continue downhill or planting farther uphill from an obstruction can prove significant.

Buffering tender fruit buds from the cold winds of winter can be as simple as a spacious evergreen stand planted on the windward side.

borderline areas. Use a nudge of common sense with that last recommendation, however: Growers in far northern zones don't need to set back bloom, and in fact putting trees on a north-facing slope may end up proving entirely detrimental to growing a productive tree.[6] In the next chapter we'll be discussing management techniques to deal with cold that potentially have more usefulness when the temperature plummets within a certain range. Protection from the hot summer sun in southern zones can be found by favoring a northerly aspect. Partial shade during the warmest part of the day can improve the texture of apples and protect fruit from sunburn; pruning for a denser tree canopy or using a reflective spray of white kaolin clay can help achieve the same result for those who have limited options in terms of site location. Pome fruit trees to be espaliered (trained in two dimensions on a trellis) will do best if planted on east- or north-facing walls in hot climates, while a west- or south-facing wall may be preferred in cooler climates.

Soil structure

Soil type is what it is to start. However, both an extremely sandy soil and a heavy clay muck can be positively influenced by soil biology and additions of organic matter. Mulching and composting over time go a long way toward improving unfriendly ground. The ratio of calcium to magnesium has relevance when nudging the biology toward certain achievements regarding soil structure (see "Cation balance" in chapter 3, on page 66). Having the proper mixture of minerals, organic matter, air, and water in the upper layers of the soil—the area where plants grow—is ultimately more important than feeling limited for the rest of your life by poor soil structure.

Were I to write a suspense novel about all this it would absolutely be called *The Glomalin Factor*. This soil superglue permeates organic matter, binding it to silt, sand, and clay particles. Not only does glomalin contain 30–40 percent carbon, but it also forms clumps of soil granules, called *aggregates*. Glomalin gives soil its *tilth*, that subtle textural quality that enables experienced growers to judge great soil by crumbling a handful through their fingers. A sandy soil's moisture-retention capacity can be increased, just as a clay soil can be unbound (to drain better) by this substance. Here lies the key to improving soil structure. And so, you eagerly ask, where can you buy this wonder product?

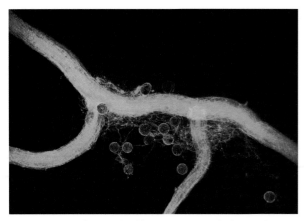

A microscopic view of a mycorrhizal fungus growing on a feeder root. The round bodies are spores, and the thread-like filaments are hyphae. The substance coating them is glomalin, revealed by a green dye tagged to an antibody that reacts against glomalin. Photo courtesy of Sara Wright, USDA Agricultural Research Service.

Mycorrhizal fungi are the exclusive producers of glomalin.[7] The arbuscular strains of these fungi use carbon from the plant to grow and make glomalin. This is the other half of the mutually beneficial pact between mycorrhizae and the roots of fruiting plants (the first being providing nutrients and moisture to the colonized roots in exchange for photosynthate sugars). Glomalin is secreted along the outside of the hyphal filament to provide enough rigidity to span the air spaces between soil particles and contain nutrient flow.

The fungi follow the root, continually forming new hyphae to colonize feeder root expansion. Hyphae higher up on what become permanent roots stop transporting nutrients eventually, at which point the coating of protective glomalin sloughs off into the soil. It then attaches to soil particles, minerals, and organic matter. The resulting aggregate soil structure becomes stable enough to resist wind and water erosion yet remains porous enough to allow air, water, and roots move through it. Any soil becomes capable of hosting a greater diversity of beneficial microbes, holding more water, and resisting crusting on the surface as glomalin levels build.

PERMACULTURE PRINCIPLES

The mutual dependency among various plants—the backbone of any ecosystem—reveals permaculture principles we should consider. Every life interacts with untold other lives. The microbe world certainly points the way in this regard. Similarly, permaculture is a framework we humans can use to comprehend plant and insect interactions that help us achieve our fruiting goals.[8]

Every plant serves at least one niche function. Some offer food, others medicine, and obviously for more than just our two-legged species. Certain plants abet mycorrhizal association, even going so far as to play a role in the production of edible mushrooms. Others provide shade or fix nitrogen or offer sanctuary for tiny allies. Still others make an array of nutrients available, be it by taproot or as cut-and-drop neighbors destined to become mulch. Fuel, fiber, and fodder elements are often desirable as well. Consideration for how such multiple functions support the bigger picture begins the permaculture design process.

Every plant fills a certain space as well, both aboveground and below. Fruit trees call for a good share of direct sunshine in order to be productive. Ergo, we have the top layer of an edible forest garden. Overshadowing nut trees become a longer-term part of some designs by introducing a succession factor—a dozen years of interplanted sour cherries makes many a pie before the overstory phase of nut saplings dominates light dynamics. A shrub layer woven throughout serves as a natural habitat for spiders and birds, provides a low-lying windbreak, produces berries in the partial shade, and even defines pathways for visiting friends. Kiwi vines can find sunlight enough as well, whether growing up an arbored pavilion or a neighboring shade tree. Herbs and wildflowers create important pocket communities of diversity. In a similar vein, root systems seek different plateaus in the soil in becoming active trading partners on the *Soil Food Web Exchange*. Far more space in a diverse orchard planting can be productively utilized than you might otherwise think is possible from listening to the conventional party line, which says that trees must be isolated in rows for maximum production.

To speak of "planting a guild" captures the harmony inherent in a permaculture-inspired layout for the home orchard. I discuss *orchard architecture* with fellow fruit growers working on a commercial scale, but here you and I will explore the concept of the *fruit guild*. A natural community of plants achieves a balance among recycling nutrients, resisting disease, and keeping pests in check while conserving water and attracting beneficial insects and other animals into the fold. Such an ecosystem hums with an inner graciousness. Humans can readily disrupt such scenes—all the more so when we come in with talk of monoculture and high yields and allopathic medicines to take care of problems we ourselves induce with our agricultural precepts. We can't do that kind of thing in a guild, however. Now the pulse of the whole guides us surely toward sustainable means. Our stewardship becomes more and more refined as we learn to trust an integrated tapestry of beneficial relationships. I get almost as much out of this term philosophically as I do in contemplating what to plant next to what! Which, of course, is where this permaculture term intends to shine the light.

We have many varietal tree size considerations to speak of in the pages ahead. Still, let's visualize planting three apple trees to start you down the fruiting path. Three trees in a row in the midst of regularly mowed grass does not make a guild. But reposition those trees to form the three points of a triangle, say on the order of about 20–30 feet apart for vigorous stock. Soil prep has already provided the beginnings of a biologically rich fungal duff, mulched principally with ramial wood chips, extending slightly beyond this cluster of apple trees in all directions. The light space bordering the trees calls for currant bushes and gooseberries. Perhaps a contained bed of raspberries bulge this island planting outward on the far side. Woodsy herbs and wild greens fill in hither and thither in the

This Asian pear guild at the Central Rocky Mountain Permaculture Institute includes buffaloberry, comfrey, lovage, horseradish, and Siberian pea shrub—to creating a self-sustaining system. Photo courtesy of Eric Toensmeier.

mulched ground at the feet of the trees. Clusters of flowering plants create a meandering horizon within the tree triad, some of these chosen specifically to attract helpful insects and support pollinator populations. Deep-taprooted plants (placed in the anticipated dripline of the fully grown tree) are chosen as living mulch because of their mineral-rich growth habit. Juneberries planted nearby provide a delicious treat for hungry birds, which in turn detour from the blueberry bushes that dominate another island bulge. A comfortable chair waits for you under a large apple limb. Yet even before you actually begin to plant, you decide to stretch open the trees to the facing sun, adding a few more apples to complete a fan layout, and just in front of those go the very peach varieties that your grandparents gobbled as kids. We're here

A FRONT-YARD ORCHARD

Exemplary home orchards can be found in many places. Yet the passionate work of Jana and David Ulmer in Sebastopol, California, truly knocks my socks off. Perhaps it was that first taste of a tree-ripened pluot. Perhaps it was flipping the notion of backyard orcharding right on its head—this is an orchard of prominence, filling the whole of the *front yard* with nearly every fruit imaginable.

The ecosystem created in this mixed orchard and garden scene provides diversity aplenty. Every view features different fruits of choice, from multi-variety peach trees and the blueberry cage to espaliered apples and grapes dangling beneath neatly trellised vines. A fruiting horizon like this can be honed only by decades of experience.

David started grafting persimmons, plums, pears, and you name it in northern Mississippi in the late 1970s. That first orchard spread steadily over 5 acres, providing tree-ripened fruits every Saturday morning for the local farmers' market. Yet life leads on, and he found his next home on the northern California coast, ground that noted plant breeder Luther Burbank once described as the greatest place to grow fruit on this continent. Wow. The new orchard, while every bit as Zone 8 as before in terms of winter lows, offered vaster harvest prospects—the relatively cool summer climate of coastal California ripens to perfection many varieties that in the hot and humid South would bake on the tree. David was leaving bacterial leaf spot and extreme fire blight behind . . . not yet knowing what he might find this second time around.

Most of his stone fruits are now planted four trees to a hole, about 18 inches apart in the planting circle, in a sense becoming one tree in form. The advantages of this are immediately clear:

Seedling rootstock can be budded in place to different varieties, open center pruning results from letting each variety fill its quadrant, and having four trees in proximity tones down vigor. Peaches, pluots, apricots, and plums planted thusly allow for many varieties in a small space, spreading out the harvest while at the same time giving enough, but not too much, of each variety for the family. One critical insight for a West Coast orchard was quickly learned: Stone fruit pruning needs to be done here in late summer in order to shortcut bacterial canker. This disease determinedly spreads onto tree wounds in the wet dormant season of California, whereas good drying breezes right after harvest deter infection. Sharing his grafting passion has been somewhat tempered by this new reality as well—taking scionwood in winter favors canker, so now David removes green buds only in early August (when it's bone-dry) to give to fellow fruit enthusiasts.

This dynamic gardening couple opted to keep the pome fruit closer to the earth. A rail fence on the perimeter of the planting area defines the orchard bounds. Apples, primarily on Bud.9 rootstock, are located halfway between the posts (spaced 8 feet apart) and trained to a rail cordon espalier. A pear at every other post is trained to be more columnar, grafted primarily onto OH×F 333 and OH×F 51 to limit excessive vigor. The apples are deliberately steered toward the non-pear post. Mucho pinching of shoots back to a bud or two takes place on a regular basis to keep this system both productive and contained. Winter apples that are desired in greater quantity—Lady Williams, Pink Lady, Sundowner, GoldRush, and Hauer Pippin—are grown as free-standing trees where the chickens can be brought in for bug duty down below.

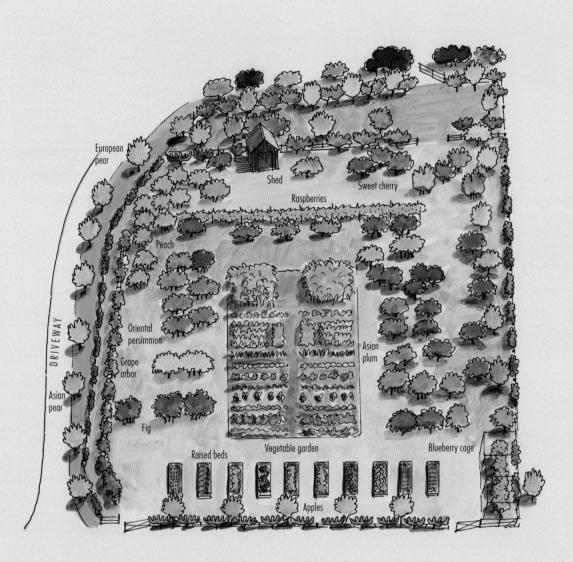

European pear

Shed

Sweet cherry

Raspberries

Peach

DRIVEWAY

Oriental persimmon

Grape arbor

Asian pear

Fig

Raised beds

Vegetable garden

Asian plum

Blueberry cage

Apples

All sorts of fruits can be integrated in beautiful ways. The Ulmers seem to have it all, from first berries and mayhaws in late spring to juicy peaches and pluots at the height of summer to the very best California heirloom apples come fall.

This land thirsts for sufficient moisture every growing season. Accordingly, drip irrigation cycles on for twenty minutes a day in the root zone of each tree and down the row of berry beds and vegetable plantings. Tons of mulch greatly improves drought tolerance. Ramial wood chips brought in by commercial landscapers constantly renew the original mulch put down over cardboard in establishing the orchard. A local coffee roaster saves bean chaff at the rate of two barrels a week, which in turn gets spread to provide a soft landing pad for ripe peaches. Greensand mixed into each planting hole also helps condition the soil to hold moisture. Soil pH runs slightly alkaline, but because the irrigation water is highly acidic, all ends up in good stead.

Pest and disease dynamics center foremost on codling moth and peach leaf curl. David smiles and says "Not enough" when asked about the steps he takes to ensure a bountiful crop. Using a battery-powered sprayer (pulled by hand on cart wheels) takes the better part of a morning. Two applications of copper along with dormant oil go on the peach trees prior to budbreak to address curl fungi. Rains continuing into May underscore how much better the resistant varieties such as Avalon Pride fare in this particular battle. David long used wettable sulfur for brown rot on peaches

David Ulmer and his Almaden Duke sweet cherry tree. Photo courtesy of Jana Ulmer.

and scab on the apples but has happily switched over to pure neem oil. These botanical applications have had a positive impact on generational moth pressures as well.

now, right in the midst of an integrated fruit guild . . . right in the midst of your orchard.

The actual layout that you come up with will be driven by the pleasure you derive from weaving beauty into your surroundings. Certainly you can integrate raised beds for vegetables into the design if that's desired. The concept of an island can literally become a forest garden filling the whole of your property, with patches of bright sunshine left for the benefit of more food plantings. Espalier-trained fruit trees along a rail fence can give definition to boundaries. Medicinal herbs interspersed in a rock garden at the feet of a noble grandfather tree create intriguing terrain. More traditional orchard layouts of trees aligned in a meadow setting are fine, too—desirable ecosystem dynamics can arise by virtue of all sorts of other plantings in the vicinity. Visiting others with thoughtful orchard designs often will generate additional ideas, such as incorporating meandering paths and hidden nooks.

Food, beauty, and diversity all come together in appropriate landscaping. An orchard based upon these three primary goals will be stunning whatever the season. Some varieties have especially spectacular spring bloom, while others load on the fall colors. A golden leaf carpet lies under the nectarines; cherries turn a mix of red and yellow; blueberries radiate whatever the season. Shades of green from unexpected plants below add delightful contrast to the trees all summer long. The variety of insects encountered marks every day as a marvel. Winter settles serenely on barren apple limbs while the jay calls: *All walk in beauty in this place.* This is the full circle of integration, a permaculture-based ecosystem that not only hums with balance but delights our hearts in every moment of the year.

THE BUZZ ON BIODIVERSITY

Permaculture people speak of two classes of plants to encourage within any gardenscape. Recognizing the role of *dynamic accumulators* and *beneficial*

1. Asian Pear; 2. buffalo berry; 3. comfrey; 4. lovage;
5. horseradish; 6. pea shrub; 7. daffodil; 8. marguerite;
9. lemon balm; 10. wood chip ground cover.

This polyculture of fruit trees, berry plants, and taprooted herbs shows how light space above and root space below can be fully utilized in a guild planting.

accumulators helps us bring specific plant interactions into focus.

Companion planting is far more than an old wives' tale. All plants contribute to the ecosystem, even those we mistakenly call weeds. Deep-taprooted species draw minerals up from the subsoil; green tops die back at season's end; root systems eventually pass on; fungi and company decompose the once vibrant botany. Minerals become available through the organic matter to other plants; these minerals have been "accumulated," and so we now become conscious of the dynamic accumulator class of plants.

Similarly, a flowering plant like sweet cicely (*Myrrhis odorata*) provides nectar for an adult syrphid fly, which means that the adult female will be around in the ecosystem to lay a random egg on a fruit tree leaf to hatch into a syrphid larva that will consume aphids on the order of forty a day. The flowers of one

have acted as a draw for certain pest-eating insects to the tree—thus accumulating the populations of good bugs—leaving you and me with an impressed awareness of the diversity brought on by beneficial accumulator species.

Plant allies

One medicinal herb serves as an understory superstar in my orchard around freestanding apple and pear trees. First, however, we require the inevitable disclaimer: You are about to hear the many benefits of this particular plant . . . just know now, right off the bat, that once introduced to your ground, comfrey will likely be an indomitable force for many years to come.[9] Digging it out—if you ever come up with a biological reason to change your mind—will be difficult. Please: Do not come back and blame me!

The marvel of comfrey from a fruit tree perspective

The broad reach of comfrey around this apple tree keeps grass at bay throughout the summer months.

begins with its deep-reaching root system, which effectively mines potassium, calcium, and other untapped minerals. Its leaves and stalks are flush with nutrient wealth, producing a lush plant that blossoms just after petal fall on apple trees in a cascading series of delightful pale purple-pink umbel florets. Bumblebees delight in this subsequent nectar source. As comfrey starts to set seed, it becomes carbon-heavy—and thus top-heavy—and soon falls in every random direction as living mulch, thereby suppressing grass growth and preventing it from becoming the dominant ground cover. A new round of herbal shoots from comfrey's insistent roots responds to this sunlight opportunity, repeating this same cycle at least two times more in a given year. The circumference of a comfrey circle grows as the mother plant expands outward. The soil here becomes deep brown, even black, brimming with life force. Fruit tree feeder roots find this an irresistible

invitation, totally unlike the reception provided by a dense sod where high carbon dioxide levels produced by fine grasses (in the process of root transpiration) proves disagreeable.[10] Comfrey leaves room in the humus for trees to find full mycorrhizal connection. And to think—all you had to do was plant comfrey starts (root crowns) around the anticipated dripline of the tree to launch this self-renewing orchard plan.[11]

A broad mix of species belongs under and within the vicinity of fruit trees. You can make deliberate choices here to reflect a certain look, or you can trust serendipity (enhanced by introduced species left to go to seed) to bring a diverse understory to the fore. Red clover has nitrogen-fixing capability, being a legume, which ties in nicely to comfrey's need for high nitrogen . . . which in turn will be made available to fruit tree roots in the form of ammonium by the action of soil life. Legumes are noted as well for raising available phosphorus levels. The humble dandelion is especially adept at drawing potassium up. Chicory's specialty is twofold: This plant accumulates zinc, and, when it dies, the hole left by the decaying root is an act of soil aeration in itself. Other plants like nettle, yarrow, and horsetail contribute similarly to this crescendo of specific nutrients. Are we tuning in to how a diverse understory contributes homegrown fertility to the orchard through organic matter cycled through the soil food web? Minerals are being mined and brought to the surface by this array of taprooted plants, and this will go on for a long, long time.

Woodsy herbs abet the fungal dominance we seek directly in the tree zone. In a sense, we could invent a new permaculture term here for plants like thyme, marjoram, and lavender, calling these *mycorrhizal accumulators* in their own right. The neatness of low-lying herbs will appeal to some of you more than the wild look found on my orchard acreage, and that's okay. Less stout perennials will be smothered under the shovelfuls of crumbly compost thrown at the base of fruit trees each fall, whereas these woody-stemmed herbs can stand up to greater biological depths. Aromatic herbs also allow us to see the trunk, unlike tall lush growth right up against the stem of each tree. Daffodils planted in a ring, bulb touching bulb, about a foot out from a young sapling, serve this same purpose and more. These spring flowers absorb their light share before the tree reaches full leaf, after which the green growth from the bulb quickly fades away, leaving more openness right around the base of the tree. Daffodil bulbs turn out to be disagreeable to voles as well, which are basically voracious mouse cousins inclined to eat apple tree bark in late fall and winter, given the opportunity.[12] Other culinary herbs including mints and chives are reputed to help with peach leaf curl and apple scab, but for the life of me I can't envision how this lore relates to fungal disease cycles. Still, *diversity rules*, and I have planted less woodsy herbs out under the dripline of some of my fruit trees—the point being, yes, you can integrate an array of kitchen herbs in the orchard if you wish.

Bitter herbs like wormwood, southernwood, rue, hyssop, pennyroyal, and gentian have long been used for tree protection in still another way.[13] These highly aromatic plants are sensed by fruit pests, creating olfactory confusion within the fruit guild. Such plant allies can be used more effectively in smaller fruit plantings than in more extensive commercial blocks. Plant knowledge like this can come into play in protecting highly desirable fruit or even in funneling insects toward sacrificial trap trees. Tansy and sage have a high camphor content that has been observed to deter codling moths. Nasturtium has a similar influence on woolly apple aphid, so if you happen to have susceptible rootstock, plant several around your apple and pear trees and enjoy a peppery nibble to boot.

Insect allies

Numerous plants attract beneficial species of insects to the orchard ecosystem. Biodiversity comes into its own now, revealing all sorts of fascinating nuances. Consider the self-contained world of an angelica plant in flower. Hundreds of pollinators—including an array of tiny wasps that parasitize the larvae or eggs of larger insects—feed on the nectar and pollen offered by angelica and similar wildflowers. It's the *other plants* in the fruit guild that deliver balance in the populations of fruit pests by providing habitat for the good bugs.

Savvy commercial orchardists plant diversity strips of specific flowering plants within a solid block of trees to draw the predators and parasitoids that help keep other insect pests in check. The home orchard, on the hand, flourishes with diversity advantages by virtue of plants you're already inclined to grow in garden areas. Wild corners should be granted due diligence—a dear friend once told me to always leave a place for the fairies to dwell. Hers was a diversity message, celebrating what we humans tend to dismiss as unsightly and unmanaged. Yet it's the wildlings that truly shine as beneficial plant allies.

The richer the diversity in and around the fruit orchard, the higher the rate of natural control.[14] A

Daffodils near the trunks of fruit trees prove disagreeable to voles.

richly flowering under-vicinity in spring might include wild strawberry, lungwort, buttercup, hawkweed, dandelion, and violet to go with bordering shrubs of willow and chokecherry. Summer flowers noted in healthy orchard settings include wild carrot, dill, mountain mints, white daisy, swamp milkweed, sweet clover, alfalfa, joe-pye weed, and boneset. The glory continues into autumn with sunflower, goldenrod, aster, and sneezeweed. We could get downright mathematical here: *Plant diversity plus bug diversity equals biodiversity.*

This ecological formula takes on an exponential component beyond the "flower-attracting good bug" dynamic explained so far. Let's look at one specific interaction surrounding apple maggot fly. This ubiquitous pest lays its eggs in midsummer into ripening apple fruit, resulting in interior destruction of the flesh. Certain flowering shrubs—winterberry, dogwood, and blueberry among them—attract a range of other fruit-feeding flies not interested in apple. Braconid wasps parasitize these flies as well as the resident apple maggot fly. Braconid numbers rise with prospects of increased host resources, leading to reduced apple maggot fly pressure overall.[15] All this takes place based on the proximity of neighboring plants like winterberry.[16]

Mixing up different types of fruit trees also plays into beneficial advantage. Peach, cherry, and apricot trees have extrafloral nectar glands on the base of leaf blades. Lady beetles are able to feed on this nectar and thus get a jump start on controlling rosy apple aphids on nearby apple trees.

Also lending a helping hand here are spiders, the populations of which are supported by plants that you might not consider relevant to growing fruit. One of my very first discoveries as an orchard observer took place lying beneath an apple tree, taking a break from scything high grass. A tarnished plant bug glimmered in the hot sun, caught in a spider's web. I watched the spider immobilize this minor pest of tree fruit, knowing that numerous wildflowers like goldenrod and dogbane in the plant understory had given this

Some species of braconid wasps seek out moth eggs in which to lay their eggs, while others opt for a fleshier nursery to rear their young. This gypsy moth larva is a definite goner! Photo courtesy of Scott Bauer, USDA Agricultural Research Service, Bugwood.org.

predator a chance to establish big plans for those who might damage *michael's apples.* (I take all this very personally!) Ground juniper, rugosa rose, and all those berries we'll be talking about ahead make for more permanent spider cover near fruit trees.

Syrphid flies—the larvae of which were introduced earlier as aphid-eating machines—have short mouthparts. These insects require flowers with an open structure such as cow parsley, dandelion, buckwheat, golden alexander, and sweet cicely. Stinging nettle is useful in the orchard environs because it has a host-specific aphid that builds up early in spring, in turn encouraging populations of predators to build up before other aphid species show up on young fruit

The spined soldier bug captures many a soft-bodied pest while hunting from leaf to leaf. Photo courtesy of NYSAES.

Spiders are important predators in all ecosystems. This cobweb weaver spider may well be planning her next intricate web, often made visible in the morning dew. Photo courtesy of Joseph Berger, Bugwood.org.

trees. Come fall, the dry stalks of nettle and other tea herbs like lemon balm provide good habitat for overwintering ladybugs. Small-flowered plants seem especially attractive to tiny parasitic wasps including valerian, Queen Anne's lace, butterfly weed, and hardy marguerite.

So many interactions, so many friends. An orchard ecosystem designed around diversity provides front-line answers that make pest challenges far more manageable.

CHAPTER THREE

Orchard Horticulture

Visions of orchard grandeur need to be backed with a solid foundation in basic horticultural skills like choosing acclimated varieties, planting, soil fertility, and pruning. In this regard, words on paper can prove useful as a guide, but at some point these lessons must be translated into the realm of direct experience. Seeing someone demonstrate firsthand what needs to be done helps, but know this: Confidence in holding those pruning shears simply waits around the corner. Theory begins to become ingrained the moment you decide where to make that very first cut. Why? Because at that point you've moved beyond mere words to learn directly from the true teachers—namely the trees and the other plants in your home orchard and garden. Think about what it means to stretch roots into rich soil, to develop fruit buds with vigor, to close cambium tissue across a graft. It's that oneness with the tree that accomplishes far more than descriptive words alone can achieve.

CHOICE OF VARIETY

Descriptions of many delectable fruits are coming soon. Let's start with understanding how to choose cultivars in the broader sense for the place where you live.

Climate zones are the first tool to guide wise selection for a particular area. Perennial plants must be able to survive the lowest temperature each winter in order to live into the next growing season. A hardiness zone map takes into account what to expect on average where you live—a highly unusual cold snap every century can always undo the best-laid plans, of course. Shifting climate has introduced changes to these maps in the last two decades, suggesting that less hardy varieties can now be planted farther north. Similarly, growers in southern zones need to account for the effect of excessive heat on fruiting prospects. The USDA plant hardiness zone map, along with the American Horticultural Society's heat zone map (see the appendices for web links), will give you the roughest idea to get started. The Cooperative Extension in your state or province might have more detailed hardiness zone maps available that better account for local variations.

One way or another, you now have a zone number to speak of as we begin this search for the best fruit trees and berries. Keep in mind that all notions of threshold temperatures are influenced yet again by *microclimate*. Your unique location may have a significant influence that the general zones fail to pinpoint. Local topography, proximity of neighboring shelter, aspect to the sun, subtle local variations in snow cover, and extended warmth in fall (from a nearby body of water, for instance) definitely affect fruiting prospects. Such variations may make it possible for you to boldly plant what no neighbor has planted before . . . allowing you to trial a cultivar rated one or even two zones colder than otherwise might be advised in a nursery catalog.[1]

Other fruit growers nearby know far more about what grows dependably in your region than anyone else. Lessons learned over the course of a lifetime are priceless—being able to tap into such knowledge is a great reason to seek out new friends. A number

2006 arborday.org Hardiness Zones Map

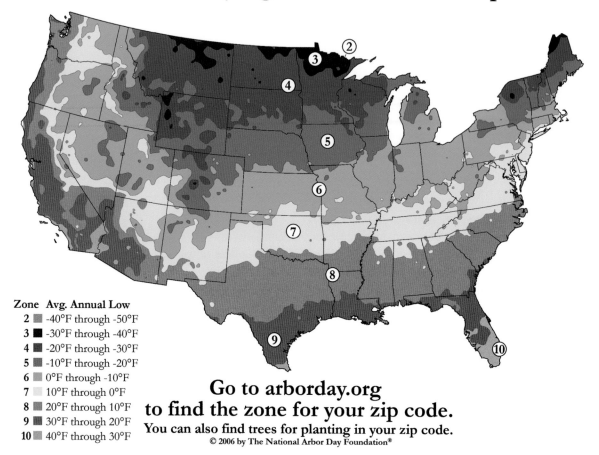

**Go to arborday.org
to find the zone for your zip code.**
You can also find trees for planting in your zip code.
© 2006 by The National Arbor Day Foundation®

Zone	Avg. Annual Low
2	-40°F through -50°F
3	-30°F through -40°F
4	-20°F through -30°F
5	-10°F through -20°F
6	0°F through -10°F
7	10°F through 0°F
8	20°F through 10°F
9	30°F through 20°F
10	40°F through 30°F

Hardiness zone maps provide a generalized idea as to varietal hardiness, but they cannot begin to account for microclimate potential.

of cultivars may easily *survive* the lowest temperature where you live; the bigger question is, which are the ones that will *thrive*? Superior cultivars in terms of flavor, annual bearing, vigor as a function of soil type, and growth habit are revealed through hands-on experience. Talking with the proprietors of local nurseries is part of this conversation. Regional fruit groups like the Backyard Fruit Growers (in southeastern Pennsylvania) hold scionwood swaps for grafting purposes—you can get all sorts of varietal advice at such gatherings of local experts. Truly pertinent information about bloom dates, chill factor, inherent disease resistance, and the normal harvest window needs to be considered in making good choices.

Blossom time

Bloom refers to the time of season when fruit trees and berries produce flowers. Many types of fruit require an overlap of bloom times in order for two varieties to pollinize each other. That's the general rule—specific cultivars may well be self-fertile, partially self-fertile, or self-sterile (apple triploids, for example). We'll broach such dynamics more thoroughly when we begin talking about each fruit. Synchronizing pollination is more of a consideration in warmer zones, where the overall bloom season may be spread over the course of six to eight weeks, especially when jump-started by a warm spell followed by a cold snap that delays later-blooming varieties. Trees in the North seem to know to wait until all vestiges of winter have passed . . . and then bloom for most fruit types will likely overlap. Nurseries identify particular cultivars as early, mid, or late bloomers; although it is wise not to rely on a variety listed as early to pollinize a variety listed as late, much of this can be taken care of by planting more than two varieties of a particular fruit.

Tender blossoms ask one other thing, especially of growers in the middle growing zones. Generally speaking, late bloomers will do better over the years than the earliest bloomers. The odds are simply that much higher that a killing freeze will come earlier rather than later in spring. No guarantees here, but there's a reason commercial fruit growers in the Midwest and the Mid-Atlantic bet the farm on apple varieties like Melrose, Ralls, and Fuji. We'll account for this with stone fruit cultivars as well, yet because peaches and cherries often bloom before apples, some tricks of the trade may be in order (see "Dealing with spring cold" further ahead in this chapter).

Chill factor

Apples and other deciduous fruits require a chilling period to break their winter rest. Buds do not emerge from dormancy until a certain number of hours between 32°F and 45°F (0°C and 7°C) have accumulated between November and February (in the Northern Hemisphere). Apples, pears, and stone fruits have chilling requirements that range from two hundred to seventeen hundred hours at these temperatures. This adaptive feature prevents plants from breaking dormancy on warm winter days when tender green tissue would be subjected to freezing temperatures. Conversely, if the buds do not receive sufficient chilling temperatures during the winter to completely release dormancy, trees may develop physiological symptoms such as delayed and extended bloom, delayed foliation, and reduced fruit set. Growers in the

warmest zones accordingly are advised to plant *low-chill varieties* that need four hundred hours or less of official downtime.[2]

Standing up to disease

Whether a cultivar is resistant or outright susceptible to disease is influenced by what you do to support ecosystem health. Still, when push comes to shove in a rainy growing season, it's wise to have chosen varieties that are somewhat adapted to the major disease challenges of your location. Many so-called heirloom varieties came into favor, in part, because such trees possessed an innate ability to stand up to regional pressures, be this apple scab, the rust diseases, or peach leaf curl. Similarly, modern varieties have been developed through deliberate cross-breeding work to find the right combination of resistant parent genetics. All this leads to commonsense recommendations of what to plant, yet it's equally important to note that even the "immune varieties" face an ever-adapting world of fungi and bacteria that are finding ways around our supposed ingenuity. I cannot emphasize enough that real-time disease resistance as delivered by health-centered orchard management trumps the temporal claims of any new super-variety.

Harvest window

Having time enough to allow fruit to fully ripen makes or breaks an orchard choice. Stone fruits and berries appropriate to your location (other than the fall-bearing types) will ripen in the summer months. No problem there. Early apples and quite a few pears never face a hard freeze either. Late varieties, on the other hand, can survive as trees in northern locations but may not have a long enough harvest window to dependably produce flavorful fruit. Pome fruits (apple, pear, and quince) can withstand a light frost in fall—such moderate cold actually helps bring on coloration and increases fruit sugar levels—but fruit starts to lose its long-term keeping ability once air temperatures dip much below 25°F (−4°C). Nights in the teens spell doom in terms of texture gone rubbery and flavor heading toward vinegar.[3] The length of the orchard growing season between a blossom-killing freeze in spring and a substantial harvest freeze in fall determines which varieties can be expected to set fruit and ripen in any given zone. One personal gain from a warming climate here in northern New Hampshire has been an extended fall season, which allows as much as a month more time to ripen classic winter apples like Golden Russet and Northern Spy.

Nursery source

Where you get your fruiting plants plays a huge role in what takes place after you put your selections in the ground. Regional nurseries are the best source, for three distinct reasons. One, the trees and berries will either come bareroot if being shipped in the mail or be freshly dug with soil somewhat intact.[4] Such plants are youthful and rarin' to go, rather than having become rootbound in a pot while waiting to sell for a year or more. Two, purchasing from a nurseryman in a similar climate zone puts you in touch with someone who knows the better varieties to suggest and probably carries some less-well-known selections for precisely that same reason. (You do not receive sound orchard advice from the kid at the national chain store, which features the same handful of varieties across the country.[5]) Finally, plants acclimated to approximately the same latitude as yours are in sync with seasonal rhythms. Reputable mail-order nurseries are listed in the appendices, but please know that many small neighborhood nurseries—usually run by fruit growers in their own right—deserve seeking out and often will answer more questions than the trees you're buying are worth.

Organic nurseries exist but are relatively few and far between. How a tree is grown after budwood has been grafted to rootstock to become a marketable sapling matters with respect to how the soil at the nursery has been revered. Large operations are likely to rely on fumigation to prepare planting beds, fungicides to ensure fewer setbacks, and soluble chemical fertilization to push branching or feathered growth.

A smaller, more hands-on operation will have a wider range of heritage varieties available, will rotate planting fields and cover crops to prepare soil anew, and may even apply mycorrhizal root dips to colonize baby trees with beneficial fungi. The rootstock nurseries are definitely not organic—a question of mere economics—so the reality is that no nursery tree (unless it's been grown from seed by the nursery itself) will be untouched by industrial agriculture. I am very glad to say that no one yet offers genetically modified cultivars.[6] Ultimately, the tree's time with you in the years ahead will be the most telling of all.

ROOTSTOCK

Every seed inside every piece of fruit represents an entirely new cultivar if we were to grow it out to maturity.[7] Peaches come somewhat *true to type*, but a cross-pollinated apple can often prove radically different from its two parents. Thus orchardists maintain a desirable cultivar through grafting, this ancient art being the means by which we create the "top" of a named varietal tree. The rooted "bottom" of any grafted tree comes with similar expectation, only now the goal shifts to controlling vigor by using *rootstock* with known qualities.

Different rootstocks provide options for everyone to enjoy the thrill of growing tree fruit. People with limited growing space can opt to choose dwarf rootstock, which limits the height of a tree to as little as 6–8 feet. Such could be the case with apples, cherries, and some hybrid plums. Pears, on the other hand, zoom to more substantial size, as pear rootstock retains a degree of untamed vigor. Peaches, nectarines, and apricots fall in between when it comes to root selections. And let's not forget that apples, cherries, and domesticated plums can be substantial trees in their own right. I tend to be a guy who likes a tree to be a tree . . . as a degree of vigor in the choice of rootstock will often be biologically advantageous and ensure a longer-lived tree to boot.

A chief virtue of dwarfing rootstock is improved light distribution to the fruit. Assertive pruning is required to achieve the same in larger trees.

Deciding which size-controlling rootstock to use involves a number of horticultural considerations. Nurseries often simplify much of this by informing home orchardists to choose a small, medium, or large tree—sometimes expressed slightly more accurately as a choice among dwarf, semi-dwarf, semi-standard, and standard (full-sized) trees. Buds from a particular apple cultivar can be grafted onto different rootstocks, giving *one-and-the-same* apple trees in name and characteristics, yet with varying degrees of oomph. Similarly, different varieties of a fruit type can be grafted onto all the same rootstock, resulting in mature trees that size differently, despite a consistent vigor down below. Thus a vigorous cultivar on semi-dwarf rootstock could be classified as large, whereas a less vigorous cultivar on the same rootstock may even be classified as small. Pruning also has an undeniable impact on size when it comes to maintaining a certain tree height.

Tree health ramifications definitely tie into this choice of rootstock. Apple and pear rootstocks should exhibit resistance to fire blight bacteria and crown rot fungi. Stone fruit rootstocks need to circumvent issues with root lesion nematodes and latent viruses. Certain roots do better in lighter, well-drained soils; others can tolerate heavier clay. Ability to deal with drought is very much a function of vigor. Winter hardiness certainly matters the farther north you go. Graft compatibility between the variety and the rootstock comes down to an agreeable scion-to-root combination: A brittle graft union may grow a tree but then snap under a full load of fruit not many years later. Nurseries take all this into account when promoting their selections.

The freestanding tree

The roots of any tree anchor what we see above to its spot of earth. Roots range far and deep seeking nutrients and moisture to sustain growth. The vigor of this action determines which rootstocks have the ability to stand on their own without staking or other physical support.

Every trademarked rootstock originated from a single seed, grown to maturity, and then selected for particular traits. Those with extreme dwarfing attributes are genetic runts, in truth, with less thrifty root systems that will require help throughout the life of that tree. Granted, commercial growers find an advantage in being able to manipulate smaller trees at less cost per tree, and thus you'll hear countless arguments as to why dwarfing stock is the way to go. Others make the case that less than full vigor is a lifetime compromise and thus argue that all rootstock should be *seedlings* grown from cross-pollinated seed—unique genetic specimens in every respect. Propagating a specific rootstock again and again for grafting purposes is done by cloning the original tree. This can be accomplished by pruning a sapling to produce side shoots, which when mounded in moist sawdust establish their own roots. Snap off these

Staking is not always just for dwarf trees. Leaders, frankly, don't necessarily cooperate with vertical intent. This freestanding tree needs central support in the form of a temporary stake to abet upward training as lean toward the sun has proven too alluring.

the ability to grow above deer browsing height will be reason enough for some of you. Good anchorage in the face of strong winds completes this package of potential advantages.[9]

The health divide in my mind comes down to whether a fruit tree requires lifetime support or whether that tree can be freestanding. There's plenty of room for diversity in this statement. Community orchardists know that having a mix of selections provides a form of "rootstock insurance" where the same variety has different degrees of harvest success in different years. Trees can range from half-sized to full-sized, with all these considered to be freestanding. The efficiency of biological management in the long run means more than all that fanfare for dwarf advantage from the commercial crowd.

Dwarf tree circumstance

A garden setting lends itself to a more intensive scale of management, so let's look at why some home orchardists might decide upon dwarfing rootstock nevertheless.

- The space issue is critical when you have a very small yard. Trees trained to *espalier* are confined to the plane of a wall or fence, and deliberately shaped by pinching shoot growth several times during the growing season (see "Zeroing in on espalier" in the pruning section ahead). No grower wants an overly vigorous rootstock working against this plan.
- Row management in the garden accommodates dwarf trees. Woodsy mulch defines a 3-foot-wide bed where the trees are staked at a spacing of 5–8 feet apart. Perennial herbs can be planted between these trees, but don't overdo companion planting with dwarf stock. Open garden ground lies beyond the permanently mulched area, be it for potatoes, garlic, or peas. These require cultivation anyway.[10] An oat cover crop follows the vegetable

rooted shoots and, voilà, you have *clonal rootstock* with one and the same genetics as the original parent (that indeed first grew from a seed).

My rootstock bias is defined by what you need to do as a grower to properly care for a tree.[8] Dwarf trees require limiting vegetative competition, the medicinal support of fungicides, regular irrigation, and trunk support in the form of a stake or trellis. Semi-standard and seedling trees, on the other hand, require far less fuss in maintaining fungal duff; they procure balanced nutrition and moisture through a vaster root system and thus are more likely to succeed with holistic approaches to disease. Simply having trees with harvest in late summer. Such management accounts for the timing of the trees' feeder root flush (learn more about "Root happenings" just ahead in this chapter) going into autumn. The oats winter-kill, perhaps allowing a no-till planting of squash or pickling cukes . . . which favors the late-spring feeder root flush of the fruit trees.

- Others might want to stack that guild design. Permaculture seeks to utilize all niches within an ecosystem. Fruit trees insist on sunlight access. This creates justification for going ever smaller on the edges. Many of the stone fruits suit here, but if you want apples in this sunny edge space, consider individually staked dwarf trees.

- You may want only a bushel or two of a certain variety at most. Dwarf trees certainly keep yields down.[11] But here's a caveat to remember: Learn to graft and you can have a dozen kinds of apples on one tree instead of a dozen demanding small trees.

Rootstock precepts

We're going to focus in on several good rootstocks for each fruit type in the chapters ahead. Nurseries often do the same, highlighting the roots that best serve their bioregion based on soil type, hardiness, and disease concerns; then they whittle even that selection down to a vigorous root and a more dwarfing type at a minimum. Offering every Malling, Mazzard, and Farmingdale cross would be too overwhelming to manage—and in the case of fledgling orchardists too overwhelming to even think about.

Apples offer a wider array of rootstock choice than any other fruit, with dozens upon dozens selected by research stations across the globe. Runted trees found in the wild in Asia in the time of Alexander the Great got the ball rolling and led to medieval gardens featuring the golden fruits of the small-growing Paradise apple. Plant breeders at the East Malling Research Station in England gathered many

Trees trained to espalier *are kept that way by pinching back shoot growth several times during the growing season. Photo courtesy of Denita Wallace.*

such selections in 1912 to classify more precisely. The semi-dwarf rootstock we know as Malling 7 (abbreviated as M.7) traces its cloned lineage back to an apple called Doucin Reinette that originated around 1688 in France. Further research at the Merton Research Station, also in England, involved crossing Northern Spy genetics into Malling progeny, in hopes of developing rootstocks resistant to woolly apple aphids. The semi-standard rootstock we know as Malling-Merton 111 (abbreviated as MM.111) was chosen as one worthy of commercial propagation from the numerous numbered selections started in 1952. Are we catching on to rootstock lingo here?[12]

Peaches are often put on seedling roots, so naming peach rootstock after the parent cultivar (whose pits were planted to provide relatively uniform roots) makes sense. You'll also see botanical names used on occasion, such as *Prunus americana* for wild plum seedlings. Sometimes there's a fascinating story to tell, such as that of Professor Reimer's discovery of two blight-resistant pears on the old Buckman homestead in Farmington, Illinois: Neither was quite perfected as a rootstock in and of itself, but together they have allowed nurserymen do all sorts of promising things with the crosses made between the original Old Home and Farmington cultivars.

Growing roots

Some of you might decide to graft your own trees. Rootstock can be purchased, be it in bundles of a hundred direct from a rootstock nursery or in less daunting amounts from a regional nursery selling grafted trees. A few inspired homesteaders among you invariably ask about doing this on the cheap.

The options for creating your own rootstock revolve around seedling genetics. Planting seeds results in baby trees. You won't have a known entity necessarily, but chances are such rootstock will be packed with vigor.[13] Fruit tree seed requires *stratification*, being the softening of the seed coat by variable weather in winter to enable inner germination. Seed thrown on the edge of a compost pile in fall will sprout come spring; similarly, seed placed in a ziplock bag in a slightly moist growing medium in the fridge for sixty days before being potted up will respond successfully.[14] Digging up a root sucker from the type of fruit tree you wish to graft is another way to get rootstock. Heading off a sapling and burying the resulting shoot response in well-composted sawdust should produce independent roots on those shoots in a year's time. Snap off the shoots with roots and you have rootstock.[15]

Don't overlook wild seedlings that pop up in the pasture or along the fence line. Such trees can be moved or left in place. John Bunker of Fedco Trees in Maine showed me a 150-year-old apple tree that had been grafted to Grimes Golden. The graft union was still evident, about 3 feet above the ground, where this apple variety had ever-so-slightly outpaced its understock in circumference.

GRAFTING

Here's an orcharding skill that will vastly enhance your fruit exploration horizons. Grafting involves a sharp knife and the mind-set of a surgeon—but don't let that intimidate you! Budwood from one cultivar (called the *scion*) is either attached or inserted into the growth tissue of a rooted tree; branch structure growing from beyond that graft point will now be the desired cultivar. This shift in varietal genetics at the graft union works with all fruits, noting that fruit type to fruit type is generally essential.[16]

Orchardists can propagate a new tree of the same exact cultivar only by grafting (as every seed represents a new variety as a result of cross-pollination). Rootstock can be *bench-grafted* in late winter for planting out in nursery beds in early spring. The resultant growth from a whip-and-tongue union can provide a suitable tree for transplanting out in the orchard the following spring, though less vigorous shoot response will likely require another year of growth in the nursery bed. All this happens from getting one of two scion buds to sprout forth beyond where the graft was made. Bench grafts make a dependable union that grows upright and straight. Not all your grafts will necessarily succeed, but no matter. Often buds down low on the rootstock will send forth several survival shoots. Select one of these (by snipping off the weaker ones early on) and the favored strong shoot can be grafted anew the following spring.[17]

Home orchardists can have much more fun than that, of course. Different varieties of a fruit type can be grafted onto one and the same tree. This might include transforming a branch to an effective pollinizer variety (like an edible crab apple), particularly if the trees you already have are not quite in tune pollination-wise, if not outright self-sterile. *Bridge grafting* can save the day when rodents girdle unprotected trees. Scions taken from watersprouts are grafted around the trunk to span the missing cambium zone. *Topworking* comes into play when you realize your fickle nature and decide to change varieties on an otherwise productive root system. New roots can even be put onto a stunted tree by *inarching*: Plant another rootstock as close to the base of the tree in question as possible; then, when the bark is slipping, splice this sapling into the trunk to maximize cambial contact. You'll see no increase in vigor the first year, but after that expect that tree to be back in business.

Opportunities abound for learning how to graft.

Regional fruit groups delve into the basics in annual workshops held every spring. Fruit enthusiasts generously share scionwood of all sorts at these gatherings, and rootstock will be available for sale. Members of the North American Fruit Explorers share advice online and in their quarterly publication, *Pomona*. Nearby growers simply need to be asked for their advice. We will start here by detailing what it takes to get a successful take with two of the grafting techniques most frequently used in orcharding. Despite all the words, keep in mind that grafting is fundamentally simple. You can indeed do this.

Grafting success

The odds for successful grafting go up considerably when you pay attention to detail. Cambium alignment involves matching up the green growth cells of the inner bark on the exposed scion to the same on the exposed rootstock. Take a first-year shoot and slice it open across the diagonal. Look closely. Between the heartwood and the dark outer bark is an inner green layer called the *cambium*. This is literally where the tree grows, nutrients are transported up and down, and water flows in the form of sap, and, yes, it's where growth cells can bond across a grafting cut and form *callus* tissue. Maximizing contact between the cambium of both the scion and the rootstock is what gives your graft its potential for future growth.

It all begins with an exceedingly sharp knife. A true grafting knife is flat on one side and honed on the other. This allows the blade to slide through supple shoot tissue and leave a completely flat plane in its wake. The angled cut used in grafting exposes more of the cambium zone: A straight cut across a shoot has nowhere near the elongated surface area of an angled cut. A practiced hand can make this cut on the order of 1½ inches long. The key word here is *practice*. You need to achieve a smooth plane on each cut so that bulges and raggedness alike do not interfere with cells touching and thus forming a bonding callus. Look through a magnifying glass and you will quickly see what I mean. Inexperienced people seemingly stutter while making this cut, concocting a series of angle-changing pull strokes rather than a confident single slice through the center of the shoot. (Note: One-year-old wood slices far more readily in this regard than two-year-old wood.) I hold the knife firmly, my index finger behind the blade and my thumb snugged tight to the base of the handle, coming in toward my body for more control. I hold scionwood at its top end and the rooted shoot at its base so as to have outward-bound growth when the resulting two angle cuts are aligned. Dwell on that point a moment: Scionwood doesn't have roots to reveal which end is up; you'll need to pay attention to upward-pointing bud growth to avoid putting buds on backward. I'll talk about size matching between shoots for the whip-and-tongue graft, but that won't be at all relevant for the bark inlay.

All this should be done with minimal human contact with the plane of the cut. Oils from our hands can interfere with cambium bonding.

Quality scions are integral to grafting success. Scionwood can be gathered anytime after the tree has gone dormant, though most growers wait till January and February.[18] Shoot size should be 3⁄16–5⁄16 inch in diameter; pieces that are too small tend to dehydrate quickly, and those any larger will not work up well.[19] If scionwood has been dehydrated or mildewed while in storage, the odds will be reduced that the graft will take. Budwood allowed to freeze (once off the tree) prior to grafting can be worthless.[20] Using wood older than the past season's growth also lessens chances. Be sure to tag the bundled wood from each variety clearly before wrapping it in lightly moistened newspaper, tucking it into a plastic bag, and storing it in the refrigerator or a cooler kept in an unheated space. Dipping the cut ends in paraffin (melted wax) seems to keep the cambium slightly more "juicy" for when the splices are made. Do not store scionwood with apples, as the ethylene gas from the maturing fruit may cause buds to abort.

The timing of grafts depends on whether you're working inside or outside. Bench grafts can be made as soon as you receive a rootstock order from the nursery throughout that final month or two of winter. Otherwise rootstock needs to be stored in a cool place and kept lightly moist until you are ready to get to work. Field grafting requires waiting until closer to budbreak to take knife in hand. Once sap starts to flow, the bark on smaller shoots will seem to slip, and that is your cue. I think of the week before that first peek of green tissue (in a growing fruit bud) reveals itself to as much as two weeks beyond as the ideal window for grafting outside. This period allows time for dormant scion tissue to set in place before being taxed by an activated growth process when the days fully warm up.[21] Sooner is better with apples and pears, as the resulting shoot growth that summer will be that much greater. Experience has also shown that successful takes will considerably outnumber failures if you work within this window, whereas ever-later grafting will see the odds reverse exponentially. Peaches and nectarines demand more warmth for callusing to occur, which is the reason summer budding is preferable with the larger stone fruits.

What you do with those completed bench grafts has import as well. A healing temperature of 50–60°F (10–16°C) is ideal for growing callus tissue with apples, pears, and even plums. This is cool enough to keep buds from waking up too quickly and yet far warmer than the temperatures late winter offers outside at night. Peaches and nectarines require around 70–85°F (21–29°C) for dormant grafting. Hold the bench grafts in a suitable space for about a week. If the ground is still frozen after this time, find a cooler location in an outbuilding to slow down the pace of bud development. I pack completed bench grafts into flat trays, keeping the roots lightly moist in a woodsy mulch or shredded newspaper. A seaweed solution is best for wetting the roots, as cytokinins in cold-processed kelp contribute to the growth of callus tissue. Should bud growth begin before you get these young'uns in the ground, which is not a bad thing at all, harden off this nursery stock for a day or two in the outside air, just as you would garden transplants coming out of the greenhouse.

Whip and tongue

The common whip-and-tongue graft relies on the cambium zones of both the scion and the rootstock making intimate contact along bark edges that are matched in size. Hold the scion along the rootstock or the shoot on an existing tree. Height of grafting on the bare rootstock is usually 4–8 inches above ground level. Move the scion up or down the rootstock until you see the spot where the relative diameter of each is about the same. Snip off the scion stick about 2 inches below this matching point, but leave the top long (more than two buds' worth) so you have more of a handle when making the angle cut on the scion. Now *do what needs to be done* with that confidently held knife of yours, taking care to make cuts on both shoots so that the relative length of exposed tissue is approximately the same.

Let's assume nearly full alignment has been achieved when holding the two cuts together. Maybe one cut has a longer tail; maybe the other cut narrows at its base more than the other. Make it your goal to have 80 percent visual contact. Keep in mind that getting too fussy often, makes things worse.

A locking mechanism can be achieved with a whip-and-tongue splice by making a slight receiving notch in the plane of each angle cut. Position this approximately halfway down on the scion cut and halfway up on the understock cut. Wiggle your knife into each cut at a slightly steeper angle than the cut itself, going into the shoot wood ⅛ inch or so. These notches interlock when the two shoot pieces are pulled together and are spaced so that the outer cambium "perfectly" aligns. Some grafters skip this step, particularly when attaching smaller scionwood, but that puts the onus entirely on the wrap to hold the scion in place while callusing occurs.

The scion should be trimmed to two buds in length before making the actual joining. Otherwise the long end tends to get in the way of wrapping the union. Never leave more than this, as excess buds will require too much in the way of water and nutrient support. Often a shoot will develop from both buds, and once

GRAFTING SUPPLIES

Every grafter has a preferred way of doing things. The supplies you need follow from there.

Cut. You can jump right in for less than $20 with a Victorinox folding grafting knife. The blade is honed on just one side to achieve that smooth cambium cut. Some folks manage with a bulkier razor utility knife. Whatever you use, keep it sharp!

Wrap. Rubber grafting strips pull the edges of a whip-and-tongue splice together exceedingly well. Hold the band on the understock with your one thumb and then wrap upward. I leave space between wraps going up, so to be able to see that side-to-side alignment hasn't slipped, go for full closure on the way back down the length of the union, and then overlap the other end of the grafting strip to knot the two ends together. Don't be afraid of pulling the rubber too tight, as this optimizes cambium closure. The frustrating aspect is when the band slips out from under your finger and quickly unwinds. Electrician's splicing tape will be self-fusing and, if given a stretch before wrapping, works nearly as well. Masking tape is cheaper and flexible enough. Grafts covered in parafilm (a clear, stretchy polyethylene tape that deteriorates in sunlight) are not going to dry out but still require a more substantial wrap underneath to hold pressure on the union.

Seal. Trowbridge's Grafting Wax smells great, seals well, and doesn't crack, but requires heat to liquefy. Doc Farwell's latex grafting compound goes on easily with a brush, doesn't get brittle when dry, stretches as the graft grows, and remains in place for years at a time, providing a bright yellow marker to the graft union. Treekote (a black asphalt emulsion) works in the cold, dries quickly if it's going to rain, and comes with a brush attached to the container cap for smearing directly over the grafting rubber and onto cut surfaces. Long ago a graft would have been tied with cotton string, then straight cow manure slathered on to cover the entire works.

---

you decide which is the stronger response (the first to reach 2–4 inches in length), prune the other off so all growth the rest of that first summer concentrates in the chosen one. Similarly, any shoots developing along the rootstock should be rubbed off as well.

Wrap the graft union with a rubber grafting strip so as to pull all cambium edges tight against one another. Some orchardists opt for using black electrician's tape or parafilm instead. Do not extend the wrapping over the scion buds. Apply a sealant to make sure cut surfaces will not dry out, including the naked tip of the scion. I coat over the grafting rubber as well, just to be sure any gaps in the wrap coverage aren't exposed. This special rubber will begin to decompose in several weeks, so, for all intents and purposes, the whip-and-tongue union is launched on the day it's made. Those using other wrap options need to come back in a month or two to carefully snip away the tape (about the same time you choose the stronger shoot response) so as to prevent the unyielding tape from girdling into new growth.

One last thing: *Label each graft as you complete it.* Mixing up scion varieties happens quickly unless you are meticulous in the order you go about all this.

Bark inlay graft

A fruit tree can be changed over to a new variety by bark-grafting its central leader and principal lateral

Making a slight notch on the scion piece and the corresponding understock helps to lock the graft union in place while callusing occurs. Photo by Mark Rawlings.

branches right at the plane of the removal cut. Commercial growers *topwork* entire blocks to a current market favorite at much less cost than replanting. Fruiting often begins in the third year after converting such trees, as the growth emanating from established root systems can be phenomenal.

Select branches of the tree that are 1–4 inches in diameter for *bark inlay* grafting.[22] This is best done in those immediate weeks following the appearance of green tissue when the bark is slipping on the bigger wood of the tree.[23] Make a clean heading cut where the stem is smooth and free of knots, being careful not to tear the bark when the weighted branch falls away. Take your knife and firmly scribe a vertical cut about 1½ inches long into the bark. Be sure to go deep enough to slice through the cambium layer. Make two such slits on opposite sides for branches that are 2 inches in diameter or less, adding one more slit for

each inch of increase in branch diameter—thus a 3-inch branch would see three slits made so that three scions can be inserted. You can use the tip of the knife to ever-so-slightly wedge open the bark at the top of the slice for receiving each scion.

The scions are cut just as for a whip-and-tongue union, but with some added refinements. Very carefully peel off a fine strip of outer bark on both edges of the angle cut to reveal sideways cambium—this will make fuller contact with the surrounding bark cambium. I also like to nip off the point of the scion angle—this helps in pushing the scion into place while also exposing a nudge of cambium outward toward the bark cover.

This scion wedge can now gently be pushed into place behind the bark of the branch, being careful to keep it centered between the two flaps of bark as they slide apart to receive the scion. The cut surface of the

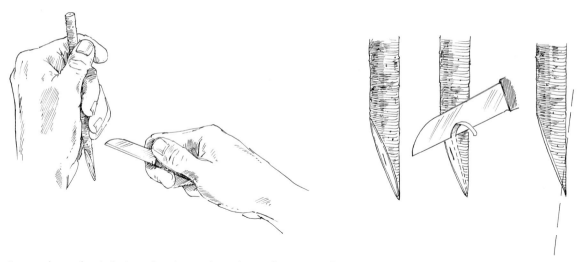

Preparing the scion for a bark inlay graft involves visualizing where cambium contact will best occur. Edging both sides of the smooth cut and beveling a chip tip at the point reveals additional surface area where that can happen.

scion faces the inner wood of the branch. Push the scion in so that hardly a vestige of its cut surface can be seen above the plane of the cut branch.

Parafilm tape (½ inch wide) is ideal to wrap this type of graft. Wrap the branch circumference tightly to ensure good contact between bark and scion. Do this the whole way down the length of the slits, around and around the branch. I strive to catch the rim of the cut with the parafilm as well to help seal the exposed bark edge of the branch. A simple tuck of this stretchy tape over itself and then pulled tightly will hold these wraps in place. The clear plastic acts like a solarium to provide a good callusing temperature as well as preventing desiccation. The remaining exposed surfaces must then be covered completely with a sealant. Be sure to dab gook into any space where each scion meets the cut plane of the branch . . . and don't forget coating those scion tips above the requisite two buds per scion. Plan on coming back to your bark grafts in eight to twelve weeks to lightly snip away the plastic once the tissue integration is complete.

Choosing which shoots to keep for the long haul shifts somewhat with this type of graft. Each scion will likely take—but if not, there's some degree of assurance that at least one will. Treat each scion as before, choosing the stronger bud response once the shoots

get to be 2–4 inches in length. Let a single shoot from every scion grow out at each branch location that first summer. This is necessary to eventually produce a full callus ring around the pruning cut itself. Next spring, depending on what you see, you can either remove the extra shoots entirely (on smaller-diameter cuts) or head back all but one shoot at each branch location to further develop the closure callus for an additional growing season or two. Many years down the road you won't even be able to see where this process was done on a vigorously growing tree.

One last trick of the trade comes into play in further assuring topworking success. Leave at least one nurse limb as a photosynthesis sink for the roots during that first season if you're doing over an entire tree structure. Such limbs can be pruned away the following year or left to serve as a pollinizer for the new grafted variety.

Multi-variety tree

Henry Lang up in Milan, New Hampshire, had a single apple tree with nearly 230 varieties grafted onto it. Tags fluttered throughout this tree in an attempt to keep track of which branch bore which fruit. It's a complicated undertaking—imagine pruning under the constraint of mistakenly clipping off all the budwood of Magog Red Streak with a single snip—yet

The scion buds on this completed bark graft are just beginning to swell.

Four peaches planted together form a varietal vase with nicely suppressed vigor. Photo courtesy of David Ulmer.

any home orchardist can have a lot of fun putting a modest number of varieties on a single tree.

Graft scionwood of different varieties onto an existing tree in early spring. A young tree in training could readily have the chosen varieties spliced onto each pencil-sized scaffold branch. A vigorous wild tree has the advantage of established maturity, particularly where borers are numerous and browsing deer devastate young plantings. Such a tree may be beautifully shaped and healthy and, given a few well-positioned grafts, could begin bearing palatable fruit.

Look for small wood near the trunk on which to place whip-and-tongue grafts, be it a watersprout in need of spreading or lateral growth with good scaffold potential. Grafting in the tree's interior allows a whole branch to eventually become a new variety, which is much easier to keep track of than twig wood in the outer canopy. The bark inlay graft is useful on more sizable branches. Time this transformation to when bark is definitely "slipping" on the tree during those weeks following green tip. Be sure to place a tag on each grafted branch-to-be so you'll know what's what later on.

A successful graft might grow 3 feet or more that first summer if tree vigor is good and competing shoots have been somewhat pruned away to allow sunlight to the new wood. Chosen shoots can then be bent under

an existing branch or tied into place that next winter for greater lateral reach. Prune away the undesired portions of the tree slowly as each grafted branch fills in its envisioned space. A few years down the road the wild branch structure will be gone, leaving you an apple tree with Arkansas Black, Fireside, Dudley, and Ashmead's Kernel forming the lower scaffold; Oriole, Rambo, and Melrose midway; and an entire new top of St. Edmund's Russet.

A multiple-variety tree provides a good way to test different fruit cultivars at your site as well as grow scionwood to graft onto rootstock. The example above was apple, but this mixing of varieties works just as well with pears and the stone fruits. I'll be making the case for the plum thicket ahead: Here, hybrid plum varieties are grafted onto individual root suckers to form a pollinator's paradise within the thicket. Dave Wilson Nursery out in California advocates a four-in-a-hole plan for all stone fruit: Four growth-compatible cultivars are planted together (about 18 inches apart in a square pattern) in a large hole, thus forming a varietal vase offering four types of mouthwatering apricots, nectarines, and wonderful crosses like the pluot. Similarly, you could create a high-density hedgerow with a dozen different peach cultivars planted 36 inches apart. Sunlight envelops this varietal hodgepodge as a single tree in its own right.

Heeling in bareroot trees can buy a couple of weeks' time when life simply gets too frantic. Be sure to tamp the soil well and water generously to eliminate air pockets around these waiting roots.

PLANTING CARE

The best time to plant a tree was twenty years ago; the second-best time is now.

—Chinese proverb

Fruit trees and berries should be planted as early in the spring as possible after the soil has dried out sufficiently. Soil preparation the year before helps in getting nursery stock planted that much earlier. Cold soil temperatures will promote the development of calluses at the tips of any torn roots. Normal spring rains will then settle the soil around the roots before leaf growth occurs. Catch this timing right and your trees will slide into full gear with nary a backward look. Planting delays do happen, however, and in that case orders from the nursery can be tucked away in moist wood shavings or the like in a cool place for a week or two. If it's going to be longer (you're off to the Bahamas!) bareroot plants should be *heeled in* the garden until proper planting holes can be dug. Trees planted after leaves have started to grow will experience transplant shock, in part because feeder root growth has begun. This can potentially stunt both the upper tree and root development, so don't wait too long. Heavy pruning can help, and reliable irrigation is better—but respecting tree dynamics is the best strategy of all.

Growers in Zone 6 and south should take advantage of fall planting. The root growth that takes place in mild winters gets the young tree established and raring to go by spring. Fully dormant trees can be transplanted from mid-November through December. Larger two-year nursery trees suffer less transplant shock when fall-planted and thus retain a head start on one-year whips. Roots continue to grow even though tops are dormant in regions where soil temperatures remain above 40°F (4°C). Damage to the roots is more likely to occur in northern zones from the frost-heaving of recently disturbed soil. Mulching a new tree after the ground freezes can alleviate this concern . . . just be sure to wrap tender young trunks to protect them from voles.

Trees can be purchased directly from nurseries as bareroot stock or already potted up at a local garden center. You might even be able to obtain trees of bearing age from a local orchardist (admittedly, a big-bucks proposition suitable mainly for those without patience). I recommend the bareroot option hands down: Young whips do not go through transplant shock like more sizable trees that have been waiting, rootbound, in bundled soil for a year or more. People tempted by the bigger tree right there that very day frequently end up making a less-than-stellar variety choice, transplanting a tree that's in full leaf (definitely not recommended), and then compromising future growth for years to come by not loosening up the roots so they can reach out beyond the matted disaster often found in the pot. Repeat after me: *I will plan ahead and arrange for bareroot stock to plant out at the right time.*

Prior to planting, you should never allow the roots of any plant to dry out. Soaking the roots in a bucket of seaweed solution will help reduce transplant stress; do this the night before planting and pledge not to leave roots soaking for more than twenty-four hours. A relatively calm, cloudy day is preferable to a sunny, windy day for planting. Be sure each tree and fruiting shrub is individually labeled to identify who's who in the planting plan. Brambles often come bundled in tens for planting out in beds. Digging holes ahead of time for a planting session can be more efficient than a "dig then plant, dig then plant" routine.

A proper hole

The tree hole obviously needs to be large enough to accommodate the root system. However, digging a hole significantly larger than that preps the immediate soil zone for root outreach. A 3-foot-diameter hole generally fits the bill. I will trench out a channel for an excessively long root rather than curl it in toward the trunk. Loosening the subsoil in the bottom of a 16- to 20-inch-deep hole provides additional leeway in setting the height of the graft union aboveground. A buried graft union will eventually establish its own roots, which override the desired dwarfing effect of clonal rootstock. I aim to keep the graft union 4 inches above the soil line, planting only slightly deeper than the tree may have grown in the nursery. Keep in mind that the settling of looser soils may bring the graft union down another inch or so. Trees on seedling roots are the one exception: The graft union can be buried if you wish to encourage self-rooting of the scion cultivar.

Do not mix massive amounts of compost with the soil in the planting hole.[24] The roots will soon extend much farther into the surrounding earth for long-term

sustenance. A super-enriched planting hole gives roots little reason to leave the home base. I prefer to backfill the tree only with the soil that came out of the hole, with the more friable topsoil placed against the roots and the subsoil used to finish filling the hole.[25] Tree nutrition in the years ahead will come from above in the form of orchard compost and ramial wood chips to build that desirable fungal duff, where 90 percent of the feeder roots will be found. Extension advice to load young fruit plantings up on nitrate fertilizers for the first several years will work against the fungal connection we seek for long-term tree health.

Roughly serrating the sides of a hole dug in heavy soil with a digging fork helps fracture a too-smooth clay finish. Growing roots need to readily penetrate into the surrounding soil; otherwise they may circle around the glazed bowl that can inadvertently result from clay particle adhesion caused by digging the hole. Piling good soil to one side of the planting hole and less loamy subsoil to another side as you dig allows you to systematically plant without compacting the turned earth as you maneuver about. I sprinkle a pound of rock phosphate (for early root development) and the same amount of Azomite (for trace nutrients) onto these soil piles and into the tree hole itself, stirring all together in the planting process.

Berries are more straightforward (not having been grafted in the first place), because the soil line evident from nursery days marks the very goal for planting day. Preparing the bed during the previous year makes planting a quick task, particularly for brambles. Use a hoe to create a deep-enough planting furrow, then line out cane stock at the recommended spacing.

Trees and fruiting bushes planted in containers will require much more frequent watering and feeding with compost tea and herbal brews. Porous-walled pots will lose moisture rapidly compared with a thick-walled tub or whiskey barrel. Drainage holes are a must to prevent roots from sitting in standing water; a gravel layer at the very bottom is strongly suggested to facilitate this drainage. Suggested soil mix for potting up: equal parts compost, perlite, peat moss, and decomposing forest leaf litter. Ramial mulch atop this soil is the right biological touch. Containerized trees eventually get severely rootbound but can be a fun novelty while the plants thrive.

Mycorrhizal root dips

A young tree with fungal allies from day one has that much better a chance of succeeding. A wee bit of mycorrhizal root investment is a worthy idea, because all commercial rootstocks lack this basic biological connection. Planting fields are fumigated, tilled, and otherwise manipulated as a matter of course. Very few nurseries in turn choose to inoculate the trees created by grafting onto rootstock purchased from these big commercial propagators. The soil where you're planting an orchard doesn't necessarily lack the mycorrhizal species needed for fruit trees—that depends on landscaping history and the proximity of other tree roots. Yet jump-starting a barren root system makes sense to me, as it can take several years for disturbed soil to otherwise be restored in this important fungal respect. You have two options to ensure mycorrhizal presence from the get-go: one to be purchased, the other to be gifted.

Root dips contain spore inoculum of a number of widely adapted mycorrhizal species suitable for deciduous trees. Rarely is there just one fungus type per root system, and at least one species in these products will work for any soil/plant/climate situation. The dormant spores will become activated once they come in contact with the growing roots of your fruit trees. These horticultural hydrogels cling to the roots, dipped right at planting time. Fungal mycelium persists within the roots that first year and then grows out into the surrounding soil the next spring and every year thereafter.

Quality inoculum is key. Mycorrhizal Applications in Oregon has earned a reputation for putting out reliable products.[26] Home orchardists can find numerous brands at local garden centers whose spore inoculum comes from this company.[27] Be aware that cheaper products in chain stores are often made with hyphal

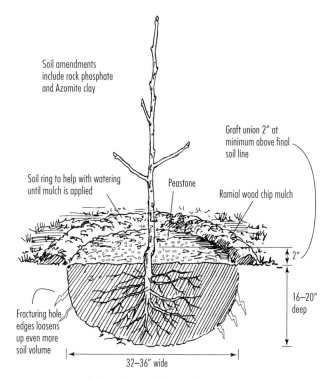

Soil amendments include rock phosphate and Azomite clay

Graft union 2″ at minimum above final soil line

Soil ring to help with watering until mulch is applied

Peastone

Ramial wood chip mulch

2″

16–20″ deep

Fracturing hole edges loosens up even more soil volume

32–36″ wide

Digging a generous hole for planting a fruit tree allows a greater volume of soil to be loosened and prepped for root growth to come.

fragments rather than genuine mature spores. I've long worked with BioOrganics in California, another reputable source, but probably more for community orchardists, as each 3-pound container of their root dip contains enough inoculum for several hundred trees.[28] Humic acids are a good fungal food when mycorrhizae are getting established.[29] Another underlying purpose of this root investment is to set a fire under you to foster this fungal ecosystem year after year with woodsy compost, liquid fish sprays, and ramial mulch.

Soil from a healthy forest ecosystem can be used to inoculate existing home orchard plantings as well. Think of this as akin to Grandma's sourdough bread yeast: A small ball of dough is set aside each time to enliven the next batch. Similarly, a small amount of topsoil taken from the root zone of a wild apple tree (or any young hardwood stand for that matter) should gift your recently planted fruit trees with mycorrhizal species absolutely suited to

Take time to spread root laterals in all directions to both anchor the young tree and maximize nutrient reach. Upper-level roots should be held up with one hand while the first layer gets backfilled with the other. Photo by Mark Rawlings.

empowering a new friend that may well be here for generations to come. Shall I just stick it in the ground, oblivious of the way of roots? I think not. Envision what's at stake here as you gently introduce these roots to Mother Earth once again.

A slight mound of loosened soil in the bottom of the planting hole helps in spreading out the roots. The very bottom roots are laid out across this mound. Press soil firmly on top of these as you backfill, taking care to recognize that the next layer of roots should be held up with one hand as you do this. That second layer of roots now goes atop the soil in between—and being thus supported won't tear off the rootstock. People who plop all roots in a single downward direction simply don't understand that a living tree is not a mere fence post. The roots should radiate in all directions around the tree just as they grew in the nursery bed, thus improving anchorage and nutrient access from the outset. With a little forethought, a rootless pocket can be left for a stake 6 inches from the trunk on the leeward side of dwarfing stock. Puddle water in the root zone to collapse any remaining air pockets before replacing the top level of soil. *Dancing a happy jig* is one way to approach a final tamping-down of moist soil and the straightening-out of any errant lean to the newly planted tree.

your bioregion. Subtleties need to be observed in this process to assure success.[30] Hyphae (brought in from other soil) have a limited capacity to grow and will die within a few days if they do not encounter a susceptible root. The upshot here is you can bring a quart of soil for each of your trees and immediately spread it beneath decomposing wood mulch, where the finer part of each tree's permanent root system will be found. Think of this as a mycorrhizal side-dressing for fruit trees planted a year or two before you learned of this advice.

Spread those roots

Every time I plant a tree I'm aware of the intimacy of this moment. That root system in my hands will be

Heading height

Nursery whips are headed back at planting time to encourage specific growth in the young tree. Shearing off the leader shoot at a certain height will do two things. The buds immediately below the cut will be invigorated to shoot for the sky, with anywhere from three to five shoots forming sharp vertical crotch angles. Shortly you will choose one of these to become the new leader. *Auxin hormone* flow is significantly affected by the *apical dominance* of this multiple bud response, by which I mean that the additional *terminal buds* now involved will strongly suppress *lateral growth* in the buds immediately below. (I know these terms are challenging, but hang in there!) Farther down on this pruned whip, other buds will respond to a buildup

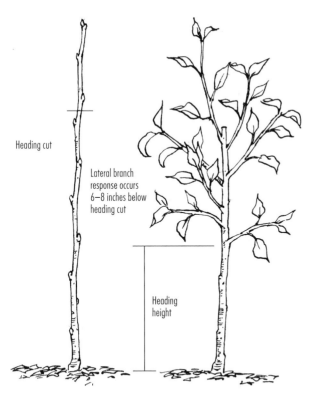

Heading cut

Lateral branch
response occurs
6–8 inches below
heading cut

Heading
height

You determine the height at which first branches will radiate off the trunk by making a heading cut to whips at planting time. Bud response up high will come in the form of a crow's foot, causing laterals to push out a handspan below the heading cut and these upper vertical shoots.

A well-shaped tree from the nursery comes with a selection of lateral branches (called feathers) already in place at a reasonable height.

of *cytokinin hormones* that reverse the inhibitory effect of auxin on lateral growth in the buds above. This is exactly what you want for this young whippersnapper! All this horticultural gibberish points to our ability as orchardists to choose at what height scaffold branches are going to be encouraged on the tree-to-be. Let's go for the clincher: *Heading height* marks the distance aboveground where the first layer of fruit-bearing branches comes off the trunk.[31]

A one-year whip is snipped at 28–42 inches above the ground, based on the vigor of the rootstock and the vision you have for a freestanding tree. The eventual branch structure being sought here will happen 6–8 inches below this heading cut. This helps compensate as well for any broken roots (lost in digging up the tree or the shipping process) that needed to be pruned away prior to planting. When

newly planted trees are not headed severely enough, they will develop first laterals well above the desired heading height. Scaffold branches on a full-sized fruit tree that start around 3 feet above the ground are just about right.[32] A portion of the fruit will be able to be picked without a ladder, and yet most fruit buds will be above deer browsing height and up in the breezes that help deter fungal disease.

Every tree coming from the nursery is not necessarily going to be a whip. Advice about heading height accordingly calls for some refinement when you are planting a *feathered tree*. Prime nursery stock often will have substantial side branches already, particularly if the grafted tree took two growing seasons to come of size. Choose a few of the strongest and best placed of

The vertical bud response of trees headed at planting time will need to be corrected when upper shoots reach several inches in length. Select a strong shoot to keep as the leader; remove the other vertical shoots by pinching, or with hand pruners.

these laterals to stay as permanent branches at a desirable height. If the reach of these side shoots seems out of proportion with the diameter of the leader, growers will cut such "feathers" back to an outboard-facing bud. On the other hand, leaving an excessive amount of small side shoots this first year will divide the energy of the tree and thus hinder strong side branches from forming. The heading cut to the leader itself will be made 8–12 inches above the uppermost lateral left on more developed nursery stock.

There's one last thing to do this first growing season. Choosing a central leader from that crow's foot of three or so vertical shoots induced by the initial heading cut is important. I come back to all

newly planted trees in late June to pinch off all but the strongest of these shoots with narrow crotch angles. These uppermost shoots need to reach several inches in length before doing this to allow the excess auxin being produced (by the collective terminal buds of the crow's foot) to work its will on the buds below. The chosen leader can now focus on its singular upward mission while the developing laterals below do their thing.

Growing productive wood

Fruit trees do better without immediate sod competition when first planted. Clean cultivation of the entire orchard was recommended at the turn of the last century, with a soil-building cover crop planted in late summer to provide winter cover. Mulch is the more biological choice, as we can add substantial organic matter in the process. Enabling young trees to grow wood through heavy mulching or shallow hoeing will mimic what canopy shading will eventually do in the bearing years of the tree. There's simply not enough branch structure yet to shade the ground below to suppress weed growth.

Ring mulching a newly planted tree differs from the haphazard mulching described earlier. The prime choices for mulching material remain either ramial wood chips or spoiled hay. Yet because we specifically want to knock back sod intrusion for several years, it's worth going to some extra trouble. Thick layers of newspaper or cardboard beneath the mulch cuts off light to any competing plants that still may be root-invested and capable of making a comeback in the immediate area around the tree planting hole.[33] The diameter of this ring should start at a minimum of 5 feet for the first-year tree and extend to as much as 6–8 feet several years hence to accommodate the growing tree. Keep in mind that peastone should fill the inner ring of such a mulch doughnut, creating a weed-free inner circle some 2 feet in diameter around the trunk. Organic mulches right up against the trunk of the tree will retain too much moisture. The peastone can be replenished anytime if subsequent forking out of root

Maintaining openness at the base of the tree over the years is especially critical with young trees. A garden fork can be used to loosen the soil for weeding out grass runners, peastone can be renewed as desired, and trunks can be checked for borer intrusions all at the same time. Photo by Mark Rawlings.

runners from stubborn quack grass penetrate the outer ring mulch.[34]

Investing in organic fertilizer these first years to build wood is highly recommended. A basic organic blend like Pro-Gro (5-3-4) ups the nitrogen ante to ensure solid growth. Hold back the fertilizer in the first year of planting—let those roots get established with the soil at hand—and begin the mineral feeding program in subsequent springs. A quart-sized yogurt container (or a 1-pound coffee can) tends to be my official measure. A mix of protein meals, nitrate of soda, humates, and rock dusts gets sprinkled across the mulch zone and the peastone. Stirring this into the topsoil takes place only if I have a need to fork out excess dandelions or encroaching sod . . . otherwise the organic elements will wash down to the waiting microbes and thus the feeder roots of the young tree.

The rate here builds over the years, starting with a half-full container and increasing threefold by year five. That amounts to 1–3 pounds, increasing by ½ pound per year. The radius of spread increases accordingly as well, from 4–6 to 8–10 feet, anticipating the roots radiating out farther and farther with each new season. Orchard compost gets applied each fall out in the mulch zone (but not over the peastone) to boost organic matter levels. This feeding program needs to be adjusted according to the tree in front of you, of course, as rich soil in some locations may fuel plenty of growth without additional measures. Annual shoot growth exceeding 24–30 inches would be considered too rampant. Less vigorous trees, on the other hand, that come into bearing late would benefit from carrying on this plan (at the 3-pound plateau) for another year or two.

Watering

Once leafed out, all fruit tree and berry plantings need regular watering throughout the first growing season. The rule of thumb here is 1 inch of rain a week. That translates to a 5-gallon bucketful per first-year tree in my roundabout mind, perhaps half that on a blueberry bush. You do need to water in such a way that the water goes into the ground where the tree sits. A mulch ring around individual trees helps prevent surface runoff. Home orchardists in southern zones are advised to provide such a drink at least twice a week in hot weather because of evaporation.

Fruiting plants in containers need to be checked almost daily.

Let's look at the hierarchy of roots in the soil. Woody plants have a framework consisting of primary and secondary permanent roots, transport and storage roots, nonwoody feeder roots, and root hairs.[35] The feeder roots and root hairs are the most important part of the root system for uptake of water and nutrients from the soil. These are particularly sensitive to drought. Keep in mind that practically all of a tree's overall root system is located in the top 3 feet of the soil, and a good portion of that resides in the top

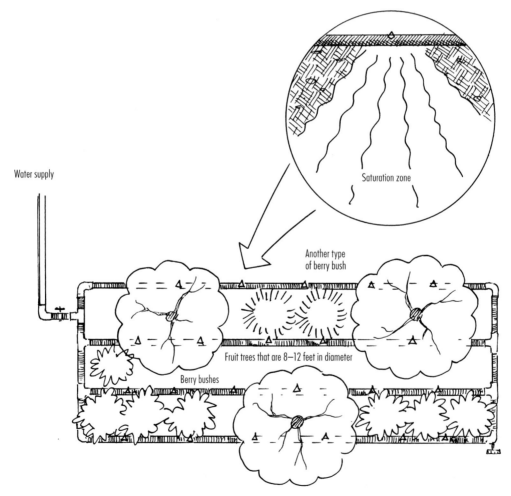

Water supply

Saturation zone

Another type of berry bush

Fruit trees that are 8–12 feet in diameter

Berry bushes

Drip irrigation provides an inverted moisture cone at each emitter. Although substantial areas of the surface may appear dry, the moist areas at each drip site merge beneath the surface of the soil. Proper planning for irrigation lines typically will involve straddling tree rows in order to provide moisture throughout the full root zone.

foot. This is especially true of the feeder roots. Dry soil causes feeder roots and root hairs to shrivel and become nonfunctional. As a consequence, water deficit develops more quickly than we might be inclined to think.

Mature trees on semi-standard and standard rootstock can likely be dry-farmed in deep soils, but dwarf rootstock will need regular watering unless it rains consistently throughout the summer. Let's zero in on that prescribed inch of rain per week for those of you who require long-term irrigation of fruit plantings. It turns out that 0.6 gallon of water per square foot provides that rainfall equivalent. Consider a single tree for a moment. Roots extend beyond the dripline by half again the height of the tree, and likely go considerably deeper than the tree is tall. So water requirements for mature trees that are calculated on the basis of dripline square footage should be doubled to account for root reach. Surface application will cover the "true diameter" of the tree, whereas drip irrigation is definitely a matter of thinking in terms of *point application*.

Drip irrigation systems are efficient water users but can result in more localized wet spots, leading to confined root systems and localized leaching of nutrients. A good half of the root area needs to be wetted at a minimum, which is why split-row application should be considered in an irrigation layout for fruit plantings. The ground surface may appear mostly dry, but it's the inverted moisture cone from each point of application that counts. Irrigating in the late afternoon and through the night increases water use efficiency.

Overwatering creates anaerobic zones. Oxygen being transported to the root system becomes negligible; alcohols produced in such a saturation fermentation of the soil kill beneficial organisms outright. Planting advice to avoid wet ground in the first place springs from wanting to keep orchard ground under fungal protection. Good fungi need their living conditions to be aerobic, just as you and I do. However, bacteria dominate along with pathogenic fungi when the soil stays saturated. This in turn leads to problems with various root and crown rot conditions. One common mistake first-time orchardists make is literally drowning trees in the first season, especially apricots and cherries. Stone fruit species are the most sensitive to flooding, which can be seen by wilting of the leaves within several days' time followed by dropping of the leaves and outright death if the roots of these trees remain underwater for much longer than a week.

Nutrient exchange depends on proper moisture levels as well. Calcium, which is the foundation of all biological systems, requires water to move up through the xylem of the tree's trunk. Post-harvest irrigation in dry regions helps increase calcium levels in the fruiting spurs for next season.

SOIL FERTILITY

The nutrition taken up by the fruit we grow in turn nourishes us and our families. And yet *soil fertility* is too often viewed as solely a means to pump up yields . . . sending the concept of nutrient density for health's sake out the window. Orchardists need to understand the place of soil chemistry in this bigger picture. Nutrient balance is a dynamic achievement that ties to many factors beyond what comes in a bag from the fertilizer store. Our role is to get the house in order so that the soil biology can then run on cruise control.

Biology rules!
The soil food web in all its diversity and complexity trumps reductionist soil chemistry many times over. New orchardists reading this book are by now up to speed, but those of you with fixed notions about fertilizer may have some cultural and generational brainwashing to overcome.

A healthy soil consists of a surprising amount of porous space, a nearly equal volume of pulverized rock, and 5 percent (give or take) organic matter. This *living skin* of our planet rests on a solid bed of rock—the parent material from which the mineral

FUNGAL DUFF ZONE

The root reach of a fruiting tree is impressive, stretching out beyond the dripline and going as deep as the permanent water table allows. This entire rhizosphere is rich in biological activity, especially in the humus layer found at the surface of the soil. Extending fungal duff management slightly beyond the dripline is all about knowing where the roots be.

portion was formed. The trillions upon trillions upon trillions of organisms within this medium are what make life possible on earth. Biologists describe soil as a marriage between the mineral world and the organic world. Many of the elements essential for plant life are provided by the molecular structure of the minerals. It's the organic partnership of the microorganism community that transforms these nutrients into bioavailable forms.

Bacteria, fungi, nematodes, protozoans, and arthropods are constantly shuffling nutrients back and forth. The inorganic ions dissolved in water and/or making up mineral molecules become attached to organic compounds within these living organisms and eventually get banked in humus. When organisms take up mineral elements to construct cells, enzymes, and other organic compounds necessary for growth, they are said to be *immobilizing* nutrients.[36] When organisms excrete inorganic waste compounds, they are said to be *mineralizing* nutrients. This back-and-forth process keys upon available carbon (the energy source provided by organic matter) to fuel shifts in microbe populations. Plenty of carbon allows a diverse biomass to increase dramatically, resulting in soil nutrients being absorbed and thus immobilized in the cells of fungi and bacteria. When the balance tilts the other way—with not enough carbon to support the microbial biomass—the population drops and cells die, releasing soluble nutrients in unbound mineral form that can be taken up by plants. Feeder roots with mycorrhizal association have a healthy affinity for microbe-derived nutrients. Yet there's more to this story.

The proximity of microbial action in the rhizosphere is what makes mineralized inorganics far more bioavailable than the soluble inorganics commonly provided by modern-day chemical fertilizer.[37] A dead, inert soil (biologically speaking) has only the latter to offer—its mineral nutrient value basically being determined by the use of such fertilizers in the first place. Under this scenario, a vast proportion of mineral salts drain off into the water table, as roots are capable of absorbing only the tiny bit that enters the rhizosphere. The odds of the plant's roots benefiting from much of a chemical fertilizer application are not unlike your chances of winning a big lottery jackpot . . . and thus the constant call for more and more fertilizer to be applied as a crutch in an impoverished agriculture system.

Here's the ace up the sleeve offered by vibrant soil biology: Mineralization is a two-way street. Those soluble nutrients produced by the microbes but not taken up immediately by the roots go right back into the next generation of microbes. There's rhythm here—a responsive beat, a tidal sensibility even. Plant roots in turn exude carbon, which keeps microbe diversity and the immobilization/mineralization balance humming right along. It's the life aspect of the soil that introduces and enforces the whole concept of balanced nutrition, as opposed to the overstocked flooding of the reductionist chemical approach.

Let's zoom in even closer. The real story behind weathering mineral rock to release nutrients includes numerous bacteria that live in association with mycorrhizal fungal hyphae. These bacteria secrete acids that can etch rock, thus securing it for uptake by the mycorrhizae to be sent on to the plant. Protozoans eat bacteria primarily, releasing additional nutrients that stimulate the growth of more bacteria and fungi. When soil scientists say *bacteria mineralize nitrogen in soil*, what's really happening is that protozoans release nitrogen as waste in consuming bacteria. Similarly, nematodes release excess nitrogen in the form of ammonium when consuming either bacteria or fungi. All this happens in the vicinity of the root system of the plant, where feeder root hairs absorb the proffered nutrients. Organically derived elements rarely leach away, even when mineralized in soluble form, as some hungry critter is always on hand awaiting its next meal.

Healthy soil is a biological factory that with time gets richer, increasingly complex, and absolutely sustainable for the long haul. The assumption by chemical advocates that a larger pool of a given nutrient, whatever the form, will enhance plant growth is very unrepresentative of what actually happens in the soil. The total amount of a nutrient in the soil is nowhere near as important in terms of the soil's fertility as is the *availability* of that nutrient. That is the proprietary function of soil life and the reason organic growers emphasize the copious use of organic matter. The untapped minerals in almost any soil—once accessed by a healthy humus complex—are more than sufficient to revitalize every sensible orchard, year after year after year.

Soil testing

Our role in starting an orchard is simply to check that the pantry basics utilized by all these forms of life are in relative balance. A soil test that emphasizes biological parameters is the best tool by which to gauge this. Certain soil amendments will likely be called for to achieve a proper starting point for the biology. That

ORCHARD COMPOST

Organic farmers and gardeners alike use compost to return goodness to the soil. Nutrients get restored, organic matter levels build up, and microorganism communities for the plants being grown receive a diversity boost. But wait . . . that last proves valid for fruit trees only if the grower knows to distinguish between *garden compost* and *orchard compost*.

Compost serves as an inoculum of not just bacteria but also fungi, protozoans, nematodes, and often microarthropods when properly made. Much has been made of the enzymes and plant growth hormones produced in compost, but in truth these materials are everyday by-products of the biology. Compost turns out to be a darned good way to reinvigorate the soil food web. Biologically rich compost will nudge an acidic pH situation slightly more in that direction, but this will be counterbalanced through microbe inducements in the feeder root zone that are definitively alkaline. Composted organic matter is Nature's buffer in its most essential form.

The amount of nitrogenous "green" material (fresh manure, grass clippings, alfalfa meal, and vegetable wastes) available determines the ratio of fungi to bacteria that will flourish in finished compost. The carbon-to-nitrogen ratio expresses how nitrogen stands in relation to carbon content in the organic debris being composted. Achieving a C:N ratio of 25:1 promotes rapid decomposition through high heat, resulting in a bacteria-dominated compost just right for the vegetable garden. Leaf mold, straw, cornstalks, woodsy brush, and moderate amounts of sawdust (from stable bedding) are much higher in carbon than nitrogen and thus are recommended as "brown" material. A simple recipe for garden compost is alternating layers of green and brown ingredients in equal proportion, turning weekly to generate bacterial heat, and winning some sort of speed race for getting finished compost to the garden in ten weeks or less. Doubling up the brown aspect boosts the C:N ratio to 40:1 to make orchard

---

life system in turn will provide a well-balanced meal for the feeder roots of our fruiting plants.

It's easy to feel anxious looking at the numbers presented on a typical soil test. Values for different nutrients will be recorded as low, medium, or high. Different labs use different extraction solvents to approximate either total nutrient reserves or what's most likely available to plant roots.[38] The recommendations that follow reflect the bias of the lab doing the test. Most state university soil labs plug chemical options. On the other hand, the biological labs listed in the appendices not only will speak organics but will emphasize the *percent base saturation* of those elements that determine soil acidity. Those numbers hold great relevance for health-oriented growing

according to William Albrecht, a Missouri soil scientist whose work in the middle of the last century has influenced many in the ecological agriculture movement today. Let's look at the more meaningful parts found on a soil report from the holistic perspective and then follow that with a discussion of important macronutrients and micronutrients.

Getting an initial read on your soil is strongly advised. A follow-up test a year or two later provides feedback on how any initial adjustments actually played out in improving base saturation, particularly with respect to calcium.[39] Giving attention to fungal duff management from here on in now takes precedence—growing healthy fruit will never be about constant soil manipulation once the grower compost. Incorporating deciduous wood chips and even the occasional layer of living soil helps achieve this goal. Orchard compost is not turned, and in fact it is aged for many months before being spread beneath the trees and on berry beds. Some people make bacterial compost and then add ramial wood chips, whereas others layer in more brown matter from the get-go. The passage of time is what's key.

Fungi thrive on nondisturbance. Roughage high in lignin content creates air passages, providing oxygen for the aerobic fungi that will thrive in a woodsy medium. Spraying the pile on occasion with liquid fish will feed a diversity of fungal species. Soil amendments forked into the pile in late summer—greensand, granite meal, rock phosphate, Azomite, kelp, and gypsum—will be taken up by the compost food web and the nutrients made bioavailable for feeder root uptake when the matured compost gets spread later that fall.

How much compost to use per tree is tied to a number of factors. Let's assume the soil-buildup phase has been completed with respect to mineral amendments and that organic matter levels in the soil are satisfactory. Fungal duff management beneath bearing trees calls for deliberately decomposing leaves and prunings in place. A maintenance rate of compost to complement this orchard recycling would amount to 2 tons per acre, which in turn looks like a pile that's 4 cubic yards in volume. Let's further assume free-standing trees with a dripline area on the order of a 16-foot diameter. This spacing amounts to approximately 120 trees per acre. That 4-cubic-yard pile would contain 108 cubic feet, so about a cubic foot of compost per tree hits the mark. That amounts to one and a half 5-gallon buckets' worth per tree per year. Compost doesn't need to be spread tight to the trunk, and extending the application a few feet beyond the dripline is good by the roots.

understands that it's a vibrant soil food web that gets the job done right. By all means take a soil test every few years beyond this initial soil-building phase if you wish to keep a finger on the pulse of regional nutrient concerns . . . though simply following the deep nutrition advice that follows this chapter should stand you in good stead from here on in.

Sampling the soil
Gathering soil to send to the lab for analysis requires care. One spot of ground may look like all the rest, but then again it might have been influenced by some factor in the recent past and may have a unique character or composition. That's why a *representative soil sample* consists of twelve to twenty slices of earth

randomly selected from the area under consideration for planting. Zigzag throughout your orchard ground to gather the samples so as to get a broad survey of the situation. Berry patches and tree ground can be treated as one if they have similar history. I like to use dripline locations when testing the soil in bearing blocks of trees, as this is where root action takes place and compost has been spread over the years.

A stainless-steel soil-sampling tool delivers a consistent core each time, but you can achieve reasonable results with a clean spade.[40] Testing the top layer of soil requires that each sample be a uniformly thick slice down through the top 4–6 inches of soil. (Wriggle the spade into the ground to create an initial opening, and then slice behind this plane ½ inch back to the desired depth.) Brushing away the plant matter at the very top is good practice. Mix all the individual samples together in a clean pail. Two cups' worth of this mix will be sent to the lab for analysis, either in a new ziplock bag or in the sampling bag provided by request. The requisite sampling form can often be downloaded from the Internet. Here's where you provide the lab with the soil's description, intended crop plans, and any recent history of liming or other soil work.

Organic matter

The percentage of organic matter (OM) in your soil eventually reflects your commitment to a living soil system. This number will vary in different regions, primarily because warmer growing zones consistently face an accelerated pace of microbial decomposition. Still, when it comes to keeping up with the Joneses, trust me: Organic matter means more than that new car or designer kitchen any day.

Organic matter supplies low to medium concentrations of nutrients, and almost always in well-balanced quantities. Furthermore, decaying plant matter and organisms have a slow-release mechanism, allowing nutrients to become available to plants over a period of several months, if not years. Nor will such nutrients leach away as readily as happens in dead soils. Lastly, organic matter gradually improves soil structure as earthworms and other soil organisms interact and feed.

A diverse understory of plants is the principal means of replenishing organic matter from one growing season to the next. Orchard compost and/or a variety of haphazard mulches contribute here as well. The soluble lignins in ramial wood chips fuel the biology that produces humus, the best type of organic matter of all. Humus is a highly stable material providing for long-term nutrient storage. This ability of a particular soil structure will be expressed as *cation exchange capacity* (CEC) on soil tests. Humic and fulvic acids made available through humus banking are what improve micronutrient assimilation across the board.

The addition of purchased humates to poor soils helps jump-start the biological action required to process more and more organic matter.

The relevance of measuring total nutrient levels in a soil gets addressed in the organic matter department as well. What counts—and this is what a good biological soil lab will insist upon—are the levels of available nutrients. Legitimate debates as to how best to determine such levels are ongoing, but guess what? Simply having a good OM score indicates that sufficient carbon and nitrogen reserves are on hand. Organic matter at 5 percent provides a potential of 120 pounds per acre of nitrogen yearly.[41] A healthy soil with a good mineralization rate (on the order of 2–4 percent) provides more than enough nitrogen to sustain good orchard yields. This recognition of what biological diversity alone can do with a sustained supply of organic matter is going to become very pertinent.

pH daydreaming

Everybody seems to talk about soil pH as the cat's pajamas. Understanding this measure of soil acidity calls for a holistic sense of what's really going on here.

Acid soils are low in fertility because too much of the cation exchange capacity is occupied by either hydrogen (which is not a plant nutrient) or aluminum (which can be toxic to plants), all of which is indicated by a soil pH range running between 3.5 and 6.0. Liming soils affects who's on first by the substitution of calcium and magnesium for a hydrogen ion on the humic acid chain. Some acidity in the form of hydrogen ions is necessary to make other nutrients available, which is why fertile orchard ground has a pH range somewhere between 6.3 and 6.7.[42] An alkaline soil, on the other hand, is oversaturated with calcium and/or magnesium. Southern salty soils are usually very alkaline, with pH ranging between 8.0 and 9.0. The application of acid salts (such as iron or manganese sulfates) results in a complex chemical reaction that literally pulls calcium and magnesium out in a leachable form.

BIO-SYSTEMS SOIL ANALYSIS REPORT

FARM NAME: LOST NATION ORCHARD -
CLIENT NAME: MICHAEL PHILLIPS

DATE: 8/25/10
FIELD: North Block **ACRES:** 1.5
CROP: APPLES

(NUTRIENTS AND RECOMMENDATIONS ARE EXPRESSED IN #/A UNLESS OTHERWISE NOTED.)

TEST DATE	8/25/10	8/16/10		ORGANIC RECOMMENDATIONS	AMOUNT APPLIED
LAB	A & L	BIO-TEST			
% O.M.	4.9		GOOD	High Carbon/Low Nutrient Compost	
NITRATE		60	GOOD		
AMMONIA		3	MEDIUM		
AVAIL. P2O5		175	MEDIUM	300# Soft Rock Phosphate	
P1/P2O5	161		MEDIUM		
P2/P205	386		GOOD		
SOLUBLE K2O		480+	EXCESS	Limit Potash sources	
K2O	293		GOOD	Maintain with High Carbon Compost	
MAGNESIUM	220		GOOD	Ok	
SOLUBLE Ca		5600	VERY GOOD		
Ca	1900		LOW	1000# Coarse Ground High Calcium Lime	
pH SOIL	6.1	6.8	MEDIUM/ VERY GOOD	(Apply after the Phosphate (AND) Gypsum	
pH BUFFER	6.9			are applied)	
C.E.C.	7.2		MEDIUM	Organic Matter	
ENERGY		500	VERY GOOD	On the verge of being excess	
% BASE SAT.					
K	4.4		VERY HIGH	Limit	
Mg	12.8		VERY GOOD	Ok	
Ca	66.2		MEDIUM	High Calcium Lime (AND) Gypsum	
H	16.7		TOO HIGH	High Calcium Lime will lower	
S - ppm	17.0		LOW-MED	400# Gypsum (apply after Phosphate)	
Zn - ppm	4.2		MEDIUM	7# Zinc Sulfate-35% Zn	Foliar
Mn - ppm	14.0		LOW	12# Manganese Sulfate-28% Mn	Kelp w/
Fe - ppm	1.0		VERY LOW	15# Iron Sulfate-20% Fe	Trace
Cu - ppm	1.3		MEDIUM	2# Copper Sulfate-25% Cu	
B - ppm	0.6		LOW	10# Borate-10% B	

7876 South Van Dyke Road ~ Marlette, Michigan 48453 ~ (989) 635-2864 phone ~ (989) 635-3888 fax ~

Here are the critical aspects to consider on a soil test:

Organic matter ties to nitrogen resources

Phosphate to potash ratio affects Brix potential

Calcium baseline begins at 2000#/A

Cation exchange capacity determines cation balance ratio

A ratio of 70:12:4 for this particular soil is the goal as determined by the C.E.C.

Trace mineral needs are very relevant to good-flavored fruit

The important biological components of a soil test include the cation exchange capacity, base saturation values, and certain nutrient ratios that in turn indicate the need for specific soil amendments.

The key question to ask here is: What do the microbes think about all this? Excessive manipulation can be harmful to the everyday functioning of the soil food web. The pH created by ongoing nutrient exchange in the rhizosphere and amendments added by the grower influences what types of microorganisms live in the soil. This has impact on the form of available nitrogen and other biological functions that affect how plants grow. The microbes desired in an orchard soil appreciate a proportional salad bar, and it's in achieving this goal that up-front compromise to adjust pH in a significant way becomes acceptable when preparing orchard ground. Establishing desired ratios between certain mineral elements ensures that the biology being fostered for fruit trees will keep such matters in line thereafter with far less intrusion on our part.

Cation balance

What truly counts are exchangeable nutrients in the right places. Cation balance is a question of having proportional ratios among calcium, magnesium, and potassium (somewhat determined by soil type), backed by a similar rule of thumb involving phosphorus and potassium. These are the numbers to be addressed with soil amendments prior to establishing a fungal-dominated food web and planting out fruit trees and berries.

All soil elements carrying an electrical charge are referred to as ions. Ions with a positive charge are called *cations* (pronounced *CAT-ions*), and those with a negative charge are called *anions* (*AN-ions*). What soil scientists call the *cation exchange capacity* represents the sum total of exchangeable cations that a soil can adsorb. Clay soils and soils high in organic matter have higher cation exchange capacities than sandy soils. The CEC number revealed on a soil test indicates how porous a soil is nutrient-wise and therefore how soil chemistry can be used (in addition to organic matter) to begin to improve this. A light-colored sandy soil will have a CEC around 3–7; a fine-textured loam will have a CEC of 8–14; a clay soil will have a CEC of 15 or more. That sets the stage for balancing calcium and magnesium levels in relation to each other.

Magnesium serves to pull soil particles closer together, whereas calcium will spread the particles farther apart. See where we're going with this? Slightly more magnesium is called for in a porous soil, whereas clay requires higher levels of calcium to improve drainage and aeration. The percentage of base saturation for each of these elements provided on a soil test is how we compare the relative levels of each. The Ca:Mg ratio for a sandy soil can be targeted at 5:1 (noting that the structural need for magnesium may skew this even lower). This same ratio for the soil of your dreams—that fine-textured loam—should be close to 7:1. The heaviest clay soils benefit from even more calcium, so now a slightly higher Ca:Mg ratio becomes appropriate. The calcium pushes soil particles apart—that's good for clay. The magnesium pulls soil particles together—that's bad for clay, but ever so good for sandy soils that lose water too quickly, which is when a higher proportion of magnesium is desirable. You determine which ratio range to use based on where the CEC number falls for your soil.

This ratio business really has to do with balanced plant uptake of these important macronutrients. An excessive amount of one cation can block the availability of another cation. Ratios that stray too far from these ideal numbers lead to calcium and magnesium deficiency symptoms. Potassium enters in here as well, tagging along on the heels of calcium at no greater than a 14:1 ratio.[43] The percent base saturation numbers that represent cation balance for a loam soil with respect to Ca:Mg:K are on the order of 70:12:4. These numbers shift for a sandy soil to more like 65:16–18:3–4 and for a clayey soil to more like 76:10:4–5. Don't be wrapped up in rigidity around this and carry a calculator out to the orchard . . . proportional guidelines are fluid at best in addressing the needs of soil structure, nutrient exchange, and microbe efficiency.

Here's why we just undertook that mathematical plunge. Modern growers have a cultural tendency to overemphasize pH and then add any ol' lime to favorably alter soil acidity. Ground limestone introduces substantial amounts of calcium and magnesium to a soil profile to replace those excess hydrogen ions. The type of lime used has a Ca:Mg ratio of its own to be considered.[44] The recommended rate should not exceed 2 tons per acre that first year, with or without tillage,[45] and even that amount will stifle microorganism activity for a spell. If additional lime beyond this is recommended, soil food web proponents favor making additional applications in fall on the order of 200–400 pounds per acre (rather than a tonnage basis) per year after this. Lime added by way of a substantial compost pile is taken up more efficiently, if given time, reducing the amount needed to a quarter of what might be called for as a surface application.[46]

- **Dolomitic limestone** is about 20–25 percent calcium and about 10–15 percent magnesium. Local garden centers generally carry this type of lime. All for the good if you have a strong Mg deficiency, but totally the wrong choice if you have too low a Ca:Mg ratio to start. If you're not sure, choose the other lime; overdoing magnesium will cause a portion of nitrogen reserves to be lost to the air or leaching.
- **Calcitic limestone** is about 38 percent calcium and around 0.2 percent magnesium. *Hi-cal lime*, (as it's also known) may be available in a farm supply store and most certainly can be special-ordered. Use calcium carbonate—this sedimentary rock's molecular name—wherever magnesium levels are close to sufficient. (Other soil amendments like Sul-Po-Mag can be used to up magnesium levels instead.) Oyster shell lime is a sea-derived source of calcium carbonate for those located closer to the coast.
- **Carbonized limestone** comes in pelleted form only and includes low levels of humates and sugars added in as carbon sources. This biological rendition of calcitic lime allows

calcium to be taken up by the microorganisms that much quicker and thus makes it available to fruiting plants more efficiently.

- **Gypsum** (23 percent calcium) is the right choice to boost calcium levels when no adjustment to pH is needed. The sulfate portion of "land plaster" reacts with water to form a weak sulfuric acid solution that releases the calcium into the soil—the abundant calcium ions then secure more of the exchange sites, thereby shoving excess magnesium and potassium back into solution. Gypsum is a powerful tool for regaining cation balance in messed-up soils! This rock dust also does wonders to improve the permeability of clay soils. A tonic rate of 200–400 pounds per acre (which translates to 5–10 pounds of gypsum per 1,000 square feet) can be used each year until calcium reserves reach an optimum level. The sulfur in gypsum will help slow the nitrate release of decomposing organic matter as well.

Macronutrients

The essential soil nutrients that plants need in substantial amounts are calcium (Ca), magnesium (Mg), nitrogen (N), phosphorus (P), potassium (K), and sulfur (S). Plants also need carbon (C), hydrogen (H), and oxygen (O), derived from air and water. All nine of these nutrients are collectively referred to as *macronutrients.*

Emphasizing cation balance highlights calcium's premier role in the scheme of things. The desirable level to see in terms of total calcium on a soil test report is a bare minimum of 2,000 pounds per acre.[47] That sets a calcium baseline for where base saturation ratios should begin. Orchard soils coming in below this gross figure will produce fruit with weakened skin and cell strength, leading to bruising susceptibility of that fruit and impacting its keeping ability. Strong fruit, so to speak, also has better membrane integrity to resist pathogenic fungi throughout the growing season.

Viewing the soil as a regenerative living system is

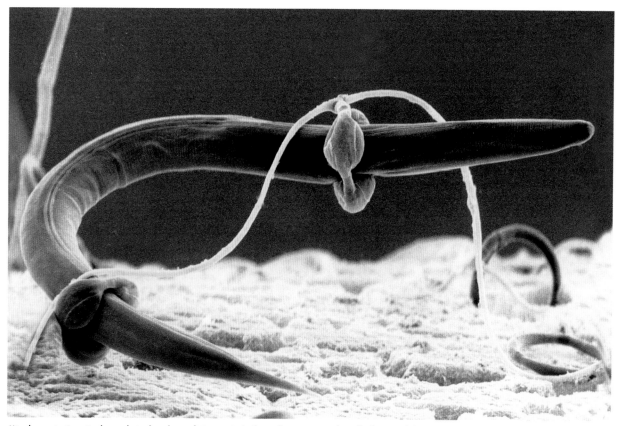

Microbe consuming microbe results in the release of nitrogen in the form of ammonium. A fungally dominated rhizosphere allows nitrogen to then be taken up in that form by feeder roots, resulting in a more disease-resistant fruit tree. Photo courtesy of George Barron, University of Guelph.

one big kick in the pants for anyone who has been taught that chemical NPK fertilization is more relevant than soil biology. Don't be fooled by the prevalence of that attitude! Nutrient balance certainly depends on nitrogen, phosphate, and potash—these being the three numbers provided on a bag of fertilizer to indicate its relative value—yet we shouldn't stress this part of the picture over the rest.[48] Biological growers view the "npk perspective" as merely another means of complementing the soil food web. Accordingly, organic soil amendment choices to address additional testing shortfalls still tie in to the calcium dynamic and what we know of soil life contributions in these areas. Do not shortchange the nutrient density of fruit by using soluble chemical fertilizers. Investing in rock powders where mineral needs become apparent is the healthier investment.

Nitrogen

The majority of nitrogen in any soil needs to be converted from locked organic nitrogen to mineral nitrogen that can be used by the plants. The protein forms of this element in organic matter must first be *ammonified*, and then a portion of this might indeed be *nitrified* in order to be taken up by the feeder roots. Fungi and bacteria drive these processes. The available levels of ammonium and nitrates constantly bounce back and forth between immobilization and mineralization as the soil food web in its entirety cycles nutrients.

A fungally dominated soil delivers the right nitrogen to fruit trees and berries, which in turn allows these plants to better resist disease. (Brace yourself for one of those moments when *big-time truth* reveals itself.) Feeder roots are taking in the nitrogen made available by one microorganism consuming another. The release of plant-available ammonium results from that everyday digestive process. In a bacterially dominated soil, nitrifying bacteria rapidly convert the ammonified form of nitrogen into nitrate. In a fungally dominated soil, something else entirely is taking place. The enzymes produced by fungi are decidedly acidic. This lowers the pH in the rhizosphere . . . which greatly reduces the amount of these special bacteria, as nitrifying bacteria absolutely favor an alkaline root zone. More ammonium therefore remains as plant-available ammonium in a fungally dominated soil instead of being converted to nitrates.

No fruiting plant flourishes on a diet of straight nitrate. Admittedly, the trees get very green and grow fruit that are humongous yet empty (nutritionally speaking), but this comes at the cost of not being able to stand up to environmental pressures. Susceptibility to disease skyrockets whenever an orchard tree takes in nutrition in a form that undermines immune function.[49] One of the principal reasons that chemical orchards require so much medicine to control disease is to compensate for the fact that chemical fertilizers are nitrate-based. And one of the principal reasons that certified organic orchards using sulfur and other mineral fungicides require more and more of that medicine to control disease is to compensate for the fact that fungal dominance shifts in the soil—thereby allowing a greater portion of the food-web-derived nitrogen to be nitrate-based. The picture becomes clear now, eh? Our precious fungal duff, the heart and soul of holistic orcharding, delivers the right form of nitrogen all by itself and in the quantities needed (thanks to abundant organic matter) for sustainable fruit production.

It's totally fine to call upon inputs in the process of gearing up for long-term fungal dominance. Poor soils simply do not deliver good wood growth in those important early years. Nor is the surrounding understory particularly lush and thus able to contribute organic matter. Additional nitrogen from an organic

BASIC SOIL VALUES

Seems like a whole lot of shaking is going on here with this soil-testing business, eh? Every orchard soil has parameters established around organic matter content, cation exchange capacity, and the geological history of the place where you live.

Some basic values can be articulated for those who are not quite ready for the full monty of soil considerations. Keep in mind that these generalized guidelines aren't as optimum as it gets. The purpose here is simply to give your trees ground to stand on with a reasonable chance of success.

- Get the pH in the 6.3–6.7 range.
- Do this in the context of cation balance based on the CEC number for your soil.
- Organic matter fuels the biology. Get OM to 3 percent at a bare minimum.
- Strive for total phosphate (P_2O_5) and potash (KO_2) readings of at least 200 lbs./acre.

This checklist defines clear goals for the soil-buildup phase in preparing any orchard. Holistic methods are not going to work as well if the basics of mineral nutrition in the soil are not up to snuff.

fertilizer blend can be applied directly to the soil surface.[50] Don't overdo this, of course, as too much nitrogen knocks many things a-kilter.[51] Other soil amendments offering nitrogen may be an ongoing component for making high-quality compost, because not every home orchardist is going to have access to decent manure to mix with those ramial wood chips.

- **Fish meal** (9-3-0). Excellent source of slowly to moderately released nitrogen. The N is tied up in proteins, so there's no risk of burning young trees. The fish essence may attract animals, but for the most part its odor has been stabilized with hydrogen peroxide. This nitrogen charge will supplement very poor orchard soils after the year of planting and boost compost potential.
- **Alfalfa meal** (2-1-2). A plant-based source that releases nitrogen relatively fast to feeding soil organisms. Useful in the nursery as a side dressing for an early-summer boost and for renewing haggard-looking berry beds.
- **Feather meal** (14-1-1). This protein source works very well where phosphate and potash soil test levels are good but organic matter is low.
- **Soybean meal** (6-1-1). Seed meals are an economical source of N for organic growers because they are the best value except for manure. The nitrogen is moderately available because the plant proteins can be mineralized by the biology slightly faster than fish meal.
- **Composted manure** (approximately 1-1-1). Woodsy compost made in part with animal manure maintains orchard nutrient levels and boosts fungal diversity. Its relatively stable organic matter will be broken down steadily over the growing season. Trace minerals can be delivered through the compost by adding kelp, Azomite, and so forth while forming the pile. Fresh manure (without composting) should never ever be used in any orchard.
- **Organic fertilizer blends** (N-P-K varies by manufacturer). Organic slow-release plant food made with various protein meals, rock phosphates, sulfate of potash, greensand, kelp, and so forth. I use higher-N blends like Pro-Gro (5-3-4) to develop wood structure on young trees and maintain berry plantings, and lower-N blends like Pro-Start (2-3-3) to support return bloom on heavy-bearing trees.

Phosphorus

This complex soil nutrient is made available by the surface feeding of decomposing fungi and then delivered to the plant by the hyphal reach of mycorrhizae. Biological management of the fungal duff addresses the phosphorus availability challenge faced by chemical growers. Still, a net phosphorus deficiency in holistic orchard ground often proves to be the missing link in increasing the nutrient density of fruit, particularly with respect to calcium. Paying attention to soil test ratios is pertinent.

Phosphate (chemically notated as P_2O_5) requires time to get functioning organically.[52] Ecological ag people have suggested that a phosphate-to-potash ratio of 2:1 is necessary to sustain crop refractometer readings above 12 degrees Brix (the Brix scale being the measure of soluble solids in plant tissue, indicative of overall health). Yet often the reverse is true in biologically managed soils, as potassium levels get renewed constantly by decomposing organic matter. Indigenous soil attributes vary widely across the continent as well.[53] Getting this ratio to toe the line nearer to 1:1 can be challenging enough.[54] Soil test readings of 200 pounds per acre for both phosphate and potash define an achievable goal for every soil. Supplementing phosphate more often than not proves to be a biological imperative, especially in the development years when the fungal system isn't yet what it should be.

This essential nutrient plays a significant role in root development. I incorporate rock phosphate into the soil when planting trees as a matter of course. Surface application of colloidal phosphate (on the order of 1–2 pounds per tree) in the second and fourth years to the fungal duff zone in late summer serves to improve P-challenged soils until bearing begins. That's the point when I expect cation balance to be spot-on, and a follow-up soil test will reveal how orchard-wide phosphorus levels are looking with respect to potassium.[55] Bearing fruit trees remove relatively little phosphorus from the soil each year when leaves and prunings are dutifully returned. Phosphorus can be tied up by excess calcium and magnesium in alkaline soils (leading to purple margins on leaves), but that's more about the need to restore a degree of acidity than it is about adding P.

- **Black rock phosphate** (0-3-0) is about 30 percent phosphorus, of which a tenth part at most becomes available each year. It is generally used to build up a reservoir of phosphate, spread atop the orchard floor every ten to twelve years for slow release. This sand-like amendment has less available P than colloidal phosphate offers for immediate root uptake. Black rock phosphate is about 48 percent calcium (as CaO) as well, giving it approximately one-fifth the neutralizing power of lime.
- **Colloidal phosphate** (0-3-0), also known as soft rock phosphate, averages about 18 percent phosphorus, of which a fifth part becomes available each season. The bony structures of prehistoric marine creatures mined in Florida are the source of this fine clay-like dust. The solubility of colloidal phosphate makes this a good choice in the early years while building the fungal ecosystem.
- **Tennessee brown phosphate** (0-3-0) is neither a colloidal nor a rock phosphate, but rather the consistency of rich soil. It comes from the washing piles that were left behind when high-grade ore was extracted to produce superphosphates in the early twentieth century. Levels of available P were regularly over 6 percent when tested in midwestern labs, making this amendment a fine alternative for root-development needs and sprinkling onto compost piles.
- **Bonemeal** (2-11-0, with 22 percent calcium) is an immediately available source of phosphorus that's good for side-dressing berry plantings early in the season before biological activity gets going. Steamed bonemeal has more

nitrogen than precipitated bonemeal (which is not considered an acceptable organic soil amendment) and tends to be a good choice where phosphate levels are seriously low from the get-go. A biochar version of bonemeal is a recommended biological alternative: **Bone char** (0-16-0) brings considerable calcium and mycorrhizal benefits to the action as well. This dusty by-product of refining cane sugar has more than five times the concentration of available phosphate and almost double the total phosphate of colloidal phosphate.

Potassium

Potassium is needed to renew what has gone into the fruit and to increase tolerance to winter cold and spring frosts. This mineral also strongly influences fruit color and fruit size. A huge heaping of organic matter, whether through generous composting and/or aggressive mulching, may nudge potassium levels too high relative to Ca and Mg, especially in dry land soils. Orchardists with shallow soils are the ones most likely to run short on the K score. The term *potash* (being potassium oxide, KO_2) is often used to refer to various mined salts that contain the element potassium in water-soluble form.

- **Wood ash** (0-1-5). Potassium in this form is readily available, and so wood ash should be applied only once active growth has engaged.[56] Wood ash has two-thirds the liming power of limestone and acts very quickly. Its calcium content runs between 20 and 30 percent, but magnesium tends to be quite low. Wood ash contains various trace minerals, including boron and zinc. Different woods vary in these respects, with denser hardwoods tending to offer the most, nutritionally speaking.
- **Greensand** (0-1-7, with 3 percent magnesium). This naturally occurring iron-potassium silicate, also called glauconite, is released over time as the mineral breaks down. It has the

consistency of sand but is able to absorb ten times more moisture, making it an exceptional soil conditioner. Many other nutrients occur in greensand, principally magnesium, iron, phosphorus, and as many as thirty trace minerals. The potash in greensand is insoluble (until taken up by the biology), so it can't be claimed in the fertilizer analysis without qualifying it as insoluble.

- **Granite dust** (0-0-6). Ground rock is widely used to remineralize soils, providing both potassium and micronutrients. Granite releases nutrients very slowly—the coarser the grind, the slower the release—and greatly enhances soil structure. This rock dust regularly features in my compost piles for both garden and orchard, given its long-term nature.
- **Sul-Po-Mag** (0-0-22, with 11 percent magnesium). Langbeinite ore mined near Carlsbad, New Mexico, is the most economical source of available potassium for organic growers provided magnesium is needed as well. Its 22 percent sulfur content helps the soil food web process nitrogen properly. Another common brand name is K-Mag. The nutrients are immediately available to plants, so apply only once growth has begun.[57]
- **Sulfate of potash** (0-0-50). This mineral application tends to be expensive, because the natural process used to precipitate magnesium from langbeinite involves high heat. Sulfate of potash adds K to the soil without any other cation contributions. It is very soluble and should be used only when trees are growing; otherwise the potassium will be lost to leaching.
- **Organic matter**. It goes without saying that the biology benefits most from potassium delivered in the form of rotting hay, ramial wood chips, and compost. Lots of nutrients come this way!

Micronutrients

The essential soil nutrients that plants need in very small amounts are iron (Fe), manganese (Mn), boron (B), molybdenum (Mo), copper (Cu), zinc (Zn), and chlorine (Cl). These *micronutrients* are sometimes referred to as trace minerals. Soil tests may reveal a strong need to supplement one or two of these throughout certain regions—and that can be done—but for the long haul I prefer using broad-source soil condiments in my orchard and garden on an ongoing basis.

- **Kelp meal** (1–5 percent N, 3–10 percent potash). Seaweed has a variety of micronutrients in addition to the macronutrients, especially boron, copper, iron, manganese, and molybdenum. The organic matter of seaweed breaks down quickly in soil because its enzymes and amino acids stimulate the soil food web across the board. Kelp meal can be sprinkled atop different layers in building a compost pile or added en masse near the end of the finishing process (forked into the pile a month or two before fall application). Needless to say, foliar kelp added to the spray tank offers similar assurance.
- **Azomite** (0-0-2.5, with 5 percent calcium). This ancient deposit of aluminum silicate clay with marine minerals is named after its A-to-Z of more than fifty minerals beneficial to plants and animals. Use in the planting hole, regularly in compost, and to boost severely disease-stricken trees (as much as 10–15 pounds per tree) by applying throughout the dripline area in late summer.
- **Florastim.** The micronutrients in this mineral clay base come with a host of beneficial microbes (over four billion organisms per pound) and fulvic acids essential to the recovery and maintenance of healthy soil. These trace minerals are spread directly atop the soil and should not be plowed under.

A deficiency of any of the essential trace minerals can interfere with nutrient flow. Yellow leaves, poor fruit set, and limited return bloom are among the possible symptoms. Holistic growers are going to see less of this simply because our stewardship efforts center upon deep nutrition. Still, let's review a few possibilities to give you a basis of concern that may suggest the need for a soil test checkup and/or leaf tissue analysis.[58]

- Southern clays and moist ground farther north often exhibit a **boron deficiency**, whereas dry areas out west aren't likely to lack this trace element. Severe boron deficiency can result in stunted shoot growth that looks like a virus infection, apples cracking about a month after fruit set, and internal corking. Boron plays a key role in calcium transport in the plant . . . so without enough boron, calcium deficiency symptoms result. The soils lab will pinpoint such a need, making a recommendation for 2 pounds (say) of boron per acre. Rarely do they specify which compound of boron to apply; the recommendation is for *actual boron*. Boric acid is about 16.5 percent boron, and borax is about 11.3 percent boron. Let's use the latter (a commonly available laundry soap) to clarify this: Applying 17.7 pounds of borax to that acre of ground meets the soil requirement identified in this example. Here's the rub, though: Excess boron is toxic to plants, so this application must not be overdone. Boron is sprinkled on like fairy dust, approximately 2.5 ounces per freestanding tree for this example, spread quite thinly around an anticipated circumference of 16–18 feet per tree. Check in every few years to keep a firm hand on the proper availability of boron if this turns out to be a regional concern. Sites with bedrock relatively near the surface and significant annual rainfall tend to be depleted of boron fairly rapidly. Other places may be verging on boron toxicity, due either to overly enthusiastic application or high boron levels in the subsoil.
- Severe gummosis on stone fruit trunks and summer leaves that appear as having undergone drought damage can be symptoms of **copper deficiency** in trees. Leafing out late, particularly in apple and pear, may indicate this as well. Foliar applications of copper are going to reach the soil, suggesting that application timing be in early spring when a degree of bacterial disease control might be garnered as well. Reluctant buds will often start to break dormancy (with green showing in the buds) within a few days following a copper application, especially if accompanied by a soaking rain.
- When a plant has **iron deficiency**, you will usually see chlorosis at the tips of the branches, with the newest leaves turning yellow first and older leaves below staying green longer. This situation gets reversed by **magnesium deficiency**—the new leaves at the tips stay green, with the older leaves at the base of each branch turning a chlorotic yellow first. This rule is not hard and fast, but it does help us figure out which mineral element might be of concern. Excessive phosphate content and a low level of potassium may also be contributing factors in causing iron deficiency. While the ideal is to fix the soil, foliar applications of manure tea (enforced with dollops of blackstrap molasses in the brew) or Epsom salts (magnesium sulfate) can help the immediate situation, respectively.

Short-term mineral deficiencies can also be dealt with using quick-fix medicine based upon organic chemistry principles. *Chelation* makes this possible by fixing the inorganic ion (the mineral in question) to an organic acid chain. A highly synthetic compound (EDTA) is used to form chemical chelates, so organic

Bud progression of sour cherry includes side green going to white bud going to bloom.

Bud progression of pear includes bud swell going to green cluster going to white bud (with a happy touch of pink!).

growers are advised to seek out foliar formulations made with natural lignosulfonates, which are wood-processing derivatives. Chelate combinations can include iron, zinc, manganese, copper, sulfur, boron, and/or molybdenum, all chosen to meet the situation at hand.

TREE DOINGS

You will quickly discover that your relationship with the orchard becomes a year-round affair. All sorts of wonders get revealed by visiting your trees often. Nor is this simply about looking for problems. Paying attention to how buds grow, when roots are in full gear, and what tree health looks like deepens your understanding as a steward. Take time in the early morning to observe what's changing as each season progresses. Come back again in the evening to listen and share a glass of cider. The pleasures of orcharding go way beyond the fruit.

The unfolding bud

Orchardists share a common language to describe the season at hand. The trees are at rest in the dormant season. Bud stages distinguish tree awakening and associated pest activity nicely. Silver tip, green tip, quarter-inch green, half-inch green, tight cluster, open cluster, pink, first bloom, and full bloom are very observable benchmarks of the apple's spring. This progression varies slightly in stone fruits that blossom without spur leaves. Peaches start at first swell and proceed through calyx green, calyx red, and first pink into full bloom. Cherries go from full swell to side green before tight cluster shows. Pears straddle a line of their own, as bud scales separate to show a fruit bud cluster, which quickly moves along to first white and then full bloom.

Bud progression allows me to speak to you about when certain tasks need doing, despite the fact that I live in northern New Hampshire and you live elsewhere. What day it is on the wall calendar isn't nearly as important as the pace of warming in the place each of us grows fruit. Orchardists in Zone 8 may observe first bloom in February, whereas this far north in Zone 4 things get going only come May. The month is in fact irrelevant—tree time is revealed by what's going on with the buds.

The *orchard calendar* is based on solar revolutions of a different kind. Actively growing plant tissue requires warmth to do its thing. Growth happens at a much slower pace in a cold spell than when the thermometer rises to 70°F (21°C) or more. Longer and longer days allow our precious sun to warm one half of the planet once again and thereby break winter's grip. Expectations at any given site can actually be tracked mathematically by keeping score of minimum and maximum temperatures each day. Each bud stage occurs only when enough *degree-days* have accumulated to achieve that next point of growth.[59] Apple buds, averaged across cultivars, will show pink after 300 degree-days, and the whole pollination shebang will end when the blossom petals fall to the ground 240 degree-days later.[60]

This probably seems silly—you just have to look at the tree to see what's happening, right?—yet such tracking ability has definite use. Community orchardists use pest-specific benchmarks to set the orchard alarm clock as regards the need to act. Some of you growing at home may relish precise knowledge about codling moth egg hatch, scab ascospore maturity, and plum curculio's last stand. Others will be pleased to simply have a general idea of such critical events . . . based on the degree-day observations of researchers who started with the unfolding buds.

Flower buds are larger than those that leaf, whether placed on the end of a fruiting spur or the longer shoot of a tip-bearing variety. Next year's potential crop can be seen throughout the winter months strictly by attuning your eyes to these rounded buds distributed throughout the tree. Leaf buds, on the other hand, are triangular-shaped and appear of far less consequence, essentially a mere bump on the shoot. Terms like *bud swell* indicate what's happening as sap starts to flow once again. The potential fruit crop becomes more and more obvious as the dormant season ends. You will find that being aware of visual fruit prospects becomes very important when those pruners are in hand.

Two practical spray applications tie in to early bud progression. That same liquid fish being recommended for holistic disease management provides a foliar nitrogen boost just prior to bloom. Such a fertility boost keeps the flower viable that wee bit longer, giving bees a better shot at successful pollination when conditions are less than ideal. The pink bud stage attracts the attention of others as well. Watch for chewing on the edges of fruit buds and tender leaves that have been wrapped shut. Both of these visual cues indicate the presence of bud caterpillars (the larvae of leafroller moths), which can easily be discovered with further investigation. The inclusion of Bt (*Bacillus thuringiensis*, a biological toxin for caterpillar species) in the spray tank mix at pink (going into bloom time) will be directed at these surface feeders if deemed abundant.

All of us at one time or another absolutely should play at being a bee when fruit blossoms open. I mean this in several ways. Breathe deep . . . the scent of plum blossoms alone makes up for almost everything that is aggravating or disappointing in life. Now

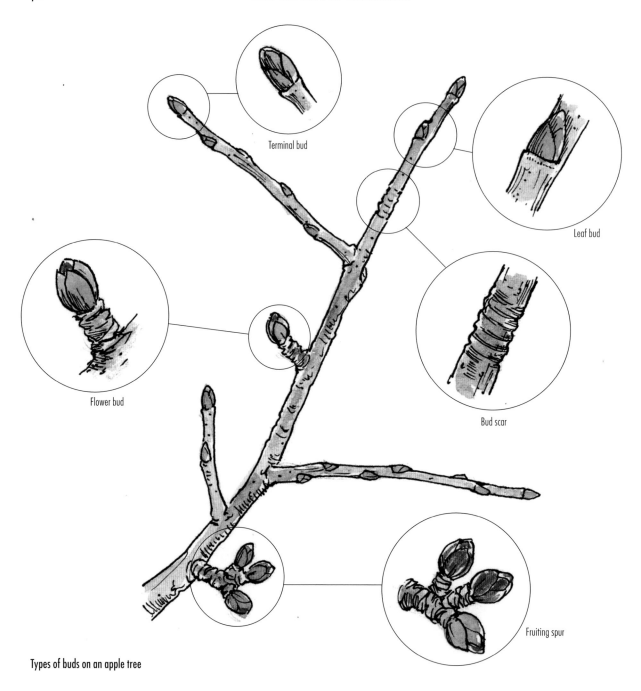

Terminal bud

Leaf bud

Flower bud

Bud scar

Fruiting spur

Types of buds on an apple tree

look closer than you ever have at a single fruit tree flower with the help of a magnifying glass. The center flower parts lead to the seed ovaries of the fruit; this is where a bee graciously delivers pollen while gathering nectar. The flower of any stone fruit has a single pistil, whereas the flower of pome fruit has multiple pistils. Think about it. How many pits are there in a peach? How many seeds in an apple? Bees know what the flower reveals. But we're not done yet. Go to a neighboring tree—same fruit type, different variety. Roll the golden pollen grains of a vibrant flower onto your fingertips. Now buzz back to that first tree. Brush one of its open blossoms ever so gently, dropping pollen grains into the flower in the process. The

Bud worms will be found in rolled leaves and tucked away in unopened blooms. One such culprit in New England includes larvae of the green pug moth. Photo courtesy of Alan Eaton, University of New Hampshire.

human bee can pollinate too, you see, working in the same thankful spirit of all bees.

Root happenings

You are about to learn the why behind doing certain orchard tasks at specific points in the growing season. So much of the biological hubbub we need to undertake as organic fruit growers relates entirely to what's up with the roots of our fruiting plants.

Roots can be thought of as the inverse of the tree above. We find a supporting trunk in the quasi-taproot structure of the larger-sized rootstocks. The brown transport roots are akin to lateral branches, sharing a brisk trade in photosynthate carbon and sugars. White feeder roots are ephemeral, much like leaves in this regard, and charged with the task of acquiring nutrients for the plant as a whole. I find it invaluable to visualize being the tip of a root when thinking about

understory management in the orchard . . . knowing that the search for rich humus begins with understanding what's taking place beneath the ground.

The absorptive roots of the tree are born in the spring, die, and are reborn in staggered fashion later in the growing season. Feeder roots live as little as fourteen days—perhaps up to sixty days where nutrient supply warrants—growing on the order of mere centimeters in the search for phosphorus and other nutrients. These fine white roots access new nutrient zones with the help of mycorrhizal fungi. The job early on is to find sustenance for fruit production in the current year. Once the harvest is under way, feeder roots focus entirely on supplying the cambium fuel that will drive leaf and shoot growth the following spring.

The first flush of root growth in every growing season kicks into full gear following bloom. A second flush of new root growth comes in late summer and early fall, often of greater duration and deeper down than what's seen in late spring. The competition for carbohydrates above- and belowground determines that shoot growth and vigorous root growth rarely overlap. Watch for this. This year's vegetative shoot reaches for the sun not long after blossoms unfurl. Tip expansion comes to a stop by the time fruitlets begin to noticeably size. Shoot growth essentially takes a few weeks off at this point precisely because that first flush of feeder root growth has begun in earnest. An unobserved autumn occurs out of our sight next . . . the feeder root system shuts down and sloughs away prior to the summer solstice . . . allowing top shoot growth to resume for the next month or so. Terminal bud set in late summer marks the end of growth and subsequent hardening off of all buds in preparation for winter's cold. Once again, unbeknownst to us, things are stirring down below, as the root system engages on a massive mission to store nutrients in bud and twig to drive next year's growth cycle.

As growers we have our own missions correlated to this intimate understanding of root purpose. Catalyst sprays directed at the ground in early spring stimulate mycorrhizal fungi into action. Biological mowing is all

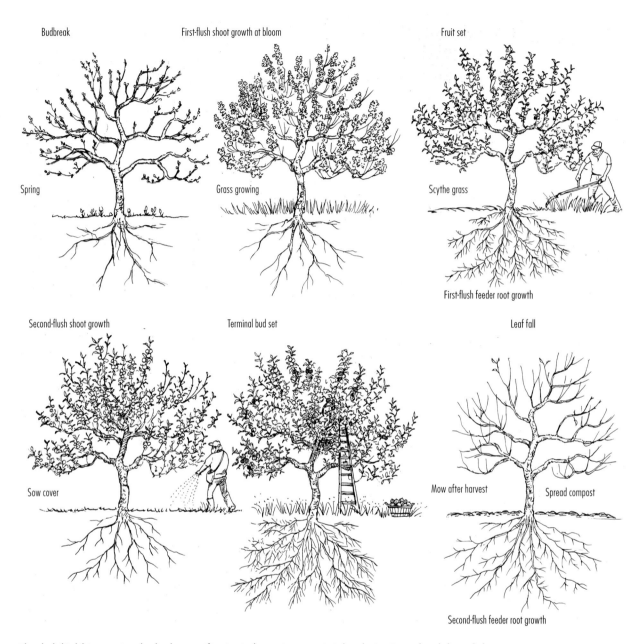

Budbreak

First-flush shoot growth at bloom

Fruit set

Spring

Grass growing

Scythe grass

First-flush feeder root growth

Second-flush shoot growth

Terminal bud set

Leaf fall

Sow cover

Mow after harvest

Spread compost

Second-flush feeder root growth

The why behind doing certain orchard tasks at specific points in the growing season is tied to what's going on down below with the roots.

about waiting to cut the grass until that first flush of feeder root growth begins. Disease suppression, room in the humus, nutrient availability, and fungal happiness are all related in how and when we cut the orchard understory (see "Mowing as a biological act" in chapter 4). Shallow tillage and cover cropping around dwarf

trees in midsummer direct the hardening-off progression of buds. The feeder root system takes a recess in that month prior to terminal bud set, thereby allowing the more aggressive management (any form of cultivation) from which smaller trees in a garden setting can benefit.[61] Leaf decomposition on the orchard floor is abetted when we spread orchard compost in fall when about half of the leaves have fallen off the tree. Fungal-rich compost provides a plethora of bioavailable nutrients just when that second flush of feeder roots runs at full bore.

Orchard tasks at ground level are sensibly tied to root happenings.

Trunk care

Welcome to the home orchard health spa! Maintaining a healthy-looking trunk and scaffold structure for many years down the road is the goal. While the human species may get concerned with wrinkles and chin sag, trees have winter injury, cankers, black rot, borers, and the incessant sapsucker to worry cambium flow.

A young fruit tree has bark vigor that bespeaks *supple and smooth*. Pruning cuts on a healthy tree readily callus over in several years' time. Age leads to a rougher bark appearance, going outright flaky on some varieties and fruit types, but still retaining a solid degree of adhesion and an invigorated appearance in its tan-to-gray coloration.

Biodynamic tree paste helps maintain these youthful attributes. This slurry mixture of a native clay and fresh cow manure helps wounds to close properly by introducing friendly organisms so that decaying rots do not win out in the long run. I find that putting trunk care in the context of a health spa helps rookie orchardists better understand this earthy technique. Application of a clay face mask restores elasticity, tightens up pores, and brightens our human skin . . . so why not the same for tree bark? Granted, the cow's contribution would be a stretch in renewing our personal radiance, but the diversity of microbes found in barnyard manure can be integral to bark health when it comes to fungal and bacterial blights.[62]

You will find different recipes and suggestions for applying biodynamic tree paste in an Internet search, but basically it comes down to slathering the tree structure going into the new growing season. The paste can be brushed thickly onto the trunk and branch scaffolds

as a general curative treatment.[63] At the very least find time to apply this mudpack to areas with obvious bark stress that caught your eye while pruning. A slurry mix of half clay and half cow manure works; adding a few handfuls of sand adds a crystalline bond to this earth poultice. I gather gray clay from a vein exposed on the banks of a nearby stream—going native here (provided you find a similar source) is desirable. I also fully understand that it will be a rare home orchardist who pastures a milk cow. Keep in mind this is all about introducing microbe diversity: Understory humus or rich compost can be used in a pinch instead if fresh cow manure isn't your thing.

Blistering, peeling, splitting, cracking, sun scald, sunken cambium, blotchiness, sooty mold, sap ooze (gummosis), sporulating fungi, and outright *dieback* describe myriad sad bark conditions. Sometimes experts can tell you exactly what's taking place, even naming a specific disease pathogen . . . but the truth is we often don't know. Injuries happen to trees, from winter cold and careless mowing to innocent openings in the vascular system (from, say, hail bombardment) and sun exposure following severe pruning. Infectious organisms take such opportunities given the chance. Tree paste gives a big leg up in overall trunk care, but other specific situations call for additional action.

So-called **southwest injury** occurs when the winter sun is closer to the horizon and thus strikes the tree almost perpendicular to the trunk in late afternoon. The tree bark warms up, thereby thawing sap and cambium cells alike . . . and then all freezes when the sun goes down. Vertical cracks down through wood may occur at the time of freezing, though it's far more likely to see surface splits in the bark. Less noticeable injury may appear as flattened, darkened cambial areas under the bark that will become more apparent during the growing season. Snow cover accentuates the risk by bouncing the light up into the "armpits" of branch unions. This type of freezing injury can be prevented! A whitewash applied in late fall makes for a reflective trunk and branch structure; it's the very darkness of the bark that makes it a solar collector. Diluted

A trunk whitewash should include the undersides of the lower scaffold branches. Sunlight reflected up from snow cover into these "armpits" can cause winter injury otherwise.

latex paint should be applied to all young trees (by the third season for sure) until such time as the bark gets flakier and lighter in color. Use a cheap interior grade of white latex, adding enough water (50 percent by volume) to obtain a whitewash consistency.[64] Paint all sides of the trunk up to 3 feet high, and do include the undersides of the lower branch scaffolds. This is a fall chore, best done after the harvest has been completed but before it snows.[65] Choose a warm, sunny day when the air temperature is above 50°F (10°C) to facilitate fast drying. Adding milk powder to the tree paste recipe, along with using light-colored clay, may well suffice to protect from southwest injury.[66] Scraping off loose bark scales before painting—it's back to the spa for a loofah rubdown!—provides surer coverage and helps eliminate hiding places for caterpillar larvae.

Canker diseases are common and destructive. These cause wilting and dieback of nearby shoots and can structurally weaken branches so much that limbs snap off in a wind- or ice storm. Cankers allow a progression of organisms to run amok by slowing the normal closure of wounds, thus providing easy entry for black rot and eventual wood decay. The *canker* itself is a dead area or lesion in the bark of a woody plant that often results in an open wound. All begins with a small, sharply delineated dead spot, usually round or oval to elongated in shape. You will notice this more when the canker enlarges and then girdles the cane, shoot, branch, trunk, or yes, even a root.

Fungi cause the majority of cankers. *Perennial cankers* on pome fruits establish themselves in mechanical wounds in the bark (such as a branch stub or mowing bruise) when opportunistic fungi move in at the start of the dormant period. The host plant tries to limit invasion by producing a layer of callus cells around and over the edge of the invaded tissue; the fungus invades the callus tissue at the end of the growing season; the host then forms new callus tissue. This cycle of fungal invasion and formation of concentric layers of callus tissue by the plant may repeat itself for many years. Pruning out a perennial canker on a redundant branch is no big deal; breaking the disease cycle on an integral branch may require supplementary preparations of certain herbs.[67] Early signs of peach perennial canker on any of the stone fruits (a different beast entirely) should be dealt with similarly. *Annual cankers* contain little or no callus and increase rapidly during a single growing season. Branches or even entire woody plants, especially young ones, may be girdled and killed in one growing season by severe cases of anthracnose canker. Holistic nutritional sprays are going to help prevent all this.

Bacteria enter the canker scene as fire blight on pome fruits and as bacterial canker on cherries and plums. Evident cankers should be pruned several inches below obvious infection during the winter when temperatures are below freezing (learn more about pruning out infected tissue in "Bacterial woes" in chapter 4). Chemical control of bacteria-spread disease is based on protective copper sprays just as fruit trees come out of dormancy. Copper limits initial infections but cannot prevent the canker phase once infection has begun.[68] All fruit crops are sensitive to copper, and injury is common. Here, as always, I prefer

Bacterial canker on a cherry twig. Photo courtesy of Alan Jones, Michigan State University.

Borers of all persuasions feed primarily on the sapwood of trees. Larvae of the roundheaded appletree borer (a beetle) spend a full two years at this task, often killing a young tree in the process. Photo courtesy of NYSAES.

to place my bet on the diversity of microbes found in an enhanced arboreal food web.

Let's talk now of pruning cuts that conspicuously blacken in subsequent growing seasons. The unhealthy-looking coating on the exposed cut and extending down on the surface of the bark can often be attributed to **sooty mold**. These superficial fungi grow off sap that oozed from pruning cuts made in previous years. Sooty mold never becomes directly parasitic.[69] The fact that sap continues to ooze from such cuts is indicative of cold injury and/or the gaining of a foothold by **black rot**. These fungi are another class entirely, moving in to form a sporulating canker edge that can eventually lead to extensive dieback of the entire branch.[70] Don't worry so much about surface mold, but definitely bring on the biological mudpack at any sign of rot. Pruning a badly infected limb may prove the only recourse.

Any fruit grower down on his or her knees at the trunk should be absolutely aware of **borers**. Varietal pests in this category include the roundheaded appletree borer, flatheaded appletree borer, dogwood borer, peachtree borers, shothole borer, and American plum borer. Some are beetles; some are moths; all are bastards. The grub stage of all these insects consumes both cambium and sapwood. Badly infested trees are girdled by the chewing and then die. The culprits will be anywhere from egg-slit big to a hefty half inch of

destruction long by the end of autumn. Probe any suspicious spot on the trunk, often marked by an orange-reddish protruding frass. Follow every crooked corner with a sharp-edged probe (like a pocketknife or your bypass pruners) until all edges of the damage are revealed. Remember, the tree survived grafting . . . it will also survive this surgery. A mass infestation can be treated with a biological mudpack of a different sort. Parasitic nematodes—sprayed in solution with a hand mister to the problem area, then protected with moistened topsoil packed around the soil line or farther up where limb damage occurs—will seek out the grubs in the next seventy-two hours and end the battle.[71] Some growers will have no borer pressure, while others (apparently those of you with karma like mine!) will have to do yearly penance. Luckily, drenching the soil zone at the base of each trunk with neem oil (applied at a 1 percent concentration) a couple times each summer has proven quite satisfactory in negating the roundheaded threat faced here.

Yellow-bellied **sapsuckers** attack living trees, with apples and cherries definitely high on the preference list. These birds drill a series of beak-deep holes in the bark, usually in regularly spaced, horizontal rows. Unlike woodpeckers, sapsuckers are not searching for grubs, intending instead to drink sap as it oozes into the holes. As one row of holes dries up, another row is drilled. A branch, or even a whole tree—depending on the height of the drilling—can eventually be girdled and then die. Sapsuckers are a migratory bird, passing through in early spring and again in fall. These birds seem to have excellent memory, zooming in on favored trees year after year.[72] Trees may survive a couple sessions of incessant drilling, but this cannot be left unchecked indefinitely. Hanging fluttering objects (old CDs quiver best of all) can help deter repetitive damage. Wrapping the trunk and major branch unions with burlap is ponderous but worth considering if it's one particular tree. Some sapsuckers will be content to feed on orange halves put out to attract nesting orioles. Owls living nearby change sapsucker dynamics dramatically. Slathering over areas of fresh drilling with biodynamic tree paste will facilitate bark closure and perhaps make the bird ponder why anyone would cover a tasty tree with unpalatable muck.

PRUNING OVERVIEW

A calm yet fruitful tree is the overarching goal of orchard pruning.

There's a directing order to my pruning mantra: *Framework first, then the thinning; lastly see the fruit and how it grows.* Nothing too mystical, but it's a beat that keeps me to task and includes all the important details. An intuitive pruner works in several years at once: seeing the fruiting prospects of the current year; training a new scaffold branch to eventually replace old wood; making a stubbing cut to encourage laterals farther back on a pole-like branch; visualizing how the sunlight will reach within the tree when the leaves are full; and providing good access when it comes time to pick the fruit. These things aren't deliberately thought through as much as felt. Such oneness with the tree comes with years of experience and confidence.

Approach each tree with an introductory intake of the breath. This meditative pause is when you take in the tree's framework and overall shape. How does it fit alongside its neighbors? Are some branches too low? Is the leader beyond reach? Are the scaffolds properly spaced? Where does a new branch need to be developed to fill an empty hole? These questions answer themselves quickly in a well-worked orchard. Restoring years of neglect is another matter.

- **Sunlight interception** is a function of tree spacing and height. The light environment throughout the tree canopy must be no lower than 30 percent of the available sunlight to produce high-quality fruit and spurs for successive cropping throughout the tree. Probably no other statement better describes why we prune apple trees annually.
- **Good tree structure** ultimately is as much about seeing the space left between scaffolds—so that sunlight and drying breezes can reach every apple—as it is about considering the limbs themselves. Learn to look at your tree as if wearing a pair of polarized glasses that gives emphasis to the inverse: First you see the tree structure; put on the glasses, and now you see the *light space* between the limbs.
- **Future fruiting prospects** depend entirely on allowing/encouraging/abetting new and renewed shoot growth to develop young fruit buds. Fruiting spurs are best developed by a light pruning touch rather than invigorated into long, unfruitful shoots by heavy pruning. Be very generous about leaving the pencil-thin laterals radiating off structural wood that will bear in future years. Our ideal as orchardists is to grow pome fruit on three- to ten-year-old wood. We cultivate such youthful wood by keeping a balanced percentage of shoots to develop spurs.
- **Tree calmness** is the result of striking that delicate balance between excessive pruning

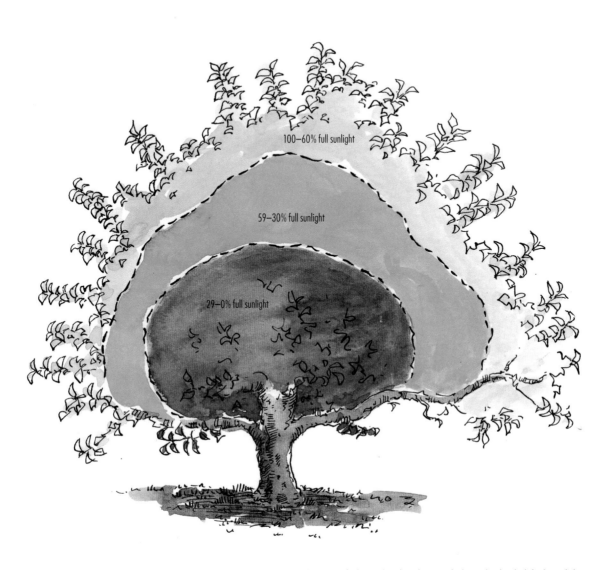

100–60% full sunlight

59–30% full sunlight

29–0% full sunlight

Distribution of sunlight within the tree is a primary goal of the intuitive pruner. I keep specific horticultural goals in mind when I decide which limbs and shoots to remove in any fruit tree.

and pruning enough to ensure an annual crop. Try not to eliminate all vertical growth in one fell swoop when taking back the central leader and/or thinning out the top of the tree. Some shorter vertical shoots are always necessary to satisfy the tree's desire to reach toward the sun. Scalping a tree in its entirety subsequently calls forth a forest of watersprouts. If you remove all of the watersprouts, just as many come back. Some vertical growth

is necessary to *apically dominate* the branch structure below in order to keep the tree calm.

- **Renewal pruning** in the top portion of the tree is an ongoing process of removing larger laterals while at the same time growing out replacement branches to renew the bearing surface of the tree. The primary tenet of *diameter-based pruning* is to remove any upper lateral branch that gets to be one-third to half the size of the trunk where it joins. While this

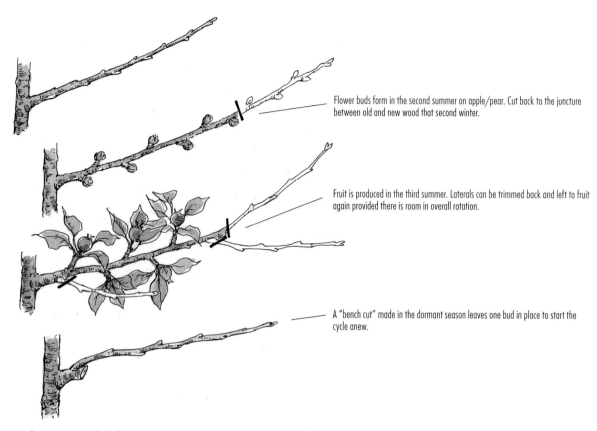

Flower buds form in the second summer on apple/pear. Cut back to the juncture between old and new wood that second winter.

Fruit is produced in the third summer. Laterals can be trimmed back and left to fruit again provided there is room in overall rotation.

A "bench cut" made in the dormant season leaves one bud in place to start the cycle anew.

Renewal pruning suits apple and pear cultivars that produce flower buds on unpruned two-year-old laterals. A bearing limb outgrowing its allotted light space in the top portion of the tree can be cut back to a short stub on less vigorous (dwarfing) trees. A new lateral will develop from the single bud left on the underside of that stub in response, developing fruitfulness two seasons hence.

may sound severe at first reading, it's a sure way of judging when higher laterals have to make way so smaller shoots can develop to replace them.[73]

Pruning 101

We always begin with a vision of tree shape and branch spacing.

An apple grower will speak of maintaining a *central leader* within a framework of three scaffolds. Like a conifer, the base is kept broad and the top more upright to allow sunlight to reach the fruit buds on the lower branches. A *scaffold* consists of three to five limbs radiating out from the trunk within a 1- to 2-foot span of the trunk. Having approximately

3 feet between scaffolds is a goal on larger-sized rootstock, with the first scaffold starting 3 feet or so above the ground on a semi-dwarf tree kept to 12 feet high. Branches originating much lower than this won't produce high-quality fruit. Good tree structure ultimately is as much about seeing the space left between scaffolds—so that sunlight can reach every apple—as it is about considering the limbs themselves.

Pears are overly enthusiastic about this central leader business. Nearly every shoot will tend toward being vertically inclined on most pear varieties, and this growth habit makes defining scaffold layers a tad more complex. Cherries, plums, apricots, and the like often are initiated as central leader trees but quickly

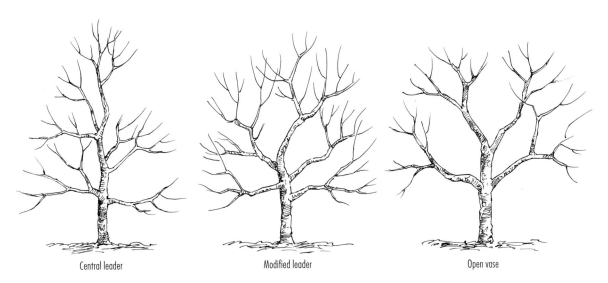

Central leader   Modified leader   Open vase

Growth habit and floral initiation (where fruit develops) are important factors in choosing a pruning style for particular fruits. Choice of tree shape—be it a central leader, a modified leader, or an open vase—is all about maximizing sunlight to suit.

opt to go in a *modified central leader* direction. Here the top of the tree naturally branches off to form several tops. This is often easier to maintain than other forms of pruning, as this is what fruit trees do given their druthers.

Peach trees in particular lend themselves to the *open vase* style of pruning. Creating an open center allows a bowl of sunlight to reach the inside of the bearing canopy. The branch structure of an open vase tree tends to be weaker, which results from favoring steeper crotch angles to create this shape. Lighter-weighing stone fruits help compensate for this style, as does renewal pruning of bearing limbs. I find my plum and apricot trees oscillating (in a sense) between having a multiple top and then having a more open center as a result of righteous branch removal every few years.

I'll address pruning specifics for each fruit type more thoroughly in the varietal chapters ahead. Knowing *why you do what you do* in making any pruning cut is what matters now. A tree responds to different cuts in different ways, and an understanding of these variables is what will make you a proficient pruner.

Use a **thinning cut** to remove a branch that is no longer desirable because of excessive crowding. Anytime a branch is removed at its juncture to another branch, the resulting vegetative response is considerably reduced from that of shearing the branch midway. Such cuts will help in maintaining those calm trees that do not put excessive energy into shoot development . . . thus keeping fruit production to the fore. A properly made thinning cut will readily compartmentalize to form a barrier zone within the wood, thus preventing rot organisms from entering deeper into the vascular system of the tree.

- Thinning from the top down is a good idea, because this way you follow the path of the sun's rays to the fruit. It's easier to thin the lower scaffolds—they're within reach—but more critical to achieve the topwork. Too many vigorous watersprouts that shoot vertically upward to the sun block the light that should be allotted to fruiting buds in the interior of the tree canopy.
- Overly tall leaders, crossing branches, and those limbs growing back toward the center or with narrow crotch angles always make the hit list.

Pruning in a very real sense is like time travel, projecting several years ahead as you see the fruit and how it grows in response to particular pruning cuts. Photo by Mark Rawlings.

- Another problem situation develops when too many limbs radiate off one section of the trunk. Crossing side branches then tend to be trimmed off in order to maintain each scaffold member, resulting in *blind wood*, where fruit buds are found farther and farther out from the trunk the longer you let this go on. Learning to thin excess limbs early on will save a series of painful decisions later.

- Spent wood results when bearing branches bend under the load of successive harvests. The most obvious thinning cuts are these understory branches, which have become too shaded to fruit well. The newer growth naturally arising over these branches keeps the fruiting canopy renewed.

A **heading cut** is made across the branch, out from the branch union, thereby exposing the vascular flow of the tree straight-on. Any pruning cut unveils sap flow, of course, but a heading cut tends not to shut off quite as readily as a thinning cut. The terminal bud has been removed, thereby eliciting a vigorous hormonal response (described earlier in this chapter with regard to the "Heading height" of nursery whips). Healthy closure of the pruning wound becomes far less likely as the diameter of the heading cut increases.

- The leaders on young trees entering the "teen years" (just before bearing begins) can be stiffened up by a heading cut. This pushes back fruiting for a year or two but often is necessary with lanky, upward-reaching growth.

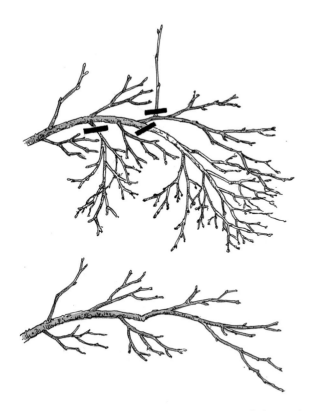

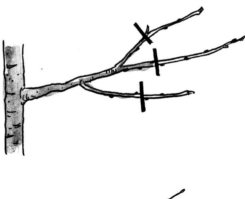

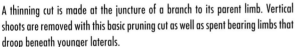

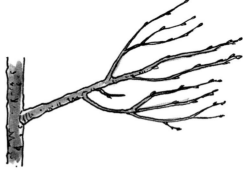

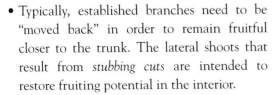

A thinning cut is made at the juncture of a branch to its parent limb. Vertical shoots are removed with this basic pruning cut as well as spent bearing limbs that droop beneath younger laterals.

A heading cut shears a branch midway and by doing so interrupts the flow of auxin hormone, thereby inducing lateral bud development.

- Typically, established branches need to be "moved back" in order to remain fruitful closer to the trunk. The lateral shoots that result from *stubbing cuts* are intended to restore fruiting potential in the interior.
- Varieties that tend to develop fruit at the end of shoots benefit from heading back excessively long shoots (more than 9 inches) to encourage compactness and lateral branching.
- Once the tree extends beyond a desired height, the dominant leader will need to be cut back to a weaker lateral. Ofttimes this heading-cut-by-default will induce numerous watersprouts, despite having been made at the branch union. Summer pruning most of this new growth response helps keep the tree fruitful.

- Don't make a heading cut if you can't envision a specific need to work with tree vigor in these ways.

Knowledge of how to use these two horticulturally distinct pruning cuts brings us to the actual deed. This is the big step, from theory to doing a good job by your trees. One last pep talk, methinks, before you head out the door.

Light space psychology

Good light penetration is needed to ripen and sweeten fruit. Air movement between branches helps considerably in preventing disease. Evaluating the light space between branches and competing shoots—and thereby considering how the chosen limb will develop to fill this space—has helped me more than any other pruning parameter in making good decisions. Pruning rules (about vertical shoots and the like) are useful up to a point. But it's only when you grasp what happens beyond the moment of the cut that you truly become effective from the tree's point of view.

Heed this advice given to me by a Vermont hill farmer: *You done a good job at pruning if afterward you can take the family cow and fling her between the branches.* Words like that certainly paint a vivid image of just how much to open up a standard-sized apple tree to the sunshine. Rookie pruners tend to do one of two things. The very timid never come close to removing enough, whereas ax-minded literalists follow pruning rules to the extreme. Neither will realize the fruiting potential of the tree standing before them. And that's a shame.

Pruning a tree properly (or a bramble or a fruiting shrub, for that matter) requires empathy. You project your mind into the buds before you and feel how additional sunshine and room to breathe will allow a chosen branch to become fruitful. Another branch competing for the very same light in a given space means neither can send out laterals and develop fruiting spurs throughout. I'm very serious here. Feel the warmth of the sun. Stretch out into this newly freed space. Be the bud. Understanding how to prune correctly involves consciously crossing the line between species and feeling what it's like to embrace photosynthesis.

Some of you will miss the gift attempted here. That's fine; go back to the rules; purchase more extensive pruning guides. A good many of you, on the other hand, might now be ready to grasp the core tenets of pruning. I've dealt with the psychic boundary around teaching this skill to novice orchardists for years. You need confidence. It comes from projecting your mind into the light space surrounding a branch. It comes from *being the bud.*

Growth habit

Every fruit tree has a natural growth habit. This tendency to grow in a such-and-such a way sometimes makes pruning easy as pie, while other trees defy all notions of ruly behavior. A bit of vocabulary is in order to further additional pruning advice related to tree vigor:

- *Compact.* The tree tends to grow tightly and close together within itself.
- *Erect.* The tree has distinct upright growth, favoring a vertical configuration.
- *Spreading.* The tree readily directs branches out to all sides.
- *Twiggy.* The tree droops numerous whippy branches downward.

The degree of vigor in a tree—whether this vigor stems from the innate nature of a particular variety or exceedingly fertile ground—accentuates the pruning task. Part of the fascination with dwarf trees is in keeping *tree reach* to a certain height through the use of runted genetics in the root. However, you actually can also restrain a full-sized tree to a reasonable height through knowledge-based pruning. Earlier we established a goal of keeping a tree calm, of striking that delicate balance between excessive pruning and pruning enough. Growth habit enters in here in a big way. The compact tree cooperates nicely. Pruning to favor outward growth will create a reasonably open limb structure. Erect trees with severe upright tendencies tend to be the most vigorous. Allowing a small percentage of weaker shoots up top to provide shading helps in training other shoots to adhere to a more horizontal position below. Spreading trees grow just like you might hope, though long branches might need to be braced under a full crop and occasionally trimmed back to a branch juncture. Twiggy types require substantial thinning of branches on the outer canopy.

Understanding where the flowers develop for different fruit types is equally apropos. Apples and pears initiate fruit buds either on short spurs found along the branch or toward the end of shoots, or some combination of the two. *Spur-bound* trees result when tree vigor is low, so thinning older spurs helps encourage new shoot growth. On the other hand, being too aggressive about branch thinning with *tip bearers* can quickly remove too many fruit buds. Stone fruits initiate fruit buds on young shoots in the node positions, the details of which will determine pruning tips specific to each fruit type.

The time to prune

Dormant pruning should be done in late winter before any sign of growth begins. How soon you begin depends on where you live. Northern growers run the risk of winter injury as long as subzero temperatures are still a possibility, and thus the suggestion to wait until February and March.[74] Orchardists in warmer zones can start in right after leaf fall, if desired. Ideally each of us wraps up the pruning season before budbreak, but . . . truth be known . . . you can persevere up till bloom if necessary.

Early summer marks the beginning of a shift in vegetative response to pruning. This is not the time for any major pruning cuts, but rather what I would call *training cuts* on young trees and *directed intent* on espalier stock. You can shorten the time to fruit production when working with young trees in this window (around the time of the summer solstice) rather than in the dormant season. Vigorous shoots can be nipped in the bud and often pushed into a fruitful direction by pinching off the growing tip.[75] Coming back to deal with the crow's-foot response to a heading cut now reclaims a single guiding shoot as the central leader. Similarly, thinning the tops of vertically inclined apple trees (like Gala) now will tone down that rocketing-upward response to cuts made in the dormant season. Supple vertical shoots can be literally snapped off should you find unwanted interior growth while thinning the fruit crop.

Late-summer pruning differs significantly from dormant pruning in that leaves actively involved in photosynthesis are being removed. The trees have entered physiological dormancy by the end of July and therefore will not respond with renewed growth.

The shoots being thinned out have contributed starch and sugar to terminal bud formation by this point, so taking away these excess growing tips leaves photosynthates primarily for the fruit-manufacturing end of the tree.[76] The sun has been granted time enough to reach fall-ripening varieties. Thinning out vegetative watersprouts in early August improves light penetration, thereby increasing fruit color throughout the canopy. These same pruning cuts also reduce the incidence of sooty blotch and flyspeck (summer fungal diseases) on light-colored pome fruit by as much as half.[77]

Growers in warmer zones—especially where "winter" implies a rainy season—will find the drier weather following harvest helps promote faster closure of pruning cuts for stone fruits. Cherries and apricots particularly are prone to bacterial canker and gummosis, which are abetted by damp weather. Late-summer pruning of these fruits makes a world of difference in keeping those diseases at bay.

Fall pruning of pome fruits before the leaves have dropped is the wrong thing to do, however. These trees are in hardening-off mode now. Stimulating any growth response at this time, including callus to close the wound, will set up cold injury in the winter months.

Zeroing in on espalier

You can have all sorts of fun in a backyard setting by training fruit trees to a two-dimensional plane against a sunny wall or open fence line. Apples, pears, and plums lend themselves to *espalier* more readily than the other stone fruits. The emphasis in this traditional pruning style is as much on artistic form in a small space as on fruit production. Keeping the tree in flat mode along a supporting trellis limits the overall harvest on account of the missing third dimension, but where else do you get to pluck tasty fruit from a candelabra-shaped tree? Nor need your imagination be limited—train a cherry tree into a figure eight; create corkscrew limbs by continuously wrapping selected shoots around the wire; graft in multiple apple varieties so all six branches of the horizontal

RENOVATING AN ABANDONED TREE

Every pruning season people ask me how to care for a long-abandoned apple tree. The journey back to a manageable-sized tree is doable. The quality of the fruit is another matter, for a chance seedling has about a one in ten thousand chance of being pomologically worthy. Your tree may have been a named variety grafted a century ago, or it may be a pasture tree once valued for its bittersweet cider potential.

The leaf canopy of a tree supports a vast root system, and vice versa. Going in with a pruning saw to undo decades of overgrowth all at once can be disastrous to an old tree. It's far better to approach this task over the course of a few growing cycles. Year one is the time to think big. All dead and broken branches can be removed first to clarify what's going on in that tumbled confusion of limbs. Next seek out three or four cuts either back at the trunk or on major scaffold limbs— overly tall leaders and crossing branches will be the chief targets. An overgrown tree likely has a structure of its own that defies orderly notions of a single leader. You're the one who needs to adapt and recognize the virtue of an elder's decision to fill its light space in artistic ways. Properly made cuts are important, as a stub of deadwood is an entry point for rot-causing organisms. Nor cut too deeply: The *branch collar* will produce callus tissue needed to close the wound.

The year ahead provides plenty of opportunity to ruminate on the shape of your tree. Heavy pruning invariably results in an abundance of watersprouts, vegetative vertical shoots that can keep your tree in a nonfruiting mode for years to come. These suckers should be summer-pruned in early August to stimulate the tree to put more energy into fruit buds the following spring. Limit your summer cutting to upright shoots less than an inch in diameter, leaving the weakest 10–20 percent of these to provide a modicum of shading.

Midsized pruning cuts resume when the late dormant season (January through April, depending on your latitude) comes around again. One or two big cuts may still be in order; otherwise focus on those weak crotch angles and excessive growth that blocks sunlight between scaffolds. Stop short of removing more than a third of a tree's canopy in any one year.

The focus on young wood capable of bearing fruit happens in year three. Improved light penetration will have initiated a shoot response throughout the tree that's now ready to form fruiting spurs. This same energy can be channeled by bending supple watersprouts (the ones you left!) beneath an existing branch the growing season before. Vertical suckers, if held to a lateral position, will develop fruit buds for the next growing season. Moderate thinning cuts aimed

cordon are lined out in mysteriously amazing colors along the trellis; create the initials of your one true love. Tree art knows no bounds.

The support structure for the trees should be placed slightly away from a solid wall to allow some air movement behind the branches. Sturdy posts (set every 12 feet) hold up the wire trellis: The first wire runs 18–24 inches above the ground, with three additional wires above that at 18 inches apart. End posts will need to be braced to prevent the wires from eventually sagging. Plant each tree just in front of the trellis plane, spaced as pairs 6 feet apart between the two at removing the spent portion of branch ends helps make room for this new wave of fruitful growth. The days of large limb removal should be behind you. Fertilizing a tree during these years of invigorating pruning cuts is usually not advised if terminal bud growth is 8 inches or more and the leaves are a healthy dark green hue. Woodsy compost and a widespread sprinkle of borax (in regions typically deficient in boron) in the fall of year two are appropriate for what should now be a productive and beautiful apple tree.

Year one

Year two

Year three

Renovating a long-neglected apple tree begins with a few major cuts in year one followed by progressive fine-tuning in the years ahead. You can indeed restore fruit production with new wood while at the same time respecting the beauty of a free-form tree.

posts (which puts each tree 3 feet from each post). Start with a one-year-old whip so you can train each chosen branch as it grows.

Dwarfing rootstock best suits espalier by far.[78] Whatever the vigor of the trees chosen, frequent pruning and pinching will be needed every year. Only shoots growing in the desired directions are kept, and these are tied to the trellis with twine or plastic wire ties as growth extends.

Here's the method to create a *horizontal cordon*. A heading cut made just above the level of that first wire on the whip at planting time will induce a crow's-foot

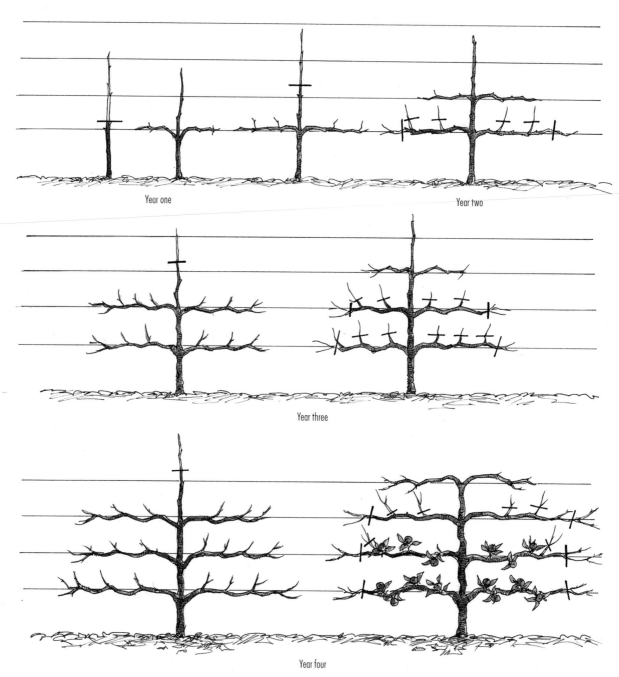

Year one   Year two

Year three

Year four

Horizontal cordon training involves a series of repeated steps over the first few years to develop the desired lateral structure. Fruit production on such espaliered trees will begin in the third or fourth season.

growth response. One of the resulting shoots will be selected as the leader, while two others will be trained to radiate sideways along the first wire. Tie these into place while the shoots are still supple, at about 10–12 inches in length. Bending a shoot to the horizontal position reduces vegetative vigor. All outward-bound shoots perpendicular to the fruiting plane are kept pinched back.

During dormant pruning at the end of the first winter, cut the central leader off at a bud just below the second wire. Repeat the process of the previous spring by developing two scaffold branches to tie to the second wire and allow the central leader to grow above the third wire. This process is repeated during the next two seasons as well, after which time a total of eight scaffolds (four on each side of the tree) should be firmly established. The leader will be bent to form one of the upper scaffolds, rather than being cut off at the top wire.

By the end of the fourth season, the trees will definitely be in production. All pruning from here on in will be done during late spring and through the summer. Distinguishing between the stubby spurs that will bear fruit and outright vegetative shoots now becomes critical. When new growth at the end of each scaffold (think terminal bud) in spring gets to be about 2 inches long, cut it off, as well as removing about a quarter of the previous season's growth. Vertical shoots developing along the scaffold are left untouched for now. As soon as this shoot growth begins to become woody at the base (the shoot will be on the order of a foot long), snip it back to the whorl of leaves at its base. Repeat four to six weeks later if a similar upright shoot response occurs. This basal snip encourages fruit bud formation and calms the vegetative urge of the tree.[79] Root pruning—done by jabbing a sharp spade into the earth at the outer edge of lateral growth in early spring—can be useful to check vigorous top growth.

Northern growers will want to try espalier against a south-facing wall to maximize solar gain for pome fruits.[80] In warm climates, try choosing a spot that doesn't get direct sun through the late-afternoon hours. A white wall helps reflect excess heat that would otherwise wither leaves. Whitewashing exposed bark areas on lateral branches will prevent severe sunburn damage. Espaliered fruit ripens slightly earlier than its varietal counterparts exposed in the open. Keep in mind from whence the fruit springs in choosing cultivars for espalier: Tip-bearing apples, for instance, will bear little fruit because of the type of pruning needed,

Late spring

Midsummer

Next spring

The *basal snip* is used to induce the production of fruit spurs close to the main stem on an espaliered tree. New growth is cut away when shoots start to get woody at the base, leaving a whorl of leaves. More pinching follows according to the vigor of the vegetative response. The result is a spur system ready to bear fruit the following season.

while more spurring types will keep you pleased as punch.[81]

Training a freestanding tree

Branch training in the early years of a freestanding tree's life is critical to building a strong bearing structure for the future. The primary goal now is to grow wood by maximizing photosynthesis output from shoots and leaves. This can be done best by leaving the pruners in the house (for the most part) and

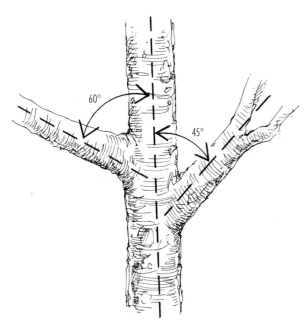

The strongest branches on a fruit tree radiate out from the vertical leader into the horizontal plane at a 45- to 60-degree angle.

A clothespin clipped to the stem above a supple shoot will spread that shoot laterally to form a decent crotch angle that holds in place by the season's end.

focusing instead on spreading tentative lateral shoots to a proper crotch angle.

The strongest branches on a fruit tree radiate out from the vertical leader into the horizontal plane at a 45- to 60-degree angle. Limbs that develop with narrower crotches form a weak union with the trunk because of included bark, and years later, be it under a heavy fruit load or in an ice storm, severe injury to the trunk is likely to occur when the two split apart. Perfectly flat branches are strong but don't have quite the loft to hold up future crop loading. Shoots, of course, do what shoots do: Some will angle off from the leader just perfectly, while others require a shot in the arm in the form of a limb spreader.

Appreciating how a shoot can be manipulated to a desirable branch position requires some understanding about *annual growth rings*. The cross section of any tree trunk at stump level reveals circumferential rings, which you can count to determine that tree's age. Each one of these rings represents the extent of woody growth achieved by the cambium in a given year. The supple growth of the shoot in spring lignifies to become wood by fall. Similarly, a whippy lateral

held in place by a spreader in spring stays in that new position when the limb spreader gets removed in fall . . . because that year's ring of growth is now insistent wood. The branch has thickened and become locked in place.

Laterals are best spread in spring when flowing sap makes wood tissue pliable. Orchardists have an array of limb spreaders that can be employed, depending on the size of the limb being spread downward. Jutting a clothespin above new growth forces that shoot to push farther out, thus forming a wider crotch angle. A toothpick wedged between a newly developing shoot and the leader achieves similar effect.[82] Red plastic wyes in incremental lengths from 3–12 inches are available commercially. I have bucketfuls of lathes

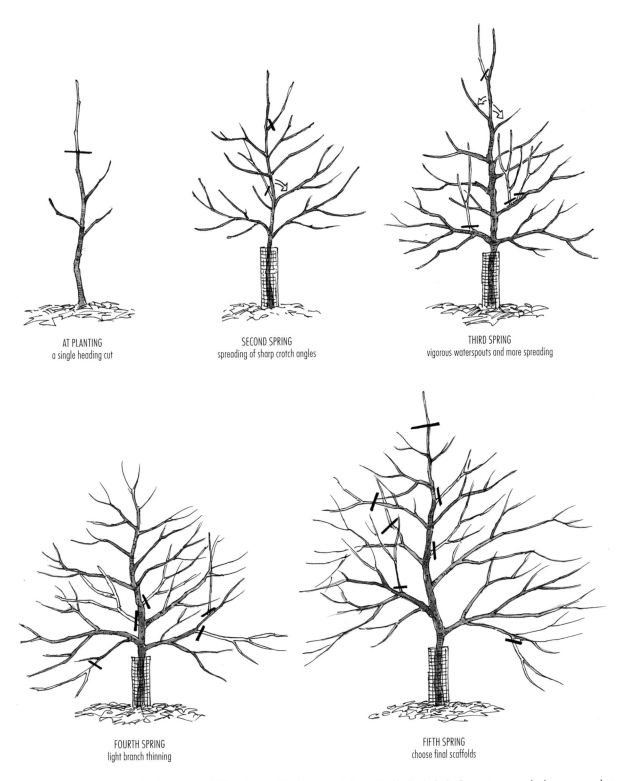

AT PLANTING
a single heading cut

SECOND SPRING
spreading of sharp crotch angles

THIRD SPRING
vigorous waterspouts and more spreading

FOURTH SPRING
light branch thinning

FIFTH SPRING
choose final scaffolds

Training trees in the early years makes for strong scaffold branches capable of bearing a full crop. Head back a lanky leader on vigorous stock when necessary, but leave more compact trees alone. Good training minimizes the use of pruning cuts until the trees start to bear.

(notched on each end in the form of a receiving vee) of various lengths for spreading even larger branches. An upper branch in more mature trees can be tied to a lower branch with stout cordage . . . the locking principle remains the same.[83]

One clever trick can be of use with a vertically inclined shoot that you'd really like to keep on a particular spot on the leader. When the shoot in question becomes too stiff to spread, a desirable limb option can be salvaged with a *bench cut* to restore fruiting prospects. A single bud on the small piece of shoot remaining from this horizontal pruning cut (made relatively tight to the leader) will then produce a more suitable crotch angle for the shoot that grows anew.

Let's walk through the first several years of a tree's life to make sure you have a clear idea of how to establish that envisioned central leader tree.

Come the spring after planting, before growth resumes, select those laterals at a desired height you intend to keep and remove any others from the lower span of the trunk. The three to five limbs left should be as evenly spaced around the trunk as the growth whorl allows. Use spreaders appropriate to the size of the shoot to establish good crotch angles. Don't head (prune) scaffold branches unless one is significantly larger than the others and needs reining back. Doing as little wood pruning as possible these first years will bring the tree into fruit production that much sooner. Shorter laterals up high should be left to maximize leaf surface area for photosynthesis. Remember to check throughout the summer for sharp-angled shoots that develop along the upper portion of the leader. Pinching off this upright growth (within 6 inches of the growing tip) will prevent competition and stunting of the central leader. This technique is used in first-, second-, and sometimes third-leaf trees to keep the leader rapidly growing upward.

The permanent framework of the tree begins to show itself in the third growing season. Lanky leaders on freestanding trees may need heading again (though hopefully not as regards fruit production) to stiffen up the tree. Each scaffold branch should be of equal vigor and have a strong crotch angle between 45 and 60 degrees. Now's when you need an ample supply of longer limb spreaders on hand. Go easy with stouter shoots, which will tear off the tree if spread too far. Continuing to pay heed to crotch angles will save split trunks years down the road. Scaffolds are separated by 1 foot to as much as 4 feet of trunk growth depending on rootstock. Interim laterals can be left in trees trained to a wider spacing until the permanent scaffold fills its envisioned light space.

The fourth and/or fifth and sixth growing seasons are the "teenage" years of the tree. The first crops are light compared with the harvests that will come at full maturity. Continue to allow scaffold branches and the leader to grow with as little pruning as possible. Dwarf and semi-dwarf trees will have started to bear, and the weight of their fruit will add greatly to the spread of the tree. Spreading laterals up high in standard trees helps the scaffold branches below reach outward in search of sunlight until annual crop loading begins.

A properly trained tree will need only minimal corrective pruning over the years to maintain this naturally spreading shape that you've diligently trained from year one. Ultimately we can hold faith in even the most vertical-growing of trees, because its branches will bend down beneath the weight of a good harvest.[84] Let me repeat: You get to the bearing years that much sooner by respecting a no-touch policy as much as possible with young trees. That's achieved by keeping those pruners at bay, spreading branches into position, and preferably pinching off unwanted shoots in early summer. Got it?

Some quirks to the plan above are called for when deliberately crafting an open vase tree shape for stone fruits.[85] A goodly number of potential scaffold branches will have grown on a peach or nectarine that first growing season. Keep three or four vigorous shoots evenly spaced around the trunk at about a 45-degree angle from it, all within 6–8 inches of one another. Prune these back to 2–3 feet in length, leaving small shoots along these branches to provide sunburn protection for the scaffold limbs

Assorted limb spreaders hold branches in position based on the premise that this year's growth ring will lock desired tree structure into place by fall.

and to possibly produce early fruit. During the second dormant season, select two or three vigorous lateral branches growing outward from each of the primary scaffold branches. Avoid selecting lateral branches situated on top of each other. Remove other branches and cut back the secondary lateral branches to 20–36 inches long. Leave smaller shoots, especially on the north and east side of the tree, to provide some shade for the scaffold branches.

The same basic pruning methods are used in the third and fourth dormant seasons, as peaches and nectarines are pruned to an upright but lateral canopy with an open center having three or four primary scaffold limbs branching out to five or six secondary branches each. Maintaining an open center in this way

will allow light penetration throughout the canopy to stimulate production of new fruiting wood and enable picking that perfect peach without a ladder.

Berry renewal

Bramble, bush, or shrub . . . pruning goals continue to be good sunlight penetration and renewing the bearing surface, only now for berry production. Working with cane fruit calls for a tad more aggression on an annual basis, but, truly, all this is so much simpler than pruning full-sized trees.

Aboveground, brambles are woody biennials, springing from a perennial root system. The canes of raspberry and blackberry grow to full height in a single season. The following year these bear fruit, then die back by fall. Next year's canes have grown up in this second season, therefore keeping an expectant rotation in step. Cutting out old canes soon after harvest is the most important part of bramble culture. All but the fall-bearing *Rubus* species require this of us to maintain maximum production year after year.

Blueberries, currants, and the like are even easier to maintain. Each can be encouraged to do better by simply removing a percentage of older branches. Don't get sentimental about those four- to six-year-old has-beens, which overcrowd the entire plant with additional side branches. Younger shoots will have plumper fruit buds and thus produce bigger berries. The farther north you go, the less pruning will be required to open up the canopy of a fruiting bush or shrub. Pruning cuts are made at ground level, either in late fall or early spring. Doing this every two years will keep these berry fruits productive and thriving beyond your lifetime.

POLLINATION

Fruit cultivars can be self-fertile, partially self-fertile, or blatantly self-sterile. Some sense of who's pollinating whom among varieties can prevent fruiting disappointment, even with those cultivars that don't seem

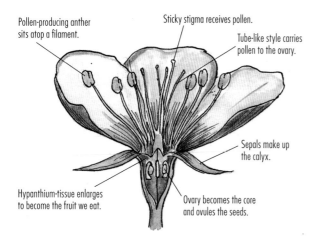

Pollen-producing anther sits atop a filament.

Sticky stigma receives pollen.

Tube-like style carries pollen to the ovary.

Sepals make up the calyx.

Ovary becomes the core and ovules the seeds.

Hypanthium-tissue enlarges to become the fruit we eat.

The anatomy of an apple blossom includes both male and female attributes. The *stamen* consists of the male pollen parts while the *pistil* refers to each stigma, style, and ovary combined.

to need a dancing partner. The straightforward advice to plant two varieties of any fruit type will always up the odds of improved pollination. Still, when all is said and done, it comes down to receptive blossoms meeting up with willing bees without deep cold upsetting the fruit cart.

Blossom dynamics

Fruit trees want to produce seed. The fruit is merely part of the marketing package from the tree's perspective. Seed development hinges on pollination. The transfer of pollen from the male anther to the female stigma of the flower can be done by either wind or insects. The cross-pollination required by fruit trees is performed by numerous bees, wasps, and syrphid flies, which are attracted to the showy flowers. Upon reaching the stigma, the pollen grain germinates and grows a tube down the style to the ovule. Each seed that grows in an apple or pear is the result of the separate pollination (often by several bees) of five stigmas leading to two egg cells apiece. Stone fruit have a single pit enabled by a single pollinator visit.

Getting pollen deposited on the fruit blossom soon after it opens is critical. The female ovule has a viable life of between two and three days at best. The honeybee

Some orchardists in Japan rely primarily on pollinating the fruit crop by hand. Partly this is about fruit spacing, but more so it's about a lack of native pollinators. All of us need to be involved in supporting pollinator diversity. Photo by Jane Alden Stevens.

will be active for seventeen hours of this fertility period (daylight shift, short day, and only then if the weather is good), suggesting that multiple pollinator species had better be on the scene.[86] The first flower to open in a pome cluster is referred to as the *king blossom* and produces the choicest fruit. Orchardists blessed with calm, warm weather at the very start of bloom know that king pollination ensures a full crop even if the weather shifts for the worse later in the week.

Cool weather during bloom complicates matters in two respects: Honeybees lie low when temps drop below 50°F (10°C), lessening overall prospects. More critically, pollen tube germination slows to a withering

Bumblebees are among the best pollinators, working from dawn to dusk. The early blooms of lungwort provide nectar for overwintering queens to establish a first brood.

crawl. This can make even the limited pollination that does occur during a cool spell unsuccessful. The pace of pollen tube germination is affected by temperature, and when slowed down significantly by daytime highs in the low 40s (4–7°C) it may well fizzle out with respect to delivering vibrant pollen to a vibrant seed ovule in the time allotted. This dynamic occurs more often than not with early-blooming hybrid plums, which depend on lightweight pollinators to work the bloom (hence the plum thicket pollination strategy to buffet gusty winds) and a minimal degree of warmth in the days that follow.

Bee attractants may make a difference if you experience poor pollination even when the sun shines. Applying Bee-Scent Attractant to less appealing pear bloom or that disappointing raspberry row might change pollination prospects dramatically. This liquid formulation of orientation pheromones and sugary attractants (sprayed on target plants during bloom) encourages the foraging behavior of honeybees and other wild pollinators. A homemade bloom spray consisting of molasses and whey will help save a crop seemingly threatened by bee disaffection as well.

Gauging pollination success in that immediate week after full bloom can be surprisingly difficult. An unfertilized flower slowly dries up as its petals fall away. The revealed fruitlet starts off green—a good sign—but then yellows and abscises (falls off) in a matter of days. Viable fruit will keep its color and slowly start to size. The ideal balance between the two would be a mere 5 percent of all those sweet-smelling blossoms on the tree having taken, evenly spaced along the branch, sentinels of the full crop we think we deserve. While there's little to be done about lost opportunity, excessive pollination is more often Nature's way

The blue orchard bee lives an industrious life centered on fruit tree bloom. This female is capping off a bamboo nesting tube where individual eggs have been placed that will hatch the following spring. Photo by Mace Vauhagn, courtesy of the Xerces Society.

Nesting condos for blue orchard bees take many forms. Community orchardists can encourage a substantial number of bees with this high-end model. Photo by Eric Mader, courtesy of the Xerces Society.

of ensuring abundance . . . which gets addressed by thinning the crop by hand in those immediate weeks following petal fall.

Bee consciousness

Focusing on providing habitat for a diversity of pollinators throughout the growing season is the best way that orchardists have to achieve successful pollination of fruiting plants in spring. The humble bumblebee and its solitary cousin, the blue orchard bee, are front-line allies. Tiny wasps and hovering flies can be especially important with early-blooming fruit. Even hummingbirds can play a role. Allowing nectar and pollen sources to flower throughout the season is what builds up a broad base of pollination support.[87]

Bumblebees start every day soon after first light regardless of the weather and work late into the evening to gather pollen and nectar. Honeybees are more inclined to keep bankers' hours and then only if the weather is nice. The first bumbles of spring in the orchard are the young queens seeking a nesting site. Boxes filled with upholstery stuffing might entice a young queen, but so will undisturbed compost piles or rotting hay bales. The early brood is critical to fruit blossoms, but it's the happiness of the bumble population throughout the summer that assures a guaranteed return. Simply put, the more flower sources, the more bumblebees.

You'll definitely want to encourage *Osmia lignaria* to claim your orchard environs as home. Blue orchard bees (also known as orchard mason bees) are very efficient pollinators, with each female effectively visiting sixteen hundred flowers on a good day. Like bumblebees, these solitary bees are better at reaching the pistil of the fruit

Syrphid flies are often seen hovering over blossoms (like this blackberry) in anticipation. Then these beneficial pollinators do one more thing . . . lay a solitary egg on shoot tips, which becomes a voracious aphid-feeding larva. Photo by Mace Vauhagn, courtesy of the Xerces Society.

blossom than honeybees, resulting in fewer misshapen apples due to incomplete pollination. Crocuses planted on the orchard floor bloom early and can attract these bees before any fruit trees bloom. Providing nesting condos gives them all the more reason to stay. Housing for blue orchard bees consists of a series of holes where eggs can be laid and subsequently protected. One design consists of PVC piping cut to short lengths to hold cardboard tubes of the preferred diameter of ⁵⁄₁₆ inch for the rearing female *Osmia*. The other involves drilling holes 4–6 inches deep in the end of a wooden block or even a nearby fence post, capped with a metal cover to keep it dry. Either will entice this native species to increase its numbers in your orchard. Face the nest toward the southeast in the crotch of a fruit tree or atop a post, securing it at least 3 feet above the ground. The bees will find such places quickly and get to work settling in.

You'll know they've been successful when you observe the holes plugged with mud immediately following the tail end of bloom. A series of eggs have been laid behind each sealed entry (provisioned with nectar and pollen); these will hatch out the following

spring. One last job on your part can make a significant difference in survival rates. Certain parasitic wasps begin flying at about the same time that this year's bees have completed both this task and their relatively short life cycle. Bringing the nest houses in to an outbuilding or the cellar a week or two after bloom ends (and storing these inside a box or cooler with ventilation!) prevents any incursions. This should be a dark place that experiences moderate temperatures at the height of summer and then much the same cold and humidity as would be found outside come fall. The goal is to keep bee awakening in sync with everything else when the nest houses are put back out in the orchard sometime later that winter. And should all else fail in attracting blue orchard bees in the first place? Starter progeny can be purchased from bee suppliers listed in the resources at the back of the book.[88]

Frankly, more of us should also be vested in keeping honeybees. These vital pollinators need stress-free places to thrive and be healthy in these days of colony collapse disorder, caused by overuse of agricultural chemicals and unnatural living conditions (including long-distance transportation). Backyard beekeepers can offer a gentler, more normalized lifestyle for the honeybee while sharing in a safe honey harvest.[89] Top bar beehives especially intrigue me as a healthy alternative to traditional frame hives that emphasize extraction efficiency of the honey over the bees' innate sensibilities.

Dealing with spring cold

It goes without saying that spring frosts do serious harm to fruiting intentions. Locating trees and berries in a safer place on your property with respect to air drainage can help to some extent. Strategies to deal with borderline cold may get you through such nights. And as a last resort, there's always next year!

Planting on higher ground can help with a marginal frost. Cold air will settle to the lower places on those crisp, clear nights when radiational cooling literally sucks the heat from the land. Location can also be used to delay bloom. The advice to plant stone fruits (which can bloom as much as several weeks before apple) on a north-facing slope or elsewhere with wintertime shade has validity. Similarly, mulching tender cultivars heavily in the fall after the ground has frozen will delay the onset of spring bloom by as much as ten days. Chances are, though, you still might awake to frozen petals in an erratically cold spring.

Pear buds are slightly hardier than those of apples, and, contrary to what might be expected of the tender peach buds of winter, so are the stone fruits upon resumption of growth in the spring. A tightly held apple bud can withstand temperatures dropping to 20°F (–7°C), but once the flower opens, temperatures below 26°F (–3°C) will kill 90 percent of the bloom.[90] Preventive measures can make the difference between getting a crop and no crop at all. After the harvest, prolonged cool weather slowly increases bud hardiness in preparation for the winter ahead. All can fall short, however, when a deep freeze follows on the heels of a warming spell in December, January, and February—resulting in flowers that open nevertheless, but can never be pollinated. Bud hardiness issues (fully examined within the "Peach tree hardiness" section of chapter 6) can best be dealt with by choosing cultivars wisely and siting those trees with uninterrupted dormancy in mind.

A moist, open soil surface can contribute as much as 3°F (2°C) to the air temperature within the tree canopy. Take heed, for within that statement lies the surest way to protect tender blossoms. Both sod and heavy mulch retard the upward flow of ground heat on frosty nights. More open ground, on the other hand, can be wetted down (really saturated) with a hose, and the heat from the water will rise during the night to warm the air surrounding the tree. And where does that open ground come from? Trees sharing the dripline space with a living mulch plant like comfrey have an open understory in early spring before the herb springs forth anew. Additionally, an enhanced biology will have decomposed a good portion of those wood chip piles and forked-over hay mulch from the

year before. Watering the ground to protect against a moderate frost is different from sprinkling the tree itself. Overhead irrigation works by coating tender plant tissues with an insulating layer of water against the ice that forms on the surface, keeping the bud within from actually freezing.[91] The risk of severe limb breakage from ice buildup needs to be considered, however. Water protection works best (with radiational cooling rather than an arctic front) when only a few degrees of protection are needed and you wet the ground.

Orchard heat—be it in the form of coal baskets hung from branches, a series of small bonfires around your island planting, or even propane stack heaters—can help on those nights when thermal updrafts are strong. Cloth covering (be it cotton sheets or floating row covers) can help too, provided the wind doesn't tear this away from protected plants. Just be aware that sometimes you will lose more blossoms to rub-off than the potential harm of marginally freezing temperatures. Plastic sheeting will not be that helpful, as poly doesn't insulate worth a darn. Stringing holiday lights in the boughs of tender trees (longing for a lemon, are we?) will add extra warmth beneath the more insulating cloth option.

A foliar application of liquid seaweed on the afternoon before an expected chill will impart a couple degrees of frost resistance by means of nutritional alchemy. The polysaccharides in cold-processed kelp are absorbed by plant tissues, thereby displacing water in those tissues.[92] This helps plants tolerate the cell-rupturing pressure from frost that would normally cause significant damage. Using molasses with the liquid kelp will enhance protectant effects yet again by temporarily upping sugar levels and thereby lowering the freezing point in buds-at-risk.

Don't despair the morning after if temperatures hovered right near the danger point. Buds yet to open may be unscathed; pollinated flowers are believed to be slightly hardier than yet-to-be-pollinated ones. Look to the all-critical pistil for blackening to see if freeze damage is severe. Some apples and pears will persist in growing, though no seeds or cores may ever develop. Frost-bitten fruitlets may show unusual crimping marks at maturity. Another way to think about all this is that severe cold has allowed you to get rid of constantly sensitive fruits in favor of varieties more suitable for your location. Some lessons to be learned are more painful than others.

THINNING THE CROP

We have come to the numero uno task in growing good-looking fruit. Timely thinning achieves three things: decent fruit size, good return bloom the next season, and one-on-one pest control.

This is transcendental work, requiring nothing more than a steady rhythm to remove excess fruitlets by hand. I focus upon one tree at a time, spending as much as a full hour per full-sized tree to do this job well, including topwork off a ladder. Other times I view a quick bout of thinning as a pleasant opportunity for a break. Perhaps I've broken a sweat with scythe in hand, it's hot . . . and so I head into the canopy of a nearby apple tree to thin the crop, cooling down in its shade, and leaving the deerflies to find some other head to bother.

Hormonal investment

Pollination success soon becomes revealed by actual fruit set. Heavy croppers may set the majority of all blossoms in an on-year, while more sporadic varieties maintain annual bearing by setting one in eight blossoms, if that. The normal failure of the tree to set every blossom is due to underdeveloped fruit buds, missed pollination, and winter injury to the pistils that cannot be detected by the eye. Take heart—if every tree actually set its full potential, thinning would be more than daunting.

A properly thinned tree can produce as many bushels of fruit as one that is not thinned, fruit size making up the difference. Most important, the tree's energy is conserved, as seed production can exhaust nutrient and hormone reserves. Removing two-thirds of the fruit removes two-thirds of the potential seeds. The energy saved is put into sizing up the remaining fruit and creating next year's flower buds. A balanced crop load helps a fruit tree harden off for winter as well. In young trees, this energy is needed for root development . . . leave yourself an apple or two for tasting in that initial bearing year, but don't be so eager for a sizable early crop that you stunt structural growth.

Fruit trees sense when pollination has crossed the overachievement mark . . . and will naturally abort a portion of excess fruitlets in response. The selection of fruits that will be retained to maturity causes the *June drop* of the weaker fruitlets. This hormonal decision is driven by photosynthesized cues—the need for unobstructed sunlight, to be exact. Cloudy weather in those immediate weeks following petal fall increases the percentage of castoffs. This is all about green leaves producing sufficient carbon sugars and growth hormones to grow fleshy fruit and support seed production at the same time. It comes down to so many leaves serving as a photosynthesis factory able to provide for each individual fruit.[93] Trees tend toward keeping more rather than less, thereby leaving it up to the grower to manipulate fruit counts a tad further.

Return bloom

Wild fruit trees naturally fall into *biennial bearing*, by which is meant producing a crop every other year. You might assume this to be the genetics of the variety, but more often than not it's the off-year having been overwhelmed by the on-year that sets up this cropping sequence.

Look at a developing pome fruitlet in that first month following petal fall. Now consider the spur wood where the stem attaches the fruitlet (in effect) to the vascular system of the tree. Cells are being formed right before your eyes at this connection point that will become a fully developed flower bud next spring if all goes right. These actively dividing cells are the *meristem* of the fruit tree. This embryonic tissue reacts

A generous pear set needs to be thinned to a single fruit from each blossom cluster.

negatively to hormones produced by an excess of developing seeds.[94] To put it bluntly, an overly bountiful crop—with too many seeds in the pipeline—prevents fruit bud initiation for the following year. The fruit tree has overcommitted itself. *Return bloom* the next growing season is unlikely . . . and that's what sets up the on-year, off-year cropping cycle.

Balancing these two competing dynamics is our job. Thinning the crop enough within thirty-five days of bloom allows the development of both seed and bud. Later thinning can still be useful for sizing the fruit, but the time has passed to assure return bloom. No one does this for wild trees, and that's why biennial cropping is the norm. Let's add *annual bearing* to the lists of benefits resulting from timely thinning of the tree fruit crop.

Hand-thinning

You can start hand-thinning as soon as fruitlets reach a workable diameter. That can be as little as ⅜ inch if you have significant canopy surface area to get done, while up to quarter-sized (the coin, that is) will still be timely. Early-setting peaches can be done fairly quickly. Apple and pear trees with the heaviest fruit set are thinned next, as an overbearing tree will have the least to invest in next year's fruit buds. Varieties like Gala, Fuji, and Macoun have particular reputations for setting way too much fruit. Plums, apricots, and quince can be left alone unless you think a high crop load will lead to breaking limbs. And no one thins cherries or berries.

Start by leaving the largest and best-looking fruit, typically one per cluster. Rot is more liable to spread in any peaches left to grow side by side, while surface-feeding caterpillars really like the hiding place provided between touching apples. The excess fruitlets are simply pinched off along the stem, noting that snips might be useful on varieties with short stems. Use two hands to prevent breaking off entire spurs . . . those are next year's fruit buds, mate! Grasp the limb nearby in one hand, and remove the extras with the other. Some of you will master not bothering with the stem at all, finding it much quicker to roll off the fruitlets between thumb and fingers.

Here's where good judgment plays a big role in improving the crop. Imagine five fruitlets have set in a cluster. The king blossom is slightly larger than the others and likely smack-dab in the center. If you see no apparent insect damage or disease spotting, that's the one to keep.[95] On the other hand, if it's apparent that sawfly or a codling moth or curculio has wreaked its havoc, then leave the next biggest fruitlet. All infested culls can be thrown into a hip bag or waiting bucket and disposed of later—this is one-on-one pest control in action! Doing this before the tree itself takes action (aborting excess fruitlets at June drop[96]) is all the more helpful, as any damaging larvae inside the fruitlet are unlikely to have as yet "parachuted" to the ground below for the insect's next molting stage. I dump badly infested fruitlets on a country road where car tires soon splatter the works into oblivion. You don't want to directly compost this collection effort in a sitting (left alone) compost pile, whatever you do, as larvae with access to soil-like conditions will pupate and then successfully come back as second-generation adults.[97] Support your local chicken flock instead.

Believe it or not, you're not quite done with this thinning yet. Reducing crop load to one fruit per cluster is satisfying, but with heavy-setting varieties this isn't always enough to assure respectable return bloom. This job now takes a radical turn—so radical that some of you may not believe I'm serious. You really should thin to leave select fruit every 6 inches (on average) along the branch.[98] I often wait a week or so to make this subsequent pass to catch more apparent disease damage. Work systematically around the tree, and then do the top from a ladder. Don't be saddened by what seems like a waste of potential fruit—the fruit left will size better and honestly match a poorly thinned crop, bushel for bushel. A properly done job gets fully revealed only the next season when blossoms open anew . . . leave too much fruit this year and you probably won't see much for flowers next year.

These trollius flowers add "radiant beauty" to a long list of virtues rooted in diversity throughout the orchard ecosystem.

Chapter Four

Orchard Dynamics

Stewarding *what needs to be right* while intelligently setting limits on *what might go wrong* describes health-based orcharding to a tee. You alone will decide the means by which you go about safely producing a reasonable-looking crop. Being aware of the appropriate use of organic spray options to balance pest and disease dynamics is important. Still, the bigger picture of how you manage orchard diversity and support soil biology remains paramount. Ecosystem dynamics are utterly fascinating to watch and nurture . . . the orchard can look so perfect going into bloom, but then, one month down the road, suddenly everything seems to have veered completely. Your job is to know when to act preemptively, in the gentlest manner possible.

Together we will work up an orchard checklist of tasks based on biological priorities that need doing in order to grow good fruit at your place. Much of this will become far more real when you start to get your hands in the soil. You'll come back here many times and find yourself now ready to hear that next bit of guidance about a particular challenge. Just as trees grow slowly, you too are developing a strong branch structure as an orchardist over the course of time.

ORGANIC HEALTH MANAGEMENT

There's revealing purpose behind the words chosen to describe one's choices in life. Take the term *integrated pest management* (IPM)—so rightfully in vogue for determining management guidelines for chemical orcharding. The concept of integration is unquestionably worthy. The word *pest* makes sense with respect to dealing with the many challenges one faces in producing a viable fruit crop. But it does demand a certain focus, no? In fact the term suggests that *problem upon problem* drives management choices in modern-day orcharding. Making a slight word shift unveils IPM more realistically to be a commercial approach focused on *integrated problem management*. Pest situations are solved to a rational economic extent through discerning chemical application based upon monitoring the actual situation. That's a far better approach, with less environmental impact, than commercial orchards took throughout most of the last century. Some home orchardists opt to go this way as well.[1]

You and I, however, are going to purposely put the emphasis elsewhere. Approaching orchard dynamics from a holistic perspective sets a new focus entirely. The phrase I'm going to suggest will play on that first framework, and is specifically selected to highlight the other side of the coin. Don't be confused and think the power lies in the first word. That could just as well have been *biological* or *ecological*. Our foremost task in the home orchard and the community orchard is to build health. Even when we deal with pest challenges and outright woes, let us never forget that we do this work by building system health. Our framework is *organic health management* (OHM)[2] . . . and with that we have established the paradigm shift that makes organic orcharding viable.

Semantics are important. The language orchardists

FUNGAL DUFF MANAGEMENT

The case has been made that fungal-dominated biology supports orchard health. We enable subtleties that keep pest and disease pressure in balance by managing the ground beneath our trees and berries as *fungal duff*. Compost, deciduous wood chips, raked leaves, rotting hay, and taprooted plant allies set the scene.

- Saprophytic fungi decompose all sorts of organic matter. Nutrients are made available to plants through a mineralization process. Long-term humus to hold that fertility in place is built through a humification process.
- Feeder roots find room in the humus where a dense sod is kept tamed with woodsy mulch. This in turn makes for a thriving relationship with mycorrhizal fungi.
- Wolf spiders, predatory ground beetles, and many other beneficial species complete their reproductive cycles in a diverse duff ecosystem.
- Holistic approaches to disease work best when fruiting plants procure balanced nutrition by means of fungal friends.

listening to the fungi and the parasitic wasps and the taprooted dandelion and the trees we revere.

This is the point where we not only choose how we will grow fruit but determine whether the entire venture will prove satisfactory from start to finish. Conversely, to undermine the biology induces disease problems and ecosystem dysfunction that can be negated only with the use of stronger and stronger medicines. I am talking here of soluble chemical fertilization, herbicide convenience, symptom-dissipating fungicides, and all those insecticides that severely compromise biodiversity. Alternatively, an organic-minded fruit grower can do much the same damage through the use of hot (bacterial) compost, flame weeding, excessive use of copper and lime sulfur, and even applications of broad-acting botanical toxins like pyrethrum to zap numerous species—all of which can technically be approved as certified organic techniques. Just because certain practices are acceptable under federal standards doesn't mean they are healthy for the orchard as a whole. So-called deep organics goes beyond substituting natural materials for synthetic chemicals and recognizes that ecosystem dynamics are best supported by prioritizing soil health.

The words *weed* and *pest* do not show up in ecology books. These common agricultural terms have far more to do with human ignorance than integrative thought.[3] Recognizing that determines the smart means to address orchard dynamics. Honoring diversity in the orchard ecosystem is a must. Let's move along now to practice what we preach.

Mowing as a biological act

Let's start with something as simple as mowing grass for those of you who have chosen a meadow-like setting for your fruit trees.

This common chore demonstrates the many tie-ins between seemingly benign actions and ecosystem response. We're about to go a bit deep . . . again, anyone expecting me to now write about merely keeping grass to a certain height, please recognize that the

have used over the course of this past century bespeaks the need to control, to wage war on the ecology in order to obtain perceived goals. The chemistry employed today underscores this: Product names like Ambush, Assail, Last Call, and Pounce sure sound like human-oriented certitude to me. What we need is a language of balance that speaks to honoring all species, one that recognizes human understanding as still in discovery mode when it comes to biological truth. We've shifted paradigms. Now we need to be

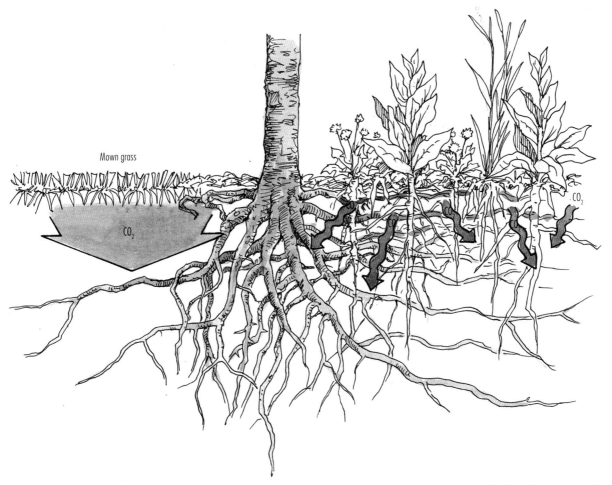

Root density of a regularly mown lawn can be as much as twenty times greater than that of a taprooted understory. Root respiration of either results in a corresponding carbon dioxide density that has relevance for tree feeder roots seeking friendly ground in the humus.

planet insists we understand how things really work if we're to "get it" when it comes to biological advantage in the orchard.

Still, some cultural norms are quite insistent: Regularly shorn grass is considered an appropriate résumé for being respectable in this culture. Many of you probably think this human precept has little relevance whatsoever to growing tree fruit. On the contrary, you might be inclined to view regular mowing around fruit plantings as a way to reduce vegetative competition for moisture and nutrients. Perhaps you're focused on religiously clipping nearby dandelion of its yellow bloom to limit competition for pollinator attention.[4] Perhaps you simply enjoy the

look of fruit trees straightly aligned in the midst of a neatly kept lawn.

Practicing what I call *biological mowing* instead helps make healthy fruit production possible. Waiting to cut the grass until that first flush of feeder root growth begins —and leaving all that organic matter to pile up as mulch—will impact the fungal world in a number of positive ways. Hear me out: The wild and woolly look may not be appropriate for every yard,[5] yet letting go of those golf fairway tendencies has import for tree nutrition, and ultimately for the ability for fruits to resist disease from within.

A quick lesson in root density and respiration explains the reasoning here. Plant roots "breathe" and in that process give off carbon dioxide. A mown lawn consisting entirely of grasses has twenty times the root density per unit volume of soil. Dig up a hunk of outright sod and those upper inches of soil seem to consist of grass roots alone. This differs considerably from the comparative space found in soil where mixed species curry favor on the forest's edge. Accordingly, substantial levels of carbon dioxide from the denser grass roots discourage fruit tree feeder roots from finding equal footing in the humus—the very place where mycorrhizal fungi supplement nutritional access for plants a hundredfold. Feeder roots are instead directed downward due to excessive carbon dioxide—exactly where mycorrhizal connection falls short. The root competition that fruit trees face when the surrounding environs are managed to favor grass (through regular mowing) becomes a fait accompli. Such trees live and grow, but they don't necessarily thrive and produce respectable fruit. That requires balanced nutrition delivered by the biology to feeder roots granted room in the humus to build full internal resistance to disease.[6] Otherwise you're back to reaching for more medicine in the form of fungicides to maintain some semblance of fruit production.

Allowing an orchard understory of high grasses and broad-leafed plants to grow tall in spring contributes to disease suppression in yet another way. It's the height of the greenery that blocks a portion of scab ascospores from being released up into the tree canopy when it rains. These disease-causing spores will come from the remnants of leaves still found on the soil surface from the season before.[7] The fungal duff zone under the tree is a decomposing paradise, but any stubborn leaves remaining in the pathways of your orchard or along neighboring fence lines will be the prime source of disease inoculum. Early-spring mowing not only frees up spore access but often drives secondary pests like tarnished plant bugs to feed on fruit buds because preferred ground cover in the out-of-the-way places has been pulverized.

All of which begs the question: *Should you mow at all?* Absolutely, only now based on root timing and fungal decomposition rather than notions of what looks good. The series of illustrations depicting tree growth phases (see "Root happenings" in chapter 3) shows a man with scythe in hand on the far side of the third tree. Not only has fruit set by this point in the season, but so has the grass. The carbon-to-nitrogen ratio of the plant understory shifts in favor of fungal dominance just as seed begins to set.[8] The storage of potassium in a carbonized understory (held within the tall grasses and wildflowers) can be especially relevant in organic systems where soluble K levels often run high from good mulching and composting habits.[9] Timing corresponds with when dairy farmers traditionally make their first cutting of hay—sometime between fruit set and as many as three weeks following. This wide window allows you to stagger bloom by not necessarily mowing everywhere at once, thereby supporting those bumblebees who are now finished with fruit tree bloom. Leave any comfrey in flower unmowed, as it will indeed fall over soon from becoming top-heavy through its own seed formation.

The mowing tool itself has relevance as well for this first orchard cut—and yes, once again, it's for the benefit of fungal allies. Grasses and wildflowers are laid down with a scythe as dripline mulch, and thus not chopped to bits by a machine, in order to suppress understory growth in two respects. This single mowing causes root mass in perennial plants to shed just as the spring feeder root flush begins. This enhances access to new nutrient zones for the tree—with the help of mycorrhizal fungi, of course—for the purpose of sizing the fruit in the months ahead. The swaths of carbon-rich organic matter left behind by the swoosh of a sharp blade suppress the pace at which understory plants recover as well. I circle each tree in my orchard counterclockwise (being a right-handed guy) so as to direct each swing of the scythe toward the vicinity of the dripline of the tree. Adding to the outer edge of the fungal duff this way feeds the saprophytic fungi, which in turn make even more nutrients available to the feeder roots through decomposition of all that plant matter.

Subsequent mowing can be done however you wish now that the biological imperative has been served. I use a walking brush hog to maintain aisle access on my hillside trees in late summer just before harvest begins. I come back with the same attachment on my two-wheel tractor after harvest to literally flatten the ground cover in order to reduce vole (meadow mouse) cover and chop up fallen leaves. We'll be discussing leaf decomposition techniques more thoroughly (see "Stirring the biological stew" on page 154) when we look at fall sanitation techniques to reduce overwintering disease inoculum.

One thing I especially want you to take from this in-depth mowing discussion is the recognition that whatever we humans do in the orchard ecosystem has ramifications running far beyond what seems obvious. Grass grows and so we cut it . . . but beneficial fungi, feeder roots, nutrient cycling, and tree immune function are involved too.

Spray notions

I like to spray my fruit trees. You won't hear many commercial orchardists say that, regardless if the plan is certified organic or tailored IPM. Applying toxins to the world in which we live is not a soul-honoring event for anyone. Personal risk obviously enters into this territory too, no matter how protectively we suit up. But we are shifting gears here . . . and dealing up front with any lingering reluctance around spraying will be pivotal for your success as a health-focused orchardist.

Choosing to spray to build system health is far different from choosing to spray to kill. I'm aware that I myself am nowhere near pure enough to be making such a statement for all times in all circumstances, but the gist of what I do in the holistic orchard is radically different from what the current consciousness around spraying would suggest. I want to zero in on *making things happy* in the orchard ecosystem in order to encourage you along a similar health-based path.

First let's visualize what's happening on the surface of the leaf when herbal remedies and arboreal nutrition

A walking tractor with brush mower attachment proves very useful on steeper ground for keeping aisleways open and performing fall cleanup of the orchard.

are applied. Projecting your consciousness like this every time you spray helps you "see" what's taking place and thus feel good about what's being achieved. A typical holistic brew in early spring includes liquid fish, pure neem oil, effective microbes, and seaweed extract. Let's throw in fermented nettle tea for tonic effect and *Bacillus thuringiensis* (Bt) for budworm control, to broaden the scope of this example. The fatty oils in the fish and neem fuel microorganism colonization on the leaf surface. The effective microbes in the spray will supplement this population, ensuring full competitive coverage against disease prospects. Certain constituents in the neem oil prime leaf chemistry to counter the enzyme chemistry necessary for disease establishment. Other constituents in the neem oil coat insect

POISON IVY

No one wants this creeping vine in the orchard understory. The allergic agent in poison ivy is an oily substance called *urushiol*, which is found in all parts of the plant and can be transported by wind or smoke as well as through direct contact. Symptoms of poisoning range from mild itchiness and redness to severe oozing lesions. Scratching will spread the reaction if the oil has not been washed from the skin. The fluid from blisters caused by the oil will not spread the reaction, however, once the skin has been thoroughly washed with a degreasing soap. The oil can remain active on footwear, clothes, and tools for as long as a year. None of this is any fun even when you know about good herbal remedies like jewelweed and a soothing oatmeal poultice.

This plant can eventually appear in a woodsy ecology that is not often mown. Undermining photosynthesis for poison ivy by regularly scything away its green leaves will serve much like a mechanical goat—all roots need the sun's good energy to continue into the long term. You need to be persistent and cut ivy back to the soil line several times a year to ultimately win this battle. Be sure not to touch the scythe blade after a mowing session before washing it completely with soapy water. And don't be tempted to use a weed whacker instead—any powered device just increases the likelihood of splattering urushiol all over the user. You can remove a single young plant or two by grasping it through a plastic garbage bag and pulling it up, root and all. Turn the bag inside out over the plant, and you should be safe. Any potential growth from broken roots can be gotten rid of with a very thick newspaper mulch. And should the vine be thick and gnarly and working its way up an old apple tree, nip it at the base with long-handled loppers and wait a full year to remove the now dismembered vine from the tree.

We should recognize one last thing about this "nasty plant," and I say this to emphasize a core point: Every species has a place in the holistic paradigm. Certain wild areas (like the dunes running behind a sandy shoreline) or spots in need of healing from man's abuse are guarded quite effectively by the shiny, three-leafed flag of poison ivy. Birds and other critters need sanctuary places that are protected from our incessant development.

eggs tucked into bark crevices and get ingested by larvae feeding directly on the tree . . . which causes the molting cycle of certain pests to crash. Green nutrients from kelp and the nettle tea are absorbed through leaf stomata, thereby strengthening leaf, flower, and fruits-to-be. Tiny caterpillars chewing on unfurling leaves ingest the protein crystal encapsulated in the Bt and stop feeding. The organism cycling of a healthy arboreal food web further stimulates tree resistance mechanisms and abets nutrient exchange. Whenever I spray I see all of this, and I want you to as well.

A few key points come out of that visualization. Timing matters, in that leaf cells are far more receptive to absorbing foliar nutrition early in the morning and again at twilight—cellular exchange more or less takes a siesta during the midday hours.[10] This notion shifts when applying refined kaolin clay, however, because this material needs to dry quickly as a particle barrier on plant surfaces. Drying applications should ideally be made when the sun is high in the sky and winds are ever so slight.

Considerable *tank-mixing* went on in this example

Nutritional orchard sprays should be applied to both the top and underside of the leaf canopy. Gauge full coverage by when spray droplets begin to run to the ground. The bark throughout will absorb nutrients as well. Photo by Frank Siteman.

as well—this won't always be the right thing to do with all materials. Applying a sticker with the white clay and consideration for biological antagonists are where limitations come up.[11] The order in which materials are applied can matter as well, especially as regards pure neem oil and the effectiveness of clay.[12]

Pay attention to the degree of coverage on the leaf surface and precisely where a particular spray should be directed. Spraying to the *point of runoff* implies ample wetting; the coverage is such that droplets just begin to run off the leaf. All nutritional sprays and all protectant sprays should be done this way. Organic orchardists rarely engage in *airblast misting* in the same way as large commercial growers. Synthetic chemistry packs a systemic punch, which allows fine mist particles to permeate the tree canopy and achieve the desired end with far less water in the spray tank. There

will be occasions when some orchardists target a *spot application* at tent caterpillars or to bait apple maggot flies on especially attractive varieties, both of which are easily accomplished with a backpack sprayer.

The term *full coverage* means wetting both the top surface of the leaf and a good portion of the underside. Buds, twigs, and limbs get wet as well. The bottom portion of the tree is easy, but pay heed to doing a good job up high when spraying too, as here is where codling moth and friends usually first alight and disease spores drop from the sky. I completely saturate the trunk with the two earliest sprays of the season, which are equally directed at the fungal duff zone beneath the tree as well.

Spray rates are initially confounding for new orchardists. Generally speaking, product manufacturers recommend so many pounds or fluid ounces of material per acre. It takes approximately 100 gallons of water to get full coverage on each acre of my midsized trees (trees kept pruned to no more than 14–16 feet tall).[13] As you might guess, I'm quite delighted to have a sprayer with a 100-gallon tank capacity. This volume works in early spring when I target the ground but there's far less leaf in the canopy, and it works equally well through the summer months, when nutritional sprays assist every tree in full green.[14] The typical backpack sprayer holds 4 gallons of water, which happens to be a reasonable weight for most folks to strap across the shoulders and carry. The rates given in this book for that "standard backpack" are simply acreage rates based on 100 gallons of water divided by 25 to get down to a 4-gallon tank capacity. This will provide the proper concentration in each backpack tank mix so you can happily spray your trees in the home orchard to the point of runoff—no more, no less—and thus achieve the same rates used on an acreage basis in a more sizable orchard. It's you who will have to determine how many backpacks' worth it will take to get full-saturation coverage for however many trees you have.[15]

The OMRI Lists are one tool to gauge acceptable organic options.[16] I have a goal to minimize off-farm inputs as well as build the health of the orchard ecosystem. Knowing how best to optimize a spray application, and whether I even need a certain something in the tank mix at all, is part of that process. Using monitoring traps, trap trees, and feeding attractants (like molasses) to boost the draw to biological toxins (like Bt) helps me stay cost-efficient. I'm aware that refined kaolin clay can be used to advantage by overcoating sulfur to lessen sun degradation, if I determine a mineral fungicide is needed in those weeks after petal fall in a particularly wet year. The holistic spring sprays I'm strongly recommending for home and community orchards alike go a long way toward simplifying decisions like that.

I can't emphasize enough that what happens at your place will be unique in terms of the disease pressures and particular pests faced. Knowing what options are available to call upon (in a discerning manner) when particular challenges are revealed is an important skill. Resist the urge to spray *something* until you clearly identify the problem at hand. It may well be too late that first time around to achieve a satisfactory result, as the damage has already been done. Shift to preventive mode in the future if a certain pest proves determined; many organic options, and especially repellents, work best if they're put in place before pest numbers build.

It's irresponsible not to know the mechanism by which any spray works. Does it need to be ingested by the insect? Is it even effective against members of the sawfly family? Kaolin clay needs to flake off onto the curculio weevil so the irritating particles make its life a misery. There's a time in the season when that's relevant, and many other times when applying anything will be absolutely meaningless. Disease cycles require knowing the beast you face and from whence it comes. All of this is why orcharding isn't necessarily simple . . . and yet remains so absolutely fascinating and determinedly doable.

Our mutual leg up is that we work with healthy trees and berries planted in a diverse ecosystem. The sprays that are most needed support wellness. So don't be reluctant to embrace the spray aspect of healthy orcharding, okay?

Innovation

Embracing big-picture thinking has allowed me to make the discoveries regarding holistic orcharding that I have. Much discussion with grower friends and open-minded researchers has opened up further horizons. My exposure to the world of healing herbs through my wife, Nancy, and her herbal sisters really got me turned on to the idea of using plant medicines for plants. The certified organic farming movement has helped in bringing more effective spray alternatives to my door; the deep organic farming movement has never deviated from the message that soil health is where we always begin. These many threads make up an evolving tapestry. This is not a work to ever set limits upon. You too will have ideas that make inherent sense for your trees and the localized dynamics you face. Take what we understand as of this moment and don't be afraid to tweak it.

BUGS AND MORE BUGS

Learning to identify who's who and then zeroing in on the when and where of pest vulnerability (based on family groupings) defines the crux of the matter when it comes to bugs in the orchard. There are some helpful ones and a few deservedly notorious ones, but most species are in truth absolutely innocent. Detailed specifics about the chosen few at your site will be found in the applicable fruit sections and in tree fruit guides listed in the resources. Our immediate goal is to understand how to balance potential pest situations.

Insect consciousness begins with paying attention. Seeing early signs of chewing on the edges of a bud or a light-deflecting pinprick (indicative of a feeding sting or an inserted egg) on developing fruit should put you on alert. Probing for details beyond this first impression leads to finding a tiny caterpillar curled within the sepal leaves at the base of a flower bud or looking for suspected culprits when cool morning dew finds curculios sluggish but not yet in hiding. One grower in Nebraska could not figure what was eating the leaves on his cherry trees . . . until he went out at night with a flashlight and found that june bugs had come up from the ground to feed with abandon. Different things will happen in different places— what's constant is the need to discern what's actually going on so you can then take intelligent measures to achieve a happy resolution.

Insect injury to fruit offers an important learning opportunity. The ability to distinguish one fruit scar from another more often than not reveals who's actually behind the deed. Consulting with an experienced grower or Extension adviser, looking at regional pest guides, and perusing the words in this book are all

A russeted, fan-shaped scar speaks to the presence of plum curculio in the orchard. The female makes a crescent cut above each inserted egg as a means of preventing fruit cells from crushing her reproductive artistry. Seeing scars on maturing fruit indicates that the apple won the race. Photo courtesy of NYSAES.

tools for getting your detective credentials in order. Knowing the name of the guilty party—if indeed the damage is significant and thus calls for specific action in the next growing season—leads to learning about the life cycle of a particular pest. This in turn reveals points of vulnerability where trapping, repelling, certain beneficial allies, and specific spray strategies have relevance.

But first let's do the numbers. You need perspective to know the difference between tolerable damage and a pest situation rapidly ratcheting out of control. Research that tracked the damage done in wild apple trees in Massachusetts over a twenty-year period gives a fairly accurate picture of what's out there. Plum curculio and apple maggot fly can afflict as much as 90 percent of the fruit in a bad year, with codling moth and one of its close cousins getting digs into about half of these yet again. Additional damage from all other fruit-feeding pests tallies below 10 percent . . . not something to get concerned about by any means. Overmanaging this situation to have all fruit left untouched will have far too great an impact on beneficial populations and thereby induce additional pest challenges. It's not worth the expense or craziness of doing this. Determine your must-do priorities around those significant pests and grant that a small portion of the crop belongs to the natural world. The concept of balance works both ways.

SPOTLIGHT ON THE JAPANESE BEETLE

Prepare to be dismayed when this insect hits your fruit plantings. Let's unveil the thinking process required to cut to the quick with Japanese beetle.

Story line

Larvae of *Popillia japonica* came to this continent with a shipment of iris bulbs from Japan sometime before 1912, when commodities entering this country started being inspected. In its native land, this beetle was much less of a pest than it was to become here. Hold that thought. The combination of well-watered turf for larval development, warm summer temperatures, and the lack of a specific natural enemy has favored the buildup of beetle populations.

The life cycle of any insect reveals certain points of vulnerability to an inquiring mind. Japanese beetle spends the greater portion of the year in the soil: The female burrows into moist soil to lay her eggs 2–4 inches deep. Larval grubs hatch out to feed on grass roots, eventually going into pupation before emerging as next year's hungry adults by midsummer. The first emerging beetles seek out suitable food plants and initiate the feeding frenzy. These early arrivals will release a congregation pheromone (odor) that is attractive to other adults, essentially calling the whole horde to come dine . . . on your trees and berries!

Preferences

Japanese beetles have definite favorites in the green world. The leaves of grape, raspberry, juneberry, autumn olive, rose, and (surprise, surprise) the Honeycrisp apple especially appeal. Red clover, zinnia, common primrose, and string beans can be surefire diversions as well.

Soil pupation

An insect species committed to a long spell in the soil risks being undone by certain biological strategies. Milky spore is a native bacterium (*Bacillus popilliae*) that can be applied as a onetime soil drench to infect grubs for many years to come. Parasitic nematodes (*Heterorhabditis* spp.) can be watered in beneath especially attractive plantings in early fall to consume all comers. But in truth? Everyone in the neighborhood needs to employ one or the other for guaranteed effect.

Beneficials

Recall how Japanese beetle was held in check in its homeland? Parasitic wasps and tachinid flies were at work. The winsome fly has been brought here from the Far East because of a desire to attach its eggs to the thorax of adult beetles. Things get rather gruesome after that. Spring tiphiid wasps (*Tiphia vernalis*) specifically hunt for Japanese beetle grubs, lured by scent alone to tunnel into the soil to lay a single egg on the beetle's larval membrane. Each female wasp parasitizes one or two grubs daily in this manner and can lay a total of between forty and seventy eggs over her life span of thirty to forty days. You encourage the right tiphiid species by providing adult habitat like forsythia, peonies, and tulip poplar.

Who, what, and when

Every insect goes through a molting cycle that starts from the egg. The larval and pupal stages subsequently lead on to adulthood and the reproductive urge. Damage to fruit trees is to either the foliage or the fruit itself. Some of this consists of adult feeding, but

Hands-on solutions

One long-standing remedy is unabashedly gross: Take a few handfuls of gathered beetles, macerate, and then spray onto plants you wish to protect. Interestingly, this may work as more than just a repellent due to an entomopathogenic fungus in some of those captured beetles now being sporulated into the environment. But let's face it: The most straightforward solution to burgeoning beetle numbers is a daily scouring of valued plants. Persistently knocking these invaders into a bucket of soapy water morning after morning eventually has to make headway. Pheromone funnel traps won't accomplish as much as vigilance. A mixture of the aggregation and sex pheromones draws 90 percent of the beetles within sensory range of the trap, but usually catches only 60–75 percent. But hey! What a nice gift to give the neighbors, eh? Again, an area-wide approach is the ticket to success. Then there's this permaculture nugget: *You don't have a beetle problem, you have a duck deficiency.* Folks with roaming poultry have yet another ally in the orchard.

Sprays

Surround WP kaolin clay spray works by clogging adult beetles with a coating of refined kaolin clay picked up when crawling across leaf surfaces. This can be used to protect fruits that are easily washed (like that Honeycrisp apple) but will turn berries into a white mess. Pure neem oil gets my highest recommendation as a feeding deterrent by causing a vomiting sensation in the feeding adult. Of course, neem works best applied as a preventive prior to the beetles arriving. Last resort lies with PyGanic sprayed on *trap plants* chosen from the beetles' known preferences. Powerful toxins—even organic ones—should not be applied ecosystemwide.

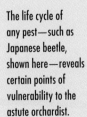

The life cycle of any pest—such as Japanese beetle, shown here—reveals certain points of vulnerability to the astute orchardist.

Not all players in the orchard are necessarily known . . . but without a doubt this twig looper belongs in the orchard moth complex, which includes dozens of species. Photo by Mark Rawlings.

more often than not it's the egg hatching out a very hungry caterpillar or grub. Let's look at family groupings within the insect world relevant to orcharding as a quick means of getting a handle on potential pest situations. The goal here is not so much entomological precision as identifying similar patterns to discern possible responses to a pest dynamic deemed unacceptable.

Every fruit grower will experience the **orchard moth complex** in some form or another. This ubiquitous force can involve dozens of species, but it always means tiny caterpillars munching away on some part of the tree. Internal-feeding larvae go for the seeds in developing fruit, often risking a mere twenty-four hours of vulnerable leaf exposure before getting safely tucked away inside. Look for a small hole in the side of the fruit and often in the calyx end from which

orange-brown frass (poop) protrudes. Surface-feeding larvae are content to nibble upon the skin of the fruit, hiding beneath an overarching leaf or where two fruit touch. Many of these are second-generation leafroller species, which in the spring larval phase were intent on feeding on buds and unfurling leaf tissue. Any resulting fruit damage at this early stage often appears as corky indentations.

Let's key in on this generational concept, for therein lies both the amplification of the moth problem and the timing of extremely targeted solutions. A given species overwinters as a hard-to-find egg mass, perhaps as larvae (in a dormant state known as *diapause*), some in a pupal cocoon, and some even as adult moths where mild winters allow for feeding and procreation. Location specifics vary as well, but mostly orchard moths favor laying eggs on leaves and

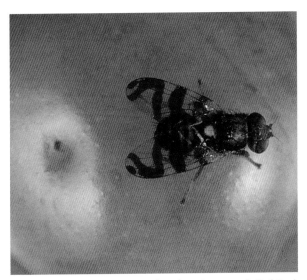

The cherry fruit fly attacks cherries throughout the eastern half of North America. Don't worry, however—closely related cousins will find the rest of you! Photo courtesy of NYSAES.

twigs where larvae can subsequently feed. These go on to find some secluded place to pupate: in crevices in the bark, litter on the orchard floor, or sheltered nooks provided by a nearby fence or wall. One way or another, with adult emergence in spring dependent on the development stages still to be achieved, *first flight* takes place when females get impregnated and then proceed to lay eggs on the new season's growth. That hatch initiates what is considered to be the first generation of the orchard year—limit this generation and all subsequent generations will be fewer in number. Some species are content with a single round of action, whereas others will achieve as many as five or six generations of egg laying and larval feeding in the extended growing season of warmer climes. The vulnerability points with moths lie in adult attraction around the times of feeding and mating, the need for eggs to respire, larval ingestion and/or contact with biological toxins, and exposing pupae hiding on the tree trunk for physical destruction.

Fruit-oriented flies affect chosen fruits across the spectrum. Fly larvae are called maggots, which I expect reveals the gruesome scene about to be revealed.[17] The female adult lays her eggs directly into the yielding flesh of ripening fruit, with specific preference by maggot fly species for apple, cherry, blueberry, and so forth. All such fruit becomes a maggoty mess of meandering tunnels and decay. Feeding attractants are used to manipulate adult flies to a deadly meal instead, along with sticky sphere traps that promise the perfect nursery for junior on which to lay an egg. Soil pupation suggests additional vulnerability points. Pick up early drops biweekly to prevent larvae from ever getting into the ground. Spraying the ground beneath badly infested trees with *Beauveria bassiana* in fall can help reestablish a clean starting gate: These parasitic fungi consume the fly pupae waiting in the soil for next season. Even more deliberately, plant a Dolgo crab tree to draw apple maggot flies in droves . . . use this as a trap tree to protect other apples, and then apply beneficial nematodes in early fall (the *Steinernema feltiae* species is recommended for AMF) to seek out the pupae in the ground below.

Sawflies are a different category of critter altogether. Wasp aspects seem to have been incorporated with fly-like behavior in this insect, resulting in a pollinator that in its larval form just happens to bore into developing fruit or strip gooseberry branches of all greenery. Pear slugs (aka pear sawflies) look pretty much like fleshy blobs designed to skeletonize leaves. The vulnerability points here lie with sticky card traps, desiccants like insecticidal soap and diatomaceous earth, and knowing precisely when a certain biological toxin will come in contact with apple sawfly larvae moving from a first fruitlet to the next.

The thing about **hard-backed beetles** is that the majority of these species pupate in the soil. (Those that opt for wood tissue will get a separate designation.) Most infamous of all are the curculios, which decimate most any tree fruit in the eastern half of North America.[18] Repellents form the backbone of an organic plan for dealing with these small weevils, with trap trees providing an effective diversion to curtail an otherwise prolonged window of activity. Applicable organic spray options along with ground-level strategies become cost-effective when a species

Green june beetles have an affinity for apples and all stone fruits, whether immature or fully ripe. Feeding damage tends to be sporadic across southeastern states and into the Lower Midwest. Photo courtesy of NYSAES.

can essentially be funneled to far fewer unprotected trees. More innocuous sorts like earwigs and click beetles contribute back to the ecosystem, reminding me that tolerance has a place. The accompanying sidebar directed at Japanese beetle is this book's example of taking a particular pest through the biological wringer in order to fully understand what all might be done. Rose chafers are noted for having similar desires for peaches. Out west, look for green fruit beetles emerging from unturned (big clue, right there!) manure piles to wreak havoc on nearby soft fruits.

We blur species lines in mentioning the unspeakable evil done by **fruit tree borers**. The reason for lumping certain beetles with certain moths applies to across-the-board damage to wood tissue. Grub consumption of cambium and sapwood eventually does in whole trees. Physical inspection and removal involves a great deal of work on your knees with a knife or similar grub-seeking tool like a drill spade bit.[19] Some of the moths can be deterred by pheromone trapping, but reducing beetle numbers often involves limiting nearby alternative hosts. Sending an army of

parasitic nematodes into badly infested bark tissue by means of a mudpack may rectify extreme situations (see "Trunk care" in chapter 3, page 79), and even if you lose a favored tree, you may ultimately save others by having eliminated the next round of destruction. Botanical trunk sprays made with pure neem oil are especially promising, acting as an oviposition repellent and adding an element of insect growth inhibition to all such borer wars.

True bugs exhibit an occasional hankering for fruit. These include assorted plant bugs, stink bugs, mullein bugs, apple red bugs, and hawthorn dark bugs. Conventional recommendations for removing the alternative plant habitat for such bugs from the orchard environs go against a diversity plan intended to attract and hold important beneficials. Bug damage often takes the form of a feeding sting, which develops into brownish rough blotches or even outright dimples on the skin of the fruit. Pure neem oil will deter feeding and interrupt the molting cycle on all these guys, which—truthfully—are rarely an all-out force of devastation.[20]

I'll mention a few **insect erratica**, as certain regional curveballs can and do show up on occasion. The *leaf-curling midge* is a tiny fly whose larvae set back young apple tree growth by tightly curling terminal leaves on the ends of shoots. Less photosynthesis means less growth. *Red-humped caterpillars* seemingly are Moths from Mars that attack apple, pear, cherry, and quince, defoliating entire branches in just a few days in late summer. Next year's buds will make a comeback, but meanwhile you can practice the fine art of handpicking off a fleshy meal for the chickens. *Pear thrips* attack all deciduous fruit trees by feeding on flower clusters, causing a shriveled, almost scorched appearance if the clusters don't fall off the tree altogether. Early-season neem oil applications will prevent the majority of thrips invasions. *Scale insects* are like tree barnacles in that they select permanent feeding sites on branch twigs and limbs. Heavily infested trees appear to be undergoing water stress, with leaves yellowing and dropping. Parasitic wasps often keep scale in check

Lesser peachtree borer initially makes its presence known by pushing frass out entry holes in a frenzied assault on cambium tissue at branch junctures. Photo courtesy of USDA Agricultural Research Service.

The resulting gummosis surrounding that larvae is the tree's attempt at turning out the varmint. Photo courtesy of USDA Agricultural Research Service.

(use a magnifying glass to look for holes drilled through the hard shell of mature scale), so unless you've chosen to kill everything in sight, don't expect much trouble from either San Jose or oystershell scale.

Last but far from least we must give heed to the **foliar feeders**. Allowing mites, aphids, psylla, and leafhoppers to run amok can set back tree vigor considerably. The good news is that much of this is indeed taken care of by numerous beneficial species given a little time. Commercial orchardists have far more problems with soft-bodied invaders because many of the chemical toxins used for significant pests kill the good guys that would otherwise checkmate foliar feeders, thus increasing these sorts of problems dramatically. It's far simpler to count on natural dynamics like predator mites to get the job done. You can pinch aphid infestations off terminal shoots on young trees if necessary, or shut down the ant highway by applying sticky goo to plastic wrap on the trunk.[21] If a certain plum variety appears overwhelmed by honeydew secretions from aphids and thus accompanying sooty molds cover most of the canopy, I rely on pure neem oil applications (made at a 0.5 percent concentration every four to seven days) on that particular tree while an especially severe problem persists. Woolly, rosy, or plain green . . . aphids do not like neem. Leafminers (the larvae of a small moth) tunnel into the cellular layers of the leaf to feed, but you will rarely see much

Tarnished plant bug damage to buds and developing fruit is typically minimal—provided these bugs are not pushed up into the fruit trees by exuberant mowing of all nearby ground cover in spring. Photo courtesy of Alan Eaton, University of New Hampshire.

of this damage in a home orchard because certain braconid wasps know their duty. That's the rub in a sense . . . we actually *need* low numbers of foliar feeder populations to maintain helpful species to a sufficient degree to keep those same foliar feeders in balance. Let's consider that next.

Beneficial mathematics

Natural predators are too often judged as being insufficient at providing complete control of a pest problem. What an appropriate moment to say *poo pah*! Dismissing helpful allies in the orchard ecosystem for not providing a complete solution on a species basis is exceedingly shortsighted, and frankly arrogant. How much better it is to understand that several partial solutions add up to substantial biocontrol. And that this might just be diversity's way of doing higher math.

Let's consider the codling moth—almost anyone anywhere will deal with this pest of apples, pears, quince, and even some apricots and plums. Eggs are laid singly in proximity to the developing fruit, often on a nearby leaf if not on the fruitlet itself. Each female moth will deposit thirty to a hundred pinhead-sized eggs. These sit exposed for six to fourteen days before hatching. Certain parasitic wasps can sense precisely where they are and will lay their eggs inside each moth egg to provide a feed for their young. Call that a 20–60 percent advantage . . . provided plenty of flowering diversity exists to support the presence of plenty of adult wasps.[22] Just-hatched codling moth larvae have significantly better odds of avoiding beneficial predators than most moth caterpillars, as this

Green peach aphids are the main vector of plum pox virus in the East. Spring applications of neem oil (part of the holistic spray mix) and numerous beneficials keep foliar feeders like these guys in check. Photo courtesy of NYSAES.

internal-feeding species bores into the fruit generally within twenty-four hours. A spined soldier bug or an especially astute chickadee might end this passage, however. Still other parasitic wasps lay their eggs in the larva itself to provide a feed for their young.[23] Score that 5 percent given the short duration of exposure. Codling larvae eat the seeds in the fruitlet and then exit some two to three weeks later, either by dropping to the ground in a fallen fruit or by crawling back toward the trunk. Yellow jackets gather such caterpillar meat for their young . . . spiders weave, pounce, and otherwise frolic . . . ground beetles never let creamy flesh walk on by. Let's take away another 5–20 percent. Surviving larvae spin a cocoon in which to pupate beneath bark scales on the trunk or in a sheltered place at the base of the tree. Woodpeckers

and nuthatches work this situation; tachinid flies aren't averse to sticking an egg within that cocoon to facilitate a pupal feast. That puts codling moth down another 10–20 percent.

Beyond letting all this happen by fostering biodiversity, our job on the insect balance front should be considered blessedly small in comparison! The advantages spoken of here apply to all pests to varying degrees. Spend some time getting to know your friends and revering their limited contributions in the grand scheme of things.

Pest options

Nudging the remaining portion of problematic pests in line with a human take on reasonable balance for fruit production is up to us as orchardists. The organic toolbox to do just that is filled with cultural methods, specific sprays, and outright physical barriers. Choosing the appropriate action to take and timing it correctly comes from understanding how things work. Preferring not to have to think is the principal reason that you might screw up.

Trapping

Certain insects can be attracted to a definitive end through the use of insect traps. Appropriate scent lures cue in on either mating or feeding preferences. Sometimes the draw is simply visual. Providing a place for moth larvae to hide rounds out trapping logic. Some traps must be purchased, but the more applicable ones can be home-sourced.

Pheromone wing traps are used by community orchardists to monitor the peak flight timing of moths. The draw is the chemically synthesized scent of the female moth (each species has its own distinctive *pheromone*), which attracts intrigued males to enter into a folded canopy with a sticky bottom. Home orchardists could use this concept to confirm the presence of a particular species, but otherwise monitoring traps are not really for lessening overall moth numbers. Pheromones that attract the female are expected to be on the market soon, and these may make a more meaningful dent.

Sticky white cards mimic the color of apple blossoms. These are hung at the early pink bud stage at head height in the outer edge of the tree canopy to draw European apple sawflies to investigate. The bugs get stuck rather than flitting about laying eggs at the base of blossom clusters. Leave the cards up through bloom, but then remove them in order to save other innocents (like ladybugs) from getting caught.

Sticky red spheres offer maggot flies a bigger "fruit" on which to lay their eggs. A fruit essence lure entices these shortsighted flies into the vicinity of the Tangle-Trap-covered ball (that's the brand name of the sticky goo), where they alight to do business . . . but then never have the opportunity to leave. These should be hung at head height in the vicinity of actual fruits and

Everything does indeed have a purpose . . . bulk supermarket apples (especially Red Delicious with its fruity aroma) make an enticing trap for apple maggot fly.

in such a way as to glisten in the sunlight. Timing is mid-June through August in the case of apple maggot flies and a full month earlier for cherry maggot flies. Another homesteading innovation to consider using would be bulk Red Delicious apples from the grocery store. It's the perfect job for an otherwise disappointing commercial apple. Project a wire through the fleshy middle to use as a branch loop, cover all but the stem end with sticky stuff (thus allowing the odor of ripening fruit to escape), and then dispose of the entire mess in the trash once it's covered with flies. Complete trap-out requires anywhere from one to six traps per apple or cherry tree, depending on tree size.[24]

Pyramid traps utilize a plum-essence-like scent to draw plum curculio to a visually familiar place.

The black silhouette of the pyramid tower design is intended to resemble the trunk of a tree. Adult curculios driven by finding the scent crawl up "the trunk" and end up in a backward funnel situation, much like a lobster trap. These come with no guarantee but may be relevant for some of you with no desire to make your trees white with repellent clay sprays. A safety yellow version of this plan has relevance to assorted stink bug species. You can make a rigid version of the tower from plywood painted the appropriate color, but the lure and funnel trap will need to be purchased from an IPM supplier.[25]

Cardboard trunk wraps pick up where we left off with codling moth a few pages ago. This idea comes straight from the late 1800s: Twists of hay rope tied at certain heights on the trunk were chosen by codling moth larvae for pupation, and the ropes could be searched through the summer months in order to destroy developing moths.[26] Using corrugated cardboard bands makes this task easier to accomplish and thus easier to justify disposing of between moth generations. Rub loose bark off the trunk to eliminate traditional hiding spots of codling moth. Wrap a couple of 4- to 6-inch-wide strips of corrugated cardboard snugly around the trunk, one just below the first branch crotches and the other several inches above the ground. Hold these in place with twisted wire, hay twine, or even duct tape. These two wrap positions account for larvae crawling down from the fruit as well as larvae journeying to the trunk from fallen fruitlets. Cocoons will inevitably be spun within the tube-like creases of the cardboard. Waxed cardboard can be peeled in half, allowing corrugations to be put directly against the trunk, thus making larvae presence that much easier to detect.

You gain decided impact by disposing of these bands just before the next generation of adult moths emerges. The timing is as follows: Put the bands on when blossoms appear, let three weeks pass by, then inspect and subsequently destroy if cocoons are in abundance. It may be another week or two to the most opportune moment in places where summer starts on

Two bands of corrugated cardboard — one placed immediately beneath the lower scaffold branches and the other at ground level — prove a pupation trap for codling moth larvae.

the cool side. Weekly inspections are required to keep the majority of successful pupations from becoming second-generation adults. Another round of cardboard bands put in place by late July will ensnare those last-generation larvae that otherwise would lie in place until next season; these can be destroyed immediately after harvest.

Vinegar jug traps deserve a quick overview. Take a plastic milk jug and cut away an opening in the upper half, leaving the handle intact for tying to an overhanging branch. Make up a mixture of cider vinegar, some water, and a dollop of blackstrap molasses or other sweetener. Pour this into the intact bottom of the jug, 2 inches deep. The resulting fruity odor and tempting nectar will invite numerous species in for a taste. A multitude of bugs will drown. If you're lucky, a significant percentage may be fruit moths, but there will be pollinators and beneficials in this brew as well. You really have to play around to determine if this simple trapping device has any relevance to growing fruit at your site.

Repellents

Spray applications that result in an insect not wanting to feed, lay an egg (referred to as *oviposition*), or otherwise hang out on particular fruiting plants have repellent qualities. The mode of action of repellents determines which insects will be affected, so pay attention please.

Refined kaolin clay forms a particle film on the surface of the plant, which acts as a broad-spectrum crop protectant, reducing damage from various pests. Picture your own body coated with tiny irritating particles that get into your eyeballs, your nostrils, your underarms, even your reproductive parts . . . that's what crawling bugs face on a tree covered with Surround (the official product name). Kaolin particles on the leaf and fruit as well as on twigs and bark rub off readily when insects like curculio are on the prowl, just as fruitlets start to grow. The upshot is such pests stop feeding and laying eggs in the fruit, instead spending their time incessantly grooming and searching for a friendlier place to be. Flying insects, on the other hand, experience this tactile strategy entirely differently. A female moth alighting on a treated branch feels (with foot pads and antennae) for various cues to confirm she's come to the right place—a slippery clay finish atop that apple leaf tells her otherwise, and so she moves to find a "real fruit tree" instead.

Several things are to be learned from that quick synopsis. The clay particles need to be small enough to get into that insect's underarm, which is why the word *refined* must be stressed. Pottery-grade clay does not work like Surround, period. Attempting to stick kaolin to the tree surface (with any type of oil) so it stays in place better through a rainstorm is the wrong

Happiness reigned that first year when the kaolin clay strategy allowed Gracie and I to finally pick a decent plum crop. Photo by Nancy Phillips.

thing to do, as Surround has been engineered to flake off and thus be a full-body experience for any insect plowing its way toward the fruit. Distracting first-generation moths at the same time curculio is active—the weeks starting immediately after petal fall when fruitlets start to size—requires thorough coverage from the get-go. It will take three applications of full-rate clay in that first week to build up a proper base coat that deters both types of insect pests. This will need to be renewed weekly, and perhaps even more often if an especially heavy rain comes during the peak time when developing fruitlets are being damaged.

Full-rate clay in the backpack sprayer amounts to

Refined particles of kaolin clay cover the fruitlets, leaves, and twigs of the tree to completely alter access dynamics for curculio. Learn the nuance of this barrier protection strategy and you will indeed win the battle!

stone fruits is especially desirable.[27] Having a trap tree nearby allows curculio to do its thing and thus shortens the window when clay coverage is required on all tree fruits—a concept I'll be covering in more detail just ahead.

Growers in the western half of North America have an entirely different use for refined kaolin clay. You folks don't have the infamous curculio, and there are other means for dealing with codling moth without quite so much mess. But you do have plenty of hot sunshine, which can lead to sunburn of fruit and on exposed branch surfaces of espaliered trees. Think of the clay for this application as a white reflective barrier, keeping the fruit cooler and thus less subject to overheating injury in the summer months. A light coating of Surround (one application) every fourteen to twenty-one days as exposed fruit matures will serve this purpose.

If it's breezy out when you apply the refined kaolin, I recommend you consider wearing a paper respirator mask. Breathing in tiny particles of anything is not conducive to long-term lung health.

Pasteurized garlic, to be blunt, does not impress me, despite all the wonderful herbal hype. The notion that strong-smelling constituents in the garlic will be systemically taken up by the leaf and thus fool the insect into believing, *Gee, I must have the wrong plant*, has validity only if those medicinal compounds are not compromised by heat processing. A fermented tea made from the flower stalks (scapes) of garlic or an outright garlic clove beer has some potential here, and both these preparations can be made from garlic you grow in your garden.[28] Conversely, purchasing the slick barrier product from a mail-order catalog is not recommended by this kid.

Hot pepper wax brings capsaicin (the compound that gives heat to cayenne peppers) to the surface of the tree to up the heat factor for pesky mammals like rabbits and squirrels, and it even temporarily deters browsing deer. A fiery feeding experience will help keep away thrips, leafhoppers, and aphids as well. If you ever rubbed your eyes after chopping up

1–2 pounds of Surround in those 4 gallons of water; the clay powder is stirred into the water and not vice versa. Follow-up applications can be made as soon as the first coat has dried. This is going to make your fruit trees appear white, white, and even more white! Apples and pears alike in curculio country should be treated once pome blossom time has ended (average this out across varieties). Stone fruits may require a slightly earlier application to encourage the bugs to zero in on an alternative home. Cherries and apricots are relatively small, peaches are often hairy, plums are lusciously soft—and all get harvested relatively soon compared with pome fruits—which is why curtailing clay applications sooner rather than later on hot peppers while making homemade salsa, you will totally understand how this works. The food-grade paraffin wax in this spray holds the hot pepper to plant surfaces for up to twenty-one days and is not washed off by rain.

Pure neem oil acts as a feeding deterrent for leaf-chewing insects in addition to inhibiting the molting cycle necessary for larval development. A leaf treated with neem oil produces a regurgitation-like reaction in the insect, causing it to temporarily lose the ability to swallow. Accordingly, that insect will no longer try to feed on the neem-treated surface. Another way in which neem helps repel pests is as an oviposition deterrent. Mating as well as sexual communication can be disrupted by certain constituents in neem oil, leaving the female confused as to even the final step of the reproduction process, being the laying of her eggs in such an apparently inappropriate place. Sensory cues as well as the bug's positive sense of well-being are subtly affected, all of which works best when repellent neem is applied just prior to known problem insects showing up in the orchard. A trunk saturation of 1 percent neem in late June and again in mid- to late July seems to successfully knock back borer aggression in this regard.[29]

Sexual frustration

Human ability to identify and synthesize the pheromone cues of the female moth used to attract males in droves led to the **mating disruption** strategy. Saturating the orchard air with the hot scent of the female leads to extreme male confusion, as promising trail after promising trail leads everywhere and nowhere at once. The net result is that the ladies cannot be found, which in turn means no fertilized eggs are going to be laid in the vicinity. Mating disruption lures are species-specific; codling moth lures are required for codling moth, and so forth. The typical dose is approximately two hundred to four hundred twist-tie lures to the acre, and that introduces the area requirement behind making this strategy work. Effective mating disruption requires that a full acre

of orchard be protected at a minimum.[30] Impregnated females coming from nearby wild trees need to be discouraged at the border with a spray of lightweight oil or kaolin clay. Orchardists with relatively few trees must find other means to counter those wild nights in the moth boudoir.

Trap trees

I'm a big proponent of including *trap trees* when laying out a community orchard, as a way to utilize repellent strategies like the kaolin clay spray to its utmost end. The basic premise is simple enough: All species have a biological imperative to feed and reproduce. If we recognize that any life-form is going to find some way to eat and definitely some way to carry its species forward—and we grant it that right by not using dangerous chemicals and other scorched-earth policies—then we can funnel those innate desires in order to protect the greater portion of the fruit crop that we deserve for all our hard work.

Let's make this advice practical for an orchard setting. The idea of repellent-treated trees pushing and pulling an insect toward an untreated tree indeed suggests sacrificing a portion of the crop in order to protect the greater portion. But we can be wiser than even this. Curculio is attracted to some varieties more than others—plums in general, lush-leafed edible crab apples, sweet cherries, and, oddly enough, the disease-resistant Liberty apple. The draw factor varies in different parts of the country, with larger stone fruits getting more attention the farther south you go and sweet cherries getting the nod in the Great Lakes region. Waiting to prune the chosen trap tree until just prior to bloom releases volatile odors that boost the allure, even before repellents are applied to the other trees.

Once blatant curculio activity starts on the trap tree, on the order of a week after petal fall (and slightly longer if it's a cool spring), the trap tree can now be dealt with by entirely different means. Laying tarps or sheets on the ground and vigorously shaking the tree very early in the morning and again at dusk each day will cause considerable numbers of this somewhat clumsy pest to fall, and they can then be carefully swept off the ground cover for destruction. This way you make a significant dent in the adult pest population while needing to tend to only one or two trees in this manner. Keep this up for a week or so (until bug numbers take a definite nose dive) and you will find it's no longer necessary to continue applying clay to the other trees.[31] Conversely, let the adults run amok on the trap trees, but plan on intercepting the resulting larvae and prevent them from pupating in the soil with a barrier strategy.

Physical barriers
Directly blocking an insect pest from its intended meal or stomping ground sounds simple enough. The labor-intensive art of **bagging apples** started in Japan, not so much for pest protection as to enhance the appearance of the fruit. Waxed paper bags of different hues block varying degrees of midsummer sunlight, which in turn results in a pale-skinned apple, which in Japanese society is valued a hundred times over the price paid for deeply colored fruit. Getting fruitlets wrapped before bugs have done the damage comes with its own range of finesse . . . which will be detailed in the apple chapter with respect to bagging choices, timing, and how disease control dovetails with all this. Home orchardists with a limited number of trees have reason to be intrigued by this potential end-around of significant pest damage on the larger tree fruits.

Hand-wrapping individual fruits early on doesn't play out quite as well for most stone fruits. Here's where **wrapping branch scaffolds** with nylon tulle can prove effective for some growers. Putting clear plastic bags on plums and peaches is problematic, because these fruits split open in a humid enclosure and are then more subject to rot disease. On the other hand, wrapping a branch (or even the entire tree while it's still small) with breathable netting fabric works to prevent curculio and vinegar fly access when the fruits are just forming in that first month after bloom. Beyond that, the fabric starts to overly confine shoot growth.[32] The

nylon tulle should be removed at that point, the crop load thinned, and drawstring-style organza bags tied around each fruit if deemed necessary to keep away later generations of Oriental fruit moth.[33] The timing for putting on 108-inch-wide sheets of standard white tulle is immediately following pollination, and be sure to give each branch a hearty shake to roust any curculio already on the scene—you don't want to wrap the bugs in with the fruit! Clothespins serve to hold a branch wrap in place. Organza bags are made of similar fabric and come in whatever sheer color suits your sense of orchard aesthetics.

Trap tree thinking enables yet another pest-balancing barrier. Plum curculio needs to pupate in the soil—a definite vulnerability point provided you understand certain options. Here's one. Eggs laid in fruitlets hatch out as grubs that eat the seeded core, which in turn causes the fruitlet to abscise and fall off the tree, from whence the curculio larvae makes their way several inches down into the soil to pupate before emerging again in late summer as adults with overwintering plans to come back the following spring. If you didn't have the time or inclination to shake the tree for curculio adults, then lay old carpeting out beneath heavily afflicted trees in order to block access for the larvae from abscised fruitlets to the soil. Such a **pupation blockade** needs to be in place beginning two weeks after petal fall and left there for a full month. Fruitlets will shrivel up in the hot sun, and so will the curculio larvae. Other growers employ "the ladies" to get this job done—chickens confined around favored trees just as the June drop begins. Throwing a handful of cornmeal across the dripline encourages an inspection of the soil surface for anything that moves. Curculio larvae that reach the soil even get scratched from what seems like certain pupation and are never heard from again.

Introducing beneficial allies
Habitat diversity encourages many beneficial species in the orchard ecosystem. Getting a wide range of flowering plants in place does the trick better than

A roving flock of bug eaters can be moved about the orchard by means of this chicken gypsy wagon.

purchasing a particular insect from a beneficial insect supplier to release among your trees. If you do feel compelled to order green lacewings or trichogramma wasps or minute pirate bugs, you will still need to have the right surroundings to keep that investment from petering out. You need to introduce specific beneficial species at the first sign of known pests (knowledge of *who eats whom* matters here) and, in some cases, make periodic releases to effectively control infestation rates. It's definitely more economical to simply trust biodiversity.

Parasitic nematodes can be of value if certain pests exceed tolerance levels. These microscopic, nonsegmented worms occur naturally in soils all around the world. Once they are released, the nematodes seek out host insects and enter their prey through body openings, injecting them with lethal bacteria, resulting in a yucky goo for the meal ahead. The nematodes reproduce and their offspring feed within the insect cadaver and emerge to seek out new hosts. This underground strategy can make a dent in next year's returning pest populations provided the target in question pupates in the soil and you have a handle on exactly when and where. Which isn't as hard to discern at it may sound.

European apple sawfly, plum curculio, and various maggot flies pupate in the ground at the base of the fruit tree. That reveals timing based on when those critters are buried in the soil and thus vulnerable: A nematode release four to six weeks after petal fall would be right for sawfly and curculio, with immediate post-harvest timing spot-on for cherry maggot and apple maggot flies.[34] Using trap trees to direct curculio makes it possible to employ nematodes on far less surface area. Perhaps you have one particular apple variety that gets hammered by apple maggot year after year . . . sending in an underground attack force of nematodes that fall will help knock back the pressure to where traps alone suffice.[35]

Nematodes are easy to use. These organisms are shipped by the millions either in a dry powdery clay formulation or in a wet sponge to be mixed with water. The solution can be applied using a watering can or a backpack sprayer directly to the ground beneath targeted trees. Release at dusk when temperatures are cooler and the nematodes won't be exposed to the drying effects of the sun. Choose a showery day if possible; otherwise moisten the soil before application and lightly water the area again afterward.

Beauveria bassiana (a soil fungus sold as a spray under the trade names Naturalis and Mycotrol) can also be used to limit insect pupation in the soil. These fungal spores attach themselves to the insect's covering and then secrete enzymes that dissolve the skin to allow hyphae (think fungal roots) to enter the body of the pest. Robbed of moisture and nutrients, the insect pupa dies. Choosing a showery day for soil application helps the spores penetrate farther down to where larvae-becoming-pupae await.

Organic sprays for bugs

Time now to sort through catalog claims to determine what's useful in the orchard and what's not. No one likes to spend money unnecessarily; on the other hand, you need to anticipate what may be called for in the season ahead, as chances are you won't be able to buy many of these products locally on the very day you notice a problem.

Lightweight oils may be mineral- or vegetable-based and can be used at any point in the season. The principal use involves smothering, be it insect eggs or fungal beginnings.[36] Stylet-Oil has shown some efficacy against powdery mildew, rust, and aesthetic summer diseases. I'd keep Golden Pest Spray Oil in mind for an unexpected gypsy moth outbreak and for the product claim of delaying bloom on peach trees when winter ends suddenly. Traditional **dormant oil** is petroleum-based, and unless you have a particular problem with scale or pear blister mites, I would leave this product on the shelf. Keep in mind, neither of these types of oil makes any contribution on the nutrition front whatsoever.

Insecticidal soap basically works by sucking a soft-bodied insect dry. The potassium salts in fatty acid soaps act on direct contact but have little residual effect. Phytotoxicity to leaves can occur, which is why I prefer other approaches for heavy aphid infestations. The one exception (and thus the reason I keep a pint of Safer Insect Killing Soap on hand) is to deal with gooseberry sawfly.

Sugar esters give fast-acting control for soft-bodied insects like aphids, mites, thrips, and leafhoppers by causing rapid dehydration on contact. SucraShield works quickly by using the esterized link of the sucrose chain to dissolve holes into the insect's cuticle (skin). Moisture escapes from the insect's body, causing it to expire. Any residual spray biodegrades into sugar and water in the environment. This would be an especially targeted approach to use if a foliar pest gets way out of hand, especially on young plantings.

Bacillus thuringiensis is just as often referred to by its brand name, Dipel. Protein crystals found in this natural insecticide attack the digestive tract of lepidopterous caterpillars—thereby leaving beneficials, bees, and orchardist unharmed.[37] Moth larvae must eat the bacterium endospore containing the toxin, which then neutralizes the enzymes protecting the stomach lining from its own digestive juices. Holes are quickly eaten through the target organism's stomach wall, with a resulting poisoning of the bloodstream. The caterpillar stops feeding within hours of ingesting the Bt (long live simple nicknames!), and it dies by the next day. This biological toxin is viable for only approximately three to five days, because it breaks down in sunlight. Multiple applications are needed to get the upper hand with codling moth, as its egg hatch period extends over two weeks. Bt works far more efficiently with surface-feeding caterpillars.

Dipel application rates vary with the concentration of the formulation used. Using a dollop of molasses as a feeding attractant can help increase caterpillar desire to take the medicine. Half an ounce of Crocker's Fish Oil (per backpack spray tank) helps to adhere the bacterium to the leaf surface and has UV-screening properties that can prolong viability an additional day or two.

Spinosad is a compound derived from a Caribbean strain of *Saccharopolyspora spinosa* (these are filamentous bacteria that give soil its sweet, healthy smell) under aerobic fermentation conditions. This fast-acting, broad-spectrum material can kill an insect through ingestion (the primary mode) or on contact when it meanders across a treated leaf surface. Spinosad causes a significant range of fruit pests to die of nervous exhaustion within one to two days—that list includes all moth caterpillars, sawflies, thrips, leafminer larvae (even within the leaf), maggot flies, and even curculio to a lesser extent. Care must be taken when applying spinosad when bees are foraging, but once residues dry on understory plants it is far less toxic to bees. Organic brand names include Entrust (the very expensive commercial concentration), Monterey Garden Insect Spray, Bull's-Eye, and Captain Jack's Deadbug Brew. The beauty of spinosad-containing products is a longer-lasting residual than Bt, on the order of ten days rather than three. This often proves helpful when dealing with a multiple-moth situation going into harvest. The shelf life for a spinosad product is stated to be no more than three years (take that to mean two years!), so don't purchase a larger amount than you will actually use in that time.

Granulosis virus will be used mostly on a commercial scale, but it's a biological tool that home orchardists should know. This baculovirus encapsulates itself in the natural environment until it is eaten by the codling moth larva. Formulations of granulosis (Virosoft, Cyd-X) contain more than a trillion viral capsules per ounce of product, allowing orchardists to make this a surer encounter. Applications are necessary every ten to fourteen days beginning at first-generation egg hatch until oviposition ceases (two sprays per generation). Granulosis virus kills a hefty majority of codling moth larvae—on the order of 96 percent—along with half of the Oriental fruit moth larvae present in the same time frame. Each infected insect dies and subsequently "melts" apart on foliage, thereby releasing more virus into the ecosystem. Treatments aimed at reducing in-season codling moth numbers result in significant mortality in overwintering larvae as well. Such a reduction in the emergence of next season's population is what makes granulovirus an excellent *precedence strategy* for softer control methods to follow in the next growing seasons.

GF-120 NF Naturalyte is a protein bait concentrate that emits ammonia-like odors that attract both fruit flies and maggot flies. The flies in turn ingest the bait, laden with spinosad and sugar, which has been sprayed onto the foliage of selected cultivars. Applying this product during the fruit fly pre-oviposition period is important for optimum performance. Individual trees are spot-sprayed with approximately 1–3 ounces of GF-120 per tree (the mixing ratio being an additional 1.5 parts water to each part bait concentrate), and blueberry bushes at an obviously lesser rate. Accurately placing the film on foliage and not fruit—such would be a sticky mess at harvest—allows you to coat the undersides of leaves, which in turn protects the toxicant from washing off as quickly. GF-120 is active for at least seven to ten days after initial application. It can be stored for up to two years without degradation.[38]

Pure neem oil used as an insect growth regulator owes its primary action to azadirachtin compounds that strongly inhibit the development of insects that consume neem directly. The insect larva feeds and, as it grows, sheds its old skin and again starts growing. This shedding of old skin (known as *molting*) is activated by an enzyme hormone called *ecdysone*. Azadirachtins suppress the production of this important juvenile hormone, so the larva fails to molt and therefore remains trapped in the larval stage until it ultimately dies. If the concentration of azadirachtins is not strong enough, the larva can enter the pupal stage but dies before coming out of its cocoon. If the concentration is still less, the adult emerging from the pupa is malformed, sterile, and without any capacity to reproduce. Some patience is required here, as the use of pure neem oil will not give immediate results like chemical toxins.[39]

Beneficials are not directly harmed by neem compounds, as these species are not ingesting the treated plant. Those early-spring holistic applications (that include pure neem oil) directed at the trunk and branch structure of the tree have the same end result for foliar pest eggs as traditional dormant oil . . . only now with an entirely different mode of action. I can't stress enough that patented neem products do not have the same effectiveness as the unadulterated oil![40] Sure, raw neem is a bit trickier to use (follow those instructions coming up just ahead), but you benefit from its multiple virtues only by using the whole plant medicine.

Pyrethrum refers to the dried, powdered flower heads of certain chrysanthemum daisies. Sounds innocent enough, right? This contact insecticide rapidly paralyzes many different species of insects. Direct hits on honeybees and beneficial wasps are likely to be lethal. This *natural botanical* should never be used orchardwide in my opinion.[41] Reserve all pyrethrum products for targeted applications like knocking back significant pest presence on trap trees. West Coast orchardists might keep this card in hand for overpowering spot outbreaks of rosy apple aphids. Pyrethrum has an incredibly short residual effect (on the order of four hours)—it breaks down rapidly on exposure to sunlight—so twilight applications are recommended. The better organic formulations like PyGanic include canola oil as a carrier that helps spread the toxin more evenly across the leaf surface. Tank-mixing with diatomaceous earth ups the ante on more challenging insects like stink bug: The sharp-edged shell particles

are breathed in by the insect, resulting in micro cuts that facilitate "injection" of the pyrethrum.

Essential herbal oils of rosemary, wintergreen, clove, and so forth can overpower a fairly wide range of insects. The concentration of commercial preparations is on the order of 10 percent to as much as 30 percent (prior to spray tank dilution), causing a quick knockdown of pest numbers by hindering insect metabolism and death by direct suffocation. The residual repellent attributes of herbal oil products will help keep migrating pests like leafhoppers from coming right back from afflicted host plants elsewhere in the neighborhood. Clove oil has fungal applicability as well.

HOLISTIC APPROACH TO DISEASE

Truth goes through three stages.
First it is ridiculed.
Then it is violently opposed.
Finally it is accepted as being patently obvious.
  —Arthur Schopenhauer, German philosopher
                                    (1788–1860)

Tree fruit diseases can be fungal or bacterial in origin, even outright viral if grafting contamination occurs, all gaining a foothold at different points in the year when conditions warrant. What you need to know as an orchardist is how infections occur, what can be done preemptively to prevent rampant disease, and additional biological measures aimed at lessening overall disease pressure. Keep in mind that having healthy trees and berry plantings capable of warding off disease organisms *from within* sets the stage for requiring less medicine (in the form of fungicides and antibiotics) to make up for what stressed plants are less able to do. All that's been said so far about soil health, microbe health, and balanced nutrition makes the biologically connected tree that much stronger. These various diseases are not some sort of manifest destiny for fruiting plants as much as an indication

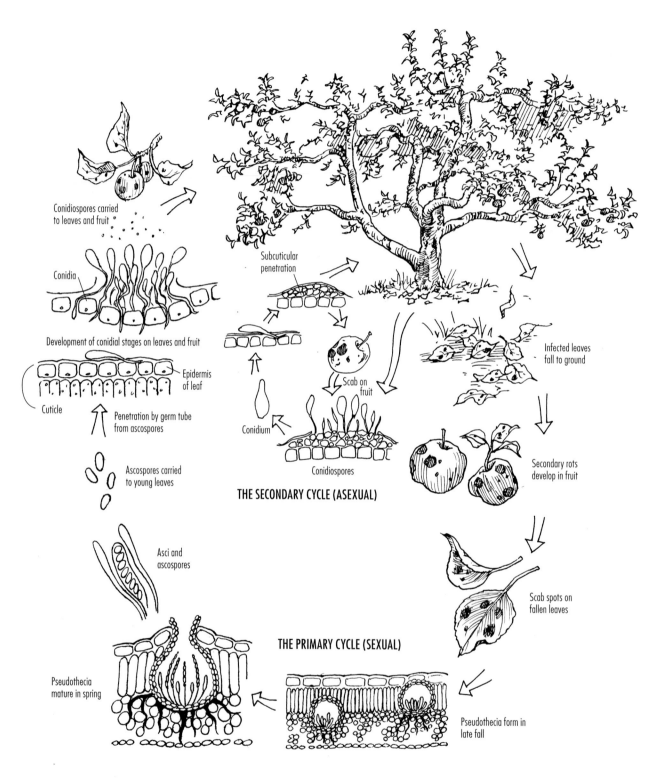

Conidiospores carried to leaves and fruit

Conidia

Development of conidial stages on leaves and fruit

Epidermis of leaf

Cuticle

Penetration by germ tube from ascospores

Ascospores carried to young leaves

Subcuticular penetration

Scab on fruit

Conidium

Conidiospores

THE SECONDARY CYCLE (ASEXUAL)

Infected leaves fall to ground

Secondary rots develop in fruit

Asci and ascospores

Scab spots on fallen leaves

THE PRIMARY CYCLE (SEXUAL)

Pseudothecia mature in spring

Pseudothecia form in late fall

The disease cycle of the apple scab fungus reveals precisely when we need to boost the immune response of the tree and be sure to have competitive colonization fully engaged.

Sporulating brown rot can be bad news for sweet cherries when rains just prior to harvest spread infection prospects throughout the tree. Photo courtesy of Alan Biggs, West Virginia University.

that the opportunity to stay healthy has somehow gone awry.

Fungal disease progression

The most immediate tree disease pressures are going to be fungal in origin. Potential infection occurs when pathogenic fungal spores come in contact with the susceptible surfaces found on young leaf tissue and developing fruitlets. A number of things can happen to keep such infections from going any farther.

Let's zero in on the life cycle of apple scab—the *Venturia inaequalis* fungus—to get a fuller grasp of the situation. Ascospores erupt forth into the air on a rainy spring day from mature spore sacs (called *pseudothecia*) on fallen leaves and fruit that didn't get decomposed from the year before.[42] Significant odds guide this harbinger of fungal disease to an unfurling leaf, where prolonged wetness facilitates hyphal growth of the spore. Enzymes are required to crack the cuticle and thus access nutrient resources within a single leaf cell. An infection occurs if everything goes along for a long enough time (the so-called wetting period) and nothing interrupts the pathogenic intrusion. Good drying weather immediately following a quick rain release of spores can sometimes prove sufficient in curtailing fungal spores from getting a foothold and becoming an outright disease lesion.[43]

Other names for this fungal affliction of apple are *black spot* and the rather ominous-sounding *sheet scab*. The latter conjures up the full image of scab run amok. Primary infections will continue to release asexually produced spores (referred to as *conidia*) through the summer months, which can literally sheet the fruit surface with crusty, blackened non-growth and outright cracking.

These details shift just slightly when dealing with fungal-caused rust diseases, fruit rots, powdery mildew, leaf curl, and the like. Still, a spore overwinters nearby or parachutes in from afar; wetness is present to facilitate an infection taking hold; the internal phytochemistry of the tree along with weather patterns either defeat this intrusion or not. The cultural specifics for fungal diseases of particular fruits will be forthcoming . . . the point now is simply having a sense of this fungal progression. Typically for these past hundred years or so, we humans have chosen to use a fungicide that proves toxic to the disease fungus at this point, thereby short-circuiting the inner fortitude of the plant itself and knocking off friendly microbes that have a role to play in the holistic quest to produce decent-looking fruit.

The holistic whammy

A number of tangents lie exposed in that spore scenario that suggest health-based courses of action rather than the use of allopathic fungicides.

- Hyphal intrusion initiates production of secondary plant metabolites within the leaf that provide a **systemic immune response** for the tree. This phytochemistry can be stimulated by applying certain plant extracts and foliar nutrients.
- Numerous microorganisms play both a competitive role and a symbiotic role through **full arboreal colonization** of the tree canopy. This presence can be renewed with microbial brews and deep nutrition.
- Balanced tree nutrition can be brought about only by **fungal duff management** favoring symbiotic relationships between tree roots and beneficial fungi.

Stimulating the immune response of the tree can be done by introducing the very compounds a healthy tree produces in response to disease presence. These so-called phytoalexins are various terpenoid and isoflavonoid compounds . . . which can also be found in pure neem oil and other plant-based preparations.[44] Similarly, the *cuticle defense* of the leaf, which must be overcome by spore enzymes, can be supported by boosting foliar levels of silica. Fermented herbal teas of horsetail and nettle are premium sources of bioavailable silica for the summer months.

Sustaining critter health throughout the tree canopy requires that we understand what depletes arboreal colonization as well as what nourishes this critical holistic force. I utilize activated effective microbes to introduce biological reinforcement to the scene; others choose to do this with aerated compost teas, à la Elaine Ingham of Soil Foodweb, Incorporated. But the fundamental missing link sought by purists has been additional food resources that will keep arboreal communities running in full gear. The fatty acids in unpasteurized liquid fish and pure neem oil are the fuel behind prolonged beneficial colonization. Equally apropos, pathogenic species prove more resilient whenever foliar nutrition proves limited.[45]

Ecosystem relationships at ground level also have absolute relevance to how the tree stands up in the face of environmental disease pressure. Here we emulate the forest edge with respect to fungal dominance of the soil microorganism community. Healthy fruit trees rely on both mycorrhizal and saprophytic fungi to access balanced nutrition, which in turn creates that internal fortitude I spoke of earlier. You simply can't buy this kind of nutrition in a bag! Fungal duff management is all about feeding fungal allies through the use of woodsy mulches and those fatty acids of fish and neem dripping to the ground when sprayed to the point of runoff.

The fungal curve

All fungal events—both the desirable ones and those of a disease persuasion—can be correlated with *root timing* down below. We already looked at how the fruit tree experiences two phases of root growth that follow

IMMUNE RESPONSE OF PLANTS

Trees have an immune system for warding off invading pathogens (different from ours, to be sure, but in process very similar). Polysaccharide compounds are produced when hydrolytic enzymes first contact fungi and bacterial membranes on the foliage surface. These in turn activate an internal defense mechanism in the plant that scientists designate *phytoalexin* compounds. These consist of isoflavonoids and terpenes (varying for each unique plant species), which, when produced in sufficient abundance, can resist the invading pathogen. Plant stress, the overuse of synthetic agrochemicals, and climatological factors work against this natural defense mechanism process found in healthy plants.

on the heels of observable shoot growth aboveground. The spring flush corresponds with soils warming up, the garnering of nutrients for fruit development, and the formation of next year's flower buds. The fall flush kicks off the expansion of the tree's permanent root system and the all-critical storage of nutrients in bark tissues for spring. Overlaying a visual sense of fungal happenings to what we've already recognized with root cycles should help you see the logic of holistic disease management all the more clearly.

Bioactivity of numerous decomposers on the orchard floor is represented at ground level on this fungal curve in early spring and again in fall when leaf drop begins. Many of our practices aimed at reducing disease inoculum in the understory are really about supporting these decomposers, which include numerous species of saprophytic fungi.

We address our fungal fears around disease when we consider the rising portion of the curve. True enough,

fungal disease spores arise from the ground surface and bud crevices to infect tender growth tissues. The primary infection period for many diseases like apple scab, rust, and an assortment of rots corresponds perfectly with the uplifted curve. Peach leaf curl settles in during the dormant months but infects just at the start of this uprising. Meanwhile, beneficial fungi and bacteria also arise and establish on the foliar surface during this outreach time. Supporting this arboreal food web will be one of our chief playing cards in countering disease mechanisms.

The descending portion of the fungal curve amounts to celebrating and abetting the role of mycorrhizal fungi in the orchard ecosystem. It's these intricate interactions of the soil food web that make animated life above the ground possible. The flush of feeder root growth is trumped a hundred times over by the hyphal reach of these symbiotic fungi. Nutrient balance for the fruit tree very much depends on the health of this life-support system. We in turn are going to support the mycorrhizal network with fatty-acid-based nutrition just as these beneficial fungi come into full gear.

Biological reinforcement

The interplay of microbe communities on the surface of the leaf and fruit is finally getting the attention it deserves. I am jump-starting orchardists (by way of this book) to the cutting edge of biological fruit growing . . . and trying to keep things relatively reasonable at the same time! This is a microscopic world where numerous species of fungi and bacteria consume and become food resources; leaf phytochemistry is stimulated by the presence of trillions of organisms; and disease-causing fungi and bacteria have to compete every step of the way.

Canopy colonization depends first of all on food resources being available, be this from leaf exudates, the bodies of fellow microbes, the food-generating capability of photosynthetic bacteria, atmospheric contributions, and whatever we supply additionally as growers. A number of other factors work against

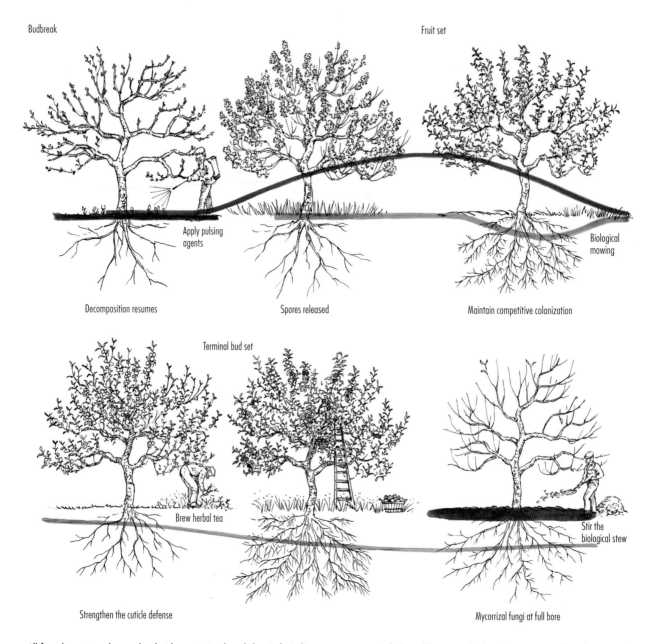

Budbreak

Fruit set

Apply pulsing agents

Biological mowing

Decomposition resumes

Spores released

Maintain competitive colonization

Terminal bud set

Brew herbal tea

Stir the biological stew

Strengthen the cuticle defense

Mycorrizal fungi at full bore

All fungal events can be correlated with root timing down below. Holistic disease management is facilitated by seeing this fungal curve as a guide to the timing of specific tasks.

full colonization of competitive organisms on all surfaces of the fruit tree. Ultraviolet degradation, acid rain, ozone depletion, extreme heat, and dry spells have to do with natural decline. Additional impact comes from agricultural choices to use fungicides and high-nitrate fertilization to up yields. The upshot here is that maintaining a competitive arboreal environment calls for regular biological reinforcement provided with appropriate food resources.

Effective microbes

An outgrowth of the nature farming movement in Japan has been the development of a special culture of beneficial microorganisms known as *effective microbes*, which are used as a probiotic inoculant to promote ecosystem health. Effective microbes increase the species diversity of both the soil food web and the arboreal food web—thus enhancing the growth, yield, quality, and disease resistance of crops. These cultures of microbial species occur naturally in environments worldwide but have decreased in many soils due to overfarming and chemical fertilizer and pesticide use.[46] The microorganisms in an effective microbes culture fall into three principal groupings.

- **Photosynthetic bacteria** are self-supporting microbes that synthesize useful substances from secretions of roots and foliage, organic matter, and/or atmospheric gases, by using sunlight and the heat of soil as sources of energy. The food resources developed by these bacteria include amino acids, nucleic acids, bioactive substances, and sugars, all of which promote plant growth and development. The metabolites developed by these micro-organisms are absorbed directly by plants and act as substrates for increasing beneficial populations. Mycorrhizal fungi in the root zone, for example, benefit from nitrogenous compounds (those amino acids) secreted by the photosynthetic bacteria, thus bulking up this symbiotic system for tree roots.[47] Needless to say, it's these photosynthetic bacteria that form the backbone of effective microbes working synergistically with all the other microbes, both those in the applied culture and those already indigenous to the orchard ecosystem.
- **Lactic acid bacteria** produce lactic acid from sugars and other carbohydrates that are proffered by photosynthetic bacteria and yeast. Common foods such as yogurt and pickles have been made with lactic acid bacteria for centuries. Lactic acid is a strong sterilizing compound in its own right, able to suppress disease-causing microorganisms, be it in the pickle jar or on the surface of a leaf. Down on the orchard floor, lactic acid bacteria promote the decomposition of material such as lignin and cellulose, thereby making the nutrients in otherwise difficult-to-decompose organic matter bioavailable. Most telling of all, for tree fruits struggling to absorb foliar calcium, these bacteria improve the utilization of calcium, phosphorus, and iron.[48]
- An assortment of **yeasts** synthesize anti-microbial and other useful substances required for plant growth from amino acids and sugars secreted by photosynthetic bacteria, organic matter, and plant roots. The bioactive hormones and enzymes produced by these single-celled fungi promote active cell and root division. These secretions are also useful substrates for lactic acid bacteria and actinomycetes, the earthy-smelling bacteria found in healthy soils worldwide.

Other organisms found in proprietary probiotic cultures may include specific actinomycetes and various fermenting fungi. One nice thing about actinomycetes is their ability to produce anti-microbial substances that suppress harmful soil fungi such as *Phytophthora* root rots. Fermenting fungi decompose organic matter rapidly to produce alcohol and esters that suppress odors and thus change the cues that attract certain insect pests like maggot flies.

Phew! That's a whole lot of interdependent rock 'n' roll showing up in a relatively invisible world! Effective microbe cultures allow us to consistently introduce these synergistic organisms via the sprayer to our fruiting plants and the ground in which they stand.

Home orchardists can keep this simple by using the *mother culture* as it comes prepared by the manufacturer. You'll find contact information for two reputable suppliers (SCD Probiotics and TeraGanix) in the resource section of this book—quality matters here![49] Community orchardists have to be more economical about this, having far more trees to cover, and thus activate effective microbes through brewing in order to increase batch size twenty times over. The premise behind this is simple: Critters awaken and then multiply when given food resources and the right temperature range. Planning ahead is essential, because the activation process takes as much as ten days. Activated effective microbes must always be brewed directly from the mother culture; microbe populations begin to shift upon subsequent batch brewing.[50]

The basic recipe for activating effective microbes is as follows:

- Measure ¾ cup of unsulfured molasses. Organic sweet sorghum is often recommended, but I opt for using a good blackstrap, which is more economical for orchard use.
- Pour the molasses into a clean gallon jug two-thirds full of hot water from the tap, up to a temperature of about 120–125°F (49–52°C). The water should definitely not be chlorinated.[51] Use a plastic jug rather than glass to allow for gaseous expansion. Shake well to dissolve the molasses.
- Measure ¾ cup of the mother culture and pour this into the sweetened water. Shake well. Top off the gallon jug with lukewarm water.
- Put aside in an insulated box or other warm place, such as by the woodstove. The goal is to keep this anaerobic brew close to 90–95°F (32–35°C) for the first two to three days. The lactic acid bacteria are the first to kick into gear, provided the jug or water was not contaminated with a more aggressive organism. The initial pH of the brew will drop from 5.5 or so to around 4.0 in this time period, indicating that active production of lactic acid has begun.
- You will need to ferment the batch for another five to seven days after this to mature the complete culture. Normal room temperature

Activating effective microbes requires little more than a week's lead time and a warm place to brew. The volume of mother culture can be increased twentyfold this way . . . providing a grower with biological reinforcement aplenty. Photo by Mark Rawlings.

is fine at this point, though slightly warmer conditions (72–78°F, or 22–26°C, is considered ideal) will accelerate the process. The photosynthetic bacteria are the last organisms in the brewing progression to grow. A slight gas expansion in the jug can be observed when you loosen the cap during this bacterial bloom phase.

- Check the pH of the solution to determine when microbe populations have stabilized. Dip a strip of pH test paper into the jug, then check the resulting color with the dispenser chart. Mother culture comes at a stable pH in the 3.0–3.5 range—but I will use an activated batch once the pH drops below 3.8, knowing that photosynthetic bacteria are now hale and hearty. Your nose is perhaps the best indicator of all: Activated effective microbes are ready when that characteristic sweet earthy smell of the mother culture has been reestablished.

• It does not matter at all whether effective microbes are brewed in the dark or in light.

This biological component of the holistic spray recipe is applied to straddle the primary infection period of most fungal diseases in spring for all the reasons given already. Some probiotic companies warn not to spray on open blossoms, as the microbes might prove detrimental to flower viability, but this is debatable.[52] Summer use of effective microbes can be continued along with the fermented herbal teas if growers in humid areas feel more protection is needed from summer rots on peaches or problematic surface fungi like sooty blotch on apples.[53] I especially want orchardists to be aware of the virtues of fall (post-harvest) applications of effective microbes as a means of denying certain disease-causing bacteria and fungi access to overwintering spots within fruit tree buds. This is the means by which copper and lime sulfur (applied post-harvest and again prior to budbreak) for use against diseases like bacterial spot and leaf curl in stone fruit and, yes, fire blight in pome fruit can be left behind.[54] Arboreal health should indeed be promoted year-round.

Compost tea

The life diversity found in the compost pile can be employed to do similar work. The nuances of using *aerated compost tea* for disease suppression have been thoroughly explored by Elaine Ingham and its use promoted by her many protégés. The basic premise is wonderful: Craft a fungally dominated compost pile for orchard use, brew an aerated tea with it to favor the further propagation of aerobic organisms, spray this on the trees to crowd out pathogens, and change

the food resource dynamic. The same tea can be used as a ground spray to replenish depleted soils. All to the good, and a homegrown proposition at that. The trick, however, is getting a righteous brew.

A rather pricey brewer is used to keep substantial volumes of tea aerobic and at a desired temperature. Many tips are shared to use specific fungal foods to guide the culture in a fungal direction. Compost quality is absolutely critical. All these steps require the power of the magnified eye to confirm the types of organisms in the brew. It's fascinating, fun, but downright finicky . . . and thus simply more than the average home orchardist is going to do. Compost tea consultants can supply you with know-how: you can get a light microscope to confirm the presence of desirable species; trial and error might eventually make you a preeminent brewer; and the tea alone may indeed counter tree fruit disease, as its most adamant proponents claim.

However, I'm going to stick with my integrated scheme for now, using effective microbes for a somewhat consistent diversity component in spray applications to build orchard health. Those of you embracing the tea approach should be in touch so I can pass word along of successful nuance. Some of you might even want to try a combined approach, using the aerobic premium of a proper compost tea with the photosynthetic bacteria that give effective microbes their holistic credentials.

Nonaerated compost tea won't satisfy purists, but I do see a place for this simple brew in orchard culture. This liquid extract of compost requires none of the fussiness of the aerated version. A few shovelfuls of rich compost soaked for a day or two in a 5-gallon bucket, stirred on occasion, then strained, yield a less defined yet still helpful range of organisms to enhance leaf decomposition beneath the trees in the fall.

Deep nutrition

Supporting these microbial reinforcements on the plant surface while at the same time building up inner plant fortitude comes down to deep

THE FOUR HOLISTIC SPRAYS OF SPRING (PART TWO)

Let's have that discussion about timing and rates for this approach to abating disease. The bud stages given here are for apples but can be bounced a week or two earlier for stone fruits with specific challenges. Apple timing is absolutely correlated to the primary infection period of most fungal diseases and is appropriate for berries as well.

Week of quarter-inch green. The soil is a sleepy place coming out of the dormant season, even after sap flow has begun in the tree. This first application of neem oil, fish, and microbes works in part as a catalyst spray to get both soil and arboreal food webs engaged. Buds are showing solid green tissue, somewhere between green tip and half-inch green. Pick a day that's warmer than not within this time frame to thoroughly wet down the branch structure and trunk and ground surface within the dripline of each tree. Target any fallen apple and pear leaf piles from the previous fall to facilitate scab decomposition. Both the liquid fish and neem rates can be doubled for this application only (as exposed foliage is minimal) to boost fatty acid concentrations in the bark crevices.

Early pink. Leaf tissue has filled out considerably at the base of blossoms, with that first smile of pink revealing itself in the apple flower. We're still in catalyst mode as regards the trunk and ground, but we're also tuned in to the competitive benefits of arboreal microbe communities on the leaf and flower cluster surfaces. Don't wait too long for this; the fatty oils in neem and the fish should never be applied directly on open king blossoms.

Petal fall. Spraying to the *point of runoff* is now the name of the game, with lots of leaf and fledgling fruitlets to cover thoroughly. This is an important renewal spray to time correctly, as the bloom period may have been extended by cool weather. You will need to average what marks orchardwide petal fall between early varieties that finish blooming well before later varieties. Weather plays a big role in this interpretation as rain tickles the fancy of pathogenic fungi, especially at this moment in the season.

First cover. Ditto. But wait . . . many of you may not realize what an orchardist means by the term *cover spray*. This marks seven to ten days following the petal fall application. Spray strategies for certain pests (particularly the use of refined kaolin clay for curculio) may overlap at this time.

Home orchard rates. This assumes a 4-gallon backpack sprayer is used to cover so many trees to the point of runoff. Mix 2.5 ounces of pure neem oil with a generous teaspoonful of soap emulsifier to achieve a 0.5 percent neem concentration. Use 10 ounces of liquid fish and 6 ounces of mother culture of effective microbes for this backpack volume. Dissolve as much as half a cup of blackstrap molasses in warm water to launch those hungry critters. These backpack applications also should include 5 tablespoons of liquid kelp or 0.5 ounce (dry weight) of the seaweed extract.

Community orchard rates. This assumes a 100-gallon spray tank capacity to cover 1 acre of trees. Half a gallon of pure neem oil mixed with ¼ cup of soap emulsifier mixed into 100 gallons of water achieves a 0.5 percent neem concentration. Seaweed extract is a given: 8 ounces (dry weight) goes in the tank. Two gallons of liquid fish and 1 gallon of activated effective microbes complete the brew.

nutrition by way of foliar sprays. Food resources for the microbes subsequently will be made bioavailable to the plant by the interactions of the arboreal food web. Foliar uptake of certain spray nutrients occurs directly through the leaf stomata but to a less certain degree.[55] Absorption is increased when sprays reach and coat the undersides of leaves, as this is where most stomata are located. Foliar nutrients cause an increase in photosynthesized plant sugars, a portion of which (research suggests 25–30 percent) are used to feed the soil biology, which then has enhanced gumption to provide more soil minerals back to the tree. Wowser! Here we cover the nuance of biologically attuned leaf foods that play important roles in holistic disease management.

Pure neem oil

The cold-pressed oil of the seeds of the *Azadirachta indica* tree (common throughout most of Africa and India) makes possible many healthy orchard happenings. We've already zeroed in on its attributes as both an insect repellent and an inhibitor of the molting cycles of various pest species earlier in this chapter. The constituents in unadulterated neem oil that play a huge role in countering disease are the immune stimulants and the fatty acids.[56] My first encounters with this whole plant medicine on the organic marketplace suggested its role as a leaf polish . . . and in a very real sense neem continues to be just that by way of nutrient pathways galore.

The raw seed oil tastes bitter and smells garlicky, if not nutty, at its freshest. More to the point, this herbal remedy contains vitamin E, essential amino acids, and secondary plant metabolites called terpenoids and isoflavonoids. The fatty compounds in neem are derived from palmitic, stearic, linoleic, and oleic acids primarily; all of these contribute considerably to microbe health as well. Pure neem oil also contains trace amounts of nitrogen, phosphorus, potassium, zinc, copper, iron, magnesium, and manganese.

Stimulating tree immune response in the orchard with an herbal remedy from another tree seems especially appropriate. The phytochemistry in pure neem oil induces fruit trees to up leaf production of those very same terpenoid and isoflavonoid compounds used by all plants to overwhelm fungal hyphae and keep them from getting an infection foothold. Healthy plants do this all the time. We're simply timing the holistic spray schedule in spring to straddle those weeks when fungal disease pressure peaks . . . thereby upping the resistance factor when it's most needed.

The fatty acids come into play in different ways. Providing this ideal biological fuel to sustain arboreal colonization should be clear by now. Mycorrhizal and saprophytic fungi in the soil respond to this food resource, which is especially useful when the ground begins to warm in early spring. The healthy sheen left on bark and leaf alike helps protect plants from climatic stresses. The ability to disrupt pathogens from overwintering in bark and bud crevices—backed with biological reinforcement to close the deal—holds particular promise for growers faced with bacterial spot or fire blight buildup. Canker infections will be somewhat checked by means of this fat nutrition providing a leg up to competing organisms. Pure neem oil is used in body lotion products in the herbal trade, in part because the fatty acids regenerate our skin. In a nutshell, healthy biology of any sort thrives on fatty-acid-based connections.

Early-season neem goes on at a 1 percent concentration when used as a fungal catalyst directed at the ground and major branch structure of the tree. Little leaf tissue shows the week of quarter-inch green, and it's generally quite cool at this time of year; the risk of phytotoxicity is low. This same 1 percent concentration is also used to totally saturate the trunk zone in the summer months to deter various borers from laying eggs. All other foliar applications of neem oil during the growing season are made at a 0.5 percent concentration. Don't overdo a hand wand application (by lingering too long on a particular branch)—you might see leaf damage and possibly even fruit russeting as a result.[57] That pathogen disruption nudge to the bark and bud crevices in fall can be made at a

2 percent concentration once the majority of leaves have dropped from orchard trees.

Raw neem seed oil will be anything but easy to spray unless you know the tricks of the trade. Due to its high levels of natural vegetable fats, unadulterated neem becomes as thick as butter at temperatures below 60°F (16°C). Planning ahead is a must when it comes time to spray: Place the container in a warm room (but not directly in sunlight) for a day until the consistency reverts to a homogeneous liquid. Placing semi-thawed neem in a pot of warm water on cool mornings may be necessary as a final step. An emulsifying agent can be any biodegradable soap.[58] This must first be mixed directly into the neem oil, on the order of 1 tablespoon of soap per 6 ounces of oil. This mixture will quickly become greenish yellow and opaque as the large globules of fatty oil are broken down into smaller globules. Pour this oil/soap blend into warm water in a bucket and stir vigorously before adding the completely emulsified mixture to the spray tank and its full volume of cooler water.[59] Applying such a mix as soon as possible goes without saying.

Neem oil can be stored into the start of the subsequent growing season, but generally try to obtain a fresh supply for each new season. You may notice a sludge factor at the bottom of the container after long-term storage. Pure neem oil is mainly composed of glycerides of fatty acids, and in this way it is similar to palm oil. Both oils deposit stearin at low temperatures (below 41°F, or 5°C) and especially after they solidify. This occurs all the more with each cycle of warming. The stearin deposit can be filtered out if needed without representing a loss, biologically speaking. The best plan around this: Purchase the quantity that suits your orchard needs for the season ahead; "thaw" the original jug amount when you're ready to make the first spray in spring; bottle up the rest of the neem in batch sizes required for each subsequent orchard spray (pints, for example); and store the batch sizes back in a cool place (like the cellar) to best preserve constituents, bringing out one at a time as needed for your holistic intentions.[60]

Pure neem oil requires a soap emulsifier to properly mix into water. Follow instructions carefully and you will see only the tiniest globules of oily fats floating to the top of the mixing bucket.

Liquid fish

Three distinct types of fish products are offered on the organic marketplace, but only one has vast biological value.

Liquid fish fertilizer is made from the first pressing of genuine fish parts and has not been pasteurized—and thus contains the fatty acids and enzymes so important to beneficial microbes. This nutrient-rich formulation of biological fish will sometimes be called *hydrolysate*. Fish emulsion, on the other hand, consists of liquid wastes (after processing fish for other purposes) that have been heat-treated and thus biologically deactivated.[61] Refined fish oil falls into its own niche as a sticker-spreader used to overcoat biological toxins like Bt and thereby protect the active ingredients from ultraviolet radiation.[62]

The bottom line is you want a liquid fish fertilizer that contains those desirable fatty acids. Recommended brands in North America include Organic Gem, Neptune's Harvest, Eco-Nutrients, Dramm, and Schafer Fisheries. These processors use an enzymatic, low-heat process to ensure that organic compounds are left intact while eliminating bacterial breakdown (and thus strong odor) by adding a trace amount of citrus extract or phosphoric acid. Heat destroys the vitamins, amino acids, enzymes, and growth hormones that act as biostimulants to the soil and arboreal food webs. Powdered versions of hydrolyzed fish (drying anything to a powder involves heat) are not in the same biological league.

Liquid fish has been included in the four holistic spring sprays not only for the benefits of its fatty acids but for its nitrogen boost as well. Foliar nitrogen serves to prolong pollen viability, helps hold fruit set, and strengthens meristem development to ensure good return bloom the next season. Orchard use of fish in the growing season ends with the first cover application, as excess nitrogen in the summer months will delay the hardening-off process of fruit trees. I apply fish one last time as part of the holistic fall application, now utilizing the nitrogen to boost decomposition forces on the orchard floor.

Liquid fish rates might seem to be determined by the applicator based upon the price paid per gallon. Home orchardists are at a retail disadvantage here: A single gallon will cost four times as much as the same gallon drawn from a barrel shipment. Recommended community orchard rates are 4 gallons per acre for ground application and 2 gallons per acre for foliar application. The backpack equivalent for foliar use amounts to 10 ounces of liquid fish in each tank mix.

Molasses

Unsulfured blackstrap molasses contains all sorts of nutrients that get beneficial microorganisms up and running. Its complex sugars are a carbon source with humic-like properties that are consumed by fungi and bacteria alike. Which is why it's so important to use molasses as a feed when activating effective microbes to increase batch size (see brewing instructions in "Effective microbes" earlier in this chapter). That same principle applies to direct foliar application of the mother culture; a dollop of molasses has been included in the home orchard spray mix accordingly. Molasses in the spray tank will help "stick" the introduced microbes to the leaf surface as well.

Adding blackstrap to applications aimed at increasing nutrient density is worth considering as well. The complex sugars in molasses help maintain high levels of Brix in fruiting plants. This measurement of soluble solids in plant tissue (which includes a combination of sugars, amino acids, and proteins) is made with a refractometer using a scale expressed in degrees Brix. Fruit grown with deliberate intentions of maintaining a higher Brix will be more nutrient-dense and of better quality. Plants with a Brix reading of 12 or more are said to be unlikely to attract insect pests, to have increased disease resistance, and to better withstand climatic stress. A jump in Brix levels not too long after applying a health-oriented spray mix serves as a legitimate indicator that foliar intentions have been met. Adding molasses to foliar applications has been shown to help achieve this.[63]

Carbon sugars are the principal source of energy to stimulate soil bacteria so that the process of decomposition can get off to a good start. Spraying red clover residues with molasses and liquid fish after mowing in both fall and spring (when prepping new ground for planting) helps bring on the bacterial flush that precedes greater fungal presence. A similar transition situation occurs when tilling out beyond the dripline in midsummer to break up heavy sod or to maintain dwarf trees. Molasses provides that requisite bit of extra energy for the soil microorganisms to rapidly break down residues just before sowing cover crops alongside the tree rows.

Table molasses is not nearly as good for horticultural use as the darker blackstrap molasses. The latter is the syrup left after the final extraction of cane sugar, with nutrients galore that include potash, iron, and B vitamins.[64] The natural sulfur component found in blackstrap made from mature sugarcane is a useful nutrient, but do avoid sulfured versions made from young sugarcane, which have sulfur dioxide added as a preservative. Rates vary between 1 and 4 quarts of blackstrap per acre for ground application.[65] Use 1–4 pints per acre for foliar purposes, which translates to ¼ cup of molasses in the standard backpack tank mix.

Whey

Milk nutrition enters the orchard in the form of whey. The liquid remaining after milk has been curdled is a by-product of the cheese industry that can be dried into whey powder. This excellent source of proteins, lactose, vitamins, and minerals can be added to any holistic foliar mix on behalf of leaf nutrition and arboreal mycology. And whey contributes directly to disease suppression to boot!

Calcium has been shown to inhibit fungal spore germination. Conversely, low calcium levels along with excess nitrogen in leaf tissue set up conditions for disease. Australian growers using foliar sprays of milk (diluted 1:10 with water) have successfully reduced powdery mildew levels on grapes. Reconstituted whey achieves similar effect, only more economically. What's not clear is the mechanism behind all this. Lactose intolerance on the part of opportunistic fungi? Competition from arboreal organisms boosted by milk nutrients? Foliar calcium uptake by leaf cells, resulting in stronger cell walls? Very likely it's all of the above.[66]

Similar observations come from South America, where the teachings of a brilliant French biologist have been brought to growers' attention. Francis Chaboussou proposed that susceptibility to pest attack is intimately tied to protein synthesis in plants.[67] Long story short, disgust with the high cost of chemicals left a number of fruit growers willing to try an all-out nutritional approach. Herbicides, fungicides, and excessive nitrogen fertilization were let go in favor of rock phosphate applications and spraying orchards every two weeks with whey (at a 2 percent concentration). That was the constant. Different growers of different crops used fermented manure tea, trace minerals, liquid fish, molasses, and humic and fulvic acids as well. Various fruits, from guava to apple, turned out impeccable and delicious, free of blemishes and infestations alike.

Herbal teas

Homegrown remedies excite any herbalist, so perhaps you can imagine the passion I hold for using fermented herbal teas in the orchard and berry patch. These summer brews follow right on the heels of the four holistic spring sprays. Other disease-causing organisms arrive on the scene just as fruit begins to takes form. Specific herbs can be used to beef up the cuticle defense of the fruit tree with silica and to supplement calcium to ensure strong fruit that stands up to summer and post-harvest diseases. This part of the holistic plan is semi-optional, but probably a good idea for fruit growers who want to fully capitalize on all the good work of spring.

Arboreal brews go totally herbal following first cover.[68] Pure neem oil continues to be at the heart of an ongoing nutritional spray program aimed at boosting immune resistance to various fruit rots and other surface diseases like sooty blotch. (Neem will also be interrupting the summer moth complex for those with multigenerational issues.) The assorted herbal teas fit in somewhat sequentially with the neem tank mix. I follow a ten- to fourteen-day application schedule for these holistic summer sprays in order to achieve a respectable fruit finish.[69] You will have to gauge the realities of summer disease pressure and overall plant nutrition at your site to determine if these arboreal brews really should overrule other plans on certain mornings.

Making a fermented herb tea is simple. Fill a 5-gallon bucket with fresh herb, lightly packed. Boil a pot of water to pour over the leaves (as opposed to boiling the herb in the water), as this helps maximize

Silica levels in the *Equisetum arvense* plant—commonly known as horsetail—rise appreciably when the fronds spread apart.

three times in my sprays following petal fall, including that final holistic spring application at first cover. Horsetail (*Equisetum arvense* being the preferred species) is 15 percent natural silica. It turns out that silica plays a role in the cuticle defense against particular summer fungi that smudge the surface of apples and pears and others that rot the lot.

You'll find this ancient plant in undisturbed moist places such as streambanks, drainage ditches, and marshlands with partial to full sun. Whorls of long brittle stems radiate out from the nodes of jointed hollow stems that grow 10–14 inches high. Its slender leaves start off reaching up but recline to a horizontal position as silica levels rise in the plant, a transition that determines harvesttime for orchard use. A non-seed plant, horsetail is usually spread by spores (just like fungi), though transplanting by root division is possible. I have an extensive patch growing on the north side of our farmhouse right along the foundation, making the gathering of horsetail for my orchard sprays a cinch.

The fermenting tea of horsetail exudes the smell of the sea . . . so says the poet . . . while its telltale rotten-egg smell reveals the full truth of a ready brew. Its anti-fungal qualities verge on the energetic for biodynamic practitioners, who include horsetail tea (made from dried herb) in ground applications in early spring and again in fall.[71] Our plan focuses solely on the bioavailable silica and its uptake into the cuticle. Summer fungi landing in that month after petal fall take some time before appearing. It's easy to miss the beginnings of rot, but in another few weeks peaches and the like can become a discouraging mess. Sooty blotch and flyspeck require 250 hours of accumulated wetting before becoming visible on apples at harvesttime. Preventing a fungal foothold early on is what wins these ball games. One last fascinating note about *Equisetum* for those of you enthralled with aerated compost tea: A significant increase in beneficial fungi counts has been noted when horsetail is added to the tea brewer.[72]

nutrient extraction.[70] Now fill the bucket to the brim with unchlorinated water. Let sit for seven to ten days somewhere outside, loosely covered to prevent significant evaporation. This fermentation period makes the constituents that much more bioavailable for foliar absorption. These teas are diluted in that I add the strained tea from each bucket for each herb being used to each 100-gallon batch of spray. Backpackers might consider adding a quart of each herb tea per spray, as you honestly can't overdo herbal nutrition used in this way for tree health.

Three plant friends in particular meet my summertime needs in the orchard, with the tops of another adding a gourmet touch.

Fermented teas of **horsetail** are included two or

Fermented teas of **stinging nettle** could actually

Stinging nettle in the seed stage has increasing levels of silica. A fermented tea of this herb helps boost the cuticle defense of the fruit tree.

Comfrey can be used as a homegrown foliar calcium source by simply brewing an herbal tea with its leaves and letting this ferment five to seven days.

be used anytime, but I wait to do this in conjunction with horsetail starting at first cover and then on through the month of August. Nettle is pure tonic nutrition for plant and food web alike. Trace minerals (like zinc, iron, and selenium) abound, along with nitrogen, calcium, potassium, and almost every vitamin named. Silica levels in *Urtica dioica* go skyrocketing up when seed formation on the plant becomes obvious . . . which coincides perfectly with the time I make teas for the fruit trees to ward off summer fungi and to perk up the vegetable garden.

Nettle leaves are covered with tiny hairs—hollow needles actually—that sting upon contact and then cause a mild burning sensation for hours afterward.[73] Unmanaged pastures might be one place to look for

this stinging herb, but it's simple to start nettle from seed in the greenhouse, from which you can then plant a home nettle patch. Trust me. You will come to treasure the gifts of this migrating plant for spring greens, for your own medicinal use for almost every condition, and as a green remedy for fellow plants renowned above all others. One suggestion is in order to keep your relationship with nettle on an even keel: Wear gloves when harvesting this plant.

A proper fermented nettle tea can be even more powerful with respect to the hydrogen sulfide (rotten-egg) smell. Interestingly, this is the brew that slugs by the dozens choose to sip and invariably drown in . . . an observation that has led me to set out shallow servings of this particular tea wherever slugs currently seem to have the upper hand in the garden. Don't worry—you'll be filtering out any slugs that make it into the tea bucket along with the nettle residues prior to making those successive orchard sprays.

Comfrey packs a wallop of calcium in its deep green leaves. This superstar of the orchard understory (see "Plant allies" in chapter 2) is known botanically as *Symphytum officinalis.* The chemical compound allantoin in this herb encourages bone, cartilage, and muscle cells to regenerate in our bodies.[74] Naturally, comfrey is a powerful stimulator of all cell multiplication and thus growth in plants as well. I rely on this herb especially as a source of supplementary calcium, a mega-nutrient required for all fruit production.

Calcium translocates somewhat poorly from leaf to fruit, especially when there are dramatic fluctuations in rainfall patterns or it's a light crop.[75] This can lead to calcium deficiency in the fruit—even when soil levels appear adequate—causing a disease condition known as *bitter pit* in apples or *cork spot* in pears. Certain varieties are more susceptible to this late-season spotting of the skin than others.[76] Commercial growers rely on summer foliar sprays to get more calcium into the fruit to prevent bitter pit. Young fruitlets are best at absorbing calcium, as eventually the waxy cuticle of the ripening apple will interfere with absorption. My homegrown solution to this perennial challenge is the bioavailable calcium found in fermented comfrey tea, applied every other week after petal fall.

Garlic extracts are considered to be *systemic*, which means that leaf tissues readily absorb the proffered plant constituents. We grow a substantial amount of garlic on our farm, a process that involves removing the flower stalks (scapes) on hardneck varieties, and it's these scapes that I invariably include as a gourmet topping in my height-of-summer brews. We cut the scapes from the garlic in June, about a month prior to the bulb harvest, and throw a handful of these into each bucket of herbal brew from that point on. The fact that the organo-sulfur compounds in garlic serve as synergistic carriers of silica and other nutrients from those teas into and through the cuticle simply rocks my herbal boat.

The process of brewing nutrient-rich teas for the holistic orchard requires little more than brewing buckets for each herb. Garlic scapes are added to facilitate the uptake of bioavailable constituents into the fruit leaf.

This concept of plant medicines for plants is expanded upon the world over—anywhere modern spray concoctions aren't necessarily desired or affordable.[77] A few last orchard tidbits might intrigue you enough to try other teas as well. Aromatic herbs like wormwood are used to ward off female codling moths (which rely on sensing nearby fruitlets by smell) during the period of egg laying. Tansy is reported to be effective at preventing fungal rusts. A fermented decoction of horseradish roots prevents various rots on light-colored apples, cherries, and plums. Undiluted fresh teas of nasturtium or broad-leafed dock can be used on existing cankers and to protect young trees from the same. Grasshoppers will not nibble on wild lettuce—a bitter slurry of this plant sprayed onto fruiting plants will indeed deter descending hordes of these foliage destroyers.[78] Sometimes the most sensible solutions grow right in our backyard!

Seaweed

The tenets of whole plant medicine invariably lead to the sea. Those brown and green seaweeds that grow in cold, nutrient-rich water and along rocky shores are various kelp species. These large ocean algae contain a wide range of naturally chelated nutrients, amino acids, and other growth-promoting substances such as cytokinins.[79] If you live near the ocean, you can harvest washed-up seaweed on the beach to take home as a great addition for the compost pile or even as haphazard mulch.[80] Growers who use kelp regularly as a foliar application report increases in fruit quality, shelf life, and resistance to environmental stresses such as drought and extreme heat, as well as pest and disease problems.

Cold-processed liquid kelp has been enzymatically digested to preserve the complete range of hormones and proteins that go with all the important trace minerals in seaweed. A quality dried seaweed extract retains a significant share of those growth-regulating hormones as well while saving considerably on shipping costs.[81] Researchers have noted that it's the cytokinins that allow the fruit tree more time to increase its resistance response to disease-causing organisms.[82] Both seaweed products contribute in that respect.

I add seaweed to every spray opportunity as a megavitamin for healthy growth once foliage is showing. Higher concentrations of chlorophyll result, and that means photosynthesis is enhanced. The tonic rate for seaweed extract is 8 ounces (dry weight) per 100 gallons per acre on a biweekly schedule, which is equivalent to the recommended 2-quart-per-acre rate for liquid kelp. In backpack terms, this amounts to 5 tablespoons liquid kelp per 4-gallon spray volume. Many of the liquid fish manufacturers offer a mixed product consisting of biological fish with cold-processed kelp, but because I want to continue using seaweed all summer long, I purchase these two products separately.

Old-school organics

The traditional organic approach to defeating orchard diseases utilizes copper early on, then various formulations of sulfur and/or lime sulfur. Copper works like a blunt barrier by unfavorably altering surface hospitality for overwintering organisms. Sulfur works as a protectant fungicide in altering solution pH, thereby inhibiting the production of spore penetration enzymes. Lime sulfur brings an eradicant edge by penetrating the leaf tissue and thus whacking that hyphal start-up out of the ballpark if applied within the first twenty-four to thirty-six hours following actual infection. All these mineral fungicides will have significant impact on soil and arboreal organisms, return bloom, beneficial insects, yield, fruit finish, and perhaps even your happiness.

Organic fruit growers have accepted the shortcomings of using an allopathic approach, as rampant disease would be a far worse scenario. The full skinny on all these mineral fungicides is provided in my first book on organic orcharding, *The Apple Grower*. Please go there to understand how to obtain respectable results using micronized sulfur and the like (if I haven't yet convinced you to work with an enhanced biology instead). What we will do here is briefly talk about several specific challenges to healthy expectations that invariably arise in some places in some years.

Wet springs will always be a fungal challenge. **Scab-prone apple varieties** in a holistic orchard ride into bloom time as clean as can be, but ever-increasing odds of fungal infection make the tail end of the primary infection period more problematic. A looming rain after a significant dry period (which allows scab ascospores to mature and thus accumulate in number) at the tail end of bloom and within those next ten to fourteen days can overwhelm even a primed immune defense. A micronized sulfur application just before such a rain can make a difference, all the more so

The *Venturia* fungus that causes pear scab overwinters in twig lesions as well as on fallen leaves. The need to deal with tree-sourced inoculum cannot be overlooked. Photo courtesy of Alan Jones, Michigan State University.

Peach leaf curl establishes at the end of harvest in bud crevices. A fatty acid knockdown after leaf fall followed immediately by competitive colonization offers a holistic alternative to the more typical copper strategy. Photo courtesy of Alan Biggs, West Virginia University.

when this needs to happen midway between holistic sprays.[83] Each season offers up changing variables with which you need to learn to dance. Keep in mind that supplemental microbe applications (especially within a long bloom window) hold equal portent for trees no longer empowered to quite the same degree by that holistic spray made at pink.[84]

Occasionally, **pear scab** establishes on a certain pear variety, setting up a potential disease vector for surrounding pears in the years ahead. This particular fungus (*Venturia pirina*) differs from apple scab in that conidia overwinter on twig lesions as well as in the form of ascospore potential on leaf litter. Both vectors jump into the new growing season beginning at bud swell. A copper application to lesion-inflicted trees at that point may be a necessary pill on the heels of severe infection the previous season. This medicinal one-shot goes hand in hand with diligent attention given to leaf decomposition throughout the pear block.

All diseases have a dormant-season component, some more vulnerable than others. **Peach leaf curl** establishes at the end of harvest in bud crevices. A post-harvest application of copper is a long-standing recommendation to knock back these problematic fungi. Full coverage of the exposed buds comes only

once the leaves have fallen off. A follow-up application of copper or lime sulfur before growth resumes in spring is not at all unusual. A similar plan can be implemented for **bacterial spot** just prior to budbreak to prevent its spread from overwintering twig lesions. An alternative approach for holistic growers lies in a fatty acid knockdown followed by biological reinforcement a day later.[85] Conversely, some of you may opt for cleaning up the orchard every few years with a harder-hitting fungicide strategy during dormancy in order to clear the deck for reasonable holistic harvests in subsequent seasons.

Fire blight on the rampage in apple and pear trees is something to fear. Warm, humid conditions when blossoms literally open the door to the tree's vascular system can lead to severe trouble. Copper gets recommended to limit the spread of this bacterial assault force just when buds start to show green tissue in spring, usually in conjunction with horticultural oil as a spreader to carry the heavy metal particles deep into bark crevices. The high-risk period for actual infection invokes the call for antibiotic medicine, and, yes, streptomycin is allowed (albeit rightfully questioned) under current organic certification guidelines. That's something you will have to learn about elsewhere, as the competitive colonization approach to countering

Bacterial spot launches right around budbreak. The timing shifts, but the holistic plan remains the same—heavy dousing with fatty acids followed by effective microbes colonization. Photo courtesy of Megan Kennelly, Kansas State University.

fire blight bacteria will be detailed as a far more sensible alternative just ahead.

This option as organic fruit growers—to reach into our own allopathic toolbox for mineral fungicides—is legitimate in certain circumstances. We knowingly compromise the biology to address problematic symptoms by doing this . . . much like facing health decisions for ourselves. Tempted to take a proton pump inhibitor to quell severe acid reflux? You've gone allopathic. Has the doctor got you on blood-thinning medication because of a heart condition? You've gone allopathic. How about chemotherapy for cancer, God forbid? You've gone allopathic. We face such medical conditions relieved to know we have such choices. And yet all this can be worked with holistically as well, using herbs and nutrition and lifestyle change. You—me—and you again believe what we each believe. That's a part of the picture. I know I'm on one of *michael's big leaps* but this is relevant. There are times in the organic orchard when you may think it best to reach for old-school ways. That's okay in the short term. Just understand there will be more and more biological ramifications the farther you go down this road.

Bacterial woes

Bacteria work openings in the tree's vascular system by different means. A fungal infection indicates that hyphae have accessed food resources from the plant, and the resulting lesion is clearly "dis-ease" on the plant. Bacteria literally take over from within once an entry point has been successfully colonized. It's all about the numbers as an array of microbe species compete for food resources and ultimate dominion. Keep that distinction in mind as we look at particular bacterial afflictions of fruiting plants.

Possible actions against bacterial disease in the holistic orchard fall along three lines, often used in conjunction:

- Pruning out visible affliction and overwintering cankers
- Eliciting specific anti-bacterial response for and by the plant
- Enhancing competitive colonization

But first let's do a roll call of the possibilities growers might face in different orchards given the right conditions. Pome fruits have fire blight, blossom blight, and blister spot with which to contend. Stone fruits engage bacterial spot and bacterial canker (aka bacterial gummosis). Brambles can come with crown gall, but that's very unlikely if planting stock comes from a reputable nursery. Timing may vary but the *creeping-into-the-ecosystem* and *point-of-entry* mechanisms remain paramount.

Reading descriptions of these various bacterial woes reveals the entry mechanism clearly. Driving rains typically play an early role in how bacterial spot afflicts the leaf tips on stone fruit trees. Blossom blast to apple and pears on the West Coast follows on the tail of frost injury at bloom time. Fire blight can take advantage of untimely pruning cuts, open blossoms, hail injury, sucking insects, or even strong winds tearing leaves.

Early surgery is one answer to limiting fire blight, as it's easy to spot. Infected blossom clusters look a bit water-soaked, then quickly wilt, shrivel up, and turn brown. Snapping off the entire spur as soon as possible prevents the bacterium from getting farther into the tree. Fire blight can strike through the growing tips of succulent shoots almost as readily and then move down toward the limb, making the shoot turn black. Almost as if someone came along and scorched the shoot, hence the name of this disease. A shepherd's-crook bend to the end of the shoot provides another telltale sign. Prune out infected shoots going back along the limb to make the cut at least 8–12 inches beyond the place where the blackening stops. Don't be hesitant; the disease can eventually prove fatal as it progresses farther and farther into the main scaffolds, trunk, and roots. Nor is this the time to be concerned about thinning cuts versus heading cuts. In fact, the latter can be helpful on bigger limbs, as chances are good the cut itself will be infected on the rebound by blight bacteria in those weeks immediately following fruit set.[86] The resulting ugly stub can be marked with flagging tape and then properly pruned away at a branch juncture in the cold dormant season, thereby removing lingering fire blight prospects safely. If you need to make multiple cuts in the growing season, especially when going from tree to tree, sterilize your pruners with rubbing alcohol.[87] Otherwise you run the risk of inadvertently spreading the disease.

A summer spent dealing with fire blight means you will want to be on the lookout for cankered bark tissue when dormant pruning time comes around again. Such cankers appear as slightly darker, water-soaked areas in the wood, with flaky bark along the edges. These produce amber-colored bacterial ooze, offering up tens of thousands more bacteria when the growing season resumes. This new army of infection will subsequently be spread by rain splash and leaf-feeding insects to other parts of the tree, all waiting for that point-of-entry moment when conditions are right for a new round of fire blight. Limbs with visible cankers obviously need to be pruned out, removed, and destroyed.[88]

The pivotal question to be asked here is what can be done to prevent blight bacteria from gaining this upper hand in the first place. The growing season arrives in all its glory. Bloom is in full swing, and you're rightfully concerned about warm, wet weather.[89] The second holistic spring spray at pink will not necessarily deliver full colonization to flowers that open several days to a week later. The race is on as to which microorganism species will claim that tantalizingly exposed opening into the heart of the tree. Supplemental sprays during bloom time have biological components that can direct the odds in your favor against fire blight.

Plan A involves a spray product called Serenade. This biological formulation contains anti-bacterial compounds derived from a natural fermentation of a particular strain of *Bacillus subtilus* bacteria found in a California peach orchard.[90] These *iturins* are capable of destroying pathogenic bacterial cells directly as well as stimulating the immune response of the fruit tree itself.[91] Here's vital information: Spray applications of Serenade must come prior to fire blight bacteria making their warm-and-humid move onto the open blossom. (In football terms, this would be called a "prevent defense"!) The first spray should be made when 1–5 percent of the king blossoms have opened, then again every three to seven days as blossoms continue to open and conditions dictate. I would definitely include seaweed in all these bloom-time sprays for the cytokinin boost.

Plan B involves specific antagonistic colonization of the opening flowers. A particular strain of *Pseudomonas fluorescens* bacteria are known to aggressively outcompete *Erwinia amylovora* (fire blight) bacteria for the nutrients on flower stigmas. Honeybees have been used to deliver these microbial allies when foraging for nectar in the orchard. (The bees pick up the bacteria when crawling through a "dust foyer" to enter and exit the hive.) These benign *Pseudomonas* rapidly claim the flower as their own, thereby preventing fire blight from becoming established. When blossom inoculation gets done on a daily basis by the bees . . . fantastic . . . but, realistically, most home orchardists are not beekeepers. There are sprayable versions of this treatment, including one called Blight Ban.[92] Timing once again is tricky and critical—the fire blight competitors must arrive on each round of opening blossoms before fire blight does. Recommended applications are at 20 percent bloom, repeated again at full bloom, and perhaps even again at the tail end of bloom if weather conditions warrant.

Plan C takes an entirely different tack on the microorganism front. A nutrient-based tree wash consisting of hops extract and a vegetable oil (along with kelp, molasses, and yucca extract) is applied as buds become active in spring and then every ten to fourteen days thereafter throughout the bloom period. Resin acids found in hops are known to be anti-bacterial. Commercial growers in the lower Yakima River Valley in Washington were the first to discover the synergy of these plant-based ingredients in keeping both fire blight and bacterial canker from occurring on apple and cherry, respectively.[93] Advocates explain that "the bacteria are deprived of their food source," which to my mind is just another way of saying that the arboreal food web—given deep nutritional support—does indeed outcompete bacterial pathogens.

Yeasts have shown potential here as well. Another bacterium, *Erwinia herbicola* (strain C9-1), produces a natural antibiotic of its own that inhibits the multiplication of the pathogen.[94] Here's the thing: All these specific bioantagonists are very likely a part of a healthy orchard ecosystem already. Such are the gifts of biodiversity! Isolating products from the biology has its usefulness commercially, but keep in mind you're already in a relatively good place enhanced by holistic doings. Choosing fire-blight-resistant varieties of apples and pears to go with some combination of these approaches can be the smartest move of all in humid regions. Stone fruit growers can feel comfortable planting cultivars with moderate susceptibility to both bacterial spot and bacterial canker given this understanding of competitive dynamics.

Stirring the biological stew

Enhancing leaf decomposition right where the leaves fall makes sense in holistic disease management. Often we refer to reducing overwintering disease inoculum as good hygiene practice. This involves a combination of leaf liming, aggressive mowing, spreading compost, and spraying fatty acid compounds to facilitate leaf decomposition. All important and useful techniques . . . I just prefer calling this "stirring the biological stew" in order to keep the concept of fungal duff support up front in my conscious efforts to always build biological connection.

Choose any three, but under no circumstances skip these steps!

- **Leaf liming.** Sprinkling a quart container (or so) of calcitic lime per bearing tree atop fallen leaves interrupts an essential reproductive act of fungal scab in late fall necessary to form pseudothecia spore sacs. Time this when a third to half of the leaves have fallen off the tree.

- **Aggressive mowing.** Chopping leaves up into smaller bits by mowing the orchard area ensures that a far greater percentage will be decomposed by spring. The mere act of flipping a leaf puts potential pseudothecia in a downward-pointing direction . . . a scab bummer if ever there was one.

- **Spreading compost.** Compost spread atop such a leafy grass mix hastens the decomposition of any remaining fungal inoculum on the ground. Earthworms and microorganisms carry out the work from this point on until the earth freezes solid. The trees should be fully dormant at the time of spreading compost.[95]

- **Fall holistic spray.** The biology awards triple value for this particular effort when approximately 40–60 percent of the leaves have fallen off the trees. Pure neem oil and liquid fish increase the decomposition to a crescendo on the ground with fatty acid compounds. I spray the entire tree and remaining leaves up top as well to facilitate microbe diversity (be it with effective microbes or compost tea) in the bud crevices and on potential twig lesions for the

The fungal duff zone finds its heyday when it comes time to stir the biological stew each fall. Accomplishing three of the four steps aimed at maximizing leaf decomposition beneath each tree also ties to nutrient uptake by the fall root flush.

A modicum of lime sprinkled on the first fallen leaves ensures that a hefty majority of the current year's scab lesions will be unsuccessful at establishing pseudo-thecia (spore sacs) to spread disease anew next spring.

dormant months ahead. The fall root flush has hit full stride in the gathering of nutrients—like the nitrogen in that fish—to store in cambium tissues that will launch spring growth. This spray is the most essential step of all.

Let's talk briefly about raking up all the leaves instead. This might seem to be sound thinking at first reading, knowing it's the fallen leaves within the orchard that will retain the greatest share of scab inoculum for next spring. But in truth, taking the leaves away undermines the very biology we want to encourage beneath our trees. Leaves are organic

matter from which nutrients will be recycled through the collective mouth of the soil food web. Putting leaves in a plastic bag to be hauled away is plain dumb. Composting those leaves can be considered (knowing you will return the result to the orchard floor), but why not let the action happen in place, right in the fungal duff zone? I do rake leaves out from the trunk to clear that peastone circle. And I do rake leaves that the mower may have missed inward from pathways back to the dripline. Orchard compost then anchors the works.

We are emulating forest-edge ecology by building up humus and increasing biological activity in all these ways. Wrapping up the orchard year with what amounts to a celebration of earthy promise always feels good.

DEER AND OTHER UNINVITED GUESTS

Animals can make quick work of a promising crop and even damage the trees themselves. A wee bit of sharing is fine, perhaps even called for, but there are definite actions to be taken on three particular fronts by orchardists. Who actually comes to your orchard door is anybody's guess. It might be raccoons stealing peaches or jays pecking pears up high. It might be a marauding beaver that decides to fell half a dozen trees in one night. It might be a wily coyote sampling the few apples of a new variety you've been eagerly awaiting. It might be gophers making entire root systems disappear. Very likely it's your favorite songbird scoring those blueberries. All I know is it will be someone.

The stories I hear from other fruit growers about animal woes make me appreciate all the more that moose that got into our south orchard (through an open gate) and then required *only* a dozen or so full-body slams into the high-tensile electric fence before breaking enough batten supports to get out between the wires . . . no trees were lost! On the other hand, deer really rip into fruit trees and can prove a constant battle. Voles will girdle tree after tree if trunk guards aren't in place for the winter months. Some years squirrels seem determined not to pass by a single piece of fruit, but luckily birds can be tricked. What follows is a range of possible solutions to all sorts of critter situations, from fencing tips to live trap-out advice to providing food alternatives. Much of this takes diligence. Some calls for compassion. Other times it's legitimate to put an end to an overwhelming vermin population. The choice of what to do is entirely yours, as, again, I'm just pointing out the options.

Bark nibblers
Take away enough bark and a fruit tree dies.

Pine voles and meadow voles are the two principal rodents to watch out for in any orchard.[96] The pine vole lives underground and feeds on fruit, tubers, and the roots of certain trees (especially apple) in burrows. The extensive burrow systems radiate out from the trunk to the dripline of the tree, with the tunnel runs averaging a few inches deep. A large root being gnawed by these rodents will send up a row of suckers. Thick surface litter prevents tunnels from collapsing, so it's better to spread ramial wood chips completely (1 inch thick rather than as a weed-suppressing pile) in pine vole country. The meadow vole prefers to construct networks of runways in sod right at the soil line. It feeds on grasses, legumes, seeds, and tubers; but when these are scarce, it's the cambium layers on the trunk that become a vole's munch. Much of the girdling damage by these so-called meadow mice occurs under the cover of snow.

Thorough mowing in the fall reduces run cover—thereby helping predators to find more voles. A family cat or two can do wonders here. You should also learn to appreciate the role of foxes, coyotes, and pine martens in the neighborhood. Skunks are especially accomplished vole hunters in a mulched understory. Sharp-eyed hawks will watch for any sign of prey movement as well.

The peastone mulch at the base of young trees helps keep the immediate area of concern open, but you absolutely should put up trunk guards starting in year one. These should be 18–24 inches tall, with limited space (no more than an inch) between trunk and guard, and absolutely expandable to allow for increasing girth over the years. Spiral tree guards on young trees are a temporary solution, in that these tighter wraps need to be removed during the growing season.[97] Galvanized hardware cloth or plastic mesh secured around the trunk (with wire twist ties or nylon plugs) offers year-round insurance against any lower bark nibbling. Allot some sliding-up space between the mesh guard and the lowest branches to allow you to check for borer issues at the soil line. The loose peastone at the base of each tree comes in handy here for piling around the base of the guard—an

Providing critters with an alternative source of browse ofttimes saves the tree. These rabbits are quite content to clean the bark off prunings thrown into the aisleway.

inch deep is plenty to block surface access. Another option: Check with your local hardware store for used window screening (left over from repair jobs) that can be double-folded into a tube-like protector from voles and borers alike.[98] Trunk guards will be necessary until the flakier bark of the mature apple tree makes this meal far less desirable to the meadow vole.

Outright trapping to kill is used in commercial orchards with bearing trees that have outgrown the trunk guard stage. Trapping methods apply to serious pine vole issues from the get-go. Rampage mouse bait, which has vitamin D_3 as its active ingredient, is the only acceptable organic poison option. Glue PVC pipe together to form an accessible tee in which poisoned bait can be securely positioned in vole runs. Elongated

wood frames with mouse-hole entrances cut into both ends can be equipped with standard mousetraps and then positioned to straddle an established route. Peanut butter makes for irresistible bait. A board lid (secured by the weight of a brick) will keep out prying hound noses and allow access for resetting traps. Juicy Fruit chewing gum provides a folkloric approach— half a stick placed every 4–6 feet along a vole run has been reported to cause voles to abandon the area.[99]

Growers in snow country can create an ice collar by stamping snow down around the trunk. This also prevents surface access into the otherwise impervious trunk guard from the top. Snowshoeing from tree to tree will also block runways made in freshly fallen snow. Simply scattering some early prunings on the ground provides voles and rabbits alike an alternative on which to nibble.

Young trees that get completely girdled need to be replaced.[100] Plastic wrap or a grafting sealant may be all that's needed on vigorous trunks that haven't been completely girdled (no more than halfway around) to hold moisture in while the tree closes the wound in early spring. A bearing tree with large areas of wintertime chewing can sometimes be saved by *bridge grafting*.[101]

Gophers intensify these matters all the more. Growers in western states cannot hesitate when tunneling starts to veer near fruit trees. Gophers push dirt forward in excavating new routes, going up to the surface to deposit the dirt, then plug the temporary exit hole. Disdain for direct openings into the underground highway system makes possible the effectiveness of the Black Hole gopher trap. These are placed in active runs (readily located below the backside of excavation piles) so as to reopen the air passage . . . prompting an irate gopher to come see who left the door open . . . and that's that. Owls, bull snakes, and coyotes do their part to keep things in balance farther beyond the tree zone.

Rabbits can be harmful, especially with dwarf trees that have scaffold limbs trained low. These animals cut off twigs and may even pull bark off trunks in shreds. Bud.9 apple rootstock seems to be especially appealing, perhaps because the bark is sweeter.[102] Groundhogs can do similar damage. Porcupines enjoy climbing up into trees and eating the bark at the base of scaffold limbs. Growers with these kinds of animal problems ultimately need a mesh-type fence down low to keep all sorts of critters out of the orchard proper. Hot pepper wax might help as a taste repellent in the short term, but a damned fine aim will bring the most unacceptable situations to a certain end.[103]

Fruit thieves
Masked bandits in your orchard? Gangs of delinquent squirrels on the loose? Such problems can be far worse

in a lean year when there's very little natural food for critters out in the woods.

Blocking trunk access up to the fruit is the place to start. Aluminum roof flashing comes on a roll in various widths. This can easily be stapled onto the trunk of sought-out fruit trees, ideally for a length of as much as 4 feet to hinder a leaping squirrel. Raccoons look upon 3 feet to be enough of a get-a-grip challenge. (Choosing a relatively high heading height to start the first branches on a full-sized tree is going to help with deer too.) A gooey band of Tangle-Trap paste formula—spread 3–4 inches wide over plastic wrap to protect the bark just above where the roof flashing ends— completes this aluminum trunk sheath to take care of the more persistent jumpers. Trees need to be spaced such that squirrels can't travel from treetop to treetop. High vegetation helps more than you might think, as squirrels veer away from locations where a quick getaway isn't as assured.

The big issue here is that squirrels don't share. They'll destroy an entire tree's worth of almost-ripe peaches at the rate of one bite per fruit. The same goes for apples and pears. These rodents can carry a significant-sized piece of fruit away as well, so don't dismiss the "cute squirrels" too quickly in the balance of things. Growers rightfully get mad, opting for one of two means to protect the crop.

Elimination traps range from walking the plank to a rather gruesome recipe to a just-takes-a-peek design that squirrels seemingly cannot resist. (Warning: Softhearted folk will want to skip this section.) Pirate-types have devised a simple 2x4 arrangement where a horizontal arm extends 3–4 feet off the trunk on which a low-cost rat trap awaits at the very end. A single peanut placed as bait is often more than a greedy squirrel can ignore. *Plaster-of-paris bonbons* are made by mixing peanut butter with dry plaster powder into a stiff dough-like consistency to form marble-sized balls. Do not use any water in this mix. These are placed in the crotches of the trees and other strategic places sheltered from rain. Once eaten by the squirrels, the dry plaster reacts violently with gastric acid in the squirrel's digestive tract, potentially causing gastric rupture, shock, and death.[104] The Kania 2000 trap settles matters by means of an inescapable head lock. These need to be safely set so only the target species finds the bait. Pecans work well, pushed through the wire mesh to release that delectable nutty essence, with bits of pecan that a squirrel can see waiting just an arm's reach away inside. Therein ends that story.

Let's now consider seemingly more gentle means. Live trapping involves the removal of a pest animal to somewhere else. Havahart traps consist of a levered bait platform inside a rectangular cage; this gets jiggled when the animal takes the bait, causing the doors on both ends to slam shut. You simply need the right-sized live trap for the animal being targeted, along with effective bait. Peanut butter works well with squirrels and chipmunks; raw cabbage snags most groundhogs (if placed near a woodchuck entrance hole); and no raccoon can resist a marshmallow. But here's the thing about live trapping: Wildlife biologists strongly recommend against relocation of most unthreatened species. Moving problem animals to a new home potentially pushes the population at the release site over its natural carrying capacity. The relocated animal is frequently at a disadvantage with regard to competing for available food, nest sites, and mates. Being aware of such prospects makes it hard to feel totally smug about the limited live trapping that I have done here at my farm.

Birds can play a significant role in this battle for the harvest as well. All tree fruit up high will be pecked for a taste by jays and crows in that month before harvest, especially in a dry year. The small-fruit harvest can be stolen from under your nose if robins or waxwings set sights on your cherries or berries. A physical barrier over the berry patch and even whole trees (see the "Bird netting" sidebar in chapter 6) can block fruit access entirely. But there are subtler means to trick birds as well.

Scare-eye balloons—printed with oversized eyes on all sides and foil streamers dangling below—might be effective in some situations as a quiet deterrent.

These can be hung from poles alongside the topmost foliage of cherry trees to make smaller birds think a *large something* is on the prowl. Each balloon casts its shadow over a radius of some 30 feet if it's put in place just as the fruit begins to color fully.

Availability of other berries seems just as important to keep the birds busy with an alternative. Neighborhood wildlife plantings are a big part of a successful strategy. Look at the unkempt edges of your property as an opportunity to provide fodder for others. Mutual fruits need to ripen at about the same time for this to be of help. Juneberries and mulberries generally score high on any bird's Top Ten list, with red currants and pin cherries not far behind.

Setting out a decoy crop before the fruit-in-contention comes ripe takes an entirely different tack. I think robins actually get disgusted at being fooled three times too many. Decoy fruit consist of red beads from a craft store that are approximately the same size as the real fruit (and appropriately spray-painted a different color if you're working with dark-colored berries). These are hung right after flowering throughout the fruiting plant (a couple dozen at least) on cherry branches and bramble tips, with thin wire run up through the bead hole. Robins and company come to investigate . . . find nothing palatable . . . and eventually get bored with the whole affair. Adult birds will leave the real cherries and even those delectable blueberries alone when color comes to the actual fruit.[105] Decoy fruit can even be left in place year-round provided you check on occasion that the attachment end of the wire isn't girdling its way into a desirable limb.

Bud browsers

Deer rarely seek out the fruit on orchard trees. The actual damage done is longer-lasting and can happen year-round. Browsing the buds and shoots of a young tree shifts the hormonal growth toward bush mode. This takes a full growing season (if not more) from which to recover—provided you deny ongoing opportunity to the perpetrators.[106] Browsing of fruit buds on bearing trees in the winter results in an aggressive loss of next year's crop within 6 feet or so of ground level. Bucks will rub young trees during the rut season, stripping away bark in the process, if not snapping the tree entirely. Deer can never be taken lightly, no matter how beautiful such animals are in a forested glen.

Taste repellents often help if extreme hunger isn't driving deer to desperation. A soap/hot pepper/raw egg combination made at home can be sprayed onto trees,[107] with commercial blends available as well. Odor repellents like deodorant soap bars and cotton bags of human hair are best rotated on occasion to keep deer from getting used to one scent. Visual strategies (like aluminum pie plates) are a stopgap measure at best and must be moved about regularly to keep deer wary.[108] Drawing coyotes onto the scene with meat scraps might avail in rural areas where predators can be appreciated. Still, if you're serious about wanting to nurture fruit trees for many years to come without overwhelming loss to browsing deer, you ultimately need to consider fencing.

The least intrusive approach is to fence each tree, much as you see shade trees protected in a horse pasture. Figure on a diameter of 6–8 feet, with the fence on the order of 4–5 feet high to limit overreach. Mesh fencing can be wrapped around several stakes (sapling poles will do) to create a temporary fence around individual trees.[109] Split rails or stacked logs (on the order of 3–4 inches in diameter) can be crosshatched to create a more frontier look. The goal is to get those trees up above browsing height, deliberately starting first branches around the height of the temporary fence. Individual tree barriers need to be kept in place for as long as ten years to achieve a relatively deer-proof tree.

Some growers are able to block the ways deer get into the orchard, assuming buildings and hedges funnel access to a degree. Deer get spooked by walking into seemingly invisible fish line strung tautly across the path. Sometimes a single electric fence wire baited with peanut butter (smeared onto aluminum foil strips) at nose height can be enough to convince the animal that this isn't the place to be right now. Motion detectors that activate lights along with high-pitched sound effects can be especially useful provided the deer are not already educated that tasty buds await beyond the monitored zone.[110] Continually blinking solar lights, advertised as resembling the eyes of a predator, seem to attract deer (in my experience) to see what all the fuss is about.

Long-term deer fencing is the best option for anyone with an exposed planting. Many of you will resist this advice, I know. No one wants an unsightly fence if it can be avoided, but I promise you will come to love those 6- to 8-foot-high posts and high-tensile electric wires. Especially once you've seen how bad a deer-ravaged orchard can look! A solid mesh fence is even better, because deer prefer to go through rather than over a barrier unless driven by fear. Fence strategies are discussed all over the web and in manufacturer literature, so I'll let you take this from here. Whatever you do, a family dog goes a long way in guaranteeing any and all fencing plans.

All of which brings us to a partridge in a pear tree. Or maybe it's turkeys. Big birds are known for browsing fruit buds on occasion, settling into various fruit trees en masse for a winter feed. A regular morning stroll with that same dog can alter roosting habits quickly. Hanging a few CDs to spin in the wind on favored trees won't hurt either.

GEARING UP

A few good tools up the pleasure of orcharding considerably. Spending several hundred dollars for quality equipment makes sense when you think about fruit trees being with you for a lifetime. Hand shears, loppers, and a limbing saw meet the full spectrum of pruning needs. A backpack sprayer is requisite for building orchard health. You get into the swing of biological mowing with a European-style scythe. Lastly, a tripod orchard ladder gets you around about and into the tops of freestanding trees.

Deer must absolutely be kept from browsing buds on the young tree. Individual tree fences work in small orchards to provide the tree with years enough to grow above browsing height.

Pruning tools

Bypass hand shears are a must for training work, gathering scionwood, and finer thinning cuts. Felco-brand shears fit the requisites for me: comfortable to hold, easy on the wrist, replaceable parts, and a handy holster for the belt. These Swiss-made tools offer a choice of right-handed or left-handed versions, better leverage for making slightly larger cuts (up to ¾ inch), and even a model designed to hold the snipped limb in the shears so it doesn't drop. The steel used to make Felco blades holds its edge and thus requires less sharpening. It would be nice if more local stores carried this and other quality brands of tools, but, alas, the inexpensive item drives the market. The orchard suppliers listed in the resource section of this book carry pruning tools worth buying.

Short-handled loppers (up to 2 feet long) are just right for making those prime thinning cuts of whole branches but too big for getting involved with overly fine detail work—an attribute that can speed you up quite a bit if you tend to be overly fussy about snipping away too many smaller shoots. Loppers take care of medium cuts (up to 1½ inches) and handle well with heavy gloves on those cold pruning days. Crucial for those who don't already know is the importance of choosing bypass- rather than anvil-style shears, whatever the size. This choice determines how tight you can make the cut to a branch union. The anvil design results in crushing the limb on both sides of the cut, thereby leaving more of a pruning stub than is desirable. A sleeker bypass-style shears tightly parallels the branch being kept and makes a far cleaner cut.

Limbing saws are used to make branch cuts up to several inches in diameter. The Wheeler pruning saw is well known in New England. This modified hacksaw (design-wise) makes only a tiny kerf with almost no tear to the bark. Set the blade to cut on the pull stroke by aligning the teeth back toward the

Felco hand shears and loppers, a Wheeler saw (with a custom bandsaw blade), and the mighty Silky limbing saw make up my pruning kit.

handle, as the push stroke direction tends to vibrate. Changing the tensioned blade requires some torque be applied to the supporting arch of the frame. This can readily be achieved by pressing down the tip of the Wheeler saw along the edge of any flat, hard surface. Japanese pull-stroke saws by Silky also make a fairly clean cut (as there is no set to the teeth), remain sharp for a long time, and fit in a holster worn on your belt. Substantial scaffold branches can be cut with little effort.[111] Folding models of these pull-stroke saws have shorter blades and work well as long as the hinge mechanism doesn't tend to buckle when in use.

Pole saws and pole pruners are used regularly in commercial orchards to efficiently reach the tops of larger trees. Good stuff if it's a Japanese-style blade or a bypass-style cutting hook on the end of the pole. Home orchardists have no need to up the level of investment in more pruning equipment, however, as the case will soon be made for obtaining a ladder especially designed for orchard work. Trees kept to 14–16 feet tall are easily accessed from the right sort of ladder . . . and that makes your loppers and limbing saw all the more apropos. Climbing up close ensures that cuts are both neat and in the right place relative to the branch collar.

A small chain saw will be appreciated when renovating an overgrown apple tree long left untouched. I can recall many such "cuts of my youth" made from a precarious position amid a jungle of intertwined limbs. All you need from me now is a reminder to be exceedingly smart about the inherent risks involved.

Sprayers

Choosing to spray to build system health is far different from choosing to spray to kill.

Have we gotten that by now? Spraying herbal remedies and insect repellents effectively pivots on having reliable spray equipment appropriate to the scale of your orchard. A hand-pump backpack sprayer will meet everyone's needs early on when the trees are young and probably will still suit many of you years later. A powered backpack sprayer achieves consistent pressure and thus can provide more thorough coverage up high for less work on your part. Trailer-type sprayers will have both higher pressure and more tank volume to begin to cover a greater number of trees with a handheld spray gun. Tractor-mounted hydraulic sprayers meet the needs of community orchardists with an acre or more of fruit.

Manual backpack sprayers with shoulder straps free up both hands, one for maintaining pressure by means of a waist-high pump lever and the other to hold the spray wand. These will generally have a 4-gallon capacity, which when full can be considered a reasonable weight.[112] It helps to have a waist-high shelf to set the unit on so you can just step into the harness rather than lifting it onto your back up from the ground. Tank caps are sealed with O-rings, so spilling onto your back should not be an issue. Piston-type pumps achieve more pressure than diaphragm-type pumps— just be aware that you need to pump rather furiously to get anywhere near those rated pressure potentials of 90 psi and 60 psi, respectively. A brass adjustable nozzle provides better tree coverage than the plastic fan nozzle provided for garden use. Couple this with a brass wand extension to get spray up high. I've used the Solo brand all these years and appreciate how all parts are replaceable. Plus, the pump handle can be attached to work from either side depending on which arm you want to give a workout. A tad of *aerobic hopping* is called for as you move about with a backpack sprayer to keep kaolin clay and the like well mixed. I still use a backpack sprayer on occasion to spot-spray tent caterpillar outbreaks or when certain trees call for special treatment. A quality backpack sprayer is a hundred-dollar (give or take) investment that will hold its value regardless of how big your orchard grows.

Powered backpack sprayers achieve excellent coverage by providing an even flow rate. Motorized versions come at twice the weight, but because the tank size is limited to 3 gallons, the overall heft required is just about the same as for a manual backpack sprayer. The relatively quiet gas engine on these provides a maximum operating pressure in the 120–140 psi range, thus achieving a finer misting spray. Battery-powered versions are obviously silent, have no emissions, and can offer tank sizes up to 5 gallons. The pressure offered by a gel-cell-powered pump is typically in the 40–60 psi range. Here's the clincher in making a decision: A quality powered backpack sprayer costs three to six times more what a hand-pump type costs. That up-front investment in consistent pressure will be worth it in the long haul only if you decide to limit your orchard planting to a dozen or so trees forever. (And even that remains doable with a manual backpack sprayer!)

Trees eventually require considerably more spray upon reaching bearing age, and that's when larger tank volume saves on considerable refilling of the ol' backpack to obtain full coverage. Trailer-type sprayers basically fall into one of two genres. Decent utility models (around three to six hundred dollars) have a 15- to 40-gallon plastic tank; feature operating pressures in the 40–60 psi range; and can be pulled by a lawn tractor or mounted up back on an all-terrain vehicle. The diaphragm pump on these runs off the 12-volt battery of the carrier. These often do not have a recirculation loop into the tank, so settling can be an issue unless you drive in quick stop-and-go fashion. Skid sprayers are intended for the back of a pickup truck or can be put on trailer wheels. These are agricultural grade (starting at nine to twelve hundred dollars); they typically have a 50- to 70-gallon plastic tank with a working operating pressure that can reach 120–140 psi. That's ideal for nutrient spray applications with a handheld spray gun.[113] A 5-horsepower gas engine powers a diaphragm pump mounted on a shelf off one end of the skid tank. Recirculation should be a given at these prices, but be sure to ask.

Tractor-mounted sprayers operate off the power take-off of the tractor and attach by way of its three-point hitch. One, let's assume you have a small farm tractor in the 30- to 45-horsepower range. Two, the cost here (eighteen hundred dollars and up) can really be justified only by stepping up from the home orchard level to seriously growing some fruit for your community. Tank sizes now range between 50 and 150 gallons, thereby allowing for an acre of coverage with a single tank. The recirculation loop along with mechanical tank agitation keeps pure neem oil and everything else evenly mixed. My Rears PAK Tank features a stainless-steel tank and a powerful diaphragm pump that will last for decades, so I guess I'm committed!

THE VENERABLE SCYTHE

I have an abiding love for good hand tools. Here's my chance to turn folks on to the straight-handled scythe.

As a home orchardist, you probably have occasion to mow the grass, be it the yard areas between your gardens or a traditional orchard layout complete with flowering meadow. A scythe readily lays down a swath of high grass around fruit trees, just when biological timing suggests that dripline mulch will abet a late-spring feeder root flush. This tool also reaches safely beneath fence lines and pulls away tall growth leaning against tree trunks in fall. A scythe requires no gas, so you can even maintain your yard in ecological fashion once you get into the meditative swing of the thing.

Distinguishing between the back-bending rendition from American frontier days and the straight-handled European scythe is key to the enjoyment of this fine mowing tool. Check out the Scythe Supply website in the resources, and pay particular attention to blade selection. An all-purpose *ditch blade* is best for the varied undergrowth of an orchard, originally having been crafted for the annual clearing of drainage swales. A *bush blade* is essentially a stockier version made for root suckers, not unlike a short machete on a stick. The *grass blade* is what you need to keep a semi-even plane of green stretching to the distant horizon.

Biological mowing with a scythe is about feeder root timing and mounding up that good organic matter in the dripline zone.

Ladders

Traditional orchard ladders are tapered such that the side rails meet at the top, so they can be leaned into the crotches of tree limbs. A tripod stepladder also tapers to a point, only here the idea is to position the ladder top between neighboring branches. Its wide base gives more stability on uneven ground, with the tripod support leg swung over and through lower branches to gain access to all sides of the tree. (You'll learn to think about ladder access while pruning.) Stability is gained when the leg is swung out farther than the ladder is wide and the front base is relatively level despite the terrain at hand.

Home orchardists are best off making the tripod their first ladder choice. One that's 6–8 feet high will be easier to maneuver than one that's 10–12 feet. This

A tripod orchard ladder and a traditional pointed orchard ladder (which sets into a limb juncture) give me all the access I need to get about my fruit trees. Photo by Mark Rawlings.

gains access to the majority of the fruit for picking—when the solidity of the tripod can also be used to help support the crop load being transferred from the tree to your picking bucket. This same ladder will come in handy for pruning, thinning the potential crop, and hanging insect traps. Don't think for a minute that a house stepladder will do, for you won't be able to access the fruit tree nearly as well. Nor are four legs ever as stable as three in the orchard! A straight orchard ladder (on the order of 12–14 feet) will have a place when fruit trees reach full height.

The handcrafted wooden orchard ladders from Baldwin Apple Ladders in Maine have a sturdy feel I prefer to the cold of aluminum. The rails are made from lightweight aspen; the rungs are durable white ash. Some argue that aluminum ladders can be left out in the rain . . . to which I counter that a quality

wooden ladder can be left out in the rain for each phase of the work to be done, too. Protecting the wood with a yearly rub of linseed oil makes eminently good sense. Straight aluminum or wooden ladders cost eight to twelve dollars per foot of height; shorter tripods cost fourteen to eighteen dollars per foot. Regional orchard suppliers may offer both types, and you can certainly try making your own.

Bringing in the harvest

You'll need a picking bag of some sort, bushel boxes or baskets in which to put the fruit, and either that recommended ladder or a pole picker to snag the best-looking fruit higher up.

An efficient picker needs both hands free for the task at hand. Which isn't to say you can't hold a tray basket on one arm and glory in picking one fruit at a

Select fruit stores best for the long term in single-layer trays that can be stacked in a cold storage area.

time. Still, the day will come when being able to pick bushel upon bushel with some degree of efficiency might matter. The options range from crafting a large hook to hang over a ladder rung for a basket handle to investing in a professional picker's bag. These range from peach bags made of Cordura fabric with a snap-held bottom to polyethylene picking buckets with a closed-cell-foam liner and a rope-release canvas bottom. All types unhook beneath so that the picked fruit can gently slide into bushel containers set on the ground. Shoulder straps free both hands for picking. The smaller-sized buckets—½-, ¾-, and full-bushel are the options—don't allow you to bring as much fruit away from the tree at one time, but then having a 50-pound weight around your torso when coming down an orchard ladder with a full bushel may not be convenient either. Buckets are more effective than sacks at protecting picked fruit from bruising against a tree limb or ladder.

I admit to not being versed in the art of using a *pole picker* but concede it has its place for those not as able to get up into a fruit tree, even on the best of ladders. The standard basket-type picker comes on a wooden or fiberglass pole. Fiberglass poles are lighter, don't splinter, and can be found extending to as much as 12 feet. Spending more for an extension pole picker allows you to harvest the very top of a 16- to 18-foot tree. Softer stone fruit are best snagged in a cloth bag (look for models that allow the basket head to be replaced on the extension pole). Just keep in mind that you can't use pole pickers to prune and thin taller trees—those other needs merit that all-purpose tripod ladder.

Wooden bushel boxes have the advantage of being able to be stacked when full with fruit. Heavy-duty plastic crates can be more thoroughly cleaned and, given the right lip design, should also be stackable. Traditional harvest baskets with wire bail handles come in four sizes, from ½ peck to bushel. Any of these can be brought up to the house in a garden cart or a lawn-tractor trailer. What you put your fruit into also depends on what you plan on doing with that fruit. Woven ash baskets are pricey but sure pretty on the kitchen counter filled with peaches intended for preserves. Cherries seemingly belong in colanders, just as any bowl can hold berries bound for a custard pie. Cider apples need a place to sweat before pressing, which can be done neatly in open bins. Stacking ability may or may not matter in your cold storage area, depending upon whether shelves are available. Premium dessert fruits merit flat-tray treatment where singly wrapped fruits maintain holiday perfection.

The sheer abundance of an apple or pear tree makes life good.
Sweet Sixteen apples ripen to perfection in Lost Nation Orchard.

CHAPTER FIVE

Pome Fruits

Amulti-seeded core distinguishes pome fruits. Botanists get a bit more involved in describing fertilized carpels surrounded by fleshy "accessory" tissue . . . the latter being what it's all about from a grower's perspective. The most important genera of pome fruits—family Rosaceae, subfamily Pomoidae—are *Malus* (apple), *Pyrus* (pear), and *Cydonia* (quince). Medlars, hawthorn, and serviceberries fall into this grouping as well. The science that deals with the cultivation of fruit is called *pomology*, thus making each of you an amateur *pomologist* in a sense.

The goddess Pomona watched over the orchards and saw to the flourishing of fruit trees in Roman times. She didn't spend her time up in the skies with the more powerful deities but rather reveled in spring blossoms and earthy things. Like us. Let's step along now with this lusty wood nymph to the best of fruit.

APPLES

Apples likely originated in the Dzungarian Alps, a tall mountain range separating Kyrgyzstan, Kazakhstan, and China, in an area still hailed today as the original wild apple forest. We'll leave the lore of how this fruit became a cultural mainstay across the globe to others.[1] Choosing from among the thousands of named cultivars of apples may seem daunting at first, so let's make a sensible plan for your home harvest.

Apple varieties ripen over a period of months, ranging from midsummer to the far end of fall. Spreading out the harvest across this time gives your family a

The goddess Pomona, as depicted in an oil painting by Nicolas Fouché

chance to enjoy a number of different varieties in their prime. The potential for bushels of fruit requires envisioning all the ways you might enjoy this bounty, whether for pies, apple butter, dried slices, cider, or crisp keepers for fresh eating and baking in the winter months. The number of apple trees you plant should be tied to these expectations as well as the space you have available.

Summer apples tend toward tart and are rarely noted for having keeping ability. On the other hand, a number of these homestead classics were considered perfect for sauce and made surprisingly good early-season pies. Some newer introductions on the early end offer more crunch and a satisfying complexity, keeping as much as four to six weeks with refrigeration, and yet even these should not be overplanted. One multivariety tree (see "Grafting" in chapter 3, on page 44) of several summer apples will be a happy choice in a tight home orchard.

Midseason varieties ripen in September through mid-October. The many fresh-eating varieties in this harvest window have decent keeping ability and can be processed in all your favorite ways. Fall apples make a sweet cider with tangible body, with righteous blending of course. Choice of rootstock and thus size of tree determines the number of bushels you might expect, but do keep in mind that any varietal tendency toward biennial bearing will likely create an on-year, off-year dynamic. A generous selection of flavorful varieties in this category—up to half of your apple trees—will ensure you stay well fed despite whatever vagaries the season at hand offers.

Late-season varieties come on toward the end of October and through November. These winter keepers make the best cider (both sweet and hard), because sugar levels develop fully with long ripening time and a touch of frost. The most celebrated apples especially achieve this balance of sweet and tart, acidity and mellowness. That last attribute is best brought out by a month or more in storage, as flavor complexity in later varieties develops only once the fruit is off the tree. A good third of your varietal choices will want to be winter apples.

Apple varieties to consider

Why do we need so many kinds of apples? Because there are so many folks. A person has a right to gratify his legitimate tastes. If he wants twenty or forty kinds of apples for his personal use, running from Early Harvest to Roxbury Russet, he should

Apple connoisseurs don't bat an eye when asked to name one of the top dessert apples in the world. Ashmead's Kernel makes one of the best single-variety ciders as well.

be accorded the privilege. There is merit in variety itself. It provides more points of contact with life, and leads away from uniformity and monotony.
—Liberty Hyde Bailey, *The Apple Tree* (1922)

That is indeed the spirit to be shared as we enter this varietal exposé! Apples spoken of here are among the flavor elite and exemplify considerations across the bioregional spectrum. Many more could be recommended . . . but I want to get you excited now with the select promise of some extremely wonderful apples.

That said, not every cultivar is going to be right for every place. Flavor is influenced by the living soil, the weather conditions of each season, and what I call the

Early-season apples realized full dessert potential with the introduction of Zestar from the University of Minnesota. This one's crunchy, juicy, with a sprightly sweet flavor and a tang of citrus to boot. Photo courtesy of Stark Brothers.

North–South continuum. Maritime conditions are a must for some varieties, while others become special only when grown in a warm climate or at cooler elevations. People often set their sights on well-praised apples and then plant them a zone too far—beyond where local experience has revealed a particular variety to be outstanding. That's where neighborly advice goes a long way in steering you toward what does well (and what does not!) in the place you live. No apples like sweltering temperatures above 100°F (38°C), but they can tolerate such in an immature state. Heat that occurs in the final week or two before harvest matters the most, and it can turn even classic keepers soft and greasy. Apples that cook on the tree never develop as good a quality. The secret lies in looking for varieties

that mature when the days are bright and cool and the nights are crisp. Yellow varieties tend to work better than red in warmer climes unless tradition has pointed out otherwise. Northern growers need to recognize limits here as well, as the longest-to-ripen varieties will not make it if there's a deep freeze before fruit fully matures.

One last caveat, if I may. Many of today's sweet-and-nothing-more varieties found in the supermarket and sold through home garden centers didn't necessarily make the grade here. Commercial fare tends to be disease-prone and requires aggressive thinning, so unless another attribute like fantastic texture simply can't be overlooked, these won't be recommended. A number of these varieties have been taste-neutered by

Rhode Island Greening is one of America's older heirloom apples. What was good in the 1600s remains outstanding today. Photo courtesy of Richard Borrie, Orange Pippin.

the trade over the years as well. Sport mutations occur (naturally, mind) that bring on fuller coloration and spur-type fruiting habit—traits that markets deem of greater value than knock-your-socks-off flavor.[2] Luckily, we can set the priorities straight in our own orchards.

Akane (aka Prime Red, Tokyo Rose). Jonathan × Worcester Pearmain, 1970. Bright red fruit with crispy, juicy, white flesh. Sprightly flavor resembles Jonathan. Outstanding dessert fruit, with good cooking and drying qualities. Tree is precocious and winter-hardy. Thin well to get decent size. Mid to late bloomer. Better keeper than most early fall apples; flavors well in warmer places. Harvest timing makes it attractive to apple maggot fly. Broad disease resistance includes fire blight. Requires eight hundred hours of chilling. Zones 4–9.

Arlet (aka Swiss Gourmet). Golden Delicious × Idared, early 1980s. Medium-sized fruit with bright orangish red blush over a green base. Fine-grained, creamy, white flesh; crunchy, yet melts in the mouth. Mild flavor with hints of melon along with enough tartness to rescue this apple from sugary banality. Fully ripens starting in mid-August and through September, depending on your location. Moderately vigorous, spreading tree. A healthy Arlet shows disease tolerance in humid climes and is said to rebuff curculio. Best in Zones 5–8.

Ashmead's Kernel. Now three centuries old and still regarded as one of the very best dessert apples. Underlying bright green skin is almost entirely covered in heavy russet. Crisp, yellowish, juicy flesh with elegant nut-like flavor; each bite offers an intense aromatic sting of sharp and sweet. Look

That first bite of a red-fleshed apple takes everyone by surprise! Pink Delight is one of many varieties with this sparkling trait. Photo courtesy of Karen Mouat.

for a warm-hued pink on sun-touched fruit in late October to know when ripe; flavor sweetens to perfection by the holidays. Stores into March, better than most russet types in this regard. Light and erratic cropping tendency can be helped with extra compost. Tree is very vigorous and relatively disease-tolerant. Zones 4–8.

Belle de Boskoop. Introduced in the 1850s in the Netherlands. Large blocky fruit with a dull red-orange flush overlaid with russet. Firm, tangy, highly aromatic flesh. Outstanding for dessert and culinary uses. Every chef in Europe reveres Boskoop: Slices of this apple stand up well in pie. Tolerant of everything, including scab. Vigorous tree (grows relatively large even on dwarfing rootstock) with open and drooping branches. Triploid, so needs a pollinizer. Ripens beginning in late September. Best in Zones 5–6.

Black Oxford. Rare Maine heirloom. Medium-sized, round fruit is deep purple taking on a blackish bloom. A real treat reminiscent of an exotic tropical fruit; exceptional sauce apple; stunning drying apple. Slow to come into bearing, with a tendency toward biennial bearing. Tree is moderately vigorous with a spreading habit. Seemingly resistant to insect problems. Ripens in late October into November. Zones 3–5.

Cortland. Ben Davis × McIntosh, 1915. An intentional cross aimed at improving the keeping ability of a popular apple, resulting in one of northern America's favorite pie apples. Medium-large red fruit underlain with stripes. Fine-grained, crisp, tender, juicy; sprightly flavor when grown in a living soil. Slow-oxidizing white flesh is very good in salads. Sub-acid mainstay for a fall cider blend. Fully ripens

Holstein has Cox's Orange Pippin in its lineage. This highly aromatic apple has a good sugar–acid balance with a slight pineapple flavor. Photo courtesy of Trees of Antiquity.

beginning in late September; fruit does not drop readily. Annual in bearing habit. Twiggy branch structure challenging to prune. Best in Zones 3–6.

Disease-resistant cultivars (DRCs). The truly big deal in these apples is a resistant gene that activates a hypersensitive response to apple scab.[3] Spore penetration is met by the death of the cell being infected, thereby stopping scab in its tracks. Yet we're dealing with Nature . . . where everything constantly evolves . . . and new strains of *Venturia inaequalis* have indeed made an end run around this singular defensive mechanism here in North America. I have included two DRCs on this list that have exceptional qualities, but others like William's Pride, Pixie Crunch, and Liberty can be just as good. Treating these varieties as holistically as the rest will make for happy results.

Esopus Spitzenburg. One of the favorite apples of Thomas Jefferson, and named after the settlement of Esopus in New York, where it was found around 1790. Large oblong fruit is crimson red covered with yellow specks and gray dots. Sweet and nutty, with the spicy aromatic flavors more commonly associated with European apples, backed by a lively acidity. Juicy yet dense yellow flesh. Susceptible to all the common diseases, especially fire blight . . . but remember, we have a plan! Spitzenburg needs good levels of sunshine to fully develop its flavor.

Moderately vigorous tree with willowy growth habit. Ripens unevenly, beginning in late September. Best in Zones 5–6.

Fuji. Red Delicious × Ralls, 1962. Reliable producer in low-chill areas. Pink-speckled flush over a lackluster yellow-green background. Crisp and juicy, with a wonderful snappy texture, so don't let its dull exterior fool you. Flavor is predominantly sweet and that's about it. Best eaten slightly chilled. Vigorous tree tends to be somewhat bushy; requires attentive pruning annually. Crop load must be aggressively thinned. Stores exceptionally well as skin doesn't shrivel. Matures toward the end of October and into November. Fruit often develops watercore if picked late. Zones 5–10.

GoldRush. Co-op 17 × Golden Delicious, PRI 1994. The best of the disease-resistant cultivars for taste and storage. Yellow-green, round-conic fruit. Flesh is hard, very crisp and breaking, flavor intense and memorable. Quite tart off the tree, but heavenly come the start of the new year. Keeps through all of spring if stored in perforated plastic to lessen shriveling from dehydration. Good drying apple for its flavor wallop. Field-immune to scab, susceptible to cedar apple rust, moderately resistant to fire blight. Ripe when green turns to yellow to gold with red blushes in November—extremely high sugar levels help protect down to a 22°F (–6°C) freeze prior to harvest. Slightly upright tree sets a heavy crop but is easy to thin to achieve good-sized fruit. Zones 5–9.

Gravenstein. Originated in Italy in the 1660s and brought to California by Russian settlers in the 1820s. Crisp and juicy, with exceedingly thin skin. Refined sprightly flavor unexcelled for pies, applesauce, and early sweet cider. The red sport of this variety (Red Gravenstein, no less) does better in the North as far as Nova Scotia. Large, vigorous tree. May need extra attention for scab in a wet year. Pick frequently because of uneven ripening and tendency to drop. Triploid, so needs a pollinizer. Ripens late July into early September. Zones 4–8.

Grimes Golden. Believed to have sprouted from one of the seeds planted by Johnny Appleseed (John Chapman) in West Virginia.[4] Medium-large yellow fruit with scattered russet freckles. Crisp and juicy, spicy sweet fruit. Thought to be a parent of Golden Delicious. Needs to be picked slightly early for best aromatics and texture, as Grimes turns soft before ever dropping. Its fragrant flesh registers 18.8 percent sugar and its juice ferments to 9 percent alcohol, making it a superb cider apple. Moderately resistant to fire blight and cedar apple rust. Ripens midseason. Zones 4–8.

Hardy Cumberland. Detroit Red × Lyons, 1961, released by the University of Tennessee. Medium-sized fruit washed with carmine over a greenish yellow base. Semi-tart, sweet-tasting apple. All-purpose. Good choice for the Southern Appalachian highlands, showing broad resistance to disease, including cedar apple rust. Excellent storage qualities, showing no sign of bitter pit. Ripens early to mid-October. Best in Zones 6–8.

Heirloom cultivars. All open-pollinated apples discovered prior to the beginning of the twentieth century are considered antique varieties. Some fourteen thousand named cultivars flourished in far-flung orchards and backyards across North America by 1900. A number of these time-honored apples are staging a comeback, and for good reason. Many offer distinctive flavor. Some are unsurpassed for specific uses. Heirlooms as a general rule stood up to the insect and disease pressures *in a given region* at that time. That will still play in your favor, especially in a healthy ecosystem. Tapping into history can be a fun part of home orcharding. A good dozen heirloom apples are being recommended here, but you can also check out state and provincial listings at GrowOrganicApples.com and other resources given in the appendices.

Holstein. Progeny of Cox's Orange Pippin discovered in Germany in 1918. Large, orange-yellow fruit. Highly aromatic with a good sugar–acid balance and slight pineapple flavor. Often proves a favorite at Home Orchard Society apple tastings. Very vigorous tree with a spreading nature, producing numerous fruiting spurs. Triploid, so needs a pollinizer. Ripens late September to mid-October. Flavors best in cooler zones and the Pacific Northwest. Quite resistant to scab. Zones 5–8.

Honeycrisp. Keepsake × unknown variety, 1991, by the University of Minnesota breeding program. Fruit is mottled red with explosively crisp flesh. That's the ga-ga factor, to be sure. Honeycrisp has a honeyed sweetness in its good flavor years. Blooms midseason. Relatively low-vigor tree with upright-spreading tendency. Annual bearing if not overcropped. Fairly resistant to apple scab and fire blight. Foliar calcium sprays to counter leaf yellows are strongly recommended. Two-week harvest window begins in mid-September in middle zones. Phenomenal keeper in the fridge, coming out just as crisp even five to seven months later. Best color and flavor in Zones 3–5.

Hudson's Golden Gem. Unknown seedling found in Oregon, 1931. Large, conical, elongated fruit with deeply russeted skin. Pear-like qualities: rich, nutty, cloyingly sweet with an unusual crunchy texture. Quite scab-resistant. Exhibits various degrees of cracking in its early years, which appears by harvesttime as healed sutures; older trees produce apples that are beautiful and uniform. Harvest in October. Adds a special aromatic touch to a cider blend. All russets make nice dried apple slices. Zones 4–9.

Kidd's Orange Red. Red Delicious × Cox's Orange Pippin, 1924. Small to medium apple with an extensive orange-red flush. Flesh is a light yellow-cream color and quite dense, but firm rather than crunchy. Deep aromatic overtones surpass its rich sweetness. Parent of Gala. Best suited to warm inland climates. Very spreading growth habit. Resists scab and cedar apple rust. Fairly reliable cropper on the light side. Harvest begins mid-September to October farther north. Zones 5–9.

King David. Thought to be a cross of Jonathan × Winesap or Jonathan × Arkansas Black, 1893. Medium-sized, pale green fruit overlaid with deep

dark red. Firm, crisp, juicy yellow flesh. Sprightly flavor much like Winesap. Versatile apple for cider, pies, and sauce. Pick when the red color becomes complete for best fresh eating, as fruit never seems to drop. Late bloomer, so avoid early frost. Resistant to scab, cedar apple rust, and fire blight, but has black rot issues. Ripens late October to November. Zones 5–10.

Melrose. Jonathan × Delicious, 1931. One of the finest tart apples with a touch of original Hawkeye (Delicious) sweetness. Large, dark red fruit. Rich flavor and coarse, juicy flesh. Good fresh-eating apple, especially when left to mature and develop its flavor for a while after picking. Excellent baking apple, retaining its shape and flavor in the oven. This apple attains its highest quality only when it fully colors in a mild fall with cool nights and when the tree is starved for nitrogen. Grower-friendly tree, somewhat willowy. Above-average keeper. Ripens mid-October. Zones 5–8.

Mollie's Delicious. Introduced in 1966. A summer apple for low-chill zones and the humid South. Good size, slightly conic shape. Light yellow background about half covered with a red blush with a glossy finish. Colors well despite the summer heat. Snappy, high-quality flesh with pleasing aftertaste. Vigorous, spreading tree has decent disease resistance. Great pollinizer for early and midseason bloom. Ripens in late July to mid-August depending on your location. Stores for about eight weeks in refrigeration. Requires four hundred chill hours. Best in Zones 6–9.

Newtown Pippin (aka Yellow Newtown, Albemarle Pippin). Originated in Newtown, Long Island, in 1759. All-around apple, with firm, crisp, aromatic yellow flesh. Packs a refreshing wallop for tart-apple fanciers, with full sugar and rich flavor developing by the winter months. Remains delightfully firm in storage through April; excellent culinary and cider-making qualities. Large, self-fertile tree tends to bear biennially. Susceptible to scab, notably on clay soils; prone to watercore without adequate calcium. Harvest mid-October to early November. Zones 5–10.

Pink Lady (aka Cripps Pink). Golden Delicious × Lady Williams, 1973. Especially good for hot climates. Large pink fruit with sweet-tart flavor; exceptionally crisp. Fruit will store for six to eight months in common storage. Tree is very vigorous and hangs on to its leaves well into winter. Relatively self-fertile. Scab-susceptible, but surprisingly good resistance to sooty blotch. Needs only four hundred chill hours to set fruit and so flourishes on the Pacific Coast, in the Mid-Atlantic, and in the Deep South. Strong sunlight in autumn is vital for the pink coloration to develop. Ripens in October. Zones 7–10.

Pristine. A premier summer apple with Yellow Transparent and Russian hawthorn in its heritage, PRI 1994. Widely adaptable. Glossy lemon-yellow fruit with high sugar content. Excellent for fresh eating and applesauce. Moderately spreading tree, somewhat twiggy in habit. Immune to scab; moderately susceptible to cedar apple rust; definite fire blight issues. Good keeper for an early apple. Ripens mid-July into August. Best in Zones 4–6.

Ralls (aka Ralls Janet, Jefferson Pippin, Neverfail, and dozens of other names). Developed in Virginia in the early 1800s. Late-blooming variety to plant in a cold pocket as it blooms two weeks later than most other varieties. Medium-sized fruit with thin greenish yellow skin covered with pinkish red and overlaid with dark red striping. Yellowish flesh is fine-grained, crisp, and juicy, with a sprightly balance of flavor. Moderately vigorous tree with considerably twiggy growth and a tendency to overbear. Slight susceptibility to scab and bitter rot. Ripens in October; excellent keeper. Zones 6–8.

Red-fleshed cultivars. This apple grouping comes with a color explosion on the inside. You'll enjoy the reaction of friends taking an unsuspecting first bite. Most are somewhat tart, are scab-susceptible, and color best in northern zones. Pink Pearl ranks high in popularity, with an aromatic hint of grapefruit to be found in its startling bright pink flesh. Red-fleshed varieties make a tasty pink applesauce and give cider a rosé blush. Even the blossoms get in on the pink theme!

Rhode Island Greening. Seedling variety that dates back to 1650. Among the top three most widely grown varieties in the Northeast at the end of the nineteenth century. Large, uniform, grass green, waxy fruit. Firm, crisp, juicy, tart, versatile flesh. One of the best cooking apples available. Tree form is ideal. Prolific, vigorous, good resistance to insect damage, bears every year, adapts to most soils, stores well. Does well in the South only at higher altitudes. Triploid, so requires a pollinizer. Harvest October into early November, depending on location. Best in Zones 4–8.

Roxbury Russet. Early 1600s. Possibly the oldest named variety in America. A classic russet with high sugar levels (12.8 percent). Medium to large in size; elliptical in shape. Green skin is tinged bronze and overspread with a brownish yellow russet. Apples need to hang on the tree as late as possible, at which point they take on wonderful sweet–sour balance. Lots of flavor, rich and aromatic; just juicy enough. Sharp, rich cider. Spreading tree tends to be crooked-growing when young (consider a training stake). Resistant to scab. Mid to late bloomer; tends to be a biennial bearer. Reliable cropper; stores well. Ripens in October. Zones 5–8.

Rubinette. Golden Delicious × Cox's Orange Pippin, 1966. An outstanding Cox-style apple from Switzerland, with perhaps the most perfect balance of sweet and sharp of any modern apple. Orange with dull red streaks over a light green background. Medium-sized fruit, but only if aggressively thinned. Prone to fire blight, but said to resist scab and mildew. Slow-growing tree does better on vigorous rootstock. Favorite of organic growers in Europe. Ripens in mid- to late September. Zones 4–10.

Sandow. Open-pollinated seedling of Northern Spy, 1912. Bright scarlet stripes over red flush. Sweet, juicy, crisp flesh; definite flavor of raspberries. Quality very high. Midrange keeping quality. Lanky tree requires occasional heading back. Hardier, definitely bears sooner, and less troubled by scab than its parent. Ripens mid-October. Best in Zones 3–5.

Spartan. McIntosh × Newtown Pippin, 1936, developed at the British Columbia Station. Beautiful, medium-sized, so dark a red as to be almost a mahogany dessert apple. Pure white flesh, crisp, sweet with some acidity. Firmer than McIntosh. Highly aromatic with a distinctive wine-like flavor. Precocious and consistently heavy bearer. Tolerant of scab, mildew, and fire blight. Quite hardy. Ripens mid-October. Best in Zones 3–5.

Spencer. McIntosh × Golden Delicious, 1926, developed at the British Columbia Station. Medium to large, nearly solid red/carmine striped fruit. Very sweet with creamy, juicy flesh. Fun fruity flavor. Picks late and keeps fairly well until March; vigorous, upright, spreading tree. Slow to begin bearing, at which point requires moderate thinning. Hardy to –50°F (–46°C) with occasional winter injury. Ripens mid-September into early October. Zones 4–8.

Sweet Sixteen. Northern Spy × Frostbite (MN 447), released in 1978. Large, red-striped fruit. Firm, crisp, aromatic flesh. Moderately acidic. People have described its flavor as ranging from a deeply spiced apple pie and licorice candy to a shot of fine Kentucky bourbon and vanilla. Finest flavor develops only where summers are not too hot. Hardy and vigorous tree. Tolerant of scab and fire blight after the early years. Mid to late bloomer. Easily goes biennial unless thinned in a timely manner. Fruit matures over a period of three weeks starting in late September. Best in Zones 3–6.

Wealthy. Cherry Crab seedling, 1860. Yellow skin is flushed and striped carmine. Greenish white flesh with a slight pinkish stain under the skin; soft and coarse-textured. Refreshing vinous flavor with a hint of strawberry. Classic all-purpose homestead apple for incredible sauce, pies, cider, and fresh eating (when tree-ripened to all-over scarlet). Compact tree bears young and heavily. Long blooming period

makes it a good pollinizer. Begins ripening in mid-September. Best in Zones 3–5.

White Winter Pearmain. Old English apple dating back to the 1200s. Fruit is medium to large with smooth, waxy, greenish yellow skin with numerous dots. Yellowish, aromatic, tender, crisp, and fine-grained flesh. Prized across the South and Midwest for its fresh-eating qualities. Extremely vigorous tree bears regularly. Excellent pollinizer. Ripens in October. Fairly good keeper. Needs only four hundred hours of chilling. Zones 4–9.

Winesap, original strain. One of the most revered of all American varieties, originated in New Jersey around 1800. Medium-sized, round, dark red fruit with crisp, juicy, yellow flesh. Rich, vinous flavor is like an explosion in the mouth. Tart reddish juice excellent for cider. Also considered outstanding for pies. Adaptable to many soils and climates. Resistant to cedar apple rust and fire blight. Showy pink flowers require a pollinizer. Harvest in October. Keeps until early spring. Zones 4–8.

Zestar. State Fair × MN 1691, released in 1999 by the University of Minnesota. Large, crunchy, juicy, hazy red fruit with a sprightly sweet flavor. Tang of citrus. Excellent for both fresh eating and cooking. Fruit will store for six to eight weeks with refrigeration. Vigorous, upright tree with spur-type habit. Susceptible to apple scab; good resistance to fire blight. Blooms early season. Ripens mid-August to early September. Best in Zones 3–6.

Rootstock for *Malus*

The work that has been done over the years to find and propagate the perfect apple rootstock has yielded dozens of choices. Freestanding trees are better suited to fungal duff management in the long haul, but dwarf trees (which require staking—no exceptions granted) will be more manageable in tightly restricted landscape settings like urban and small backyard gardens, especially if you're using espalier training. Soil type comes into play when choosing rootstock, as does winter hardiness and resistance to crown rot and burr knotting. The roots listed here are the cream of the crop in terms of fire blight resistance in each size class.

Seedling rootstock produces a standard-sized tree . . . noting that *full vigor* from the genetics of every apple seed can never be guaranteed. Certain parent varieties give more consistent results; thus you will find a proven track record for Antonovka, Ranetka, and Beautiful Arcade seedlings, to name a few. Always a good bet for winter hardiness in far northern zones where a shorter growing season keeps tree size more controlled. Spacing ranges 25–35 feet, depending on pruning intentions. Trees grown on seedling stock will endure beyond your lifetime: Plant a few for the grandkids.

Bud.118 produces a tree 80–90 percent of standard size. Well anchored, precocious, good productivity. Moderately resistant to fire blight; no burr knot issues. Red leaves make it clear what shoot comes from the rootstock in the nursery. Winter hardiness goes without saying for this Russian immigrant. Spacing of 16–18 feet in the row.

MM.111 produces a tree 75–85 percent of standard size. Growth tends to be upright with wide crotch angles. Well anchored; stands up to drought and high soil temperatures. Excellent semi-vigorous rootstock for heavy soils. Moderately resistant to fire blight. Bears fruit in four to seven years. Resistant to woolly aphids. Disadvantage can be heavy burr knotting. Spacing of 14–16 feet in the row.

MM.106 produces a tree 70–80 percent of standard size. Good productivity; induces wide crotch angles. Moderately resistant to fire blight; no burr knot issues. Susceptible to crown rot: Use in light soils, as it is sensitive to wet feet. Resistant to woolly aphids. Spacing of 14–16 feet in the row. Unsuitable for Zones 3–4.

M.7 produces a tree 50–60 percent of standard size. One of the first monastery roots, with origins going back to the late 1600s. Moderately resistant to fire blight and crown rot. Root suckers can be heavy. Requires staking in heavy soils, as it does a poor job of anchoring in clay. Plant with graft union low to the ground to avoid cold-tenderness issues. Spacing of 12–14 feet in the row.

G.30 produces a tree 45–50 percent of standard size. The Geneva series was deliberately bred to be resistant to fire blight and crown rot. Very precocious (comes into bearing early) and productive. Staking is an absolute must because of brittle graft union issues under both leaf and crop load. Modest vigor would allow freestanding treatment otherwise. Spacing of 10–12 feet in the row.

G.935 produces a tree 35–45 percent of standard size. Its extra charge of *dwarf vigor* makes possible tighter spacing in a competitive understory. Good fire blight resistance. Forms wide crotch angles and has impressive productivity. Winter hardy. Staking recommended to direct upward formation of canopy. Cultivar-determined spacing of 8–12 feet in the row.

G.11 produces a tree 30–40 percent of standard size. Heavy production starts early. Moderately resistant to fire blight. Very few burr knots and minimal suckering. All varieties must be staked or trellised. Vigor advantage of this root allows for taprooted plants to grow in the vicinity. Well adapted to moist soils because of crown rot resistance. Do not overcrop in first years to ensure good tree structure. Spacing of 6–8 feet in the row.

Bud.9 produces a tree 25–30 percent of standard size. Grows fast and furious in warmer zones. Production begins in the third year (pinch off any blossoms in the second year). Shows positive influence on return bloom. All varieties must be staked or trellised; good choice for mulched espalier. Moderately susceptible to fire blight. Spacing of 4–7 feet in the row.

Yield potential of these various rootstocks depends on many variables. Site fertility, allotted height, renewal pruning, proper thinning, and then the variety itself all enter in here. Still, it's useful to have an idea of harvest potential based on tree size. A seedling tree can yield on the order of 20–30 bushels of apples when it's fully grown, though this will be more

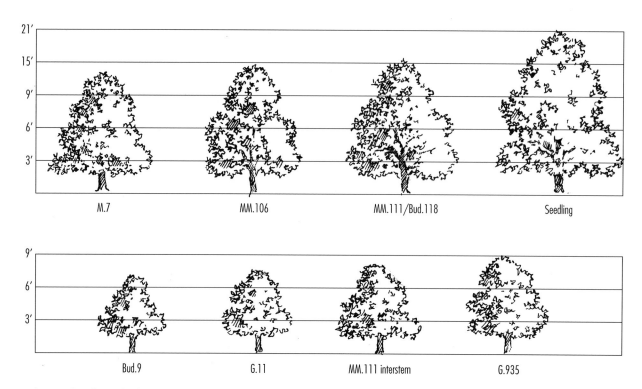

Apple rootstocks with semi-dwarf vigor and up produce freestanding trees that don't require support and additional coddling to make up for a more runted root system.

like 10–16 bushels if the tree's growth is kept more contained by pruning. A tendency to bear biennially in the variety may well mean these numbers apply only every other year. Figure a semi-standard rootstock like MM.111 will offer 5–10 bushels when it comes into its own. A semi-dwarf tree averages more like 3–6 bushels. Dwarf trees will yield 1–2 bushels, with crop load assistance from the stake or trellis absolutely required.

Pruning tips for apples

Different varieties of apples have different growth habits that somewhat correlate to where the fruit buds can be found. Cortland and Jonathan types tend to be twiggy and want lots of thinning out at the branch tips. Sweet Sixteen, Winesap, and Fuji grow more upright, requiring attentive training to prevent weak crotch angles. Vigorous heirlooms like Northern Spy branch heavily and seem to turn toward the sun even after initial training. Pink Lady grows like a house on fire. Strong, spreading trees

like Rhode Island Greening, Arlet, and Mollie's Delicious grow just as you might hope, though long branches often need to be braced under a full crop load. Varieties like Liberty and Macoun that bear heavily can stand to lose more than a few fruit buds when you're thinning out laterals. Working with similar varieties back-to-back helps you focus on particular growth habits.

Now let's zero in on the fruit buds. Outright **spur types** require less branch pruning overall. Limbs on these trees readily develop an excess of spurs, however, and that calls for thinning out older spurs after several years of production. These develop multiple fruit buds in successive seasons and eventually start producing smaller apples. Overlong, overlapping, complicated spur systems can be cut back to the two or three largest buds or completely removed if new upstarts are nearby on the limb. You'll be able to judge how many spurs are right to keep for a given variety once you hand-thin an overabundant fruit set.

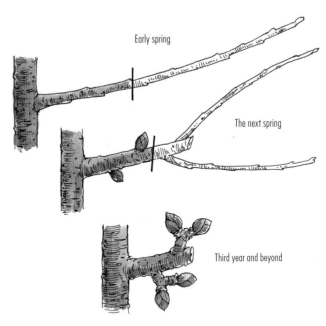

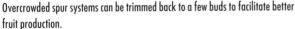

Overcrowded spur systems can be trimmed back to a few buds to facilitate better fruit production.

Fruiting spurs can be induced on a lateral shoot by a series of timed pruning cuts.

On the other hand, **tip bearers** should be pruned lightly with respect to lateral thinning. Fruit buds on the ends of shoots aren't quite as obvious earlier in the dormant season as those on spurs. Any maiden (one-year-old) shoots less than 9 inches in length should be left untouched, because they will likely have fruit buds at their tips the coming season. Longer shoots are pruned back to two or three buds to stimulate the production of short tip-bearing shoots for the following year. You can convert watersprouts in this way (that you otherwise might fully remove) should a relatively bare branch be in need of increased fruiting potential. Observing how a certain variety responds from year to year to such cuts can be essential for getting a full crop on what otherwise might seem to be a light-bearing tree.

Many apples, in truth, are a combination of these two types. The basics of crafting a central leader apple tree—branch structure, light space, and leaving a percentage of the smaller shoots—should deliver good results without the need to get highly involved in fruit bud shenanigans. Inducing spurs on unproductive shoots can be done by cutting back the shoot to three or four buds in the first dormant season, then removing the more vigorous response to that cut in the following dormant season, just beyond where fruit buds formed at the base.

Trees on dwarf rootstock can be pruned within the heart of the growing season, when the danger of invigorating excess vegetative growth is less (such being the genetically weakened nature of the root) even after bloom. Ninety percent of the pruning and training on dwarf trees can take place between petal fall and early August, with only 10 percent corrective surgery left for the dormant season. The basal snip technique (see "Zeroing in on espalier" in chapter 3, on page 89) is fundamental to redirecting vegetative growth on smaller apple trees not being confined to a single plane as well.

Apple pollination

Most varieties require cross-pollination for optimum fruit set. This occurs when one variety crosses with a second variety, not a second tree of the same variety. If you have three or more varieties of apples, pollination will probably not be a problem. That said, certain related apples will not pollinate each other well, and triploid apples definitely have sterile pollen. Nurseries can a big help here in pointing out such considerations. Selecting a good pollinizer as one of your favored varieties helps, for these varieties have both an extended bloom time and attractive pollen (to the bees) to offer other apple flowers. Edible crab apples like Chestnut, Trailman, and Dolgo are especially good in this respect. Bloom overlap becomes of greater concern the farther south you grow. Selecting one early-blooming variety, one late-blooming variety, and a triploid would most likely get you nowhere pollination-wise. Early bloom usually overlaps with midseason bloom, which usually overlaps with late bloom . . . so a tad of awareness here should keep you on course for a good apple harvest.

Insect pests of apples

Knowing *who done it* and the timing involved defines the challenges on your particular orchard ground. Any of the recommended field guides will provide species specifics and photo identification to go with established *point-of-vulnerability* insights:

- Internal-feeding moths often seem to work as tag-team partners in the destruction of the apple crop. Growers in different regions experience either codling moth paired with **Oriental fruit moth** or codling moth paired with **lesser appleworm** or, in a warmer zone, extra generations of **codling moth** to make up the difference. Limiting the first generation of all three sets up smooth sailing in the summer months. Knowing that the first round of egg hatch keys to fruitlets being available not too long after bloom is the ace up our sleeve.

- Surface-feeding moths come in many incarnations. **Red-banded leafroller** and **green pug** afflict northeastern America, while **orange tortrix** and **fruit tree leafroller** feature more prominently on the West Coast. **Tufted apple bud moth** and **oblique-banded leafroller** come on strong following fruit set. **Green fruitworm**, **apple pandemis**, and **tent caterpillar** work this beat as well. Supporting biodiversity and thus numerous beneficial species keeps much of this group in check.

- Growers in the Northeast down through the Mid-Atlantic and across to the Great Lakes (just you wait!) need to reckon with **European apple sawfly**. This relatively recent immigrant lays eggs at the base of blossom clusters. The larvae go on to eat the seeds in multiple fruitlets. Loss of as much as a third of the crop can occur by the time of June drop. That's when sawfly burrows into the top inches of soil at the base of the tree to pupate for next spring's return.

- Draw a line from the headwaters of the Mississippi River down through the Ozarks, step to the east, and you are in **plum curculio** territory. This humpbacked brown weevil with a curved snout can devastate apple crops. Eggs are laid at the rate of four or five per day when spring warms and sizing fruitlets are in evidence. A curved scar at harvesttime, either grown out to a russet spread or smushed inward like puckered cheeks, is a surefire sign of curc at work. But mostly fruitlets are destroyed and drop to the ground with larvae ready to move on below. Pupae will spend a couple of weeks in the soil before emerging in midsummer to head for forest leaf litter to overwinter. Up and down, back and forth, it's this migratory habit that offers orchardists certain opportunities for control.

- Borers weaken if not outright kill trees. **Roundheaded appletree borer** is the absolute

Now, here's an apple no one is going to want to eat! This codling moth larva is on his way out to seek a place to pupate. Photo courtesy of Elizabeth Beers, Washington State University.

worst offender, but it is localized, so not every grower in eastern North America has to deal with this nefarious beetle. Grub frass extruding from bark tissues at the soil line is a dead giveaway. Growers out west find **flatheaded appletree borers** drawn to trees that are afflicted by sunscald or other structural injury. The **dogwood borer** is a small moth especially drawn to burr knots on exposed rootstock.

- **Apple maggot fly**, also known as the notorious railroad worm, makes a maggoty mess of the flesh of the apple. Adults emerge in early summer just as early-ripening varieties give off ripening volatile odors. This emergence

continues off and on for about two months—very dependent on moist soil conditions—and thus midseason varieties become the target by late July. Female apple maggot flies seek out the very best apples in which to insert the egg. Successful larvae move from the destroyed fruit (which eventually drops) to the soil to pupate in three to nine days.

Organic solutions

The whole of the moth complex is interrupted by regular applications of pure neem oil. Persistent codling moth numbers can be brought down with cardboard banding in combination with granulosis virus. All budworms succumb when you include Bt in the holistic spring sprays at pink and petal fall. Pheromone traps and/or vinegar jug traps may be enough to nudge you over an acceptable threshold. Mating disruption is a prime option in larger orchards.

White sticky cards hung out at pink—one to four per tree, depending on diameter of canopy—will catch a significant portion of apple sawfly. Watch for signs of winding scar damage on pea-sized fruitlets—if it's unbearable, apply spinosad. Release parasitic nematodes beneath heavily afflicted trees in late June or early July to feed on vulnerable larvae in the soil.

Keep curculio at bay with full-rate refined kaolin clay coverage in the immediate weeks after petal fall. Keep in mind trap tree dynamics to shorten the coverage period. The old-fashioned option involves shaking the tree early each morning to cause adult weevils to fall onto ground tarps . . . keep this up until catches diminish.

Borer strategies call for intensity. Clay-based trunk slurries (with a tenth portion of plaster of paris added for steadfastness) need to be heavily dribbled around the base of each apple tree and brushed up over burr knots in early summer to repel egg-laying females. Heavy dousing of neem oil into bark tissues (up to the height of the first scaffold branches) and drenching the soil right at the base of the tree contributes a similar bad vibe. *Spade-bit diligence* in digging out the larvae needs to be done in late summer, backed with a spring checkup. Avoiding limb injury of any type deters the flatheads in this crowd of nasties.

Red sticky sphere traps properly placed in the summer months catch apple maggot flies. Removing early drops twice a week going into harvest catches larvae in transit. A ground-directed *Beauveria bassiana* spray on a warm, rainy day not too long after harvest under trees that were badly infested cleans up larva-turning-to-pupa potential.

Disease concerns of apples

Holistic orchardists indeed have a plan to deal with disease. We'll add some twists and requisite timing notes here to our general understanding of how tree health keeps fungal and bacterial pathogens in check.

- **Apple scab.** Widespread fungal disease, leading to severe black spotting and cracked lesions on the fruit. Infection in spring hinges on last year's fallen leaves not being decomposed on the orchard floor. Wetting by rain releases the ascospores, which in turn require moist conditions for a temperature-dependent amount of time on young leaf tissue to take hold. Growers in warmer zones must be wary of conidia overwintering in bud crevices as well.

- **Cedar apple rust.** Fungal disease sharing an on-year/off-year association with eastern red cedar trees. Severe orange leaf spotting can lead to early defoliation and eliminate return bloom. Spores from the rust galls (gelatinous orange blobs found on the cedar) are released by rain in spring between pink and three weeks after bloom. Infection occurs if the leaf wetting period lasts long enough. No round of secondary infection takes place on the apple tree. Eradicating nearby red cedars helps reduce rust pressure considerably.

- **Powdery mildew.** The *ghostly fungus* colonizes developing shoots on certain apple varieties, more so in warm semi-arid regions. Overwinters as fungal strands in leaf and fruit buds that were infected the previous season (temperatures below 18°F, or −8°C, will do in the majority of these). The powdery white appearance on affected shoots consists of many thousands of spores that will cause secondary infections and reduce the vigor of the tree by late summer. A baking soda solution (add 4 teaspoons per gallon of water, along with 2 tablespoons of Stylet-Oil as a spreader) will work on contact if mildew begins to establish on new leaf growth in spring despite the holistic applications.

The goal throughout the primary infection period each spring is to prevent apple scab lesions from establishing on fruitlets and foliage alike, as this sets up a secondary infection sequence all summer long. Photo courtesy of Alan Biggs, West Virginia University.

Summer disease fungi such as flyspeck feed solely on the surface of the fruit. Photo courtesy of Bill Turechek, USDA Fruit Lab, Beltsville, MD.

- **Fire blight**. Beware the shepherd's crook! Pruning out blackened shoots (gone limp and thus looped over) and blossom clusters is important sanitation work to prevent the spread of this bacterial disease in early summer. The best preventive plan going is biological reinforcement and deep nutrition. Serenade or Blight Ban can be used during bloom to up the oomph factor on that front.
- **Summer fruit rots**. Various rot fungi are at work here. The brown, slightly sunken spots of bitter rot expand rapidly when temperatures stay over 80°F (27°C). White rot is most severe in the Southeast. Black rot has a leaf phase (called frog-eye leaf spot) and causes decay in the seed cavity and pimple-like lesions on the skin of the fruit at harvesttime. Beefing up the protective cuticle with herbal teas and competitive microbe colonization is sound advice for anyone experiencing rot problems on apples.
- **Sooty blotch and flyspeck**. Another set of surface-feeding fungi that affect the appearance of the apple, but little more. This condition becomes visible only once 250 hours of accumulated wetting (be it rain or fog) has occurred. These fungi feed on wax platelets in the cuticle layer. Expansion cracking of the cuticle as the apple grows is natural. Keeping these micro-cracks fully colonized with competitive microbes supplied with fatty acid nutrition in those immediate weeks after bloom lies at the heart of lessening sooty blotch and flyspeck discoloration. Growers of mid- and late-season yellow apples in humid regions face even greater pressure. Successive spray solutions of coconut oil (made every ten days in late July and August and even into September) might help abate serious problems with these aesthetic fungi.[5]

Harvest notes

Apples approaching ripeness go through a period of rapid cell expansion, growing daily by as much as 1 percent. The base skin color gradually changes from green to light green to yellow; the fresh inside turns

A gentle lift and the slightest twist is all it takes to pick tree-ripened apples.

from greenish to a creamier white; the seeds start to turn brown. The stem of a ripe apple will break easily and cleanly when its calyx end is tipped up toward the spur from which it hangs. Most telling, ripe fruit tastes good.

You should take an early taste or two in order to find the flavor pinnacle for any apple variety new to you. Calendar date can be surprisingly accurate with midseason and late varieties. Summer apples can run ahead from year to year, depending on the start of bloom and daytime temperatures. Fruit ripening in September and October almost always plays out more consistently . . . allowing you a sense of normal picking dates. Do keep harvest records, taking note of flavor impressions, and you will be able to peg tree ripening to a given week after a few seasons have passed on by.

Fruit are picked with the slightest lift-and-twist motion. Reach for the apple so it rests in the curve of your palm. Lift its weight slightly upward and turn your wrist so the stem pivots off the branch. If the fruit hangs on to the branch, use your thumb as a fulcrum point against a woody stem. A straightaway pull often strips off next year's budwood contained in

the fruiting spur or rips the stem out of the fruit. Such stem pulls are to be avoided because open wounds cause the fruit to spoil sooner. Skin punctures result from rough handling in the branches and from the stems of fruit colliding in the picking bucket.

Many apple varieties ripen unevenly over a two- to three-week period. Spot-picking the best-colored fruit on the outside canopy of the tree allows sunlight to enter and color the inner apples for picking several days later. Tuning your eyes to the *right shade of undercolor* will hasten the picking of the best-tasting fruit each time through. Some cultivars are worth picking three or even five times to maximize color and size, whereas with others strip-picking the entire tree at once seems right. Collecting recent drops before picking allows you to set aside the better of those for processing.[6] Field grading as you pick can save some time sorting later on—smaller apples and the less-colored fruit hanging down low are bound for the cider press (probably), so why not make the distinction from the get-go?

PEARS

Plant pears for your heirs. The right interpretation of that saying reflects the longevity of the pear tree. The Endicott pear tree has been producing fruit for well over 370 years since being planted by the first governor of Massachusetts back in 1730. The second interpretation comes from impatient fruit growers wondering when that new pear tree is finally going to bear some fruit. Let's see if the wait can be worth it.

European pears (*Pyrus communis*) are native to central and southern Europe. One variety or another now grows in most of the temperate regions across the globe. As a rule, pear trees grow faster and get larger than apple trees. Some wild pear trees are known to exceed 50 feet at maturity. Pears take longer to come into bearing than apples, usually on the order of eight to twelve years at most. Spreading limbs will help bring bearing on a year or two sooner. Pear trees can tolerate damp, heavy soils, often being located where

IDENTIFYING HEIRLOOM APPLE VARIETIES

No doubt you've wondered what kind of apple that big tree in the backyard might be. It's been there as long as anyone can remember, yet the folks who planted it have long since passed. There are ways to figure out if that apple tree is an Aunt Penelope Winslow or a Brushy Mountain Limbertwig or merely a wild seedling. So come along, Watson, and let's see what we can do about this varietal conundrum.

Every heirloom apple variety springs from seed cross-pollinated under the auspices of serendipity: A tree grew, and people liked the fruit, subsequently gave it a name (if not several), and then started sharing scionwood to propagate more such trees. Word-of-mouth of such regional favorites led to more than ten thousand named varieties by the close of the nineteenth century. Apples were selected for taste, preferred use in cider or cooking, and keeping ability. Books like Beach's *Apples of New York* (published in 1905) provide detailed descriptions of each fruit's characteristics as well as color plates for confirming varietal identity. A new compilation put together by orchardist Dan Bussey in Wisconsin correlates many such historical references—with original watercolor plates commissioned by the Department of Agriculture way back when, no less—to provide stunningly thorough varietal descriptions.

Zeroing in on the heirloom varieties known to have once been grown in your area sets a plausible stage. John Bunker of Fedco Trees does a phenomenal job assisting people with this in New England. His descriptive "wanted posters" make plain which varieties John intends to rediscover. This diehard fruit explorer displays more than a hundred named apples at the Common Ground Fair every fall in Unity, Maine, where people can bring in mystery fruits to compare and then request further proclamation. Lee Calhoun and Tom Brown do similar things in Appalachia, often seeking out the tree in question to gather scionwood to propagate rare finds like Southern Crow Egg anew.

The first clue about any apple's history lies with the tree itself. Large trees set at a seemingly consistent spacing (on the order of 25–35 feet apart) indicate grafted origins. Seedlings that have sprouted beyond the dripline are likely windfall progeny of the mother tree—fruit from such trees should be tasted with that genetic potential in mind, yet understand that any seedling has yet to be given a name. Other clues help fruit detectives discern if a tree has been grafted and is therefore a once-noted variety. Trees near an old farmhouse or stone wall have good potential of being an heirloom if you see a single trunk. An unmanaged tree tends to have multiple trunks, often due to animal browsing in its heyday. Sometimes a graft will still be visible as a swelling on the trunk many decades later. A plausible branch structure hidden within a jungle of massive watersprouts speaks to a tree having once been pruned. An overly tall apple tree with no evidence of lower limbs having been broken off is absolutely a wild seedling that spent its entire life reaching for the sun in the woods.

other fruit species wouldn't necessarily survive. Being less attractive to pests—*you* try taking a bite out of a dense green pear—means that this fruit actually requires few control measures. This perfect dessert fruit ("paired" undoubtedly with a good cheese) tastes nearly as good preserved in the canning jar. And for

The Orcas pear is a great dooryard variety for maritime regions. Photo courtesy of Raintree Nursery.

those who know perry (the pear equivalent of hard cider) . . . ahh, yes, a toast to the noble pear!

All this would seem to make pears relatively easy and desirable to grow. However, a few caveats are in order. Pear blossoms are quite unattractive to bees, so pollination isn't always good. Its early bloom dances with early frost many a year. The fruit itself is trickier to pick and then subsequently ripen properly. Lastly, fire blight can wreck the best-laid plans in a quick, devastating manner.

Obviously a number of things need to be understood to successfully grow pears. But to hold that soft juicy pear in your hands, to be able to say *I grew this*, that's what makes the teachings ahead so valuable.

Pear varieties to consider

Why bother growing grocery types like Anjou, Bosc, and Bartlett—many of which are fire-blight-susceptible—when you can explore a diversity of flavors and sensational textures better suited to your bioregion?

Northern growers have a comparatively limited range of hardy choices. Few of these will keep much more than a month or two. First pears will be edible beginning in late August, and the last ones will have to be eaten or processed by the end of October; otherwise they will be lost. Canning and drying are necessary to preserve pear goodness for the winter months. All of which leaves a fairly short season and, hence, a warning not to plant too many trees for home use. On the other hand, a number of doable pear varieties (ones that will crop annually farther south) tend toward being biennial in the North. Seckel and Summercrisp will bear almost every year in Zone 4, whereas Magness and Tyson will likely be every other year. All are exceptional cultivars and worth what it

Very rich, sugary, and aromatic flesh makes Magness among the very best when fully ripened. Photo courtesy of Adams County Nursery.

The Potomac pear has a moderately fine and buttery texture, very similar to Anjou . . . only this new variety shows superior fire blight resistance! Photo courtesy of Edible Landscaping.

takes. Crafting a multivariety tree is a good way to hedge your bets if space is tight.

Orchardists in the South need to reckon with hot, humid weather during bloom. Fire blight prospects increase dramatically where bloom temperatures incline toward warm. Looking for a strong degree of innate resistance to this bacterial disease is advised in selecting varieties.[7] Multiple strains of fire blight make this more complicated than it might seem. A nursery catalog that speaks glowingly of seeming immunity in one location won't necessarily correspond to the experience of a grower across the country, even one in the same zone. Pruning out some blight isn't going to be the end of the tree, of course, but rarely having to deal with this scourge is even better.

Growers in maritime regions need pear varieties that develop good quality in the salt air. Blossom timing becomes the most pertinent in the Midwest and across the Mid-Atlantic due to the increased odds of freeze damage in middle growing zones. Likelihood of hail will be a fire blight vector everywhere. Dry inland areas along the West Coast are the commercial heart of North American pear production for good reason: Here blight-prone varieties can seemingly be grown with abandon.

The pear must be approached, as its feminine nature indicates, with discretion and reverence; it withholds its secrets from the merely hungry.
—Edward Bunyard, *Anatomy of Dessert* (1933)

Atlantic Queen. Maritime pear brought to America several decades ago from France. Fruit is firm, of immense size, weighing up to 1½ pounds. Yellow-green skin is refined. Very juicy, sweet, melting flesh, with a most delicious aroma all its own. A robust cheese pear for the after-dinner plate. Tree thrives under the most adverse conditions, including proximity of salt water and intense summer heat. Seemingly immune to fire blight unless grafted on quince. Prolific bearer. Ripens in September. Zones 5–8.

Ayers. Garber × Anjou, introduced by the Tennessee Ag Experiment Station in 1954. Small to medium golden russet fruit with a rose tint. Juicy, sweet, sub-acid. Excellent fresh-eating quality. Vigorous, columnar-shaped tree. Resistant to fire blight. Partially self-pollinating. Modest chill requirements. Matures in early August. Best in Zones 6–8.

Blake's Pride. Recent USDA-ARS release from West Virginia. Light golden color, glossy finish, with a smooth russet covering about a quarter of the fruit surface. Moderate in size, averaging almost 3 inches in diameter, with a short, upright stem. Aromatic, rich flavor; juicy flesh. Moderate-vigor tree with upright-spreading habit. Moderate to high yields, with the first crop three or four years after planting. Produces viable pollen and will pollinize most other European pear varieties except for Seckel. Stores four months without core breakdown. Eight hundred chill hours. Matures in September. Zones 4–8.

Burford. Selection from renowned fruit expert Tom Burford's great-grandfather's orchard in Virginia dating back to the late 1800s. Round pear with outstanding flavor. Texture is similar to an Asian pear but without any grittiness. Natural semi-dwarf tree with branches that are extraordinarily limber under crop load. Resistant to fire blight and pear psylla. Ripening time for harvest is forgiving, as even windfalls are usable for dessert, canning, and pickling. (Tom recommends pear-pineapple jam especially.) Pick through September. Best in Zones 6–8.

Comice. Outstanding winter pear dating back to 1849. Classic pear shape with narrow neck. Greenish yellow fruit has soft, buttery texture. Premium sweet dessert pear. Large, vigorous tree comes into production slowly. Fruit forms without seeds when temperatures between 70 and 85°F (21 and 29°C) occur during bloom. Needs a month of refrigerated storage to flavor to perfection. Four to six hundred chill hours. Does best on the West Coast. Zones 6–8.

Duchesse d'Angouleme. First propagated in France in 1808 and then named in honor of the lady who savored its fruit. Fruit large, even exceedingly large. Greenish yellow skin, changing to pale dull yellow, covered with freckles of pale brown russet. Buttery, melting flesh, with a rich flavor when well ripened. Resistant to fire blight. The secret to success lies in sandy loam, plenty of compost, and growing this tree against a south- or west-facing wall for heat. Perfect for espalier on dwarfing rootstock. Zones 5–8; Zone 9 with elevation.

Flemish Beauty. Originally known as Fondante des Bois (melting pear from the woods) in Belgium around 1830. Large, roundish pear, uniform in size and shape. Clear yellow skin with a red sunblush. Sweet and aromatic with a slight musky flavor. Hardy, strong-growing tree bears abundantly. Good pollinizer. Somewhat susceptible to blight, so suggested mainly for northern zones. Pear scab will be an issue farther south as well. Matures mid-September. Best in Zones 4–5.

Harvest Queen. Introduced by the Agriculture Canada Research Station in Harrow, Ontario, in 1981. Flavor and musky perfume of a tree-ripened Bartlett, but this variety has slightly smaller fruit and is hardier and far more resistant to fire blight. Like pure sugar with pear essence. Excellent for fresh eating, canning, and preserves. Fruit size improved by thinning. Fruit keeps on the tree very well. (Harrow Sweet and Harrow Delight are similar cultivars from this breeding program.) Ripens in September. Zones 5–8.

Kieffer. Asian sand pear × Bartlett, introduced by Peter Kieffer in 1863. Yellow skin with prominent rusty lenticels. Firm, crunchy, juicy, flavorful, and gritty. Folks either love this pear or impugn it as inedible. Outstanding for canning (better than

Bartlett because it retains its firmness). Hardy, vigorous tree bears young. Tolerates fire blight well, with neglected homestead trees still producing loads of fruit years later. Self-fruitful. Widely grown in the South. Four hundred chill hours. Matures from mid-September to mid-October. Zones 5–9.

Luscious. Introduced by the South Dakota Agricultural Experiment Station in 1973. Medium-sized, bright yellow fruit with a red blush. Firm flesh, fine-textured, melting, very juicy. Flavor similar to Bartlett, only more intense. Broad-oval, vigorous, moderately productive tree. More tolerant to fire blight than most varieties. Requires a pollinizer. Brilliant red foliage in the fall. Cold-hardy. Matures mid-September. Best in Zones 3–5.

Magness. Seckel seedling × Comice, 1960. Medium, oval fruit is russet green when ripe. Very juicy flesh, almost free of grit cells. Very rich, sugary, and aromatic. Among the very best when fully ripened. Tree very spreading for a pear. Extremely fire-blight-resistant in leaves and flowers, but blight-susceptible in trunk and larger limbs (hail damage is a concern). Hard summer skin deters insects. Requires a good pollinizer nearby. Graft-compatible with quince. Relatively slow to bear. Ripens in Maryland in early September. Zones 4–7.

Maxine (aka Starking Delicious). Bartlett type discovered in Ohio in 1845. Medium to large golden yellow fruit with firm, juicy, snow-white flesh that is free from grit cells. Reminiscent of Asian pears that are sweet but not rich. Flavor peaks when ripened five to ten days at 70–75°F (21–24°C) after picking (no post-harvest chilling required). Vigorous, upright tree is relatively hardy and productive. Fire-blight-resistant. Cross-pollination recommended. Matures in early to mid-September. Zones 5–8.

Nova. Discovered by Bill MacKentley of St. Lawrence Nursery in upstate New York and named after his daughter. Large, round, good-quality fruit. Juicy flesh is buttery and grit-free. Can be used green or ripe. Hangs well without premature drop. Moderate fire blight resistance works in the North. Self-fertile.

Hardy to −40°F (−40°C). Ripens in mid-September. Zones 3–5.

Orcas. Seedling discovered along the roadside on Orcas Island, Washington, in 1966. Medium to large fruit, elongated, with broad base. Yellow skin with green dots and red-orange blush. Juicy, mild flavor, small core. Good for fresh eating, canning, and drying. Upright, becoming a spreading tree. Resistant to pear scab. Partially self-fruitful. Great dooryard pear for maritime regions. Matures in early September. Zones 6–9.

Potomac. Moonglow × Beurré d'Anjou, released in 1993. Ripens to a glossy, light green. Flesh texture is moderately fine and buttery, very similar to the Anjou pear. Pleasingly sub-acid flavor with a mild aroma. Moderately vigorous tree shows superior fire blight resistance. Relatively slow cropper. Matures early September; keeps eight to ten weeks in refrigerated storage. Best in Zones 5–8.

Seckel (aka Sugar Pear). Chance seedling from fruit brought here by German immigrants around 1800. Small olive-green fruit with a russeted red cheek when ripe. Fine-grained, smooth, extremely sweet, very juicy flesh. Distinctive, spicy, rich flavor, mostly in the skin. Outstanding for fresh eating and so sweet it dries beautifully. Natural semi-dwarf tree is widely adaptable, reliable, hardy, and heavy-setting. Some fire blight resistance, but can jump on the scab bandwagon. Ripens during September. Zones 4–8.

Shenandoah. Bartlett type released by the USDA-ARS, Kearneysville, West Virginia, in 2002. Large fruit with excellent perfumed sweet qualities. Higher-than-average acidity gives it a snappy flavor balanced with a high level of sugars. Mellows after harvest. Very blight-resistant. Stores well (if properly chilled) for about four months. Matures mid- to late September. Zones 4–8.

Summercrisp. Discovered in Minnesota in 1933. Produces medium-sized, red-blushed fruit that is mild and sweet with a crisp texture. Dessert and canning pear. Medium-sized tree. Free from fire blight. Dependable annual bearer. Very hardy.

Harvest when still green with red blush to keep for a month in the fridge. Pick in mid-August. Best in Zones 3–5.

Tyson (aka Early Sugar Pear). Discovered in Jenkintown, Pennsylvania, about 1794. Deep yellow fruit with no blushing. Fine-grained, tender, and melting; very juicy, sweet, and aromatic. Vigorous tree, upright-spreading. Graft-compatible on quince. This description from the early 1900s stood out: "Resists better than any other the black scourge of blight." Productive once bearing begins. Best pear of its season for the home orchard. Matures in late August. Zones 4–8.

Warren. Introduced by horticulturist T. O. Warren in Mississippi in 1976. Medium to large, dewdrop-shaped fruit is faded green with an occasional red blush in full sun. Flavor-wise, it's a Magness for the Deep South. Sweet, very juicy, smooth flesh with no grit. Spreading tree. No fire blight despite extreme heat and humidity. Flowers appear to produce no pollen or nectar, so a bee-favored pollinizer (like Harrow Delight) needs to be very close. Requires six hundred chill hours. Ripens in October. Best in Zones 7–9.

Rootstock for European *Pyrus*

Pears have long been the giants of the orchard. The word *vigorous* almost seems redundant in this context, as so many European varieties literally shoot for the sky. Standard domestic pear rootstock does little to quell this nature. All things evolve in time, however, and seedling trees with taming tendencies have been identified. The Old Home and Farmington cultivars found in Illinois have advanced the search for suitable devigorating stock considerably. Interstem grafts and using pome cousins such as quince and serviceberry as roots have potential here too.

Climatic conditions affect more than just vigor. Fruit size and return bloom—and thus overall production—are influenced by the root as well. Researchers in different parts of the country report entirely contradictory results for the newer rootstock. I'll weave in a bit of such commentary . . . but you still might want to seek out neighborly opinion on this score to find the right dwarfing root for pears.

Pyrus communis (domestic seedling). Common pear rootstock produces full-sized standard trees. Very vigorous with good productivity. Well anchored; tolerant of both dry and wet soils. Bears fruit between six and twelve years, and grows to 25–30 feet tall. Can be more variable than desired due to its seedling nature and natural genetic variability. Hardy to –50°F (–46°C). Bartlett seedlings are the most widely available but do have fire blight issues. Winter Nelis seedlings are thought to offer more "refined vigor" (you gotta love nursery catalogs!) and have slightly more blight tolerance.

Pyrus calleryana (Callery pear). Probably the most widely used pear rootstock in the South because of good anchorage, general disease resistance, and ability to support both European and Asian pears. Heavy-bearing at a young age. Tolerates wet soils. The challenge is that it exhibits even more vigor than a domestic seedling. Most strains are not winter-hardy. Zones 6–9.

Pyrus ussuriensis (Siberian pear). The hardiest seedling pear. Used as a rootstock for Ure pear and other far-northern varieties. Zone 3.

OH×F 87. Produces a tree that is 85–90 percent standard size. One of the most precocious of the Old Home series. Promotes early spurring. Tolerant of blight and pear decline. Trials consistently show high production and good fruit size. Proven hardiness through Zone 5.

OH×F 40. Produces a tree of 60–80 percent standard size. Resistant to fire blight and pear decline. Precocious, well anchored. No suckers. Worth trialing everywhere.

OH×F 333. Produces a tree of 50–70 percent standard size. Resistant to fire blight and pear decline. Hardy, well-anchored tree with no suckers. Tolerates a broad range of soils. Bears fruit between three and four years, and grows to 12–16 feet tall. The general consensus, however, is that this root reduces fruit size due to excessively heavy fruit set. Zones 4–8.

OH×F 51. Produces a tree of 40–50 percent standard size on heavy soils. Moderate fire blight resistance. That said, it has a bad rap for poor productivity in the Northwest. Yet growers in Zone 9 deem it to be excellent. Getting the idea yet? *Bioregion matters*.

PyroDwarf. German introduction from an Old Home cross. Produces a tree 40–50 percent of standard size. Very precocious, with fruiting beginning in two to four years. Uniform fruit size. Promising reports come from midrange growers (Zones 5 and 6) but not very impressive in the Deep South or Pacific Northwest because of low vigor. Root suckering can be severe. A second selection given the trademark name Pyro 2-33 has been far more productive in western trials.

Quince. This series is the most fully dwarfing root-stock available for pears. Quince A produces a tree of 50 percent standard size and Quince C, 30 percent. Fruit matures as much as a week earlier than on seedling stocks. Several problems crop up here. Not all pear varieties are immediately compatible with a *Cydonia* cross (but interstems of Warren or Conference can be used); long-term compatibility issues also arise. Quince readily succumbs to fire blight. Perhaps most damning, this pome root is as susceptible to roundheaded apple borer as any apple root, whereas true pear stock holds no borer interest whatsoever. Lastly, quince rootstock lacks the hardiness required for northern regions in low-snow years.

Pruning tips for pears

Here's a fruit that deserves a new botanical name derived solely from its growth habit: *Pyrus erectus*. I made that up, but it sure sets the stage for what needs doing.

Pears are worked in much the same way as apples—trained to a central leader followed by years of annual yet moderate thinning. The degree of pruning depends on the vigor in particular orchard ground. Cutting out too much brings forth an aggressive vegetative

Limb position can be improved on vertically inclined trees over the course of a single growing season. Poly twine holds the branch in question to a more horizontal position, whether tied to a lower branch or to a tire at ground level. Come fall, a new ring of growth will have locked the limb in place.

response. That in turn ups the odds for shoot blight. Pruning is often limited to removing suckers and those branches that are out of bounds. It's usually necessary to do some thinning out of smaller branches to allow better sunlight penetration to improve size and color of the fruit as well. Annual shoot growth of 12–18 inches is a good indicator of balance. Much more than this and you're either pruning excessively or leaning too heavy on the nitrogen.

Young pear trees often appear too dense because of a more upright growth habit. Once these begin to fruit, however, the branches will spread naturally under load. Limit pruning of young trees to those cuts necessary to maintain the dominance of the central leader. Limb spreading promotes fruiting at an earlier age. Position lateral branches to achieve a crotch angle of 60 to no more than 75 degrees from the vertical if the variety indeed allows such manipulation. This can be difficult to achieve with limb spreaders alone when the branch immediately curves back skyward. A *teenage limb* (prior to fruiting) can be further secured with poly twine tied to a stake driven into the ground or an abandoned tire if necessary.[8] Certain pear branches will seemingly stretch for the horizon. Heading back longer limbs to an outward-facing bud (toward the base of last year's growth) as deemed necessary will encourage a desirable compact habit.

A continuous call for action will be ongoing up top. Pear trees will grow very tall if you allow it. Yet maintaining a status quo is easily manageable. Some growers simply cut back the current year's growth (in the dormant season) once the tree reaches the height deemed acceptable. I prefer to cycle my topwork over the course of a few seasons, letting the pear achieve a degree of apical dominance beyond this height (say, 18–20 feet on standard rootstock), only to whack that back to a weaker side shoot below this height once things start to get ridiculous.

Nor can ground-level pruning be ignored with pears. If a rootstock produces suckers (as some seem to do) and that particular rootstock is susceptible to fire blight, the disease may enter the root system through tender sucker growth and do in the entire tree. Keeping root suckers pruned to the soil line is critical.

Pear pollination

Much ado is made about the unattractiveness of pear blossoms to mainstream pollinators and varietal incompatibility. You can see this glass as either half full or half empty. Here's what you really need to know.

Pears come into bloom earlier than apples, though not as early as many of the stone fruits. The spring air in many parts of the country tends to be on the cool side at that time, resulting in down days for pollinators (specifically the honeybee). The nectar of pear flowers is about 10 percent sugar, as compared with the bloom of other fruit crops, which may be up to 60 percent sugar. Native pollinators don't have the same snooty standards as the honeybee—face it, beekeepers—and that's the integral factor here. Tiny wasps, certain flies, and solitary bees are delighted by the gifts of a pear blossom, but these little ones tend to often be less observed. This pollinating force is in place by virtue of your biodiversity stewardship throughout the year. Now for the follow-up punch. Bumblebees are just coming up to speed when pears bloom. Overwintering queens are certainly on hand, and the very first vestiges of early brood may be exploring their territory in a warm spring. Bumbles tend to pears later in the afternoon (when nectar concentrations build) and make a good team coupled with the little pollinators. Still air can actually be the most important factor of all—this so that native pollinators can freely move about up high. Pear pollen grains are relatively large, so transfer of pollen by the wind rarely occurs.

Some pear cultivars are self-infertile or poorly self-pollinating. These require that a pollinizer with abundant pollen be within 12–24 feet. Attractive cultivars (to a bee) in the home orchard mix such as Blake's Pride, Flemish Beauty, Maxine, and any of the Harrow series assure that viable pollen delivery can be made to such trees.[9] Other pears like Seckel and Kieffer are self-fertile, though having another pollinizer on hand will help set even more fruit. Pollination charts on the web and in certain nursery catalogs can help with all of this. Most recommended pear cultivars flower in the same time frame, making for satisfactory bloom overlap for effective cross-pollination. It's not so much about early bloom versus late bloom with pears as it is about using proven cultivar combinations (Bartlett being more finicky than most in this respect). Selecting a few different sorts of pears with just the slightest attention paid to this issue should ensure success.

An unattractive tree to bees may simply be in need of a little bit of help. Using a *honeybee attractant* like

Nectar levels in pear bloom build by late afternoon to attract those persnickety pollinators that always seem to have something better to do earlier in the day.

Bee-Scent (a sprayable combination of orientation pheromones and sweeteners) might shift pollination dynamics in your favor.[10] Young bees, seeking a food source for the first time, rely heavily on odors to which they have been introduced in the hive by the experienced foragers that recruit them. Such bees are as likely to be taken in by nectar essence as by pheromone scent signals. Even more pertinent, I think, is how native pollinators are drawn in droves to disaffected fruits of all types immediately after application. A bee attractant should be applied at early bloom (5–30 percent open flowers) on a problematic tree to help improve foraging patterns of all sorts of species.

Varieties like Magness and Warren are notorious for having blossoms with very little drawing power and thus inconsistent fruit set. Here's a way to bypass the bee scene entirely if you feel so compelled.[11] Gather extra bloom at the height of its glory from other pear varieties, perhaps at your place, perhaps from somewhere else. Mash up those flowers into a sprayable slurry in a blender. Spray this sweet nectar (so to speak) onto the variety in question when it's in full bloom, spreading viable pollen in the process. Check off *mission accomplished*. Pretty cool, eh?

One other thing to note as pear trees slide into the bearing years: First flowers do not necessarily mean first fruit. A tree too young to hold fruit simply aborts those first efforts, pollinated or not. Don't think for a minute that you did something wrong or that fate is out to get you. Your tree knows better. Give it another year or two and the pears will be yours.

Insect pests of pears
Knowing *who done it* and the timing involved defines the challenges on your particular orchard ground. Any of the recommended field guides will provide

The larvae of pear sawfly take off the top layer of chlorophyll, leaving just the veins of the leaf behind. Pure neem oil in the holistic sprays has ongoing impact on these fleshy slugs. Photo courtesy of Elizabeth Beers, Washington State University.

species specifics and photo identification to go with established *point-of-vulnerability* insights:

- Pears have many of the same pest and disease problems that apples have, but usually to a considerably lesser degree. **Apple culprits** include codling moth most of all, followed by curculio and even maggot fly. Leafrollers don't seem to zone in on pears given a choice of apples in the vicinity. The foliar pest scene is slightly more involved, as new variations on old themes crop up specific to pears alone.

- Pear growers are familiar with sooty molds because they commonly grow on the honey-dew secreted by **pear psylla**. Fruit and leaves alike can quickly become blackened on psylla-infested trees. Photosynthesis may be seriously

reduced if this goes unchecked. Adult psylla hibernate on the trunks, in crevices, and under bark. These small insects start flying and (presumably) laying eggs when several nice warm days in a row occur early in the growing season.

- New growth curling upward on the edges of the leaves and developing red blisters that eventually blacken? The culprits behind this are **pear blister mites**. The adults are very small and cannot be seen without a hand lens. This mite causes two other distinct types of damage: During winter, the feeding of the mites under the bud scales is believed to cause the bud to dry out and fail to develop. Fruit damage results when mites come out of infected leaves to feed on the developing pears, from the green-tip stage through bloom, causing sunken russet spots.

- **Pear slugs** skeletonize the leaves of pear, cherry, and plum, leaving only a framework of veins. These slimy, nondescript olive-green to orangish blobs are actually the larvae of the pear sawfly. The first feeding period lasts two to three weeks following the full leaf stage before the slugs drop to the ground to pupate in the soil. Generational comeback allows a second round in late summer. Greater damage occurs in wetter seasons when the slugs are less likely to dissipate from lack of moisture.

- Given a spike in populations and/or loss of preferred habitat, **stink bugs**, **lygus bugs**, and other **true bugs** (insects in the order Hemiptera) will sporadically feed on pear fruits in the late-spring and summer months. Early feeding damage may result in a pucker or dimple in the fruit. Mid- and late-season feeding results in the development of so-called stone cells immediately beneath the feeding site, usually toward the stem end of the fruit. Adult bugs often migrate to fruit trees in midsummer from surrounding edges in search of moisture when uncultivated vegetation starts to go dry.

Organic solutions

Basic pome strategies for controlling curculio and codling moth apply equally to pears. The first year I sprayed the refined kaolin clay for barrier protection on all my apples and plums, curculio indeed made its way to the otherwise less desirable pears. That was a lesson learned, and now all but the trap trees in my orchard get clay coverage. Second-generation codling moth (coming from the other fruits) will succeed better with maturing and thus softening pear fruit. Orchardwide efforts to protect against first-generation moths will checkmate the second rounders.

Did you take note of where pear psylla overwinter? Spring emergence from bark crevices spotlights the course of action. A dormant oil application can be useful against pear psylla at the swollen bud stage by smothering adults and nymphs that are contacted directly. Pure neem oil in the holistic spring sprays will alter nymph maturation as well as providing a repellent effect on adult females looking to deposit their eggs. Refined kaolin clay gives great psylla control all season long (always spray pear trunks when applying Surround), with residues from the previous season being sufficient to kick off the new season. One good natural ally here is the misunderstood earwig, which actually preys on psylla rather than eating pristine fruit as too many wrongly believe.[12]

Similar strategies are relied upon for pear blister mites. Dormant oil or pure neem oil (the preferred biological choice) needs to be put on at bud swell before the mites can enter the leaves. Once they're within the sanctuary of foliage tissues—those leaf blisters being *home sweet home* to these guys—quick-acting insecticidal soap is said to do some good, but do be aware of phytotoxicity issues with repeated applications. Relying on green lacewings, predatory mites, and various species of ladybird beetles, as well as minute pirate bugs and predatory thrips, will usually be the surest summertime ticket of all.

A number of parasites and predators go after pear slugs as well. Neem ramifications here include deterring oviposition by the female sawfly immediately after bloom, interfering with larval development as the eggs are exposed for seven to eleven days before hatching, and inducing "slug lockjaw" by means of being an effective feeding deterrent. A spray of rosemary-oil-based Ecotrol directly on feeding larvae will knock back situations that seem especially out of hand. A desiccant such as diatomaceous earth can be sprinkled on young trees when damage is first observed.

Stink bugs are easy to see on trees because of their large size. They see you too, however, and will quickly move to the opposite side of the fruit when disturbed. Being underhanded—by placing a cupped hand beneath the fruit as you reach for the bug from above with the other hand—improves the odds of capturing such felons. Crab spiders are especially adept at capturing all bugs. But really? Just cut around any spot-specific damage on a European pear and be done with it.

Disease concerns of pears

Holistic orchardists indeed have a plan to deal with disease. We'll add some twists and requisite timing notes here to our general understanding of how tree health keeps fungal and bacterial pathogens in check.

Pear scab overwinters as spore inoculum on the orchard floor and as conidia in twig lesions on the tree. That dual-carryover mechanism makes this disease all the more challenging to keep in check on susceptible varieties. Photo courtesy of Alan Jones, Michigan State University.

- *Fabraea* **leaf spot**. This fungal disease gets its dibs on both pears and quince. Susceptible cultivars, which include nearly every European pear, can be defoliated, resulting in reduced buds and smallish fruit. Infections first appear as small, purplish dots and gradually enlarge to form circular, dark lesions up to ¼ inch in diameter. The fallen leaf cycle and cankers on shoots carry *Fabraea* forward to the next season. The minimum wetting period for infection runs twelve hours at 50°F (10°C). This can continue into the summer months, especially in the eastern half of the country. Holistic summer sprays just might be a must-do for some pear growers. Refined kaolin clay is registered and labeled for suppression of *Fabraea* leaf spot as well.

- **Fire blight**. Let's take the high road in adding to what's already been discussed about this bacterial disease. Pear adversity to blight begins with choosing varieties that have a fighting chance toward achieving that promised longevity. Many great selections are available, so that's doable. Cultural practices that favor moderate growth of pear trees are recommended as well. These include using only half as much compost as for apples, never using fresh manure, and avoiding heavy populations of clovers (which supply extra nitrogen) around the base of the tree. Limited pruning will lessen any succulent shoot response. Irrigating "just enough" does the same. Avoiding rampant growth in turn prevents *enhanced susceptibility* on the part of even genetically friendly cultivars. Do all this properly and you will probably find that you actually prune out more fire blight strikes in apple than you will in pear. Nor will fire blight necessarily rear its ugly head again and again as a permanent presence in your orchard once strikes occur. Aggressive disease surgery coupled with biological reinforcement wins this battle eventually.

- **Pear decline**. This girdling disease causes bark strangulation of tissues at the graft union, which in turn causes slow or rapid decline and death of the tree. Pear decline is transmitted by pear psylla, a common insect pest of pears. Most nurseries no longer use rootstocks susceptible to decline, so this disease is rare.

- **Pear scab**. The pear variant on *Venturia* fungi overwinters in fallen leaves as well as conidia in afflicted twig lesions. The spore sacs mature slightly later than those of apple scab, provided that pear leaves overwinter. It's the conidia washing directly onto leaves and fruit that escape biological decomposition in the fungal duff. Pear scab is not serious except on certain varieties, which can differ in different parts of the country depending on the prevalent strain of this disease. Should a bad year occur that results in obvious lesions on an errant tree, be prepared to deal with pear scab more universally on other varieties the next season if conditions warrant. Prune out any afflicted shoots (if that's feasible) and add an extra holistic spray to the plan when bud swell begins.

Harvest notes

European pears are picked when *physiologically mature* and then temperature-conditioned to allow the fruit to *ripen to perfection* off the tree. Letting these pome fruits stay on the tree until things "look ripe" is a big mistake. Euro pears actually ripen from the inside out. Most tree-bound pears become a packet of gritty brown mush within a week or two of when the fruit should have been picked. The trick, of course, is knowing how to tell just when that moment occurs.

Pears are ready to harvest when the base skin color turns from dark green to a lighter green, but definitely not yellow. You'll usually be able to observe the dots in the skin (called *lenticels*) change from white to tan to brown. Use your thumb to pressure-test the flesh near the stem end every few days. When there is a slight give, the fruit should be picked. First fruit falling to the ground at this time confirms matters. Lift each

pear from its normal vertical orientation to a horizontal position, putting your index finger along the stem, and then give it the slightest of twists. Mature fruit will pop loose cleanly. If you find that pears in the shaded interior of the tree need to be wrenched off—breaking the fruiting spur in the process—you might want to wait another day or two to pick those, but not much longer. The most important thing is to get all fruit off the tree before grit cells begin forming.

Harvested pears should be promptly refrigerated. Pears store best at or near 35°F (2°C) at about 85 percent humidity. A minimum post-harvest chill period of five to seven days somehow enables the pear to ripen evenly throughout. Individual fruits can be removed as needed after this and allowed to sit for two to four days at room temperature. The pear will take on a more golden color as it fully ripens to peak flavor and that wonderful melting texture. Longer-term storage is best done either in perforated plastic bags (to keep good humidity around fruit being left in the fridge) or layered out in flat boxes for slow ripening in the cellar or some other cool place. Fully ripe pears will not keep, so keep an eye on your wares.

Now for the varietal quirks. Certain pears like Summercrisp and the recently introduced Green Jade can be picked on the green side for exceptional crisp eating. Other varieties can actually be tree-ripened for a different degree of flavor perfection. Harvest Queen, Magness, and Seckel are among those reputed to have this dual ripening nature.[13] This is really about experimentation to find out where your own preferences lie. Learning the ropes of particular pear varieties with respect to picking date and post-harvest chill nuance is ultimately the work of a lifetime.

ASIAN PEARS

More round than the traditional pear, delightfully crunchy and juicy, and having less to do with aromatics than other pomes, the Asian pear (*Pyrus pyrifolia, P. ussuriensis,* and other intercrosses) has claimed the

BAGGING FRUIT

Orchardists in Japan traditionally bag apples for aesthetic reasons—color hues are toned down with waxed paper liners, allowing a stenciled pattern to be imbued into the skin of the fruit (by blocking the sun's rays) when the bag gets removed a few weeks prior to harvest, thereby creating ceremonial apples that sell for more than a hundred dollars apiece. Here on America's shores this idea has taken a more pragmatic turn. The concept seems simple enough: Place developing fruit in a protective wrapper so insect pests are rebuffed from the get-go. Let's look at what home orchardists have learned to date so you can decide if this approach makes sense for any of your fruit trees.

Pest particulars

The question of who's out to get particular fruit determines everything as regards bagging prospects. Making this substantial effort to protect fruit individually is based on forgoing insect sprays and/or trapping particular pests with a promise of a perfect crop in return.

Curculio gets its dibs in relatively early when fruitlets move from pea-sized to marble-sized to quarter-sized, depending on how quickly the season warms. Potential damage from codling moth initiates in this same window . . . but in truth it's the subsequent generation that leads to finding a worm inside harvested fruit. Other moth species renew their assaults throughout the summer as well. Stink bugs and apple maggot flies come on strongly now too. The stage is always set by the incursions faced in your specific location. Bags will need to be secured in those first weeks following pollination (right when you properly thin the fruit crop) and kept in place up until nearly harvesttime.

Both bird and squirrel damage will be reduced considerably on bagged fruits. Just don't expect this to deter Rocky Raccoon—hands that can open an ear of corn can just as readily yank a bag off a ripe peach!

Most disease dynamics are established by the time fruit is of sufficient size to bag. The holistic spray plan directed at priming tree immunity in spring and providing biological reinforcement against blight will still be necessary. Higher moisture levels in nonfabric bags actually will make matters worse for stone fruits.

Choice of bag

Paper bags can easily be stapled snugly around the stem of a developing apple or pear. It's a decent

In Japan apples are bagged to deliberately pale the fruit through the growing season. Once unveiled in late summer, color gently fills in around an overlaid stencil, revealing a stunning artistry emblazoned within the very skin of that apple. Photo by Jane Alden Stevens.

barrier against curculio, codling moth, apple maggot, and secondary scab. No interior condensation means rots don't get a leg up. The fruit won't color up well, however, if you don't remove the bag a few weeks prior to harvest. Bleached white bags will keep the ripening schedule closer to par, whereas brown paper bags will push the harvest back a week or so.

Plastic sandwich bags must have both bottom corners clipped off to allow respired water to drain. Minimal condensation in these bags won't be harmful to pome fruits but often will split plums and peaches down the middle. Twist ties are an effective fastening method. Ziplock bags are a slightly more expensive option, with name brands (that offer deeper grooves to ensure the seal) staying in place better. The lock is never so tight that it bites into the stem, but invariably some fruits fall off when you're attaching these bags.

Cloth drawstring bags need to be appropriately sized for the fruit-to-come. A 4 × 6-inch cloth

Bagging fruitlets to protect them from insects and disease will be effective for some home orchardists. Everything keys to the timing of the pests at your site and the right choice of bag.

bag should prove roomy enough for stone fruits; go with a 5 × 7-inch bag for everyday apples and pears, opting for 6 × 8-inch bag for vigorous triploid apples. Fabric is likelier to stay on at windier sites, whereas the sail effect often will grab paper and plastic coverings on weaker fruitlets in the early stages.

Footies stretch as the fruit grows. Think nylon pantyhose cut into fruit-sized sections and you've got the concept. Drawstring organza bags can be purchased online. These polyester fabric options breathe well—which helps limit summer disease—but can be penetrated by insects later in the season when the covering stretches tight around the fruit.

Other considerations

A portion of bagged fruit inevitably falls from the trees soon after bagging. The stem may have been broken during the bagging procedure, but more often this is a normal drop response to excessive crop loading. Thinning aggressively prior to bagging should limit such loss.

Sunscald on bagged apples is rare, but you may discover fruit with a split in the skin on the southwest side of the tree. High daytime temperatures are the cause.

The medicinal attributes of all fruit result from direct sunshine and immune phytochemistry engaged by a modicum of disease pressure. Bagging limits this positive exposure to the environment!

Once you get the hang of it, you can bag one or two fruits in about a minute's time. Multiply that by a hundred fruits minimum on a mature dwarf tree. That's the time balance to consider in the overall scheme of things.

sweet spot in today's gourmet palate. These pears have been cultivated in China, Japan, and Korea for centuries. Chinese miners introduced the first Asian pears to North America in the wake of the California Gold Rush of 1849. The fruits are also known as Oriental pears, nashi, sand pears, apple pears, and salad pears. More than a thousand varieties range widely in shape, color, and taste . . . but only a handful of these are commonly grown in commercial orchards in North America.

Asian pears are more labor-intensive to grow and harvest than their European cousins, primarily because aggressive hand-thinning is a must in order to grow desirably large fruit. Certain varieties are traditionally grown inside opaque, wax-lined bags in Japan, which allows for very thin skins and a delicate flavor. Unlike European pears, Asian pears ripen on the tree. The ripe glow of this translucent fruit offers one intriguing clue to knowing when to pick. Asian pears are easily bruised and therefore require careful handling.

Asian pear varieties to consider

The range of where Asian pears can be grown comes down to hardiness and proper heat for flavor ripening.

All varieties are slightly less cold-hardy than European types, potentially suffering fruit bud damage once temperatures drop below –10°F (–23°C). The trees are generally hardy to –20 to –25°F (–29 to –32°C), making them adapted through Zone 5. Most Asian pears bloom slightly earlier than their European counterparts and may lose some blooms or buds to freezing in areas with a highly variable spring climate.

Flavor is admittedly subjective, but most growers agree: Asian pears absolutely need summer heat to become something special. Positive flavor descriptions can run the gamut from surprisingly nutty to more butterscotchy than butterscotch. Other people report that Asian pears have no taste, little sugar, and not enough acidity to count. "Crunch, yes, but too bland to bother," as one friend says. The difference lies in

Shin Li is a recent Asian pear introduction from the University of California. Photo courtesy of One Green World.

growing this fruit in places that experience a majority of hot summer days in June, July, and August.

Asian pear cultivars fall into three groupings based on skin coloration. Many of the apple-shaped fruits with bronze-colored skin verging on copper-russet originated in Japan. Round fruit with a greenish yellow smooth skin come from either Japan or Korea. Both types ripen at various times from late July into October. True Chinese cultivars are more pear-shaped (pyriform) with smooth green skin, generally ripening late in the season.

Chojuro (aka the Rum pear). One of the oldest varieties rates among the most flavorful of all. Firm, brown to orange, thick-skinned, flat-shaped fruit. Rich rum-like flavor. Not quite as juicy as many newer varieties. Highly productive tree. Apparently resistant to pear scab and *Alternaria* black spot. Ripens in mid-August. Fruit is subject to severe bruising and skin discoloration if picked late.

Daisui Li and **Shin Li**. Recent hybrid introductions from the University of California breeding program. Very large fruit, light green in color. Trees are extremely vigorous and will pollinize Chojuro. Limited pruning is essential in the second and third seasons to slow growth and encourage spur production. Both ripen in late September and early October. Will store for six months at 32°F (0°C) while maintaining both flavor and firmness.

Hosui transcends *merely sweet* to win taste tests across the country. Photo courtesy of Trees of Antiquity.

Hosui. Hard to miss with this russet. Very large, copiously juicy fruit with papery golden skin. Taste-test winner by a significant majority in California and Alabama. Sugar content usually 12 Brix or higher, but less sweet/more tart in the North. Extremely vigorous on *P. betulifolia* rootstock, with a wild, loose growth habit. Good resistance to pear scab. Ripens in early August. Stores for six to eight weeks.

Nijisseiki (aka 20th Century). Originated in Japan about 1900. Very popular with those preferring less sweet fruit. Medium-sized, round, yellow-skinned fruit. Branches grow straight up, but once full of fruit will bow outward somewhat reasonably. Can be a thinning nightmare. Old trees need spur removal and rejuvenation pruning to maintain fruit size. Susceptible to black spot. Fruit ripens in mid- to late August. Stores up to six months.

Olympic (aka Korean Giant, A-ri-rang). Very large, attractive orange fruit with a russet coat. Appealing texture resembles a crisp melon. Tree has a delightful branching structure. Tolerance to fire blight in some locations. One of the more cold-hardy nashi in two respects: Fruit buds survive winter cold better than most and pears hanging on the tree late in the season will withstand 26°F (−3°C) nights. Thin to 15 inches between fruits for full size. October ripening. Develops enhanced butterscotch flavor after a month in refrigerated storage.

Pai Li (aka Peking pear). Most popular pear in China, where sweetness rates far higher than tartness and sub-acidity. Medium-sized, slightly oblate fruit. Light lemon color, with many small, inconspicuous cinnamon dots. Skin is smooth, shiny, and quite thin for an heirloom variety. Flesh is firm at picking time but becomes tender and juicy like a European pear when ready to eat. Excellent keeper for the early winter months.

Shinko. Seedling of Nijisseiki, introduced in 1941. Medium-sized, round, golden-russet fruit with a radiant skin. Fruit flavor is excellent in hot climates. Well-shaped tree is extremely productive and an annual bearer. Far less susceptible to fire blight than all other Asian pears. Shinko must be properly thinned to mature its fruits. And then give it plenty of hang time to ripen to perfection throughout September and into October.

Shinseiki (aka New Century). Nijisseiki × Chojuro; introduced in 1945. Round, yellow-skinned, firm fruit. Juicy, excellent taste with a hint of tartness near the core. Dependable production and great size. Good pollinizer for other cultivars, even self-fruitful in warm zones. This Asian pear is ripening in Zone 4b for those who like to push hardiness bounds. Relatively low chilling requirement, so applicable throughout Zone 9 as well. Earliest to ripen. Stores fantastically well for three to four months.

Ya Li (aka Duck Pear). Old cultivar from northeast China. Pear-shaped with green skin. A bit mild for most tastes. Aroma is more like incense than fruity. Vigorous, spreading, dense, productive tree. Blooms very early, so needs another early bloomer such as Tsu Li to set a decent crop. Requires cross-pollination with Nijisseiki, Chojuro, or Shinseiki to yield fruits. Cold-hardy, yet has a low chilling requirement, about two to three hundred hours. Ripens late in August and early September. Stores well into February. Sparkling fall colors makes this an ornamental as well.

Yoinashi. Large, orange-brown fruit with edible skin. Crisp, richly aromatic, firm flesh. Outstanding flavor, suggestive of brown sugar and butterscotch. Tree is upright and medium in vigor. Resistant to *Pseudomonas* blossom blast and tolerant of fire blight. Begins ripening in late August with Nijisseiki but sizes much better.

Rootstock for Asian *Pyrus*

A pear's a pear when it comes to grafts merely taking hold—a number of the rootstocks suitable for Euro pears can be used here—but there are Oriental caveats. Breeder emphasis continues to be on manageable tree size while keeping production from tapering off after relatively few years. While Asian pears can be dwarfed by grafting on common domestic rootstock, that dwarfing results from genetic incompatibility. The tree lives, but fruiting peters out over time. The roots listed here have positive correlations to Asian pear productivity based on grower experience.

Harbin pear (*Pyrus ussuriensis* strain) brings long-term hardiness to northern varieties. This particular wild Manchurian seedling will not die out at twenty to thirty years of age like Asians put on common pear rootstock. Moderate fire blight resistance. Definitely the right choice for Zone 4.

OHxF 97 with standard-sized vigor is a good candidate for weaker-growing Asian varieties such as Hosui. Otherwise this relatively thrifty root proves a bit too invigorating. Fire blight resistant. Zones 5–8.

OHxF 513 produces a tree with two-thirds the vigor of a standard. Resistant to fire blight, crown rot, and woolly pear aphids. Has a reputation for supporting Asian pears without the problem of pear decline several years down the road. Zones 5–9.

Pyrus betulifolia is a hardy Asian rootstock immune to pear decline and resistant to fire blight. Exceptional vigor, so recommended for marginal land. Produces a tree 15–20 feet tall when used with Asian varieties. Reported to enhance fruit size. Can suffer damage in climates consistently below −10°F (−23°C). Piling dirt up over the graft union for the winter could be helpful. The recommended spacing for plantings on this rootstock is 12 feet between trees.

Pyrus calleryana has a slightly dwarfing effect on Asian pear varieties. Bears heavily at a young age. Strong, vigorous root system tolerates wet soils. Resists fire blight. Not especially winter-hardy, therefore to be used in Zones 6–9.

Interestingly, the Winter Banana apple enters the Asian pear rootstock picture due to its apparent cambium-friendliness with apple and pear alike. Researchers at Oregon State University grafted Asian pears to M.26 apple rootstock, using an interstem of Winter Banana between the root and the pear above. The resulting trees are fully dwarfed, productive, and showing no signs of graft incompatibility after five years of bearing.

Pruning tips for Asian pears

Here's a twist. Asian pears are generally grown as central leader trees in most areas of the world. Yet in California things always seem to be done a bit differently. An open vase hybrid style is preferred instead in order to renew young wood growth for better production. This recommendation is worth considering given the growth habit of the Asian pear.

Nursery trees are headed about 26–32 inches high at the time of planting. Select three or four main limbs from the growth response that have relatively sharp crotch angles to keep. Head these new limbs about halfway once buds have awakened the following spring, leaving 12–24 inches of growth depending on the length of the growth that occurred. This results in six to ten fairly low secondary limbs that are headed to 30–36 inches long the next spring. Pruning Asian pears after growth has commenced encourages lateral shoots to develop with a wider angle to the branch. After fruit production starts in the third season, these secondary limbs are allowed to elongate about 18 inches per year and then headed back partway every season thereafter. Some limb spreading to further open tree centers will be desirable with certain varieties. Flexing shoot growth in the direction you want to spread it (whenever you happen to walk by) will instill "limb recall" in otherwise brittle wood so that you can subsequently tie it into position a year later.

The best Asian pears are borne on spurs on two- or three-year-old wood. Older spurs give smaller fruit than those on younger wood. All pruning cuts should be smooth so no stubs are left to rub and damage large-diameter fruit. Down the road, aggressive spur thinning may be just as important as hand-thinning the actual fruit.

This more or less modified leader tree should help keep fire blight at bay by promoting tree calmness. Managing the cycle of upright growth with a *grow-fruit-remove* rotation of the outer laterals every three years or so will direct actual fruiting to stay within reach of the ground. One nice technique for training replacement limbs is to tuck new wood (a shoot farther back) within the branch slated to be removed to gain the desired fruiting angle. Peering ahead into future seasons like this makes simultaneous goals achievable.

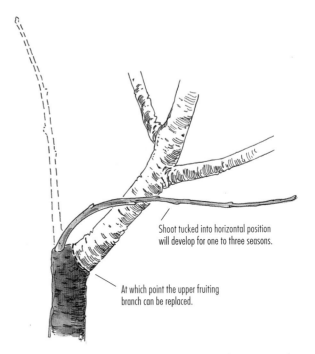

Shoot tucked into horizontal position will develop for one to three seasons.

At which point the upper fruiting branch can be replaced.

A vigorous shoot tucked beneath an older branch in spring becomes secured in that horizontal position by the next growing season. The older lateral can then be pruned away, leaving young wood in place to fill that light space and produce fruit for the next cycle of years.

Asian pear pollination

Asian pear varieties are considered partially self-fruitful, being able to produce up to a 15–25 percent crop from self-pollination at best. Planting at least two cultivars is the means to ensure cross-pollination and thus full cropping potential. Cross-pollinated fruit with a full seed cavity tend to be larger and more uniformly round than fruit with few seeds due to inadequate pollination.

The early-blooming Chinese varieties kick things off and thus run the greater risk of frost in early March through early April, depending on your location. The majority of Japanese and hybrid varieties are later-blooming and show no incompatibility with one another. Most years the last third of Chojuro bloom will overlap with the first third of Nijisseiki bloom. Thus, most Japanese cultivars overlap adequately to pollinate one another. A later-blooming Asian pear will pollinate with an early-blooming European pear (and vice versa), so that option can work in a small home orchard as well.

Aggressive hand-thinning

Asian pears require heavy thinning to obtain good fruit size, to ensure annual cropping, and to avoid limb breakage. All thinning is done by hand, even in commercial IPM orchards. Some growers *blossom-thin*, by snipping off all but two flowers per cluster. Most growers wait for fruit to set and then cut off all but one fruit per spur. (Suggestion: Leave two fruits per cluster to start if you fear significant codling moth damage early on.) This first fruit thinning is best done as soon as possible with small hand shears. A second follow-up thinning is done about ten to fourteen days later to achieve generous spacing for good fruit sizing and to fix any Asian pear doublets not properly thinned the first time. (That's when you choose the ones not damaged by codling moth.) Well-thinned Asian pears

Codling moth complicates matters by coming in generational waves throughout the growing season. Targeting the very first round of hatching larvae not long after bloom is what prevents the proverbial worm in the fruit come harvesttime. Photo courtesy of Jay Brunner, Washington State University.

will be spaced 6–8 inches apart and even more for cultivars like Olympic. Young trees will size pears well if carrying no more than 100–150 fruits per tree after thinning is finished. Crop loads of two to four hundred fruits per tree are the right amount on trees ten years down the road. Asian pears that size fully will develop better flavor and sugars, so this is indeed worthy work.

Insect pests of Asian pears

Knowing *who done it* and the timing involved defines the challenges on your particular orchard ground. Any of the recommended field guides will provide species specifics and photo identification to go with established *point-of-vulnerability* insights:

- **Codling moth** can be severe on Asian pears starting with the first generation. This may require well-timed sprays of Bt or granulosis virus for control of this serious pest if other methods appear to be falling short at your site. Let's get very specific as to how this is done. Knowing the timing of first egg hatch determines when the first application goes on the tree.[14] The larvae will be safely inside the fruit in as little as twenty-four hours, so having a tasty feed in place is paramount. A dollop of molasses in the Bt spray serves as a feeding attractant, while a shot of fish oil helps prolong the viability of this biological toxin (specific to moth larvae) to a full five days. Reapply the Bt every five days over the course of two weeks to fully coincide with the extended spread of hatching larvae.

- The usual foliar crowd for *Pyrus* species may

show up on occasion. **Pear psylla** will cause sticky fruit. Neem oil directed at bark crevices early in the season will help. **Two-spotted spider mites** can become serious on Asian pear trees at some sites, especially if the trees become water-stressed. The sugar ester spray (when this is evident) and frequent irrigation clean up a mite flare-up.

- Many types of **stink bugs** cause feeding injury to Asian pears. This can be far more serious than what is experienced on harder-fruited European varieties. Accordingly, let's look at the latest in stink bug trapping. Adult stink bugs produce aggregation pheromones. The chemical mimic available from IPM suppliers is methyl(2E,4Z)-decadienoate. Funnel trap jars are placed atop a yellow pyramid tower. You might expect two to four visitors a day to take up residence with normal stink bug influx.

Disease concerns of Asian pears

Holistic orchardists indeed have a plan to deal with disease. We'll add some twists and requisite timing notes here to our general understanding of how tree health keeps fungal and bacterial pathogens in check.

- *Alternaria* **black spot**. The *Alternaria* group of fungi produces host-specific toxins that kill infected plant issues. There's a whole lot of genetic shakedown going on here as these fungi continue to evolve and migrate. One strain has developed an affinity for Asian pear, first becoming known as Japanese pear black spot. Stories like this never end, of course, and the disease has since reared its head in isolated places in North America and Europe. Leaf symptoms are small, round black spots that can lead to severe defoliation. The fruit spots are deeply penetrating, leading to uneven fruit growth that causes the fruit to crack and drop prematurely. Primary

infection is initiated in spring by spores from overwintered shoot infections and leaf debris. Secondary spread carries on into late autumn. May the holistic force be with you.

- **Fire blight**. All Asian pear varieties except Shinko may develop fire blight. Ya Li, Chojuro, and Yoinashi are among the moderately resistant varieties. Shinseiki has been rated resistant in Kentucky but susceptible in Alabama. Olympic and Shin Li are listed as resistant in nursery catalogs, but grower experience with heavy fire blight pressure in Arkansas indicates that they are at best only tolerant. This is all about varied growing conditions and localized strains of the *Erwinia* bacteria that cause fire blight. Grow the cultivars that appeal to you with a full complement of biological reinforcement.

- **Blossom blast**. *Pseudomonas syringae* bacteria may afflict pears as a blossom cluster blight resulting in reduced fruit set. Twig dieback and bark cankers can follow from there. The presence of blossom-blast bacteria allows ice crystals to form at higher-than-normal temperatures, thereby increasing the incidence of freeze damage during cold, wet weather. Asian pears are especially affected because their early bloom makes them more susceptible to frost injury. Western growers at elevation are the most likely to encounter blossom blast, but sporadic cases in north-central states and the Northeast have occurred as well. This disease twin of fire blight differs in that bacterial ooze will not be observed coming from infected tissues.

- **Pear scab**. Russet cultivars like Olympic and Hosui fare best with this fungal disease. Add an extra holistic spray to the plan when bud swell begins if you experience increasing conidia pressure from twig lesions over the years.

Harvest notes

Asian pears ripen on the tree. When the fruit tastes good, you pick it. But here's the rest of the story . . .

A translucent skin seems to be a good indicator for many varieties. Spotting those fruit that seemingly radiate a *ripe readiness* comes quickly with experience. Going out at night with a flashlight can actually help build your confidence around this. Hold the shining light right up to the back of the pear. An Asian pear will be more opaque than not before it's actually ripe. But once sugar levels reach that varietal zenith, that same pear will literally glow with the anticipation of lip-smacking goodness. This is orchard magic at its finest.

Select picking is part of the Asian pear landscape. Fruit exposed to full sunlight on the outside of the tree will ripen days, if not weeks, before interior fruit. Picking everything at once is a good way to turn your family and extended community off to Asian pears. Get out there every few days to pick each individual pear in its moment of glory to ensure that never happens. The base color of russet-type fruit changes from green to brown when ready. Green fruit of a round nature moves toward yellow. The smooth green Chinese types and newer hybrids do not change color much at maturity.

All Asian pears must be carefully handled to minimize bruising and outright stem punctures. Ripe fruits quickly show fingerprints and other signs of rough handling at harvest. Picking directly into single-layer packing trays is wise. The earliest-picked fruit of a given variety will generally store longer; later picks often show internal browning sooner.

Heirloom varieties of Asian pears are best enjoyed peeled. Most Chinese and Japanese traditionally peel this fruit—thick pear skin having been the norm for centuries. Modern breeders consider a finer skin one of the desirable traits in developing a new Asian pear cultivar. Those are the ones to eat like an apple right off the tree.

QUINCE

We have come to the "golden apples" of the ancient world. The common quince (*Cydonia oblonga*) is one of the earliest known fruits. For more than four thousand years quince trees have grown in Asia and the Mediterranean. Mythology holds that these are the fruit that Hercules was sent to obtain from the garden of the Hesperides as part of his epic twelve labors. Paris gave his golden apple to Aphrodite for the promise of Helen . . . and thus precipitated the Trojan War. And the fruit that tempted both Adam and Eve in the Garden of Eden? Indeed, it was a quince![15]

Quinces typically aren't eaten fresh (one exception being the Aromatnaya cultivar) but make wonderful marmalades, jellies, chutneys, and preserves. A quince or two mixed into applesauce or an apple pie leads to transcendence. Many chefs complement meat dishes with quince. Simply baking them like apples will bring out quince's pleasant tart qualities beneath a drizzle of sugar and cognac. The fruits are so fragrant that a single fruit can fill a room with its rich fruity scent.

Plutarch wrote that a Greek bride would nibble a quince to perfume her kiss before entering the bridal chamber, "in order that the first greeting may not be disagreeable nor unpleasant."

Quince varieties to consider

Many farmsteads had at least one quince tree at the turn of the previous century. Perhaps, since the quince is seldom (if ever) eaten fresh, it fell out of popularity as home canning did. A hundred years later and it's comeback time for this mostly forgotten fruit.

Quinces are generally hardy to Zone 5, perhaps even Zone 4 given a microclimate advantage, but have a very low chilling requirement of 150–300 hours. Buds waking up too soon rightfully worry northern growers, but this trait extends the range of some quince cultivars to Zone 10. A quince tree flowers later in the spring than pears, as some vegetative growth must occur before the flowers appear.

Assorted quince varieties from the germplasm collection at the USDA-ARS National Clonal Germplasm Repository in Corvallis, Oregon. From the top down, Van Deman, Cooke's Jumbo, Ekmek, and Quince A, a rootstock variety used for grafting pears. Photo courtesy of Stephen Ausmus, USDA Agricultural Research Service.

Besides producing edible fruit, quince makes a splendid ornamental tree. Part of its natural beauty comes as the tree ages and develops very attractive exfoliating (peeling) bark similar to that of crepe myrtle trees. The naked tree looks not unlike a bonsai version of the mighty oak. Finding a place for such elegance in the home orchard shouldn't be too hard, despite the insect and disease dynamics that lie ahead.

Aromatnaya. Among the best of thousands of varieties from the Black Sea region of Russia and Turkey. Lemony yellow skin. Pineapple flavor with a citrus aroma. One of only two quince varieties sweet enough to eat fresh (the other being Karp's Sweet). Dense flesh is best when thinly sliced. Medium-sized fruit is picked in October and softens to a pear-like texture after harvest. Relatively disease-resistant for a quince.

Meech's Prolific. Selected and later popularized by the Reverend William Meech in his definitive book *Quince Culture* (1888). Pear-shaped fruit is a lively orange-yellow color. Bright strong taste with a pleasant piney tartness, like a mango, with caramel and pear notes. Uniformly prolific. First fruit in two years after planting. Immensely productive tree requires vigorous thinning to prevent limb breakage. Ripens in October.

Orange (aka Apple Quince). Produces a fruit about the size and shape of a large navel orange. Ripens to a brilliant yellow. Flesh very tender, yellow-orange turning red on cooking. Scents the entire house with a sweet fruity aroma. Heavy-producing tree. Good in cooler summer regions. Ripens early in October. Zones 5–10.

Smyrna. Originated in Turkey, 1887. Very large fruit with lemon-yellow skin. French chefs bake and serve slices of the Smyrna quince with quail, because the quince passes on its fragrance to the fowl. Attractive multistemmed shrub (essentially) with dark green foliage and very showy blossoms in late spring. Widely adapted. Stores longer than other varieties.

Van Deman. Large, oblong pear-shaped fruit. Bright yellow-orange when ripe, with pale yellow flesh. Spicy flavor. Early-ripening. Heavy-bearing tree grows 15–20 feet tall. Considered among the hardiest of quince cultivars. Does well in cool summers. Ripens late October to early November. It took seven hundred crosses of Orange × Portugal for legendary plant breeder Luther Burbank to develop this cultivar.

Victory (*Chaenomeles japonica*). Ornamental flowering quince with edible fruit. Scarlet-red flowers in February and March produce medium yellow fruits, which hang on the tree until late October. Makes exquisite preserves. Requires cross-pollination for fruit production. Southern growers with extreme fire blight issues will find an end-around with *Chaenomeles*-type quince. Zones 5–9.

Rootstock for *Cydonia*

Quince rootstocks are generally used for quince. Both Quince A and Quince C make a slightly dwarfed tree (though not quite to the same degree as when used for pears). Pear rootstocks—those that are compatible—make a larger tree and have no susceptibility to roundheaded appletree borers. Quince seedlings will work, of course, although the tendency to sucker will likely be more pronounced.

Quince C. Moderately vigorous. Makes a bush quince tree about 8–12 feet tall, bearing fruit within several years. Suitable for highly fertile soils but not where conditions are poor. Old stocks of Quince C may be infected with a virus, so care should be taken to obtain certified virus-free stock.

Quince A. Medium vigor. Slightly more vigorous than Quince C. Bears fruit between four and six years, making a tree of some 10–16 feet in height and spread. Suitable for multistem or central leader training.

Pruning tips for quince

Quince trees are naturally compact and broadly spreading, therefore requiring less maintenance than apples and pears. This fruit can be trained to a single trunk to make a small tree, or it can be grown as a bush with multiple stems. Quince will lend itself to espalier against a wall if you truly feel called to dominate an obedient tree to the nth degree.

Quince grows stocky. Newly planted trees should be headed severely to 24 inches high to start branching at about 18 inches from the ground. Initial framework training consists of winter pruning to cut back the leader(s) by a third to half of the season's growth to an outward bud. Do this for three to five years.

First flowers will mark the shift in this plan, as fruit will be carried on spurs and on tips of the previous summer's growth. Very little pruning is required once the desired framework has been established beyond basic thinning cuts to keep the center of the tree open. Concentrate on keeping branches that are attached with strong U-shaped joints over weaker narrow connections. Occasionally, and without any apparent cause, individual branches will die off and should be removed.

Fire blight is its own beast with respect to highly sensitive quince. Aggressive bacterial spread is likely to occur in humid regions in any fresh cut made once the growing season has begun. Lush new growth stimulated by heading off any limbs will further fuel disease prospects. Limit quince pruning to structural thinning (whole branch) cuts made in the depth of winter.

Quince pollination

Fruiting quince trees are self-fertile, for the most part, with a good set in both cool and hot climates. Pollination is via all sorts of bees drawn to the fragrant blossoms. Varietal cross-pollination never hurts with *Cydonia* species, of course, but you actually can have a single tree and get fruit. You will need two distinct *Chaenomeles* types, however, if you're growing an ornamental flowering quince like Victory.

Insect pests of quince

Knowing *who done it* and the timing involved defines the challenges on your particular orchard ground. Any of the recommended field guides will provide species specifics and photo identification to go with established *point-of-vulnerability* insights:

- Certainly **codling moth** knows a good quince when it sees one. Larvae entry points on the fruit favor the stem end and can be hard to see initially. **Quince curculio** may be of concern in the East.[16] Maggot fly should be deterred by the hairy reception of the immature fruit. Ecosystem basics apply here.

San Jose scale establishes itself in barnacle-like fashion throughout the fruit tree. Any holes drilled into the sides of their waxy shells tells you that parasitic wasps are on top of the situation. Photo courtesy of Alan Eaton, University of New Hampshire.

- Another internal moth can be as much a nuisance in some locations as the codling moth. The **Oriental fruit moth** has a definite affinity for the peach but happily moves back and forth to pome fruits like the quince. First-generation larvae bore feeding tunnels into succulent shoots, while later generations get dibs into maturing fruit at the stem end. This species overwinters on the lower portion of the trunk and leaf litter on the ground. Holistic applications in spring have relevance, as does Bt in the weeks immediately following petal fall.
- Entirely new challenges for fruit growers come on the scene when moths with slightly different timing drift in from afar. Such is the case with **winter moth** from Europe. The Canadian Maritimes experienced the first infestations on this continent in the 1930s. Now this fruit tree pest is just as likely in the Pacific Northwest and throughout coastal New England. It's the jump start of winter moth that befuddles orchardists. Hatching caterpillars gnaw out holes in buds just as growth begins. The notion of a dormant oil spray in midwinter or applications of Bt (or spinosad) just as buds start to open is unheard of, but that's exactly the timing required.[17]
- **San Jose scale** commonly infests quince. Left unchecked, a large infestation can cause branch and even shrub death. These barnacle-like insects begin to feed as the sap starts to flow. Females give live birth to tiny, bright yellow crawlers in June. The young crawlers

quickly settle in, inserting their long mouth-parts into twigs and branches to suck sap. As they grow, the crawlers secrete a waxy filament that becomes a permanent scale covering. Overlapping generations are present from June through September. Dormant oil suffocates the majority of a serious scale problem if numbers get far ahead of natural parasites.

The ultimate organic solution?

Russian lore holds that a single quince tree in the orchard possesses a pivotal influence in reducing insect pressure for other fruit trees. The friend who told me this, Lou Lego in western New York, was able to pass along only the threads of vague recollection. Pliny the Elder, who spoke at length of the medicinal virtues of the quince in Roman times, says that the fruit warded off the influence of the evil eye.

How I would love to have a conversation with an ecosystem-minded grower from the steppes of Asia, from whence this tale arises. What I do know is that Lou grows some of the most impressive organic fruit I have ever seen in the East with minimal reliance on sprays of any kind . . . and the man has a few quince scattered about the farm.

Something about that quince is going to be the one bit of folklore I pass along in this book with not a single iota of biological understanding. Some of you will counter, "Sure, that's because this tree is a magnet for codling moth and the like." The implication being that traditional people knew a good trap tree when they saw one. On the other hand, it may be that the secret of quince lies in a subtle masking odor that changes the cues by which insects find other fruit nearby. Subtleties like this have been hidden before in traditional wisdom.

Disease concerns of quince

Holistic orchardists indeed have a plan to deal with disease. We'll add some twists and requisite timing notes here to our general understanding of how tree health keeps fungal and bacterial pathogens in check.

- The beat goes on with **pome afflictions**. Look back to read about *Fabraea* leaf spot, powdery mildew, sooty blotch, and pear scab. *Cydonia oblonga* species have serious fire blight tendencies in the Southeast—making biological reinforcement with competitive microbes a must. Don't plant common quince unless you're more than willing to be proactive.
- **Quince blotch**. A relatively minor disease of apple called Brooks spot (caused by *Mycosphaerella pomi* fungi) appears on its pome cousin on occasion under a different name. Spots appear on the fruit in July and August, deeper red on the colored face of apples, darker green on lighter fruits. The spots are irregular, slightly shrunken, and more abundant near the calyx end of the fruit. The symptoms on quince are more a blotch than a definite spot. It's most severe in the eastern part of the country but also appears in the Great Lakes region. Fungal duff action aimed at leaf litter and holistic spring sprays should keep this under wraps.
- **Quince rust**. These fungi have an association with the eastern red cedar tree (as does cedar apple rust). The elongated canker in the cedar phase extends along an infected twig and develops a ridge of gelatinous spore horns. Quince leaves are most susceptible when three to nine days old and may show orange-spotted lesions. Infection on the fruit appears as dark green fruit distortions extending to the core. The brilliant orange spores are borne in very small-toothed cups on the pocked surface of the fruit. Infected quince will drop before harvest. Holistic protection is needed from pink to three weeks past petal fall.

Harvest notes

An immature quince fruit has a fuzzy covering similar to a peach. When the fuzz rubs off, the fruit ripens and turns from green to yellow. Quince should be left on the tree as long as possible to achieve the best flavor, but it must be picked before all but the lightest of frosts. The fruit stem lacks a well-defined abscission layer, so quince fruit should be cut from the tree to avoid tearing the stem out of the flesh. Handle the fruit carefully—bruises show up easily despite the apparent hardness of that golden orb in your hands.

Quince should be stored in a single layer, preferably not touching, on slanted shelves or cloth-lined trays. Kept in a cool, dry place, the fruit should store for two to three months. Peak quality comes about four weeks into this mellowing phase . . . make that marmalade then unless you're saving fresh fruit for a holiday feast. Never store quince with apples or other fruit, because those will take on a quincey flavor surprisingly quickly.

The radiant glow of stone fruit can be yours by choosing the right varieties for your place. Photo courtesy of Dave Wilson Nursery.

CHAPTER SIX

Stone Fruits

A single pit encased within distinguishes stone fruit. The botanists refer to such fruits as *drupes*. The outer fleshy part surrounds the pit (also called the stone), which is actually a hardened endocarp with a seed inside. Trees and shrubs of the *Prunus* genus include cherries, peaches, apricots, plums, and almonds. These are traditionally placed within the Rosaceae or rose family, like the pome fruits, but in a different subfamily, the Prunoideae.

The practical side of encountering a pit can further be defined by how the fleshy fruit holds to the stone. *Freestone* varieties of these fruits have a pit that is relatively free of the flesh and thus can be removed with ease. Plums with this quality dry nicely as prunes, just as freestone cherries make an encouraging pie. *Clingstone* varieties of these fruits have pits that are well attached to the flesh and, in that sense,

are more time-consuming to process. Stone fruits of this nature are preferred for fresh eating and jams, because clinging flesh tends to be more tender and juicy throughout.

CHERRIES

Dozens of species make up the cherry family. The most preferred ones are derived from either *Prunus avium*, the sweet cherry (sometimes called the wild cherry), or *P. cerasus*, the sour cherry (sometimes called the pie or tart cherry). These fruits have become synonymous with the best of the best throughout our language: Life is just a bowl of cherries, *mon chéri*, and indeed . . . make that with a cherry on top. It's the fragrant blossoms; the irresistible harvest; that exquisite red goo bubbling out from a freshly baked croissant. And

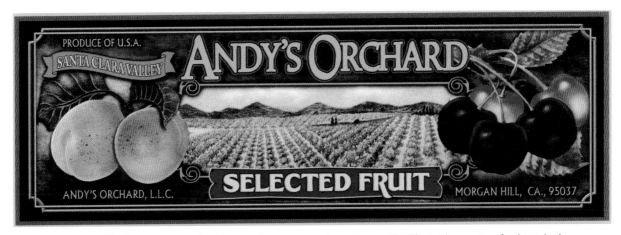

Andy Mariani is renowned for the sumptuous stone fruit he grows at his community orchard in Morgan Hill, California. Photo courtesy of Andy's Orchard.

cherries are good for us.[1] Darker cherries have higher anti-oxidant and vitamin levels than lighter ones, but sour cherries, which are generally bright red rather than a darker red-purple in color, have far higher levels than sweets.

Success with cherries requires having several things in your favor. These fruit trees thrive in soils that are well drained yet retain moisture. Heavy clay and wet pockets in the terrain foster root diseases that lead to certain demise. The risk from late frosts will be far greater for sweet cherry blossoms. A warmish growing season without an abundance of rain will sweeten those up nicely, while sour cherries prefer cooler weather. Sour types embrace real winter—requiring more chill hours and having innate hardiness down to –40°F (–40°C)—thus giving northern growers a legitimate shot at a piece of the pie. Choosing varieties adapted to your area and on advantageous rootstock is integral to a long and fruitful life. Only a few of us will be in a spot where both types of cherries thrive, to be honest.

Let's put all that in perspective. The hardiest varieties of sour cherry will crop in Zone 3, with the whole shebang especially suited for Zones 4–6. A chilling requirement of up to fifteen hundred hours to break dormancy is not a problem in the North. Sweet cherries, on the other hand, can be grown well in Zones 6–8 where their moderate chilling requirements get met—provided their earlier bloom doesn't get taken by an untimely spring frost. Siting trees on north-facing slopes with some elevation improves prospects considerably. It's the in-between zones where the challenges stack up. Sweet cherries grafted to a sensible rootstock in Zone 5 will be fine with respect to winter hardiness, with select microclimates in Zone 4 worthy of trial for the hardiest varieties. Dormant blossoms survive down to –20°F (–29°C), and that's what sets a non-negotiable limit on sweet cherry production as you head north. Sour cherries will be of respectable quality farther south given elevation and thus a cooler spring.

Fruit cracking is a big problem on nearly all varieties if rains are heavy going into harvest. Extreme heat added to any humid situation ups the prospects of fruit rots. The dry-climate advantage that guides commercial cherry production to certain regions cannot be understated! Longevity issues seem to pop up almost anywhere with significant wild cherry in the vicinity (be it pin cherry reclaiming abandoned pasture, chokecherry in nearby hedgerows, or black cherry standing tall in the woods), as unexplained tree loss often gets blamed on wild disease vectors. Orchardists need to embrace all the facts before tapping into that particular vein of thought. A *varietal best shot* given its chance in full sun on well-drained ground—with overall health boosted through deep nutrition—will likely reap satisfactory rewards regardless of wild influences. Everyone should give cherries a try.

Cherry varieties to consider

That regional prospectus certainly points the way to which type of cherry to consider growing. Yet even more factors enter in as we turn our attention to specific cultivars.

> I have a deep compassion for our town dwellers who know so little of fruit at its best. How many of them have ever tasted a ripe cherry, one of those we gather on a July day, so full of juice and tender of skin that it would burst at the very sight of a bushel basket? No, cherries at their best are for the garden owner.
> —Edward Bunyard, *Anatomy of Dessert* (1933)

Sweet cherries

Most sweet cherries are firm, dark, and luscious, the ones you gobbled as a kid from the supermarket . . . only now the flavor of homegrown will far surpass the visual expectation of store-bought. The soft-fleshed ones often come in paler shades. Sweet cherries are generally not self-fertile, so cross-pollination dynamics do come into play. Knowing it takes two to tango means you will want to select two varieties with compatible bloom times to ensure a bountiful sweet cherry harvest on the order of 100–200 pounds per tree.

The heart-shaped fruits of Black Tartarian sweet cherry vary from purplish black to deep red depending on the growing site. Photo courtesy of Dave Wilson Nursery.

Angela. Black sweet cherry from Utah. Firm, dark red flesh. Vigorous, heavily productive tree. Resistant to Western X virus. Offers good crack resistance and late blooming. Blossoms are more frost-hardy than most. Seven hundred chill hours. Zones 4–8.

BlackGold. Stella × Stark Gold, introduced by Cornell University. One of the new self-fertile varieties of sweet cherry. Dark red, firm fruit. Blooms late; will pollinize other sweet cherries. Resistant to bacterial

canker. Tree hardy to –30°F (–34°C; winter injury to flower buds from deep cold is another matter). Easy to grow, with fruit expected within four years of planting. Zones 4–8.

Black Tartarian. Large, heart-shaped fruits vary from purplish black to deep red depending on growing site. Exceptionally juicy, dark red flesh. Full-bodied flavor. Vigorous tree with waxy green foliage. Old trees exhibit canker, but vigor enables these to go on producing full crops of up to 4 bushels per tree in a single season. Early bloomer, so requires another early bloomer for pollination. Eight hundred chill hours. Best in Zones 5–7.

Early Rivers. Seedling of Early Purple Gean. Long regarded as one of the finest English cherries. Large, unevenly shaped, reddish black fruit. Soft, dark flesh. Seldom cracks in wet weather. Ripens early. The fruits ripen in succession, giving two or even three pickings. Introduced in 1872 by the famous English nurseryman Thomas Rivers of Sawbridgeworth.

Hedelfingen. Old European variety. Large black fruit with softer flesh. More resistant to cracking than most. Exceptional quality. Used for fresh eating and canning. Vigorous, healthy, early-bearing, and reliably productive. Blooms early, ripens midseason. Best in Zones 5–7; especially recommended for eastern growers.

Hudson. Oswego × Giant, originating in New York State in 1935. Medium-large black fruit. Very firm, sweet flesh. Crack-resistant. Hangs well and keeps its quality. Open, moderately productive tree. Ripens late. Considered to be one of the hardiest sweet cherry cultivars, in a class by itself. Zone 4 growers would need to count on a run of mild winters for regular fruiting.

Kristin. European Francis × Gil Peck, introduced in 1982. Glossy, 1-inch-diameter purplish black fruit. Tender skin. Firm, meaty, juicy flesh. Sweet, richly aromatic flavor. Large, vigorous, winter-hardy tree. Heavy cropping. Resists cracking and bacterial canker. Ripens mid-July. Proven winter-hardy throughout Zone 5.

Lapins. Van × Stella, a 1983 Canadian introduction now well on the way to replacing Bing as a commercial standard-bearer. Firm fruit as large as Bing, but with excellent crack resistance. Heavy producer. Trees grow only 15 feet on standard rootstock and 8 feet on dwarf stock. Self-fertile, thanks to that Stella lineage. Ripens late July into August. Best in Zones 5–8.

Merton Bigarreau. Knight's Early Black × Napoleon, introduced in 1947 by the John Innes Horticultural Institute in England. Large, round, dark red, thin-skinned fruit. Juicy, firm, light crimson flesh. Superb quality. Heavy crops.

Rainier. Van × Bing. Large yellow fruit with a considerable red blush. Firm, clear flesh. Distinct flavor, but not at all watery like some blush cherries. Vigorous, upright-spreading tree. Tendency to overbear, reducing fruit size but not quality. Resists cracking. Exceptional holding ability after harvest. Ripens midseason. Tolerates hot summers. Zones 5–9.

Royal Lee. One of the "low-chill twins" (**MiniRoyale** being the second) recommended by the Dave Wilson Nursery for Zones 8–10. Medium to large, heart-shaped, firm red fruit. Both flower at same time, two weeks before other cherries, and thus will pollinize each other. Zaiger introduction.

Sam. Developed at Summerland, British Columbia, in the early 1950s. Medium-large, firm, jet-black fruits. Vigorous, upright-spreading tree with a desirable framework. Blooms later than most sweet cherries and so may escape spring frosts. Self-unfruitful, but a good pollinizer for other varieties. Shows some resistance to canker and cracking. Ripens early. Zones 5–9.

Stella. First self-fertile sweet cherry. Large, heart-shaped, dark red fruit. Sweet, juicy flesh. Productive tree grows 25–30 feet tall. Moderate cracking susceptibility. Fine pollinizer for other varieties. Fruit buds are relatively tender. Ripens in mid-June. Zones 5–8.

Van. Introduced in 1944 in Summerland, British Columbia. Large, shiny, reddish black fruit. Exceptional flavor. Fruit clusters are slow to dry out after rains due to short stem; therefore rot can be an issue in the East. Thrives on dry summer weather with plentiful irrigation. Excellent pollinizer. Ripens from mid-June to early July depending on location. Withstands harsher climatic conditions than other sweet cherries. Zones 4–9.

WhiteGold. Emperor Francis × Stella, developed by Cornell. Yellow skin blushed with red. Firm yellow flesh. Consistently productive. Resists cracking and bacterial canker. These self-fertile trees will

WhiteGold sweet cherry has firm yellow flesh that resists cracking and bacterial canker. Photo courtesy of Edible Landscaping.

The English Morello sour cherry tolerates heat better than average. Photo courtesy of Trees of Antiquity.

pollinize other sweet cherries. Ripens midseason. Hardy down to –30°F (–34°C). Zones 5–8.

Sour (pie) cherries

Don't be fooled by the word *sour* in considering pie cherries. Tree-ripened sweetness backed with puckery attitude doesn't mean these are any less delectable for eating fresh off the tree. You might eat fewer per session, it's true, but keep in mind those latticed pies and crumbly crisps perfected by this broad flavor reach. Sour cherries have a bright tang that, when tamed with sugar, is hard to duplicate in the world of fruits. These also make the best dried cherries.

Every sour cherry tree will give a decent crop without having a pollinating partner on call. Being self-fertile holds for both distinct groupings of sour cherries. The *amarelles*, like Montmorency, have

yellow flesh and almost clear to light amber juice. This is the standard American pie cherry (which in truth originated in France) preferred by canners. The *morellos* have red flesh and dark juice, adding delightful color to all cherry desires. The latter group makes smaller trees in general, and thus they are easier to net and thereby ripen fully. One tree will provide plenty of fruit for a family, but I'd recommend at least two to ensure a respectable harvest. You can expect twenty to twenty-five years of productivity from sour cherries given proper maintenance.

Balaton. Introduced by Amy Iazonni of Michigan State University in 1984, who found it in Hungary when searching for new genetic resources. Dark-skinned cherry with a robust sweet-tart taste. Larger pits than other sour cherries. Makes a dark red juice.

Northstar sour cherry retains its quality on the tree up to two weeks after ripening. This trait in turns allows you to lift the bird netting far less often. Photo courtesy of Edible Landscaping.

Bud development begins early and therefore is more susceptible to spring cold. Slightly more vigorous than most sour cherries. Best in Zones 5–7.

Danube. A European morello hybrid from Hungary. Medium to large dark red fruits straddle the sweet–tart divide. Firmer flesh than most sour cherries. Crack- and spot-resistant. Typically grows 12–14 feet high with a 10- to 12-foot span. Ripens in early July. Zones 4–8.

English Morello. Brought to America prior to 1862. Medium-sized, dark reddish pie cherry with semi-firm flesh and deep red juice. Extremely tart. Use the fruit for cooking and preserving rather than eating fresh. Very productive. Cold-hardy. Tolerates heat better than average. Small tree with drooping branches. Five hundred chill hours needed. Zones 4–9.

Evans. Russian-heritage tree found near Edmonton, Alberta, and first promoted by Dr. Ieuan Evans in the late 1970s.[2] Bright red fruit. Precocious producer, yielding 100–150 pounds of fruit per tree. Does well in light soil; not a sure thing in clay. Evans (also know as **Bali**) trees propagated on their own roots are hardy down to –45°F (–43°C).[3] Wood hardens off better and breaks dormancy later than other sour cherries. Variable root suckering. Best in Zones 3–5. Fruits subject to severe curculio pressure farther south.

Jan, **Joel**, and **Joy**. These Korean-cross bush cherries yield Montmorency-type fruit.[4] Early-fall-bearing and so tend to be overlooked by birds. Resistant to powdery mildew, Japanese beetle, and cherry fly. Hardy to –30°F (–34°C). Mature size is 4 feet high and wide. Cross-pollination highly recommended to increase yields—plant more than one! Subject to severe blossom blast in the Pacific Northwest. Zones 4–6, with microclimate prospects in both directions.

Mesabi. Hybrid seedling from Duluth, Minnesota, 1964. Long-stemmed, red-fleshed fruits with sugar content halfway between pie cherries and Bing sweet cherry. Pyramidal tree grows to 12 feet tall. Fruit resembles Meteor, but pit is smaller. Blooms mid-May; ripens mid-July. Zones 4–8.

Meteor. Montmorency × Russian variety, introduced in 1952. Large, oblong, bright red fruit. Juicy, dense flesh. Natural genetic dwarf grows 8–10 feet tall. Large leaves help shield fruit from sunscald. Requires less pruning than average. Resistant to leaf spot. Spur type. Zones 4–8.

Montmorency. Sweet cherry × *Prunus tomentosa*, originated in France in the 1600s. The standard pie cherry in commercial production. Medium-large, bright red fruits. Firm, yellow flesh and yellow juice. Rich, tangy flavor when fully ripened to a dark mahogany skin color. Spreading tree insists on good drainage and root aeration. Seven hundred chill hours. Tree hardy to –40°F (–40°C). Zones 4–9.

Northstar. Siberian cherry × English Morello. Developed by the Minnesota AES from a seedling found in Yugoslavia, introduced in 1950. Large fruit with thin, fire-engine-red skin. Red flesh with a small freestone. Retains quality on tree up to two weeks after ripening. Resistant to both cracking and leaf spot. Natural dwarf tree grows 8–12 feet tall. Often bears in second year. Begins to ripen by mid-June. Hardy to –40°F (–40°C). Best in Zones 3–5.

The Saskatchewan Six. These Mongolian-cross bush cherries come out of breeding work done originally by Dr. Les Kerr in the 1940s, and later by the University of Saskatchewan, crossing *Prunus cerasus* with *P. fruticosa*. Fruits are large, with a flesh-to-pit ratio of 5:1. More flavor and sugar than a Bing sweet cherry, along with a touch of acid to provide some bite. **Valentine** offers light red, semi-sweet fruit, from a very dwarfing bush that ripens earlier than the others, in the middle of July. The other five cultivars—**Carmine Jewel**, **Romeo**, **Juliette**, **Rose**, and **Crimson Passion**—offer darkly colored, semi-sweet fruit, from plants reaching 6–8 feet at maturity, and ripen in August. Each bush yields up to 20–30 pounds of fruit by the fifth year. Tolerance to clay and/or alkaline soil makes these cherries quite well adapted to prairie conditions. Hardiness extends into Zone 2.

Surefire. New York State introduction. Bright red skin and flesh. High sugar content. Blooms about a week later than other sour cherries, thus it's the best bet to miss spring frosts. Crack-resistant. Semi-upright, vigorous tree. Zones 4–9.

Rootstock for cherries

The right rootstock can make a great cherry variety everything that's been promised . . . but choosing wrongly may guarantee an unhappy end. Obtaining your trees from a reputable nursery ensures that you know what's what. The degree of dwarfing will probably need to be balanced with tolerance to wet ground: Talk of productivity and early fruiting is nice, but keep in mind that a long, fruitful life will be attributable to the root's inherent resistance to viruses. Cherry trees are notorious for dying before their time otherwise. Cold hardiness enters in for anyone pushing northern bounds.

Sour cherry trees on seedling rootstock grow to a manageable 10–14 feet, but sweet ones can reach 40 feet or more. Mahaleb rootstock, the standard choice for sour cherries, requires well-drained soil but dies in heavy, wet ones. Mazzard rootstock, propagated from the seed of a wild sweet cherry species, produces a huge tree and tolerates wet ground but bites the dust if the thermometer drops much below 0°F (–18°C). Recent breeding work has unveiled an array of promising dwarfing options, but it remains up to each grower to select wisely for a given climate and soil.

Colt (*Prunus avium* × *P. pseudocerasus*) was developed in England based on this root's ability to reduce tree vigor by about 25 percent. Fruiting comes three or four years after planting. Tolerates wet soil, but needs regular irrigation if planted in dry ground. Produces wide branch angles on a well-anchored tree. Resistant to bacterial canker and root rot, but susceptible to crown gall. Gophers do not like Colt. Hardy only down to –10°F (–23°C).

The **Gisela Series** (*Prunus cerasus* × *P. canescens*) from Germany produces dwarf trees that fruit fast, within three years of planting. This precocious trait encourages early flowering, by two to four days, thereby exposing emerging fruit buds to the threat of frost. Gisela is suitable for both sweet and sour cherries. Shallow root systems do make irrigation necessary. Commercial growers who can count on a reasonable spring are quite keen on these roots . . . the popularity of such which accounts for their significantly higher cost compared with other options.

• **Gisela 5** produces a semi-dwarf tree about 45 percent the size of Mazzard. Tree induces wide branch angles, good lateral branching, and early and heavy production. Good scion compatibility with both cherry types. Not susceptible to virus problems. Does not perform well in heavy soils and needs good drainage. Tree support recommended. Imparts more winter hardiness than seedling rootstocks.

• **Gisela 6** is slightly dwarfing, sizing about 70–90 percent of Mazzard. Excellent yield precocity, with full production possible by the fifth leaf. A good choice for sandy soils that dry out easily. New commercial plantings in both Oregon and Turkey feature this root. Premium fruit quality is possible with cultivars of moderate to low productivity. New shoots keep on coming. No varietal incompatibilities. Resistant to bacterial canker.

• **Gisela 12** produces a tree 55–70 percent the size of Mazzard. Excellent disease resistance in well-drained ground. Good fruit size and quality are possible with proper pruning. Adapted to a wide range of soils. Open and

spreading tree structure with new branches forming readily.

The **Krymsk Series** from the Black Sea region of Russia shows reasonable tolerance for clay soils. These multiple-hybrid rootstocks are well adapted to cold climates but also can deal with extreme heat, because the leaves cup far less than others under temperature stress. **Krymsk 5** produces a tree 60–80 percent the size of Mazzard, while **Krymsk 6** knocks back seedling vigor just slightly more. Tree form is good, with wide crotch angles. Issues with bacterial canker and necrotic ring spot virus may affect longevity in some locations. Commercial orchardists on the dry side of the Cascades in the Northwest are planting extensively on both. Krymsk rootstocks are easy to propagate by cuttings and layering.

Mahaleb (*Prunus mahaleb*) provides a seedling root exhibiting standard vigor for sour cherries and a slightly dwarfing effect for sweet cherries. Should be used only in well-drained soils. Resistant to crown gall, bacterial canker, and some nematodes. Hardy to Zone 4. Bears fruit in three to five years and grows 20–30 feet high. Mahaleb is also popular worldwide, particularly in Spain and Italy, with its use first reported in the mid-1700s. Incompatibility and variability problems. Attractive to gophers. Sweet cherries tend to be much shorter-lived on this root.

Mazzard (*Prunus avium*) is the most popular rootstock worldwide, with a history dating back some two thousand years. This sweet cherry seedling produces a well-anchored tree that grows 25–40 feet high. Tolerates heavy soil provided drainage is adequate. Resistant to oak root fungus and root-knot nematodes. Provides excellent compatibility and good fruit quality. Lack of precocity means a bit of a wait: First cherries come in the sixth leaf, with full production arriving by the twelfth. Easily and inexpensively propagated. Hardy only down to –10°F (–23°C). A vegetatively propagated selection of Mazzard known as

F.12/1 is used in many locations instead of the seedling-propagated rootstock due to its resistance to bacterial canker. This clonal version comes with drawbacks, however, being appreciably more vigorous than the seedling itself and sensitive to crown gall. Zones 4–8.

The **M × M Series** compromises deliberate crosses made between Mahaleb and Mazzard seedling stock. Improving resistance to root rot problems was the goal here. Growers with soggy ground find M × M rootstock one of the better bets.

• **M × M 2** is more vigorous than Mazzard and more precocious. Does well in drier and sandier soils than the others in the series.

• **M × M 14** (*Prunus mahaleb × P. avium*) originated in Oregon from an open-pollinated Mahaleb tree. This semi-dwarfing rootstock controls size to about 60–80 percent of Mazzard. Good yield precocity and fruit quality, with little suckering. Resistant to iron-induced chlorosis caused by calcareous soils. Also known as Maxma 14 in the nursery trade.

• **M × M 60**. Slight dwarfing ability and well suited for sweet and sour cherries. Moderate disease resistance to root rot, even in heavy clay. Tolerance to bacterial canker. Hardiness compares to Mahaleb.

Cherry trees grown from pits (directly seeded) are not quite true to the parent variety and can take up to ten years to fruit. That said, cherries on their own roots will defeat many of the seemingly insurmountable problems spoken of above. Planting a grafted cultivar deep enough to bury the graft union—some 2–4 inches below the soil line—eventually leads to the variety sending out roots of its own. Fruiting isn't delayed, because the rootstock dominates until the scion grows those roots. Real-time benefits lie in improved hardiness (through burying a tender rootstock) and an uninterrupted connection to the soil over the long haul.

Pruning tips for cherries

Cherry trees rarely get caught up in out-of-hand vigor. Strong scaffold choices need to be made in the development years with both sweet and sour types, of course. Once fruiting begins, pruning consists mainly of thinning out modest growth each year to allow sunlight to filter into the canopy. A tendency toward stoutness in cherries makes for less whippy growth overall in the tree's upper reaches.

Sweet cherry is trained to a central leader system quite similar to that of apple. Its one *Prunus* caveat applies to yearly thinning back of the leader to a less vigorous, upright side shoot. The years ahead eventually see each scaffold branch developing a somewhat helter-skelter claim on leadership status as the trees reach 15–25 feet in height, which is fine. A modified leader system suits mature cherry trees quite well. Opening up the center eventually (by removing the original leader) is a legitimate means of keeping the upper quadrants from hedging into neighboring turf.

Scaffold junctures on sweet cherry can be prone to splitting at the point where the limb joins the main stem of the tree. Such winter injury can be abated to a degree with diluted white latex paint, but far better is assertive training from the get-go. Crotch angles kept as wide as possible will acclimate (harden off) that much more quickly in the fall. Serious limb spreading in the beginning will counter the seeming insistence of sweet cherry whips to direct most shoots in an upright direction. Cutting back young trees to 30 inches high at planting forces a more lateral response. Scaffold branches are selected from the second year on, until there are a total of five or six scaffold limbs well distributed along 3–4 feet of the main stem above the lowest branch. Prune these chosen branches with the lightest touch (if at all) until the trees start to fruit.

The cherries that set from blossoms formed at the base of the previous season's growth (nicknamed *wood cherries*) are generally the largest and sweetest of the cherries on the tree. Leaves on the current season's growth pump photosynthate sugars directly to these first-in-line fruits. Additional fruits will be found on young fruit spurs on two-year and older wood.[5] Those spurs can be productive for years provided you prune with good exposure to sunlight in mind.

Sour cherry produces a more compact tree. Select three or four permanent lateral limbs along the leader in year two, some 6 inches apart and spaced evenly around the main trunk. The very first limb selected should be 18 inches or so above the soil line. Do not head these back, as this will stunt terminal growth and delay fruiting. Sour cherry trees are often well branched when planted, so simply removing excess laterals with narrow-angled crotches achieves the goal. Develop a second scaffold layer above this over the next few years, allowing no more than 2 feet of trunk space to intervene between branch levels. The leader will pace its upward progress accordingly but can be nudged back to a weaker lateral when deemed necessary.

Floral initiation for both types of cherries takes place not long after the crop is harvested. The principal difference is that sour cherry forms new floral buds farther along the length of a first-year shoot rather than just at the very base. Trees lacking vigor tend to overflower, leaving too few leaf buds to properly support a quality crop. There are two options here. Heading such branches back no farther than third-year growth can be useful to stimulate dormant vegetative buds to shoot forth and thus regain a rightful proportion of green. Alternatively, scoring through the bark to the inner hardwood on third-year growth with a sharp knife at bloom time just above a dormant bud often stimulates that bud to grow.[6] Do either in conjunction with spreading extra compost on weak trees that very same spring.

Pruning during the dormant season in regions where winter tends to be rainy increases the risk of bacterial canker in cherry, which can kill limbs prematurely. Post-harvest pruning in late summer is recommended in such places.

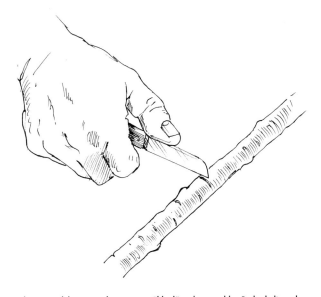

Cherrywood has a tendency to go "blind" rather quickly. Buds dedicated to flowering one season no longer are in the game, so to speak. Scoring above a dormant bud (cambium-deep is plenty) along a three-year-old limb going into bloom time can stimulate regrowth at seemingly spent node positions.

Cherry pollination

Sour cherries are on cruise control with respect to good pollination. All cultivars are self-fertile and the flowers generally open late enough in spring not to be bothered by frost. Sweet cherries, on the other hand, require more consideration.

All sweet cherry cultivars—excepting Stella, BlackGold, WhiteGold, and Lapins, which are self-fruitful—need a pollinizer. Even then certain cultivar combinations won't work out due to specific incompatibility issues. Nor will early bloomers necessarily coincide with late bloomers, especially in warmer zones where the bloom period plays out over a period of weeks. The one thing in every grower's favor on those cool spring days without an insect pollinator in sight is that cherry pollen is light enough to wind-pollinate. Tree placement matters here as much as having at least two different varieties, and preferably three for the best pollination. Nurseries and your state Extension Service have cross-pollination charts available. Placing a variety in need of pollen assistance downwind from a proven pollinizer, or even in between two self-fertile types so as to catch variable breezes, is answer enough.

Growers making a serious global warming bet in choosing sweet cherry varieties for more northern zones will need two mild winters to see fruit—one to form spurs and another to see spring flowers come to fruition. Deep cold in either dormant season (temperatures below −20°F, or −29°C) may set back that plan and cause winter injury to the fruit buds. Having no crop under those circumstances is not a pollination issue. On the other hand, winning this bet results in absolute pleasure. Be bold, my friend!

Insect pests of cherries

Knowing *who done it* and the timing involved defines the challenges on your particular orchard ground. Any of the recommended field guides will provide species specifics and photo identification to go with established *point-of-vulnerability* insights:

- **Cherry fruit flies** are the soft-fruit equivalent of apple maggot flies. All are *Rhagoletis* species, the ones with the clear wings with distinct markings, drawn by the ripening odor of the targeted fruit. These particular flies pierce the still-green cherry to insert eggs singly just below the skin. Larval feeding separates the pit from the pulp and causes the now-coloring cherry to brown. Infested fruits will not drop prematurely (unlike apples), and thus brown rot can get a foothold to make matters worse for noninfested fruit. Preventing the female fly from achieving step one marks the primary course of action.
- Since landing on the West Coast several years ago, **Japanese vinegar fly** (*Drosophila suzukii*) has set its immigrant eyes on cherries, other smooth-stone fruits, raspberries, and blueberries. These small flies are very much like the fruit flies flitting around a bowl of overripe fruit in the house. Only now the problem gets magnified as these new kids in town attack immature fruits. Eggs are laid in ripening fruit; maggots hatch out at picking time; a mess falls to the ground to start things anew. These spotted wing flies have up to thirteen generations per year, establishing them as a phenomenal threat.[7]

- **Cherry tree slugs** are in truth the very same progeny of the pear sawfly discussed earlier. Curiously, feeding on *Prunus* species results in slug larvae having a different range of coloration that's more dark green in wet weather to orangish brown in dry times. These wet-looking worms focus first up high in the cherry tree and then migrate downward. The upper surfaces of the cherry tree leaves are chewed between the leaf veins, leaving a lacy layer of tissue that begins as translucent and quickly turns light tan to brownish in appearance. An extreme case of cherry slug damage can cause the entire cherry tree to become defoliated.
- Moth-wise, **cherry fruitworm** and **winter moth** in the East and **western tussock moth** and the recently introduced **cherry bark tortrix** and **cherry ermine moth** in the Pacific Northwest enter the fray in their own species-specific ways. The options for all Lepidoptera tie to larval timing based on spring emergence.
- The thing to understand about "**cherry curculio**" concerns the oviposition preferences of the pest, more properly identified as plum curculio. These weevil-like foes have learned through evolutionary zeal which fruits favor reproductive success in different parts of the East. It's in the Great Lakes region where the strongest preference for cherry shows.[8] Cherries elsewhere might be targeted, of course, but more or less in passing rather than as a prime focus.

Organic solutions

Sticky traps hung out in mid-May can be effective for cherry fruit fly. Home orchardists can use red ball traps (à la apple maggot fly), but even better is to change both the color plan and the lure attractant. Immature flies are attracted to bright yellow, and if this scheme is coupled with the right feeding lure, it can continue to draw mature adults as well. Take a plastic soda bottle, first cutting open a substantial side opening and fashioning a wire tie around the cap end. Spray-paint the bottle yellow, then coat the outside with sticky Tangle-Trap. Pour equal parts ammonia and water about 1½ inches deep inside the soda bottle for immature flies—this imitates the smell of bird poop, which is a primary food for maggot species. A second liquid bait entirely replaces this as cherries start to size. Mature flies are drawn to a mixture of cider vinegar and sugar water—both males and females will either drown or get stuck in the process of finding the window on the side of the bottle. Keep this bait renewed weekly up until harvest. Hanging one to four pint-sized traps per tree should be quite satisfactory.

Community orchardists can utilize that spinosad formulation created specifically for these types of flies. GF-120 NF Naturalyte (see "Organic sprays for bugs" in chapter 4, on page 131) effectively draws the cherry fruit fly to the undersides of sprayed foliage to lick the sugary bait laden with biological toxin. Remember, this is spot application with a backpack sprayer; never apply directly to fruit. Renew every seven days up until harvest.

Many of these same strategies will help lessen vinegar fly numbers as well.[9] Discarding fallen fruits as soon as possible and prompt harvesting must both accompany any trapping efforts. Vinegar traps with a few drops of dish soap added to the brew (to lessen surface tension) will snare a portion of these tiny fiends. Netting entire cherry trees with tulle works—just keep in mind that so many other fruits are being targeted here too. Avoid open composting, as kitchen scraps become an egg-laying vector as well. Field trials in California indicate that a single application of Entrust is good for close to a full week of knock-down.[10] A variant strain of Bt (*Bacillus thuringiensis israelensis*) is specific for *Diptera* larvae, which include mosquitoes and fungus gnats. The vinegar fly, being

Yellow sticky cards—with ammonium bait in the goo itself—snag a hefty share of immature fruit flies. These purchased traps are hung while the preferred fruit is green and therefore before any damage gets done.

a distant cousin, may be subject to applications of Bti starting at fruit set.[11]

The neem plan remains the surest bet for cherry tree slugs. These sawfly larvae feed on the foliage for approximately one month's time, at which point the "slugs" drop to the ground and burrow into the soil. Ingesting the azadirachtin compounds in neem oil is assured by all that leaf chewing, thereby interrupting the desire to keep on keeping on.

Those ripening cherries in late May and early June are right on cue with the initial sizing of pome fruits for curculio to do its thing in the middle growing zones of the East. Severe pressure on cherries occurs when the weather warms substantially just before

The looming eye of a predator may keep birds from the cherry crop—but then again the results inherent in human logic may mean little to savvy birds. Scare-eye balloons are best hung so as to wave directly above the laden branches.

apple petal fall. This challenge is best addressed by an early touch of Surround kaolin clay on these stone fruits. These branch structure applications will indeed occur before apples and pears are protected in similar fashion.[12] Another strategy here is to use pure neem oil with garlic or a homemade *Allium sativa*, brew as a sensory repellent before curc settles on a cherry haven.

Birds eventually find most cherries. Placing a decoy crop of red beads out well before the actual fruit begins to color is one means of averting focused attention from robins. I find the scare-eye balloon distracting to waxwings and starlings, but not enough in itself to

challenge a determined claim to the crop. Coupling it with a taste repellent (liquid fish applied the same day you put up balloons) and the occasional Teddy Roosevelt charge (as the first scouts return to the scene) can encourage these marauders to find somewhere less nuts to hang out and feed. Netting the trees, of course, is the most effective measure.

Disease concerns of cherries

Holistic orchardists indeed have a plan to deal with disease. We'll add some twists and requisite timing notes here to our general understanding of how tree health keeps fungal and bacterial pathogens in check.

- **American brown rot**. We start with the fungal challenge for all stone fruits in the humid East, attacking blossoms, spurs, shoots, and fruit. It is spread from blighted twigs and mummies (the dried-up brown-rotted fruit from the year before) either hanging or fallen beneath disregarded trees. The potential for brown rot on cherries increases as the fruits mature, and all the more if stings of cherry fruit fly provide an entry point. Sweet cherry is considerably more susceptible than sour cherry. Holistic sprays between fruit set and when the fruits start to color are essential.

- **European brown rot**. The varieties most affected are Meteor, English Morello, and Balaton sour cherries. This fungus infects and kills open blossoms and then moves down into the spur. Elliptical cankers form on the limb at each infection site—these carry conidia over to the next season to renew the disease cycle. Plant trees where good drying breezes prevail in spring.

- **Black knot**. Talk about a perfect description for this affliction of sour cherry and certain plum varieties. Microscopic spores produced by the fungus on two-year-old knot tissue provide the inoculum for this disease to spread in spring. Prune out and burn these

Alternaria fruit rot can set in near to harvest on maturing cherries throughout eastern North America. Don't let down your guard when it comes to competitive colonization, especially in a wet year. Photo courtesy of Alan Jones, Michigan State University.

coarse-textured galls growing on the twigs of orchard trees and surrounding wild fruit hosts in late winter.

- **Cherry leaf spot**. This fungus infects the foliage of both sour and sweet cherries in the Mid-Atlantic and Great Lakes regions. Reddish to purple spots appear, then turn brown, resulting in yellow chlorotic leaves that abscise before harvest. Fruit bud formation for the following two seasons will be severely impacted. Young trees become less cold-hardy and often die the following winter. This disease overwinters on fallen leaves (think decomposition), with ascospore discharge occurring from early bloom to about six weeks after petal fall (think holistic coverage).

- **Bacterial canker**. Cherries are highly susceptible to this bacterial disease when conditions are wet. Remember that advice about pruning during the dry time of your year? Bacterial canker enters the plant chiefly through exposed pruning cuts. The organisms responsible (assorted *Pseudomonas syringae*) are always present on the surface of the tree. Leaf scars and stomata are additional points of entry. Limb and trunk cankers result when infection occurs, often exhibiting a distinct vinegary odor. Branch crotches are particularly susceptible. Trees with good vigor—be generous with the compost and avoid overly acidic soils—have the health advantage. Dormant copper applications at leaf fall and

BIRD NETTING

Birds love small fruit. Berries and cherries may need protection if you're to get your fair share. You'll quickly become aware if you need to invest in netting to protect a particular crop at your location. Robins are voracious feeders with a territorial inclination to claim a fruit planting for weeks on end. Cedar waxwings, on the other hand, have an uncanny ability to swoop down in a marauding flock the day before you envision picking.

Plastic bird netting typically comes in ¾-inch mesh in widths ranging from 7 feet to as much as 30 feet for trees. This material is totally suitable for sliding over a frame but has a real tendency to snag branch ends whenever the netting is placed directly on the plant. More expensive soft nylon netting (having a smaller mesh size) will not get as tangled up on itself and lasts longer.

A supporting frame helps considerably. The design in turn depends on the growth habit of the fruit being protected. Blueberries are relatively tame and thus often put within a permanent cage with headroom—a 2 × 4 box frame with netting stapled tautly down to the soil line being the most common. Brambles are more pokey and wantonly spreading. An arch frame allows the netting to easily be pulled back to pick the berries and can quickly be removed in its entirety post-harvest to allow edge work. Freestanding cherry trees might seem to provide a perfectly viable branch structure to hold up netting, but shoot growth will become matted down and a portion of the crop always gets caught in the net. A tee frame is little more than a roll bar held just above the tree canopy to support the net.

The white piping used in construction for drainpipes is plenty rigid to hold up lightweight netting. This particular plastic (called PVC) can be joined together with a solvent—a standard tee fitting and two 3-foot arms create that "roll bar" to stretch the netting up over a small tree. Available caps for the exposed end of each arm will prevent snagging. I prefer using 1½-inch-diameter pipe, keeping the full 10-foot length intact for the leg. This could be shortened up for dwarf trees, as the net needs to be suspended only a tweak above the canopy. This framework in turn can be tied to the tree trunk in one or two places to hold it in place.

The foremost challenge is getting the netting up and over something taller than ourselves. Enter the two-person team, more lengths of rigid piping, and duct tape. Lay the netting out on the ground, securing the width ends to the lifting pipes with a minimal amount of tape. Stand apart from each other, raise the pipes up, and then walk the netting over the cherry tree. Undo the lifting pipes once the netting is centered over the tree, and then bring all the draping edges inward to tie around the trunk. The netting will touch branches lower down but not nearly as snugly if the roll bar didn't hold it above. Access comes by untying the edges to pick fruit within. The netting will be removed as soon as all the cherries have ripened by simply

again in spring are the traditional medicine, but do know that copper residues reduce fruit set on treated trees.[13] Biological reinforcement is the righteous way to go.

- **_Prunus_ necrotic ringspot.** Why is it that viruses always get the coolest names? This one occurs on sweet and sour cherry, peach, nectarine, and plum. Leaves on affected limbs taping the netting back onto the lifting poles and raising it back off the tree.

The simplest means to secure an arch frame over brambles and gooseberries involves inserting pairs of 24- to 30-inch lengths of steel rebar into the ground (a foot or so will do) to straddle the row every 5–6 feet. These stakes provide a foothold for polyethylene water pipe, being the flexible black plastic piping used to move drinking water underground. Lengths of 1-inch-diameter pipe cut on the order of 8–14 feet long (to be determined by row width and desired height) will slide readily over ½-inch rebar to create each arch. Wire ties can be used to hold a center pole in place to support the netting between arches. Berry pickers work from one side of the row at a time by draping the netting up over the center. Net edges should be secured at ground level with loose boards or bricks at all other times to prevent bird access.

Two people can lift and carry wide netting up and over an individual tree to protect ripening cherries from birds. Rigid piping or board strapping works well for lifting handles. The roll bar attached to the trunk minimizes branch snagging.

are small, often with depressed arc-like rings on their surface. The centers of these necrotic rings fall out, giving the leaves a tattered appearance. The virus is spread through grafting (vector alert!), with contaminated pollen then reaching otherwise healthy trees. Both vigor and crop will be reduced for two years, after which trees typically recover.

• **Fruit cracking.** The disorder is characterized by a splitting of the cuticle on cherry fruit. Susceptibility to cracking varies with each variety.[14] It most commonly appears around the stem bowl, where water can accumulate. Late-season rain or humidity accompanied by higher temperatures can cause osmotic pressure to increase to a point beyond the expansion capability of the cuticle. That same roll bar (used to hold up bird netting) can do double duty by supporting poly sheeting over susceptible varieties when a rainy stretch precedes a promising harvest.

Harvest notes

Carrying a bowl into which to pick cherries up a tripod ladder entails a predictable risk. A fly brushes your cheek, the ladder tilts, you reach quickly to reaffirm your grip . . . and that forlorn bowl tumbles down to the ground, spewing its precious contents across the fungal duff. Enter the basic peck basket with a bail handle that can be held by a hook secured to the ladder leg. This isn't so much about the need to have two hands free for picking as it is about the precariousness of it all. Reaching between branches to pluck clusters of cherries makes it plumb difficult to continually grasp that bowl!

Stem pulls are not a concern if the fruit will be consumed immediately, and, in fact, it's quite advantageous to take time to destem sour cherries as you pick. The deepest-colored fruit will come cleanly off the stem, while not-quite-so-ripe fruit will be more snugly attached. The need to pick for a range of ripeness will be driven to a degree by whether you chose to protect individual trees with netting—and thus have to unsnug the whole works each time you're ready to pick. Sweet cherries should be pinched off at the tree end of the stem (this means each fruit will retain its stem) in order to have a longer shelf life.

Cutting out pits with a paring knife is tedious work. Perhaps a single pie warrants such Zen-like attention, but an ever-increasing harvest will eventually lead to mechanizing for cherry bounty.

A punch-type cherry pitter works great, especially if intact fruit is important in your canning plans. A small stainless-steel punch drives the pit down through one cherry at a time by means of a levered arm. A silicone rubber gasket pulls the pit off the punch on the upstroke, thereby allowing it to fall into a waste bin. The cherry itself is automatically lifted and dropped into a bowl placed in front while the next cherry rolls into position. Pit. Pit. Pat. And then you're done. Cherries come out whole and virtually undamaged with only a small hole down the center, just perfect for prizewinning pies, cobblers, and preserves. Twenty-five pounds of fruit can be pitted in just under an hour. It takes a bit of practice to make sure each cherry is pitted, so do check for missed pits when you're first learning the ropes.

A crank-style cherry pitter delivers restaurant-volume results, so if you don't mind crushed or split cherries, this one may be a better choice for serious jam and winemakers. A crank wheel forces the fruit through a narrow channel, squeezing out pits from the resulting slurry. Seldom does a pit get missed. The xylon-coated cast body gets clamped to the countertop, standing just over 7 inches tall, with its send-off bowl holding a pint of cherries at a time. Lehman's Hardware store in Ohio offers both types of cherry pitters at a reasonable price.[15]

PEACHES

The wonderful flavor of fully ripened peaches—so delectable you can hardly do anything but stand at the tree and eat away—makes local peach culture a must.

The peach tree (*Prunus persica*) comes from China. Peaches were first mentioned in Chinese writings more than three thousand years ago and were a favored fruit of the emperors. The peach made its way to India along the Silk Road before Christian times. Alexander the Great introduced the fruit into Europe after he conquered the Persians. That pivotal moment in peach history led to some botanical confusion—the name *persica* was derived from an early European belief that peaches were native to Persia (now Iran). Spanish explorers brought peach pits to the Americas, a move seconded by the British in the founding of the colonies. Various American Indian tribes are credited with spreading the peach tree inland, taking pits yet again for planting this delectable fruit.

The fundamentals of peach horticulture shift significantly from how apples and pears are grown. Siting for bud hardiness, pollination strategies, pruning rules, effective thinning techniques, and spray timing for peaches and nectarines (a fuzzless cousin) call for new perspective. Peach trees are not nearly as long-lived, for one. Take heart in the fact that these trees are vigorous and precocious. Good crops will come quickly and for several years, maybe a decade, maybe even two decades in ideal climates and conditions. The blessing lies in the fruit you do harvest being so very, very good. Peaches are absolutely worth the risk and the work.

Peach varieties to consider

More than two thousand named varieties allow for all sorts of taste and firmness preferences. And yet in the supermarket a peach is just a peach, as varietal identification is rarely provided. We know apples by name . . . and now the time has come to cross the peach divide.

California peach grower David Masumoto immortalized the Sun Crest peach in his book *Epitaph for a Peach*. Listen to the taste cadence flowing in his words:

> *Sun Crest tastes like a peach is supposed to. As with many of the older varieties, the flesh is so juicy that it oozes down your chin. The nectar explodes in your mouth and the fragrance enchants your nose, a natural perfume that can never be captured . . . This is a real bite, a primal act, a magical sensory celebration announcing that summer has arrived.*

He goes on to explain why this exquisite peach has become obsolete and its trees bulldozed from commercial memory. Like many an heirloom, it lacks marketable fortitude. Its delicate skin can be readily bruised. Why, Sun Crest even tastes peachy! Modern peach breeders, in contrast, typically strive for super-sweetness in fruits that can be packaged like baseballs for a trip to market.

Each of us decides where passions lie. And to be fair, modern peaches can indeed be wonderful . . . in the hands of a grower who insists on picking only tree-ripened fruit. Heirloom peaches are often softer; sometimes the juice factor can be like a dip in the pool; disease susceptibility should be reckoned. And yet watching people's eyes light up as they bite into an Indian Free peach—the very same enjoyed by Thomas Jefferson at Monticello in the early 1800s—speaks volumes for flavor subtlety. This old-time peach happens to have natural resistance to peach leaf curl as well.

Being able to stand up to disease pressure matters considerably in choosing good peach varieties for your geographic region. The telltale woes of bacterial spot, brown rot, peach scab, leaf curl, and canker are best checked by the innate ability of the tree to resist any pathogen in the first place. But know this: Varietal resistance shifts somewhat from region to region, not unlike how peak flavor correlates to soil type and that season's weather. All indicators are only that. Given the advantage of across-the-board health resulting from deep-nutrition choices, the peach you love may well be the right peach for you to grow.

Most peach cultivars are self-fertile and entirely suited to Zones 5–8. Low-chill considerations enter into the equation when selecting varieties to grow farther south. Northern peach cultivars will have to offer proven bud and wood hardiness. Growers in the Northwest are best advised to seek out curl-resistant varieties, while growers throughout the East will appreciate a modicum of resistance to bacterial spot and brown rot. While peaches require well-drained soil, the trees are more tolerant of wet feet than cherries or apricots. Budded whips are sensitive to water stress during transplanting, so be vigilant with the

The Baby Crawford peach has an intensely rich flavor verging on mango. Photo courtesy of Trees of Antiquity.

watering can. Peaches have a high nutrient requirement, needing more nitrogen than most other fruit trees. A charge of composted poultry manure immediately after harvest will benefit shoot production right when next year's fruit buds initiate. Summertime heat is required to mature the crop, with mean temperatures between 68 and 86°F (20 and 30°C) in the month prior to harvest ideal. Weave in the usual dance around spring frosts and you should be all set.

Augustprince. Very firm fruit softens slowly while on the tree, allowing picking over an extended period. Large, round fruit is nearly 3 inches in diameter. Yellow flesh, with some red coloring when fully mature. Developed by W. R. Okie at the ARS Southeastern Fruit Tree Station in Georgia. Ripens in late July to early August.

Avalon Pride. Chance seedling found in Washington in 1981. Highly flavored, yellow-fleshed, semi-freestone fruit. Resistant to peach leaf curl. Reliably ripens in mid-July. Patented variety with royalties used to support fruit research at the WSU Mount Vernon station.

Baby Crawford. Fruit connoisseurs call this one the best-tasting peach. Intensely rich flavor verging on mango. Delicate freestone with golden-orange flesh. Vigorous tree. University of California selection

nurtured by Andy Mariani. Superb flavor whether eaten fresh, preserved, dried, or canned.

Contender. Firm, large, bright red over yellow freestone. Sweet, aromatic, delicious. Sets fruit throughout the continent. Resists browning when canned. Released by North Carolina State University in 1988. High chilling requirement of 1,050 chill hours. Escapes late-spring freezes with a late bloom. Moderately resistant to bacterial spot. Ripens in August. This is the new kid on the block for northern growers in Zone 4.

Coral Star. Lots of zing in this peach! The backdrop of acid gives it almost a nectarine quality. Firm, softball-sized freestone. Every bit as good as Ernie's Choice, but with a bit more fuzz. Resists bacterial spot. Holds well on the tree. Multiple pickings required.

Ernie's Choice. Snappy flavor of a nectarine and the bouquet to back it up. Practically fuzzless. Good size. Rot- and crack-resistant. Considered too juicy and too melts-in-your-mouth tender by the trade . . . which scores one for Ernie in my book! Gets rave reviews all over. Developed at the New Jersey Experiment Station.

Flamin' Fury Series. Fruit breeder Paul Friday in Coloma, Michigan, stresses bacterial spot resistance in all his peach selections. The twenty-five varieties already introduced to commercial growers cover the full gamut of the ripening season, with accommodation for different geographic locations. Other breeding goals are more open-ended, with most varieties exhibiting high red color, roundness, firmness, good size, and shipping quality.

• **PF7**. Ripens with Garnet Beauty, two weeks before Red Haven. Large, beautiful fruit, unblemished, with probably fewer split pits than any other peach. Very firm. Biggest percentage of number ones imaginable. Hangs well on the tree.

• **PF Lucky 13**. Ripens one week after Red Haven. Very classy, radiant, freestone peach. Fruit remains on the tree more than ten days, stays very hard, and keeps growing past when

Vista exemplifies superior peach qualities all around. Photo courtesy of Dave Wilson Nursery.

you originally thought it should have been picked, just getting bigger and bigger while remaining very firm. Spreading, productive tree. Bacterial spot resistance invaluable for eastern growers.

- **PF 24C**. Ripens twenty-four days after Red Haven. Highly colored fruit with excellent flavor. Very cold-hardy. This extraordinary peach requires thinning where other varieties freeze out in a challenging winter or spring. Buds have withstood –16°F (–27°C). Late-blooming. Strong, right-angled branch structure. Worthy of trial in Zone 4.

Frost. Flavorful, yellow-fleshed peach. One of the most curl-resistant varieties. Split pits do not occur. More prone to bacterial canker on the trunk than most. Reliable in the Pacific Northwest. Seven hundred chill hours. Ripens mid-August.

Garnet Beauty. Bud mutation of Red Haven. Medium to large, slightly elongated, almost fuzzless red fruit. Firm, yellow, semi-freestone flesh streaked with red. Smooth texture. Vigorous, productive tree. Resistant to split pits, which commonly occurs in early varieties. Quite bud-hardy. Discovered in Ontario in the 1950s. Eight hundred fifty chill hours.

Gold Dust. Earliest top-quality peach. Yellow semi-freestone with exceptional flavor. Superb for fresh eating. Ripens mid- to late June in California. Good reports from the Mid-Atlantic with respect to

Saturn is a peento-type peach—flattened like a doughnut, only without the hole. Photo courtesy of Adams County Nursery.

disease. Zero peach scab. Not an early bloomer. Five hundred fifty chill hours.

Harrow Diamond. Medium-sized yellow fruit with red blush. Freestone when picked ripe. Deals well with leaf curl in most years. Resists brown rot and bacterial spot. Moderately tolerant to perennial canker. Found at Cummins Nursery in New York. Ripens about three weeks before Red Haven. Cold-hardy through Zone 4.

Indian Free. Large, aromatic semi-freestone. Red skin with white flesh marbled with crimson stripes. Rich, distinctive cranberry-like flavor. Highly resistant to peach leaf curl. Moderately susceptible to bacterial spot and brown rot. Requires another peach or nectarine as a pollinizer. Ripens late season. Best in Zones 6–8.

Madison. Bright red freestone with excellent flavor. High-quality orange-yellow flesh. Tolerates brown rot. Recommended for northern conditions. Very wood-hardy so recovers quickly from winter injury if pushed a zone too far. Considerable bud tolerance to spring frost. Ripens in late August. Released by the Virginia Station in 1963.

New Haven. Freestone with yellow flesh. Strong, spreading, productive tree. Very resistant to bacterial spot; moderately resistant to leaf curl; tolerance to brown rot. Cold hardiness equals that of the more disease-prone Red Haven. Ripens twenty-four days before Elberta. Nine hundred fifty chill hours.

Raritan Rose. Large, round, freestone fruit. Bright red over very light creamy white background. Melting, tender, honey-sweet white flesh. Vigorous tree with hardy blossom buds. Excellent bacterial spot resistance. Rot-tolerant. Introduced by the New Jersey AES in 1936. Ripens early to mid-July. Nine hundred fifty chill hours.

Red Baron. Large, round yellow freestone up to 3 inches in diameter. Sweet, juicy flesh. Zesty, rich flavor rates among the best when given a hot summer. Tree features large double red blossoms. Ripens mid-July to mid-August. Very low chill at 250 hours. Zones 6–9.

Saturn. Peento-type peaches are shaped like a doughnut, without the hole. Large, yellow fruit has melting white flesh. Hint of honeyed almond taste. Showy, double pink flowers. High bacterial spot resistance. Brown rot issues in the East. Four hundred chill hours and thus early blooming. Heavy set requires excessive thinning. Ripens early midseason.

Slappy (Slappey). Large, yellow freestone with thin skin. Distinctive, clean flavor reminiscent of the Newtown Pippin apple. An outright juice bomb that will soak the whole front of your shirt! Appalachian favorite for home canning. Ripens in late August.

Veteran. Medium to large yellow-fleshed peach. Highly flavored. Easy to peel. Freestone when fully ripe. Hardy buds and wood. Ornamental tree, with large, pale pink blooms. Originated in Canada in 1928. Reliable producer in cold, wet weather. Ripens midseason.

Vista. This luscious, bright-red peach ripens in late June in California. Yellow-fleshed, semi-freestone. Vista exemplifies superior qualities all around with large size, good skin color, and a balanced, acidic-sweet flavor. Chilling requirement of six to seven hundred hours.

White Lady. Medium-large red-skinned freestone. Very firm white flesh. Low-acid/high-sugar flavor profile. Widely adapted around the nation. Long harvest season. Zaiger introduction in 1986. Needs eight hundred chill hours.

Rootstock for peaches

Let's be clear about one thing from the start: Plant a pit from a good-tasting peach, it sprouts and grows, then this "root" can be budded to a specific cultivar two years later out in the orchard. However, chances are high that this natural seedling tree will yield a decent peach in its own right. The traditional roots listed below have particular traits that work for nurseries and commercial growers—you may want that—but in truth you've just been told enough to proceed on your own. Named rootstocks can also be propagated from root cuttings (stem-end up) once you've obtained a first tree grafted to a desired root.

Size control in peaches has been tricky to obtain. Selected seedlings with a proven degree of uniformity might reduce vigor 10–15 percent at most. Other *Prunus* species exhibit either incompatibility (making an interstem necessary) or exceedingly poor vigor. New hybrid roots made between peach and another stone fruit when used with peach do reduce scion vigor on the order of 50 percent . . . but trees tend to be significantly shorter-lived. Personally, I'd rather do a good job pruning.

Bailey seedling features the proven roots of an old peach cultivar from Iowa. Good reports come in from across middle growing zones. This rootstock is not necessarily the answer for all hardiness problems, however. Bailey grows long into the fall and induces the scions grafted on it to do so as well, delaying senescence and hardening off before winter. Best for sandy and sandy loam soils. Develops an abundant root system. Resistant to root lesion nematodes.

Citation is a complex peach × plum hybrid bred by Floyd Zaiger of California. Peach trees on Citation are slightly more than half of standard size. Strong union and well anchored. Resistant to nematodes, tolerant of wet soils, no suckers, and cold-tolerant.

Guardian seedling peach comes from a controlled cross that remains proprietary. Growers in the Southeast take note: Guardian is the best bet going with respect to peach tree short-life issues. Still, there's always a catch: It's highly susceptible to armillaria root rot (being the other problem encountered by Georgia peach growers).

Lovell seedling produces a well-anchored tree with good resistance to bacterial canker. Tolerates cold and wet soils. Susceptible to nematodes in sandy soil. Vigorous rootstock for plums, peaches, nectarines, apricots, prunes, and almonds. Unmanaged tree height of a seedling reaches 20–25 feet, by the way. Lovell delays senescence slightly.

Nemaguard induces late blooming and offers the best nematode resistance going. It produces a vigorous tree in well-drained soils. Plant on a hill on poorly drained soils, as it's extremely susceptible to wet feet. Bears fruit in three years and grows to 12–18 feet. Winter hardiness is so-so.

Myrobalan, often shortened to **Myro**, is a cherry plum (*Prunus cerasifera*) rootstock used for peaches in the heaviest soils. Hmmm . . . could better ground be found? Graft-compatible with many cultivars. Excellent anchorage. Susceptible to oak root fungus and lacks nematode resistance. Zones 4–8.

Peach propagation

Budding (bud grafting) in July through mid-August is best for peaches and other stone fruits because the warm temperatures occurring then encourage rapid uniting of the bud with the rootstock.[16] Buds cut from one-year-old vegetative shoots are either inserted under the bark of the stock (T budding) or placed where a portion of the bark has been removed from the stock (chip budding). Whips up to ⅝ inch in diameter work best for budding, as the bark of larger growth often tends to be too thick. Use parafilm to wrap the bud in place and help seal in moisture.[17] Each varietal bud settles into dormancy that fall . . . and then awakens rarin' to go come next spring. The growth above the bud union can be pruned away once swelling in the bud becomes obvious.

Bench grafting of stone fruits in late winter can be done with dormant scionwood and rootstocks from a supplier. Dependable heat to promote callusing is far more critical, however, compared with the relatively cool needs of pome fruits. Best results come from putting freshly grafted rootstocks into a mulch tray

Warm-season grafting is fairly straightforward given that the inserted bud simply needs to settle in for the end of summer that first year. The stock gets cut back just above this emerging bud the following spring.

(keep those roots moist!) held at 80–85°F (27–29°C), with fair-to-good results being obtained closer to 70°F (21°C). Rigging a poly-covered frame over this with a low-wattage lightbulb to generate a modicum of heat can help if you don't have dependable bottom heat. Those immediate weeks before stone fruit buds outside show green are the right time to do this. Several days with supplemental heat will be plenty, after which these trees-to-be should be moved to a slightly less warm place until it's time to plant them out in the nursery.

Pruning tips for peaches

An open vase tree structure suits peaches very well. That, along with flowers being initiated on one-year-old wood, sets the stage for pruning a peach tree.

Formative pruning to create that open vase form is straightforward. Newly planted trees should be headed to about 30 inches in height, just above a lateral branch or bud. Cut all side branches to one bud. If the tree is well branched when it comes from the nursery,

One-year-old peach

Two-year-old peach

Open vase training involves consistently favoring outward-growing buds during the formative years of a peach tree. Scaffold limbs should be headed slightly each spring to promote branching. Pinching misdirected buds in the growing season will save considerable pruning the next spring. The result is a low-spreading tree with plenty of sunshine access in the center.

select three or four laterals that are well spaced around the trunk for the permanent scaffold limbs. Cut these back to two buds each, and remove all other laterals. A number of shoots will develop during the first growing season, from which you can select scaffold limbs. Pinching back errant buds (those directing inward) during early summer will direct more growing energy to the buds remaining. Dormant pruning just before growth begins the second season will be round two in this shaping work.

Once the scaffold system of the young peach tree is established, scale back somewhat on pruning until the tree begins to bear. Heading back terminal growth on the scaffold limbs to outward-growing buds should be enough to keep the tree to task. An open-center form should be emerging as a result of making the right cuts. Your ultimate goal is a wide tree with a spreading frame 8–12 feet high. Continue to cut branches that turn upward back to laterals that are growing outward. This creates a much wider branching habit. Strong, upright shoots growing in the center of the tree should always be removed to maintain the open center that will admit light to the lower inside branches.

Good peach production is driven by a good amount of sunlight.[18] This is especially important in June and July for maximum flower bud development.[19] Pruning peaches annually is really about improving light distribution. The best peaches—those with good size, well colored, and with high sugar levels—result when the interior of the tree receives at least 25 percent full sun.[20] Ergo, the open vase.

The ways of peach fruit buds determine the rest of the story. These develop on "one-year-old wood," which should be understood to be the current season's shoot growth. The very shoots of spring that absorb the generous sunshine of June enter the bud initiation phase going into harvest.[21] Flowers result the next spring, bearing fruit. The node positions on that section of shoot producing peaches will not fruit again if all buds at that position produce flowers that season . . . which is often the case, and thus the reason fruiting potential peters out quickly on peach shoots beyond that first bearing season. Node positions above this will develop fruit buds for the following year—as all new growth (extending from the terminal bud of the current bearing shoot) will indeed

Fruiting prospects become obvious when early bud swell occurs on peach. The three buds at this node position represent the gamut: one dead flower bud, one conical leaf bud, and one blessedly plump flower bud. Generally, winter-killed buds will fall off the tree at about this time. Photo courtesy of Mark Longstroth, Michigan State University Extension.

be "one-year-old wood" that next season. The spent portion of the shoot becomes nonbearing forevermore excepting for any errant leaf buds with one more shot at redemption.

Peaches do not develop spurs with the ability to produce fruit for years on end. This changes everything. Bearing shoots left to grow beyond that first fruitful season are essentially moving the fruiting zone farther and farther out from the branch structure of the tree. Pruning tenet numero uno for peaches and nectarines: Spent shoots need to be replaced with new growth to prevent the tree from becoming long, willowy, and productive only at its very ends. This also ensures that

any mummified fruits (prime sources of brown rot inoculum) on the shoots from the year before are removed from the tree. An annual heading-back of the three or four main scaffold limbs is often required to keep an abundance of one-year wood growing, therefore creating lots of flowers in the subsequent year.

Two good questions follow from there. Which are the shoots to keep? And when is the right time to do this?

Fruit bud distribution on a shoot can be gauged by how much a given shoot grew. The ideal fruiting shoot is 12–24 inches long and about the diameter of a pencil at its base. Smaller-diameter twigs produce

Experienced peach growers know that the ideal fruiting shoot is 12–24 inches long and about the diameter of a pencil at its base.

small fruit because short shoots have too few leaves to support the growth of fruit. Longer, branched shoots produce fewer flower buds, because more energy gets invested in lateral shoots. The first are keepers and the other two get thinned. Balanced nutrition, irrigation, and fruit loading play key roles in producing desirable shoot growth for the following season.

Timing is very much a regional decision. Lightly thinning new growth in early to midsummer maximizes light for the shoots being kept. Growers everywhere should take note of that. Additional pruning will be completed either immediately after harvest or after that first peek of pink in spring.

Growers facing a wet dormant season in the land of extreme bacterial canker have little choice here. Pruning the peach tree following harvest when it's bone-dry means that pruning cuts can heal without risk of infection. Step one is to remove all of the dark shoots from the scaffold limbs, these being the bearing shoots of the season just passed. Thinning bright green shoots (this year's growth) would be completed now as well, especially in coastal locations.

This flips entirely where winter brings snow and ice, even the lightest touch. Pruning peach trees at the start of the dormant season (in late fall and early winter) reduces hardiness for the cold months ahead. Even just before bloom, when pink tissue shows at the tip of the buds, pruning can make those buds slightly less tolerant of frost. Delaying pruning significantly lessens the chances of peach perennial canker in the East. These fungi make headway in winter-injured bark, whereas late-spring pruning cuts heal quickly, thus slamming the door on these opportunists. Growers pushing northern bounds benefit from being able to distinguish winter-killed shoots in making final thinning selections. Pruning peach trees during bloom or shortly after bloom may not seem ideal: Fruitlets are easily knocked off; it's harder to sense light space around leafing limbs; and, frankly, this is a busy time of year. Just know you will not adversely affect the growth of the tree in any way.

Peach tree hardiness

Going dormant is a widely adapted plant strategy for negotiating the depths of winter. Yet hardiness is far more complex than minimum winter temperatures alone suggest. Much depends on how fall plays out, and no other fruit tree better exemplifies what can go awry than the peach.

Trees thought to have been killed during a deep cold snap in midwinter[22] may just as well have experienced a game-changing event earlier, when temperatures were far milder by comparison. Peach tree hardiness reveals a chink in its armor when late-fall conditions make a direct assault on the trunk zone. A tree goes dormant from the top down, with the exposed stem especially dependent upon *cold preconditioning* to harden off. Peach cambium remains active well into October in some years when nights stay relatively warm, which in turn predisposes the trunk and major branch crotches to injury when a cold snap comes along in late fall. The buds and twigs up above are hardier at this point. Relatively speaking, the temps being talked about here are not all that cold—cambium death can occur at 15–21°F (–6 to –9°C) after leaf fall, which is entirely a function of trunk cambium cells being the least prepared.[23] Bark tissue undergoes extracellular freezing, resulting in the death of the tree trunk without damaging any other part of the tree up above.[24] This explains why finding plenty of live buds in spring can never be a guarantee with peaches. Those buds will indeed start to grow but then wither abruptly . . . all because the trunk died months ago just above the soil line.

Peach growers are well advised to protect their trees from southwest injury: Dark tree trunks warm up considerably on a sunny winter day; the sun goes behind a cloud, instantly taking away that solar gain; then temperatures plummet and the bark quickly refreezes. That's especially hard on cambium tissues on the southwest side of the tree, which is exposed to a continuing on-and-off stream of late-afternoon sun. Even if the tree lives, an entry point has been made for borers and bacterial canker. Whitewashing the lower trunk and major branch crotches (see "Trunk care" in chapter 3, on page 79) to reflect the sun's warmth helps prevent this.

Dormancy issues around bud hardiness enter in for peaches as well. Flower buds are more cold-tender than leaf buds, and, in a borderline situation, the flower buds will get killed but the leaves will still come out. The flowers may even open . . . but there will be no fruit. Peaches and nectarines subject to fluctuating winter temperatures respond similarly to apricots. Temperatures in the mid-40s (6–9°C) for several days in a row during the winter months cause all fruit buds to de-harden ever so slightly. A sudden drop to subzero temperatures affects different species to a different degree. With peaches, the doom point for viable pistils (the female parts of the flowers) often occurs around –10°F (–23°C) when preceded by a warm spell. Those same buds can take it slightly colder otherwise.[25] Once the pistils in peach flower

buds are killed, there's no pollinator in this world that can perform a miracle.

What to do about all this, you rightly ask? *Not all that much*, to be honest. The pace of fall hardiness is a function of the weather. Adding seaweed to the fall holistic spray has some merit, in that cytokinins in kelp help toughen plant cell walls. Potassium availability counts here as well. Keeping soil on the dry side after leaf fall hastens the hardening-off response. The challenge of dormancy issues, on the other hand, calls for counterintuitive thinking. Siting for shade is a far different notion from creating a microclimate facing due south in hopes of assured warmth.[26] The best place to consider growing a peach is in the *winter shadow* of your house or barn, a conifer stand, or what have you. Fruit trees need to be located to receive full sun in the summer but close enough to be in the shade through the coldest months in more northern zones. The goal is uniform cold so as to not interrupt dormancy. Physical shelters to provide shading (think plywood) can be built around individual trees for the winter months, but that tends to get old quick.

Zone ratings for stone fruit trees typically reflect a cultivar's inability to resist de-hardening in a warm spell. Wood-hardy varieties designated Zone 5 often can take greater cold, provided that shading from low winter sun maintains deep dormancy during a January thaw. Keep in mind that losing upper growth in a particularly brutal winter is not the end of the world: New shoots typically arise from any part of the tree protected by snow cover. Peach trees are both vigorous and precocious—bearing fruit on one-year-old wood—which means the next crop is just one good winter away.

Peach pollination

The many attractive pink or reddish blossoms of the peach open at about the same time each spring on most cultivars. Peach bloom follows closely on the heels of plum bloom, and some years might even coincide. Peaches are generally self-fertile, thus making cross-pollination strategies unnecessary.[27] The flowers are

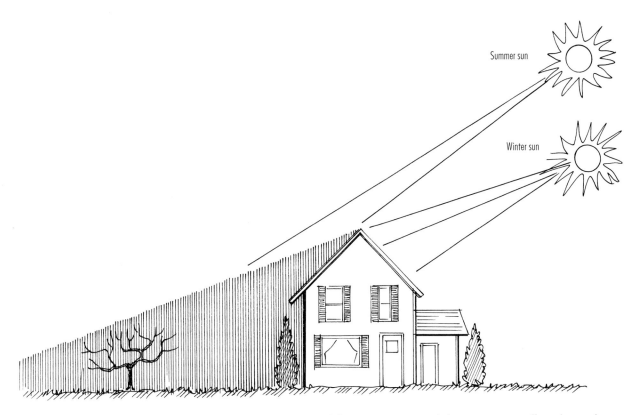

Placing a tender stone fruit tree in the winter shadow of a building helps buffer fruit buds from temperature swings. The low winter sun cannot affect such trees, whereas the higher summer sun makes things just as peachy as can be during the growing season.

highly attractive to honeybees and both pollen- and nectar-collecting insects. Wind alone does not dislodge the pollen, so seeing such allies out on a balmy spring day working the bloom is important. Fully opened flowers are receptive for about three days' time, with enough stagger in bud development to be able to count on at least one delightful day of real-time pollination.

A pollinated peach flower reveals itself when the pistil outgrows its anthers. (That's anatomical-speak for the stand-alone stalk in the middle of the flower rising above the stubby male parts surrounding it.) This happens very rapidly after pollination, with the pistil sticking up as much as ¼ inch past the anthers. Pollen from another cultivar results in even faster growth of the pollen tube leading down to the ovule and thus a greater likelihood of fertilization under adverse conditions.

The usual tricks of planting on a north slope to delay spring green-up and pumping up sugar levels in fragile bloom (with a liquid kelp/molasses spray) help get tender flowers past late frosts. A delayed dormant application of soybean oil at the earliest hint of green in opening leaf buds will delay bloom by as much as a week.[28] This can cause the death of some of the flower buds—depending on the oil rate used and the weather—so do review the research before trying this.

Thinning peaches

Severely overcropped trees will produce small fruit and will be that much more vulnerable to cold injury the following winter.[29] Return bloom dynamics are not the driving factor here as is the case with apple and pear. *Prunus* trees can literally break under the weight of too much fruit. Trust me: Those baby peaches left on the tree will get plenty big and juicy only if you do this job right.

The rising pistil of a peach flower is a recognizable sign of successful pollination. Photo courtesy of Mark Longstroth, Michigan State University Extension.

Peaches should be thinned to 6–8 inches apart on the tree to achieve proper size. This can mean removing as much as 90 percent of a particular cultivar's fruit set in an outrageous pollination year.[30] Peaches and nectarines will always be smallish if lacking rigorous discipline on your part. The same holds true for apricots and plums, only now the goal shifts to leaving these smaller fruit slightly apart throughout the tree by breaking up heavy clusters.

Stone fruit trees can be manually thinned quite effectively with a combination approach. The bulk of developing peach fruitlets can be unceremoniously removed with a good thrashing once these get to be ½–¾ inch in diameter.[31] This takes courage to do right. Thinning with a pole—be it a wooden dowel, plastic pipe, or bamboo—begins with attaching a short length of rubber hose or a cloth wrap to the end of the pole. This minimizes scarring or bruising the

remaining fruit. A well-directed whump at the base of a branch will dislodge weaker fruitlets. Follow that up with a thrust at individual fruits or stubbornly set shoots to achieve a spread-out knockdown on the order of 50–60 percent. That rule of thumb provides a twofold visual goal to those of you doing this for the first time: You are knocking off a significant portion of the crop with just enough force, while at the same time not being obsessive-compulsive about exact spacing. Don't wait too long to do this, for once leaf growth dominates the view, pole thinning becomes far less feasible on bigger trees.

Hand-thinning comes in the weeks that follow. Keep the fruits that are undamaged by insects and show the fastest growth. Waiting to do this allows the peaches remaining (after pole thinning) to show their stuff with respect to sizing vigor. Here's how this works. Pit hardening begins about fifty to

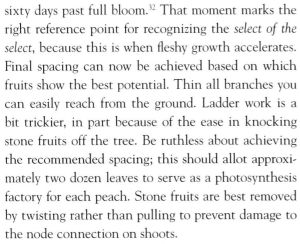

A slight twist of the stone fruitlet when hand-thinning helps prevent damage to the bearing shoot.

A stiff brushing along one side of each bearing shoot will reduce fruiting potential by approximately a third due to the triangular facing pattern of peach flower buds.

sixty days past full bloom.[32] That moment marks the right reference point for recognizing the *select of the select*, because this is when fleshy growth accelerates. Final spacing can now be achieved based on which fruits show the best potential. Thin all branches you can easily reach from the ground. Ladder work is a bit trickier, in part because of the ease in knocking stone fruits off the tree. Be ruthless about achieving the recommended spacing; this should allot approximately two dozen leaves to serve as a photosynthesis factory for each peach. Stone fruits are best removed by twisting rather than pulling to prevent damage to the node connection on shoots.

You can hand-thin entirely if you're working just a few trees, of course. Early-season cultivars are thinned heavily from the get-go so as not to have to come back that second time. Especially generous spacing causes the tree to push all its energy to the peaches left on the tree, achieving good size for all varieties ripening before or along with Red Haven.[33] Later cultivars have a longer period of time to take in nutrients, so often more fruit will be left on the tree by tightening up the spacing a nudge.

Thinning flowers long before fruit appears always seems tenuous. Yet an opportunity awaits here with peaches and nectarines that shouldn't be dismissed too quickly for the heavier-setting cultivars. *Prunus* bloom occurs somewhat regularly along shoots with respect to spacing and does so in an evenhanded way in the orientation of individual flowers as well. Some face upward, others open to either side, essentially forming three ranks of flowering potential. A stiff bristle brush tied to a stick can be used to rub the flowers off at the *popcorn stage* (when flower buds are just about to fully open) from the top rank of each shoot. One quick pass potentially reduces the thinning task ahead by a third.

Insect pests of peaches

Knowing *who done it* and the timing involved defines the challenges on your particular orchard ground. Any of the recommended field guides will provide species specifics and photo identification to go with established *point-of-vulnerability* insights:

- The confluence of **plum curculio** and peaches in the East ties to the pace of spring emergence of the bug and the choice of other fruitlets available when warm evenings kick pest activity into full gear. A second generation figures highly in the minds of southern peach growers. Freshly minted adults emerge from the soil in early midsummer.[34] Midseason and late-ripening peach cultivars fall prey after pit hardening begins. These larger fruit will stay on the tree until ripe, but the grub-damaged flesh makes the fruit worthless.

- The **peach twig borer** is a far greater problem across Texas and west of the Rocky Mountains. These larvae emerge in the spring and then bore into twigs and buds before pupating into dark gray moths. Later generations of larvae attack maturing peaches during the summer, surface-feeding near the stem end and rendering the fruit unfit. Unlike other whitish to pink caterpillars found within fruits, twig borer larvae are chocolate brown with distinct segments.

- **Oriental fruit moth** shows a definite preference for peach over apple. The first noticeable damage occurs to shoot tips. First-generation larvae tunnel several inches into new twig growth, causing it to wilt and die back. Each culprit may feed in as many as five different shoots before seeking a place to spin a cocoon.[35] Round one larvae will feed inside fruit as well, as revealed by telltale blobs of peach pectin on the sides of infested fruitlets. *We now interrupt this program for a short break for pupation.* The ensuing grayish brown adult females go on to lay an egg near maturing fruit, and second-generation larvae tunnel within on the stem end, making a rotting mess of later-maturing varieties.

- A blue-black moth with clear wings and an orange band across its midsection lays its eggs in crevices in the bark within a few inches of the soil line. The larvae of **peachtree borer** can girdle any of the stone fruits, much like roundheaded borer does to apple. This can be a serious pest in the eastern half of the country: A peach tree will live only four years if peachtree borers go unchecked. The adults emerge in late June through September, mating and laying eggs immediately, having a mere seven-day life span.

- Kissing cousins, one might assume, comes when acknowledging the work of **lesser peachtree borer** higher up in the tree. These moth larvae attack the standing trunk and branches in areas that have been injured by implements, cankers, low temperatures, or sunscald, and in split crotches or under the cracked bark of old trees. The clear-winged adults are in flight from late May through September.

- Feeding of adult **stink bugs** causes *catfacing* (dimpling) on peaches. If fruit is almost mature when injured, the flesh does not turn corky but begins to decay. Damage on peaches is more noticeable than on apples or European pears. We'll add to the list of remedial approaches under nectarines—these fuzzless peaches offer a slightly more volatile calling card.

Organic solutions

Barrier protection for stone fruits needs to be in place prior to petal fall on apples. This early application of the refined kaolin clay works to deter curculio scouts seeking peach fruits about to be revealed at shuck split. The clay is not being placed directly on the fruit at this point—remember that papery shuck—but is indeed clogging the limb highway system utilized by the pest. The need for additional applications over the next few weeks depends entirely on the lure of other fruit attractions available and the insightful use of nearby trap trees. Big hint: One sacrificial plum can be instrumental in delivering bushels of peaches.[36] Fuzzy peaches can be tenacious about holding on to that white coating if the clay barrier needs to be maintained closer to harvest.

Peach twig borers gravitate toward weaker trees, so the holistic program for disease already gives growers a healthy leg up. If you see wilting and a gummy exudate from a few twigs, snip off shoots just below the entry hole and destroy. And should the situation seem to be getting too far out of balance? Plan for the next season by looking to the life cycle of this moth. Its larvae overwinter in the limb crotches of young wood and deep cracks in the bark. Come blossom time, these brown-striped caterpillars emerge to feed on flower buds and the tips of shoots. They are not yet inside the twig (and thus protected) at this point. An application of Bt sprayed at pink and again at petal fall regains the upper hand. This strategy protects all sorts of beneficials—*Bacillus thuringiensis* being specific to moth larvae—leaving braconid wasps, lacewings, ladybugs, and minute pirate bugs to finish the job.

Bloom timing for Oriental fruit moth is all about emerging moths contemplating an advantageous place to lay eggs. Mating disruption lures put out by pink interrupt the dating game from the get-go. Neem oil applications affect both oviposition choices as well as the egg-to-larva success rate. Use of Bt or spinosad prior to peach shuck split will snag hatching larvae on the undersides of leaves before they bore into twigs to feed. Snapping off infested shoots is trickier, because OFM larvae make their way from the entry point back into the shoot several inches before flagging becomes apparent. You absolutely want to do all you can to limit the first generation.

The moth borer scene is not too different from the beetle borer scene with respect to cutting out damage (but never green cambium) to get established grubs. Caveats specific to moths come into play, however. Pheromone traps are available for both peachtree borer and lesser peachtree borer. Neem oil saturation of infested tissue has dramatic impact on any caterpillar—and stone fruit borer grubs are exactly that. Parasitic nematode mudpacks help clean up an over-the-top situation. Adding plaster of paris or diatomaceous earth to a trunk whitewash will fill in the majority of bark crevices, which females prefer for placing eggs. The old-time practice of mounding wood ashes at the base of young peach trees in late June and again in early August deters the peachtree borer from laying her eggs at the soil line.

The larvae of Oriental fruit moth can devastate late-summer peaches if the first generation of this moth escapes your notice. Photo courtesy of Clemson University–USDA Cooperative Extension Series, Bugwood.org.

Disease concerns of peaches

Holistic orchardists indeed have a plan to deal with disease. We'll add some twists and requisite timing notes here to our general understanding of how tree health keeps fungal and bacterial pathogens in check.

- **American brown rot**. Peach riffs on this primary fungal challenge depend foremost on the wetness of the season. Infection appears in its most obvious form as soft brown spots on the fruit. Peaches are susceptible not only between bloom and the usual couple of weeks past shuck split but all along through harvest. Warm rains kindle this *rot frenzy*. Neem oil sprays continued beyond fruit set and supplemented from that point on with fermented teas of horsetail and nettle are highly recommended. Boosting silica levels of the cuticle are important in turning the tide against rot organisms. The fungicidal aspect of Serenade (see "Bacterial woes" in chapter 4, on page 152) works by destroying the germ tubes and

BACTERIAL SPOT TIMING					
Bud Swell	Blossom	Midseason	Harvest	After Harvest	Dormancy
Bacteria ooze from active cankers and infect young stems and developing leaves.		Fruit develops sunken, greasy spots that may ooze.		Bacteria survive the winter months in dormant summer cankers.	
Early-spring holistic sprays reinforce competitive colonization.	New cankers appear on twigs.	Bud death	Leaves develop lesions and shothole symptoms; they become tattered.		Fall holistic spray introduces "fatty acid knockdown" and competitive colonization.

The *Xanthomonas* bacteria that cause bacterial spot disease on stone fruits overwinter in leaf scars and twig lesions. That sets the stage for holistic action on both sides of dormancy.

mycelium membranes of certain disease fungi. Combining this with biological reinforcement has reduced incidence of brown rot in peach. Research trials suggest that the use of Serenade MAX with Saf-T-Side oil can be "moderately effective" against brown rot.[37]

- **Peach leaf curl**. This fungal disease comes with a window of opportunity. The old-school approach involves applying copper (or lime sulfur) in late fall and again just before bud swell to eradicate overwintering spores tucked away in the bud scales and on the bark. Otherwise, infection occurs at bud burst to soon affect unfurling leaves with red blister-like growth, which later will curl, yellow, and drop.[38] No cultivar is entirely immune to leaf curl, but choosing resistant varieties such as Avalon Pride saves considerable angst. Biweekly kelp sprays beginning at bud swell have been found effective by some southern growers. The holistic fall spray of neem oil and liquid fish ups fatty acid levels in bud crevices, thereby disrupting existing microflora, paving the way for competitive microbes a day or so later to consume the leftovers. This sort of biology-based knockdown is as cutting-edge as it gets!

- **Bacterial spot**. Infections from the previous season launch the causative agent behind this stone fruit challenge prevalent throughout the East. Oozing leaf scars and twig cankers are one thing, but even symptomless plant surfaces play host when it comes to *Xanthomonas* bacteria. Hard, driving rains concentrate their numbers onto growing shoot tips and unfurling leaves in spring, where water congestion of tissues enables the infection to take hold. Leaves develop dark, angular spots, and the sunken spots on fruit are soon followed by cracking in the skin. A dormant copper application just before growth resumes metaphorically drops a piano orchardwide on bacterial prospects.[39] Competitive colonization and plant immune support follow from there, regardless. Even better? Plant peach varieties with noted resistance to spot.

- **Peach scab**. Earlier-ripening varieties that face less heat and humidity suffer less from scab in the Southeast.[40] Peach scab develops as black, velvety spots on fruits, shoots, and occasionally leaves. Conidial production initiates in twig lesions at shuck split and peaks two to six weeks later. Good air circulation is paramount to allay infection. Micronized sulfur applied a month after bloom and again the next week (when the fruit is going from dime to nickel in size) effectively negates this disease. The summertime holistic plan of neem oil, effective microbes, and fermented herbal teas will do similar good.

- **Peach tree short life**. Various parasitic nematodes are major factors in this syndrome,

The *crusty fruit effect* brought about by peach scab can be entirely prevented by extending holistic protection six weeks beyond bloom. Photo courtesy of NYSAES.

which results in premature mortality of peach trees in the Southeast. Short life is characterized by the sudden springtime collapse and death of young trees, typically three to seven years of age. The final killing factor is believed to be freeze injury caused by *Pseudomonas* bacteria. Guardian rootstock offers good resistance on this score.

• **Perennial canker**. Gummosis on peach trees is often caused by *Leucostoma* fungi.[41] Infection in spring goes hand in hand with a high incidence of winter injury to bark tissues. Oval or linear cankers establish and then continue to enlarge until infected limbs are girdled and die. Crotch angles are the principal port of entry, along with mechanical damage to the trunk. Delaying pruning until buds show green will help allay infection, as callus healing tissue forms rapidly once the weather warms.[42] Recognize a losing battle when you see one: Prune out and destroy any badly cankered limbs. An earth mudpack on developing cankers may turn the colonization tide back in your favor.

Harvest notes

Sugars accumulate in the peach at the tail end of the growth cycle. The fruits will not sweeten once picked but merely become less acidic with the ripening. Wait to pick those wonderful-looking peaches until they yield ever so slightly under pressure from the thumb. Picking them hard only results in a supermarket peach . . . which undermines the whole point of growing your own.

Growers in Texas and elsewhere report that high heat doesn't hurt peaches until temperatures stay in the 100s (38°C plus) for days on end. Sugar levels are not affected so much as the acid content of the fruit. A hot summer leads to peaches that are cloyingly sweet, whereas a cooler summer produces fruit of the very same variety with a more distinguished bite. The modern palate tends to veer toward low-acid fruit— and many, frankly, might not miss the taste nuance that makes for a great peach. Just be aware that peaches that don't taste as good one year as a result of low-acid heat may be absolutely smashing the next.

Depending on climate and cultivar, the peach harvest can occur from late May through the whole of September. The harvest from each tree lasts a week or more, as each fruit ripens at its own pace. Varietal ability to keep firm on the tree extends the multiple-picking window considerably.

NECTARINES

Some folks have a hands-down preference for nectarines over peaches. These fruits are a single-factor mutation of the peach—a serendipitous gene shift having brought on qualities different enough to create a fruit type in its own right.[43] Nectarines have an extremely smooth skin with no fuzz, average slightly smaller in size than the peach, and have a distinctive sub-acid flavor. Nectarine coloration runs strikingly redder. And oh, the aroma!

Nectarines arise naturally from peach trees, as either bud sports or sprouted from a pit.[44] Shaved variations of *Prunus persica* can then be grafted to grow entire new trees that retain the genetic mutation. Breeders can run with this as well, crossing nectarine with nectarine to create even more varieties.

Nectarine varieties to consider

Choosing the right nectarine ties to the particulars of the place it's to be grown. Summertime heat that ensures full flavor ripening matters, especially

Growers in less humid regions will want to pursue the exceptional flavor of Fantasia. Photo courtesy of Trees of Antiquity.

with some of the newer varieties. Fabulous nectarines are not merely about fruit buds surviving the winter months . . . though chances are you will still be pleased. There is no universal cultivar for all locations, nor for the range in grower ability.

One argument shows up consistently: Nectarines cannot be grown organically. The rationale behind this is the *fuzz factor*, and I quote: "The fuzz is your friend in the battle against the bugs, a friend you do not want to lose. Smooth skin is more prone to cracking and rot problems as well." Crikey! Sometimes I just want to grab the chemical-biased fruit advisers and crack them upside the head! Let's do the visualization thing. Be an Oriental fruit moth, be a peach scab spore, be a nasty, nasty spot bacterium. Do you really care about the presence of immature fuzz on a young fruitlet? I don't think so. A vigorous immune response with a dose of high Brix, on the other hand, changes this picture entirely in the holistic grower's favor. There. Another chemical myth staked with holly through its cheating heart.

What's true is that flavor is accentuated by a degree of water stress going into harvest. Conditions that are overly lush do not bring out the flavor profile of any fruit. Otherwise, you are certainly ready to grow some fine nectarines.

The Honey series of nectarines developed by Zaiger includes Honey Blaze, Honey Kist, Honey Royale, and the Honey Diva shown here. Photo courtesy of Dave Wilson Nursery.

Let us be thankful for that day when the downy covering of the Peach slipped her maternal memory and produced the Nectarine, one of the great triumphs of our Western civilization.
—Edward Bunyard, *Anatomy of Dessert* (1933)

Arctic Jay. Hot summers bring out the winning flavor of this white freestone nectarine. Good balance of sugar and acid, with firm flesh texture. Blooms late, but ripens midseason (from the middle of July in California to the middle of August in Pennsylvania). Five hundred chill hours. Skin speckles not uncommon. Tree hardy to –20°F (–29°C).

Fantasia. Large, egg-shaped freestone with very smooth skin. Bright red overlaid on brilliant yellow skin with yellow flesh. Exceptional flavor. Fairly small, vigorous tree. Susceptibility to brown rot, peach leaf curl, and to a lesser degree bacterial spot makes holistic support a must in humid zones. USDA introduction from California in 1969. Late-ripening. Zones 6–9.

Hardired. Classic nectarine coloration with yellow freestone flesh. Tree-ripened flavor is pure ambrosia. Tolerant of bacterial spot and brown rot. Cracking can be an issue when big rains precede the harvest. Bud hardiness makes this one more reliable in colder areas. Large, showy pink flowers. This Harrow Ontario selection is proven throughout Zones 5–8.

Honey Royale. This Zaiger introduction gets rave reviews. Very firm, large fruit. Yellow-fleshed freestone. Low acid, high sugar. Ripens late July into August. High susceptibility to bacterial spot, so drier sites preferred. Estimated chilling requirement of five to eight hundred hours. Northern growers might

Big, succulent, and juicy describes the SunGlo nectarine perfectly. Photo courtesy of Stark Brothers.

consider pot culture to get these promising buds through the winter and to better garner ripening heat.

Maria's Gold. Pure golden skin and flesh. Juicy, richly flavored, with a delicious balance of sweetness and acidity. Named after Russian horticulturist Maria Plekhanova and selected by Andy Mariani from seeds brought back from Uzbekistan. This Tashkent strain resembles the fabled Golden Peaches of Samarkand. Three hundred chilling hours. Best in Zones 8–10.

Mericrest. The hardiest nectarine. Smooth, dark red skin. Juicy, yellow freestone. Rich, tangy flavor. Blooms late. Resistant to brown rot and bacterial spot. Withstands temperatures of –20°F (–29°C). Developed by Elwyn Meader in New Hampshire. Eight hundred chill hours. Ripens in mid- to late August.

Redgold. Deep yellow peel covered with 50–70 percent glossy red. Large to very large freestone. Melting, juicy yellow flesh. Exceptional flavor. Highly crack-resistant. Not recommended for eastern areas where bacterial spot is severe. Longer shelf life than most

cultivars. Ripens middle of August. Eight hundred fifty chill hours. Zones 5–8.

Summer Beaut. Large to very large, glossy, almost all-red fruit. Firm, juicy, deep yellow, semi-freestone flesh with red around the pit. High quality. Vigorous, exceptionally productive tree grows 12–15 feet tall. Decent crack resistance. Medium susceptibility to bacterial spot and split pits. Attains good size if properly thinned. Ripens in August according to location. Eight hundred fifty chill hours. Zones 5–8.

SunGlo. Introduced in 1962 by Stark. Big, succulent, and juicy. Brilliant red over a yellow background. Hardy and vigorous tree. Long, curved leaves sometimes have purple-red hues. Ripens the week after Summer Beaut. Susceptible to bacterial spot. Zones 5–8.

Zephyr. Large fruit. White freestone flesh. Excellent flavor. Reddens inside around pit. Vigorous, productive tree shows moderate resistance to bacterial spot. Late-summer ripening checks this one into Zone 6 and warmer. From the Riviera Breeding Program in southern France.

Rootstock for nectarines

The story line for peach works entirely the same regarding rootstock selection for its fuzzless cousin. Lovell seedling seems preferred by far in the nursery trade. Still, the world of orcharding loves to offer up even more options. All these, of course, are apt for peach desires as well.

Tennessee Natural peach seedlings make a good summer budding companion for any nectarine cultivar. Uniform vigor. High yield efficiency. Fair tolerance for wet ground.

Atlas and Viking produce extremely vigorous trees. Both are peach × almond × flowering plum crosses from Zaiger's Genetics in California. Nematode resistance on par with Nemaguard. Productive; thought to increase fruit size. Atlas is intolerant of wet soil conditions, while Viking shows a modicum of tolerance.

Summer Beaut nectarine exhibits decent crack resistance in standing up to eastern conditions. Photo courtesy of Adams County Nursery.

Mature peach and nectarine trees require a substantial thinning out of excess one-year-old shoots and last year's bearing shoots.

Pruning tips for nectarines

Advice for pruning a nectarine tree is easy . . . follow the *peach plan* all the way!

- Flower buds are produced on current season's shoots.
- Thin weaker shoots in early summer to provide better light.
- Remove overcrowded laterals to provide better light.
- Remove vigorous, upright shoots growing in the center of the vase.
- Remove the previous year's spent wood.
- Remove mummified fruit from the orchard environs.
- Use heading cuts to keep tree structure contained and instill vigor.
- Reduce vigorous shoots on the framework by about a third each year.
- Young trees should be pruned after mature trees.

Nectarine pollination

All nectarines are self-fertile, so in one sense there's no need for pollinators. Still, when push comes to shove, seeing bees and other insects at work ensures that the pollen is getting spread around. The bloom period for a nectarine cultivar—when flowers are receptive and thus able to be pollinated—lasts for four to seven days, depending on the weather.

Nectarine flowers are slightly more susceptible to frost injury than peaches.[45] Spreading out the bloom among a few cultivars increases prospects for those who must have this yearly treat. Let's add one other trick to our bag for delaying fruit tree bloom: Painting trunks white in fall to lessen the chances of southwest injury also works to delay the awakening of buds in spring. This effect can be amplified with early applications of refined kaolin clay throughout the tree well before any sign of bud swell.[46] Double coverage ought to up the whiteness factor sufficiently . . . provided you find a reasonable day that early in the season to even be out with spray equipment.

Pot culture for fruit trees

Northern growers right on the cusp of nectarine nirvana—where temps invariably drop below 0°F (−18°C) on the tail of a warm spell—can take bud hardiness matters into their own hands. Simply put, an especially desirable nectarine cultivar on a dwarfing root planted in a pot can migrate. Such trees need to experience a cool winter in order to meet chilling requirements yet have a protected place where temperature extremes can be moderated. Even summertime disease pressure can be abated and the heat requirements for enhanced flavor met with a little additional ingenuity.

The notion of sheltered orcharding precedes modern trials in poly tunnels to bring about an early-season crop. Thomas Rivers, a nurseryman in Sawbridgeworth, England, first explored this method of growing fruits in an unpretentious work of a few sheets, which he called *The Orchard House*, published in 1852. Bud preservation methods shift somewhat with modern materials, but in a nutshell the plan as he outlined it is much the same today, more than 150 years later. Tender trees in large pots are left outside after harvest to harden off. The trees are moved at the approach of winter into a cellar or some sort of pit—this chilling-zone treatment

Pruning for compact tree structure is a given for a potted fruit tree. Fertility renewal comes by way of compost and nettle teas.

being essential for buds to break dormancy come spring, but also keeping the deepest cold at bay. Pots should be mounded in wood chips or straw to reduce cold getting to the rootball. The trees then enter springtime on cue, be it outside (set into the ground, still in the pot) or in a solar space such as an unheated poly tunnel or greenhouse that's open to the breeze. The benefits of overhead protection are twofold—avoiding both blossom frost and fungal disease spores. Moderated solar warmth in Zones 4 and 5 brings the flavor advantage of more temperate zones to stone fruits grown on the margins. Any growing tunnel dedicated to tree fruit should have its sides rolled up to keep things from getting ridiculously hot.

That horticultural plan comes with plenty of caveats, of course. Selecting dwarfing roots like Citation or Krymsk 1 goes hand in hand with bush mode pruning. Lots of targeted pinching (think espalier) goes into containing the tree above much like the roots are contained in the pot below. Self-fertile cultivars have a pollination edge in this setting. Compost tea, liquid seaweed, and tonic nettle tea keep things fertile, but not overly rich. Water stress facilitates hardening off. Chunks of burnt wood (think biochar) provide a fitting drainage medium at the bottom of the pot.

This passionate approach to growing elite flavor varieties a zone too far is not about bushels and bushels of fruit. Nor does it save you a dime. This is entirely about the smile on your face as you savor any of the Honey series of nectarines while gazing across your northern vista.[47] And only the truly wealthy can afford experiences like that!

Insect pests of nectarines

Knowing *who done it* and the timing involved defines the challenges on your particular orchard ground. Any of the recommended field guides will provide species specifics and photo identification to go with established *point-of-vulnerability* insights:

- All stays in the family, so be aware that the full array of **peach culprits** will indeed take note of nectarine trees. Apparently the fruit essence factor works against these smooth-skinned peach cousins; thus nectarines tend to be hit even harder by plum curculio right after bloom and assorted moth ruffians going into harvest.
- The only things that **Oriental fruit moth** likes better than peaches are nectarines and pluots. Growers in the Mid-Atlantic region and throughout the Southeast need to be especially vigilant. Damaged fruit in turn becomes the vector for the spread of brown rot—infections frequently start at the entrance and exit holes of first-generation OFM. *Concealed injury*

Are these brown marmorated stink bugs lined up for action or what? An integrated strategy involving trap crops and pure neem oil (applied to fruit trees early on as a feeding deterrent) will be needed to protect the nectarine harvest from these marauders. Photo courtesy of Tracy Leskey, USDA Appalachian Fruit Research Station.

occurs when the larvae enter the nectarine through the green stem rather than directly into the fruit alongside the stem (thereby leaving a small pile of brown frass). The short stem gets left behind when the fruit gets picked, and no one's the wiser why things went awry.

- **Stink bugs** begin feeding from the time that the fruit enters the shuck split stage up till harvest. These piercing-sucking feeders use their saliva to penetrate their food material, dissolve the contents, and then suck up the digesting mixture. The resulting feeding damage to nectarine and peach destroys part of the developing fruit. The damaged portion

of the fruit stops growing, resulting in healthy tissue riding up and over the underlying scar to produce a fruit injury typically resembling the cheeks of a cat. (You may need to be imaginative about this!) This type of injury tends to be several times greater in the upper part of the tree than on lower branches.

Organic solutions

Nectarines are more tolerant of Surround protection, as smooth-skinned fruit can be cleaned of a white clay coating more readily. That helps in counterbalancing the aroma draw of these peach cousins. Pure neem oil in the holistic applications makes life a tad dizzier for curculio while strongly addressing moth inclinations. The successful nectarine grower will find trap tree selection paramount in making organic approaches work.

A number of factors affect Oriental fruit moth abundance. Cooler temperatures during bloom (below 60°F, or 16°C) suppress egg production. Wet weather following a dry spell kills many of the shoot-embedded larvae, which drown in the flow of renewed sap. Severe winters may kill up to 90 percent of overwintering cocoons above the snow line. Creating overwintering pantries for *Macrocentrus ancylivorus* and other braconid wasps helps in the long run. A sunflower patch ostensibly left to feed the birds or a nearby strawberry bed has direct OFM relevance.[48]

Home orchardists hit especially hard by multiple generations of this fruit moth might consider bagging individual fruits after thinning. Early-damaged nectarines can be taken away and destroyed—notch one up for OFM population control—while good-looking fruits can be protected from what comes next. Thin to single fruits that show no signs of sting (entry) damage and brown rot will be abated as well.

Migrating stink bugs can be captured in yellow pyramid traps before these cumbersome pests discover the fruit tree (see "Pest options" in chapter 4, on page 123). Other ecosystem interactions will be more useful when population pressures get totally out of hand. Small plots of soybeans planted outside the orchard can be an effective detour, especially if you have a handle on where localized species have overwintered. Let's take this one step farther for the brown marmorated stink bug that seeks out houses and other outbuildings in the fall, congregating beneath siding by the hundreds. Its spring migration out to the plant world includes many crops—with the pumpkin patch always a surefire draw. That's the right trap crop for later-ripening pome fruits, but it's the summer squash family that must serve as sacrificial bait for earlier-ripening stone fruits like nectarines. Plant zucchini and pattypan squash as early as possible in the vicinity of the trees. Stink bugs will congregate on the developing squash, at which point the grower has two distinct options: Use a flame weeder to "nuke the zuke" as bug numbers peak, going out each evening over the course of those few weeks when stone fruit are coming of size. Or take the spray approach, utilizing hard-hitting PyGanic along with a hypodermic needle (of sorts) to ensure delivery of the botanical toxin. Diatomaceous earth brings a sharp particle edge to the pyrethrum application, thereby upping the efficacy on less soft-bodied pests like stink bug.[49] Count on neem oil applications as nectarines begin to size (and then renewed at least weekly) to make affairs less palatable overall.

Disease concerns of nectarines

Holistic orchardists indeed have a plan to deal with disease. We'll add some twists and requisite timing notes here to our general understanding of how tree health keeps fungal and bacterial pathogens in check.

- **American brown rot**. The nectarine can possess an affinity for brown rot fungi catching hold. Primary infection for rot starts at bloom time; therefore, don't underestimate the importance of providing these trees with holistic fortitude from the get-go. Brown rot persists in shoots, so getting through the bloom period does not mean health-supporting actions come to an end. Adding molasses in the holistic spray mix will help adhere competitive colonization to the developing fruit.[50] To repeat: *Nectarines are even more susceptible to brown rot than peaches.*

- Other story lines remain much the same. **Peach scab**, **leaf curl**, and **bacterial spot** are unwavering. Are you?

- **Powdery mildew**. Rusty spot, oh rusty spot, home sweet home to me . . . but wait a minute, that's *Rocky Top* down in good ol' Tennessee.[51] We're talking disease here, and this minor affliction of nectarine and peach in the Southeast is the result of a fungal cloud afflicting young

The most significant source of brown rot inoculum in the orchard is mummified fruitlets holding fast to the tree. All should be removed at the start of each new growing season. Photo courtesy of Tom Burr, NRAES.

fruit but then sloughing away to leave a discolored spot on the fruit. This one's easy: Neem followed by neem takes care of aesthetic fungi with ease.

- **Bacterial canker.** This can spread like fire blight from one stone fruit tree to the next via leafhoppers, weeds, rain, and even wind. Risk is as tangible on nectarine and peach in the humid Southeast as it is on the West Coast with any stone fruit. Slow-healing wounds to the bark are especially subject to pathogenic colonization. Pruning in late summer/early fall helps keep bacterial canker at bay in places where bone-dry weather can be counted upon for the four to six weeks that follow. Biological reinforcement will help counter *Pseudomonas* in areas that lack this opportunity. Make competitive colonization applications at leaf fall and again in spring just as buds swell.

- **Split pit.** Sometimes the pit within a nectarine or peach may split in half before harvest. This disorder is most serious for early-ripening varieties and for trees with light crops and very large fruit. Fibers from the flesh are attached to the developing pit. Right after the pit begins to harden (about fifty to sixty days after bloom) is when the fruit itself (relative to the pit) starts sizing rapidly. If the pit is not fully developed before this occurs, the force may pull the pit apart. Avoid irrigating around this time to lessen the damage in susceptible cultivars. Fruit with split pits are usually obvious before harvest because the diameter of the fruit across the suture appears stretched.

Harvest notes

Full flavor comes just as the nectarine yields to the slightest squeeze. That firm crop bound for the supermarket picked a week too soon may bruise less readily, but it also tastes less readily. Keep your picking mantra simple: Slow and easy does it. The slightest bump will result in a bruise, which can very quickly degrade and rot. Tree-ripened fruits will keep in premium condition for three to five days after picking. Refrigeration extends this to two weeks, though the fruit will be far from its best after serving time in the tundra.

APRICOTS

The very first apricots were developed in China thousands of years ago. Global traders brought this stone fruit to Roman hands in what we moderns would call the first century AD. Shakespeare celebrated the aphrodisiacal powers of an apricot potion in *A Midsummer Night's Dream*. Settlers in turn watched young apricot trees bloom in Virginia by the early 1700s. Some years saw a bumper crop; other years an absolute bust due to normal spring cold . . . and on that score little has changed since then.

The first tender blossoms every spring appear on apricot trees. Zone hardiness has improved since colonial times (due to the introduction of Russian crosses[52]), but it's that palpable risk of frost that remains paramount. Early demise from *wet feet* reflects apricot's other strict demand—vulnerability to heavy soil and excessive rain (where trees literally drown that same week) can be accommodated by utilizing planting mounds and ideal siting.

The plus side of apricot culture certainly makes a thoughtful attempt worth pursuing. Apricots surely have more flavors packed into each fleshy orb than any other fruit. Dried apricots shipped from a California connoisseur orchard make quite the gift, but it's a tree-ripened apricot fresh off your own tree that leads to transcendence. *Prunus armeniaca* species do not need as much early-summer heat to properly ripen as do peaches. Apricots (for the most part) are self-fertile, which helps considerably on cooler spring days when smaller pollinators do not roam far.[53] The apricot makes a good urban tree, where the heat island effect often proves the difference in warding off a blossom-killing frost.

Apricot varieties to consider

The Turkish idiom *bundan iyisi Şam'da kayisi* describes when something is the very best it can be . . . like a delicious apricot from Damascus.

Choosing the right apricot must reckon with regional considerations, perhaps more than any other tree fruit.[54] Cultivars that do well in one part of North America can be difficult to grow within the very same growing zone elsewhere. Earliness of bloom and how buds fare with respect to winter temperature fluctuations are big factors. Erratic spring weather makes crop certainty almost impossible except on the most ideal slopes in drier locations. Humidity plays a hand wherever fungal and bacterial disease lurk. Chill requirements determine southern limits. The truly cold-hardy varieties seem to size well only in colder climates. Ripening for full flavor works best where moderate heat and semi-arid conditions in the summer are the norm. Commercial apricot production in Iran, Pakistan, and Turkey suggests exactly what apricots have in mind.

Dormancy issues undermine so-called bud hardiness, regardless of latitude. This takes more new fruit growers aback than I can recount. Apricot shows this to a strong degree, which—when you think of its origins in the central steppes of Asia, where winters are uniformly cold—shouldn't really surprise anyone. Winters in North America are anything but consistent! The pistils in the apricot flower bud can be winter-killed by erratic weather patterns anytime in December, January, and even February. Deep cold on the tail of a warming spell has undeniable effect on what would otherwise seem to be a tucked-away situation.[55] Bud hardiness is exactly the kind of thing that fruit explorers look for in breeding improved varieties.

The right apricot varieties for each bioregion key to disease challenges, winter hardiness factors, and bloom timing in spring.

Apricot flowers with dead pistils will still open . . . but lack of pollination will not be the issue at hand when no fruit appears that season.

Adaptability of a particular cultivar begins with understanding exactly what regional curveballs you are facing. California undoubtedly offers the widest selection of varieties because much of California is an apricot place, not unlike Turkey. The maritime climate of the Pacific Northwest delivers wet winters and lengthy springs—thus, disease resistance and hardy bloom are required. The prairie provinces of Canada and the Upper Midwest experience subzero cold that sucks the marrow out of trees—winter hardiness and late bloom, please. The Great Lakes region

verges into the Mid-Atlantic, where fluctuating winter temperatures invariably claim buds, if not open flowers. New England and the Canadian Maritimes have moderately cold winters, followed by wet springs that carry into summer—hardiness and disease resistance, don't you know. Farther south and across the Lower Midwest it's about late bloom, disease resistance, and proper chilling. The Mountain West finds apricots back on more friendly turf, provided you protect the bloom. Look for clues in the varietal descriptions that follow and don't be afraid to push the envelope when a nearby orchardist knows more than I do.[56]

One last consideration here for grafters. Obtaining virus-free budwood is the only way to be sure an

Harogem apricots offer it all: rich flavor, fragrant pink flowers, proven cold-hardiness, and disease resistantance across the board. Photo courtesy of Adams County Nursery.

exciting new cultivar has a chance at your place. Ask your source about the history of the mother tree. Good nurseries do the very same when propagating trees for sale.[57] *Prunus* viruses not only shorten tree life and cropping potential but can also severely lessen grafting success.

Alfred. Small to medium, bright orange fruit, often with a pink blush. Fine-grained and juicy orange flesh. Late bloom along with a measure of resistance to subsequent frost injury. Wide adaptability makes this a good choice in the Mid-Atlantic through the Gulf Coast states and on to the heartland. Requires aggressive thinning to get good fruit size. Developed at the New York AES in Geneva, 1965. The right choice for Zone 4 and 5.

Blenheim. Large, pale orange fruit with red dots. Sweet, aromatic flavor sets the standard for all fresh apricots. Favorite in California for canning and drying as well. Quality issues with too much heat. Early bloom. Four hundred to 750 chill hours. British origin, going back to 1830.

Chinese Sweet Pit. Also known as the Mormon apricot. Medium-sized, golden orange fruit. Semi-clingstone flesh. Good flavor and texture. Called a sweet pit, because the kernel can be eaten like an almond. Late-blooming with frost-resistant buds, and a good pollinizer for later-blooming apricot cultivars. Precocious and very productive tree. Susceptibility to shothole fungus and brown rot points to a semi-arid location. Seven hundred chill hours. The warm side of Zone 4 through Zone 8.

Sweet, sweet Katy glows with promise in orchards that can count on a warm winter. Photo courtesy of Dave Wilson Nursery.

Debbie's Gold. A prairie-hardy cultivar developed in Saskatchewan. Medium to large, golden yellow fruit. Sweeter than its fellow hybrid Westcot, and blooms a day later. A proven annual producer "most years" in north-central regions, but not a good choice for the Northeast due to dormancy issues.[58] Ripens in mid-August. Tree hardy to −35°F (−37°C).

Harrow Series. A number of hardy apricots were released during the late 1970s and early 1980s by the Harrow Research Station in Ontario. (Big clue: Each name usually starts with the letters *Har*.) All feature late bloom and noteworthy disease resistance. A fair ability to handle fluctuating winter temperatures makes these viable candidates in the Great Lakes and Mid-Atlantic regions. Cross-pollination among siblings comes highly recommended the farther

north you go. Most of these (other than Harcot) are hardy into Zone 4.

- **Harglow**. Late-blooming cultivar with a few extra degrees of bud hardiness. Firm, sweet, flavorful fruit has a deep orange color with a red blush. Growers on the maritime side of the Cascades in the Northwest like this one as well. Widely adaptable. Resistance to brown rot and bacterial spot. Resists cracking. Ripens later than most. Eight hundred chill hours.

- **Harlayne**. Medium-sized orange fruit with a moderate red blush. Firm, orange, freestone flesh. Great for fresh eating or processing. Moderately resistant to perennial canker, brown rot, and bacterial spot. Ripens in late August. Most winter-hardy of the series, to

The home-court advantage of Puget Gold in the Pacific Northwest comes from its tolerance of wet climates. This apricot variety does equally well in the humid Northeast. Photo courtesy of Trees of Antiquity.

about –30°F (–34°C) on flower buds. Harogem and Hargrand are both effective pollinizers of Harlayne, which is not self-fruitful.

- **Harogem**. Medium-sized fruit, bright red glossy blush over orange background. Ideally suited for the fresh market. Orange, firm flesh, with rich flavor. Fragrant pink flowers. Trees are upright, productive, and very cold-hardy. Resistant to brown rot and perennial canker; somewhat resistant to bacterial spot. Skin cracking is rare.

Jerseycot. Bringing the Zard apricot from Persia into the Rutgers breeding program led to this late-1970s release. Successful fruiting has been recorded 90 percent of the time since then. Self-fruitful; blooms as much as one week later than most apricots, and can survive late frosts. Round-oblong fruit, light orange in color with a slight green suture. Melon-like flavor. Fruits ripen early, drop fast, and soften somewhat quickly. Resistant to brown rot, bacterial spot, perennial canker, and bacterial canker . . . wowser! Try it on the East Coast and farther south into Appalachia, over in the Pacific Northwest, and back across to the Great Lakes region. Winters that dip below –30°F (–34°C) will prove too much. Hardy into Zone 4.

Katy. Large, firm, freestone with a pleasing, sweet, sub-acid flavor. Delightful bright orange skin. A favorite for warm-winter climates, with an estimated chilling requirement of two to three hundred hours. Ripens around June 1 in California's Central Valley. Late bloomer in areas without early warm spells.

Precious. Exceptional ability to crop its way through a frosty spring. Later-blooming, disease-resistant, self-fruitful, and very tolerant of late frosts. Fruit size small to medium, yellow-orange skin and flesh, edible kernel, flesh soft and sweet, ripens fairly late in apricot season. Tree has a very symmetrical, upright to spreading growth habit. Discovered just south of Georgian Bay in Ontario; assumed to be a seedling of Russian apricots distributed by the Fruit Growers' Association around 1900. Growers in the humid Northeast should keep their eyes on this one. Hardy throughout Zone 3 in humid climates, and the warmer part of Zone 3 in dry climates.

Puget Gold. Chance seedling introduced in 1987 by Washington State University. Large, elongated, clear yellow, red-blushed fruit. Dense, sweet, deep orange freestone flesh with excellent flavor. Prolific. Natural semi-dwarf tree can be maintained at 15-foot height and spacing. Tolerant of wet climates, and thus its home-court advantage in the Pacific Northwest. Proven in the humid Northeast as well, with disease resistance above average. Blooms late and sizes fruit in cool, frosty spring weather. Self-fertile. Ripens in August. Zones 4–9.

Robada. Outstanding apricot from the University of California praised by all who eat it, even people who dislike most apricots. Sweet pit type. A grower's dream—good size, fantastic flavor that transcends normal tangy-sweet expectations, distinctive magenta wash over an orange base color, and highly resistant to bruising. Falls short, however, on handling disease pressure in humid locations. Fully winter-hardy throughout Zone 5.

Royal Rosa. Extremely vigorous and more disease-tolerant than other West Coast apricots. Bears young and heavily. Sweet, low-acid, fine-flavored fruit ripens very early, in late May. Six hundred chill hours. Since life is already too good, pollinize with Flavorella plumcot.

Sugar Pearls. A very promising New Jersey release. Spreading, stocky tree handles fluctuating winter temperatures well. Medium-sized fruit with full-bodied, golden-honey flavor. Exquisite, smooth texture. Lackluster color (yellowish green) for an apricot. Blooms later than most, ensuring more reliable harvests for those in Zones 4–7. Not self-fruitful; use Harlayne, Jerseycot, or another later-blooming cultivar as a pollinizer. Broad-spectrum disease resistance.

Tomcot. One of the higher-ups in the blossom-hardiness department. Lusciously huge, orange orbs with firm orange flesh. Blooms for a full two weeks—so if early flowers are bitten by frost, there's still hope. Colors up early, so wait to pick. Cross-pollination needed. Developed by Washington State University fruit breeder Tom Toyama. Does well in much of the nation except for wet coastal regions. Five hundred chill hours. Zone 5 and warmer.

Westcot. The hardiest of the prairie hybrids.[59] Showy pink flowers in mid-April. Large fruit with yellow to orange skin with a light reddish blush. Firm enough to can. Mature trees produce as much as 200 pounds of fruit. Large pit relative to edible flesh. A prime candidate for growers in Wisconsin and westward. Flower buds hardy throughout Zone 4.

Rootstock for apricots

Apricots will typically be grafted onto apricot seedlings in the North and onto peach seedlings in the South. Stone fruits readily self-seed, often producing a fruit similar to its mother parent. Plum seedlings are used as rootstock to induce a notch of winter hardiness in middle growing zones—just be prepared to stake these. Sandy, well-drained soils are fundamental to success with apricots, whatever the root chosen.

Manchurian is the nursery standard for northern apricots. This seedling strain of wild apricot (*Prunus mandshurica*) produces trees that are relatively hardy. First fruit commences after four or five years on this root. Full-grown trees can reach 20–30 feet tall after many years, if bacterial canker or something else doesn't wreak havoc long before. Produces usable fruit even if never grafted. The root itself is hardy into Zone 2.

Citation, a peach × plum hybrid whose patent has now expired, has become the favored rootstock in California orchards for pluot trees as well as for apricots. Zaiger's first interspecific rootstock holds apricots to 12–18 feet in height. Very tolerant of wet soil but not drought-tolerant (induces early dormancy in dry soil), so needs regular watering in hot climates. Resists root-knot nematodes. Induces heavy bearing at a young age. Strong and well anchored.

Marianna 26-24 makes a comparatively small tree, about 15–20 feet in height. Shallow, spreading root system earns kudos for being more tolerant of wet soils—but accordingly will not tolerate hot soils. Like many plum-derived roots, forms suckers on a prolific basis. Resistant to oak root fungus, root-knot nematodes, and root rot. Influences growth too long into the fall, thus delaying leaf senescence. Introduced by the University of California in 1926. Hardy to Zone 5.

Varietal plum rootstocks like **Brompton** and **St. Julien** are reasonably winter-hardy, especially if given a reliable and heavy snow cover. The usual plum rootstock used in commercial orchards for apricot is **Myrobalan 29C**, principally because it crops better in droughty summers than the others. Certain apricot cultivars have compatibility issues with these plum options and will require an inter-stem to proceed.

Pruning tips for apricots

Apricots are fairly easy to train and prune. A mature apricot tree is typically larger than a plum tree, but also far more spreading, like a peach. This fast-growing tree requires the usual establishment of good branch structure in its early years. All pruning beyond that is to generate adequate new fruiting spurs by removing older ones that no longer produce.

Creating a vase-shaped tree with three or four main limbs dividing into two secondary limbs is the place to start with a young apricot tree. Its spreading habit tends to produce plenty of lateral shoots with little need for heading cuts to induce this response.

Removing flatter-angled branches and leaving the more upright laterals maintains desirable onward-and-outward energy. Flowers are produced on one-year-old wood and, as the tree matures, on spurs that arise from two-year and older wood. Apricot spurs are not long-lived but will bear for three or four years.

Crowded branches that block light into the center of the tree are continually removed. This can be done in late summer right after harvest as well as in late February to March. Late dormant pruning (right around bloom) allows pruning wounds to heal faster than cuts made earlier in the winter, thus providing less time for fungal disease organisms to infect the wound. Spores of *Eutypa* dieback can cause severe gumming and branch loss otherwise. Bacterial canker is best avoided by choosing the drier season at your site to make all cuts. Utilizing both pruning windows has merit, if you can, as those thinning cuts in summer allow more sunlight into the fruiting canopy, whereas larger branch removal in spring generates more lateral response.

Bending upright shoots closer to horizontal (not completely, but not too far off) helps slow rampant growth on more vigorous trees. This should be done in early summer, with new shoots directed into the light space of a fruiting limb that's at the tail end of its productive life. This preemptive training is preferable to heading branches and waiting for new lateral branches to form.[60]

Apricot pollination

Full sun throughout the day makes this fruit, and with that caveat come a couple of slope recommendations to better ensure pollination prospects. A north-facing slope can be best because apricot flower buds will be held back ever so slightly in spring. The sun is not as high in the sky in February and March (as it will become midsummer), which in turn means degree-day warmth accumulates at a slower pace on the far side of the solstice. Similarly, an east-facing site not far from a wall or the house itself proves better than a west-facing site, as frosty mornings buffer early warmth,

Apricot buds cut vertically to expose the pistil for freeze damage evaluation. Note the blackened pistil on the right, killed by the prior night's freeze. Photo by H. J. Larsen, courtesy of Colorado State University Extension.

Pollinated fruitlets emerging from their papery shucks mean all is well in the world for apricot lovers. Photo courtesy of Mark Longstroth, Michigan State University Extension.

whereas by day's end dark branch structures facing the setting sun will absorb considerably more solar energy. Good apricot pollination begins with viable bloom getting through totally expected frost situations.[61] Temperatures of 27°F (–3°C) and below do in open apricot blooms. The length of time required to kill blooms at this degree of cold can be as little as an hour. Those few buds that have not opened or are somewhat more protected within the canopy can survive and prove fruitful if temps stay above 21°F (–6°C), the absolute kill point for *Prunus armeniaca* bloom.[62] The later-blooming the variety, the better your odds.[63] Nor are apricot aficionados out of the woods yet: After shuck split, when spent flower parts fall off the just-developing fruitlets, the tolerance point for cold rises to 28°F (–2°C). Sad to say, post-bloom frosts can steal home base as well.

Let's look at a viable apricot flower when the weather actually cooperates. Those relatively few insects out on a warmish spring day play a pivotal role. Apricot flowers are mostly white, like plum, but are not borne in clusters. Instead, these blooms are found either singly or in pairs at a node along very short stems. About thirty stamens (the pollen part) accompany a single pistil (leading to the seed ovary). Wind is not necessarily effective at lifting the slightly tacky pollen grains off the filament. A pollinator working self-fertile apricot trees needs to do one of two things. Honeybees carry pollen on their rear legs to other flowers—thus cross-pollination among apricot varieties will increase fruit set, often considerably—but this doesn't happen if the day's high temperature doesn't crest into the 50s (10–15°C). Ground-nesting solitary bees are the true troupers for apricots in early spring. Flies and ladybugs (lady beetles) provide another approach to pollination by bludgeoning pollen loose while stomping about the blossom to feed.[64] Dry weather during bloom helps considerably, because rain otherwise dampens pollen transfer and keeps the insect realm at bay.

Moderate thinning in a boom year should be done with a smile on your face: An overwhelming apricot crop could so easily have been missing in action instead! Stick thrashing works well to knock down

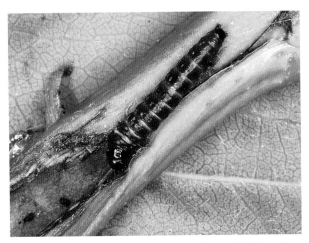

Round one of peach twig borer strikes at shoots on the tail end of bloom. Photo courtesy of Elizabeth Beers, Washington State University.

Round two of peach twig borer partakes of the fruit itself going into harvest. Photo courtesy of Elizabeth Beers, Washington State University.

green fruitlets once you've gauged what it takes to knock off approximately half or more of the set. Leave individual fruits every 3–4 inches (on average) along the branch if you're thinning more carefully by hand.

Insect pests of apricots

Knowing *who done it* and the timing involved defines the challenges on your particular orchard ground. Any of the recommended field guides will provide species specifics and photo identification to go with established *point-of-vulnerability* insights:

- Ad nauseam, ad nauseam. Both **plum curculio** and **Oriental fruit moth** get dibs on apricots, with an intensity based on emergence timing and the choice of other succulent prospects.
- Apricot trees succumb to **peachtree borer** as well. The grubs overwinter in burrows at the base of the host tree. The larvae vary greatly in size, depending on when the egg was laid the previous summer. Some are more than ½ inch in length, while others are very small, not more than ⅛ inch long. The larvae pupate in place, just beneath the bark, and begin to emerge as adults by late June. Adult emergence and egg laying will continue through September, peaking during August.

- **Peach twig borer** will tunnel into apricot shoot tips at bloom, causing them to flag, and then onto nearly ripe fruit. These "worms" feeding on the top surface of apricot fruits are not the same as moth larvae that burrow within.
- **Earwigs** are not necessarily innocent when it comes to stone fruit. (Pears were a different story, as these insects do indeed prey upon pear psylla.) The softer flesh of the apricot is especially primo for gorging. Earwigs exploit fruit cracking in a big way and then move on to whole fruits nearby.

Organic solutions

A multitude of borers at the base of the apricot trunk spells disaster. Botanical trunk sprays of pure neem oil applied every two to three weeks starting in late June will serve to both repel the ovipositing female moth and break the molting cycle of any larvae that do hatch. Preemption is far preferable to seeing frass piling up at the soil line. Should things reach that point, a nematode mudpack can be employed to restore cambium sanctity to the tree.

Apricots subject to regular twig borer pressure are best treated year after year with Bt. These biological applications at pink and petal fall can be considered essential on the checklist of orchard tasks for most western growers.

Earwigs can be trapped early on with crumpled newspaper tucked into branch crotches. These insects prefer to hide by day and then seek out soft fruits to feed upon at night. Make it a morning ritual to replace and destroy the wadded newspaper when earwig presence becomes insurmountable. PyGanic can be sprayed at dusk if things really, really seem to be getting out of hand on certain trees in certain years.

Disease concerns of apricots

Holistic orchardists indeed have a plan to deal with disease. We'll add some twists and requisite timing notes here to our general understanding of how tree health keeps fungal and bacterial pathogens in check.

- The beat goes on with *Prunus* afflictions. **American brown rot** shows up early on bloom on apricot and can become quite dismaying by the time the fruit ripens. The velvety fungal touch of **peach scab** has its own affinity for the velvety skin of apricots. The need to establish competitive colonization on both ends of the dormant season to deter **bacterial spot** is well established.

- **Bacterial canker.** Call it blossom blast on the West Coast or bacterial gummosis else-where—the different guises attributed to *Pseudomonas* bacteria affect stone fruits chiefly in the canker phase.[65] Outbreaks are often associated with prolonged periods of cold, wet weather in spring and severe storms that injure the emerging blossom and leaf tissues. An early-blooming trait makes apricot twigs and limbs all the more susceptible to canker establishment. Ever-evolving bacteria develop a resistance to copper over the years—suggesting that *going holistic* is better than *going ballistic*.

- **Shothole disease.** Ready to apply the inverse factor to your understanding of fruit tree

disease? This particular fungus afflicts apricot, peach, and nectarine and only rarely cherry and plum. The centers of the small scabby lesions that develop on young leaf tissue enlarge to about ¼ inch and then fall out. Apricots can show fruit spotting as well. You can't cure this fungus during the growing season as much as prevent initial infection of twigs and buds during the dormant season with either a fall copper application or biological reinforcement. Keep in mind that the subsequently infected leaf doesn't drop, leaving a good 90 percent of photosynthesis still operational.

- *Eutypa* **dieback.** This branch-killing disease of apricot on the West Coast initiates on wounds made during wet weather in the fall and winter, causing severe gumming at pruning cuts. Leaves wilt and die early on affected limbs and then remain on the tree for the dormant season. Symptoms become apparent one to two years after infection, often eventually killing the tree. Restrict pruning to July and August so at least six weeks of rain-free weather follows pruning. Existing lesions must be pruned out at least 8 inches below the gummosis. Make sure to prevent sunburn by leaving enough foliage to cover remaining limbs during this summer haircut. Late dormant pruning just before bloom provides a second, relatively safe opportunity to further thin out crowded branches when leaves no longer block the view of overall tree structure.

- **Cracking.** Fruit cracking can be attributed to fluctuations in moisture (as with cherry) but can also be traced to a copper deficiency. Copper gives stretchiness to both tree bark and fruit skin. Let's take this one step deeper than the usual reductionist conclusions. Quite a number of nutrients move up in the plant attached to phosphate. When phosphate is deficient, other minerals such as

A DELECTABLE CROSS

Think about everything you like in the smooth-skinned plum. Now think about the taste explosion offered by a tree-ripened apricot. Put those together to create the perfect fruit and you have the remarkably sweet pluot.

Luther Burbank was the first to cross plums and apricots late in the nineteenth century. His goal was to produce an apricot-like fruit that would bear consistently in wet coastal zones where early-blooming apricots often fail to set fruit. The plum influence pushes back the flowering date just enough where spring tends to be less erratic. Another grower named Floyd Zaiger of Modesto, California, ran with this idea to create the more than one dozen hybrids popular today.

Officially, pluots have more plum parentage than apricot—this by way of backcrossing with plum again. These fruits require another pluot or an Asian plum as a pollinizer. A pronounced susceptibility to bacterial spot results from this plum lineage. Growers back east enticed by pluot promise deal with brown rot woes as well. The results are well worth extra holistic care provided that pollination is not problematic at your site, as the so-called plum advantage isn't all that much where cold nights beckon consistently in early spring. Pluots are a worthy gamble in Zone 5 despite this—noting that the odds improve considerably in warmer regions of the zone chart.

Three things jump out when you bite into a tree-ripened pluot: the juice dribbling down your chin, the lack of bitterness to the skin, and the substantially higher sugar content than that of a plum or an apricot alone. I experienced pluot nirvana for the first time in David Ulmer's California front-yard orchard in early August. Glowing red-orange fruits beckoned . . . and I was quickly won over by **Geo Pride** and its enticing sweetness.

Other pluot varieties certainly tantalize as well. Tiny **Splash** with its voluptuously sweet orange flesh sets the orchard aglow with ripe fruit by mid-July. **Raspberry Jewel** has dark red skin with brilliant red honey-sweet flesh backed with just the slight touch of acidity. **Flavor King** provides a larger pluot with a sensational bouquet of sweet, spicy flavor beneath a reddish purple skin. The best apricot aftertaste can be found in the yellow skin and flesh of **Flavor Queen**. And then there's **Dapple Dandy**, a uniquely colored pluot with pale green to yellow skin with distinctive red dots. Its creamy white flesh, streaked with crimson no less, often rates at the top in pluot tastings put together by the Dave Wilson Nursery in California. This one also serves as a proven pollinizer for the rest of the gang.

Dapple Dandy pluot. Photo courtesy of Dave Wilson Nursery.

copper cannot reach the intended location in the plant. Balanced stone fruit fertility enters into this picture.

Harvest notes

Apricots ripen in late June to July, on the order of 100–120 days from full bloom. A long dry spell during this time can necessitate irrigating to size up the crop. Watering deeply and infrequently is preferable for stone fruit trees, especially apricot, as susceptibility to root rot and iron chlorosis goes up in constantly saturated ground.

Extreme hot weather often causes the fruit to *pit burn*—soften and turn brown around the pit—which lowers the quality of an otherwise good-looking crop. Shading might help if this gets your goat year after year.

Squirrels can become a full-time nemesis just as apricots begin to turn that luscious deep orange hue. These tree rodents eat a hole in the side of each fruit to extract the pit, leaving the remains of the fruit to wither in the sunshine. Be forthright in defending your crop, knowing what it took to get this far. Sweet pit varieties like Harcot generally fare the worst in this respect.

A tree-ripe apricot is many times better than anything picked even slightly green. Ripe apricots bruise more readily than peaches, so take your time and be gentle. Think of your hands as cupping tools rolling an individual fruit off its spur rather than as five-fingered grabbers.

PLUMS

The common plum of Europe (*Prunus domestica*) has been cultivated for centuries. Damson plums (*P. institia*) from the Caspian Sea region are somewhat hardier but vary greatly in their need for chilling. The so-called Japanese plum (*P. salicina*) is a native of China.[66] This Asian plum—name shift noted—is generally less hardy than the European plum. The

native plums of North America (*P. americana*) are the hardiest of the lot, but few have been selected as named cultivars. Crosses made between Asian and American plums resulted in selections better able to bring a dependable bloom through winter. These hardier hybrids introduced challenging dynamics on the pollination front, however, which growers have only recently begun to grasp. Keeping those various genetics straight gets complicated by an additional thirty or so species of plums that have been identified and occasionally bred into the mix. No other group of stone fruits knows such diversity!

The fruits range in color from burgundy to yellow to orange to deep purple-blue. Plum skin is always smooth, with a polished shine waiting to be revealed beneath a waxy bloom. Fruit size ranges from that of a tiny sour cherry to a modest-sized nectarine. The contrasting tartness of the skin highlights the sweetness of the flesh. Plums can be eaten fresh or dried (when we call them prunes), made into jam, baked in coffee cakes and tarts, fermented into plum wine, and even distilled to make plum brandy.

Plum varieties to consider

Plums are widely adaptable. Most Asian plums prefer warmer places with drier summers—disease challenges in the more humid East having upset this particular plum cart more often than not. The influence of a prairie upbringing gives American plums both the northern and heartland nod. European plums are less likely to be damaged by spring frosts, as these trees bloom a good week later than Asian plums most seasons. Regardless, dormancy issues for plums are not as severe as with apricots. European plums can take a heavier soil, whereas Asian and native hybrids will tolerate a lighter, shallower soil.

Plans are afoot for the insect pests and diseases that come in plum territory. Like the other stone fruits, slightly earlier timing of holistic spray applications helps in establishing resistance mechanisms. The woes of bacterial spot and canker, brown rot, and black knot can best be checkmated by healthy

The honeyed flavor of gage-type plums like Bavay (shown here) makes things right in this ol' world. Photo courtesy of Dave Wilson Nursery.

vitality across the board. One unfortunate preconception related to this is that the smaller stone fruits don't need to be thinned. This might be true of a light fruit set, which indeed happens when pollination conditions in early spring run on the cool side. A well-laden branch will likely break, however, so be forewarned: A prop for that branch sooner rather than later may be vital.[67] More to the point, it's *touching fruits* that best suit persistent moths and fungal rots. These fine fruits deserve the advantage of good air circulation. Thinning indeed matters for plums.

The pluses and minuses of each variety are highlighted in the descriptions that follow. Keep in mind when selecting plum trees that generalizations cannot be relied on absolutely. Extensive hybridization among the *Prunus* species always makes for exceptions. Read between the lines and you're sure to find a few that fit the bill.

European plums

One of the rarest fruit experiences is a tree-ripened Euro plum. Seriously. What's picked slightly green and hard in the commercial trade is little better than a winter tomato. You get to experience plum finery only by growing these Old World varieties for yourself.

The domesticated plum is distinctively rich, sweet, and aromatic. Descriptive words in the varietal name take this farther—*prune*, *gage*, and *mirabelle* being

Imperial Epineuse plums are used at the English National Fruit Trials as a standard to judge prune flavor. Photo courtesy of Raintree Nursery.

The jewel-like fruits of Mirabelle de Nancy catch the eye at farmers' markets. Photo courtesy of Raintree Nursery.

traditional groupings with particular traits. Prune plums, for instance, are dark blue, elongated freestone fruit with a heartiness that pleases those who prefer a less juicy reception in eating a fresh plum. A far less tart skin accentuates the sweetness. Inside, the flesh is yellowish to greenish yellow, turning red when baked. Prune plums can be dried to perfection owing to their relatively high sugar and low water content. Everyone got in on the act apparently, as Italian Prune, German Prune, Hungarian Prune, and the always reliable French Prune continue to be revered far and wide.

A number of European plums are self-fruitful, but even these will set a better crop if another Euro variety is planted nearby. Most fruit are borne on long-lived spurs that grow 4–6 inches in length—this determines a slightly different pruning tack. Growers in Zones 5–9 have the proven environs for these plums.

Coe's Golden Drop. Legendary, oblong golden plum. Seedling planted in 1809 at Bury St. Edmunds, England. Medium to large fruits have straw-yellow skin and golden flesh. Incredibly sweet and juicy flesh featuring flavor pockets with an intense apricot burst. Freestone fruit ripens in late summer.

French Petite. The Prune d'Agen of great renown in its home country. Very old prune plum variety propagated for its especially fine flavor. Small to medium, long, oval fruit, tapered toward the stem. Violet-purple skin. One of the best for dessert baking. Self-fertile. Ripens during September.

Golden Transparent Gage. The best late-season gage plum. Large yellow fruit dotted with red. Rich, aromatic, sweet yellow flesh. Exquisite fresh eating. Genetic semi-dwarf tree. The fruit ripens in late September. Reportedly self-fertile. Hardy to Zone 4.

Green Gage. One of the grand old "English" varieties . . . having actually originated in France as the equally famous Reine Claude. An American favorite since the time of Jefferson. Not overly attractive, as fruits are dull green, often with surface freckles, and fairly small. Its honeyed flavor, however, makes this plum special. Small, low-branched tree with deep green foliage. Susceptible to brown rot. Skin splits if it rains near harvest. Four hundred to eight hundred chill hours.

Mirabelle de Nancy. These small jewels are a hit in farmers' markets throughout France. Gold fruit marbled with red. Sugary, high-quality yellow flesh. Eaten fresh or made into conserves and tarts. High flesh-to-stone ratio. As good today as it was in 1790. Upright-growing tree. Needs a pollinizer. Ripens in August.

Mount Royal. Good-tasting freestone plum. Abundant clusters of medium-sized round blue plums with yellow flesh. Less susceptible to black knot than most. Genetic semi-dwarf. Ripens in mid- to late August. A chance seedling found near Montreal in Québec and introduced in 1903. Self-fertile. Thrives throughout Zones 3–7. Rated the hardiest tested European plum.

Rosy Gage. Unique fresh-market plum bred at the Cornell-Geneva research station. Seedling of the famed European variety Imperial Epineuse. Elegant flavor. Yellow-green skin with a pink to rose-colored blush. Hardy, consistent cropper. Tree is not self-fertile. Moderately susceptible to brown rot and black knot. Early to midseason bloom. Ripens in late August.

Seneca. Very large plum with beautiful reddish purple skin and amber-orange flesh. Sweet, delicious freestone. Regular bearer on an upright, vigorous tree. Needs a pollinizer. New York release in 1972. Proven one of the best European plums in western Washington. Resistant to cracking, brown rot, gummosis, and split pits. Tolerant of black knot. Ripens from early to mid-September. Hardy throughout Zone 5.

Valor. Late, dark purple prune plum. Just enough acid to go with all that sugar. Wonderfully rich, juicy texture. High Brix every season. An introduction from the Vineland breeding station in Ontario in 1967. Starts ripening in September and continues over a full month. Color comes on early, so you need to feel each plum individually to know when peak ripeness has been reached. Susceptible to black knot; resistant to bacterial spot.

Victoria. Trees in English gardens overflow with these large, oval pink plums in August. Typically 2-inch-diameter fruit. Golden yellow, sweet freestone flesh. Excellent variety for canning. Seedling found in Sussex in 1840. Precocious and productive. Foliage subject to powdery mildew. Late-blooming.

Asian plums

Let's up the ante on what constitutes an Asian plum. There is no such thing as a pure *Prunus salicina* plum being promoted in the variety choices that follow. All are multiple hybrids to varying degrees. Much of which has to do with Luther Burbank.

Back in 1885, this noted plant breeder imported twelve plum seedlings from Japan.[68] These "Japanese plums" were correctly named—*Prunus triflora*, which grew wild in Japan.[69] Burbank brought in plums from all over the world and intercrossed them in a giant melting pot to emphasize the best characteristics while rejecting the undesirable ones. Another Chinese plum, *P. simonii*, with aromatic yet bitter fruit, richly colored skin, and a small pit contributes significantly to this gene pool.

Asian plums typically have *Prunus salicina* in the fore of their lineage. That distinction determined this plum grouping's take on disease and hardiness issues for a long time. Recent breeding work, however, has begun to improve things in both respects.

Asian plums are predominantly red. The fruits tend to be softer than European plums and juicy, with flesh that ranges from mildly tart to indescribably sweet. These large, round plums are best eaten fresh and are not for drying.[70] Most Asian plums are not self-fertile and will require a cross-pollinizer. Blooming periods must overlap, as an early plum will likely not pollinize the later varieties. Fruit is borne on both spurs and new wood of the previous season. The trees are naturally spreading and have light-colored foliage. Full flavor brought on by dependable summer heat suggests that the majority of these be planted in Zones 6–10.

Resistance to bacterial spot, black knot, sunscald, and brown rot make Au Rosa the right Asian plum for southeastern conditions. Photo courtesy of Adams County Nursery.

Au Rosa. This plum is the highest-ranked of the Auburn University series of plums in resistance to bacterial spot, black knot, sunscald, and brown rot. Aye, this one was bred for Southeast conditions. Firm, dark red fruit with saffron-yellow flesh. Great for fresh eating, baking, and canning. Vigorous, moderately productive tree. Ripens early July. Seven hundred chill hours.

Burbank. Dark red with golden-yellow skin. Apricot-colored flesh. Firm, sweet, juicy, uniquely flavored. Clingstone type. Low-growing, drooping tree. Brittle wood. Pollinized by Santa Rosa. Needs thinning to obtain the best fruit size and quality. Widely adapted. Does okay in the East despite fungal challenges. Ripens unevenly beginning in late July and continuing through mid-August. Four hundred chill hours. Hardy in Zone 5.

Emerald Beaut. Delicious and unusual late-season plum. Ripe fruit holds on the tree longer than any other stone fruit, up to two months. Plums continue to sweeten, becoming exceptionally sweet, yet remain crisp and crunchy. The Beaut has green skin, which gets yellower as it fully ripens. Yellow-orange free-stone flesh. Requires six to seven hundred chill hours.

Fortune. Large, attractive fruit with bright red skin at harvest time. Developed in Fresno, California, in the 1980s. This upright grower wants its branches tied down. Relatively resistant to black knot and

The meaty flesh of the Fortune plum will turn a surprising dark red when fully ripe. Photo courtesy of Dave Wilson Nursery.

bacterial spot. Pollinize with Santa Rosa. Five hundred chill hours. Cambium hardiness surpasses other Asian plums. Subject to pre-harvest drop.

Kuban Burgundy. Satsuma × Myrobalan. This red-leafed tree produces flavorful red plums with a blood-red flesh. Hints of Bing cherry taste. Fruit size ranges from 1 to nearly 2 inches when aggressively thinned. Moderate vigor. Myrobalan influence offers disease resistance. Originated in the former Soviet area of Abcausia. Ripens in the Midwest in early July. Hardy into Zone 4.

Methley. Sweet, medium-sized, reddish purple plum. Red flesh; mild, distinctive flavor. Nicely spreading tree. Practically a sponge for black knot. Stands up to

bacterial disease. Crack-resistant. Self-fertile. Ripens over a ten-day period in June. Does not keep well. Two hundred fifty chill hours. Bud-hardy in Zone 5.

Ozark Premier. Large, bright red fruit. Juicy, yellow clingstone flesh with a small pit. Mildly tart flavor. Skin is tough. Horizontal growth habit. Self-fruitful. Ripens in late summer over an extended period. Best in the South. Introduced by the Missouri Experiment Station in 1946. Seven to eight hundred chill hours. Hardy in Zone 5.

Red Heart. Medium to large fruit. Dark maroon ripening over amber-green skin. Dark red flesh. Firm, meaty, sweet, with a touch of mango. Heart-shaped varieties are especially prone to pitch pockets, but

Heart-shaped varieties are especially prone to pitch pockets . . . but not the Red Heart variety! Photo courtesy of Stark Brothers.

Satsuma needs a lot of hang time on the tree to develop its rich, lively flavor. Photo courtesy of Trees of Antiquity.

not Red Heart.[71] Holds well on tree when ripe. Moderate cracking issues. One of the best pollinizers for other Asian plums but needs a pollinizer itself. Five hundred chill hours.

Ruby Sweet. Reddish bronze skin with a dark red freestone flesh. Large, about 2 inches in diameter. Received the highest score in southeastern taste tests. Tolerant of humid conditions. Moderately resistant to bacterial spot and canker. USDA release from Byron, Georgia, in 1989. Ripens early to midseason.

Santa Rosa. Very large, round-oval fruit. Purplish red skin covered with light dots. Fragrant, fine-textured clingstone flesh. Luther Burbank considered this one of the four best plums he produced. Partially self-fruitful. Shy-bearing under eastern conditions. Vigorous, upright growth. Susceptible to bacterial spot. Ripens midseason. Requires three hundred chilling hours. Hardy in Zone 5, but sensitive to fluctuating winter temperatures.

Satsuma. The blood plum has nearly all *Prunus salicina* heritage. Imported from the Satsuma province in Japan. Maroon skin. Dark red, meaty flesh. Rich, lively flavor. Reliable bearer. Needs a lot of hang time on the tree, well past when the fruits turn all red, for best flavor. Handles disease pressures of the Mid-Atlantic region. Three hundred chill hours. Hardy in Zone 5.

Vanier. Ontario release in 1983. Medium-sized, bluish red clingstone with light orange flesh. Firm and meaty. Flavor continues to improve after picking. Precocious and vigorous, with an upright growth habit. Self-unfruitful, but an adequate pollinizer for all the major Asian plum cultivars. Tolerant of bacterial spot. Late-ripening.

American plums
Prunus americana genetics give this grouping its own set of attributes. The cultivated Asian plum was crossed with the smaller, hardier wild American plum to form a series of Asian × American hybrids, which show more hardiness than either European or Asian varieties. These plums are reliably winter-hardy through Zones 3 and 4. Fruits are usually red

or yellow in color. Fruit skin tends toward the astringent side, but the flesh more than makes up for that in sweetness. Black knot is a non-issue. Warm weather increases pollination prospects considerably; accordingly, Middle zones often experience heavier crops than areas farther north. Bloom times are similar for all varieties, with cross-pollination a must. Ripening occurs between mid-August and early September.

Alderman. University of Minnesota, 1985. Oval to heart-shaped fruit, notably larger than most American hybrids. Smooth, burgundy-red skin. Medium-soft, sweet, juicy, golden-yellow clingstone flesh. Vigorous, spreading tree reaching 12–15 feet in height when mature. Profuse white flowers are a full inch in diameter. One of the hardiest.

Gracious. Developed in Mandan, North Dakota, 1957. Oval to roundish yellow-orange fruit with coral-red mottling. Firm, juicy freestone flesh. Upright-spreading tree. Rare.

La Crescent. Minnesota introduction in 1919. Small fruit with tender yellow skin. Yellow, melting freestone flesh. Aromatic and sweet; suggestive of apricots. Extremely vigorous, upright-spreading tree. Moderate cracking issues. Fruits do not keep long. Hardy to –50°F (–46°C) with occasional winter injury.

Superior. Selected for extreme size, vigor, and hardiness. Large, golden fruit turns pink, developing a deep red blush in the sun. Peels like a peach. Firm, fine-textured clingstone flesh. Very good for fresh eating. Tree grows faster and larger than most. Good pollinizer. Stands up to brown rot.

Toka. An *americana* cross made with the apricot plum (*Prunus simonii*). Reddish bronze fruit. Firm, yellow freestone flesh. Rich, spicy perfection makes this the candy plum. Erect, vase-shaped tree. Minor cracking issues. Slightly susceptible to brown rot. One of the best pollinizers for all hybrid plums. Developed by N. E. Hansen at the South Dakota Experiment Station in 1911.

Waneta. Largest of all hybrid plums. Yellow skin washed with dark red. Small pit. Juicy, deep yellow clingstone flesh. Highly fertile tree bears at an early age. Heavy, annual producer. Pollinize with Toka. One of the best for severe winter areas. Hansen introduction in 1913.

Rootstock for plums

Knowledge of your specific soil and climate will determine the right choice for plum rootstock. Suckers from an existing tree can be useful as well, especially when these arise in the midst of a pollination thicket. Such *root volunteers* are an opportunity to graft new varieties into your mix. Scattering pits on the edge of a sitting compost pile in fall results in totally compatible *root sprouts* the following year. One caveat: Euro varieties grafted onto Asian stock will be short-lived, whereas Asian varieties are more accepting of *Prunus domestica* rootstock in the long run.

Myrobalan 29-C gets the nod as an excellent, all-around rootstock for plums and prunes. Shallow but vigorous root system tolerates wet soils. Widely adapted. Trees will be vigorous and nearly standard size, reaching 15–25 feet depending on pruning severity. Resistant to root-knot nematodes with some resistance to oak root fungus. Winter-hardy in Zone 4.

Prunus americana brings the crossed genetics of any wild plum seedling into play. Grower experience varies accordingly. Native rootstock for Japanese × American hybrid plums. Does well on thin soil. Hardy in Zone 3. Root suckering can be tremendous farther out from tree.

St. Julian GF 655-2 is a clonal rootstock specifically cultivated for plums. Produces moderately vigorous, productive trees. Good anchorage. Does well on heavy, wet soils. Resistant to root rot and bacterial canker. Produces a tree about 12 feet tall at maturity. Hardy to Zone 4.

Marianna GF 8-1 tolerates poorly drained soils even better than Myrobalan. This vigorous French rootstock handles calcareous soils as well. Sensitive to common nematodes. Winter hardiness is questionable beyond Zone 5.

Kahinta hybrid plums are yet another excellent choice for growers on cooler sites. Photo by Meg Hanrahan, courtesy of Tooley's Trees.

Controller 5 is a new rootstock developed by the University of California/USDA-ARS by crossing a Japanese plum with a peach. Dwarfs plum-tree vigor by half. Keep in mind that you get a self-sufficient tree on more vigorous rootstock . . . and that containment pruning works especially well for most plums.

Krymsk 1 matches the good traits of Myrobalan plum with the dwarfing nature of Nanking cherry. The *Prunus* germplasm collection at the Krymsk Breeding Station in Russia focuses on genes long missing from domesticated fruits. Dwarfing effect on both European and Asian plums (and perhaps apricots) along with good anchorage. Tolerates cold climates and heavy, wet soils. Root-knot nematode resistance. Susceptible to bacterial canker. Fruit size enhancement an added bonus.

Pruning tips for plums

Talk about a friendly tree! Plum vigor offers new shoots aplenty to renew bearing prospects without inundating a grower with jungle-like mandates. Given time, plum trees develop into an open vase form— whether trained that way from the get-go or eventually cascading forth from single-leader intentions to having multiple leaders with the center opened up. Pruning decisions are not so complicated when a tree cooperates.

Many plums have a strong upright growth habit in the very beginning. Limb spreading when scaffold shoots are supple is called for to get anywhere near a decent crotch angle. Be compromising here—a 45-degree flattening from the vertical will be all some cultivars will provide. Cutting back to outside lateral branches from here on in will provide further tree spread.

The majority of pruning cuts for mature plums are to promote spur formation. Floral initiation in plum for the next spring occurs as early as July and as late as September. Each spur produces one to three flowers but no leaves. Node buds on new shoots also establish bloom at this time. All terminal buds will be vegetative, but it's farther down the first-year shoot where leaf action has special merit—it's the leaf buds that second season that develop into longer-lasting fruiting spurs, while first-year flower buds always cause the node involved to go blind after fruiting. Thinning is the means by which light enters the interior of the tree to both reach the fruit buds as well as stimulate replacement laterals to become the next round of fruit bearers.

The timing for plum pruning keys on where you live. Immediate post-harvest pruning is best for opening up the current year's growth and maintaining overall height. All such cuts must be done on trees at this time where bacterial canker lurks in a wet dormant season. Utilizing both pruning windows back east, on the other hand, depends on the vigor of each tree. Here's the thing to remember: Heading cuts in the dormant season tend to stimulate furious shoot growth at the expense of fruiting. Kick-starting an "old dog" (a low-vigor tree) with late-winter pruning isn't appropriate in more balanced situations.

European plums have a more compact growth habit and can be grown as an open vase or in a pyramidal form (with a central leader). The Euro growth habit lends itself to fan espalier as well. These trees grow less vigorously once fruiting begins than the Asian or native plums and thus require less pruning overall. Thinning out excessive growth constitutes the bulk of the job.

Fruiting occurs principally on semi-permanent spurs on older limbs, with the heaviest production on wood that is two to five years old. Additional fruit will set on any of the previous season's growth left in place. The emphasis stays on renewing laterals in European plums, however. Spur thinning can be used in the interim on established branches with an abundance of fruiting sites.

Susceptibility to black knot fungus adds one last Euro caveat. Thick excrescences form along the twigs, which will be especially noticeable in winter. Far better to snag these as the knots develop in summer with your pruning shears. Disposing of diseased shoots promptly helps prevent further progression of the trouble.

Asian plums have a more lanky growth habit best directed by training to a central leader. Time will change this as branches on the outer perimeter spread both outward and upward: At that point remove the original leader and, presto, an open vase form (along the lines of an inverted umbrella) reveals itself.

Ongoing vigor changes the emphasis in pruning Asian plums. These typically overgrow and overbear. Branch splitting is not unusual in a heavy crop year. These trees are best kept in balance by removing a third to half of the new wood each year by thinning and heading back. Such heavy pruning will help produce larger fruit. Keep long, thin branches headed to give the tree a stubby, wide shape.

Flowers on Asian plums initiate on both the previous season's growth and, to a lesser extent, on semi-permanent spurs that arise from three-year-old wood. Allowing a good proportion of slender shoots to grow and thus crop the next year brings peach notions into play.[72] Plum shoots are also rotated out after harvest to allow new growth to do the very same thing the following season. Any shoots chosen to stay after cropping have specific heading purpose: Removing two-thirds of the shoot length promotes eventual spur formation lower down. Spur maintenance in the interior of the tree structure produces the rest of the crop.

American hybrid plums take a similar cue—not surprisingly, because the lineage here includes considerable Asian genetics. Only now the growth habit is not quite as lanky. Fruiting plans hinge evenly on shoot rotation and spur renewal. When the fruit spurs on a lateral branch have borne for four or five years, it's time to develop a new branch from shoots farther back on that branch. The next year, remove most of the old branch, cutting it off just beyond the selected lateral. Tucking a whippy watersprout into position works well here. The horizontal position induces spur formation for future years . . . and, since watersprouts tend to arise nearer the trunk, brings the fruiting zone back inward.

Plum pollination

Read my lips: *plum thicket*. The time has come for plum growers to grasp the lessons Nature puts before our eyes. I admit a northern perspective here, as one who fruits American hybrids. Let's tackle that challenge first, as it offers sounding ground for Asian and European plums as well.

Three factors need to be accounted for if good pollination of American hybrid plums is to occur. First, a reasonably warm spring day brings the insect world out to play. Plums bloom at a time when the pollinating force consists principally of solitary bees and tiny wasps. These wee ones cannot deal so well with buffeting winds . . . wherein lies the advantage of a thick grouping of plum pollen sources. The cross-pollination factor is always important, but particularly so with *Prunus americana* genetics.

Professor Alderman of the University of Minnesota wrote this back in 1934: "Very few hybrid plums would accept pollen freely from other hybrids, but they all accept pollen from native plums." The upshot here is that not just any *americana × salicina* cross is going to pollinate another *americana × salicina* cross. Native plum pollen comes by way of varieties like South Dakota, Toka, Kaga, and pure *americana* seedlings.[73] Having these nearer at hand increases the odds of a

Growing plum trees in close proximity helps lightweight pollinators in early spring mix things up pollen-wise between cultivars.

lightweight pollinator encounter, thereby checking off the second important consideration. Planting two hybrid varieties within several feet of each other so that branches intertwine creates a pollen-sharing haven. A small rectangle of hybrid plum trees spaced 10–12 feet apart achieves the same end, and all the more so if intermediary root suckers are allowed to grow and mingle as well.[74] That, my dears, is a plum thicket.

The third factor is one the grower can't do too much about: Tender plum bloom still needs to get through those inevitable spring frosts when temperatures teeter at the 27°F (–3°C) point. Yet there's more to this story line. Let's say the weather at the start of bloom has been warmish with plenty of insect activity. Here's the rub: The transfer of pollen does not ensure fruit set. Pollen germination merely triggers the growth of a pollen tube to reach the seed ovule. If the weather turns cold immediately after pollination—and daytime highs don't crest much above 40°F (4°C) the rest of the week—then the pollen tube grows so slowly that the ovule loses its viability in the meantime. Alas, no fruit. The hardiest hybrid plums in northern zones require a warm nudge immediately after pollination just as much as that native pollen source.

European and Asian plums need pollinizer companions drawn from their own ranks. Many of these cultivars are not self-fertile; that is, no fruit will set if a tree is pollinated by its own pollen. Nor does an Asian plum work for a European plum. And vice versa. Follow nursery recommendations for suitable pollinizers if you're not sure. Better odds for even the self-fertile cultivars come with cross-pollination, such being the nature of diversity.[75] The afternoon will generally see more bee activity, and not just because the day has warmed. Nectar is secreted at the base of the style, and although quite dilute in the morning, this floral draw becomes more concentrated as the day progresses.[76] Bees seek nectar, of course, being the ones that also move pollen from one tree to the next. Plum blossoms are only moderately attractive to bees due to a somewhat condensed bloom period and modest sugar levels in the nectar.[77]

Bloom from another plum variety—standing in a jar of water attached to the trunk to keep everything fresh—introduces a different pollen onto the scene.

Self-fertile cultivars do have a significant advantage in marginal spring weather, to be sure. Pollen-eating insects alone can get the job done here. Moving pollen from one flower to the next isn't as important now as simply loosening pollen grains from the anthers. This ups the chances of wind pollination playing a more definitive role as well. Cultivars like French Petite, Mount Royal, Santa Rosa, and Methley outperform self-unfruitful varieties in a cooler spring because of this.

Insect pests of plums

Knowing *who done it* and the timing involved defines the challenges on your particular orchard ground. Any of the recommended field guides will provide

Home Sweet Home for the nefarious plum curculio is indeed the plum tree. Photo courtesy of Tracy Leskey, USDA Appalachian Fruit Research Station.

species specifics and photo identification to go with established *point-of-vulnerability* insights:

- If you were a **plum curculio**, what do you think might be your favorite fruit in all the land? These native weevils migrated from wild plum thickets to gradually become an orchardwide scourge of many tree fruits throughout eastern regions. Yet even this evolutionary zeal has never really changed their underlying affinity for plums.
- Other plum aficionados abound, of course. **Japanese beetles** go for every cultivar of every plum type. Ditto-heads like **Oriental fruit moths** and **stink bugs** don't need to be called

twice for dinner. Dark-colored **aphids** can so overwhelm shoots as to cause a serious decline in tree vigor, typically resulting in reduced bloom the following year. Even **codling moth** will cross the pome line in some locations for a bite of plum.

- Naturally, there must be an **American plum borer** to go with all the peach variants. These moths are more inclusive than the name suggests, targeting sweet and sour cherry, apple, apricot, peach, pear, plum, and nectarine across southern Canada and into the United States. This borer parallels lesser peachtree borer in many respects, even sharing the same breeding ground beneath the bark of wounded trees. The grubs are dusky white to grayish purple, going to near-black in the final pupal stage. Frass found in the midst of black knot injury is a sure sign this species is at hand.

Organic solutions

Some plums would seem to have varying degrees of resistance to curculio. Asian plums tend to have bitter skin early on, a trait passed on to crosses made with *Prunus americana*.[78] The Asian influence pushes bloom earlier relative to European cultivars as well. All such factors determine which stone fruits will be particularly attractive when curculios themselves are ready to roll. Curc activity crests when days are warm, while cooler conditions keep the horde in waiting. An accelerated stage of development makes it possible for earlier plum varieties to be less subject to curculio interest. Or vice versa in other years. Finding the right trap tree(s) to best implement the *push-and-pull strategy* keys to accommodating those fast-paced seasons while recognizing which trees in your orchard seem to hit the curculio sweet spot most consistently.

There will certainly be a plum cultivar deserving of trap tree billing for curculio at every orchard site in the East. What you do with that sacrificial draw very much ties to the long-term success of this plan. Simply abandoning the crop of such a tree to this fate would allow curculio numbers to build significantly for the following year. Compounded action is required here—whether that's a "pupation blockade" of old carpet, astute chickens working the understory at drop time, or unleashing a million-strong contingent of *Steinernema riobrave* nematodes approximately a month after petal fall.

Both Japanese beetles and stink bugs have natural enemies, most notably parasitic flies in the family Tachinidae. These parasites place their eggs directly on the thorax of adults. The eggs, when present, can be easily seen as raised white spots about 1–2 mm in diameter around the head-and-shoulder area of the bug. Biodiversity coupled with the beneficial release of

helpful species (if such are not already present in your region) eventually makes other hands-on approaches a tad less necessary. Pure neem oil may well be enough to fill the gap, given its repellent nature. Those shoot-sucking aphids will definitely experience setback from a neem bath while you await ladybugs to arrive on the scene.

Plum borer larvae tend to be somewhat gregarious; spotting as many as twenty larvae around a single wound site is not uncommon. Branch wounds often do not heal properly, as tree vigor gets diminished by cambium feeding. The full extent of larval feeding is seldom apparent because the bark above the frass zone appears normal. Larvae may be several inches beyond the visual damage and therefore well on the way to completely girdling the branch, if not the tree itself. Use a biological mudpack (with parasitic nematodes) at the first sign of frass extrusion to prevent this from happening.

Disease concerns of plums

Holistic orchardists indeed have a plan to deal with disease. We'll add some twists and requisite timing notes here to our general understanding of how tree health keeps fungal and bacterial pathogens in check.

- **American brown rot.** The potential for infection increases as the fruits mature. Spread is rapid within clusters where plums touch one another. Rotted fruits shrink into the mummified form as they dry on the tree, providing an inoculum source for the following year. Native plums show innate resistance to this fungal kingpin, making *P. americana* crosses a better choice in humid regions. Curculio wounds in this favored fruit provide an unerring entry point for rot organisms.
- **Black knot.** Limbs and sometimes whole trees can be stunted and eventually killed by the girdling action of ever-expanding knots. Good immune function from budbreak through two weeks after bloom helps check fungal disease

The girdling action of ever-expanding black knots can eventually kill trees. Keep susceptible varieties well pruned of this fungal intrusion.

development. Good eastern exposure to dry off morning dew quickly, keeping trees vigorous, and removing all knots as they appear go along with that. Susceptibility varies considerably among plum varieties.

- **Bacterial spot.** Asian plums were the first to reveal the sensitivity of stone fruits in eastern North America to *Xanthomonas* bacteria. Lesions on young fruit (established at bloom) can ooze golden sap, whereas infections that occur on fruit in the pre-harvest period tend to be superficial, giving the plum a mottled appearance. Lesions on shoots occur at budbreak as well as all summer long, thereby establishing a staging ground for the bacteria

to colonize neighboring bark surfaces in the dormant months ahead. Providing "no room at the inn" through competitive colonization lies at the heart of the holistic plan.

- **Bacterial canker.** Back to the West Coast, where this *Pseudomonas*-induced canker bothers European plums to a degree, but not Asian plums. Prune in the dry season, support good vigor through balanced nutrition, and boost microorganism allies at leaf fall and again at bud swell.
- **Plum pox.** This virus was accidentally introduced into North America in the 1990s. Its vascular reach extends to peach, nectarine, and apricot as well. Symptoms vary considerably depending on the species, age, and vigor of the tree. Plum fruits develop distinct dark spots on the skin, with red discoloration in the flesh, and tend to be tasteless due to lowered sugar content. Quarantine measures include the certification of nursery stock, removal of infected trees, and strict management of the aphid vector.

Harvest notes

Plums do not continue to ripen completely after being picked and so, just like all the other stone fruits, should be picked fully tree-ripe to taste their best. Picked underripe, plums will still soften and some of their complex carbohydrates may break down to sugars, but those changes are more akin to the first stages of rotting than the flavor changes associated with true ripening. That's what you buy in the supermarket . . . but not what you should be picking in your own *garden of eden*.

No fresh plum keeps particularly well. Those immediate days after picking the crop are for dribbling juice down your chin, but then decisions must be made as to putting up jam, drying the prune types, or letting fruit flies run amok. The point here is not to plant more plums than you can enjoy. A few varieties will be more than plenty for a family.

CHAPTER SEVEN

Berries

An integrated orchard consists of far more than trees. The very same woodsy ecology principles apply to all sorts of berries. Fruiting brambles, bushes, and shrubs are the lower-lying understory of a productive fruit guild.

The place to plant berries, in a sense, is everywhere. Garden nooks are lovely. Bushes growing by rock promontories among the orchard trees add height diversity as well as good spider habitat. Cane fruits tied to individual stakes and espaliered red currants expand the vision beyond production beds. Larger plantings are invaluable for taking advantage of growth habit, being able to protect against birds, and filling the pantry with the very best jam.

The whole biodiversity scene gains from the presence of a mix of fruiting plants. The pollinators are happy; parasitic wasps find more food hosts. Root systems interact on different levels, bringing subsoil minerals up to leaves and fruit alike. Microclimate pockets can be found for berries that benefit from shade and wind shelter. Frost insurance comes with this plan too. Various blooms occurring over a long period ensures that something misses the icy curve-balls of spring. Hardy currants and gooseberries often have fruit under way when regionwide cold strikes late tender blossoms. Juneberries provide for songbirds that indeed leave us a delightful few fruits. Beauty surrounds all in such orchard ground, as the colors and textures and branching of so many different fruiting plants provide visual artistry. And, oh, the low-lying fruit that awaits!

Berry devotees discover their true passion at a very young age.

BRAMBLE

The assorted *Rubus* genus brings a cane focus to orcharding. Broadly speaking, this naturally hybridized grouping includes an impressive number of plants found growing across the continent. From north to south, brambles are the perfect home garden plant in many respects. All are easy to get started, requiring little more than a patch of full sun and some well-drained soil. The growth habit of raspberries and blackberries varies more than you might expect, yet all gets addressed by the right cultural practice matched by cultivar. Disease problems rarely overwhelm, though viruses do indeed set regional longevity parameters. The fruits are highly perishable, often extremely pricey . . . so what could be better than going out early in the morning to pick your own berries for breakfast?

The botanical distinction between blackberries and raspberries revolves foremost around fruit characteristics. These berries are aggregate fruits consisting of multiple smaller fruits, called *drupelets*. These fleshy seed capsules are attached around a fibrous central core. This whitish *torus* remains with the plant when raspberry fruit are picked, giving each berry a hollow appearance within. Blackberry fruits differ in that the drupelets remain attached to an edible core, which comes off with the berry when picked.

Raspberries

Both red raspberry and black raspberry are somewhat insistent about home turf. Reds like summer on the cooler side, while blackcaps can take far more heat. Winter hardiness follows accordingly—red raspberry can certainly tolerate –20°F (–29°C), whereas black raspberries start to take a serious hit at –5°F (–21°C). All share chilling requirements ranging from eight hundred to sixteen hundred hours, meaning neither is going to venture too far south. That's a niche well filled by blackberry, coming up soon.

Cane terminology is required to further distinguish bramble considerations. First-year canes are called *primocanes*. These arise from ground level each spring and grow vigorously. Shorter day length and cooler temperatures in early fall signal summer-bearing red raspberries, black raspberries, and blackberries to initiate flower buds. The following spring,

the second-year canes will fruit starting in early summer and then die off after the harvest is done. These so-called *floricanes* define traditional bramble culture. Fall-bearing red raspberries, however, do this complete cycle in a single year. Once a certain number of nodes of growth are reached (genetically predetermined by variety), the fall-bearing primocane initiates flower buds from the tip of the cane downward. These then bloom and fruit, with the fruit typically ripening in early fall. Different pruning scenarios follow from here, including being able to mow down a fall-bearing patch annually and thereby ensure winter survival.

Management of brambles cues to where new canes arise. Red raspberries reproduce asexually via underground runners. These pop up and renew bed potential in a narrow hedgerow. Black raspberries rarely send out runners, preferring instead to tip-root where the growing point hits the ground. Head such canes back and you have the makings of an excellent containment plan. Black raspberries initiate new canes from the crown of the plant rather than from root suckers. Accordingly, cultivars are grown in a hill system where each plant is grown independently, with pruning done on a per-plant basis. These require summer tipping—unlike red raspberries—because individual canes would otherwise grow to unmanageable lengths.

Planting specifics

With all that firmly in mind, let's get to planting.

Red raspberries are typically planted 2–3 feet apart within the row, knowing that many new shoots will originate from root buds. Black raspberry plants do not spread far from the original plant and hence do not fill in the row in the same manner as red raspberries. That said, considerable space is needed for each plant because they produce new canes from the crown area, as well as strong lateral branches when pruned properly. Plant black raspberries about 3–4 feet apart within the row, and plant the more vigorous purple raspberries 5–6 feet apart in the row.

Autumn Britten produces a fall crop on first-year canes. Given proper pruning, those same canes make a comeback to produce more berries early on the following summer. Photo courtesy of Backyard Berry Plants.

Incorporating woodsy compost into the planting bed suits all brambles. Studies in Switzerland have shown that compost made from green material and wood chips produced the best results for nutrient availability and aeration around the roots, and the highest levels of beneficial fungi. Spread compost 2–4 inches thick across a 2-foot width down the length of the intended bed. Keep a steady hand on the tiller at this late stage of the game . . . ideally by keeping this bacterial machine at a distance! Lightly forking the compost into the soil instead will maximize the fungal advantage provided by a red clover crop sown the season prior to planting.[1]

Red raspberries and blackberries can asymptomatically (showing no outward sign themselves) carry viruses that severely affect black raspberries. Nurseries typically recommend that these bramble types be kept 100 feet apart, whether cultivated or wild. These viruses are spread by aphids and windblown pollen. Black raspberries will do fine at first but can quickly decline after a mere three to five years. The stated isolation distance, in truth, doesn't really alter eventual realty. Regional recommendations take this into account. Great strides are being made in discovering new sources of aphid and disease resistance in black raspberry germplasm, so hang tight.

Raspberry varieties to consider

I grew up loving wild black raspberries in southeastern Pennsylvania. Yet here in northern New Hampshire,

Amateur fruit breeder Pete Tallman in Colorado has his eyes set on a primocane-bearing black raspberry with good flavor and size that proves hardy throughout Zone 5. These berries from one of his recent improved selections show he's making progress! Photo courtesy of Pete Tallman.

temperatures drop to −5°F (−21°C) in combination with dry winds.[2] Red raspberries, on the other hand, love cooler days and nights. Come farther north and you will be pleased by their full potential.

Fall-bearing red raspberries go a long way toward addressing disease frustrations in viral pockets. Summer bearers in such places tend to burn out in five to seven years. The strategic advantage offered by fall varieties has to do with a later bloom time: Wild summer bearers proffer virus-laden pollen in spring, yet this vector is long gone when fruiting primocane types (maintained by annual mowing) flower in midsummer. Growers in the Pacific Northwest report red raspberry success with Heritage (the very first of the fall bearers) going on twenty-five years now, when grown in rich soil with a touch of dappled shade. Other advantages follow here: cooler picking conditions, far less berry mold, and a fuller sweetness in the fruit itself in the drier fall window.

The raspberry spectrum doesn't end with a mere two colors, of course. Purple raspberries are the offspring of a red and a black raspberry and exhibit characteristics of both. **Royalty** is an excellent purple, producing good-sized berries that shine when made into jam or an ice cream topping. The gold raspberry lost the ability to make red color anthocyanins in its breeding.[3] **Anne** is the largest and best-tasting (with banana overtones, no less) of these pale yellow cultivars. It grows well in middle zones—provided the viral challenge doesn't do in the patch in too quick a time—and ripens in fall if managed as a primocane bearer. These many-hued variations of raspberry run on the mild side flavor-wise compared with their darker compatriots, but they sure do liven up the fruit bowl with unexpected color.

hardiness alone rules out that choice (though I did try). The abandon with which red raspberry fills in openings in the woods across northern zones tells all. On the other hand, heat, drought, and yet other viruses are issues for red raspberries in the Southeast. Growers in maritime climates need to consider other parameters yet again in deciding which cultivars will make the grade in the long run. The best berry choices for each region are about far more than flavor preferences.

Some people find red raspberries boring—tart and with a small bit of flavor compared with the complexity of the black raspberry. Tellingly, that's a southern friend speaking. Black raspberries are a heat-loving crop. These brambles winter-kill to the snow line if

Allen. Bristol × Cumberland. Large, firm, juicy, very sweet, glossy black berries. Consistently productive. Uniform ripening, so harvest period is short. Disease-free. Widely adapted summer bearer. Developed at the New York Experiment Station. Ripens in early July. Zones 4–8.

The banana overtones of Anne add to the surprise of encountering
a yellow raspberry. Photo courtesy of Backyard Berry Plants.

Autumn Britten. Red everbearer from Great Britain. Bears fruit from late August through the fall, followed by early-summer production if properly pruned. Firm, coherent berry with good flavor. Winter-hardy to –20°F (–29°C). Will produce in warmer climates with limited winter chilling. Zones 4–8.

Black Hawk. Very large, nearly round black raspberries. Flavor of a rich Merlot wine. Exceptional quality. Does not crumble, even when a little overripe. Bears despite hot, dry weather. Resistance to anthracnose. Ripens late midseason on second-year laterals, with a picking window of two weeks. Introduced by Iowa State University in 1955. Zones 5–9.

Boyne. Summer-bearing. Consistently produces deep red berries with an aromatic, sweet flavor. Strong canes. Spreads quickly by suckers. Extremely winter-hardy. No disease issues. Hardy to Zone 3.

Caroline. Most productive primocane bearer. Ups the taste parameters for a red raspberry with a rich intensity. Success in many soil types and locations. More tolerance for root rot than Heritage. Does not tolerate high heat or drought. Ripens earlier in fall, thereby escaping late frosts. Zones 4–7.

Heritage. Most resilient primocane bearer. Drought-tolerant, outcompetes weeds, long-lived. Decent-sized berries. Moderately productive. Requires a long ripening season, otherwise frost gets fruit. Prone to die if it has wet feet. Best in Zones 5–7.

Jewel. Black raspberry with rich, jammy flavor. Very noticeable seeds and thorns. Canes grow up to 10 feet. Tip-roots very easily. Best choice for the Appalachians and Midwest. Hardy to –15°F (–26°C). Best in Zones 5–8.

Killarney. Bright red fruit. Good raspberry flavor and aroma. Ripens in midsummer. Upright, bendy canes require trellis support. Modest suckering. Released in Manitoba in 1961. Extremely winter-hardy throughout Zone 4.

Polana. Annual fall bearer. Heavy producer of ruby-red fruits that tend to be favorites among berry lovers who prefer a tart counterpoint to plentiful fruit sugars. Ripens three weeks earlier than Heritage, allowing northern growers to beat the frost to the harvest. Vigorous yet relatively short canes. A side-dressing of compost or protein meal in late spring is advised. Zones 3–8.

Prelude. Red everbearer that bears heavily in its second year in June (if stimulated with proper pruning). A lighter fall crop from first-year canes begins the split-crop cycle. Very large, firm fruit. Well adapted to the Coastal Plain and Piedmont. From Cornell Small Fruit Breeding Program. Zones 4–8.

Taylor. Awesome late-summer raspberry. Considered the best-flavored red variety you can grow. Medium-colored, medium to large, long-conic berry. Subject to mosaic virus (aphid vector). Sturdy canes need no support. Introduced in 1935. Zones 4–8.

Pruning tips for raspberries

Cane fruits are biennial by nature, completing the fruit cycle in two years. The crowns are perennial with respect to sending up new canes from buds at the crown each spring. Early in the fall, summer-bearing red raspberries initiate lateral buds at the base of leaf nodes on the primocane. Early in the second season, short fruit-bearing laterals grow from these buds. After fruiting, the old canes die, leaving the bed to the vigorous canes that grew all summer. Call this scenario number one.

Back at the midpoint of the last century, breeders made use of a wild raspberry strain that fruited in its first year. Initially, results were meager—small fruit with an abundance of seeds, yet ripening from late August on first-year canes. This introduced the advantages of later bloom not subject to spring frosts and mowing down the entire planting after every harvest season. Welcome to scenario number two. The modern raspberry revolution arrived with the development of these primocane-bearing cultivars.

One more notion tripped its way into grower consciousness not long after this: Fall bearers become *everbearers* with proper pruning based on understanding the fruiting primocane. The top third to half of the cane fruits in year one, but the portion below reserves

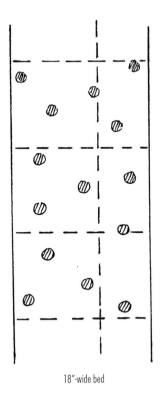

18"-wide bed

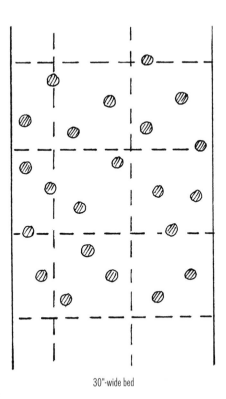

30"-wide bed

Light enhances growth; ergo, favor stronger canes and thin out the rest. Cane density should amount to two or three canes per square foot across the width of the bed.

its fruiting potential for the second year. That sets up scenario number three for certain varieties that yield particularly well from a split-crop production approach.

Summer-bearing red raspberries, black raspberries, and purple raspberries are pruned to increase production and bed longevity. Many growers do this entirely in the dormant season (immediately following snowmelt in early spring). Others tip canes considerably lower—or maybe not at all—depending on the vigor of the variety. Black raspberries should be *summer-topped* to encourage stouter growth.[4] This plan espoused by Nourse Farms especially suits the traditional red raspberry:

- The spent fruiting canes are removed soon after harvest. They should be cut off close to the base of the plant, removed from the planting, and destroyed.[5] Good air circulation helps reduce disease pressure on first-year canes.

- Selecting the more vigorous canes to keep has merit at this point in late summer. Production potential increases for the next season by letting more sunshine in for lateral bud initiation in fall. Thin to leave canes ½ inch or more in diameter (by removing weaker live canes) on a square-footage basis of two or three canes across the width of the bed.

- Once the canes have seen a few killing frosts, summer red raspberries are topped at 6 inches above the trellis wire. Having a top wire at 54 inches above the soil means the canes are being pruned at 5 feet tall for the winter ahead. The fall laterals on black raspberries are cut back to 12 inches at this same time. This trim in late fall results in the virtual elimination of winter damage.[6]

Two crops a year can be picked from the same raspberry planting. Allowing a fall bearer such as Prelude to crop again keys to the ability of the lower part of the cane to fruit that second season.

Primocane-fruiting red raspberries are cut to ground level after the harvest in fall. A heavy brush mower gets the job done, or you can use a pair of loppers to cut canes down individually. One-inch-diameter canes will probably prove too much for a lawn mower. Winter hardiness issues become a moot point when cane survival rests in the crown. The row can be narrowed to 16–18 inches wide at this time by tilling. Mulching the bed edges heavily with cardboard covered with ramial wood chips is a biological alternative . . . with a light dressing of wood chips in the cane area as well to help limit weeds the following season.

And that brings us to red raspberry scenario number three. Every primocane bearer can theoretically be managed for split-crop production if a grower so chooses. Prelude should definitely be held to the everbearer pruning plan, as its berry production the following June dwarfs a lesser fall crop.[7] Home orchardists with limited space find this the way to go,

being able to count on a couple of handfuls of berries every few days in early summer as well as through the fall from a single planting.

- During the winter or early spring, prune the standing canes at about chest height (about 4 feet high). Multiple fruiting laterals or additional cane development from the top auxiliary buds will result. Basically, this cut removes the top portion of the cane that produced fruit the fall before and initiates lateral branching on the remaining portion of the second-year cane that remains.

- A new batch of primocanes that will produce the next fall crop will grow in the meantime. The net result is two crops in the same year from two different sets of canes. Bed crowding occurs to some extent—so be sure to remove the June-bearing canes when the early fruiting cycle ends.

Insect pests of raspberries

Surprisingly few insects bother brambles in any one place. Cane borers get their dibs in almost everywhere, while the rest of the field might visit only on occasion. Which makes berries pretty friendly when you compare this with the pest prospectus of fruit trees!

- Sawdust-like frass at the base of suddenly dried-up canes literally shouts that **raspberry crown borer** is at hand. Spindly cane growth and reduced leaf size in the bramble patch are also indicative. The adult is a clear-winged moth that resembles a medium-sized yellow jacket in coloration and size. Eggs are laid singly on the undersides of the leaves in late summer. These hatch in about a month's time, and then the larvae crawl down the cane to tunnel beneath the soil line to feed on roots—hence its other name of **raspberry root borer**. The following spring, each cream-colored grub will tunnel into a selected cane to complete its development. Moths emerge from July through September to begin the cycle anew. Keep an eye out for ¼-inch tunnels in the base of canes when pruning. Soil drenches of pathogenic nematodes (the *Heterohabditis bacteriophoba* strain) in fall will successfully clean up overwhelming numbers.

- The beetles that attack brambles are much like dueling banjos playing the same tune. The **raspberry cane borer** causes tip dieback followed by eventual cane death. Oviposition damage can readily be identified by two rings of punctures about ½ inch apart and located 4–6 inches below the growing tip of primocanes. The work at hand becomes more insidious the following season as the larva continues to burrow to the base of the cane, causing the entire cane to die before the fruit matures. The adult culprit is a slender, long-horned beetle, black in color except for a yellow-orange thorax, measuring about ½ inch long. The first-year grub will overwinter about 2 inches below its girdling entrance point. Watch for girdled tips wilting in June and July. Pruning cuts made a few inches below the oviposition rings take this borer out of the arena.

- Adult **rednecked cane borers** attack foliage, often feeding on the upper leaf surfaces during the day, leaving irregular holes. These metallic, slender beetles are approximately ¼ inch long and all-black, with an iridescent coppery red thorax. The larvae feed on primocanes, resulting in irregular swellings between 1 and 3 inches in length that often split the bark of the cane. These *galls* are mostly found at ground level but can also be as much as 4 feet above the ground. Larvae normally tunnel upward into the pith, but tunnels may extend 6 inches below to 25 inches above the gall. When looking for overwintering larvae, it is best to split the cane at the gall and follow the brown, discolored tunnel from the gall to its end. Live larvae are rarely found in the gall. Infested canes either die or become so weakened as to be unable to support a crop the following season. These borer beasties may infest as much as 50 percent of the canes when left unchecked. Parasitic wasps are good allies here. The stewardship nudge required of you calls for astute observation: Look for a faint brown-green line circumventing unhappy-looking stems in midsummer. Snip these wilting stems off just below the problem area. Separated from the plant, the stem will wither and dry up, thereby killing the grub. Otherwise, after a day or two of wilting, the stem will repair itself and continue growing. A slight S curve marks infested canes, with a leaf or two often crippled nearby. That provides a second chance to snare these rednecked fiends. Opportunity knocks a third time come spring when entire canes with obvious galls need to be removed and destroyed.

- The larvae of **winter moth** feed on the buds and blossoms of cane fruits as well in early spring. Leaves and flowers are often webbed together with silk. An early-season application of Bt is the ticket here as soon as green tissue shows.
- Brambles are subject to the whimsy of **Japanese beetle** and **stink bugs** as well. Let's hold **rose chafer** in similar regard. These insects are noticed most often in very sandy soils where the breed can multiply quite rapidly. Chafers attack flowers primarily, resulting in far less fruit. Feeding damage to leaves and remaining fruits follows from there. Handpicking always makes a dent; pure neem oil repels from the get-go; play the pyrethrum card if you have to on especially appealing varieties.
- **Tarnished plant bug** becomes problematic only if nearby forage crops (especially alfalfa) are mowed when raspberry flowers or fruits are present. A conscious approach to ecosystem dynamics addresses this.
- Organic growers typically rely on high rates of parasitism to hold aphid numbers down. One exception to make here relates to **raspberry aphids** and viral spread from nearby wild brambles. Here's yet another reason to be directing the holistic spray combo—which includes pure neem oil—at berry plantings as well as fruit trees.

Disease concerns of raspberries

Holistic orchardists indeed have a plan to deal with disease. We'll add some twists and requisite timing notes here to our general understanding of how plant health keeps pathogens in check.

- **Bramble viral woes**. Mosaic, leaf curl, tobacco streak, and tomato ringspot are the principal viruses that afflict cane fruit. Vectors include aphids, pollen from nearby wild plants (that appear absolutely healthy), and dagger nematodes working the root zone. Misshapen leaves indicate something is amiss, and, not too long after that, progressive stunting of growth with undersized and crumbly fruits establishes viral infection as fact. A few years pass and the entire planting goes kaput. Standard advice is twofold: Purchase certified virus-free plants and remove all wild raspberry from the vicinity. Good calcium levels in the soil help slow viral progression. Floricane types are especially prone to pollen sharing—primocane bearers (if mowed down annually) have the advantage of blooming after wild raspberries. Healthy plantings will remain productive for decades in regions where viruses are less prevalent.
- **Anthracnose**. Black and purple raspberry varieties are more often affected by *Elsinoe veneta* fungi, but the disease can be significant on red varieties as well. Symptoms appear on canes, leaves, and sometimes the fruit. Infected canes show tiny purple spots, which progress to larger spots (¼ inch in diameter) with ash-gray centers and purple borders. These lesions will appear sunken and the borders raised as the canes age. Leaves develop similar small spots that frequently drop their centers, leaving a shothole appearance. Unchecked, the fruit becomes worthless. The fungus survives the winter in infected canes and produces spores (both conidia and ascospores) in the spring at the time of leafing out. Abundant rain in late spring and early summer will ramp up fungal prospects. Destroying old fruiting canes after harvest is good hygienic practice. Holistic support in spring takes care of the rest of the story.
- **Verticillium wilt**. This soilborne fungus reduces raspberry yields by wilting, stunting, and eventually killing individual fruiting canes. Black and purple raspberries are especially prone, with red raspberries and

CANE SUPPORT

Trailing blackberries and floricane-fruiting red raspberries need support in order to maximize berry production. These may be grown on a trellis, trained along a fence, or tied to individual stakes. The simplest trellis consists of two wires stretched at 30 and 54 inches high between posts set 10–16 feet apart. Pairs of cedar or metal fence posts 2–3 feet apart can be used to straddle the bed, or a tee brace can be constructed from milled lumber. Holes can be drilled through the two horizontal arms of this central post arrangement to hold the wires up and slightly offset so that the top wires are outboard. Upright fruiting canes are loosely tied over to these top wires in spring, leaving the midway open for primocane growth in the current season. Canes of trailing varieties are best fanned out at a diagonal from the ground, tied where they cross the wire, and then trained horizontally. Individual stakes for singular plantings (no bed intended) need to extend 4 feet or more above the ground. Tie the more vigorous canes to the stake with a loop at a point about midway between the ground and the tips of the canes, and again near the top of the stake to support the weight of the fruit.

Those inclined to skip all this fuss should be willing to get scratched reaching for berries in the midst of a thicket. Providing space to let summer-bearing red raspberries, black raspberries, and traditional blackberries run amok works best if you have the wherewithal to whack back the edges. Mow down access paths to open up bigger thickets. Canes will be more crowded as a consequence of limited pruning—and thus produce less fruit on a per-cane basis—but there still will be plenty for bears and family alike.

Fall raspberries that ripen on primocanes may require a temporary string trellis to keep laden canes upright. This consists of a 4-foot stake driven into the ground every 15–20 feet, with one string tied to either side at about 30 inches high. The canes are trained in between the strings as growth reaches skyward in early summer. Allow a little slack in the strings to accommodate bringing a foot-wide swath of canes into line.

Two wires on each side of the raspberry bed supported by tee braces go far when it comes to keeping canes erect for easy picking.

blackberries susceptible to a lesser degree. Wilt is most severe on fruiting canes in cold, wet springs. Symptoms on new canes frequently coincide with hot, dry midsummer weather. Go figure. Recommended practice is to avoid replanting in an area where cane loss has been a problem.

- **Raspberry root rot**. The formation of coated spores allows *Phytophthora* fungus to survive ten to fifteen years in infected soils. Raspberry varieties are never completely resistant. Water-saturated soils prevent the necessary root growth to overcome infection, pointing the way to raised beds to help prevent water-logging in heavy soils. Liberal use of woodsy compost helps by improving soil structure. Good aeration around the roots, backed by a competitive food web, will block sites of potential infections. Keep young roots thriving and this one's outta here!

- **Spur blight**. Infected canes release fungal ascospores in May and June during rainy periods. Conidia release continues throughout the growing season during wet weather. Purple spots appear around the nodes on the lower portions of the canes. These areas turn brown, causing both leaf and flower buds to shrivel and die. Leaf lesions appear as brown wedge-shaped areas. Diseased canes dry out and crack as they mature, with the lesions turning brownish purple and covering much of the cane. But hey! We know how to deal with fungal progression, right?

- **White drupelet disorder**. Ripening berries exposed to ultraviolet radiation and high temperatures develop normally, yet occasionally individual seed capsules on the berry remain white. These white drupelets may occur singly or in groups. Since berries with white drupelet disorder differ from normal fruit only in the absence of pigment, they remain suitable for processing but are usually unacceptable for fresh market sales. Shading susceptible cultivars to reduce "too much sunshine" may lessen the problem.

Blackberries

Imagine a plant that can be used as an impermeable hedge throughout the year, with showy blooms that come in late spring and fruit starting as early as May. Imagine a plant that scoffs at most insects and disease, while producing one of the best jelly, jam, pie, cobbler, and wine fruits known. One fruit alone boasts all these attributes—the uncommonly common blackberry.

Blackberries are native to Asia, Europe, and North and South America. They've been enjoyed for hundreds of years for eating, for medicinal purposes, and, yes, as hedges to keep out marauders. Various *Rubus* species have been important in developing northern cultivars, including thornless types. *R. ursinus* is native to the Pacific Northwest and the prime driver in the development of trailing cultivars grown in that region.

Wild blackberries abound, so it's a legitimate question to ask why specific cultivars should even be introduced to the home orchard. (The same could be said of wild red and black raspberries.) Mother Nature's offerings are certainly a boon in a good year, and therein lies the crux of the matter. Wildlings don't produce all that well from year to year, are relatively small and often quite seedy, and even fall short on the flavor front. Carefully selecting wild fruits has allowed humans to bring forth better and better traits.

Blackberries adore intense sun, heat, and humidity. That statement has not been made throughout this entire book. Fruit growers in Zones 6–9 absolutely appreciate the blackberry blessing. Growers farther north are coming up to speed, in part, by looking to the past.

Planting specifics

Most thorny blackberries produce suckers profusely and should be planted 3–4 feet apart to form a uniform hedgerow of canes. Thornless blackberries do not produce many suckers, but their growth is vigorous and new canes develop from the original crown. Plant thornless blackberries in a hill system with each plant set 4–6 feet apart within the row.

Blackberries particularly thrive in warm, mild climates. These plants do well in sandy soil with a pH between 4.8 and 7.2. Iron chlorosis in the form of yellowing leaves shows up where blackberries face more alkaline conditions. Watering weekly to keep the soil evenly moist, but not soggy, becomes all the more important when mature plants are producing fruit.

One looming issue in preparing berry ground centers on aggressive perennial weeds like johnsongrass, Bermuda grass, and quack grass prior to crop establishment. Sites with these grasses need to be either avoided or properly cover-cropped for two years prior. A raised-bed system provides a third option. Lay down a thick layer of cardboard and newspaper mulch as a soil foundation upon which to build a boxed bed a minimum of a foot high. Imported soil mixed with woodsy compost and the usual planting-hole soil amendments (like rock phosphate and Azomite) fills this frame. Those invasive grasses can be kept mowed along the base. Blackberries thrive in this deep, rich soil coupled with a drip irrigation system. Choose a cultivar with an erect growth habit that, once laden with fruit, will direct the tops of its canes outboard against a top trellis wire. These will continue upward and then droop back down to eye level at a perfect picking height out over the aisleway.

Blackberry varieties to consider
The more complex flavor nod generally goes to the thorny. Still, management preferences based on less bloody forearms suit many growers. Thornless varieties seem more resistant to diseases like crown gall and viruses than the thorny varieties. Paying attention to the growth habit of chosen cultivars is key to the pruning challenges that lie ahead. Primocane-bearing blackberries present an easier alternative for those equipped with enough mowing oomph to skip winter cane management altogether.

Arapaho. Erect, thornless canes. Large, short-conic, firm, aromatic fruit with small seeds. Harvest begins in early summer. Doesn't require trellising. Resistant to rosette. Heat-tolerant and relatively cold-hardy. Originated in Arkansas in 1993. Hardy into Zone 5 with winter wind protection.

Balsor. Sweet, small berries for the northern grower. Many suckers. Nova Scotia origins. Impressive winter survival rate, down to –30°F (–34°C). Hardy throughout Zone 4.

Black Diamond. Thornless, trailing selection for the backyard connoisseur. Sweet, earthy flavor of the marionberry, but with a larger, firmer berry. Highly productive. Disease-resistant. Bears for several weeks in late July and August. Developed in Corvallis, Oregon. Zones 6–9.

Chester. Starts its huge production right when Triple Crown leaves off. Very large, flavorful berries start ripening in August and continue up until frost. Vigorous, thornless, semi-erect canes show resistance to cane blight and tolerance to rosette. Berries stay firm in the heat. Spreads by tip-rooting only. Well adapted across the country. Hardy throughout Zone 5.

Kiowa. Largest of the Arkansas varieties. Wickedly thorny. Splendid grape-like flavor when dead-ripe. Six-week picking window begins in June. Semi-erect growth habit accommodates either training scheme. Lower winter chill requirements stretch its bounds across both the Southeast and the Southwest.

Loch Ness. Semi-trailing, thornless blackberry from Scotland. Large, shiny black fruit with a richly tart bite. Highly productive. Can be grown like raspberries (with little support) or trailed outward along a fence rail. Ripens late for a blackberry, beginning in mid-August and through September. Zones 5–9.

Nelson. Commercial blackberries are not hardy enough to fruit regularly in Zone 4 above snow line. And yet this old-time variety has been surviving Maine winters and fruiting for at least a century.[8] The inch-thick canes are sturdy and upright, reaching 8–9 feet tall. Moderately large, quite juicy fruit

A semi-trailing, thornless blackberry from Scotland absolutely deserves the name of Loch Ness! Photo courtesy of Raintree Nursery.

has a sweet, true blackberry taste. Robustly prolific, with as many as sixteen to eighteen flowers on the central blossom stalk. Disease resistance bar none. Slight tip dieback occurs at –25°F (–32°C). Ripens in mid-August over a two-week period.

Ouachita. Thornless variety from the University of Arkansas in 2005. Firm, quarter-sized berries. High Brix puts these among the sweetest. Erect canes with intermediate vigor. Resistant to anthracnose and orange rust. Recommended for trial in the Mid-Atlantic, West Coast, and South. Ripens in midsummer. Zones 6–9.

Prime Ark. Newest primocane blackberry that bears on first-year canes. Cut the canes just above the ground and allow them to grow back each year. More flavorful than its predecessors. Erect growth habit. High temperatures during bloom (above 86°F, or 30°C) will reduce yields. Harvest begins in September up until frost. University of Arkansas release. Zones 6–9.

Triple Crown. Very sweet, shiny blackberries. Produces as much as 30 pounds of fruit per plant. Supercharged canes, up to 2 inches in diameter and potentially 15 feet long. Semi-erect, thornless type. Grow it like a vine, at 8-foot spacing, or create a fruiting hedge. Fruiting arms should be kept relatively short to prevent snapping off under excessive crop loading. Ripens in mid-July to early August. Hardy into Zone 5.

Pruning tips for blackberries

Growth habit determines the pruning method for these brambles. Cultivars with an *erect* nature can be managed like freestanding raspberries. *Semi-erect* is much the same as *semi-trailing* in nursery catalog lingo—the latter having slightly more limber canes. These can be either topped to form a fruiting hedge or trellised on a wire, depending upon regional considerations. A true *trailing* blackberry is the Northern Hemisphere's counter to kudzu vine. Erect, thornless blackberry varieties such as Arapaho are generally easier to maintain than semi-trailing, thorny types. That said, all blackberries require proper pruning and training to maintain productivity for years to come.

Fruit bearing is induced by tipping first-year blackberry canes to induce a lateral growth response. More side shoots means more accessible fruit. The height at which this is done ties to the winter ahead. In areas that can anticipate strong cold and biting winter winds, like Kansas or Indiana, it makes sense for growers to keep the canes shorter and stiffer. Heading in the growing season is done accordingly at 3–4 feet. In Georgia or Texas, with milder winters, hardy canes could be kept twice as tall for larger plants and thus higher productivity. Growers wishing to bump tender varieties into Zone 5 and even farther north generally need to face winter protection in an entirely different manner (see "Winter cane protection" just ahead).

The mechanics of tipping blackberries involves removing the top inch of the cane (think terminal bud) when it reaches the desired height. This encourages lateral branching—you'll be picking fruit at the end of each lateral next year instead of just at the very tip of the upright cane this way. Clip side laterals as well when these reach 16–20 inches. This results in an even bushier plant that indeed forms a self-supporting hedge (more or less) on a neighborly footing with other canes in the bed. Excess suckers that overly crowd the

Prime Ark is a primocane blackberry that bears on first-year canes, making annual pruning as simple as mowing canes down to the ground after harvest. Photo courtesy of Berries Unlimited.

keepers or that extend the width of the bed beyond your worst nightmares can be removed as necessary. Leave approximately three or four shoots per running foot of row (across a narrow bed width) for hedge management. Height parameters are enforced again with dormant-season pruning, now at around 5 feet for the stoutest of beds.

Having a wire trellis in place for semi-trailing types introduces variations on this theme. Fruiting canes for the blackberry season ahead can all be tied to one side of the trellis, leaving the other side open for new

Call it the trellis flip-flop . . . this year's fruiting canes are tied to one side, allowing primocanes to develop freely; they are then tied accordingly the next spring.

primocanes.[9] These would typically be pruned for lateral development at a higher point than in a hedge. The end result segregates first-year canes from second-year canes for easier management. More limber cultivars can even have their canes laid down en masse for winter protection, where deemed necessary.

Individual plants supported by a central pole require little pruning. All spent canes should be removed after harvest or at the dormant pruning time. Leave five to seven of the best canes per hill, cut no less than 5 feet in length, and quasi-tied by twine loops to the stake. Selecting the more vigorous replacement canes throughout the summer months grants more elbow room for these to develop fully.

Everbearing cultivars such as Prime Ark that fruit on first-year canes should be tipped early in the summer, according to the University of Arkansas. When canes reach 3–4 feet tall, take off about 6 inches of growth. The soft new growth will be just going hard at the correct spot to make this cut. This should create two to four strong laterals per cane. You'll need to attend to your planting several times to catch individual canes at the correct hardening stage.[10] Don't bother tipping canes too late, however. The tip of a cane can show flower buds surprisingly early in warmer regions—removing a single flower bud in the act of tipping these cultivars reduces yield considerably.

Winter cane protection

Desiccation due to cold winter winds makes quite a few blackberry cultivars marginally winter-hardy with respect to bud survival—sometimes even in zones recommended by good nurseries without a wink! Winter protection then becomes necessary if you want to count on a crop every year. Without some effort aimed at protecting next season's floricanes, you might get a full crop in only two of five years, with no crop at all one year, and the other two years good for a partial crop. Such straggler berries will be found down low where canes were less damaged by winter winds.

Blackberries straddling the hardiness divide between Zones 5 and 6 are the ones that begin to suffer cold damage when temperatures dip below 0°F (−18°C). Part of the challenge for these cultivars is their requiring as little as two to six hundred chill hours—thus readily breaking dormancy during a January warm spell, and thereby being set up badly when the next polar front comes along.

Laying trailing canes (preferably thornless!) down on the ground and mulching them isn't as impossible as it may sound. Areas with reliable snow cover in the coldest months will be all set from that moment on. Otherwise, it's a question of layering leaves and/ or straw down under a protecting tarp or going high-tech with foil-faced bubble wrap, all held down with wire ground staples around the edges. Weighting this down further with a collection of wooden posts and old plumbing won't hurt. This isn't going to work with erect or even semi-erect varieties that lack a more limber cane, of course.

Another method leaves erect canes standing. Once leaves have dropped and the blackberry plants have surely gone dormant, a cylindrical wrapping of chicken wire can be put around hill stands of canes. Straw and/or dry leaves can then be stuffed into this cage for insulation, which then gets wrapped around the top with a stout plastic tarp to keep things relatively dry until spring. Rose growers do the very same to protect tender plants from harsh winter winds. Driving a few stakes into the ground to hold down each wire cage ensures your efforts stay in place.

Others rightfully call all this excessive work and seek out old-fashioned cultivars like Nelson instead.

Insect pests of blackberries

Blackberries are subject to the same localized insect challenges as raspberries. **Crown borers** and **cane borers** head the list, particularly rednecks. Pruning vigilance for damaged canes continues to be the foremost approach. Congregating crescendos of **Japanese beetles** and the like are ecosystem situations that can intelligently be dealt with through a range of means discussed earlier.

Disease concerns of blackberries

Holistic orchardists indeed have a plan to deal with disease. We'll add some twists and requisite timing notes here to our general understanding of how plant health keeps pathogens in check.

- Isolating cane fruits from **bramble viruses** can indeed be difficult. Promptly removing distorted canes might help slow down varietal demise. Spreading compost generously along with deep nutrition (foliar) applications has merit as well in keeping cultivated blackberries robust. We're really just learning about the value of inner fortitude on the viral frontier.

- **Orange rust**. New growth clustered together in twisted bunches indicates that this particular bramble rust is at hand. Leaves will be oddly shaped and of a yellowish color. Soon the leaf tissue will turn white with black specks, which subsequently turn into blister-like bubbles. These bubbles then rupture and turn bright orange. Removing any blackberry or black raspberry canes that show symptoms of the rust in spring will help minimize the damage later on. Continue to look through the entire blackberry patch to remove additional leaves showing blister bubbles. Spores from these pustules, when blown to nearby healthy canes, will initiate new infections. This systemic fungus shows no quarter—infected plants will bear little or no fruit again.

- **Botrytis fruit rot**. The gray mold fungus can affect bloom, fruit caps, and berries. In wet, warm seasons—with prolonged rainy and cloudy periods—probably no other disease causes a greater loss of fruit. Fungal spores lodge in open flowers, leading to rot getting a foothold near the attachment to the stalk. The berry succumbs to mold just before harvest and if not removed can become stuck to the branch. The fungus overwinters in plant debris consisting of berry mummies and fallen leaves. Good airflow created by properly thinning canes will keep moisture levels down in the bramble patch. Picking berries at the correct stage of ripeness helps keep others from becoming moldy. Fall decomposition enhanced with compost will limit inoculum loading. Holistic applications on both sides of bloom limit further establishment.

- **Blackberry rosette (double blossom)**. Primocane buds become infected in August and September but don't show signs of fungal infection until the following spring. Distorted shoots will come from each leaf bud and be far shorter and lighter in color than normal shoots. Flower buds are longer and redder than usual, and when the flower actually opens it's larger and twisted, giving an appearance of two blossoms. Fruit quality is very poor if any berries set at all. Infected clusters of shoots and blossoms can be handpicked to control this disease. Pulling spent fruiting canes immediately after harvest helps prevent the late-summer handoff to primocanes. Holistic applications continued through the summer are called for if rosette recurs the following year.

- **White drupelet disorder**. Individual seed capsules on blackberries can lack color as a result of insect feeding as well—stink bug being one such culprit. A sunken surface affirms such as feeding damage. Heat damage will be the far more likely cause when temperatures exceed 90°F (32°C). Some things are just a fact of the season, mates.

- **Crown gall**. This bacterial disease of roots and stems occurs on a large number of plants, including blackberry. The name describes the rough galls that develop at the crown where the main roots join the stem right at the soil line. Similar knots often can be found on secondary, lateral roots as well. These innocuous growths can eventually girdle the stem, causing the plant to become stunted and sickly, with small yellowish leaves. Crown gall is caused by *Agrobacterium*, which is widely distributed in many soils. These bacteria can enter the plant only through wounds, and much infection occurs through grafting and budding scars at the nursery level. Mechanical injuries of crown and roots by cultivation equipment, animals, and insects are also important entry points. Plants having suspicious swellings at graft unions or near the soil line should be discarded.

BUSH FRUITS

Blueberries make a lovely ornamental, with attractive green foliage and bright fall color, and are blessedly long-lived, up to forty to sixty years. Gooseberries and currants are the troupers of the integrated landscape, surviving spring frosts and asking very little in return. Selecting the right bush fruits for your place comes down to varietal nuance. Add a relatively small time investment and you'll be rewarded by bountiful harvests all summer long.

Blueberries

This indigenous berry has been gathered from forests, meadows, and bog edges by Native Americans for centuries. Northern tribes revered the gift of this fruit. The blossom end of each blueberry forms the shape of a perfect five-pointed star. The elders told how the Great Spirit sent star berries to relieve the children's hunger when less game was to be found. Dried blueberries were added to stews or soups and rubbed into meat for a jerky treat.

The domestication of the highbush blueberry started in the early 1900s when a botanist in the U.S. Department of Agriculture, Dr. Frederick Coville, began considering superior plants for breeding. The very first selections came from his home farm in southern New Hampshire. Elizabeth White in New Jersey learned of this research and soon the two were collaborating. She established the first commercial blueberry planting in America and had her pickers and others look for extraordinarily fine wild blueberry bushes for Dr. Coville's cross-breeding efforts. All this resulted in the plump, juicy, sweet, and easy-to-pick blueberry cultivars we enjoy today.[11]

Planting specifics
Blueberries have three basic requirements: access to an acidic root zone, consistent moisture—both of which are abetted with regular mulching—and plenty of sunshine. Hereby lies the way to the sweetest berries in the land.

These fruiting bushes are often said to require an acidic soil with a pH between 4.8 and 5.5. This directs a couple of actions in preparing blueberry ground that are worth doing, despite the fact that we'll be examining what this fundamental supposition concerning pH really means. Blueberry roots have an appreciation for lots of organic matter . . . so amending the planting hole in this direction has merit. Sulfur—typically used to lower soil pH—wears a nutritional crown in its own right. Finally, the use of supplemental nitrogen to abet strong growth shows up on the acidifying agenda as well.

Amending the planting hole

Sandy and heavy soils alike are ideally amended with sphagnum peat moss for a blueberry planting. Peat moss will help acidify the soil as well as lighten up compaction. Shredded pine bark and well-decomposed wood chips can be substituted here, as local sourcing tends to be more economical, and, in truth, these materials are not unlike what peat moss was way back when.[12] Recommended proportions fall along the lines of a 50–50 alteration. Key here is the extent to which you amend. A good-sized hole for highbush blueberry amounts to a 3- to 4-foot-diameter circle dug a foot deep. Understand this: It isn't that the relatively small blueberry plant fresh from the nursery needs a hole this size to accommodate the rootball you see at planting; rather, this is the zone being amended in anticipation of root reach to come.

Here's a basic recipe to consider: Mix 40 percent of the native soil (removed in digging that extremely generous hole) with 50 percent sphagnum peat moss and 10 percent finished compost. Peat moss can store nutrients although it is not especially fertile itself. One cup of elemental sulfur along with the same amount of rock phosphate and double the greensand can be stirred into this mixture.[13] The peat moss should be pre-moistened by making a small hole in the top of the bag, placing the end of a garden hose in it, and filling with as much water as the bag can hold. Leave the bag to sit for a day or two so that moisture wicks fully into the core.

Heavy clay soil is trickier to amend than sand. First, there's the pot factor, followed by the fact that blueberries reject waterlogged sites. The roots of a plant growing in radically improved soil tend to be homebodies—root expansion beyond the confines of the hole into less friendly ground can be as little as nil. The sides of a well-defined planting hole represent an interface of both fertility and capillary action. Ergo, we make the hole "larger" by forking in the edges to roughly incorporate the boundary areas with the peat soil mixture. Creating a transition zone to facilitate groundwater flow allows blueberry roots to be less subject to wide swings between soggy and dry. Organic mulch up top will abet soil life to open up channels in the clay extending even farther out and down.

Highbush blueberries and rabbiteye types typically are planted at a 4- to 6-foot spacing (depending on cultivar). A commercial grower utilizes a tractor swath to achieve what's just been talked about. A deep furrow opened with a middle buster plow allows for the addition of well-decomposed wood chips and other chosen amendments. This has the added advantage of forming a slight planting berm when the native soil is folded back over and subsequently disked. Container-grown blueberries like a light soil cut with peat and aged bark chips as well. Chunks of burnt wood at the very bottom add a biochar component to good drainage via the bottom hole in the pot.

The role of sulfur

Almost everything written elsewhere about blueberry culture will stress knowing the pH of the intended soil, and subsequently driving it downward (numerically speaking) with sulfur. Important minerals for blueberry health are not readily available in alkaline conditions. When soil pH is appreciably higher than 5.5, iron chlorosis can result. When soil pH drops below 4.8, the possibility of manganese toxicity arises. Plants can struggle at both ends of this spectrum.

Deciding to incorporate sulfur when preparing blueberry ground to achieve an acidic pH reading starts with a soil test. Do this, but pay heed to our current plan. Not only is soil pH subject to considerable seasonal fluctuation, but peat moss in itself is quite acidic. (The pH of Canadian-derived sphagnum peat generally ranges 3.0–4.5.) Soils in drier regions and along the Gulf Coast tend to have a buffering reservoir of lime and thus a high pH reading. Trying to radically lower the pH of alkaline soil to create an acid one suitable for blueberries is difficult.[14] Adding organic matter, which is naturally acidic, can generally be chalked up as the right first step. Nutrients will be made available as the elemental sulfur, rock phosphate, greensand, and compost (all mixed into the planting hole as well) are taken up by the biology.[15]

Conventional advice comes with a table recommending as much as several pounds of sulfur per 100 square feet per application, depending on soil type. Spreading sulfur pellets (the granular form of elemental sulfur looks much like pale yellow lentils) again and again over the years to satisfy the pH meter should rightfully be questioned by holistic growers. Please. Being more conservative about applications of sulfur designed to alter the entire soil profile demands more nuanced understanding. Sulfur has fungicidal properties that detrimentally affect soil biology when overused. A tad, yes, maybe applied once every four or five years if leaves start to show the need through chlorosis.[16] Sulfur helps make iron available to the plant through its acidifying action. Deeper perspective will help us zero in on exactly where this requisite nutrient exchange needs to take place.

Acidifying nitrogen

Supplemental nitrogen in the early years of a blueberry planting is spot-on. Woodsy mulches are not that far along with respect to decomposition, and so fresher material may actually be tying up what nitrogen is available as the soil food web attempts to deal with significant carbon loading. All will change for the better as the mulch dynamic comes into gear in the years ahead.[17] Now, however, is now.

One economical source of nitrogen made available in the ammonium form utilized by blueberries is soybean meal. Soybean meal has little influence on soil acidity, however. That niche belongs to cottonseed meal (7-2-2), assuming you can find an organic source.[18] It's not inexpensive, but it will do the job of acidifying soil much faster than elemental sulfur. Call this another choice on the peat moss/sulfur/acidifying-N continuum, okay?

Spread an organically approved source of nitrogen a month after spring planting at the rate of 1 pound per 100 square feet. Do this again in fall, and then subsequently at a 2-pound rate every fall thereafter as the bushes come to full size.[19] Healthy blueberries should produce new shoots 10 inches or longer on older canes and should put out several new canes from the roots every year.

Moisture matters

Native blueberry soils generally have a shallow water table approximately 2 feet deep that supplies uniform moisture during the growing season. Constantly saturated soils are undesirable, of course.[20] Blueberries can certainly be grown on ground with a deeper water table provided the grower commits to providing *consistent moisture* through irrigation maintained by mulching. The upshot? Don't let a dry week go on by!

Water is especially critical in the first year or two. New plantings with lush growth may require watering every two days during dry periods. If in doubt, scoot your hand down below the mulch to see if the root zone is dry. Negligence during the growing season leads to stunting growth for a long, long time to come.

Most plants have root hairs extending the reach of feeder roots. This increases the absorptive surface area considerably for taking in moisture and nutrients. Blueberries are unusual in that they do not have root hairs. The blueberry root system turns out to be functionally smaller than that of other fruiting plants because of this. Most blueberry roots are located in the uppermost soil layer (like any other), but they rarely reach beyond the dripline of the plant. This means that the blueberry is unable to draw water from a substantial volume of soil—and thus relies upon the grower to provide water in the immediate vicinity during each and every dry spell.

One last shot across the bow to drive this point home. Early drought in spring will reduce this year's growth and fruit size. Later drought through the summer months and into fall will decrease next year's crop and growth.

True-blue acidity

Organic mulch consisting of shredded bark, ramial wood chips, aged sawdust, leaf mold, and/or pine needles applied several inches deep—and kept renewed annually—results in more uniform soil moisture for blueberries. Mulch reduces soil temperature and promotes better bush growth overall.[21] Softwood-sourced materials from pine and other evergreens are as fine for blueberry mulch as hardwood-sourced materials—perhaps even better, based entirely on the notion that blueberries are acid-loving plants. (Coniferous mulches have a pH in the 3.5–4.5 range.) The place to investigate this more fully brings us at last to the blueberry feeder root zone.

The surface of the soil beneath a decomposing mulch is where the action that rocks the kasbah lies for blueberries. Holistic understanding begins with the insights of a horticultural researcher in Oklahoma. Carl Whitcomb proved that pH throughout the entire planting zone need not be corrected for acid-loving plants; furthermore, the rhizosphere can be changed in only a small area (the soil surface beneath mulch), whereby such plants can draw the iron required for healthy growth.[22] Here's the thing. This whole pH business defining blueberry culture isn't about *overall acidity* as much as it is about the availability of iron gained through *localized acidity*.

Mulched blueberries access iron at the soil/mulch interface precisely because acids released due to the decomposition of organic mulches make iron available there. Here lies an acidic haven for blueberry feeder roots. This is where modest amounts of sulfur can be directed should chlorosis start to show—applied on the existing mulch surface, followed immediately with additional mulch.[23] This is where additional greensand—rich in iron—can be distributed after planting, prior to putting down the first layer of mulch.[24] Old-timers did much the same when they threw a handful of rusty nails around the base of blueberry plants. Feeder roots find available iron in this acidic interface even as the majority of the root system continues to function in a soil with a pH higher than typically recommended.

Blueberries indeed do thrive in soils with an overall pH well into the 6 range, if not higher. Revisiting the concept of cation balance (explained back in chapter 3) helps us understand this further. It turns out that blueberries like lots of magnesium but have a real aversion to high calcium levels. Shifting the Ca–Mg balance in blueberry soil—by nudging the base saturation of magnesium up several points relative to calcium—makes possible that higher pH, which in turn promotes nutrient density (as measured by Brix) in berries.[25] We now stand on holistic ground in the blueberry patch. Higher readings of soluble solids indicate balanced nutrition across the board. The result is a healthier plant better able to defend against disease and insects—that's also going to produce the best-tasting berries.

Blueberry varieties to consider

The genus *Vaccinium* includes more than 450 species. Blueberries share this stage with cranberries, bilberries, lingonberries, and huckleberries. The small berries of the lowbush blueberry (*V. angustifolium*) as grown commercially in Maine and up into the Canadian Maritimes are renowned for intense flavor and cultivation by fire. These are harvested en masse with a blueberry rake, being a low-handled contraption with tines, designed to scoop up uniform-ripening berries and leaves alike. Cultivated varieties are the result of selecting and breeding other regional species to emphasize highbush traits. Single berries of considerably larger size are picked from bountiful clusters by hand over the course of a couple of weeks. Choosing

Lowbush blueberries are traditionally harvested with a handheld blueberry rake.

from among northern highbush, southern highbush, and rabbiteyes begins with understanding the particularities of each. The health benefits of well-grown blueberries make this a righteous quest.

Northern highbush

Domestication of the highbush blueberry (*Vaccinium corymbosum*) of the northern forest has led to all sorts of cultivars suitable for Zones 3–8. These relatively high-chill varieties (a thousand chill hours and up) are the most widely planted. The berries range in size from ¼ inch to a full inch in diameter, and in color from almost black to light powder blue. A planting of several varieties ensures pollination as well as setting up a continuous harvest that can stretch over months, from midsummer through first frost. Upright bushes reaching to 6 feet tall experience bud injury around –20 to –25°F (–29 to –32°C); growers farther north look to half-high cultivars with lowbush genetics that introduce exceptional cold hardiness.

Aurora. Enjoy blueberries through the month of September! Moderately large, powder-blue fruit. Its fresh tang beats Elliot (the other fall variety) hands down. Rounded upright bush spreads to 5–6 feet. Named after the aurora borealis (the northern lights) by breeder Jim Hancock at Michigan State. Hardy in Zone 5.

Bluecrop. Light blue berries are very large and flavorful. Open clusters of fruit make this easy to pick. Upright growth habit. Light red wood and fiery red fall foliage. Dependable yields, year in and year out. Widely adaptable. Ripens mid-July and bears for a month.

Blueray. Early to midseason cultivar. Large, dark blue berries have a hint of the wild blueberry. Best flavor in cooler locales. Vigorous bush grows 4–6 feet tall. Tight fruit clusters susceptible to mummy berry in a wet year. Winter-hardy to Zone 4. Widely planted throughout the Northeast and Upper Midwest.

Chippewa. Half-high cultivar from the University of Minnesota. Compact bush grows to 3 feet tall and 4 feet wide. Classic aluminum blue color; excellent-flavored berries. Hardiness improves with dependable snow cover. Hardy in Zone 3.

Earliblue. First blueberry of the season to ripen. Moderately large, medium blue, aromatic fruit. Vigorous upright bush. Berries hold well in cluster. Resists cracking. Avoid planting in frost pockets. Hardy into Zone 4.

Jersey. Spicy berries with a distinctive old-time flavor. Consistent and heavy producer. Favorite for baking. Vigorous upright bush. Bright yellow fall leaf color and yellow winter wood. Fruit ripens from mid-August until frost. High temps will diminish sweetness.

Nelson. A good blueberry for the Upper Midwest. Late-season. Large, firm, medium-blue berries. Released by the Michigan State breeding program. Quite hardy. Suitable for Zones 3–7.

Northblue. Best overall fruit quality of the half-high cultivars from Minnesota. Dark blue berries with superior flavor. Propagates well; consistently productive; highly self-fertile. Averages 2 to 3 feet in height. Plan on 5–8 pounds of fruit from each bush.

Olympia. One of the West's best-kept secrets. Large fruit has a distinctive spicy flavor. Ripens in late July. Vigorous, highly productive bush with a spreading

The aromatic fruits of Earliblue hold well in the cluster for easy picking. Photo by Michael Kevin Daly and courtesy of Fall Creek Farm & Nursery.

Reka is hot! This dark blueberry variety from New Zealand offers the best early-season flavor going. Photo by Michael Kevin Daly and courtesy of Fall Creek Farm & Nursery.

Toro. Medium to large, attractive blue fruit. Figure on sixty berries to the cup. Ripens midseason somewhat uniformly. Harvest may be completed in two pickings. Tolerates fluctuating temperatures. New Jersey release in 1987. Hardy throughout Zone 5.

Southern highbush

Cultivating highbush blueberries for southern zones required that breeders reduce the chilling requirements of *Vaccinium corymbosum*. This was accomplished principally by introducing the genetics of *V. darrowii*, a pine understory native found from Florida across to Mississippi. The resulting crosses—in addition to providing lower chilling requirements—develop superior fruit quality despite high summer temperatures, offer somewhat greater drought tolerance, and are adaptable to alkaline-tending soils. These cultivars are self-fertile; however, larger and earlier-ripening berries result if several cultivars are interplanted for cross-pollination. Southern highbush bear earlier than rabbiteyes and are more resistant to blossom freezes. Chilling requirements range from 150 hours and up, making some of these suitable for even Zone 10. Growers in transition zones are advised to grow both southern and northern highbush types, as each highlights different flavor subtleties.

habit. Developed in Olympia, Washington. Tender. Zones 6–8.

Reka. Widely adaptable blueberry from New Zealand. Dark blue fruit offers the best early-season flavor going. Grows well in light sandy soils, peat, and heavier clay loams. Tolerant of wetter ground. Winter hardiness on par with Bluecrop. Best in Zones 5–7.

Rubel. Old selection from the Pine Barrens of New Jersey. Top-rated cultivar for health benefits. Sparkling, tart flavor. Good productivity, though you need to pick many more berries to fill a cup . . . smaller berry size, quite frankly, is a virtue when making good ol' blueberry pancakes! Tends to be stemmy when harvested overripe. Zones 4–7.

Cape Fear. Think berries the size of nickels. Incredibly aromatic, almost piney flavor. Early midseason. Adapted across the Gulf Coast and up to South Carolina. Tolerates heat extremely well. Three hundred chill hours.

Jewel. Large, tangy berries. Patented release from the University of Florida breeding program. Very early-ripening (beginning in mid-April in Gainesville). Low chill requirement of two hundred hours. Moderately susceptible to *Phytophthora* root rot.

Jubilee. Sky-blue berries grow in large clusters. Developed in Mississippi. Performs well in heavier soils and summer heat. Deals well with cold snaps. Upright yet compact bush. Ripens over a two-week period in midseason. Five hundred chill hours.

Bluecrop offers dependable production year after year for northern growers. Photo courtesy of Fall Creek Farm & Nursery.

Ka-Bluey. Complex sweet flavor with peach-like overtones. Crisp, purple-blue fruit. University of Arkansas selection licensed exclusively to Gardens Alive.[26] Matures in June. Bush reaches 6 feet tall. Resists root rot. Good hardiness due to a dominance of northern highbush lineage. Proven to date in Zones 5–7.

Legacy. Parentage includes *Vaccinium darrowii*, Florida 4B, and Bluecrop. Medium-large berries.

Brilliant fall foliage is bright orange and stays on the bush into the winter. Vigorous grower and heavy producer. Release from the USDA Blueberry Research Station in New Jersey. Very adaptable to different soil types across the country. Ripens late midseason. Zones 5–8.

Ozark Blue. Late-season berry with sweet to sub-acid flavor. Drought resistance of a rabbiteye. Performs well in cold country or in areas with high summer

Legacy stands out as a southern highbush blueberry that's adaptable to different soil types across the country. Photo courtesy of Backyard Berry Plants.

Sharpblue blooms and fruits throughout the year where frosts are uncommon, with foliage remaining nearly evergreen. Photo by Roanne Lavelle and courtesy of Fall Creek Farm & Nursery.

heat. Large, vigorous bush grows up to 8 feet high. University of Arkansas release for upper southern zones. Four hundred chill hours.

Reveille. Unique crisp, almost crunchy texture. Outstanding pop of flavor. Upright, narrow, easy-to-grow habit. Great hedge plant at 5 feet tall. Pink bloom yields loads of medium-sized, light blue berries. Thrives in hot climates as well as in the cool Pacific Northwest. Hardy to 0°F (−18°C). Needs five to six hundred chilling hours.

Sante Fe. Describing this berry for the Sunshine Belt as "sweet as a Texas rose" speaks to its prospects. Early-ripening, light blue fruit with a determined touch of acidity. Flowers may be slow to open in the spring. Unusual ability to thrive in soils that are low in organic matter and with alkaline irrigation water. Four hundred chill hours. Zones 8–10.

Sharpblue. Widely adaptable variety for low-chill areas. Blooms and fruits throughout the year where frosts are uncommon, with foliage remaining nearly evergreen. Medium-sized fruit. Upright bush grows to 6 feet tall. Pollinize with Misty for larger berry size.

Sunshine Blue. One of the best varieties for pot culture. Compact evergreen bush with showy hot pink flowers. Tolerates higher-pH soils better than many. Self-fertile. Requires only 150 chill hours, yet plants are frost-hardy. Suitable from San Diego up to Seattle as well as the Deep South.

Rabbiteyes

Now, don't be expecting the southern rabbiteye (*Vaccinium ashei*) to be nearly as well behaved as your everyday highbush cultivar! The common name springs from the calyx on the berry, which is said to resemble the eye of a rabbit. These taller bushes have superior drought tolerance and are not nearly so fussy about soil acidity. Rabbiteye bloom comes slightly later than that of southern highbush, which helps in evading a spring freeze. The picking season extends from late May into the first weeks of September. Regular irrigation helps prevent bursting fruit, which occurs if there is a dry spell followed by heavy rain.

Brightwell. University of Georgia release in 1983. Light blue, firm fruit with good flavor. Around eighty berries to the cup. Vigorous, upright, excellent producer. Ripens in June. Three hundred chill hours. Zones 6–9.

Centurion. Intense, jammy flavor with bright notes of acidity. Darker than most rabbiteyes. Crunchy berries are excellent for baking. Vigorous, upright bush grows 6–10 feet tall. Latest to ripen. Flower buds resistant to freeze damage.

Climax. Large berries ripen uniformly with full sweetness. Ripens early. Spreading, open growth habit, 10–15 feet tall. Leaves have a blue tinge, turning red in the fall. Susceptible to gall midge. Four hundred fifty chill hours. Zones 6–9.

Columbus. High-yielding, superior-flavored fruit. Distinctly sweet with little acid. Berry quality judged by many as the best. Slightly spreading bush grows 6–7 feet tall. Ripens midseason. North Carolina State introduction.

Powderblue. Sweet, dark blue fruit. Very reliable producer. Yields of 8–14 pounds on each irrigated bush. Hangs well with little fruit cracking. Chilling requirement estimated 250–300 hours.

Tiftblue. Medium to large, powder-blue berries. Harvest when all reddish color on stem end disappears. More willowy bush. Long bearing season starts in early July and runs into September. Most

The distinctive calyx end on these Powderblue berries makes clear how "rabbiteyes" earned their name. Photo courtesy of Berries Unlimited.

cold-hardy rabbiteye. Six hundred chill hours. Zones 6–9.

Pruning tips for blueberries

Blueberry plants typically are not pruned for the first few years. Ongoing shoot growth (from the ground up) is a sign that roots are finding balanced nutrition at the mulch/soil interface. Good. These will form a light-space-filling branch structure with keeper fruit buds by the third season.[27] During the fourth and fifth years, dormant plants should be pruned in late winter. Remove excess twiggy branches down low and thin any terminal wood with smallish buds. Crossing branches in the interior should also be removed to allow light into the center of the plant. Even though you don't yet realize it, you are now an accomplished blueberry pruner.

These rules hardly deviate in subsequent years. Now thinning out older base branches forces new growth from the root crown. Vigorous shoots appearing in early summer represent the annual tide of blueberry renewal. Sunlight will tickle these upward while eventual fruiting (starting in the third season) will spread new branches outboard. Keeping eight to ten base branches on the team at a time speaks to the pace here: Remove two or three of the oldest each year to make way for an equal number of replacements. Bud vigor begins to decline after the fifth year—making this rotation totally about robust berry production. Tall-growing branches can be

I'LL BE YOUR HUCKLEBERRY

Here's a berry packed with lore, its flavor extolled across northern continents, that continues to be virtually untamed. Mama grizzlies seek it, the gunfighter Doc Holliday invoked it, and Huck Finn won't ever dodge it. We're talking huckleberries, the small round berries found in wild places from the Louisiana bayou to the mountain country of the Rockies to the shores of Lake Michigan and throughout the woodlands of the East.

Numerous species of *Vaccinium* fall under the huckleberry banner. Berries range in color from deep crimson through eggplant purple and on to the blues. The taste of huckleberries stretches from tart to sweet, with a wild undertone that transcends every domesticated blueberry. Musky fragrance differentiates these similar-looking fruits, followed by what lies within: Blueberries have numerous tiny seeds and a whitish inner core, while hucks have ten larger seeds and deep color throughout.

A varietal overview can be found on the website of the International Wild Huckleberry Association. The most common huckleberries harvested commercially in the Northwest are the mountain huckleberry (*Vaccinium membranaceum*) and its alpine cousin, the cascade bilberry (*V. deliciosum*). Attempts to cultivate these wild species have been made but often end in failure. One improved cultivar for southern regions is Trentberry, which offers large, glossy black fruit about ½ inch in diameter from a shrub that stands 6 feet high.

The saying *I'll be your huckleberry* implies being the right person for a given job. The berry itself offers outstanding medicine for our benefit. Enhancing vision, regulating diabetes, and toning the circulatory system are attributed to the huckleberry/bilberry grouping. These deeply colored berries hold an abundance of anthocyanin compounds well worth tracking down, whether in the wild or your own backyard.

headed back to stimulate new upper shoots in those seasons when crown shoot production seems to be lagging.

Here's yet another way to understand this. Flower buds on *Vaccinium* are produced on tips and down along limb growth (side shoots) from the previous season. Thinning out at the branch tips and outright removal of spent branches means fewer flowers overall. Blueberry bushes tend to produce smaller berries when they are overloaded. Hence, it is important not to have too many flower buds. Hence, we prune.

Insect pests of blueberries

Here in northern New Hampshire problems with blueberry pests are nil. Many of you will be able to say the very same. And still others must be prepared to face what comes.

- The thing to understand about "**blueberry curculio**" concerns the oviposition preferences of the pest more properly identified as plum curculio. These weevil-like foes have learned through evolutionary zeal which fruits better favor reproductive success in different parts of the East. It's from the Carolina coast up through New Jersey where the strongest preference for blueberry shows. Kaolin clay is not a good choice on soft fruit, so use neem, liquid fish, and garlic extracts to change olfactory cues.

- The minute that **Japanese vinegar fly** set its sights on blueberry and raspberry plantings up and down the West Coast shall ever be remembered as madness unleashed. This perverse situation must be prevented ecosystemwide. All thin-skinned fruits are prospective targets, as are open compost piles. Vinegar traps with a few drops of dish soap added to the brew (to lessen surface tension) will snare a portion of these tiny fiends. Broader strategies have been discussed for protecting the cherry crop (see "Organic solutions" for cherry pests in chapter 6, on page 226.)
- A kissing cousin of the apple maggot fly in all respects but choice of fruit would be the **blueberry maggot fly**. Think clear wings with black markings, flitting about ripening berry clusters, ovipositing a single egg into random fruit, the larvae making a tunneling mash of each infested berry. Which may very well be indistinguishable until you gobble one down. Yuck. Yellow sticky cards (baited with ammonium) will catch emerging adults. Soil treatment of the mulched zone with nematodes in late summer may be necessary to regain the upper hand. Laying out old carpet beneath bushes to gather infested berries that eventually fall breaks the soil pupation link altogether. Braconid wasps are a definite ally throughout central and northeastern regions where this pest strikes.
- Tag-teaming comes into play with certain moth pests. The **cranberry fruitworm** and the **cherry fruitworm** have equal affinity for blueberry. Eggs of both are laid on unripe fruit; the larvae hatch and then enter the stem end of the berry to feed. More than one fruit can be damaged by a single worm. Finding berry clusters webbed together with silk confirms moth origins. Applications of Bt in the first two weeks following petal fall hold this incursion in check.

- Blueberries are not deeply rooted. Assorted **white grubs** establishing in the mulch have little choice as to a meal. Oriental beetle and other non-native scarab beetle larvae have especial affinity.[28] An entire plant dying with leaves on and bark shriveled up can be indicative that an excessive number of root eaters are at work. Dig down to the outer periphery of the root system. Grubs consume the small fibrous ends. This situation can become particularly bad under sawdust. A neem soil drench will change grub prospects, but it will likely be too late for the worst afflicted blueberry plants by the time you catch on.
- Clearly not all damage is caused by insects. Lack of blueberry bloom may well be traced to deer or rabbits nibbling the buds in the winter months. Paying attention year-round needs to become part of your program.

Disease concerns of blueberries

Holistic orchardists indeed have a plan to deal with disease. We'll add some twists and requisite timing notes here to our general understanding of how plant health keeps pathogens in check.

- **Mummy berry**. This affliction of blueberries can result in significant crop loss in the Northeast and across the Midwest. The fruit becomes discolored and shrivels up—like mummies—due to a fungus with a rather complicated life cycle. The causal fungus overwinters in infected berries that have fallen to the ground. In spring the dried-up berries sprout small, mushroom-like structures, with little cups on the end that produce spores. Lots of them. The spores are spread by wind to land on leaf buds and young shoots; infection occurs if green tissue stays wet long enough. Infected leaves and shoots wilt and turn brown a couple of weeks later. Fungal conidia (essentially

You'll be one of the lucky few if aluminum pie pans actually keep neighborhood birds from your berries. Photo courtesy of Alan Eaton, University of New Hampshire.

a second round of spores) now spread to nearby flower blossoms via rain splash and insect activity.[29] Infected berries turn pinkish and shrivel instead of ripening. Cultural practices can help break this annual cycle. Raking under the bushes and shallow cultivation between the rows in early spring destroys the spore cups. Applying a couple of inches of new mulch in fall will effectively bury the fallen mummies. The holistic sprays of spring address the blown-in factor.

- **Stem blight**. This vascular disease of southern highbush varieties often starts from cold injury to shoots. The leaves on blighted stems brown and wilt but don't fall off. The stem itself can be cut open to reveal a light brown discoloration. Removal of infected wood (pruning about 12 inches below the discolored part of the limb) is important in containing the damage and limiting further spread. Protect susceptible plants at budbreak and both sides of bloom with clove oil to inhibit fungal growth and spore germination of the pathogen.[30]

- **Red leaf disease**. Systemic infection requires the prompt removal of infected plants to keep this fungus from spreading to healthy plants. During the middle of summer, terminal leaves on some bushes will turn a reddish color. The undersides of these leaves will be whitish due to the development of fungal spores of the pathogen. Later, the leaves will turn black and dry up. A primed immune response is the only defense. Take care not to confuse this with red coloration in season without that underside clue—lack of available iron in the soil can lead to a similar appearance with an entirely different solution.

BERRY PICKING TIME!

A few tips make time in the berry patch that much more productive.

Color indicates ripeness, yet don't be too eager. You'll quickly learn which berries to let hang for fuller sweetness and which lose their edge after spending one day too long in the heat. Spot-picking is a better rule of thumb than stripping off less-ripe berries along with the good ones en masse. Berries do not continue to ripen once picked. Blueberries will be a deep inky blue when ready; those tinted red or a shade of lavender need more time. Gauging the depth of color in cane fruit is for the taster alone. Gooseberries picked slightly early will make a good pie, but it's the ones that escape notice that sweeten up fully for fresh eating. Processing fruit like elderberries and currants can hang in the cluster to ripen completely.

Use your thumb, index, and middle fingers to create a "harvesting rake" to gently pull berries off the plant. Raspberries will slide off the inner cone when ready—any sign of resistance indicates the berry needs at least another day to ripen fully. Blueberries and currants literally roll into the cup of your palm, usually without too much stem debris once they are delectably plump and ripe. Gooseberries and blackberries come armed with thorns, some varieties more so than others. You can't just grab a branch to strip it! These fruits warrant being plucked at a slower pace. Elderberries are snipped off the plant in the cluster and then stripped from the bitter stem at the kitchen table.

Shallow bowls or trays are preferable for picking containers, as soft berries crush under the weight of too many layers. Fastening a pail (by its handle) at waist height with some twine or a belt hook frees two hands for picking. Empty the pail frequently as you pick. Setting the bowls or trays on a garden cart lessens having to bend down, plus the cart can easily be rolled along as the family works its way down the bed. Every picker should have his or her own pail rather than having to stretch across to a neighbor with each new handful. The hand can hold only so many berries safely before berries get smushed or drop to the ground in reaching for *just one more.*

Back in the kitchen, clean the berries by delicately pouring them into a colander. Gently roll them around to remove stems, errant bugs, and any damaged fruit. Never wash berries unless you will use them immediately. Berries that are rinsed and then stored can mold surprisingly fast. Refrigerate the unwashed berries in open plastic bags or containers to allow air circulation until you make that pie or do up a batch of jam. Berries are far and away the easiest garden goody to freeze for later use. Spread the cleaned, unwashed berries on a cookie tray and freeze overnight. Once frozen, transfer the berries to a sealable plastic bag or pint box, where they will keep until the harvest comes around again.

• *Alternaria* **fruit rot**. Watery-looking berries going into harvest are indicative of this fungal rot. The earliest symptom is the presence of dark greenish sporulation on the blossom end of the fruit appearing a week or two before harvest. The causal fungus overwinters in and on the twigs and in debris on the ground.

• **Witches' broom**. This shoot-growth-run-amok disease is caused by a fungus that needs two host species to survive. Blueberry is one of them; the other is the fir tree.[31] The fungal spores that infect blueberry come from fir—in other words, one blueberry's broom cannot spread to other blueberries directly. Pruning out the excessive growth doesn't eliminate the disease from an infected plant, as the infection is systemic. Clumps of swollen, spongy shoots with short internodes and small leaves spring from the base of the plant each season. The strange twigs start out yellowish, then turn brown, and finally dark brown, dry, and cracked. Eliminating nearby fir trees helps reduce incidence. Bushes can often continue to be productive for years despite this.

Gooseberries

European gooseberries (*Ribes uva-crispa*) are native to North Africa and the Caucasus Mountains of eastern Europe and western Asia, while American gooseberries (*R. hirtellum*) are native across the northern half of this continent. The real difference lies in what humans have done to both develop and celebrate this audacious berry. Fruit size varies widely within the European types, from pea size to as large as a small egg. Color varies as well, with fruit maturing in assorted shades of green, pink, red, purple, white, and yellow. Such diversity is due to a long history of appreciation of a beloved fruit. Over the past two centuries, Europeans have developed hundreds of cultivars, with a focus on prizewinning fruit size and color.

Native American gooseberry species have smaller fruit size and admittedly less flavor, but they are extraordinarily resistant to disease compared with European cultivars. Susceptibility to powdery mildew and leaf spot, frankly, has limited the culture of the premium European types on this continent. The good news lies in crossing the two lines. Disease resistance has improved through additional breeding with American types, and several promising new European cultivars have been introduced recently in Canada.

Americans will catch gooseberry fever in part by realizing that these bushes (like currants) are such easy landscaping plants. Every small yard in Europe has a couple of gooseberry bushes tucked into a backyard garden or ornamental planting alongside the house . . . much as our culture does now with azaleas or yew bushes. How much better to grow nutritious food!

Gooseberries are typically used for preserves or pies, somewhat like rhubarb, more than for eating out of hand. Still, the better cultivars will change even that perception quickly. And then there's gooseberry butter: Heat the berries until the skins pop, then force them through a colander; add sugar in equal proportions to the pulp, and simmer until thick. Top off a toasted English muffin and you'll understand far more than mere words can tell.

Planting specifics

Gooseberries like morning sun, partial shade throughout the afternoon, and good air circulation. Northern to northeastern exposure works well because the air and soil will be cooler and moister. *Ribes* growers in southern regions must absolutely limit direct exposure from the sun starting at high noon. Light intensity in the first half of the afternoon coupled with high heat results in sunburn to both leaves and fruit. Air temperatures regularly cresting 85°F (29°C) lead to unhappy plantings in general. Full sun exposure in considerably cooler or mountainous climates, however, will be desirable to boost yields.

Gooseberry plants are less finicky about soil acidity than most other small fruits. These bushes tolerate a wide range of soils, except those that are waterlogged. Heavier soils hold an edge where summers are hot, because better fruit results when all contributing factors point toward keeping things cool. You can bet a thick woodsy mulch is in order here. Gooseberries have a fibrous, shallow root system that benefits from regular drip irrigation. Keep these plants watered throughout the season, as buds and leaves lost to drought stress will not be regenerated.

A high requirement for potassium and a moderate need for nitrogen make up basic gooseberry nutrition. An ongoing supply of woodsy mulch addresses the

Invicta gooseberry offers up its exceptionally sweet fruits at a price: Beware those prickly thorns! Photo courtesy of One Green World.

The teardrop-shaped fruit of Captivator gooseberry are very easy to pick. Photo courtesy of Vesey's Seeds Ltd.

first, and a light top-dressing of composted manure answers for the second. Don't overdo compost with gooseberries; excessive amounts of nitrogen will promote disease, especially mildew. These berry plants appreciate plentiful magnesium as well, so use dolomitic lime whenever adjusting soil pH upward into the recommended 5.5–6.5 range.

All *Ribes* plants require approximately a thousand to twelve hundred chilling hours to break dormancy. That tells you two things. No gooseberry is intended for the Deep South or Southern California, a conclusion you should have already reached with all those admonitions about high heat. Second, these bushes bloom relatively early in the spring, several weeks before strawberries.[32] Avoid low areas where late-spring frosts can injure the blossoms. Temperatures below 28°F (–2°C) will damage open flowers and thus take a cut out of that year's berry crop.

Both gooseberries and currants should be planted at least an inch deeper than they were in the nursery. Covering the lower canes with soil—to a depth of two or three buds—will encourage a larger root system and the development of numerous renewal canes. This attention to detail will maximize the life span of the plant. Head back plants at this time to 6–10 inches tall to further facilitate root and basal shoot growth. Gooseberries may be spaced as close as 3 feet apart for a hedge-type system. These bushes are self-fertile;

nevertheless, planting more than one cultivar always improves pollination prospects.

Gooseberry varieties to consider

These highly prized fruits are an important part of a well-rounded garden in Europe. The gooseberry has been sadly neglected in America, as native species tend toward the tart and mouth-puckering end of the flavor spectrum. Crossing the sweet varieties of the Old World with disease resistance from the New World has changed everything. Gooseberries generally ripen in July, with hardiness appropriate throughout Zones 3–8 unless otherwise noted.

Achilles. Old English variety noted for its large, elliptical, deliciously sweet red fruit. Ripens later than most, extending the season. Spreading, drooping habit. Unripe fruit is used for compote and ripe fruit for fresh eating, jams, and preserving. Zones 3–9.

Black Velvet. Considered the champagne of all gooseberry cultivars. Large crops of sweet, dark red fruit with an intriguing blueberry-like flavor. Hardy bushes are tremendously productive. Disease-resistant. Cooler zones produce the tastiest berries. Zones 4–8.

Captivator. Large, teardrop-shaped fruit. Deep pink and sweet when ripe. Foliage turns yellow in the fall. Mildew-resistant and exceptionally hardy. A cross of European and American species that is nearly thornless and thus easy to pick. Bred in Ottawa, Canada, in 1935. Zones 3–9.

Friend. Disease-resistant gooseberry from Ukraine. Lack of thorns makes for pain-free picking. Large, yellow, sweet berries. Recommended for the Pacific Northwest.

Glenndale. Developed by the USDA for warmer climates. Shady or partially shady location strongly recommended. Very productive despite summer heat and high humidity. Best in Zones 7–8.

Hinnomaki Yellow. Outstanding aromatics distinguishes this variety. Medium-sized, sweet yellow-green berry with a luscious aftertaste reminiscent of apricot. Low-growing bush with a spreading habit. Ripens midsummer. Mildew-resistant. Finnish lineage delivers extreme winter hardiness into Zone 2.

Invicta. Mildew-resistant selection from the Malling Research Station in England. Produces heavy yields from the get-go. Large green fruit hang in heavy clusters down the length of the branch. Exceptionally sweet. Incredibly thorny. Sunburn sensitivity best dealt with beneath afternoon shade. Magnet for imported currant worms in the South. Zones 3–7.

Jeanne. Superior cultivar with mixed European/American gooseberry pedigree. Large red fruit with thin skin. Full-bodied sweetness calls you back for more. Vigorous bush. Glossy leaves stand out. Resistant to mildew and rust. Introduction from Corvallis, Oregon.

Poorman. Highly flavored, sweet table variety. Excellent for eating out of hand. The green berries turn red with a lilac bloom when fully ripe. Sets a ton of fruit. Very thorny bush. Considered by many to be the best American gooseberry. Beware: The birds know this! Zones 4–10.

Red Jacket. Excellent in both green and red stages. Sturdy, nearly thornless bush. Self-fertile. Very disease-resistant. Hardy to –30°F (–34°C). Developed at the Cheyenne Experiment Station in Wyoming in 1930.

Pruning tips for gooseberries

A gooseberry bush is usually grown on a permanent short leg crown about 6 inches high, from which the bush is continually renewed with new shoots arising at or near ground level. Allow the more vigorous stems to grow for the first three or four years, then begin to selectively remove the oldest ones to make room for new shoots. Snap off any side branches that spring from the base of the plant as a matter of course.

Removing those older shoots with a plethora of side branches right at ground level does a couple things beyond creating light space for new gooseberry shoots to fill. I became an aggressive *Ribes* pruner myself only when it finally dawned on me that younger shoots have plumper buds. That promise of bigger berries can be fulfilled only once you heed to what amounts to a relatively straightforward rule. Keeping an older branch past its prime just because there seems to be room results in filling a picking bowl with hundreds of smaller berries that tend to ripen unevenly. Favor youthful response and the same bearing surface yields consistently larger berries with fuller flavor that ripen more uniformly. Then there's the thorn factor: Pruning out the bushiest growth opens up the center of the bush to make picking easier as well.

Gooseberries produce most of their fruit from short spurs located on younger canes. These spurs decline in productivity by the fourth year. Can you picture how the recommended cane rotation fits the fruiting habit of the plant? Having nine to twelve main stems ongoing in any one year is the goal for a mature *Ribes* bush. These consist of three or four each of one-, two-, and three-year-old canes. Don't get attached to any stems older than that. Constant renewal pruning will keep bushes cranking out a gorgeous crop for years to come.

Insect pests of gooseberries

The hit-or-miss crowd showing a preference for gooseberries includes all the typical suspects. Sawflies, fruit moths, and maggot flies have localized representation throughout the continent. Clear points of vulnerability coupled with the holistic sprays of spring keep this quite manageable.

- The larvae of what's commonly called the gooseberry sawfly feed on gooseberry and red currant leaves. Voraciously. The second generation of **imported currant worm** leaves the fruit alone entirely but can strip a bush of all foliage in under a week's time. The first sign of damage will be noticed at the base of the bushes. Eggs are placed on the undersides of leaves by an inconspicuous black sawfly female in early spring. The larvae hatch and begin feeding on the tender growth in the center of leaves down low. Round one lasts for two to three weeks; pupation occurs in the soil; and the summer tsunami that chews to the very last bite comes just prior to harvest. Take note that these green worms with dark body spots are not moth larvae—the word *caterpillar* does not apply here—and so the biological toxins in a Bt formulation will not be effective. Clip out heavily infested branches to remove the majority. An application of insecticidal soap will take care of any others that otherwise would return the following spring.
- The **gooseberry fruitworm** moth lays its eggs directly on the fruit. The larvae enter the developing berries and feed on the pulp, moving from one fruit to another. Infested berries color prematurely and fall off. Look for silken webbing tying together several berries.

Handpick infested fruits before these greenish caterpillars move to adjacent ones.

- A small yellowish fly with smoky bands across the wings can make a mess of numerous berries. **Gooseberry maggot** develops inside egg-stung fruit, making the berry inedible. Infested fruit often drop prematurely, but others remain on the bush. Infested berries show a discolored area where the egg was inserted. These insects overwinter as brown pupae (each about the size of a wheat grain) 1–3 inches deep in the soil at the base of the plant. Remove infested fruit as soon as discoloration appears. Lay cardboard temporarily under such plants to prevent future flies from pupating in the soil. Applications of spinosad will help limit severe pressure.

Disease concerns of gooseberries

Holistic orchardists indeed have a plan to deal with disease. We'll add some twists and requisite timing notes here to our general understanding of how plant health keeps pathogens in check.

- **Leaf spot**. Anthracnose can hit gooseberries and red currants especially hard. Spotting most often starts somewhere on the interior of the leaf, especially in wet, humid years. Brown spots continue to enlarge on leaves, spreading to young shoot tissue as well. Leaves lose color and abscise in the latter part of the summer. Whole bushes are defoliated other than a handful of terminal leaves that grew after the initial infection. Yes, affected leaves can be pinched off and removed early in an attempt to prevent further spread. This particular fungus ramps up fairly quickly, however, and in truth? Gooseberry bushes always survive to fruit the next season—often becoming defoliated again after that harvest as well. Renewing mulch not long after leaf drop will help in decomposing overwinter inoculum.

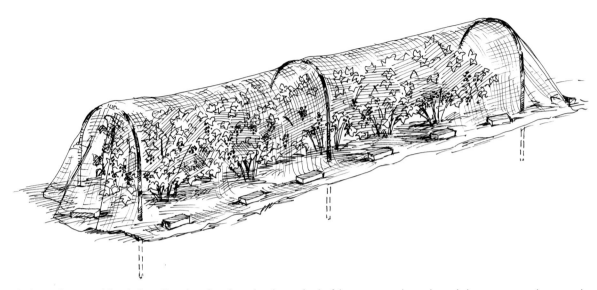

Berry bushes can be protected from birds quickly and simply: Rebar stakes along each side of the row support plastic tubing, which in turn supports the netting above the top shoots.

Nutritional fortitude certainly lessens the grip of leaf spot to a more tolerable degree.

• **Powdery mildew.** The North American variant of this fungal disease of *Ribes* species is especially problematic for European gooseberries. A whitish, powdery growth appears on the surface of leaves, shoots, and branch tips in early summer. If left unchecked, the fungus will progress to the berries themselves. Warmth and poor air circulation favor powdery mildew. Assertive pruning in the dormant season enables good airflow. The young side growth on susceptible cultivars can be shortened in June as well to help lessen vulnerable tissue exposure. Supplementing holistic sprays with herbal brews in the summer months—particularly in a dry year—puts the silica defense into play against these ghostly fungi as well.

Currants

Red and pink currants are often classified as members of the same species, *Ribes sativum*, which, upon granting consideration for additional crosses made with *R. rubrum* and *R. petraeum*, certainly covers the bases. European black currants are classified as *R. nigrum*. The American black currant (*R. americanum*) shares the pleasantly musky flavor of the European currant. Another native species, the buffalo or clove currant (*R. odoratum*), proffers yellow blossoms with a spicy, empowering scent.

Having been botanically launched, let's consider what one indeed does with this fruit. A taste for black currant seems a much more European than American thing. The berries are used mostly in jams and juices, and they are especially high in vitamin C, potassium, and bioflavonoids. A pinch of dried currants added to the teapot perks up the most bracing brew. Currant syrup can be considered on a par with elderberry syrup, whether served medicinally as an immune system booster or to add genuine flavor to sparkling water. The red currant grouping, despite that name, varies widely in color, from dark red to pink, yellow, and white; the berries continue to sweeten on the bush long after first aspiring to full color. Every gourmet treats these fruits with respect, delighting in the brightness unleashed in jelly and when used as a garnish for desserts.

Planting specifics

Currants prefer a cool, moist growing area and can tolerate partial shade. That less-than-full-sun attribute becomes a necessity the farther south you go. Planting along the east side of a building or shady arbor is all it takes. Fruit trees serve similarly well in guild plantings as a canopy or overstory for the currants. Avoid still-air sites simply to lessen the incidence of powdery mildew.

Incorporate organic matter (woodsy compost and even peat if the soil is somewhat sandy) to improve the soil. A soil pH on the order of 6.5 provides a broad nutritional pantry. Currants awaken relatively quickly once the dormant season ends and thus should be planted in late fall or very early in spring, before the plants start to grow. Space plants according to the vigor of the cultivar, 4–5 feet apart at a minimum. Red currants have the ability to climb and thus can be trained upward. Planting with cordon intentions allows for even tighter spacing, of course.

Currant bushes are heavy nitrogen feeders. Annual top-dressings of composted manure will keep production in step with harvest hopes. Spreading the rich stuff lightly around the dripline of each bush in fall and then renewing woodsy mulch atop that and farther out (to define the bed area) ties right in with biological underpinnings. Plants on poorer soils will appreciate an additional charge of an organic fertilizer blend in the early years, lightly broadcast in spring at approximately ½ pound per plant throughout its envisioned diameter.

Keeping the soil cool with mulch in the summer has the added benefit of retaining moisture. Spread ramial wood chips or shredded leaves several inches deep that first spring. Avoid sawdust unless it is already well rotted. Supplementing this with grass clippings in the summer months can be a homegrown part of the nitrogen plan.

Currant varieties to consider

Black currants claim the aromatic and more complex flavor nook. Red currants grow in exquisite clusters and make a delightful jelly. Pink currants downplay the tart side of that red heritage with a translucent sparkle. White currants tend toward the insipid in warmer zones but indeed offer novelty.

Cultivars that perform well in the eastern half of the continent can behave quite differently in the Northwest. The heat of southern regions must be countered with shading during the noon phase of high sun. The general hardiness rating for all currants falls within Zones 3–8 unless otherwise noted.

And now the rub. *Ribes* species can serve as an intermediate host for the white pine blister rust fungus. This association with a valuable timber tree led to laws outright banning the growing of currants and gooseberries in North America—black currants in particular. Other species were allowed if the grower could certify there were no valuable white pines within 900 feet of the planting site. Shipping permits for in-state and out-of-state nursery sales have often been part of the requirements. The federal ban was lifted in 1966, but certain states continue to disallow these plants.[33] The black currant cultivars Consort and Titania are completely resistant to white pine blister rust. Red currants and gooseberries rarely prove to be an intermediate rust vector. Crosses made between black currant and gooseberry are known as jostaberries. These hybrids are completely resistant to powdery mildew, fungal dieback, and white pine blister rust.

Ben Lomond. Heavy producer of berries with that traditional strong pungent flavor. The black currants of the Ben series are named after the mountains of Scotland. Upright bush grows to 5 feet tall. Susceptible to rust. Ripens uniformly. Yields increase with cross-pollination. Zones 3–7.

Ben Sarek. Black currant developed by the Scottish Crop Research Institute. Somewhat resistant to white pine blister rust. Compact bush easily maintained at 3 feet tall and 3-foot spacing. Requires two harvests about two weeks apart. Premature drying trait requires keeping this one well irrigated. Frost-hardy blossoms.

A good choice for hot, dry, windy conditions is the Crandall clove currant. Photo courtesy of One Green World.

Consort. Medium-long clusters of somewhat soft, dime-sized black berries. Prominent, musky flavor. Excellent drying quality. Heavy-bearing shrub grows 4–6 feet tall. Self-fruitful. Naturalizes readily. Resistant to anthracnose. Completely resistant to white pine blister rust. Developed in Ottawa, Ontario. Hardy to –30°F (–34°C).

Crandall. The most ornamental and the sweetest in flavor of the so-called buffalo or clove currants. Selection of *Ribes odoratum*, native throughout much of the Rocky Mountains. Large berries lack the black currant aftertaste. Delicious, clove-scented yellow flowers. Irregular ripening. Spreading bush to 4 feet. Defoliates the least in hot, dry, windy conditions.[34] Leaves turn brilliant red and yellow by early fall. Hardy into Zone 2.

Gloire de Sablons. Long clusters of translucent pink currants adorn this beautiful bush. Flavor not as tart as a red currant. Highly desirable for decorating summer desserts. Productive, upright grower. Good disease resistance. Selected in Versailles, France, in 1883.

Jhonkheer Van Tets. Red currant selection from Holland. Heavy producer of large, dark red fruit. Mildew- and aphid-resistant. Considered by many to be the best-flavored red currant variety in the world. Excellent for espalier, trained on a cordon. Less tolerant of summer heat than other reds. Early-ripening. Best in Zones 3–6.

Minaj Smyriou. Bulgarian introduction with excellent European black currant flavor. Heavy producer. Medium-sized bush. Resistant to white pine blister rust. Self-fertile. Fruit ripens before the weather turns exceedingly hot. Does well in semi-shade. Zones 4–8.

Red Lake. Large, juicy red fruit on compact clusters. Long stems for easy picking. Makes a sparkling red jelly. Vigorous, upright bush. Resistant to powdery mildew. Very resistant to white pine blister rust. Excellent windbreak plant. Introduced by the University of Minnesota in 1933. Ripens during the mid- to late season. Zone 2–8.

Rovada. Red currant with exceedingly long clusters of good-sized berries. Very easy to pick. Resistant to mildew and other leaf diseases. Developed in the Netherlands. Late flowering escapes frosts. Ripens late July into August. Zones 3–7.

Titania. Scandinavian black currant with rich flavor lineage. Very large, mildly pungent berry. Dries well. Resistant to powdery mildew. Completely resistant to white pine blister rust. Branches may break under heavy crop loading. Mature height 3–4 feet. Long season of ripening from midsummer into September. Reaches full maturity in three seasons as opposed to four or five with most other popular varieties. Zones 3–7.

Pruning tips for currants

Prune currants when the plants are dormant in late winter or early spring. Start by removing any branches that lie along the ground as well as branches that have been broken by crop loading the previous year. The road ahead diverges a bit from here, with black currants having a different take on the rest of the story than red currants.

Black currants produce best on one- and two-year-old wood. They do not fruit on spurs, as do red currants and gooseberries. Big hint there: Red currants held to bush production follow the very same cane succession as do gooseberries. It's the *nigrum* species alone that calls for a shift in thinking to accommodate fruit buds arising from node positions right on the cane. Strong one-year-old shoots—along with two- and three-year-old stems that have an abundance

Gloire de Sablons currants are highly desirable for decorating summer desserts. Photo courtesy of One Green World.

of strong one-year-old shoot side branches—are the most productive. This bearing habit brings us to yet another fork in the road (I know, I know) that allows black currants to be pruned by two different methods in both freestanding and hedgerow systems.

The first method bears a strong semblance to the method used for pruning gooseberries. Each black currant leg crown should have two- and three-year-old canes, along with one-year-old shoots, for a total of ten to fifteen canes per mature bush. Black currants are generally more vigorous, allowing more canes to be kept. Approximately half of all canes being kept should be one-year-old canes, however. Any and all shoots beyond the third season are removed at ground level.

Titania comes from Scandinavia with a rich flavor lineage and complete resistance to white pine blister rust. Photo courtesy of Vesey's Seeds Ltd.

Experts say the second method of pruning black currants both is easier and reduces insect and disease carryover. This system uses only one-year-old canes and an alternate-year production cycle. Let's be clear about the upshot here: If you desire a highly medicinal berry crop every year, then two different plantings of black currants must be maintained out of sync with each other if using method number two.

- **Year one**. Prune all bearing canes to the ground immediately following the harvest. Apply compost and water thoroughly. Small immature canes that provide no more than 12–18 inches of growth by dormancy should be kept. No flower buds will initiate on this secondary growth.
- **Year two**. The previous year's canes remain vegetative, and additional canes are produced.
- **Year three**. The large crop produced is mighty impressive. Bearing canes are again pruned to the ground immediately after harvest.

Let's revisit those red currants left so casually in bush mode at the start of this pruning discussion. That method of production certainly suits, but these particular cultivars do something all the more special when trained to a cordon. Keep in mind that the best berries always arise from spurs on two- and three-year-old wood. Such shoots grow off much older wood than that—given insightful pruning—and therein lies the wherewithal to create a fruiting vine out of an otherwise humble bush. This requires judicious removal of suckers and stem growth during the growing season, along with some means of support.[35] The advantages of a trellising system are increased yields, great air circulation, and those gorgeous clusters of fruit dangling tantalizingly before the eyes. All this comes at a cost of decreased plant longevity, however. Starting red currants that have been trained in this fashion for enhanced production anew every twenty years or so is simply part of the plan.

Insect pests of currants

The medicinal virtues of currants seem to offer a carryover effect when it comes to pest dynamics. Very few bugs mess with the currant bush—and those that do have clear points of vulnerability.

- The **currant borer** (a clear-winged, blue-black moth) appears in June and lays eggs at leaf nodes. The larvae then burrow into the pith of currant and gooseberry canes. Infested canes do not die in the fall but put out sickly growth in the spring. Removing and destroying infested canes prior to June will prevent the next generation of moths from emerging. Overwintering larvae often fall prey to a parasitic wasp and a fungal disease.
- Masses of tiny greenish yellow insects feeding under young leaves toward the shoot tips are **currant aphids**. Affected leaves will curl downward, blister, and become reddish. In severe cases, leaves become excessively distorted and fall off, while the fruit never ripens properly. These aphids overwinter in the egg stage on bark or new canes. Pure neem oil should keep this in balance. Sugar esters can be used for severe infestations. Keep in mind that many parasites and predators attack aphids, and that help is on the way.

Top-quality red currants for market are produced on a greenhouse cordon in Holland. Photo courtesy of Steven McKay, Cornell Cooperative Extension.

- Larvae of an entirely different sawfly girdle the tips of new shoots with their feeding. Each shoot will eventually die and fall off wherever **currant stem girdler** strikes. Cut off affected tips in May or June several inches below the girdle or, if left until later in the season, about 8 inches below the girdle. Females lay eggs singly, inserting each into the pith of first-year growth. After ovipositing, this sawfly girdles the shoot about ½ inch above the egg with her saw-like ovipositor. Often a portion of the shoot remains uncut, and the almost severed, wilted tip may remain attached for some time. One female can lay up to thirty eggs and therefore girdle thirty shoots.

Disease concerns of currants

Holistic orchardists indeed have a plan to deal with disease. We'll add some twists and requisite timing notes here to our general understanding of how plant health keeps pathogens in check.

- **Powdery mildew**. Currants across the varietal spectrum are subject to the ghostly touch of the *Ribes* strain of this summertime fungus. Rampant symptoms appear as the berry harvest draws near. The actual infection period began back when bloom drew to a close and the days warmed. Rain inhibits mildew spore germination, but come a relative dry spell, morning humidity can abet microscopic infections that in turn produce asexual conidia to ensure a powdery grip on foliage surfaces. Serenade's ability to destroy the germ tubes and mycelium membranes of existing mildew can be used to advantage if early conditions favor infection. Weekly applications of this *biofungicide* when susceptible currant bushes first berry up turns the tide.

- **White pine blister rust**. This disease attacks both *Ribes* and white pines, which must live in close proximity for the blister rust fungus to complete its back-and-forth life cycle. Certain black currant cultivars and white pines are extremely prone to rust, while red currants and gooseberries exhibit far less susceptibility. Symptoms begin in spring when small, yellow spots appear on currant leaves. Rust-colored fruiting bodies are now also visible on the leaf undersides. Your fruiting bush will be fine . . . it's what happens next that concerns authorities. Limb damage and outright tree death of susceptible five-needled pine species (eastern white pine, western pine, and sugar pine) occur over the ensuing years.

- **Red currant shoot blight**. This disease from the past is popping up with increasing frequency in the Northeast. Red currants experience sudden wilt and blight of the canes. Fungal infection begins at the shoot tips in the summer months. Pruning declining shoots out 6 inches below the affected tissue—and sanitizing pruning tools between all such cuts—is critical. Dormant-season copper is suggested to knock this back to manageable levels should shoot blight get established at your site. And yes, there sure is a holistic alternative to that sort of thinking!

SHRUB FRUITS

Berries spring from the wild. We go to the forest and fields to gather the small fruits offered freely to all. Varieties with improved traits slowly evolve as surprise finds and deliberate breeding lead to domestication of a particular fruit. The cultivation of bramble and bush fruits has became far better understood as regional challenges have been met with varietal nuance. Other berry plants are not necessarily as tamed, venturing into our agriculture, yes, yet often remaining just as rooted to wilder notions.

So-called shrub fruits are certainly worth growing and trialing in the home orchard and on community farms seeking a local niche. Named cultivars of juneberries, serviceberries, and saskatoons (all common names for various *Amelanchier* species) are available, with breeding for improved strains being something any inspired amateur can and should do. Aronia, highbush cranberry, black haw, thimbleberry, cornelian cherry, and huckleberry deserve and are getting similar attention. The honeyberry (native to Siberia) is the latest must-have for its blueberry-like fruit coming ripe a full month before the earliest blueberries. And that very quick survey brings us to the most prolific berry of all.

Elderberries

I work with elderberry as much in the wild as with specific cultivars here on the farm. This easy-to-grow shrub likes the moist soil along roadsides and streams—and will do equally well with regular irrigation in many home landscapes. Elder's bloom comes last of all the fruiting plants, its bright, cream-colored clusters appearing as the summer solstice draws near. The purplish black berries are highly regarded for making a rather unique country wine and an unforgettable jelly. Healing tradition especially honors these fruits, and it's on that score alone that you will want to find a spot for elderberry.

American elderberry, *Sambucus canadensis*, also called sweet elder, has the widest range of all small

MEDICINAL VIRTUE

Fruit friend and biochemist Richard Moyer in southwest Virginia has done solid research on the medicinal benefits of different berries. He surveyed more than a hundred cultivars of blackberries, raspberries, blueberries, black currants, and gooseberries. The winners for total anti-oxidants were black raspberries, followed by small-fruited blueberries. The winners in total phenolics were black currants. One paper published from his original work has been cited time and time again in the field of dietary polyphenols.

I caught up with Richard recently to see how our understanding of fruit phytochemistry continues to come into focus. He notes:

Recent research suggests that fruit polyphenols stress our cells slightly, activating our defenses against many types of damage. These compounds apparently act more like oxidants in our bodies, thereby stimulating protective mechanisms. Whole, dried black raspberries (shown very anthocyanin-rich in our work) have been used to successfully treat cancers of the digestive tract, as seen in the work of Dr. Gary Stoner at Ohio State University.

If we could figure out one or two key chemicals that we thought were the most healthy in each fruit, society might be tempted to take the easy way out by taking that chemical in pill or drink form. We aren't smart enough to know all the benefits of the hundreds of plant chemicals working together. But we often are foolish enough to think we can take a shortcut with modern, processed foods—foods more expensive than price alone suggests.

Eating the variety of whole fruits available through the season, and with preservation, all year, is the wisest course of all.

native fruits, being found from northern Québec down into Florida and Texas, and appearing again in South America. European elderberry, *S. nigra*, also called black elder or common elder, has a similar reach across zones on both sides of the Atlantic. Technically, these are so closely related that *canadensis* is considered a subspecies of *nigra* . . . yet nurseries continue to make the distinction because planting two or more of the same type usually ensures better cross-pollination. The red-berried elder, *S. racemosa*, grows throughout the cooler parts of North America, but its bright scarlet berries are not considered edible.[36]

Planting specifics
Elderberry prefers a soil high in organic material, one that can retain moisture and yet would be considered reasonably drained. The perception that these plants prefer wetland areas isn't quite correct: Look more closely at wild elderberries and you will see the knoll effect in play, with elevated mounds providing lift enough above a high water table for the relatively shallow root system. Streambank settings provide a similar clue—such meandering ground is moist, but it's only up the bank a couple of feet that elder actually puts its feet.[37] Light, sandy soils should be well conditioned with ample quantities of compost and/or peat moss to hold moisture. A slightly acidic soil suits these shrubs, along the lines of 5.5–6.5, but elderberry will tolerate a wide range of both acidity and fertility. Early spring applications of compost will go a long way in balancing out initial soil challenges.

Plantings can be done from early spring through June, but late plantings will have little first-year growth. Bareroot stock of select varieties will look much like dead sticks, but new shoots will come quickly once they're planted in the ground. Elder is not hard to propagate, with the preferred method being root cuttings. These can crop in the second year—which is quite an astounding leap into production for any fruiting plant.[38] Individual shrubs should be set at least 4–5 feet apart. Larger plantings would be done in rows 10–12 feet apart to allow equipment access. Creating an elder guild of a more circular nature emulates the way this shrub sets itself up in the wild.[39]

Placing mulch around the base of these clumping shrubs is essential in the early years; otherwise persistent grasses can readily crowd out unmanaged elder in short order. Avoid disturbing the soil once the plants are in the ground, because the slightest injury can damage the fibrous root system and kill new upright shoots. Use a combination of pulling weeds by hand, mowing, and renewed mulching to control competition without disturbing the elderberry roots. Mints, nettles, and other loosely rooted herbs make for good elder companions farther out from the shoot-renewing crown once a thick hedgerow of plants has developed. Elderberries will suppress weeds quite well and stay productive from that point on—provided you heed the pruning advice coming just ahead.

Elder accepts dappled shade but, given its druthers, produces far better with full sun. Water requirements are 1 inch per week during the growing season and half again that amount during droughts and fruit-ripening season. You can expect each shrub to reach a height of 6–10 feet in northern regions to as much as 15 feet in southern regions.

Sambucus species are partially self-fruitful, but yields often increase significantly with cross-pollination from another variety. It's best to have different cultivars of the same type—for example, two varieties of *S. canadensis*, or two of *S. nigra*—for best pollination. That said, a single cultivar in the home orchard may do just fine. (I will not let you be dissuaded even if space in your yard is at a premium!) Pollination usually occurs through wind, with all sorts of insects

playing a supplementary role. Late-spring frost rarely affects elderberry given its last-in-line bloom time.

An elder "flower" is actually a collection of many small florets arranged as a flat-topped umbel. The berries simply follow suit—fruiting in that same broad umbel, except that their weight usually causes the laden clusters to hang downward, bowing the branches. Berries ripen from green to red to black with a hint of purple over a period of six to eight weeks after pollination. Harvest involves snipping the whole cluster from the stem with garden shears. Stripping the berries by hand (a cluster at a time) into a clean bucket for processing[40] and then straining the seeds from the juice is the far bigger and more time-consuming part of the job.

Elderberry varieties to consider

Selecting named cultivars of elderberries began a mere century ago. Not a whole lot of investment in breeding work has been done since that time—especially when compared to other favorite fruits—in part because commercial growers have been satisfied with slightly improved berry size at just over ¼ inch in diameter. While the size of wild elderberries often runs half this, just know that Mother Nature can also throw some whopping surprises. The University of Missouri has unveiled two such tantalizing, large-fruited cultivars onto the scene that have commercial growers excited, to say the least.

Adams. *Sambucus canadensis.* Early-ripening with very large berry clusters. Sweeter than most American elderberries. More vitamin C than an orange or grapefruit. The standard of the earlier releases, dating back to 1926 and developed by the New York State Agricultural Experiment Station. Both Adams 1 and Adams 2 are strong, vigorous, and productive. Tolerates wet locations well. Hardy into Zone 3. Ripens late, with fruit maturing in early September.

Allesso. *S. nigra.* This lush variety is being planted commercially in Sweden and Germany. Bears large

Wyldewood elderberry is reliably prolific. Photo courtesy of Patrick Byers, University of Missouri Extension.

crops of flavorful fruit among especially dark green foliage. Grows to about 10 feet in sun or partial shade. Pollinize with Haschberg or other European varieties for best results. Known to be hardy to –25°F (–32°C).

Black Beauty. *S. nigra*. Spectacular ornamental bush for the yard. Grows about 10 feet tall with glossy, purple-black foliage. Lemon-scented, pink flowers cover the bush in early summer, contrasting perfectly with the foliage. Bears clusters of edible berries in fall. Developed at the East Malling Research Station in England. Best reserved for cooler climates.

Bob Gordon. *S. canadensis*. This recently released cultivar from the University of Missouri has a larger berry and yielded nearly triple that of Adams 2. Largest mean berry weight known, in fact. Heavy-fruiting cluster inverts downward more than other varieties, protecting berries from birds. Researchers are confident this cultivar found in the Missouri hill country (can you guess by whom?) is truly superior.

Haschberg. *S. nigra*. Austrian variety. Berries form in very large clusters on long stems. Vigorous and spreading shrub, growing to about 10 feet tall. This one combines the flavor and medicinal qualities of the wild black elder with heavy varietal production and good fruit size. Hardy to about –25°F (–32°C).

Johns. *S. canadensis*. Huge clusters of large purple-black elderberries. Slightly more vigorous than Adams, ripening about fourteen days later. Lovely fall foliage. Will grow in any soil. Originated in Canada in 1954. Zones 3–9.

Nova. *S. canadensis*. Open-pollinated seedling of Adams. Large, sweet berries lack the astringency of some varieties. Medium-sized shrub at 6–8 feet. York cultivar recommended as a pollinizer. Ripens evenly during August. Originated in Nova Scotia in 1960. Hardy into Zone 3.

Samdal. *S. nigra*. One of several newer varieties from Denmark. Plants produce long shoots from soil level in one growing season that bear abundantly the following year, thereby working quite well with the invigorating pruning approach for elder. Large fruit clusters with good flavor ripen in August. Small-sized berries are noted for their high anthocyanin content.

Wyldewood. *S. canadensis*. The first variety to reach budbreak in spring and yet the latest to ripen. Vigorous producer tends toward having three sizable umbels on each stem. Fruit set is reliable and prolific. Collected from the wild by Jack and Marge Millican near Eufala, Oklahoma, in 1995; subsequently released by the University of Missouri.

York. *S. canadensis*. Cross between Adams 2 and Ezyoff. Largest American elderberry prior to the Missouri introductions. Self-fertile, but sets better when planted as a pollinizer with Nova. Medium-sized shrubs should be planted 7–8 feet apart. Developed at the New York State AES in 1964. Hardy to –30°F (–34°C).

Pruning tips for elderberries

Fruits are produced on one- to three-year-old wood, with the best production occurring on the terminal portion of one- and two-year-old canes. Knowing that launches the right understanding of how to prune elderberries to keep plants invigorated for years to come.

Elderberries are capable of sending up many new shoot canes each year. Canes typically reach full height in one season and develop lateral branches in the second. Flowers and fruit develop on the tips of the current season's growth, often on the new canes but especially on laterals. Second-year elderberry canes with good lateral development are the most fruitful. Older wood tends to lose vigor and become weak: While canes entering a third year will be fruitful and can be left for one more summer of fruiting, removing these faithfully in early spring is what keeps the crown of the elderberry rejuvenated for especially vigorous shoot production.

Elderberry is a rather unique shrub in that it produces fruit on both primary (current-season) and secondary (older) canes. Primary canes arise each spring from spreading underground rhizomes. These end in a single large flower cluster that opens a few to several days before those on the secondary canes. Flower clusters on secondary canes tend to be smaller and more numerous than those on primary canes.

Commercial growers using mechanical equipment are taking advantage of this flowering trait through an annual pruning approach. Cutting back elderberries completely with a tractor-mounted sickle bar every winter causes the plant to totally put its energy into fewer but much larger umbel clusters. Greater uniformity of flowering, fruiting, and ripening can be achieved with pruned-to-the-ground plants because all growth on these plants will be primary canes. Annual yields are slightly reduced by this method, but it's a trade-off in terms of greatly simplified pruning and consolidated harvest.

Insect pests of elderberries

The elderberry doesn't garner a whole lot of insect attention of the pest persuasion. The pure neem oil in the holistic sprays should generally keep things all the more reasonable. Still, here's a rundown of who's who in the medicinal fruit patch.

- The larval stage of the **elder shoot borer** is a caterpillar that bores into the stems and shoots. The adult moth lays eggs in July and August in canes at least one year old. Eggs hatch the following April into May. The larvae first feed within the unfolding leaf

Elderberry bloom on the primary canes of this York cultivar makes for a happy West Virginia mountain girl. Photo courtesy of West Virginia Elderberries.

whorls, then bore into new lateral shoots. When partially grown, they migrate to the ground shoots, entering these at the bases and feeding upward into the shoots. Come mid-June, they leave the ground shoots and tunnel into dead canes to pupate, leaving small piles of frass (sawdust) on the ground at the base of the old wood. Pruning out infested shoots or canes offers up-front control; eliminating dead canes will discourage pupation.

- The **elderberry borer** is a shimmering dark blue and yellow beetle. It ranges across central North America to parts of the Southern Appalachians. Droopy-tipped shoots are a surefire sign—snap these off below the damaged area and within a foot or so you should find the grub. That's one down for the return count.

- Large caterpillars found removing substantial amounts of elder foliage during feeding are larvae of the **cecropia moth**, otherwise known as the **giant silk moth**. These are most abundant near wooded areas. Control sporadic incursions by hand removal and then do a good thing: Provide individual caterpillars of this magnificent species with a new home on lilac or maple to complete their cycle. Cecropia moth cocoons are often more than 3 inches long—the largest produced by native silk moths. They are made of tough silken threads and are always attached lengthwise to the twigs or branches of the host plant.

- **Eriophid mites** are a common pest of elderberry, yet little is known about their life cycle. It has been reported by one Czech researcher that the mites overwinter within and beneath leaf buds. The species is known to be wind-disseminated. Encountering these "elder mites" in North America is not improbable, but healthy plants can cope with them.

Disease concerns of elderberries

Holistic orchardists indeed have a plan to deal with disease. We'll add some twists and requisite timing notes here to our general understanding of how plant health keeps pathogens in check.

- **Bacterial leaf spot**. Infected plants have reddish angular spots on the foliage, usually uniform in size, occurring on either side of bloom. Entire leaves may yellow, wither, and drop as spots become more numerous. The unknown bacteria behind this disease very likely overwinter in the soil around infected plants as well as in twig cankers and on the bark itself. Just remember that *ubiquitous* does not mean *competitive* when biological reinforcement gets delivered on a regular basis.
- **Powdery mildew**. Four species of powdery mildew fungi affect elderberry by producing the typical white coating of the leaves. This really becomes a problem only when conditions so favor these dry fungi that the fruit itself gets affected.
- **Cankers**. Many different fungi cause stem cankers. These can girdle an elder shoot, causing the tissue above the damaged area to die. Stressful conditions such as winter injury, drought, and flooding are causes that can lead to infection. Cankered shoots should be removed and properly disposed of to prevent more infections.

Health benefits of elderberries

Black elderberry has been used medicinally for hundreds of years. All parts of the plant are useful in myriad ways, so much so that herbalists refer to this single plant as the *countryman's apothecary* in its own right. I especially want you to know about the role elderberries have in protecting us from viral influenza, aka the common flu.

Elderberries have been proven in quite a few recent studies to shorten the duration of cold and flu symptoms, as well as strengthening the immune system.[41] Constituents in the juice of these dark-pigmented berries work by inhibiting the amino acid chain that the virus needs to escape from an infected cell.[42] This prevents viruses from being able to replicate in more and more of your cells . . . which is why elderberry can help prevent the spread of an infectious disease in the first place, and shorten its duration if you indeed come down with the flu or a cold.

One way the goodness of elder can be preserved for wintertime use is by making a honeyed syrup from the fresh berries. Typical recipes call for using 2 parts sweetener to 1 part juice for seemingly unlimited shelf life. My wife, Nancy, reverses that ratio to up the medicinal ante, knowing actual need will see each bottle used sooner rather than later. Serving this tasty remedy in a glass of warm water adds a touch of deep purple elegance that is uplifting in its own right.

Here's Nancy's recipe: Simmer 1 gallon fully ripened elderberries with ½ cup water in a large soup pot until soft. Strain the pulp from the juice. Add ½ ounce grated ginger and a heaping teaspoon whole cloves to the liquid and simmer for forty-five minutes uncovered. The volume should reduce by half. Add 1 cup dried elder flowers (if available) to the hot juice, put the lid on, and infuse (turn off the heat) for twenty minutes. Strain out the herbs and add 1 part raw honey to 1 part juice. Bottle and cap when cooled.

This low-sugar syrup must be kept refrigerated and used within the next year. Whole berries can be frozen to make more syrup during the winter months when this anti-viral brew becomes essential community medicine. A shot-glass dose taken the evening you first feel viral tinglings and twice again the next morning does wonders.

Chapter Eight

The Orchard Year

Every orchardist needs to create a task checklist to keep biological timing of orchard tasks throughout the year clearly prioritized. Accounting for a unique pest complex and other regional variables for the particular tree fruit and berries that you are growing will be woven in and around root growth cycles, nutrient uptake, and beneficial fungal relationships. Knowing *what to do when* becomes far more manageable when you take the time to organize your thoughts on paper.

Spend time observing how each season actually plays out. Make this part of your daily routine, be it with morning coffee in hand or after the workday ends. Be flexible about that task checklist as things change from year to year.

Early-season bud moths need to be scouted and then nudged accordingly if numbers seem high. Foliar pests like aphid outbreaks on young trees will soon be handled by beneficials hot on the trail. Those immediate weeks following petal fall are curculio time for growers in the eastern half of North America, though some years this wily insect may show up as early as pink to wait for tender fruitlets . . . or then again, it may arrive a week or two late because it's been unusually cool.

Other concerns vary. Oriental fruit moth doesn't range where peaches won't overwinter, while lesser appleworm does show up in such places. Codling moth will be the dominant internal feeder regardless. Northern growers see two generations of these pests, whereas orchards with longer growing seasons might experience as many as five generations. That shifts pest priorities mightily in places like California and Georgia.

Early summer marks two tactical undertakings for most growers, though species will vary with the fruit of choice. Maggot flies afflict blueberries, cherries, and apples, all of which can be handled with baited sphere traps. Borers of both the beetle and moth persuasion need to be repelled, confused, and otherwise harassed to lessen damage to trunks and susceptible areas on tree limbs. Know which ones you face and take the appropriate action before these insects do in your trees and brambles.

Disease intensity gets determined by the weather patterns of a given year. Primary scab season for apple and pear occurs ten to fourteen days on either side of full bloom no matter where you roam—tree immune support needs to be unwavering during this time if the orchard is to be relatively free of secondary infection risk for the remainder of the summer. Fire blight danger peaks when the open blossoms offer a pandemic point of entry for infection: Competitive populations of microorganisms need to be maintained to ward off the blight bacteria during bloom. Stone fruit growers should do the very same at leaf fall and again just prior to budbreak to prevent the establishment of disease populations of bacterial spot and peach leaf curl. Keeping fruit rots to a minimum depends on maximizing nutrition and boosting silica levels with fermented herbal teas. Summer disease pressure peaks in the more humid Southeast, but rains will eventually reveal sooty blotch and flyspeck in most regions. Just remember that a little "spit polish" can clean any lightly smudged apples right up!

All this work, so many hopes, come together in a delicious way when the fruit harvest comes in. Photo courtesy of Trees of Antiquity.

Building orchard health through biodiversity and fungal duff management has an amazing long-term benefit—*all this gets easier with time.* You've planted those first trees and have more ground cover-cropped for berry patches next spring. You're excited and eager, but also nervous to do right by these efforts. Learning to prune, making woodsy compost, identifying what pests are on hand . . . none of this comes easy at first. You learn by doing. Just as a fruit tree needs to build good wood structure in those early years, you are building ecosystem understanding and personal confidence through genuine experience.

Keep asking questions that lead to those wonderful *aha* moments. What is the growth response when you open a tree by selecting to prune out a certain branch?

What tiny parasitic wasps come on the scene when you introduce sweet cicely, valerian, and Queen Anne's lace to the orchard environs? How vibrant can you make the leaf canopy with foliar nutrition, which in turn makes the fruit crop? All such things eventually become second nature. Biologically based answers fall into place, causing pest numbers to dwindle. Neighbors see that it's your trees that rise up and overcome the disease tide despite their own allopathic choices. Your fruit stays on the tree to ripen to perfection rather than dropping prematurely. Return bloom is stronger. Invigorated growth keeps the berry patch replenished.

Perhaps your children even have good teeth because they prefer homegrown fruit to empty calories.

And it's all because health works!

HOLISTIC COMPENDIUM

This task compendium doesn't tell you everything to do in your orchard as much as provide a starting place. The specifics of each orchard site and the fruit being grown have to be woven in accordingly. Writing down your orchard's schedule will deepen your understanding both of what needs to be done and of what can be improved. The timing of avant-garde holistic techniques included here will guide you in the healthiest ways I know to grow tree fruit.

Dormant season
- Check for deer incursions at least weekly; snowshoe around the base of tree trunks to pack down vole tunnels.
- Order rootstock; collect scions for grafting.
- Prune all bearing trees. You need to establish an open framework of scaffold branches that allows maximum penetration of sunlight and drying breezes.
- Remove all mummified fruit (still on the trees) to reduce rot spore inoculum.
- Complete routine maintenance on all orchard equipment.
- Order organic orchard supplies for the coming season. Be sure to include seaweed extract to add to every spray tank throughout the growing season.

Budbreak
- Chip prunings in orchard for the benefit of soil fungi. Any obviously cankered wood (a source of disease inoculum) should be removed from the site.
- Finish any compost spreading not completed in late fall. Spread deciduous wood chip mulch in haphazard fashion.
- Finish thinning canes in bramble plantings on a square-footage basis; fortify the soil bed annually with an organic fertilizer blend or compost; spread deciduous wood chips or leaves (bagged back in the fall) as bed mulch.
- Plant new trees as early as possible.
- Meet boron needs with a sprinkle of borax every few years. Most other micronutrient shortcomings can be corrected by good compost habits and using seaweed in tank mixes when spraying.
- Remove any spiral trunk guards used on young trees.

Week of quarter-inch green
- First holistic spring spray (liquid fish, pure neem oil, effective microbes) at double rate aimed at ground, trunk, and branch structure. This is a catalyst spray to wake up beneficial fungi, establish arboreal colonization in bark crevices, and interrupt the development of foliage pests now in the egg stage. Stone fruit growers can initiate the holistic sprays as much as two weeks earlier than apple timing.
- Apply an organic fertilizer blend to nonbearing trees in order to grow a strong framework of branches quickly.
- Train branch crotch angles on young trees with limb spreaders.
- Cultivate around nonbearing trees and replace shade mulch if available.
- Check all trunks for borer damage missed in fall inspection.

Pink
- Second holistic spring spray (liquid fish, pure neem oil, effective microbes) aimed at unfurling buds, trunk, and branch structure. A good amount of runoff should reach the ground as well. Direct a blast at any obvious leaf piles that are not yet decomposed from the year before.
- Spray fruit trees with Bt (added to the holistic tank mix) if unfurling leaves reveal a significant presence of bud moth larvae.

- Hang white sticky traps for European apple sawfly (EAS).
- Primary scab season has begun. Relax. The holistic applications have the trees primed to deal with early ascospore release.

Bloom

- Cut down wild fruit trees spotted in bloom within 100 yards of the orchard to prevent pest migration to your managed trees. The exceptions here are feral trees pruned at this time as an alternative draw for insects put off by repellent strategies.
- Become a honeybee steward and give three cheers for the wild pollinators. Nesting tubes need to be replaced in mason bee condos every couple of seasons to make way for new brood.
- Hang pheromone wing traps for monitoring moth presence (pheromones are species-specific) and timing of first-generation egg hatch.
- Lightly cultivate edges of dwarf tree rows in preparation for a summer cover crop.

Petal fall

- Third holistic spring spray (liquid fish, pure neem oil, effective microbes) aimed at leaf canopy and developing fruitlets. Make this application early if king blossom pollination was good, because oils may assist in smothering excess flowers. Including a light rate of Surround in this mix will help establish a clay matrix for bonding additional kaolin clay layers.
- Initiate full coverage of the refined kaolin clay. Two or three applications are necessary from the get-go to build up barrier protection from the imminent curculio invasion and to be helpful in suppressing moth oviposition (laying eggs). Repeat every five to seven days for the next two to three weeks, taking into account the wash-off factor due to a heavy rain.
- Gather EAS sticky traps. If damage to fruitlets seems apparent and widespread, include spinosad in the first full-rate clay spray to check further EAS damage to additional fruitlets.
- Primary scab season is in full force now. Some growers may deem a micronized sulfur application on disease-prone varieties necessary if spore maturity has built up and definite rain is predicted. Sulfur can be tank-mixed with subsequent Surround sprays. Take note: Mineral fungicides will compromise arboreal colonization and affect return bloom. Holistic innovation suggests a midway application of microbes and seaweed as a healthier approach to a major spore release, especially where the blooming period is more spread out.
- Prune out shoots and break off blossom spurs if fire blight strikes become apparent. Good arboreal colonization is the best offense against fire blight.
- Begin mowing of green understory (preferably with a sickle bar and/or scythe) and pile resulting mulch thickly under trees around the dripline.

First cover

- Fourth holistic spring spray (liquid fish, pure neem oil, effective microbes) aimed at leaf canopy and developing fruitlets. The fish will help meristem development for return bloom; neem stimulates immune function and hinders moths; microbes are biological reinforcement for the summer ahead. Add horsetail and nettle teas as well to this brew.
- Full clay coverage continues on bearing trees for growers faced with curculio.
- Place dropcloths under trap trees to contain infested June drops, thus preventing larvae from getting to soil to pupate. Alternatively, give those chickens a particularly rousing pep talk.
- Hand-thin crop, beginning with heaviest-setting varieties. Leave one fruit per cluster, being even

more aggressive on varieties that tend to bear biennially otherwise. Timely thinning must be completed within forty days of petal fall. Place infested fruitlets in buckets for disposal via the chicken coop or as road splatter.

- Primary scab season usually ends with a daytime rain around this time. A second micronized sulfur application may be deemed necessary on susceptible varieties in community orchards, especially if more than a week has passed since the previous rain. Alternatively, growers intending to continue with holistic sprays (which now go completely herbal) in the summer months can accelerate those applications based on weather challenges that first month of fruit set.
- Spray for first-generation codling moth according to degree-day tracking if egg-laying suppression from the clay has been gauged insufficient the previous season. Options include Bt, spinosad, and granulosis virus; any of these can be tank-mixed with fish oil as a UV inhibitor and molasses as a feeding attractant. Growers may rely on parasite control and cardboard banding if high moth pressure has been abated previously.
- Pinch off shoots on young trees to correct crow's-foot situations from heading cuts.
- Continue biological mowing with a scythe or sickle bar mower.
- Hang bird netting in place over cherries and blueberries.

Those lazy, crazy, hazy days of summer
- Hang out sticky traps for apple maggot fly (AMF) by mid-June. Target early varieties and/or the orchard perimeter. Renew Tangle-Trap coating every four to six weeks if you're using a sticky variation of this strategy. Traps should be moved to midseason varieties in late July.
- Apply thick kaolin slurry with a paintbrush for borer protection in late June and again in mid-July. Alternatively, botanical trunk sprays (at a 1 percent neem oil concentration) can be directed to saturate lower bark tissues and the soil at the immediate base of each tree. Repeat the neem application a third time in early August if borer pressure is severe.
- Summer-prune watersprouts on especially vigorous apple trees in late July/early August to increase sun penetration to the tree interior and improve fruit color.
- Spray for summer moth control according to the timing of the species attacking your fruit. A rotation of spinosad and Bt just as eggs hatch is typical. Pure neem oil may well get this job done in its own right if holistic spray options for disease are being continued in the summer months.
- Holistic summer sprays include pure neem oil and nettle tea. Horsetail tea should be included in the first two rounds as well to build up the silica defense against summer diseases. These are ideally applied every ten to fourteen days up until harvest. In addition, bicarbonates may help with sooty blotch and flyspeck on light-colored apples where humidity tends to be especially high.
- Spray foliar calcium (at biweekly intervals) beginning when the fruit reaches the size of a nickel if bitter pit has been a problem on certain varieties. Fermented comfrey tea is a homegrown source for bioavailable calcium and can be included in the holistic summer sprays.
- Mow pathways for better harvest access and enjoying your orchard. A light scything under heavily laden trees will help in keeping early drops picked up.
- Visit your trunks: Hand-weed that peastone circle, check for borers, adjust mesh vole guards, rub loose bark off, place a repellent mudpack over active sapsucker holes, and so on.
- Sow an oat (or legume mix) cover crop along the edges of dwarf tree rows.

A well-tended holistic orchard comes together with a good steward at the helm who honors Nature's ways. Fruit trees in home and community orchards— everywhere!—are integral to the good life.

- Take ongoing soil tests in mid-August every few years to check on nutrient status and thus the need to obtain specific soil amendments for fall application.
- Place intact bales of mulch hay around orchard environs. The goal here is to provide nesting sites for field mice (which are not voles) so that abandoned nests the next spring become bumblebee habitat.
- Prune out spent canes in bramble plantings immediately after harvest to allow more sunlight in to initiate fruit buds on maturing primocanes.

Harvest
- Prune stone fruit post-harvest in dry zones to lessen winter establishment of bacterial canker.
- Check for borer egg slits at soil line of trunk

and smush these in along the edges with the tip of hand pruners.
- Gather AMF sticky apples and dispose of properly; remove all other monitoring traps.
- Gather all drops twice a week to feed to the cow or other livestock. A hot compost pile (turned often, for garden use) will work to destroy larvae in infested fruitlets, whereas a laissez-faire pile will not.
- Applying soil amendments at this time works best, because the soil remains relatively warm and feeder roots are in uptake mode.
- Oh yeah . . . pick an amazingly high percentage of beautiful fruit!

Winter preparation
- Spread lime (if light applications of renewal lime were indicated earlier on a soil test) on

Fungal duff management results in mushrooms growing on the orchard floor . . . that's a proper badge of honor for any biological orchardist!

fallen leaves, mow aggressively, then spread well-aged compost.
- A holistic fall spray (liquid fish, pure neem oil, effective microbes, and/or compost tea) made when 50–60 percent of the leaves have fallen off the tree is absolutely recommended. Target the ground, trunk, and branch structure. This is important for leaf decomposition as well as competitive colonization against bacterial and fungal disease organisms within bark crevices. The nitrogen in fish should also help alternate-bearing trees shore up bark nitrogen reserves for spring bud growth.
- Remove limb spreaders.
- Install tree guards on young trees and fork thick ring mulch farther back to deter nearby nesting. Check that mesh protection from voles remains in place on all bearing trees with tender bark. Speak kindly to resident foxes and coyotes if vole numbers seem especially high.
- Renew whitewash on smooth trunks to prevent snow-line freeze injury. Growers using borer slurry in midsummer may find enough whitening still in place.
- Hang peanut butter strips on electric fence for baiting uneducated deer tongues.
- Give thanks for another blessed year on this good earth.

PARTING WORDS

Liberty Hyde Bailey compiled a series of agricultural manuals published by Cornell University around the end of the nineteenth century. One quote of his has always stood out to me as a driving philosophy in my own orcharding:

If a grower knows why, he or she will teach themselves how.

We don't need to guess about what's going right for our trees or the quandaries that inevitably pop up. We observe, we ask questions, we learn, and eventually, yes, perhaps, we even comprehend . . . all of which should lead to a deeper appreciation of this beautiful creation. That attitude alone can lead to success at procuring the gifts of this good life for family and community. Don't be overcome by learning-curve insistence on orcharding challenges. Much of this takes time. The biological lessons presented here become obvious to those eager to grasp the connectiveness of it all. Listen to what the trees and the microbes tell you to be true. Trust your inner druid to guide you in these ways. Growing healthy fruit is for thinking people who embrace being a part of something slightly more than wonderful.

Appendices

ORCHARD RESOURCES

The future of agriculture lives in those people who develop low-input, integrated systems. Economics won't have it any other way; nor will the planet. Still, growers need what they need when they need it. Keep in mind that some nurseries offer training supplies, the soil fertility folks have organic spray materials, and everybody has backpack sprayers (well, almost) regardless of how the listings pan out below.

Mail-order nurseries

Many excellent local nurseries sell freshly dug trees. Those listed here will ship bareroot stock, come highly recommended, clearly state rootstocks being used, and represent a broad swath of regional advantage.

Adams County Nursery
P.O. Box 108
Aspers, PA 17304
(717) 677-8105
www.acnursery.com

Backyard Berry Plants
3267 T.C. Steele Road
Nashville, IN 47448
www.backyardberryplants.com

Bay Laurel Nursery
2500 El Camino Real
Atascadero, CA 93422
(805) 466-3406
www.baylaurelnursery.com

Berries Unlimited
807 Cedar Lane
Prairie Grove, AR 72753
(479) 846-6030
www.berriesunlimited.com

Big Horse Creek Farm
P.O. Box 70
Lansing, NC 28643
www.bighorsecreekfarm.com

Boyer Nurseries
405 Boyer Nursery Road
Biglerville, PA 17307
(717) 677-8558
www.boyernurseries.com

Burnt Ridge Nursery
432 Burnt Ridge Road
Onalaska, WA 98570
(360) 985-2873
www.burntridgenursery.com

Century Farm Orchards
P.O. Box 271
Altamahaw, NC 27202
(336) 349-5709
www.centuryfarmorchards.com

Cumberland Valley Nursery
686 Hidden Valley Circle
McMinnville, TN 37110
(931) 273-9500
www.fruittreefarm.com

Cummins Nursery
1408 Trumansburg Road
Ithaca, NY 14456
(607) 227-6147
www.cumminsnursery.com

Dave Wilson Nursery
19701 Lake Road
Hickman, CA 95323
(800) 654-5854
www.davewilson.com

Edible Forest Nursery
E7946 Upper Maple Dale Road
Viroqua, WI 54665
(608) 782-3343
www.edibleforestnursery.com

Edible Landscaping
361 Spirit Ridge Lane
Afton, VA 22920
(800) 524-4156
www.ediblelandscaping.com

Fall Creek Farm & Nursery
39318 Jasper-Lowell Road
Lowell, OR 97452
(800) 538-3001
www.fallcreeknursery.com

Fedco Trees
P.O. Box 520
Waterville, ME 04903
(207) 873-7333
www.fedcoseeds.com/trees.htm

Greenmantle Nursery
3010 Ettersburg Road
Garberville, CA 95542
(707) 986-7504
www.greenmantlenursery.com

Hardy Fruit Trees Nursery
2999 Chemin Aquilon
Sainte-Julienne, Québec J0K 2T0, Canada
(450) 834-3060
www.hardyfruittrees.ca

Hidden Springs Nursery
170 Hidden Springs Lane
Cookeville, TN 38501
(931) 268-2592
www.hiddenspringsnursery.com

Johnson Nursery
1352 Big Creek Road
Ellijay, GA 30536
(888) 276-3187
www.johnsonnursery.com

Moser Fruit Tree Sales
5329 Defield Road
Coloma, MI 49038
(800) 386-5600
www.forfruittrees.com

Nourse Farms
41 River Road
South Deerfield, MA 01373
(413) 665-2658
www.noursefarms.com

One Green World
28696 South Cramer Road
Molalla, OR 97038
(877) 353-4028
www.onegreenworld.com

Raintree Nursery
391 Butts Road
Morton, WA 98356
(360) 496-6400
www.raintreenursery.com

Schlabach's Nursery
2784 Murdock Road
Medina, NY 14103
(866) 600-5203

Siloam Orchards
7300 3rd Concession
Uxbridge, Ontario L9P 1R1, Canada
(905) 852-9418
www.siloamorchards.com

Stark Brothers
P.O. Box 1800
Louisiana, MO 63353
(800) 325-4180
www.starkbros.com

St. Lawrence Nurseries
325 State Highway 345
Potsdam, NY 13676
(315) 265-6739
www.sln.potsdam.ny.us/

Tooley's Trees
P.O. Box 392
Truchas, NM 87578
(505) 689-2400
www.tooleystrees.com

Trees of Antiquity
20 Wellsona Road
Paso Robles, CA 93446
(805) 467-9909
www.treesofantiquity.com

Van Well Nursery
P.O. Box 1339
Wenatchee, WA 98807
(800) 572-1553
www.vanwell.net

Vintage Virginia Apples
P.O. Box 210
North Garden, VA 22959
(434) 297-2326
www.vintagevirginiaapples.com

Scionwood and rootstock

Varietal wood for grafting comes first and foremost from fruit friends nearby. Each regional network sponsors an annual scionwood exchange. Certain heritage orchards and commercial fruit nurseries oblige as well. The following growers offer budwood of heirloom varieties to the general public for a nominal fee. Please be entirely respectful of the generosity offered here and cover all costs (including a SASE) when requesting a listing of varieties available.

Nick Botnar, OR, 4015 Eagle Valley Road, Yoncalla OR 97499
John Bunker, ME, www.fedcoseeds.com/trees.htm
Davenport Collection, MA, www.towerhillbg.org/thwebscion.html
Maxine & Tony Dempski, WI, www.maplevalley orchards.com
Richard Fahey, NY, Catholic Homesteading Movement, Oxford, NY 13830
Joyce Neighbors, AL, 1039 Lay Springs Road, Gadsden, AL 35904
Bob Purvis, ID, 1568 Hill Road, Homedale, ID 83628
Walt Rosenberg, CO, www.masonvilleorchard.com

Rootstock for pome fruits and stone fruits comes from commercial nurseries out west. Orders for bundles (minimum one hundred count) are best placed early in fall. A number of fruit nurseries might provide a smaller amount of rootstock (a quantity of five, say) if you promise your firstborn. The folks organizing a regional scionwood exchange often have root choices available as a matter of course.

Copenhaven Farms
12990 Southwest Copenhaven Road
Gaston, OR 97119
(503) 985-7161
www.copenhavenfarms.com

Lawyer's Nursery
6625 Highway 200
Plains, MT 59859
(800) 551-9875
www.lawyernursery.com

TRECO Rootstock Company
P.O. Box 98
Woodburn, OR 97071
(800) 871-5141
www.treco.nu

Willamette Nurseries
25571 South Barlow Road
Canby, OR 97013
(800) 852-2018
www.willamettenurseries.com

Heritage orchards to visit
Common Ground Orchard, Unity, Maine
Eastman's Antique Apples, Wheeler, Michigan
Masonville Orchard, Fort Collins, Colorado
Seedsavers Heritage Orchard, Decorah, Iowa
Southern Heritage Apple Orchard, Pinnacle, North Carolina
Tower Hill Botanic Garden, Worcester, Massachusetts
Upper Midwest Heritage Orchard, Duluth, Minnesota

Fungal support
A biological fruit grower promotes the fungal duff and competitive colonization throughout the year. These essential fungal resources will assist you in creating a healthy orchard ecosystem.

Mycorrhizal inoculum:
BioOrganics
2153 Vista Del Mundo
Santa Maria, CA 93458
(888) 332-7676
http://bio-organics.com

Mycorrhizal Applications
P.O. Box 1029
Grant's Pass, OR 97528
(866) 476-7800
www.mycorrhizae.com

Organic Gardener's Pantry
Victoria, BC, Canada
(250) 661-0383
www.gardenerspantry.ca
A one-shop fungal source for Canadians!

Unpasteurized liquid fish:
Dramm Corporation
www.dramm.com

Eco-Nutrients
www.econutrients.com

Neptune's Harvest
www.neptunesharvest.com

Organic Gem
www.organicgem.com

Schafer Fisheries
www.schaferliquidfish.com

Effective microbes:
SCD Probiotics
1327 East 9th Street
Kansas City, MO 64106
(913) 541-9299
www.scdworld.net

TeraGanix Effective Microorganisms
19371 U.S. Highway 69S
Alto, TX 75925
(866) 369-3678
www.teraganix.com

Compost tea:
Compostwerks
487 East Main Street, Suite 160
Mount Kisco, NY 10549
(914) 837-2364
www.compostwerks.com

Keep It Simple
12323 180th Avenue Northeast
Redmond, WA 98052
(866) 558-0990
www.simplici-tea.com

Pollination
Apple Tree Pollination Compatibility
www.orangepippintrees.com/pollinationchecker.aspx

Beediverse
641 Claremont Street
Coquitlam, BC V3J 3T5, Canada
(604) 936-3913
www.beediverse.com

Brushy Mountain Bee Farm
610 Bethany Church Road
Moravian Falls, NC 28654
(800) 233-7929
www.brushymountainbeefarm.com

Knox Cellars
25724 Northeast 10th Street
Sammamish, WA 98074
(206) 849-5065
www.knoxcellars.com

Mason Bee Homes
2460 Oakes Road
Black Creek, BC V9J 1J1, Canada
www.masonbeehomes.com

Pollinator Paradise
31140 Circle Drive
Parma, ID 83660
(208) 722-7808
www.pollinatorparadise.com

Insect monitoring/trapping/beneficials
Biocontrol Network
5116 Williamsburg Road
Brentwood, TN 37027
(800) 441-2847
www.biconet.com

Gempler's
P.O. Box 44993
Madison, WI 53744
(800) 382-8473
www.gemplers.com

Great Lakes IPM
10220 Church Road Northeast
Vestaburg, MI 48891
(989) 268-5693
www.greatlakesipm.com

Green Spot
93 Priest Road
Nottingham, NH 03290
(603) 942-8925
http://greenmethods.com

IPM Laboratories
980 Main Street
Locke, NY 13092
(315) 497-2063
www.ipmlabs.com

Natural Insect Control
3737 Netherby Road
Stevensville, Ontario L0S 1S0, Canada
(905) 382-2904
www.naturalinsectcontrol.ca

Organic suppliers
Agriculture Solutions
P.O. Box 141
Strong, ME 04983
(207) 684-3939
www.agriculturesolutions.com

Agro-K Corporation
8030 Main Street, Northeast
Minneapolis, MN 55432
(800) 328-2418
www.agro-k.com
Foliar nutrients

The Ahimsa Alternative
15 Timberglade Avenue
Bloomington, MN 55437
(952) 943-9449
www.neemresource.com
Pure neem oil

ARBICO Organics
P.O. Box 8910
Tucson, AZ 85738
(800) 827-2847
www.arbico-organics.com

Gardens Alive!
5100 Schenley Place
Lawrenceburg, IN 47025
(513) 354-1482
www.gardensalive.com

Golden Barrel Molasses
4960 Horseshoe Pike
Honey Brook, PA 19344
(800) 327-4406
www.goldenbarrel.com

Organic Grower's Supply
P.O. Box 520
Waterville, ME 04903
(207) 873-7333
www.fedcoseeds.com/ogs.htm

Peaceful Valley Farm Supply
P.O. Box 2209
Grass Valley, CA 95945
(888) 784-1722
www.groworganic.com

Planet Natural
1612 Gold Avenue
Bozeman, MT 59715
(800) 289-6656
www.planetnatural.com

Seven Springs Farm
426 Jerry Lane Northeast
Check, VA 24072
(800) 540-9181
www.7springsfarm.com

Soil amendments
Fertrell Fertilizers
601 North 2nd Street
Bainbridge, PA 17502
(717) 367-1566
www.fertrell.com

Gaia Green Products
9130 Granby Road
Grand Forks, British Columbia V0H 1H1, Canada
(800) 545-3745
www.gaiagreen.com

Harmony Farm Supply
P.O. Box 460
Graton, CA 95444
(707) 823-9125
www.harmonyfarm.com

Lancaster Agriculture Products
60 North Ronks Road
Ronks, PA 17572
(717) 687-9222
www.lancasterag.com

Midwestern Bio-Ag
10955 Blackhawk Drive
Blue Mounds, WI 53517
(800) 327-6012
www.midwesternbioag.com

North Country Organics
P.O. Box 372
Bradford, VT 05033
(802) 222-4277
www.norganics.com

Orchard equipment
American Nettings & Fabric
P.O. Box 227
Custer, WA 98240
(800) 811-7444
www.americannettings.com

A. M. Leonard
P.O. Box 816
Piqua, OH 45356
(800) 543-8955
www.amleo.com

Baldwin Apple Ladders
P.O. Box 177
Brooks, ME 04921
(207) 722-3654
http://peterbaldwinarts.com/ladders

Forestry Suppliers, Inc.
P.O. Box 8397
Jackson, MS 39284
(800) 647-5368
www.forestry-suppliers.com

Kania Squirrel Traps
2345 Delinea Place
Nanaimo, British Columbia V9T 5L9, Canada
(250) 585-1800
www.kania.net

Orchard Supply and Equipment
P.O. Box 540
Conway, MA 01341
(800) 634-5557
www.oescoinc.com

Orchard Valley Supply
5243 Z-Max Boulevard
Harrisburg, NC 28075
(888) 755-0098
www.orchardvalleysupply.com

Peach Ridge Orchard Supply
8405 Fruit Ridge Avenue
Sparta, MI 49345
(800) 452-6748
www.peachridge.com

Premier Fence Systems
2031 300th Street
Washington, IA 52353
(800) 282-6631
www.premier1supplies.com

Scythe Supply
496 Shore Road
Perry, ME 04667
(207) 853-4750
www.scythesupply.com

Wilson Orchard and Vineyard Supply
1104 East Mead Avenue
Yakima, WA 98903
(800) 232-1174
www.wilsonirr.com

HELPFUL WEBSITES

Regional growing advice

State Extension services and trade publications offer tons of regional advice for commercial IPM growers as well as home orchardists. Some stand out more than others. Ignore the chemical bias where it appears . . . use these resources instead to learn more about pest life cycles, proven cultivars, and exciting new research.

Good Fruit Grower, www.goodfruit.com/
  Good-Fruit-Grower
A Grower's Guide to Apple Insects and Diseases in
  the Southeast, http://ipm.ncsu.edu/apple/contents
  .html
Michigan State University fruit IPM portal, www
  .ipm.msu.edu/fruit.htm
Midwest Home Fruit Production Guide, http://ohio
  line.osu.edu/b940/index.html
NCAT Sustainable Agriculture Project, http://attra
  .ncat.org
Northwest Organic Fruit Production, http://organic.
  tfrec.wsu.edu/OrganicIFP/Home/Introduction.html
Organic Agricultural Center of Canada, www.oacc
  .info
Pennsylvania Tree Fruit Production Guide, http://
  tfpg.cas.psu.edu
Small Fruit Horticulture portal., http://mtvernon
  .wsu.edu/Small_Fruit_Hort/SFberrylinks.html
Tree Fruit & Berry Pathology, www.nysaes.cornell
  .edu/pp/extension/tfabp/pome.shtml

Chelsea Green connections

Edible Forest Gardens (Dave Jacke), www.edibleforest
  gardens.com
Gaia's Garden (Toby Hemingway), www.pattern
  literacy.com
The Holistic Orchard (Michael Phillips), www.grow
  organicapples.com

Plant hardiness zones

United States, www.usna.usda.gov/Hardzone/ushz
  map.html
Canada, http://planthardiness.gc.ca/exmint
  .pl?lang=en
Heat perspective, www.ahs.org/publications/heat_
  zone_map.htm

Heirloom varieties

Forgotten Fruits Manual & Manifesto, http://raft
  alliance.org
Heirloom Orchardist, www.heirloomorchardist.com
Orange Pippin, www.orangepippin.com
Slow Food's Ark of Taste, www.slowfoodusa.org
Tom Brown's Apple Search, www.applesearch.org

Insect knowledge

All Abuzz About Bugs!, http://bugguide.net/node/
  view/15740
Beneficial Allies, www.omafra.gov.on.ca/english/
  crops/facts/96-029.htm
Dr. McBug, www.drmcbug.com
IPM Images, www.ipmimages.org
Xerces Society, www.xerces.org

Soil testing labs

A&L Eastern Laboratories, www.al-labs-eastern.com
AgriEnergy Resources, www.agrienergy.net
Bio-Systems, MI, bio-systems@centurytel.net
International Ag Labs, www.aglabs.com
Kinsey's Agricultural Services, www.kinseyag.com
Soil Foodweb Inc., www.soilfoodweb.com

RECOMMENDED BOOKS

Attracting Native Pollinators (Xerces Society Guide)*

Florida's Best Fruiting Plants by Charles Boning

Fruit, Berry, and Nut Inventory (Seed Savers Exchange)*

Home Orchard (University of California ARN Publication 3485)

Old Southern Apples by Lee Calhoun*

Soil Biology Primer (Soil and Water Conservation Society)

The Grape Grower: A Guide to Organic Viticulture by Lon Rombough

Apples: 200 American Varieties by Tom Burford (coming in 2012)

Tree Fruit Field Guide—Insect, Mite, and Disease Pests and Natural Enemies of Eastern North America (NRAES Publication 169)*

Uncommon Fruits by Lee Reich

The Apple in North America by Dan Bussey (coming in 2012)

*These selections are available at the Holistic Orchard Network's website. Every book order placed through the Bookshelf at www.groworganicapples .com helps support grassroots research for health-oriented, biologically based orcharding.

FRUIT NETWORKS

Conversing with other fruit growers jump-starts your learning curve!

Backyard Fruit Growers, www.sas.upenn.edu/~dailey/ byfg.html

British Columbia Fruit Testers Association, http:// bcfta.ca

California Rare Fruit Growers, www.crfg.org

Holistic Orchard Network, www.groworganicapples .com

Home Orchard Society, www.homeorchardsociety .org

North American Fruit Explorers (NAFEX), www .nafex.org

Organic Tree Fruit Association, www.organictree fruit.org

Southern Fruit Fellowship, http://southernfruit fellowship.wordpress.com

NOTES

1. THE ORCHARD ECOSYSTEM

1. The *Soil Biology Primer* put together by the Soil and Water Conservation Society offers a quick behind-the-scenes look at how everybody involved here fuels the engine of our existence. *Teaming with Microbes* by Jeff Lowenfels and Wayne Lewis goes much farther in providing practical suggestions allowing you to come up to biological speed in the organic garden.

2. A large fraction of the nutrients available to plants is a result of microbial grazing and nutrient release by soil critters like protozoans, nematodes, and arthropods (good ol' bugs). When nematodes eat bacteria or fungi, for instance, they release excess nitrogen in the form of ammonium, usually in the vicinity of the root system of the plant.

3. It wasn't until the 1980s that soil scientists could accurately measure the amount of bacteria and fungi in soils and thus start to draw life-basis conclusions. Dr. Elaine Ingham at Oregon State University and others started publishing research that showed the ratio of these two organisms in various types of soils. The least disturbed soils had far more fungi than bacteria, while disturbed soils experienced just the opposite. The correlation between woodsy plants and a preference for soils that were fungally dominated followed from there.

4. Let's recognize a holistic badge of honor when we see it. Surface manifestations of fungal dominance beneath fruit trees—mushrooms like morels and other basidiomycetes—are telling you that your mulching and composting efforts are righteous. Job well done, biological steward!

5. Ectomycorrhizae colonize the surface of the feeder roots, whereas endomycorrhizae enter the cells of the root. The latter form storage structures (*vesicles*) for nutrient exchange that branch out like miniature trees (*arbuscules*) and operate like tiny feeder roots within the feeder roots of the tree. There's rarely just one species of fungi involved with an individual root system.

6. Even the eyeballs viewing these words are a microorganism host, so get over the squeamishness, okay? Protection from pathogens begins with *good guys* in all the right places.

7. Spiders, to be specific. Fungal food readies an entire army of baby spiders that in turn will trap more than a few pest insects as adults. While this may seem to be a huge jump as regards the subject at hand, the point should be taken that all things are interconnected in the natural world . . . which is why we (the stewards) must be cognizant of how every action we take in the orchard will affect the whole. This sort of fascinating nuance absolutely rocks once you start to grasp a holistic perspective on growing healthy fruit.

8. This concept of tillage interspersed with undisturbed woodsy ground has considerable biological value. The extant root systems from which you have removed the growing tips (the assorted tree saplings cut at ground level) are very likely to have already been colonized by appropriate mycorrhizae species. Leaving the aisle portion of an orchard planting undisturbed means you are agreeing to a contract with native mycorrhizae to soon reach again into the narrow strips of tillage being made for your fruit trees.

9. Any guide to cover cropping in the organic garden will explain the choices of what to plant as regards weed suppression, deep root aeration of the soil, bulking up on organic matter, and nitrogen fixation. Different conditions call for different strategies. Buckwheat is useful to crowd out persistent grasses provided a second planting is preceded by a ten-day fallow (rest period) after plowing under the first buckwheat planting. This admittedly bacterial process will be necessary for clearing the deck in order to establish more fungal ground cover after the buckwheat one–two step.

10. Allowing seven to ten days of downtime prior to planting a cover crop helps in two ways. First, the bacterial explosion following tillage settles after a few days, making the soil environment more conducive to seed germination. Second, weed seed near the surface that just begins to sprout toward the end of that fallow week will wither when the cover crop is lightly stirred into the top inch of soil.

11. The biological wealth of ramial chipped wood was first revealed in Québec in the late 1970s when Edgar Guay

began searching for new products that could be derived from the huge piles of branches seemingly wasted after logging operations. A paper published in 1998 titled "Regenerating Soils with Ramial Chipped Wood" by the Laval University team led by Gilles Lemieux provides the detail you find summarized here.

12. Sawdust does this very same thing, of course, having originally been stem wood sawn into lumber with the dust created as a by-product.

13. Rot fungi on the soil surface are not the same as the fruit rots that growers battle in more humid zones. Don't get taken in by the mention of colors here! Botanical Latin would clear all this up for any of you who need to distinguish between decomposing brown rot on the forest floor and sporulating brown rot on stone fruit more fully.

14. Here's a nice play on ramial for the majority of you without a chipper: Fruit tree prunings are deciduous wood, and, yes, you can snip these into 4- to 8-inch segments as you stand by your tree deciding which branch to prune away next. Chances of seeing any sign of this twig wood come fall are practically nil once the decomposers zero in.

15. I like to think everyone has a particularly valuable bit to contribute to society. Here's mine. Those guys chipping that brush get mighty thirsty after a day's work. Offering them a six-pack of cold beer in appreciation for the truck coming by with a load of ramial wood chips gets their attention. And if it turns out one of your neighbors also bought this book—and thus is savvy to biological value—then up the ante: Offer a better brand of beer!

16. Good question: Does it matter if the ramial chips are fresh, or do these need to be aged as well? I currently have no reason to say one way or the other. We'll be talking about using this same treetop source as part of an orchard compost pile. Chips piled to begin decomposition on the forest edge might actually pick up a mycorrhizal spore component (being in the vicinity of extant tree roots) over the course of a year or two. But I also use freshly chipped ramial wood directly in my orchards when it becomes available in late fall and in earliest spring when I work up cordwood. I figure those ramial chips are functioning biologically like humus on a deciduous forest floor by the time the growing season begins in earnest.

17. The Agriculture Canada Research Station in Summerland, British Columbia, has done extensive studies as to the effect of different kinds of mulches on apple trees. Cross-sectional trunk diameter of fruit trees is up to 35 percent greater after using a biological mulch versus unmulched control trees. Come the fruiting years, cropping averaged

about 15 percent more fruit per tree. The overall health and vigor of the trees with mulch were noticeably increased as well.

18. The openness helps in deterring borers as well as bark-chewing rodents. The dryness lessens the chances of *Phytophthora* root, crown, and collar rot fungi establishing. Growers in the Piedmont regions of the southeastern United States especially want to keep the base of young trees clear of dead organic matter to deny southern blight fungi a food resource right by the trunk.

19. Here we should give some consideration to the bumblebee queen. A hay bale placed out in late summer is in place when spring arrives and queen bumbles awake to search for a nest site. A semi-intact hay bale offers ample opportunity for this, particularly if field mice made a nest in that bale in the fall, leaving a cozy start for an eager queen. Come fall she and her progeny will have passed their season . . . and now that fairly rotten bale can be spread apart where it sits to break down even further.

20. I'm going to state this just once: The word *conventional* used to describe orchard methodology really bugs me! Chemical proponents assume that spray choices of the last hundred years represent the norm; that not to use chemicals to grow fruit is somehow *unconventional*. The right words here are *nonbiological* and *biological* when we take Nature's perspective.

21. Buds will have sprung forth on the order of ¼–½ inch with baby leaf in the case of apple. The stone fruits do various things, some flowering before showing green, so gauge this approximate timing by the apple. Basically, we're talking about doing this first catalyst spray with pulsing agents about two weeks into the active growing season on a warm spring day.

22. Microbe diversity can be enhanced with aerated compost tea as well. More on this will be forthcoming. Many home orchardists might be tempted to forget this aspect of the plan—both effective microbes and properly made compost tea require a brewing process. Reductionist science has yet to show whether nutritional support alone can set up a healthy season ahead. Providing biological reinforcements is based on intuitive insight and the fact that more and more holistic growers are having success with these techniques.

23. Stone fruit growers in particular pay heed. A number of diseases like bacterial spot and peach leaf curl that traditionally are treated organically with copper or lime sulfur sprays post-harvest can be outcompeted by utilizing diverse biology. These mineral-based medicines work against holistic advantage . . . which isn't to say that some

of you, knowing when conditions favor bacterial spread, might not decide it's still necessary to go the heavy-hitting allopathic route in certain years. Such a thinker's option always remains on the table for growers striving to make the healthiest choices possible.

24. Non-aerated compost tea requires none of the fussiness of the aerated version. A few shovelfuls of mature compost soaked for a day or two in a 5-gallon bucket, stirred on occasion, then strained, yields a helpful range of organisms from the compost to the brew. Apply at a hefty rate, on the order of 1–2 quarts tea per backpack spray tank. The other proportions (for pure neem oil and liquid fish) for fall application follow the rates for early spring.

25. All this is in conjunction with what's already been probed to support dynamic soil life . . . remember, system health relies on *all the subtleties* being in place. The interdependent, interconnected paradigm underlying healthy orcharding being presented in this one "deep chapter" of *The Holistic Orchard* cannot be overlooked in any respect.

26. Where you live will alter such monthly proclamations, of course. Growers in warmer zones see fruit bloom as early as February and continuing throughout March and April. This creates an "orchard summer" consisting of the months of May and June when harvesting begins.

27. Laboratory tests suggest that imidacloprid can impede honeybees' sophisticated communication and navigation systems. Italy, Slovenia, and Germany banned all neonicotinoids recently after the loss of millions of honeybees.

28. Will Allen's *The War on Bugs* (Chelsea Green Publishing, 2008) provides an excellent history on how we got started on the chemical bandwagon. I realize I won't always be speaking to the choir in this guide to growing good fruit. However, I do know we all gain from having our eyes opened at times.

29. I don't know if curculios have a word for "ironic," but we humans should be aware that for two hundred years now this snout-nosed weevil has outwitted us hands-down. And should curcs ever decipher this book, we are truly in big trouble!

2. ORCHARD DESIGN

1. Soil that becomes saturated for significant periods will lose its fungal component. Anaerobic conditions occur as well in compacted soils. Fungi are aerobic organisms. Wet conditions at the feet of fruiting trees indicate another kind of welcome mat: Rather than embracing mycorrhizal and saprophytic fungi, roots and trunk collar alike are now exposed to pathogenic types that cause root rot and crown rot.

2. Branches, tops, roots, fallen tree trunks, straw, and leaves can all be used in this decomposing core. This particular method does not stress the deciduous principles established in Québec for ramial wood chips. Even woods such as cedar and eucalyptus can be chipped to become part of the berm. These species are loaded with oils that act as natural pesticides/herbicides, and so are best used after being piled outside and left to decompose in the elements for a full year. Black locust and black walnut would have similar issues. Tannins in all softwood bark inhibit deciduous growth, but pine/spruce/fir blowdowns can be used once decay is established on the forest floor. A hefty portion of deciduous branch tops would serve as an important fungal counterbalance in establishing *Hugelkultur*.

3. *Sepp Holzer's Permaculture* is now available in an English-language edition from Chelsea Green Publishing.

4. Stone fruit trees lose bud and twig hardiness due to fluctuating winter temperatures. Tender trees are best kept in deep dormancy by planting them on the north side of a shade source or by providing a winter buffer from sun and wind alike.

5. Donna Hudson in Tennessee had planted this seed in my brain at the time, however, as posted on the NAFEX discussion listserve: "I was at a garden meeting where a local guy named Jim Joyner said that gardeners spend so much time worrying about the top six inches of the soil, but that he'd seen instances where organic matter much deeper had had dramatic results. He gave two examples. One was a tropical island where a hurricane had knocked down all the coconut palms. Someone had laid the palms down in a single layer and piled dirt on them before planting a commercial avocado grove. He said that the trees in the part of the grove with palms under them did much better than those without. He said that in the Ozarks an experimental station had been trying without success to produce grapes, and finally resorted to making 4 ft deep trenches in the clay soil and filling them with woody debris. The grapes grew fine after that. I have been fantasizing about making a ditch witch across our slopes for a decade now. Because of these stories, I have let wild trees grow in my orchard so we can cut these down later after their roots have punched holes down into the subsoil for my own trees to follow. Branches of the trees we remove wind up on the ground to decompose back into the earth."

6. This applies for growers in Zones 2 and 3, and very likely Zone 4 as well depending on microclimate considerations.

Even apples may need a southerly aspect in places with a short growing season simply to grow long enough to mature fruit. Frost danger to blossoms of all sorts becomes more relevant for growers in Zones 5, 6, and 7.

7. Sara Wright, a soil scientist for the USDA Agricultural Research Service, discovered this mycorrhizal secretion in 1996. She named glomalin after Glomales, the taxonomic order to which arbuscular mycorrhizal fungi belong.

8. *Gaia's Garden: A Guide to Home-Scale Permaculture* by Toby Hemenway (Chelsea Green Publishing, 2009) will take you much farther into the sustainable design principles developed by permaculture practitioners. Toby has a way of making the whole yard bloom into a self-renewing landscape. I especially love the illustrated guild designs meant to inspire each of us to integrated thinking about diverse plantings. Fruit trees weave in and out of many of his suggestions.

9. Comfrey species include true comfrey (*Symphytum officinale*), dwarf comfrey (*S. grandiflorum*), and a hybrid cross known as the Bocking 14 cultivar of Russian comfrey (*S. × uplandicum*). The first two self-seed freely, but the hybrid does not produce viable seed and thus its spread is limited to clump expansion.

10. Roots metabolize carbohydrates photosynthesized in green plant parts by taking up oxygen and releasing carbon dioxide as they grow. Low oxygen levels coupled with high concentrations of carbon dioxide can reduce and even stop apple root growth. Dense sod produces more carbon dioxide in its fine root zone per unit volume of soil than tree feeder roots prefer to encounter. Small rootlets actually require a higher level of aeration to function normally than do larger tree roots. Carbon dioxide levels from stockier root systems like comfrey are more dilute and thus favor diversity in the underground realm.

11. Let's go into thinking-things-through mode. Comfrey is not planted right up tight against a young tree; this would simply be too competitive in those early years when we need to grow wood structure. The term *dripline* refers to the anticipated outer diameter of the tree, which for free-standing purposes can be 6–8 feet out from the trunk. I often don't introduce comfrey onto a particular tree scene until the fourth or fifth year.

12. Daffodils aside, a rigid wrap of wire-mesh hardware cloth (available at any local building supply store) can be wrapped around apple trunks to protect the bottom 2 feet of bark from voles. This comes highly advised as the ultimate vole insurance!

13. Credit for getting me started along these lines goes to Juliette de Baïracli Levy, who passed along gypsy plant observations in her wide-ranging herbals from the 1960s. These classic books have been reprinted by Ash Tree Publishing in Woodstock, New York.

14. Leius stated that mean parasitism of tent caterpillar pupae increased eighteenfold and that of codling moth larvae increased fivefold in Ontario apple orchards with rich assemblages of flowering understory plants. K. Leius, "Influence of Wild Flowers on Parasitism of Tent Caterpillars and Codling Moth," *Canadian Entomologist*, 99, no. 4 (1967): 444-46.

15. Maier observed higher rates of parasitism of apple maggot by braconids in northern Connecticut apple orchards where plants such as blueberry, dogwood, and winterberry commonly grew nearby. C. T. Maier, "Parasitoids Emerging from Puparia of *Rhagoletis pomonella* (Diptera: Tephritidae) Infesting Hawthorn and Apple in Connecticut," *Canadian Entomologist*, 113 (1981): 867-70.

16. Some botanical name-dropping will be of use to zero in on the right winterberry for a given site. *Ilex verticillata* (common winterberry) is a shrub that likes moist or wet soil and can take some shade. *I. laevigata* (smooth winterberry) shows greater tolerance to drier soil. *I. glabra* (inkberry) prefers sandy or peaty soil and all-out sun.

3. ORCHARD HORTICULTURE

1. Those same climatic variations can also work against an attempt to push a variety beyond its comfort range. Severe fluctuations in the temperatures in late fall can screw up the hardening-off of fruit trees. Add to that a warm rain in December and what that does to confound root systems in certain soils. Tree loss from winter-kill happens sometimes, no matter how safe you play it.

2. Kevin Hauser of Kuffel Creek Nursery in Southern California is "the man" to explore the possibilities of low chill with respect to apple varieties. His website (www.kuffelcreek.com) is rich in advice for temperate growers in Zones 9 and 10.

3. Fruit frozen to the core may be fine for processing and making cider in the next couple of weeks, provided it was approaching a relative degree of ripeness when it froze. Let the crop thaw on the tree before picking. Such apples (that aren't outright mush!) may seem fine at first, but over the course of several weeks they will start to soften and become off-flavored. Dense-fleshed apples like GoldRush, Fuji, and Cox's Orange Pippin, with their relatively higher sugar levels, can take more cold than other varieties.

4. Breathable-fabric root control bags are a recent introduction on the nursery front. Root systems become more fibrous as a result of feeder roots responding to the air barrier at the surface of this underground bag. The resulting tree develops a multitude of lateral roots that launch quickly into transplanted ground with practically no root loss as a result of being dug up. Tooley's Trees in New Mexico is one organic nursery reporting phenomenal success using this cutting-edge technology.

5. What's worse is that brand-name varieties may actually be something other than what the label states. Large wholesale nurseries do indeed sell overruns and mislabeled stock to national chains at a discount. The store label subsequently applied too often proves to be an unexpected surprise. The thinking goes that the buyer will probably not even know the difference or will have killed the tree long before fruit finally comes.

6. Crossing genetics between species in the name of disease resistance is taking place at Cornell and other research labs. The mad scientists are at work splicing genes from silkworms, soil organisms, and even human lysozyme into fruit tree cultivars and then using tissue culture to propagate the transformed version. None of these GMO trees have yet come to market for the simple reason that anticipated results are hard to come by.

7. Consider that seed. It's the result of cross-pollination between two different sets of fruit genetics. (The exception being—and there always are exceptions!—a self-fertile fruit type.) Just like you: There's Mom; there's Dad; making you a unique new variety of human sharing some of each parent's traits.

8. I've walked this talk with apples, trying different management systems with a wide range of rootstock. Obviously mine is a northern perspective, where growth tends to be not quite so exponential and precocity advantages (coming into bearing sooner) are not as pronounced.

9. Even a vigorous rootstock will benefit from being staked in its development years in a strong wind area or on heavy clay soil. Fruit trees in the Plains states (for instance) often develop a pronounced leeward lean unless securely staked until the trees are big. Occasional heading of the leader to stiffen up girth can help keep trees aligned with gravity rather than leaning severely toward the sun or bowed to the wind.

10. Garden skills need to integrate with fruit tree needs for this to be successful. Cultivation should be shallow, thus not disturbing feeder root outreach from the trees in May and June. Hill potatoes early and then mulch with rotting hay or straw to keep things more fungal. Tillage should be shallow, with all machine action kept to an absolute minimum to lessen soil compaction. Cover-crop with red clover every few years along the tree edges, renewing soil for vegetable and tree alike. This mini lesson could go on and on.

11. Here's an apple example. Rhode Island Greening grafted onto Bud.9 rootstock yields that single bushel. That same variety on MM.111 rootstock may yield 8 bushels or more.

12. These rootstock names refer simply to the place where the original crosses were selected with a number to indicate the particular cross that had noteworthy traits. Naming apple rootstock isn't exactly rocket science. But since those of you who actually read these notes apparently like to have fun, let's carry the story a wee bit farther. The next round of research involved heat-treating these very same roots to remove latent viruses. This collaboration between East Malling and the Long Ashton Research Station in the 1960s resulted in the EMLA series. Thus there's EMLA.7, slightly more vigorous than M.7, but not prone to unexpected decline. This goes on . . . and hopefully has made it clear why I am not covering every named rootstock under the sun!

13. Seedling rootstocks generally are started from the seeds of a mother cultivar that produces fairly uniform progeny. Antonovka is a good apple example: This Russian variety has proven itself extremely hardy with consistent vigor (on the order of 90 percent) and is fire-blight-tolerant. Pomace from a run-of-the-mill cider operation, on the other hand, will be filled with cross-pollinated prospects that may not prove as consistent.

14. Searching for *tree seed germination* links on the web can be very helpful.

15. You can propagate clonal rootstock this way, of course. If the "sapling" you began with was a bench graft that never took, and yet the root sent up a new shoot from below the attempted graft, this "new tree" is the named rootstock itself. Mounding its shoots gets you more of the original clonal rootstock.

16. Apple to apple, peach to peach, cherry to cherry, pear to pear . . . Oh, but wait, pear will indeed take on quince, and apricot is a sucker for plum. More exceptions exist, but we're not going there.

17. Don't go and dig up this tree the following spring to bench-graft it, however. Your second chance comes in the field, down on your knees, using the one and same whip-and-tongue splice attempted the year before. Only now the right diameter to make that splice might be considerably higher off the ground. It's okay to graft higher up, but you can also opt to do an offset splice with smaller-diameter scionwood. Make the full angle

cut on the scion that you would regularly, only now don't go through the center of the root shoot. Do this by making a sharper angle cut so as to expose a smaller union surface on the understock. Maximal cambium contact can be achieved without matching shoot diameters if you maintain this sense of proportion in the root cut.

18. In truth, scionwood can also be cut the very day of grafting if you are working in the early end of the grafting window. Fruit buds may be showing green tissue at this time, but the leaf buds on the one-year growth needed for grafting should not. Same-day graft unions can callus while cells above are growing . . . provided the weather stays cool enough to limit bud dehydration while the vascular connection gets reestablished. Still, most growers prefer to be sure about gathering dormant wood and thus collect scionwood a month or two before sap starts to flow.

19. Cut the shoot from the tree at a point a little bit bigger than this at the base and even leave the terminal bud intact as a desiccation buffer for the budwood that is of desirable size in between. Long shoots can be cut in half to store in the fridge, but each cut end will be subject to drying out. I never use the very end bud on the scion stick for this reason. More fastidious growers will dip scionwood in melted wax to seal all cut ends.

20. Water moves out of cells to prevent the rupturing of cell walls when budwood freezes. On the tree, water returns to these cells when things warm up. In cuttings, the water may be lost more readily since it has no means of replacement. Some people do successfully keep scionwood in the freezer, but the automatic defrost cycle tends to exacerbate the desiccation problem.

21. It's recommended that nighttime temperatures after grafting stay above 40°F (4°C) for a few days, as callus tissue exposed to 34°F (1°C) before it differentiates may die or be permanently stunted.

22. Even bigger trunks will generally be receptive to this treatment. More extreme topworking like this is structurally facilitated by "braiding" the resulting shoot response together.

23. Topworking in the dormant season (before budbreak) is done by means of a *cleft graft*, the details of which are fully explained in my earlier book, *The Apple Grower*.

24. Ideally, compost and the right kind of lime have already been incorporated into the whole of the orchard ground in the previous year as part of a cover crop plan. Truly poor soils that absolutely shout *Help me* can have compost (no more than a 5-gallon bucket's worth) sifted into the hole. Still, subsequent surface application remains preferable for most situations.

25. Previously I made the case for spreading a peastone mulch right at the base of the tree, at least half the diameter of the hole just dug. This in turn will bring the graft union "down" a couple of inches, which often proves of value for winter hardiness. Soil-building from the top down isn't directed toward this relatively small surface area at the trunk compared with what the tree root system is going to become.

26. This according to Elaine Ingham of the Soil Food Web, who checks on all sorts of microbe reality through her powerful light microscope. Biological products can come with all sorts of promises but won't be of much use unless great care is taken to assure microbe viability.

27. Plant Success, ROOTS, Kellogg's, Doctor Earth, Pennington Seed, E. B. Stone, Monrovia, Down to Earth, Garden-Ville, Fungi Perfecti, and Fox Farm are brands supplied by Mycorrhizal Applications.

28. Spore inoculum kept refrigerated will remain viable for several years, which is more than enough time to plant a small community orchard.

29. Decomposition of deciduous wood chips results in the production of both humic and fulvic acids once the biology in your orchard comes up to snuff. Early on, however, it can be worth purchasing fungal food in the form of mined humates to stir into the top inches of soil around young trees. Leonardite shale in New Mexico (formed from rain forest plant matter over millions of years) holds both humic and fulvic acids in a carbon matrix and is sold under the trade names Activate 80 and Menafree Humates.

30. Every aspect of this mycorrhizal plan involves living beings. I've learned in working with healing plants that good intentions are best initiated by honoring all the parties involved. So ask the wild apple tree for permission before taking that soil and give thanks for the life force of all concerned. Too many humans won't understand this, but it's worth sharing with those of you who read endnotes.

31. A scaffold branch started 30 inches from the ground stays put on the trunk at that height. As the branch enlarges in diameter, it will actually appear to get slightly closer to the soil line.

32. Here's another vision for a freestanding tree in a landscape setting: A heading height closer to 5 feet puts all fruit buds above deer browsing reach and makes it possible to use trunk flashing to successfully keep squirrels and raccoons out of the tree. This goal is reached by making

a follow-up heading cut in the leader at the start of the second year, on the order of 5–6 feet high. Branches that emerge too low in the first year can be pruned off either this second spring or the next.

33. Newspaper layers consisting of four to six sheets are needed to slow down rhizomatous grasses and must be spread over larger areas than you intend to open up if you want to kill off existing grass. Overlap is critical: The next bunch of sheets covers half of what you just set, then the next one covers half of that, resulting in an actual mat that is eight to twelve sheets thick. Wetting the newspaper down will help in windy weather. The covering mulch holds it in place and certainly looks more attractive. Most colored newsprint now uses vegetable dyes so it need not be a contamination concern. Do avoid using ad inserts, however, as most companies still print these with heavy metal inks, especially the glossy ones.

34. Had you only cover-cropped the year before! Replenishing the newspaper layer each spring may be necessary as well if quack grass proves this determined.

35. Blueberries are a slight exception in that these plants do not have root hairs. This means that the blueberry is unable to draw water from a substantial volume of soil—and thus relies upon the grower to provide water in the immediate vicinity during each and every dry spell.

36. Another term in vogue here is *assimilation*, which can be defined as the taking up of inorganic ions into biological tissue, be it plant, animal, or microbe.

37. Confused, are we? Organic chemistry involves carbon in the molecular matrix; inorganic chemistry revolves around carbon being out of the picture. Nutrients not attached to a carbon structure are thus inorganic and yet absolutely vital to organic agriculture. Doublespeak around these concepts is often used by chemical proponents who argue that their way is no different from our way . . . the difference lying entirely in the biological subtleties being explained here.

38. A tremendous leap of faith takes place when looking at lab determinations of soil values, beginning with which extraction method makes the most sense from the plant perspective. Lab technicians make several assumptions along the way. Choice of extraction solvent sets a somewhat dubious stage: Weaker acids are used to simulate what roots can assimilate, while stronger acids are intended to capture the total picture. The difference between the two can be as high as a factor of 30 for certain nutrients! This makes comparisons between results from one lab to another essentially meaningless. Accounting for biology is difficult and thus ignored by too

many labs. Providing "desired levels" for each nutrient on the report as the basis for recommendations rarely reckons that the needs of fruit trees are not quite the same as those of soybeans. The final rub, in my mind, is that pH and nutrient levels are constantly in flux throughout the growing season. Testing accounts for only one particular moment, and, in fact, a slight delay in analyzing a sample will show a shift in certain available nutrient levels as the biology in the soil sample invariably shifts in accordance with the changed reality. Those of you intrigued by the beguiling nature of soil testing can take this farther by checking out my report on the results from five different labs given the very same soil sample from my orchard in the research section of www.groworganicapples.com.

39. Try to take comparison tests at the same time of year. Late summer (prior to the fall root flush) is good with respect to knowing whether additional soil amendments will be needed that fall or very early next spring.

40. Iron levels will likely be higher if you're using a steel spade, such being the influence of an ordinary metal blade that can rust. A stainless-steel implement is necessary to get a true take on iron in your soil.

41. My friend Brian Caldwell in New York offered up this math: An acre furrow slice 6 inches deep is said to weigh about 2 million pounds, so 5 percent of that would mean the OM weighs 100,000 pounds. If it is roughly 50 percent carbon, and the C:N ratio is 15, then that 100,000 pounds of OM contains a little more than 3,000 pounds of total N. If 4 percent of the OM is mineralized in a year, about 120 pounds of N is made available through the biological activity of healthy soil.

42. Let's add some biological parameters to this given range for soil pH in orchards. An anaerobic and/or compacted soil is going to *act more acid* than its pH reading indicates, whereas a biologically activated soil will tend to *act more alkaline*. The first soil situation is simply not as healthy, and in such cases pushing pH up toward the 6.7–7.0 range during the soil-building phase makes sense. The second soil situation comes about when the soil ecosystem finds its fungal groove—a pH in the 6.0–6.3 range becomes totally acceptable when solubility of cations is enhanced and accessed by a healthy biology. I point these scenarios out to emphasize yet again that pH in and of itself tells but a part of the story.

43. French research suggests that a Ca:K ratio closer to 20:1 helps the fruit tree achieve optimum protein synthesis. This balance between calcium and potassium in turn seems to lessen the accumulation of a particular amino acid, asparagine, which is a preferred food of *Venturia*

inaequalis (apple scab) and a number of other pathogenic fungi. See A. Soenen, "Les traitements contre les maladies en culture fruitière," *Symposium semaine d'ètude agriculture et bygiène des plantes*, Gembloux, September 8–12, 1975.

44. Nor is the type of lime the only consideration on some sites. Irrigation water quality becomes especially relevant in dry areas. Groundwater drawn from a limestone aquifer will cause soil pH to rise to close to neutral (often inducing copper, zinc, and manganese deficiencies as a result) after a few irrigation seasons, without any lime being applied prior to planting. My friends Chris and Michelle McColl in southeast Australia initially faced a soil pH below 5 on non-irrigated pasture ground being converted to orchard but were well advised that irrigation alone in Kalangadoo would alter that situation rather quickly.

45. Typical soil test recommendations are made in tons per acre of lime. A 2-ton rate translates to 100 pounds per 1,000 square feet. Imagine a grid across your orchard ground measuring 10 feet by 100 feet. That area would receive 100 pounds (two 50-pound bags) of either finely ground limestone or slightly more expensive pelleted lime to meet this recommendation. This has a significant impact on topsoil ecology. The effect of the lime will drift slowly down into the soil, moving about 4 to 6 inches deep in three years' time. This first charge of lime (where necessary), when made prior to planting, can be incorporated throughout that full depth with tillage or harrowing. Follow this up by planting the appropriate first cover crop (recommended in the first chapter) on your way to finishing up with a red clover cycle prior to planting the trees.

46. Call this a sense and sensibility endnote. The amount of lime applied to a compost pile must be proportioned to the volume of compost incorporating that lime. The old adage that *if a little is good, a lot is better* does not apply here! Too much lime will literally stop the biology from working. The maintenance rate for compost established earlier for a holistic orchard was based on a 4-cubic-yard pile per acre application. Adding 50 pounds of lime to that size pile of relatively finished compost two months prior to spreading will be the biological equivalent of a 200-pound surface application. A bit of microorganism alchemy will enhance uptake of the calcium all the more: Stir a pound of humates into the lime first, equally distribute this across the compost pile, spray the entire surface with a backpack tank of diluted molasses spray, then fork the lime thoroughly into the pile.

47. Different labs use different test procedures to measure nutrient levels. This makes comparison talk difficult at best! The extract solution used on the Mehlich-3 test results in values give in ppm (parts per million) for macronutrients. The extract solution used on the Morgan tests was designed to obtain the same amount of nutrients from the soil that a plant can get. It's those results given as pounds per acre that reflect available nutrient levels. You can convert numbers from one method to the other with this simple Cornell equivalent: (Ca in ppm × 0.75) × 2 = Ca in lbs./acre. The 2,000-pounds-per-acre figure for calcium given here applies to a lower-CEC-value soil—this goal shifts to more like 3,000 pounds per acre and up for a higher-CEC-value soil.

48. Too much soluble nitrogen or potash will cause problems with calcium and other mineral uptake. Commercial orchardists going for high yields and ultimate fruit size by overfertilizing see a lot of this.

49. We have known about the relationship between nitrates and disease susceptibility for a long time: Several fungal diseases, such as rust and powdery mildew, are enhanced by high levels of nitrogen, particularly in the form of nitrate. Many bacterial diseases are promoted by high nitrogen levels as well. See D. M. Huber and R. D. Watson, "Nitrogen Form and Plant Disease," *Annual Review of Phytopathology*, 1974, 12:139–165.

50. Some of these organic blends will contain a natural nitrate of soda in addition to various protein meals to supply nitrogen. Organic certification agencies allow up to 20 percent of a plant's nitrogen needs to be supplied by this mineral salt, specifically in colder soils where microbial activity in early spring is suppressed. I accept this seeming contradiction in the early years of a tree knowing how important it is to grow a tree prior to growing actual fruit that will indeed be subject to disease pressures. Many suppliers offer a twin formulation made without any Chilean nitrate whatsoever, because growers in arid and semi-arid zones should avoid using this nitrogen source due to its high sodium content. Excess nitrogen in a soluble form will dissolve humic materials, so once the fungal system comes into its own, stop using Chilean nitrate entirely.

51. That nitrogen boost is often called for in the soil-building phase. However, once the biology is up and running, too much applied nitrogen, even from an organic source, can shift dynamics back toward bacterial dominance, and that in turn leads to increased disease problems. The soil-maintenance phase will always be an entirely different ball game.

52. Joe Scrimger of Bio-Systems in Michigan has been exceedingly patient in teaching me about the challenges

of bringing phosphorus levels up in orchard soils. Organic matter has to be present in quantity along with a good population of beneficial soil fungi in the presence of a balanced bacteria base (brought about by enough, but not too much, nitrogen) to get the phosphate system working. The microbes require both phosphate and sulfur to put with soluble nitrogen to form more stable nitrogen and humus. Fruits like cherries or berries that bear earlier in the summer require especially high soil phosphate levels because the release of organically acceptable phosphorus slows considerably in cool spring soils.

53. Leave it to the USDA to track regional soil attributes. Phosphorus tends to be especially needed in the northern Great Plains and middle South, while "just a tad" makes things right in the Northeast. Potassium, on the other hand, is most often needed in the Southeast and less often in the central Great Plains. Much of western North America generally has high-K soils due to the prevailing climate and dominance of soils that have developed from high-K parent materials.

54. The ratio of P:K depends entirely on the soil extraction methods that are used. This all gets simplified considerably when soil test results show total phosphorus in lbs./acre of P_2O_5 (as revealed by the Bray P1 test) and total potassium levels in lbs./acre of potash (as revealed by the modified Morgan extract). Converting results given in ppm makes matters slightly more dubious, as results given for elemental P and K have to be translated into phosphate (P_2O_5) and potash (KO_2) to get the same sense of nutrient levels in the soil. The 200 lbs./acre starting goal for each of these two nutrients then becomes a minimum of 43 ppm for P and 83 ppm for K on a CEC-centered test.

55. Potassium plays a significant role in the cation-balancing act. Base saturation of K is going to be influenced by haphazard mulching and compost applications while you work initially with getting calcium and magnesium right. Being moderate about supplemental K in those early years makes sense from the perspective of often needing higher P levels in the long run. The result of such patience here is that you are able to fine-tune the difficult P:K ratio just as the trees come into fruiting without screwing up other equally important fundamentals.

56. Ultimate timing for wood ash application occurs between the two phases of shoot growth in spring and then again in early summer. Soluble potassium can be utilized by the first flush of feeder roots specifically gathering nutrients for the current year's crop. Wood ash sprinkled lightly under bearing trees in the immediate weeks after petal fall will help both color and size of fruit.

57. Noted soil scientist Carey Reams made a number of observations that have stretched mainstream understanding. One concerns the uptake of K-Mag fertilizer broadcast in fruit orchards between July 15 and September 15, the timing correlated to the warmer part of the growing season. The molecular structure of langbeinite does not necessarily disassociate when taken up by the feeder root during that time period and will get stored in the tree bark. This is said to cause copper to function better, resulting in a less constricting bark structure and better sap flow. Jon Frank of International Ag Labs in Minnesota told me of a few success stories in freeing bark-bound trees based on this application timing, done on eight-year intervals.

58. Commercial growers have been trained to think of leaf tissue analysis as a more complete indicator (than a soil test) of available nutrient status. This laboratory view of the mineral elements found in a leaf specimen shows what's being achieved by the biology and feeder roots with exchangeable nutrients with respect to vascular flow at a given point in the growing season. Neither the soil test nor leaf analysis stands alone; both are indicators—at best—of a constantly shifting reality.

59. Calculating degree-days involves averaging the minimum and maximum temperature for each day and then subtracting a specified threshold temperature as determined by researchers for a particular orchard event. A primer on degree-day tracking and its many uses can be found in *The Apple Grower*.

60. Bud progression begins at silver tip on apple, using a base temperature of 40°F (4°C). No growth takes place at temperatures any colder than this threshold.

61. Take into account the design of your home orchard in this statement. An island planting maintained with a fungal duff mulching system doesn't require cover cropping. Other plant species permanently in that fruit guild compete for water and nutrients. Ground was cultivated generations ago in midsummer to make things less lush for that terminal bud. Following a pea or garlic crop (grown alongside the tree row) with an oat cover crop at this time is another way to temporarily make things less lush for today's terminal bud.

62. Using a diverse microbe poultice definitely works in the case of American chestnut. A fungal blight (imported on Japanese chestnut nursery stock in the late 1800s) came near to destroying this noble tree, which once dominated the eastern forest. Tree after tree would die back to the soil line, sprouting back from the roots only to be zapped again. Let's ask ourselves what happened at the soil line: The fungal infection killing the cambium aboveground

basically met up with the diverse arsenal of the soil food web: Organisms in the humus readily defeated this foreign pathogen. Decades passed before anyone realized the portent of the obvious. Finally it became clear that soil taken from the base of the chestnut tree could be applied as a biological mudpack to developing blight lesions to stop the disease entirely. This testament to microbe truth has weighed powerfully in my own understanding of seemingly invisible miracles.

63. Some fruit growers screen even wetter slurry and run it through a power sprayer, coating smaller branches as well.

64. Exterior latex paint will likely damage cambium, whereas cheap interior latex has not been formulated with the same chemical bonding agents. Oil-based paints should never be used, as these are guaranteed toxic to bark tissues. Certified organic growers do not have the house paint option under current standards and so must rely on some combination of kaolin clay, plaster of paris, BioShield milk paint, and 100 percent pure linseed oil to adhere for winter trunk protection.

65. This timing lessens the chance of injury from the paint; plus the paint will not have time to weather as much as from an earlier application.

66. Fall application of biodynamic tree paste works just as well for improving bark health, plus it helps with lightening trunk hues going into winter. I would renew the tree paste on all obvious injuries in early spring just to ensure diverse microbe colonization on trouble spots.

67. The resin of the calendula flower is anti-fungal. Herbal salves that promote this quality are available in health food stores. I have used calendula salve beneath tree paste applications in late fall and again in early spring and have saved an integral branch from being lost to perennial canker. Don't let too many years go by before treating. Similarly, freshly chopped garlic is anti-microbial by all accounts. Smearing minced garlic deep into the sides of a perennial canker is localized medicine at its finest.

68. An allopathic spray such as copper calls for discernment. Applying copper year after year is not appropriate for building a healthy ecosystem. Community orchardists will use this in reclaiming a disease-prone orchard or in following up a bad fire blight outbreak from the year before. As a home orchardist, you have much to learn before heeding conventional organic advice to use copper on a regular basis.

69. Pear growers are familiar with sooty molds because they commonly grow on honeydew from pear psylla (an insect pest) and can blacken fruit and leaves on psylla-infested trees.

70. Dave Rosenberger, a plant pathologist at Cornell, sheds more light here: "One can determine the difference between a black rot canker and a sooty mold infestation by observing the edge of the pruning cut for callus formation. If a distinctive callus is evident around last year's pruning cuts, then the wound is healing normally and the tree is unlikely to develop a black rot canker. Where black rot is present, dead bark will usually extend an inch or more above or below the cut. The dead bark may appear sunken and/or scaly. Where extensive discoloration is present below a pruning cut, one can check for green tissue beneath the discoloration by making a small cut with a pocket knife. If the cut reveals green tissue beneath the discoloration, then the discoloration is most likely caused by sooty molds and no corrective action is required."

71. Work being done by David Shapiro at the Southeast Tree Fruit Research Station in Georgia with *Steinernema carpocapsae* nematodes for peach borers first turned me on to this idea. The researchers were using baby diapers to create a moist environment on branch infestations. Knowing that nematodes are soil critters to begin with (and not wanting to invest in orchard Pampers!) led me to ask about using a topsoil mudpack instead. Cleaning up an overwhelming infestation of roundheaded apple tree borers at the soil line should work as well as it did for peach tree borers farther up. Wrapping limb damage with wet burlap (around the mudpack) would further prolong the requisite moist environment for the nematodes on their journey inward.

72. The St. Edmund's Russet apple trees garner exclusive sapsucker attention in Lost Nation for some reason. This particular variety must have some mighty tasty sap, given the array of fruitwood this shy woodpecker has to choose from in my orchard.

73. Trees lacking in replacement potential—those numerous small laterals naturally arising along a vigorous leader—call for a slight modification to this diameter-based pruning rule. Removing such a larger lateral in its entirety can mean the end of any growth response from that bud site. Leaving a short stub with one bud on its underside, however, ensures that a new lateral replacement will develop at that location.

74. A branch cut at any time stimulates cell activity at the wound. Callus tissues don't have the same degree of hardiness that first week; that's why subzero temperatures too soon after pruning will expose fresh cuts to cold injury.

75. *Pinching a shoot tip* implies the removal of the tender

growth portion of a shoot before it proceeds to lignify and harden off. This knocks back sucker growth while possibly encouraging fruit buds to form at the woodier base of the shoot.

76. Net photosynthesis remains the same as sunlight penetration to interior leaves makes up the difference. Only now fruit sizing takes precedence precisely because additional shoot growth is not induced by earlier pruning.

77. Air access always has impact on fungal presence. Summer diseases require 250 hours of active wetness before becoming visible . . . hence the benefit of drying breezes when the tree is opened up through late-summer pruning.

78. My friend Scott Bolotin in Vermont grows an apple tree on seedling rootstock up the east side of his barn in espalier fashion. Art does not need to be limited by scale! His trellis is rather ingenious: Two screws with a wire harness are used to hold shoots to whatever position desired on the wall. The limb locks into place by virtue of hardened-off growth rings, allowing Scott to move the screw support farther out before any limb girdling might occur.

79. This pruning cut when the shoot is half woody leaves a stub about ½ inch long. Fruit bud formation should result, noting that some vigorous varieties will grow a new shoot (despite this note!) in its place on the earliest cuts made. Orchardists around the world have learned to adapt this basic description in accounting for climatic nuance. If you're deeply intrigued about creating an extremely productive espalier, google the *Lorette System of Pruning* and then let the fun begin!

80. A sun-favoring wall works in two respects in northern zones. The reflected light serves to increase sugar levels in apples and pears. And the increased warmth and buffering from strong winds works wonders for more tender varieties. Folks wanting to try Asian pears in Zone 4, take heed.

81. Cutting back vertical shoots in summer to contain growth on the trellis results in the removal of flower buds out on the ends of those shoots. And that means no crop on tip-bearing varieties. Avoid apple cultivars like Grimes Golden, Golden Russet, and Granny Smith for this reason. Spur types like Empire and Zestar are better suited for espalier.

82. Don't worry about the pinprick injury caused by a toothpick or even the protruding nail used in longer hardwood spreaders. That mere blip in this year's growth ring will be completely covered over by next year's growth.

83. You need to allot stretching room whenever tying down a branch. A simple loop is easily achieved by first making

a tight half hitch in the cordage right at the spot you envision your knot. This bump prevents your loop knot from then sliding tight against the branch and possibly girdling future growth.

84. The fruiting wood of a productive tree is continuously pulled downward by annual cropping. A limb never regains its full height once bent by the weight of fruit, even after it's picked.

85. Peaches and nectarines can be trained as central-leader-type trees as well. Commercial growers in California claim greater productivity results when stone fruit trees are trained to a single leader. This necessitates ladder work, of course.

86. Research indicates it takes six or so honeybee visits to an apple blossom to achieve full pollination of all ten seeds. This is because the honeybee sometimes inserts its proboscis at the base of the flower for nectar, leaving the anthers and stigma untouched. A bumblebee, on the other hand, clambers over the anthers and stigma when foraging and cannot help but transfer pollen from flower to flower.

87. This notion of continuing bloom deserves our full awareness, because the human species is dependent on pollinating species for much of our food. The work of the Xerces Society to implement pollinator conservation projects is especially to be commended. You will learn much by going to their website via the resource section of this book.

88. Growers east of the Rocky Mountains are advised to work with the eastern subspecies, *Osmia lignaria lignaria*. The potential ecological consequences of shipping the western subspecies, *O. l. propinqua*, are unknown. More practically, nonlocal bees often do not develop in sync with local conditions and often fail to thrive in their new environment.

89. One good book to get started with honeybees is *Natural Beekeeping* by Ross Conrad. His insights on organic apiculture are critical for hive health and thus your enjoyment of this worthy hobby.

90. These temperatures are for apple buds and blossoms. Other tree fruits—pears, cherries, peaches, and plums—can withstand even greater cold. Cherry bloom, for instance, experiences 90 percent kill only at 21°F (−6°C).

91. Bud tissue freezes a degree or two below the freezing point of water because of the sugars and other organic compounds in the buds. A coating of ice would hold the bud temp at 32°F (0°C) for some time when the air temp goes slightly below freezing.

92. Dried seaweed extracts do not retain this frost-limiting

attribute, as the polysaccharides are lost in the dehydration process.

93. On average, twenty-five to forty leaves produce the green nutrition required to support a growing fruit. The range here corresponds to shoot leaves being a tad more efficient in the photosynthesis business than spur leaves.

94. The endosperms in developing seeds produce the plant hormone gibberellic acid, which in turn promotes enlargement of the fruitlets. Excess production of gibberellic acid, however, inhibits the development of next year's flower buds.

95. Don't you love exceptions? Certain varieties tend to produce very large fruits, especially in a year that has fewer blooms on the tree due to alternate-bearing tendencies. Thinning to a lesser-sized fruitlet in such varieties results in producing a reasonable-sized apple, not some giant grapefruit-like orb. Larger fruits in varieties like Honeycrisp and Braeburn tend to have more post-harvest issues such as bitter pit and internal browning . . . and can be just too much for the average mouth!

96. Aha . . . so you're the smart one asking if your thinned fruit crop will subsequently drop in the so-called June drop. The answer is no, as the hormonal adjustments that the tree seeks have already been granted through your thinning work. The strong fruitlets you select to grow to harvest are here to stay.

97. A fair number of such fruitlets dumped onto a compost pile roll down the edges, from where the pest larvae can creep out and seek refuge in the surrounding ground. All this changes, of course, if you're actively making garden compost, which requires regular turning to generate weed-seed-killing heat.

98. Temper this thinning advice with reason, please. Fruit will be sporadically clustered on some varieties, particularly tip bearers, making proper spacing more a question of the ratio of leaves to fruit rather than a given number of inches along the branch.

4. ORCHARD DYNAMICS

1. The oft-used home fruit spray (basically a combination of a broad-acting insecticide, a single-mode fungicide, and perhaps a miticide) available at garden centers is more an abomination than it is legitimate IPM practice. This chemical mix essentially promotes ignorance as a means of growing fruit through the application of toxins every seven to ten days, regardless of what's actually going on in the orchard. You should be engaged as a chemical home orchardist with respect to what you spray and when targeted applications are truly needed. To do otherwise is to do the greatest harm of all.

2. Let's call this an author's moment. I've been teaching about *organic health management* for several years now, making this very case for motivational semantics in presentations across the country. Yet I never spelled out the acronym and saw that it could indeed be pronounced. I say this knowing I will bring smiles to the faces of many respected IPM friends. We have here in OHM the *om* sound, the call for harmony and peace in meditation practice. Somehow that really, really fits with what we are doing in growing fruit holistically for our families and communities.

3. I am paraphrasing George Bird of Michigan State University here. This wise professor is one of the principal authors of *Fruit Crop Ecology and Management*, an Extension bulletin that guides commercial orchard practices in a biologically sustainable direction. George is a nematode man, one of my frontier teachers, and a respected voice in the eco-agriculture movement.

4. Dandelion pollen is gathered by honeybees to maintain hive health. This underappreciated herb closes down by midafternoon, and it's then that the full attention of all worker bees turns toward fruit blossoms. Varied nutrition is just as important to bees as it is to us—bloom consensus does not require human interference, regardless of what your local Extension adviser says.

5. The fruit guild designs shared earlier are the right alternative to a grassy understory if a "certain look" is your thing. Far more woodsy mulch is required for an island-style planting, but you still achieve species diversity with a smattering of taprooted plants and woodsy herbs within the fungal duff zone.

6. There's always more to every story. Grass by its nature is a bacterial plant. It favors nitrate fertilization, which is a function of nitrifying bacteria. An all-grass root zone tends to be alkaline as a result of greater bacterial biomass. This in turn inhibits soil fungi, which would otherwise keep available the form of nitrogen (ammonium) preferred by woodsy plants. Excess nitrates taken up by tree feeder roots leads to greater disease susceptibility . . . which directly counters one of the intended advantages of fungal duff management.

7. Raking away infected leaves suggests itself, but you rarely remove 100 percent of the leaves. It's far better to build organic matter by allowing decomposers in the fungal duff to recycle nutrients . . . and nearby grasses to block any leaf remnants that escaped notice.

8. Green growth implies being flush with nitrogen. Mowing lush grass early in the season favors bacterial dominance in the soil food web. Waiting until seed begins to set brings on increasingly higher levels of carbon. Think about a grain crop to understand this fully. The wheat plant at first is green and supple but then takes on a golden hue as the grain head ripens. You are literally seeing the shift from nitrogen to more carbon in this color change. The C:N ratio as seed formation initiates is on the order of 30:1 . . . and that is absolutely a fungal-favoring dynamic.

9. Soluble potassium levels often build to excess in organic systems through the copious use of mulches, compost, and lab recommendations early on to boost potash. Here's a beautiful nugget: Grasses and wildflowers entering the seed stage take up K (as well as more carbon) in forming a firmer stalk. The potassium in turn goes back into slow-release form and temporarily stays there, provided the mowing is not chopped to bits. The exact opposite happens in regularly mowed settings where both soluble nitrogen and soluble potassium become issues of excess, leading to greater disease susceptibility. Growers contribute to the ebb and flow of cation balance both by their choice of mowing cut and the frequency with which it is done. The upshot here is that the scythe becomes the right tool (in a very broad sense) to keep potassium levels more in tune with Ca and Mg in the biological orchard.

10. Absorption at air temperatures above 80°F (27°C) is very poor because the leaf stomata (pores) are closed. The most effective foliar feeding is done in the early morning, when temperatures are right and wind is minimal. Absorption is further enhanced when weather conditions are humid and moist. The presence of heavy dew on the leaves will facilitate nutrient uptake.

11. Mixing pure neem oil with full-rate Surround (kaolin clay) will result in clogging your sprayer. That's a practical limitation. Avoid tank-mixing biological toxins like Bt and spinosad with sulfur and lime sulfur, because product degradation occurs with more caustic materials. It goes without saying that effective microbes should never be mixed with copper or the other mineral fungicides.

12. Getting neem oil on before the initial kaolin and/or renewing kaolin coverage has relevance, in that you don't want to stick the clay beneath an oily application. Remember, it's the loose clay particles coming off onto the insect that create the barrier strategy effective against curculio. On the other hand, growers using Surround for sunburn issues may find a neem overcoat a good plan to achieve longer-term rainproofing.

13. An orchard of full-sized standard trees may require as much as 200–400 gallons per acre to spray to the point of runoff. A young orchard just beginning to bear may require only 50 gallons of spray per acre. Each orchardist takes manufacturer rates and adjusts accordingly.

14. The amount of water required to spray to the point of runoff typically goes up in the growing season as the leaf canopy fills out. That 100 gallons required for an acre of my trees is more like 125–135 gallons in the summer months if I cover every tree. Truth is, those trees with a light crop often get sprayed lighter. Summer is when I'm typically applying nutrition sprays—adjusting rates to account for this is less pertinent other than being sure to use pure neem oil at no more than a 0.5 percent concentration to prevent oil damage to the leaves.

15. One efficiency trick for those of you with an ambitious home orchard is to premix 4-gallon batches in 5-gallon buckets, then space these out appropriately in the orchard. That way you can spray as you go rather than having to return to the house to mix each next batch. Neem oil mixes will be made with warm water, so overcooling shouldn't be a problem in the buckets farther down the row.

16. The Organic Materials Review Institute (OMRI) looks at product information to determine that no synthetic ingredients are included. Growers are not necessarily privy to the various adjuncts, emulsifiers, spreaders, stickers, and so forth that are formulated with the active ingredients of a spray product.

17. Given current trends in historical literature, it's a wonder we don't call fly larvae "zombies" instead. Hmmm . . . Perhaps my next book will be *The Holistic Orchard and Zombies* if this one does especially well!

18. Regional pest reality does balance out in the end. This bit from a listserve exchange hits the nail on the head: "There is no plum curculio west of the Mississippi—that's why God gave you gophers!"

19. Check out "Borer Insights" on the biological curriculum page at www.groworganicapples.com for a complete immersion into the depths of a certain Captain Ahab's madness in seeking out badass borers.

20. Mid-Atlantic growers facing growing pressure from the brown marmorated stink bug won't concur with this statement. This invasive pest from Asia first appeared in Lehigh County, Pennsylvania, in the late 1990s. Broadspectrum pesticides are not a particularly good option for growers trying to protect beneficial species that keep other pests in check. Cutting-edge organic approaches for curtailing a localized implosion of stink bug can be found under nectarine solutions to pest challenges in chapter 6.

- THE HOLISTIC ORCHARD -

21. Ants herd aphids for honeydew (much the way we keep dairy cows for milk) by moving the aphids to untouched shoots within the tree. Ants use the trunk of the tree to access these promising pastures . . . and that's where the ants are vulnerable. Tangle-Trap is the sticky substance used on insect traps. It should never be applied directly to the tree bark, as it will suffocate cambium tissues. Plastic wrap or wide masking tape can provide a temporary surface on which to apply the Tangle-Trap. And this in turn prevents ant access to the protected tree and thus the further spread of aphids to every shoot.

22. Trichogramma wasps can be purchased from beneficial supply houses and timed for release into commercial orchards just as codling moth egg laying initiates. Research indicates as much as a 60 percent decrease in pest numbers as a result. The braconid wasp *Ascogaster quadidentata* does similar work.

23. Charles Darwin once wrote about ichneumonid wasps: "I own that I cannot see as plainly as others do, and as I should wish to do, evidence of design and beneficence on all sides of us. There seems to me too much misery in the world. I cannot persuade myself that a beneficent and omnipotent God would have designedly created the *Ichneumonidae* with the express intention of their feeding within the living bodies of caterpillars." Let's keep in mind that the father of evolutionary thought was not a fruit grower!

24. Far more could be said here regarding strategies for protecting substantial blocks of trees. One point worth making for those of you with more than a couple of trees: Apple maggot flies will be drawn to early-ripening varieties in July, then the midseason varieties in August, while winter keeping varieties will likely be left untouched (unless it's been a dry summer and thus fly emergence is delayed). The point here is to protect the early varieties, then move or add traps accordingly to midseason varieties by mid-July . . . and thus not have to do this for every tree.

25. Benzaldehyde is one of the volatile compounds being utilized by researchers as a lure to draw curculio to traps. Right, you say. Like you already have that in one of your kitchen drawers. Well, maybe you do. Artificial almond extract consists mostly of benzaldehyde. Never let a big chemical word keep you from a homegrown solution to a vexing pest.

26. Going back through old farming literature reveals fascinating detail as to what our great-grandparents once did (prior to their own fascination with toxic sprays) to deal with the very same pests we deal with today. Hay rope twists came to my attention one evening while reading through Cornell University's *Annual Report of the Agricultural Experiment Station* dating from the 1890s. Extensive counts were made of damaged fruitlets and captured pupae, resulting in a reported effectiveness rate as high as 60 percent using this method. Beneficial insects undoubtedly got the rest, as growers at that time thought the monumental expense of four cents a tree (to have orchard workers inspect hay rope twists every ten days and then remove and destroy them after harvest) was money well spent.

27. There's no reason to spray Surround on berry crops! Berries could never be thoroughly washed of this white clay, but even more pertinent is the fact that berry pests are not subject to the mode of action described here.

28. The organo-sulfur compounds in garlic can readily be absorbed by our skin—rub a raw garlic clove on the underside of your foot and it won't be long before you smell garlic emanating from your skin pores elsewhere. Similarly, use of synthesized dimethyl sulfoxide (DMSO) in medicine dates from around 1963, when a University of Oregon Medical School team discovered it could penetrate the skin and other membranes without damaging them and could carry other compounds into a biological system. Unpasteurized garlic extracts contain compounds similar to DMSO. The best use of garlic in the holistic orchard is as a synergist carrier of spray nutrients into the leaf cuticle.

29. A 1 percent concentration of neem oil applied to the trunk zone involves wetting the trunk below the lowest scaffold branches completely, and allowing excess spray to puddle up at the base of the tree to completely saturate the ground right at the base. I often make these trunk sprays with a light rate of kaolin clay included in the tank mix. The slipperiness of the clay adds to the confusion factor, while its whiteness makes any egg-laying activity that much more apparent.

30. Manufacturers actually recommend a minimum of 4 acres be protected with mating disruption. Smaller blocks are subject to greater wind dissipation of the pheromone. On the other hand, provided the orchard isn't right out in the open at the top of a hill, positive results have been obtained in plantings of a hundred trees or so in blocky formation. Small orchards that are more spread out can be protected by extending pheromone protection into hedgerows. The cost gets rather prohibitive, however, where the results will be iffier at the end of the day.

31. Manufacturer recommendations speak to the need to maintain clay coverage for eight to twelve weeks to wait out curculio. The trap tree strategy reduces the need for coverage to two to three weeks, saving you money, spray

time, and the extended effects that come with continuous *anything* on beneficial insects.

32. Nylon tulle works to protect cherries from curculio as well and might best be left in place (despite restricting shoot growth) where bird damage to ripening fruit is excessive. Leaning a support pole or two through the branches to hold the fabric slightly off the leaf canopy helps when wrapping an entire tree.

33. Glad you asked. There's a reason such bags are not used right from the start. The risk of curculio feeding through the organza fabric where it touches a sizing plum or peach often proves high. That's the reason for the one–two step with nylon tulle used as a branch wrap. On the other hand, if you deal with Oriental fruit moth by other means or have very little problem with that pest to begin with, there's no need to do any subsequent bagging. The rules here are entirely flexible and based on the pest reality at your site.

34. All these fruit pests pupate somewhat shallowly. Typically, *Steinernema carpocapsae* nematodes are chosen, because this species prefers to ambush its potential host from the surface on down to about 3 inches deep. Current trials being done at the Southeastern Fruit and Tree Nut Research Station in Byron, Georgia, indicate that *Steinernema riobrave* nematodes in particular suppress plum curculio larvae by 78 to 100 percent.

35. Using nematodes to clean up a bad maggot fly scene should be considered radical surgery employed to restore functional balance. What you really need to be focusing more on every year thereafter is picking up early drops every few days and removing that fruit from the orchard environs. Feeding windfalls to livestock is the best disposal solution. This way fly larvae are destroyed rather than left to lie on the orchard floor before leaving the fallen fruit (that takes three to nine days) to wriggle into the soil.

36. Lightweight oils can be used for thinning subsequent bloom on heavy-setting varieties as well. The basic premise remains smothering, only now it's the fragile parts of the flower. Community orchardists are more likely to try this . . . but only if it's certain the first round of bloom got pollinated!

37. This microbial insecticide is made by growing the *Bacillus thuringiensis* bacteria in a vat until it exhausts its food supply. At this point, the microbes are forced by starvation to produce dormant endospores. These contain the crystal protein toxin that proves so effective in the alkaline gut of caterpillars.

38. GF-120 is sold in gallon-sized quantities (and pricey at that) at the time of writing. That's a bit much for a home orchardist, even if it does stay viable for two growing seasons. My hope is that smaller quantities will soon be made available, as this could be a relatively simple way to keep maggot flies in check in a backyard orchard.

39. Understanding neem's mode of action also points out why a pest such as curculio isn't all that bothered by it. The adult curculio is the pest (not so much its larvae, which show up only after the damage is done) and thus lies beyond the growth-regulating effects of neem. The curculio's feeding sting made into individual fruitlets somewhat avoids the ingestion of a surface coating of neem compounds as well. These are the kind of thought connections that guide us into taking different actions for different pests.

40. The neem-derived insecticides on the commercial marketplace (like Neemix and Aza-Direct) are basically alcohol extractions of the azadirachtins. Emulsifiers, adjuvants, activators, and stabilizers are added to make the final product easier to apply and store. The oil fraction left behind by this process demonstrates a limited effect against disease, from whence come the so-called hydrophobic neem fungicides. Heat processing absolutely destroys the nutritive value of the fatty acids. The synergistic actions of the nimbin, nimbidin, ninbidol, gedunin, quercitin, and salannin compounds are left behind. Keep in mind that you get it all with whole-plant medicine . . . and that's why you need to use pure, raw, unadulterated, unrefined, 100 percent neem oil!

41. Take this one step farther and you might notice I'm not even mentioning using the other broad-spectrum botanical often touted in earlier organic orcharding books. Rotenone has been implicated in causing Parkinson's disease in humans besides killing almost everything in sight in the ecosystem the day it's applied.

42. The scab organism can overwinter as well in dormant buds in warmer zones, complicating matters in the early part of the season when spring dampness can spread conidia directly from the bud onto emerging tissue. This may make imperative an additional holistic application just prior to apple budbreak in such orchards. The fall holistic application (primarily to beef up decomposition forces on the ground), if aimed throughout the tree, would also be of help by colonizing those buds with conidia-eating bacteria from the get-go.

43. Sufficient pruning allows drying breezes to penetrate into the tree canopy, where they facilitate an end to the continuing leaf wetness required by the spore to successfully infect the leaf. The amount of time required for an infection to take place decreases with warmer temperatures. Please see *The Apple Grower* for a much more

thorough examination of wetting variables and the pace of spore maturity.

44. An overview of plant-based immune stimulants was provided in *The Apple Grower*. What's interesting is the number of products just coming onto the market that reflect the promise to be found in this holistic approach to disease management. An extract of giant knotweed (*Polygonum sachalinense*), sold under the brand name Regalia, delivers on its promise to inhibit bacterial spot, powdery mildew, and assorted blights. This all gets cooler when you know the medicinal plants and make such preparations for yourself.

45. Disease-causing organisms benefit in two respects when the arboreal food web crashes due to limited food supplies. Competitive colonization will be lacking, leaving a short-changed pantry to the more aggressive pathogen.

46. Contrary to what you might hear via the rumor treadmill, effective microbe cultures do not contain any genetically modified microorganisms. Any such efforts to undermine biological methods can be traced to those who profit from chemical agriculture.

47. The nutrient outreach of colonized roots increases as a result of increased fungal mass. The recommended spray rate for ground application is 5 gallons of activated EM® per acre, applied monthly through the growing season, according to Eric Lancaster of TeraGanix.

48. It's often said that calcium is not mobile in the plant. This is only partially true. Calcium is indeed ushered to the growing point of the leaves and the fruit itself when bonded with phosphate. This happens more readily where plants grow in soils in which the recommended ratio between potassium (which has its own relationship to calcium) and phosphorus has been addressed. Soil calcium that enters the plant in phosphate of calcium form does get integrated into the cellular structure. A similar pathway is assisted by lactic acid bacteria tending to foliar dynamics on the leaf surface.

49. Effective microbes are promoted as offering a consistent quality of beneficial microorganisms. All such claims can ultimately be proven only under the lens of a high-powered microscope. Some manufacturers sell products that appear to lack those highly touted photosynthetic bacteria when tested by Soil Food Web Inc. Microbe promise is a fragile affair, especially when product ages and species' populations invariably decline in number if not go outright dormant. Obtaining relatively fresh mother culture from reputable suppliers provides reasonable assurance that your batches of effective microbes are up to snuff.

50. An activated culture should be used within thirty days of brewing, because further microbe shift can occur when the photosynthetic bacteria eventually go dormant.

51. Let chlorinated water sit overnight in an open container to allow the volatile gases to dissipate.

52. Microbes can already be found on all flower parts, and mere spraying is not going to wash pollen off the stamens. Citrus growers using effective microbes do indeed spray when blossoms are open wide and report no problems. Any grower experiencing browned blossoms seemingly as a result of a microbe spray needs to consider all factors. The fatty components of pure neem oil and the liquid fish can smother virgin blossoms . . . whereas flowers already pollinated are beyond the clogging effects of oil. Making the third holistic spray a few days prior to petal fall could serve to reduce fruit set if you feel the pollination of the first flowers to open in each blossom cluster has been good. But it won't necessarily be the introduced microbes giving you this edge!

53. Control of brown rot on peaches has been achieved using the recommended spray rate for foliar application of 1 gallon of activated EM® per acre weekly, according to Eric Lancaster of TeraGanix.

54. Growers are just beginning to grasp the significance of competitive organisms in controlling some of the more difficult tree fruit diseases that establish in the dormant season on bud and bark surfaces. I want to add one more note in this regard concerning the fatty acids of pure neem oil and unpasteurized liquid fish in these post-harvest holistic applications. *Fatty acid compositions have been shown to disrupt existing microflora, making it more likely that desirable microbes will successfully colonize the surface under contention if applied at the same time or soon after the fatty acid composition.* I took that statement from a patent application looking to secure product registration for biocontrol organisms. The nuance here is to up the pure neem oil concentration to as much as 2 percent, along with liquid fish at the full 4-gallon-an-acre rate. Make the "fatty spray" on the dormant branch structure separate from the microbes—these can also be potentially disrupted at higher rates—then follow in a day or two with the microbe/molasses application. Fatty acid compositions do not persist on the plant at effective concentrations very long. The upshot here is we can treat trees with observed infection susceptibility with a massive dose of a biology-based knockdown before bringing in the competitive microbe reinforcement to eat the leftovers. Any fruit grower ready to grasp these principles gets my kudos for making a very impressive leap on the ol' learning curve.

55. Product literature for foliar sprays—be it calcium by way of calcium chloride, magnesium by way of Epsom salts, boron by way of Solubor, or micronutrients like iron and zinc by way of chelated mineral formulations—suppose direct absorption by the leaf stomata. That's only part of the story, however. The efficient uptake of foliar nutrient applications can depend as much on the arboreal biology being an intermediary consumer.

56. I can't emphasize enough that the benefits of whole plant medicine come only when using cold-pressed 100 percent neem oil rather than any of the patented neem extract products! Neem products that claim insect activity are isolated azadirachtin extracts; neem products that claim anti-fungal activity are basically the leftover oily portion. The immune stimulants and fatty acid chemistry have been left behind in both product groups.

57. The oily portion grabs hold as water drips off. Spraying the same branch again in a bout of rampant enthusiasm ups the net concentration left behind, resulting in potential leaf damage. This risk inherent in any horticultural oil application goes up as the temperature rises. Never spray neem oil in the middle of a hot day, even at this "safe" concentration: Phytotoxicity becomes far more likely when temperatures rise above 80°F (27°C).

58. I originally worked with Dr. Bronner's Castile liquid soap as an emulsifying agent, but that particular soap formulation seems to require slightly higher rates to completely emulsify the fatty nature of neem. Both Ecover and Seventh Generation biodegradable dishwashing liquid work better at the rates provided.

59. Sizable oil globules floating on top at this stage indicate the need for slightly more soap to completely disperse the fatty component of the neem oil into the bucket of warm water. Otherwise you might wind up with fatty residues in the spray tank that need to be scooped out by hand when you're done spraying.

60. Depending on the price savings inherent with a larger purchase volume, it may make sense to purchase pure neem oil in batch sizes from the supplier. A gallon contains 8 pints, one of which would provide six backpack tanks' worth of foliar neem spray at the 0.5 percent concentration each time. That purchase quantity would be enough for the four holistic spring sprays plus the more concentrated fall application. A case of 12 pints would make possible four additional summer sprays. All this depends on how many backpacks' worth it takes to cover your fruit plantings each time, of course.

61. The fish is first cooked in order to remove the oil portion for paints and cosmetics. Then the protein is removed and dried to make fish meal for livestock feeds. The remaining wastewater is condensed into a brown, thick liquid called an *emulsion*, which has considerably less nutritive value than liquid fish.

62. Crocker's Fish Oil has a number of uses in the commercial organic orchard. It can replace petroleum-based dormant oil to smother mite eggs and scale in early spring. Some growers use refined fish oil to increase absorption of foliar-applied nutrients. Others use fish oil in combination with lime sulfur to thin especially heavy-setting apple varieties such as Gala and Fuji.

63. The knowledge that Brix levels can be increased by adding molasses to the spray mix can be utilized to increase the attractiveness of trap trees as well. Think counterintuitively here. Protected trees are sprayed with molasses added to the holistic mix to enhance *plant sap fortitude*. Trap trees, on the other hand, can be sprayed with diluted vinegar to deliberately knock down Brix levels, thereby increasing the draw factor for pests.

64. The third boiling of cane sugar syrup results in *blackstrap molasses*. The majority of sucrose from the original juice has been crystallized, but blackstrap molasses is still mostly sugar by calories. However, unlike refined sugars, it contains significant amounts of vitamins and minerals.

65. The lower rate will promote beneficial fungal activity, while the higher rate increases photosynthetic bacterial response, according to SWEP Analytical Laboratories in Australia.

66. The lactoperoxidase system in milk has anti-microbial properties. A protein in whey produces an oxygen radical (when exposed to ultraviolet light) that is directly toxic to fungal conidia. The action of lactoferrin further collapses extant fungal hyphae. Australian researchers also noted that populations of benign bacteria, filamentous fungi, and yeasts were generally larger on leaves and berries on grapevines sprayed with milk and whey than on those either treated with sulfur or left untreated.

67. Acres USA has published an English translation of Francis Chaboussou's classic 1985 work, *Healthy Crops*. This transformational read addresses how and why pests shun healthy plants and disease need never take hold. Such invaluable research should be continued today . . . even if it's not in the interest of the chemical companies!

68. Liquid fish by any stretch of the imagination is not an herb. Pure neem oil, however, being derived from the seeds of the neem tree, is very much an herbal remedy. Microbe sprays are now optional unless you know you face high rot pressures on particular fruits and/or you

failed to deter primary scab on the apple crop due to totally unfavorable weather conditions.

69. The month immediately following petal fall calls for herbal treatments every ten days. This is when rot fungi and cuticle-feeding fungi get their start; thus the need to be more proactive. Calcium absorption is also greater on the front end of fruitlet development than it will be later. The spray interval widens in true summer to every fourteen days, when nutritional sprays and pure neem oil serve more or less as arboreal cruise control to maintain a health-based balance.

70. Effective horsetail tea can be made this way, as the silica is drawn out in the fermentation. Other sources suggest simmering this particular herb over low heat for an hour or two in order to release its hard constituents, much like a root decoction. Those sources are generally focusing on using fresh (not fermented) horsetail tea as a fungal curative sprayed three days in a row right after symptoms appear in the garden.

71. Biodynamic agriculture takes its inspiration from Rudolf Steiner, who seemingly channeled the fungi in giving instructions for the biodynamic preparations in a lecture series held in Breslau, Germany, in 1924. Steiner's instructions around horsetail centered on "sprinkling it as liquid manure over the fields . . . wherever we want to combat rust or similar plant diseases." Devotees since that time have also promoted horsetail tea, to be sprayed directly on the plants as a preventive measure.

72. This favorable fungal increase due to including horsetail in the compost-tea brewing process was reported by Hugh Courtney in the spring 2010 issue of *Applied Biodynamics*.

73. I actually like this nettle sensation, but here's the chance to share with you a plant remedy for dealing with occasional stings. Simply find any member of the dock genus (*Rumex*), break off a stalk at the base, then rub the soothing sap on the inflicted body part. See? I'm trying to keep this orchard ally and you the best of friends.

74. Let's not let use of this herbal remedy get out of sight. Next time you sprain a joint or strain tendon tissues, go out to your orchard and gather some comfrey leaves. Lightly steam these and then wrap a poultice of comfrey leaves directly over the hurt area, covered with a towel to hold in the moisture as you sit back and read more of *The Holistic Orchard*. Do this twice a day for up to an hour over the course of the next few days. You are going to be one amazed human at the turnaround time granted by this healing plant. A common name for comfrey is *knitbone* . . . but just be sure any broken bones are properly set before the allantoin in comfrey helps reestablish bone continuity!

75. Here's a fascinating bit about herbal synergy: The silica contribution of the nettle and horsetail teas helps promote the ability of the leaf (and thus the fruitlet) to absorb the calcium contribution of the comfrey. Now, aren't you glad you read this endnote?

76. Yellow Newtown Pippin and Gravenstein apples are highly susceptible to bitter pit, with Cortland, Jonathan, Honeycrisp, and Northern Spy not far behind. Calcium deficiency often appears more regularly on younger trees regardless of variety. Calcium reserves build up in the bark tissues of mature trunks and scaffold branches, which in turn helps mediate this situation down the road.

77. Check out www.frenchgardening.com for a full treatise on herbal plant remedies. Look for the "plants to the rescue of plants" page in the "Trucs d'artan" section. Barbara Wilde is a fabulous garden writer in all respects.

78. All these herbal remedies transcend mere folkloric reputation. The active constituents in each herb underlie the positive garden results found on both the insect and disease front. This grasshopper remedy correlates directly to the white milky sap of *Lactuca* species: Snapping the stem of wild lettuce in two reveals a bitter-tasting latex compound that contains sesquiterpene lactones. It may be the taste that grasshoppers don't like, or it may be the slight narcotic effect, but whatever . . . it works.

79. Cytokinins stimulate and sustain cell division, particularly in root tissue. Kelps are abundant in cytokinins, as it's these hormones that help secure the rootless algae to underwater rocks by means of cupped growth known as a *holdfast*.

80. Never clean a beach entirely of washed-up seaweed, as other life-forms depend on these homeless shelters made of kelp. A quick ocean rinse will save little crabs and the like that really don't want to be part of your compost pile. A more thorough rinse at home may be called for to wash off excess salt.

81. The principal constituents lost from dehydration of seaweed are the polysaccharides, which can help protect plants and fruit from subfreezing conditions.

82. The product literature for Stress-X (a dried seaweed extract available from North Country Organics) points this out. Cytokinins are known to increase the natural synthesis of flavonoids, which are a key part of the plant immune response. Higher phytoalexin levels in turn lengthen the wetting period (based on temperature) that the disease organism requires to cause infection.

83. The decision to use sulfur ties to all factors pointing to a major ascospore release. Do this no more than twice in the latter half of the primary infection window for scab

if experience shows certain varieties need extra protection. This use of sulfur as a targeted single application of allopathic medicine does indeed compromise the biology . . . but not as severely as in orchards where mineral fungicides are applied constantly. Now for the dose. The appropriate rate for targeted applications is 10 pounds of micronized sulfur per 100 gallons of spray. This amounts to 8 pounds of actual sulfur per 100 gallons applied just to the point of runoff. This is not an acreage rate but rather a concentration rate. If it takes more than 100 gallons to cover the trees on a single acre, then, yes, you are applying even more sulfur on an acreage basis. Don't mess around having made the decision to play the sulfur card, okay?

84. This scenario happens more often than not, actually. Some apple varieties are definitely on the downhill side of bloom; others are just opening king bloom. The second holistic spray made at pink was five days prior, say, and it's been sunny and warm since. Now a significant rain event is expected the very next day. Scab spores have been maturing all that time—so you know this coming wetting period brings a significant probability of infection. You really can't make that third holistic spray yet, as oils from the neem and the fish may prove detrimental to the new bloom. Innovation suggests a spray consisting of effective microbes, seaweed, and molasses at the full foliar rate. Such will renew competitive colonization, kindle resistance mechanisms in the leaf, up Brix levels (thereby upping the immune response as well), and who knows? The pollinators might just decide these new blooms have become especially attractive despite the rain.

85. Applications of fatty acid constituents at higher concentrations in the fall holistic spray can be used to shift microbe populations. Pure neem oil can safely be upped to a 2 percent concentration and fish applied at the full ground rate of 4 gallons per acre. This works against pathogens like peach curl fungi and *Xanthomonas* spot bacteria overwintering in bark and bud crevices. Biological reinforcement in the form of effective microbes and/or compost tea then has a leg up in colonizing those surfaces under contention when applied a day later. A molasses feed of 1–2 pints per 100 gallons per acre with this competitive colonization application will help the "new guys" establish for the winter ahead.

86. Fire blight risk is minimal if not completely gone by the time terminal buds set (harden off) in the first part of August. There is little risk for fire blight if you're summer-pruning your trees at that time.

87. Conversely, there's no need to sanitize pruning equipment in the dormant season. Bacteria infect when conditions are somewhat warm and moist. And that's just not the case in most locations in the winter months.

88. Applying copper or other chemicals will not kill bacteria in cankers. The wood that contains the bacteria has to be removed.

89. During bloom, rain and 80°F (27°C) temperatures establish fire blight conditions. On the other hand, with rain but temperatures under 60°F (16°C), there is very little risk of infection occuring.

90. AgraQuest produces the commercial formulation of Serenade for foliar application from *Bacillus subtilus* strain QST 713. Another strain of this bacterial grouping GB03 (Kodiak) was discovered in Australia in the 1930s and is applied either as a seed treatment or directly to soil. Neither strain is considered a genetically modified organism.

91. Iturins also play a role against disease-causing fungi by destroying the germ tubes and mycelium membranes of disease fungi like powdery mildew. One grower in New Jersey swears by Serenade (tank-mixed with compost tea) for reducing incidence of brown rot in his peach crop.

92. Other competitive colonization treatments to prevent fire blight would include effective microbes and aerated compost tea!

93. I was able to obtain the patent application for this herbal tree wash and thus read the initial studies. Untreated control blocks of apple and cherry were subject to the usual incidence of fire blight and bacterial canker, respectively. Western growers, needless to say, are excited about Plan C!

94. Although this bacterium is related to the pathogen that causes fire blight, it is a different species and does not hurt fruit trees. This particular strain, however, has not yet been approved by the EPA and so is not commercially available.

95. A hefty portion of leaves might still be waiting to fall on a fully dormant tree. But the phytochemical decision to abscise (to lose those leaves) has been reached and buds and shoots alike are done growing. Apple trees tend to remain green after harvest for a month or more, even after most of the hardwood trees in the forest have turned brilliant colors. You will know when it's time to spread compost, because orchard leaves yellow and start to fall. The thing is to beat the snow in northern regions so as to take full advantage of mycorrhizal action going into winter. Compost spread in the spring helps further leaf decomposition, certainly, but not in as fully integrated a fashion.

96. Other small rodents in the orchard often get confused with voles. Moles are earthworm carnivores that love to

dig—they'll aerate your soil, but they rarely damage tree roots while seeking out insect grubs. A potential ally is the short-tail shrew, which devours other small rodents along with insect delicacies. Deer mice and their white-footed cousins might nest in surface litter but cause no problems.

97. Plastic spirals hold moisture right against the trunk and provide wonderful cover for borers of the beetle persuasion. Young trees should be wrapped in late fall and then unwrapped in early spring after snow cover is gone. Of course this means there's no protection in the summer months, when cambium chewing by voles is far less likely but not unheard of. Spiral tree guards are most useful in the nursery to protect grafted rootstock through the winter months.

98. Screening out borers works this way: The top of the screen needs to be scrunched together and stapled across so as to not leave any ½-inch-size bubble openings. Each year the tightness to the trunk will have to be adjusted so as not to constrict growth. The screening must also be slightly tucked into the peastone (or earth), which you would do for voles anyway. Roundheaded appletree borer crawls down the trunk to get to the soil line, so it is possible that eggs may be laid right above the top of the screening. It goes without saying that screening needs to be put in place in the spring the trees are planted to make sure no borers have already "done" any of those trees. Do not use more than a double fold of screening; otherwise it can get too moist inside the trunk guard.

99. The suggestion has been put forth that chewing gum "gums up" the vole digestive tract, but in reality the way this works is as an odor repellent. Take away the advertising and such chemically enhanced taste treats stand revealed as little more than yucky. Just don't bother trying to convince my teenage daughter of this!

100. An investment of a few years in a young tree lost to vole girdling just isn't worth saving by grafting in a new rootstock (called *inarching*). A replacement tree will likely outpace such surgical efforts at this point. You will probably observe the buds on fully girdled trees pop forth with green growth that spring and think *Wow, my tree somehow survived*. Then all the leaves die off by early summer. That growth was fueled by nutrients stored in the cambium the previous fall.

101. Watersprout scions are wedged into the cambium layer both above and below the girdled area in early spring when the bark is slipping. Grooves can be cut into sound bark tissue to receive each end of the scion, or the gnawed edge trimmed to receive an inlay bark graft.

Be sure to insert the new wood so that upward sap flow continues in the requisite direction. These scions should be slightly longer than the span in order to ensure a binding tension. Several scions are used to bridge around the trunk, spaced every 3 to 4 inches around the circumference, with each one properly nailed and sealed into place. Small brads hold each graft in place; asphalt emulsion or latex grafting compound seals the exposed cambium cells from desiccation. Wrapping clear plastic around this entire bridge-graft zone further helps in holding in moisture while the scion grafts callus together over the next few weeks. The grafts that take will grow rapidly and, being of such succulent growth, will likely be sought out by voles again if left unprotected.

102. Some of these bits of apple lore simply need to be accredited. Who, you ask, would have ever thought to taste-sample the bark of different rootstocks? Neil Collins of Trees of Antiquity in California is that man!

103. Those of you with neighbors relatively near might opt for .22-caliber "shorts" in a single-shot rifle. These modified bullets use a gunpowder that takes a smidgen longer to burn, and thus the backfire report is low. Jerry Lehman in Indiana says his four neighbors within 300 yards don't complain about hearing his shooting. Muzzle speed is also lower with these bullets, thus reducing the distance of travel should you miss.

104. One positive aspect to this method according to Lucky Pittman in Kentucky is that there should be no worry about secondary poisoning of other animals that might capture affected squirrels or find and eat those that have died as a result of consuming the bonbons. Secondary poisoning of nontarget predators or scavengers is a significant concern when dealing with the anti-coagulant-type rodent baits (like warfarin).

105. Jim Fruth in Minnesota has probably done the most to develop decoy fruit techniques. He points out that fledglings fresh from the nest just when a particular crop starts to ripen have not yet been educated and therefore may very well undermine this plan.

106. Each one of those nips results in the removal of the terminal bud on a shoot. This causes a hormonal shift in that limb, resulting in the next several buds responding with vertical growth. Come June you want to select the outwardmost shoot and pinch off the other competing shoots at each such location on the tree. It's just a few buds that respond this way, mind, for farther down the shoot the growth will be lateral, and that's desirable. What you are doing here is restoring tree mode from the bush mode induced by heavy deer browsing.

107. One homemade recipe for deer repellent calls for ¼ cup of liquid dish soap to be mixed with two eggs and a sprinkling of powdered cayenne pepper per gallon of spray. It's okay to make a batch large enough to last for several applications, as brew gone funky seems to work that much better. This spray absolutely needs to be applied weekly to lower branches until deer pressure abates.

108. Visual strategies that seem slightly effective tie to the animal's initial perception of the situation. Tying white plastic bags on the perimeter of your property at tail height sends a familiar warning—movement in the wind mimics the blaze of a fleeing deer's tail, thereby putting other herd members on alert. Placing a colored tarp loosely over a short stepladder (held down by a weighted bucket for a "head") creates a roughshod version of you wildly flapping arms in a stiff breeze. Such unexpected presence can keep deer wary for a night or two, but these animals are smart and invariably figure out all this is nothing more than human silliness.

109. Mulch management and the like will be only slightly more difficult. Forming mesh into a ring fence requires two or three of its horizontal wires to be folded around a vertical on the other end. This can be quickly removed to get to the tree, as the fencing does not need to be tied to the stakes.

110. The Deerchaser triggers a spotlight coupled with a surprise radio to deer-proof a 625-square-foot zone. Gardeners are familiar with leaving a radio on at night to deter raccoons from the corn patch. Orchardists only need to figure out what deer like the least, whether it be opera or heavy metal or political talk radio. The Critter Gitter is simpler to install, offering a similar combination of flashing red lights and high-pitched sirens. Just know that deer even get used to motion detectors when hunger calls!

111. Relevant pruning tip: Make a first cut about a foot or two out from the finish cut at the branch union. Otherwise the weight of the full branch as it starts to fall ends up tearing bark down along the trunk. The effort of making that second cut comes easier with a good saw in hand.

112. Manual backpack sprayers also come in 3-gallon and 5-gallon tank sizes, with overall weights in the 11- to 14-pound range. Figuring in spray weight (based on water alone) means that you need to heft either 35 or 43 or 54 pounds onto your back. All rates used throughout this book are based on the "standard" 4-gallon tank size.

113. Optimum nutrient uptake is achieved when foliar sprays are finely atomized. Smaller droplets of spray mist the surface of the plant to achieve more even coverage. This can be managed by setting the operating pressure on a hydraulic sprayer to 120–140 psi.

5. POME FRUITS

1. Check out *The New Book of Apples* by Joan Morgan and Alison Richards for a rich British perspective. *Apples* by Frank Browning and the apple chapter in *Botany of Desire* by Michael Pollan go far to speak of the apple tree's role in enhancing our culture. Johnny Appleseed might add that all such reading assignments are best undertaken with a glass of chilled cider in hand.

2. Let's look at a few examples. The original apple that led to today's Red Delicious was called Hawkeye (discovered in Iowa in the 1880s) and delivered those fruity overtones that widely appeal. This first version, however, happened to be more stripey than red; it was not especially elongated, nor did it *bounce* . . . by which I mean it showed an honest bruise. Branches on apple trees go through what can best be described as a climatic mutation on occasion (early cold affecting buds) that alters the appearance or some other trait of the fruit on that particular branch. Growers take note of these sports and graft them anew to create a new strain of the original variety. Rarely do those choices have anything to do with improving flavor. The original Golden Delicious (found in West Virginia in 1905) exhibited russet flecking on its skin. Can't have that, can we? Newer strains cleaned this up and also emphasized spur habit for production reasons. But at a cost: The creaminess of today's version lost the refined spiciness and snap of the original apple. Granny Smith used to be special just a few decades ago, but that's another apple now headed for the doldrums in favor of spur habit and a lighter shade of pale. The once perfect level of subacidity in that great tart variety be damned!

3. The entire focus of breeding apple varieties for scab resistance comes down to the Vf gene that promotes this cellular hypersensitivity. Professor C. S. Crandall at the University of Illinois selected the original source of this gene from a *Malus floribunda* seedling in 1907, and that tree became the basis of propagation work picked up again in the 1940s by a Purdue/Rutgers/Illinois collaboration. The first letters of those three universities are PRI, which you will find incorporated into the names of many of these scab-immune varieties (such as William's Pride and Pristine).

4. The October 1947 issue of *Life* magazine claims Grimes Golden is "believed to have sprouted from one of the seeds

planted by Johnny Appleseed about 1795 in Wellsburg, West Virginia," on the farm of one Thomas Grimes. Now, that's some living history you can bite into!

5. Organic fruit growers in Europe use a coconut soap formulation (a 1 percent concentration of Biofa Cocana RF) that seems to help, but the foamy soap can cause phytotoxic damage to the leaves. The coconut oil portion found in coconut milk would be a more nutritional approach. My friend Jim Gallot suggests I always issue a Speculation Alert when I do things like this: I would modify this idea on the home orchard front by using a 10-ounce can of coconut milk per backpack spray tank to spray on especially susceptible varieties in a wet summer. This could be tank-mixed with all-herbal holistic summer sprays. Follow the same spray schedule as the Europeans suggest for sooty blotch and flyspeck. Chances are you will at least add to your apples' flavor profile!

6. Apple drop management has nuance as well. The very first drops tend to be early and bug-infested, which explains the advice to clean these up twice a week and destroy the fruit. That can be done in a hot compost pile, in the guts of farm animals, or by shipping this part of the harvest to your brother in Outer Mongolia. Finally comes the week of tree-ripened fruit, which is indicated in part by some mighty-fine-looking windfalls lying on the ground. These apples will not have been bruised by landing on earlier drops, assuming you have done your cleanup job. Scything a landing pad of grass mulch ahead of time can help cushion their fall as well. I don't use any drops for fresh cider, but these windfalls do go into cider destined to become alcoholic or hard cider (fermentation eliminates any harmful *E. coli* bacteria that might be present) or are used for applesauce and pie baking (cooking also destroys any potential pathogens). Sometimes such drops even have the best flavor that day, being the more tree-ripened fruit. I think you get the idea—drops can indeed be used and all the more so when you manage the situation on the ground.

7. Low-chill pear varieties for the Deep South (Zone 9) that have the ability to stand up to severe fire blight pressure include Acres Home, Tennousi, Southern Bartlett, Southern Queen, and Southern King; this according to Ethan Natelson in Houston, Texas.

8. All extra training after the limb spreader phase involving tie-downs needs to be done so as not to girdle the branch. I make the ground connection first, be it a stake or tire or even a cement block. Then I wrap the poly twine around the young (and thus supple) branch in question and pull it down to the desired position. This allows me to take

measure of where a loop should be tied. Make a simple knot in this location on the tie-down side of the twine. When you wrap the twine around the branch again to pull it to the desired position, there will be a knot in place to brace a simple half hitch against to keep it from slipping and going tight around the branch.

9. David Fried of Elmore Roots Nursery in northern Vermont reports that including one Siberian pear in a mix of domestic varieties enhances fruit production. The bloom periods overlap slightly and yet pollination seems improved. This is one of those tips that may make a difference if you've been having trouble getting a reasonable crop in northern zones.

10. Legitimate debate exists as to the degree that pheromones produced in the honeybee's Nasonov (scent) gland affect foraging behavior. Synthesized pheromones make up 20 percent of the active ingredients in a proprietary formulation. The other 80 percent are some combination of whey, sucrose, and spices. Are we ready for yet another Speculation Alert? I see no reason why a molasses spray with whey powder might not do some good in drawing pollinators to a less attractive tree. Why buy a specialized product when you can find what you need in the kitchen? Let me know what you and the restless natives figure out for a recipe.

11. Thanks to John Bunker of Fedco Trees in Maine for passing along this tidbit. John's varietal write-ups in his tree catalog are rich and compelling . . . and packed with intriguing tips like this.

12. Eric Strandberg, an organic fruit grower in the Okanogan River Valley in Washington State, relates a pertinent story about unexpected allies. "An agrichemical guy and some farmers were in our organic pear orchard. The ag-chem guy grabs a bunch of pears and some earwigs fall out. Well, he maintained that the earwigs are eating and damaging the pears and recommended an organic spray. I knew full well, though, that earwigs don't eat pears and that they were just sleeping there. They are actually beneficial as predators of the pear psylla. The other farmers didn't know that." Here's a grower who crumples up newspapers to put in crotches of pear trees to promote earwigs. The earwigs hide in the newspaper during the day and come out at night and feed on pear psylla eggs. Once again, a little understanding goes a long way!

13. European pear varieties that are good candidates for tree ripening have been indicated as such in the varietal descriptions in this book. You will find harvest recommendations based on when one pear matures in such a month versus when another pear ripens in that month to reflect

grower experience with the different varieties. The idea here is to harvest the bulk of a particular pear for post-chill conditioning, but let a portion hang to discover tree-ripened flavor in those varieties with a less gritty nature.

14. The full details of this are provided in *The Apple Grower*. A pheromone wing trap pinpoints when the first male moth has flown and thus been captured by the female lure. Degree-day tracking from that day on based on a 50°F (10°C) development threshold reveals the pace at which moth eggs are developing. Expect first hatch at 243 DD and 50 percent at 465 DD. Doing this for a season or two will provide you a sense of expected timing for future seasons with respect to petal fall on your Asian pears.

15. I know, I know. You always heard it was an apple. However, the book of Genesis does not name the specific type of fruit that Adam and Eve ate from the tree of knowledge of good and evil in the Garden of Eden. Other ancient texts suggest that the fruit of temptation was most likely a quince.

16. The principal nemesis on the orchard front is the far-ranging plum curculio (*Conotrachelus nenuphar*). This pest of apple, pear, peach, cherry, apricot, blueberry, and of course plum typically shows a regional preference for one of those fruits. What's less well known is that plum curculio has more isolated cousins. The quince curculio (*C. crataegi*) is a small gray-and-yellow curculio whose larvae live in quince. The apple curculio (*Anthonomus quadrigibbus*) roams northern zones across the continent and focuses its attention on apple, pear, and saskatoons (*Amelanchier alnifolia*).

17. Application timing is all about the life cycle of the pest being targeted. Feeding by winter moth larvae can continue all spring and as late as early June. These are surface feeders—ingestion of exposed leaf material is what green caterpillars do. This makes Bt a cost-effective choice, applied the week orior to green tip and renewed every five days up until tight cluster if necessary. Use fish oil to limit ultraviolet degradation and molasses to help the medicine go down as a bait attractant. A pricier spinosad product can be used instead, with the renewal spray made ten days after the first application.

6. STONE FRUITS

1. Emerging evidence links cherries to many important health benefits—from helping to ease the pain of arthritis and gout to reducing risk factors for heart disease, diabetes, and certain cancers. Cherries also contain melatonin, which has been found to help regulate the body's natural sleep patterns, aid with jet lag, prevent memory loss, and delay the aging process.

2. Dr. Evans believed this cherry was transported to Edmonton as a root cutting from a small town in southern Alaska, where the tree grows so profusely that the residents held an annual cherry festival. It seems logical that the origin is Russian since Alaska was first settled by Russian fur traders.

3. Most nurseries use tissue culture to propagate this cherry, thus delivering a self-rooted tree. Which brings us to a name divide, of sorts. Bill MacKentley of St. Lawrence Nurseries in Potsdam, New York, was among the first to heed Dr. Evans's enthusiasm for this northern fruiting tree. The cherry at that time did not yet have a name, and having been invited by Dr. Evans to do so, Bill called it Bali after one of his daughters. Only subsequently did others in Canada give it the name Evans and begin to propagate it in earnest. Let me emphasize this point to take down a misperception: These two names refer to one and the same cherry.

4. Okay, botanists, relax. Jan, Joy, and Joel are selections of the Korean bush cherry—which is actually a plum, *Prunus japonica*—chosen by Professor Elwyn Meader of the University of New Hampshire. The red, cherry-like fruits can be used in pies and make the best "cherry preserves" of all.

5. Cherries have single buds in the leaf axils of the current season's growth. If it turns into a flower bud, then the node goes "blind" in that it will not be fruitful again. If it's a leaf bud, then a spur can develop, which will have both leaf and flower buds in the years ahead.

6. Scoring is a technique that can be used to encourage low, fruitful branching. Sweet cherries have a tendency toward long, bare branches, devoid of fruit. Eventually these buds along the trunk and branches will die if they aren't stimulated. So it's best to do this radial slice through the bark (one-third of the way around the branch) centered just above the chosen bud on wood that's no more than three years old.

7. Let's do the numbers to assess the full threat posed by Japanese vinegar fly, also commonly referred to as spotted wing drosophila (SWD). A single female can lay as many as 375 eggs. The generational life cycle from egg to sexual maturity takes a mere eight days. A single fertile female gives rise to 22,500 egg-laying daughters after just two generations. Ready for the full crescendo? There have been estimates from California of a million vinegar flies

to the acre. Oregon State University sponsors a spotted wing drosophila website (http://swd.hort.oregonstate.edu) where far more can be learned. And lest you be smug, this pest has already made its way to Wisconsin and Michigan within five years of appearing on this continent.

8. These regional preferences by plum curculio will be duly noted with other fruits as well. This pertinent discovery by Tracy Leskey and company at the Appalachian Fruit Research Station in West Virginia reveals effective trap tree species on a statewide basis. A curculio map showing the oviposition preferences of this widespread pest can be found on page 164 in the revised edition of *The Apple Grower.*

9. Spotted wing drosophila are not drawn to the ammonium bait in GF-120. Researchers have yet to figure out an all-around lure for Japanese vinegar fly. Spinosad, on the other hand, is quite effective if you nail generational timing down to a tee . . . which frankly can get quite expensive with a prolific pest reproducing at such a frenetic pace among so many different fruits.

10. Trials of various spray formulations were used on an organically managed raspberry field in the summer of 2010. Entrust showed the most efficacy, providing five days of control. Two applications of PyGanic 5.0 (at 18 ounces per acre per treatment) provided a similar period of control. One of the patented neem extracts failed to gain headway . . . and, as is typical of university trials, whole plant medicine in the form of pure neem oil was not included in the trials.

11. Olive growers on the West Coast are successfully using Bti for the olive fruit fly. Both species are in the order Diptera—the olive fly is in the Tephritidae family, whereas the vinegar fly is in the Drosphilidae family. Chances are good that Bti may prove useful against this cherry pest, though research has yet to be done on its overall effectiveness.

12. Massively coating stone fruits with multiple applications of refined kaolin clay for curculio is less than ideal once fruit begins sizing in earnest. Cherries bloom before apples, and with far less leaf showing initially. Surround applied at this critical juncture on the just-about-to-pop flower buds delivers a message to this pest to move onward to other prospects. Curculio prefers making its way by crawling, particularly early on when temperatures tend to be cooler. The main route to developing fruit is by way of the limb highway, and thus the reason for thorough coverage on the branch structure of the tree. Two applications going into bloom will do the trick in a warm spring, with an additional application as soon as petal fall

begins probably necessary in a cooler season. The cherry harvest is six to eight weeks away at this point, meaning that little residual clay will cover fruit otherwise ready to enjoy right off the tree.

13. Copper is toxic to pollen, and the earlier flowering date for cherries as compared with apples increases the likelihood that copper residues from dormant applications in early spring could interfere with pollination.

14. Studies have shown that micro-cracks may be present in the cuticles of crack-prone cherries; these cracks are the eventual source of the splitting brought on by osmotic pressure during wet periods.

15. You can order directly online from Lehman's Hardware by visiting www.lehmans.com. Or, even better, request their fascinating catalog of homestead goods by writing to P.O. Box 270, Kidron, OH 44636.

16. Timing for budding is based on when the bark is still pliable and next year's buds (at the base of each leaf) have begun to size. Growers in southern zones will start budding peaches as early as mid-June, whereas up north this is often an early-August task. Irrigation can be valuable in extending the T-budding season, if need be. Two other precautions are commonly taken to ensure success. First, buds should not be grafted when the air temperature exceeds 90°F (32°C). Second, buds should be inserted on the cooler north or east sides of stems.

17. The beauty of parafilm is that the bud can grow right through this special stretchy plastic. Some grafters find a well-placed bud heels in fine using just parafilm, while others report the need for a rubber band wrap to secure the union over which the parafilm is used primarily as a seal. The A. M. Leonard catalog offers Buddy Tape—perforated 2¾-inch strips of heavy-duty parafilm that are just the right size for budding and plenty strong enough to hold the bark down.

18. Shoots developing in 20 percent full sun in the tree interior produce only half as many flowers per foot of shoot length as shoots developing at the tree periphery that receive more than 70 percent full sun.

19. High light levels in late July, August, and September will not influence flower bud formation. Shoot thinning in the latter part of summer misses the boat of improved peach prospects.

20. That minimum light distribution goal of 25 percent was reported by Rich Marini in an excellent article, "Pruning Peach Trees," published by the Virginia Cooperative Extension. One grower anecdote to go with this comes from a man who measures his fruit regularly for Brix. He reports that his under-canopy peaches (the more shaded

fruit) consistently read out at half the Brix of his better-exposed fruit. Peaches are the only species where he finds such a dramatic difference. Sunlight matters with peaches!

21. Look closely at the base of leaves on the current season's shoot growth in late summer. Auxiliary buds develop here during the early-summer months that can be either leaf or flower buds. Many of the nodes on the lower two-thirds of a shoot have two or three buds arranged side by side, most often in the pattern of a central leaf bud flanked by flower buds.

22. Peaches have an "existential hardiness" starting around –20°F (–29°C) and ranging to as much as –40°F (–40°C) in the Siberian cultivars. Such blunt cold kills the tree outright regardless of the influence of preceding weather and the complicated hardening-off process at work in stone fruit.

23. Peach builds cold tolerance at the rate of 1–3°F (1–2°C) a day as low night temperatures (40°F, or 4°C, or less) accumulate. This process begins with the buds and twigs, slowly working its way down toward the trunk. A warm fall prevents this from happening at the desired pace. Should a sudden and dramatic dip in the temperature come along in November or early December, bark tissues are often not prepared. Southern growers experience this vulnerability of peach just as much as growers farther north.

24. Trunk cambium at the soil line includes the graft union. Do two-piece and three-piece (interstem) genetic systems have anything to do with hardiness issues? Seedling peach trees demonstrate greater cold hardiness even when snow or soil protects the graft union of neighboring trees. Use of a less hardy rootstock would be an issue, of course, if that rootstock were exposed—which is not the case. Grower observations like this make graft influence on hardiness a very legitimate part of the equation.

25. Peach hardiness is complicated, to say the least. Fruit buds have a baseline hardiness of 29.8°F (–1.2°C) following leaf fall. Chilly temperatures in November and into December increase this by as much as 3°F (2°C) a day, eventually reaching an absolute hardiness of –18.4°F (–28°C). Consistent preconditioning by cold nights is required to reach this point, without which a given bud may achieve a minimum hardiness level of only –5.8°F (–21°C) to face winter. De-hardening, on the other hand, can occur at a rate of as much as 0.9°F (0.5°C) an hour when winter temperatures rise above the chilling requirement range. That's why days in the mid-40s (6–9°C) have impact in December, January, and February if

followed by extreme cold, whereby the buds have no time to acclimate downward again. All this accounts for the dormancy issues faced by peach buds. See E. L. Proebsting, "Relation of fall and winter temperatures to flower bud behavior and wood hardiness of deciduous fruit trees (a review)," *HortScience*, 1970, 5:422–424.

26. Creating a south-facing microclimate for stone fruits is in fact a very bad idea. Fruit breeder Dave Griffin in Minnesota provides very sound guidance here: "Don't plant a tender tree in a 'protected' site. I wish I knew how many times someone has told me about the peach that died in spite of their having planted it in this great warm and wind-protected site right up along the south side of the house. Absolute cold kills peaches, not wind-chill, unless you are in a prairie climate with dry, snowless winters, and then that is bud desiccation, not windchill. And minimum temperatures come around sunrise, way after any benefit from yesterday afternoon's buildup of slightly warmer temperatures in the tree's little heat island is long gone. Once in a while I even hear about someone who has tried to espalier a peach against the south wall of a building in an effort to get it through the winter—geez!"

27. Self-sterile cultivars have been largely or completely eliminated from the commercial peach scene, regardless of other good qualities, largely because interplanting of cultivars and insect pollination then become necessary for production. These include Alamar, Candoka, Chinese Cling, Hal-berta, J. H. Hale, Indian Free, June Elberta, Mikado, and a few others.

28. The soybean oil coating restricts carbon dioxide exchange, thus slowing down flower bud respiration and delaying bud development. See R.E. Myers, D.E. Deyton, and C. E. Sams, "Applying soybean oil to dormant peach trees alters internal atmosphere, reduces respiration, delays bloom, and thins flower buds," *Journal of the American Society of Horticultural Science*, 1996, 12:96–100.

29. Gibberellins are produced in the making of seed. Excess production of this hormone is a driving factor in delaying cold acclimation. The observed reduction in hardiness following a large crop is thought to be due to the increase in gibberellins rather than to a depletion of reserves as is so often assumed. See Melvin West, *Temperate Zone Pomology*, revised edition (Portland, OR: Timber Press, 1988), p. 318.

30. Actual accounting should help many of you grasp what it takes to properly thin a peach crop. What follows comes by way of a determined grower and a mature Elberta peach tree. "We took off just over 3 gallons' worth of

baby peaches, estimating 120 to the pint, and thus 3,600 extra peaches in all. One fruit was left every 6 inches along the branch. We harvest 300 to 400 pounds of nice peaches from this tree if we thin enough. And if not, we have broken branches and about the same weight of small so-so peaches."

31. Apples and pears don't respond to pole thinning particularly well. It actually takes quite a beating to dislodge the stem attachment of pome fruits, and that would result in significant damage to the apples or pears remaining on each branch. Peaches and other stone fruits bump off surprisingly easily, on the other hand.

32. Pit hardening is an internal developmental change in *Prunus* species when the seed takes on its stony nature. The timing of this can be tested by trying to cut the fruit in half.

33. Fruit tree catalogs often choose one variety to represent the ripening norm with which other varieties can be compared. Red Haven gets the nod when it comes to peaches. Those cultivars ripening before or along with this standard market variety are considered early-season, while cultivars ripening after Red Haven are considered mid- or late-season. Commercial growers can plan harvest succession better when ripening of other cultivars is referenced to a variety very likely being grown on the farm.

34. The early life cycle of plum curculio, from an egg inserted after peach shuck split to a newly emerging adult in midsummer, requires five to eight weeks, depending upon climatic conditions. There are usually two generations and possibly a partial third generation each year in the Southeast. Northern growers rarely see second-generation activity on fruit, as the migratory urge of curculio to return to nearby woods kicks in by August in places where nights turn cooler sooner.

35. Pruning ramifications follow as a result of severe Oriental fruit moth infestation. Each shoot taken down essentially has undergone a heading cut. The growth response of the tree is to go bushy, developing several lateral shoots below the damaged area that grow rapidly. Some of these new tender shoots may be injured by later generations, and then secondary lateral shoots will be produced. The upshot? Keep tabs on OFM and you will have far less excessive growth to deal with.

36. The Santa Rosa plum, for one, has been shown to have eleven times the draw of apple. Plum curculio has never lost its native affinity for any of these smooth-skinned fruits. Late pruning of the trap tree emits additional volatiles to close the deal. Just don't be silly and let curcs get

away with plundering all the plums on the sacrificial tree. Harder-hitting spray materials like PyGanic can used to curtail activity. Otherwise, plan on an interception strategy like fencing in the chicken flock beneath the trap tree during the infestation period.

37. This petroleum-based horticultural oil is more like an emulsion, thick like soft butter. Oil works as a fungicide by interfering with the attachment of the pathogen to the host plant by basically smothering spore and mycelium alike. University compilations of data reveal that Saf-T-Side was more effective than the chemical fungicide captan against brown rot. Serenade is added to the tank mix because of its efficacy against fungal diseases in drier conditions. That's worth what it's worth, especially considering what captan does to the food web ecosystem. But hey! Some growers really like to rely on reductionist trials, so there you go! I'd vote for the neem-based approach on healthy ground myself.

38. Let's zero in on the ramifications of leaf curl defoliation. The new growth that develops after petal fall is not affected and quickly hides the defoliation caused by earlier leaf curl. Severe infections that cause more than 10 percent defoliation, however, do result in reduced fruit size. A few scattered infections cause no significant damage to the trees but will provide overwintering inoculum to start things anew the following year.

39. Copper has a dramatic impact on establishing a healthy food web, both above- and belowground. Still, some of you might feel compelled to clean up a bacterial situation going south fast. Understanding how to utilize copper allopathy to its utmost capacity then becomes important. That application made at bud swell to peaches and nectarines should be a fixed copper formulation that includes dormant oil (2 percent concentration) or some other spreader-sticker in the tank mix to help spread the coverage. This can be followed with Mycoshield (copper oxytetracycline) at shuck split and the same again seven days later in the most severe situations. Think of this as onetime surgery . . . now get back on the holistic bandwagon!

40. Peach scab is an entirely different fungus from the one that afflicts apples and pears. Common names describe the look, whereas botanical identification keys to species differential. *Cladosporium* fungi have affinity for stone fruits, whereas *Venturia* fungi seek pome feeding grounds.

41. Fungal gummosis in peach trees can be triggered by *Botryosphaeria* fungi as well. Naming diseases by visual indications gets confusing when the tree's response to infection is one and the same. Exuding sap is an attempt

by the tree to compartmentalize the damage, whether caused by black rot or the fungi behind perennial canker.

42. Fall pruning can severely weaken and stress peach trees, setting them up for winter injury and subsequent infection from perennial canker fungi. Spring pruning, on the other hand, heals over quickly and favors benign organisms in the race to colonize the cut surface. Prune each branch carefully to leave the swollen collar at its base to promote rapid callusing. Do not leave stubs and avoid a very close flush cut. Avoid leaving weak-angled crotches, as these are potential sites of infection in general.

43. Fuzziness is the dominant trait in the peach, while a recessive gene allows for nectarines to have a smooth skin.

44. Deeper delving into *Mendel's Principles of Heredity* by William Bateson (1902) reveals that Charles Darwin looked into the relationship between peaches and nectarines. His records proved abundantly that the seeds of peaches may come up nectarines, and conversely, the seeds of nectarines may give rise to peaches. The latter situation occurs only when the nectarine flower is pollinated with peach pollen. Sport mutations of the bud are more variable, sometimes resulting in a true nectarine, other times yielding a fruit with a mix of *Prunus persica* traits.

45. Nectarine blossoms average about 1 degree less of frost resistance than peach, according to the University of California. Much of this ties to nutrition and other factors . . . so don't sweat this distinction by any means.

46. Call this an organic switcheroo. Rutgers University reports that spraying diluted white paint on peach and nectarine trees—buds and all—in mid- to late January can help delay blooming by up to five days. This can certainly make a big difference in flower survival and fruit set. Gunking up tree buds and sprayer lines alike with paint doesn't strike me the same as the use of interior latex (also diluted 50–50) in the trunk zone, however. Old-timers used a lime whitewash to delay bloom. Today we have refined kaolin clay to reflect the warmth of the winter sun on awakening buds. This earth remedy can be renewed as needed with no harm to the buds.

47. The Honey series of nectarines developed by Zaiger includes Honey Blaze, Honey Kist, Honey Royale, and Honey Diva. As one enthusiast put it, "Fruit lovers everywhere should do whatever necessary to grow one of these low-acid, yellow-fleshed nectarines!"

48. The parasite *Macrocentrus ancylivorus* is a common parasite of Oriental fruit moth larvae and peach twig borer larvae. Parasitism can reach levels of 80–90 percent by August and September to help provide long-term control of this pest. California studies indicate that growing a nearby plot of sunflowers can provide these braconid wasps with an overwintering host, the sunflower moth *Homoeosoma electellum*, which allows their populations to build more rapidly in the orchard the following season. Similarly, studies dating back to 1921 in the Northeast reveal the strawberry leafroller as a prime food host for *Macrocentrus*.

49. Thanks to Jim Koan in Michigan for this insight into pyrethrum efficacy. Residual action of this broad-spectrum botanical breaks down rapidly in sunlight, thus sprays are best made at twilight. Diatomaceous earth consists of the shells of tiny marine organisms. While its sharp micro-edges do cut into the soft bodies of aphids, the real damage occurs when this fossil-shell flour gets absorbed into the spiracles (breathing tubes) of almost any insect. That defines the injection point for pyrethrum with stink bug.

50. Foliar rates for molasses vary between 1 and 4 pints per 100 gallons per acre. The lower foliar rate will promote beneficial fungal activity against brown rot, whereas too much sugar may well favor this particular opportunistic species. Fruit-directed sprays are not so much about Brix readings in this case as the practicality of getting the holistic mix to stick to the smooth-skinned nectarine. Stirring that extra dollop of blackstrap molasses into warm water first will help make mixing more manageable in a backpack sprayer.

51. Doc Watson fans, unite!

52. Hybridization with the closely related *Prunus sibirica* (Siberian apricot; hardy to −50°F, or −46°C, but with less palatable fruit) leads the way in breeding more cold-tolerant apricot varieties.

53. Apricots generally do not require pollinizer trees. These are the exceptions: Moongold and Sungold require each other for pollination; while Goldrich, Perfection, Riland, and Rival are self-unfruitful varieties that can be pollinized by any other apricot variety.

54. The synopsis offered here on regional prospects for apricots comes from the work of the NAFEX Apricot Interest Group led by chairman Bob Purvis. The North American Fruit Explorers provides enthused growers with a round-robin opportunity to share what each has learned about particular fruits in member orchards. The apricot group stands a notch above in getting solid varietal information out to the rest of us.

55. Temperatures in the mid-40s (6–9°C) for several days in a row during the winter months cause tree fruit buds to de-harden ever so slightly. If there's a sudden drop to subzero temperatures (−18°C and under), bud kill increases

rapidly with each degree, spelling complete doom for apricot fruiting prospects around –12° to –14°F (–24° to –26°C). Offer up that same cold without a midwinter thaw preceding it and those buds can take –20°F (–29°C), if not colder. One of the goals in the New Jersey breeding program is developing apricot cultivars whose flower buds are better adapted to winter temperature fluctuations.

56. Bob Purvis detailed the depths of varietal nuance in an article titled "Apricots Around the Country," published in the fall 2006 edition of *Pomona*, the quarterly journal of the North American Fruit Explorers. Specific cultivar recommendations by region can be found posted on the web when you do a search for that title.

57. A mother tree can be tested using indicator budwood—grafting a highly susceptible variety (like the Tilton apricot) onto the desired source reveals the presence of virus in the resulting growth. Twisting, stunting, discoloration, and other symptoms show up rather quickly if the host plant is indeed infected.

58. The prairie-hardy apricots include Westcot, Debbie's Gold, Morden 604, and Brookcot. These Manchurian crosses don't deal with the stress of fluctuating winter temperatures that well and thus usually do not thrive in the Northeast. As David Maxwell in Nova Scotia puts it, these cultivars are "a sucker for midwinter thaws."

59. Westcot has survived –48°F (–44°C) with minimal injury in a Zone 2 location, just northwest of Bemidji, Minnesota, at Del Stubbs's orchard, on a north-facing slope with clay soils.

60. Generally speaking, a good selection of vertical shoots off the limb structure is the norm on a vigorous apricot tree. Bending more upright shoots in a desired direction has surprisingly good effect, with the bending principle ingrained by the time the late dormant pruning window comes around the following year. Those rarer situations where shoots are not in the offing from the growing season just passed are when heading cuts come into play to induce latent buds. This give-and-take becomes rather obvious when you start working with an actual tree!

61. Apricots bloom at the same early point in spring when forsythia provides its brilliant yellow display and the earliest daffodils are in bloom . . . when odds are 50–50 that a significant frost will settle in on a clear-sky night. Apples and blueberries have swollen buds now; red raspberries are at green tip; currants are just showing the beginnings of leaves. Those other fruits know to wait till flowering prospects improve.

62. What about enhancing freeze resistance, you say? Liquid kelp applied with molasses in the spray tank will gain a few degrees of internal oomph when sprayed in the early afternoon preceding a predicted cold night. Supplemental nutrition plays a hand here as well: Zinc applied shortly before leaf drop (as a soil amendment) apparently makes apricot flower buds better developed and able to deal with spring cold.

63. Choosing varieties with a higher dormant chill requirement can be a factor in later blooming. Bud protection can be taken up another notch by rigging tender fruit trees with miniature holiday lights on a thermostatically controlled relay. The apricot bloom, in essence, is now in the midst of a cheery microclimate during the cold of the night. Locations such as the high plains of the Southwest—where blossoms open around the third week of February—get nipped year after year. This electric maneuver allows fruit to develop in an ecosystem probably less bothered by bugs as well—no wild crops exist to sustain pest populations otherwise.

64. Pollen is high in protein, and many flies and beetle (and bees, of course) eat it. Flowers dependent on insects that eat pollen produce large amounts of pollen to ensure successful pollination. And that's the reason behind the many pollen stamens surrounding the single pistil of self-fertile stone fruits.

65. The blossom blast phase of *Pseudomonas* shows no sign of bacterial ooze on pome fruit when infection associated with frost damage occurs. Apricots and company have an entirely different response—gumming does occur on stone fruit buds and spurs infected with this bacterium. The canker phase exhibits gummosis as well, particularly in sharp-angled branch crotches.

66. The first *Prunus salicina* cultivars were developed in China more than two thousand years ago. The Japanese began refining these around AD 1700, bringing their plums along to California not too long after the Gold Rush era.

67. Any narrow board or even a forked stick makes a prop for a laden branch of fruit. A notch cut into the upper end helps keep the prop in place when the wind blows. The sweet spot to place this brace could be defined where stoutness in a limb ends and lankiness takes over. Thinning isn't always enough for a weaker branch to maintain a strong horizontal position. The need to head back such limbs in future seasons as the drooping propensity takes over (even when there's no crop load) will become obvious.

68. Burbank states in his journal that bringing in these plum seedlings was the "most important importation of fruit bearers ever made at a single time into America."

69. *Prunus triflora* plums came in many colors of skin, from white to purple, and were large and rather tasteless, but

the Japanese people pickled them while green and hard. These true Japanese plum genes have influence in many Asian plum crosses today.

70. If dried with the pit intact, an Asian plum will ferment rather than dry like a prune.

71. *Pitch pockets* are an inherited physiological disorder. The flesh grows at uneven rates in certain conditions, creating cracks that fill up with callus and pitch. Red Heart plum has similar flavor and quality to Elephant Heart, but because it's rounder, it almost never gets pitch pockets.

72. The peach shoot bears and then goes into blind wood mode, thus pushing the fruiting zone farther out from the tree structure. The Asian plum shoot, on the other hand, will go into spur mode two years hence. Nevertheless, in most situations, favoring a new one-year shoot in that relative position on the plum branch remains the better fruiting choice. This aspect of the pruning plan for Asian plum is much the same as for peach.

73. South Dakota is one of those few *Prunus americana* cultivars with select fruit in its own right. Both Toka and Kaga are *americana* × *simonii* crosses, a mix that has proven quite effective as a native pollinizer. Pure American seedlings can be dug up from wild plum thickets or very likely achieved by way of *americana* rootstock on purchased trees. A good half of such seedling stock suckers significantly farther out from the tree. Leaving select root suckers to grow as part of a wild and woolly thicket provides native pollen sources for the *americana* × *salicina* crosses being grown for fruit. These can be rotated every five to seven years (cut off at the base) to keep the underling stock from ever outgrowing the desired cultivars.

74. Think of the plum thicket as a single organism. The ecosystem/microclimate in this conceptual design expands to incorporate several trees, that's all. What's more, you can have all sorts of grafting fun by topworking root suckers to yet another variety you might want to trial.

75. Pollination tip #122: Placing bouquets of plum blossoms in other plum trees creates a pollination haven of a different sort. Waiting to prune redundant shoots (with respect to light space) until bloom begins allows you to bring different varieties together, no matter how far your trees are spaced apart. Such bouquets can be placed in mason jars tied to the trunk, with water to keep the flowers alive for the full day of insect activity ahead.

76. Personally, I consider the fragrance of a plum blossom beyond compare. Bees, on the other hand, use different parameters. The relatively low sugar content of plum nectar (reaching 21 percent sucrose by the afternoon) doesn't necessary hold sway if sweeter nectaries are available in other flowers at the same time. Orchard trees use "afternoon delight" to increase pollinator draw back toward fruiting needs.

77. Flowering periods for tree fruits differ based on cultivar and climate conditions but usually last four to eight days. This period may be extended to up to fifteen days during unusually cool spring weather. An individual plum blossom may be viable for two or three days, but it's the fact that some cultivars seem to open almost simultaneously in some seasons that limits pollinator awareness. Alternative bloom with higher amounts of nectar sucrose can distract pollinators from realizing just how *plum good* life can be when the action begins, and then it may be too late.

78. Beach plums (*Prunus maritima*) seem to have yet another mechanism for resisting curculio by encapsulating the egg in a drop of sap that quickly hardens. The little drop of hardened sap will be evident on the outside of the fruit, but no curculio infestation will be found inside.

7. BERRIES

1. Cover crop scenarios vary, as discussed earlier. The ideal finish is a red or crimson clover, as these legume species are inclined toward mycorrhizal association. A light disking in late fall where the stubble is left on the surface of the soil to decompose preps the bed area for spreading compost just prior to planting brambles in spring. Yes, maybe you do use a tiller—with tines set as shallow as possible—to reach this point. Or you can simply fork up any extant clover root systems. The less disturbance, the better.

2. Black raspberries have a backup plan of sorts when exposed floricanes succumb to winter cold. Crown laterals growing from near the base of the plant can offer a strong replacement cane that very spring, which grows and acts like a flowering primocane. These have blossoms just before the main crop would have ripened, about four to six weeks after the normal flowering time. Backup canes inevitably die back completely in the fall after fruiting. Unfortunately, basal buds capable of generating such laterals are anything but consistent.

3. Anthocyanins are the medicinal pigments found in dark-colored berries that are highly touted for warding off degenerative disease in our bodies. There are other healthy compounds in all raspberries regardless of color, such as ellagic acid.

4. Black raspberries are topped in the summer when the young shoots are about 24 inches high; purple raspberries, about 32 inches. Summer topping consists of removing the top 3–4 inches of the new shoots by cutting them with shears or a knife just above a bud. This stimulates a lateral branching response that can be looked upon as a primocane candelabra.

5. Spent canes are a source of potential fungal inoculum. Rather than burning these canes, however, the biological grower should give consideration to using this organic matter for the benefit of good fungi. Canes can be chipped to go to the compost pile. That admittedly takes a bit of doing. My preference is to flatten wheelbarrow-sized piles outside the dripline of developing fruit trees. These get brush-mowed not too long after as part of leaf-fall hygiene. I then toss a shovel or two of compost atop the brushy debris. The cane remnants by spring are few—all having gone to the benefit of the fungal duff zone of the selected trees.

6. Tim Nourse explains: "Pruning the plant mass reduces the surface area of the plantings, decreasing winter damage due to wind desiccation. I have seen virtually no winter damage in our summer red and black raspberries. Most recommendations suggest it is better to wait until spring to prune off the winter damage on summer-bearing brambles. I believe that decreasing the amount of cane the plant has to support increases the chances it has to survive the winter."

7. The majority of primocane bearers have greater fruit production in the fall. Look at the portion of the first-year cane that commits to floral initiation—cultivars with a third to half of the cane involved in fall berry production are best mowed down given the commercial advantages of mechanical management. Prelude commits itself far less, leaving more cane below to come on strong the following summer.

8. Talk about a comeback kid! Prolific bloom stands out in so-so springs when wild blackberries appear to be on sabbatical. Fruit explorers are inclined to knock on doors when potential reveals itself. Nelson Frank has a 1928 family photograph taken on their farm northeast of Farmington, Maine, showing this blackberry growing next to the barn. John Meader (son of noted New Hampshire plant breeder Elwyn Meader) got things rolling by evaluating and then propagating this northern heirloom for Fedco Trees. All of us should keep our eyes open for local heirlooms waiting to be rediscovered.

9. Commercial growers out in Oregon and Washington allow the first-year canes in the rows to flop outboard and grow along the ground out of the way of harvesting equipment. (This requires wide spacing between the rows!) Many don't bother tying up the new canes at all until early spring to gain a down-low hardiness edge.

10. If you soft-tip canes by taking off only an inch or so, the tip of the cane is less mature and often produces fewer branches. Proper tipping of primocanes to encourage branches will increase yield about threefold.

11. A number of university research stations have been involved in breeding improved highbush blueberries since Dr. Coville's original work. The current cultivated gene pool originated primarily from New Jersey northward, with a small but significant contribution from North Carolina, primarily for resistance to blueberry stem blight.

12. Peat moss is an accumulation of partially decayed vegetative matter that forms in wetland bogs and swamp forests over the centuries. Approximately 60 percent of the world's wetlands are peat, of which 7 percent have already been mined for this valuable soil amendment and fuel. Legitimate concerns exist around the sustainable use of peat. Still, when it comes to a blueberry soil conditioner, peat moss's ability to increase the soil's capacity to hold water and nutrients is truly invaluable.

13. Elemental sulfur often comes in the form of a yellow powder when used for soil acidification. When it is incorporated into soil, sulfur-oxidizing microorganisms slowly utilize the elemental sulfur and convert it to sulfate, and in the process they generate acid-forming hydrogen ions. These principally displace calcium in the soil matrix, and that's what decreases the soil pH. Be thoughtful here—growers in northern zones with an acid-tending soil don't necessarily need to add sulfur.

14. Soils have a buffering capacity that resists substantial changes in pH. Any attempt at significant change will be temporary at best and will need to be repeated frequently to maintain the desired pH. Growers focused solely on this one parameter in blueberry culture need only step back and think about those continuous applications of sulfur over the years.

15. Prepping ground months ahead of planting—and covering with mulch materials well along in the decomposition process—introduces biology back to the disturbed ground and gives all a chance to settle. Lead time isn't critical, because plant and microbes will find symbiosis regardless given consistent irrigation . . . but it sure doesn't hurt!

16. Symptoms of iron deficiency are common in blueberries. When tissue between leaf veins turns a light yellow to bronze-gold, then chlorosis is at hand. Symptoms differ from those associated with magnesium deficiency in that

the main veins and many minor veins remain green in iron-deficient leaves. Symptoms normally appear first on the youngest leaves toward shoot tips. Shoot growth and leaf size are reduced as well.

17. We need to understand the converse here: An established mulch interface of decomposing organic matter is where the biology hits the road, so to speak. Fresh mulch added up top is no longer the same player with respect to demanding nitrogen. Any new mulch will be a couple of years old before it gets down to where feeder root action can be found. Even fresh sawdust put atop a thick mulch layer will not tie up nitrogen. Incorporating fresh woodsy material into the top inches of soil is an entirely different matter, however.

18. Cotton is genetically engineered to be resistant to glyphosate products (Roundup herbicide) that are regularly used in conventional cotton fields. This is a cruel chemistry that carries over in plant residues to the next location. You want cottonseed meal? Then it had better be from an organic cotton field.

19. Some sources will tell you that nitrogen for a blueberry planting should be applied in spring—that this is when the plant takes up nitrogen in the ammonium form. Such statements are made in reference to fast-release chemical fertilization. Nitrogen uptake by blueberries in fall is about storing bud reserves for spring. Organic forms of nitrogen like soybean meal and cottonseed meal are slow-release and thus still on tap when spring roots have need once again.

20. Blueberries cannot tolerate a permanent water table higher than 14 inches below plants. Make a raised bed up to 18 inches high and 3 feet wide to create proper drainage if there is a high water table. Blueberries are not bog plants per se and will develop root rot in saturated soil.

21. Cooler soil temperatures are especially relevant in middle and southern zones. Jim Ballington of North Carolina State has stated repeatedly that excessively high soil temperatures are as damaging to blueberries as high-pH soils.

22. Carl Whitcomb's research indicated that pin oaks suffering from iron chlorosis in a base soil quickly recover after a surface application of sulfur, even though only a tiny portion of the soil has been changed. Thanks to Alan Haigh, an incredibly astute NAFEX forum contributor from the Hudson Valley of New York, for putting two and two together. Recognizing the full virtue of the soil–mulch interface changes *everything* with regard to blueberry culture. Here is where biology and nutritional tenets find common ground.

23. Granular sulfur is best applied under a layer of mulch where moisture will contact it. Do not dig into soil, as this can damage fine, hard-to-see feeder roots near the surface. A renewal rate can be as little as ¼ cup per bush throughout its allotted diameter.

24. Greensand (glauconite) has no measurable effect on soil pH. This iron potassium silicate is often used to provide a slow-release source of potassium and offset iron deficiencies. The high cation exchange capacity of greensand helps loosen and lighten clay soils as well.

25. Sul-Po-Mag (langbeinite) would be one soil amendment to consider to increase magnesium levels. The sulfur component in this naturally mined ore should help precipitate calcium out at the same time. Epsom salts, being magnesium sulfate, is another valid soil amendment here. Choice of mulch enters in here as well. Ramial wood chips from conifers contain less calcium than hardwoods. Ditto for pine needles, shredded pine bark, and sawdust from a softwood mill.

26. Ed Fackler, fruit guru to many in the middle of the country, advises Gardens Alive! and its subsidiary companies on orchard cultivars and product selection. While touring the Clarksville station in Arkansas, Ed and his wife tasted this unreleased cultivar that breeder John Clark had reserved for hybridizing purpose. The taste of Ka-Bluey was recognized as superb, but its berries were thought to be too dark. As Ed relates, "I have been convinced for a long time that some of the best fruit varieties around were the non-commercial 'rejects' from university breeding programs: Someone early in blueberry breeding surveyed consumers about what blueberries they found most appealing, and pale was much preferred to dark. This has determined the course of blueberry breeding ever since."

27. Flowers and berries are best stripped the first two years after planting to avoid stunting young blueberry bushes. Gauge this by the size of the plant you purchased, of course, as a potted bush may well be a few years old already.

28. Albrecht Koppenhöfer, at Rutgers University, found a species of nematode now named *Steinernema scarabaei* that is exceptionally virulent to all non-native species of white grubs. This nematode species can provide exceptional control of Oriental beetle in blueberries but is not yet available commercially.

29. Now here's an insidious fungal touch: The grayish tan layer of conidia at the end of mummy-blighted shoots is attractive to bees because it reflects ultraviolet light and gives off a sugary scent. The bees in turn carry residual conidia to the blueberry blossoms.

30. Sporan and Phyta-Guard EC are two essential oil formulations registered for suppressing various fungal diseases. The concentrated essential oils of clove and rosemary disrupt the cell membrane of fungal hyphae and spores. A spreader-sticker (like yucca extract) is required to enhance coverage and performance.

31. Balsam fir is the native host for this particular witches' broom fungus, but any fir tree (including Fraser fir, common in Christmas tree plantings) can do the same. Pines, hemlocks, spruces, and other evergreens are not involved with this blueberry challenge.

32. During spring migration in February and March and on into April, hummingbirds need early-flowering plants for their survival as they make their way northward. Among some of the first plants to bloom are wild plum, serviceberry, red-flowering currants, and, you guessed it, gooseberry. Hummingbirds also find small insects on pussy willows for additional protein intake. Bloom succession very much ties into the holistic worldview. Help the hummers—plant some gooseberries.

33. In 2003, following studies done at Cornell to reassess the actual risk to white pines, New York made it legal to grow red currants, gooseberries, and resistant cultivars of black currants in the state. Consult your state's department of agriculture for up-to-date regulations. Nursery catalogs make this rather clear when you see a line like this in the varietal description: "Cannot ship to DE, ME, NC, NH, NJ, WV, MT, RI & MA." Often this refers solely to black currants . . . which is just a darned shame knowing what we do about inherent resistance coupled with holistic health.

34. Humidity turns the tide back toward early leaf loss in the Southeast. Crandall was selected based on many promising traits in Kansas. Bringing a native plant beyond its comfort zone introduces new disease variables and climatic challenges. Growers reporting different results are rarely wrong.

35. A guy could go on for quite a spell about the art of training red currants to a cordon system. That said, an excellent web article titled "Improved Fresh Fruit Quality of Gooseberries and Red Currants with the Cordon Training System" by Steven McKay of Cornell Cooperative Extension will help get you started. See www.fruit.cornell.edu/berry/production/pdfs/Improvedribesfruitquality.pdf for an excellent overview of this technique, complete with all sorts of inspiring photos.

36. Some sources list all *Sambucus racemosa* species as poisonous unless carefully seeded and cooked, while others say red elderberry is far too bitter to eat regardless.

37. *Wildcrafting* essentially means the harvesting of healing plants from the wild. A significant crop for our medicinal herb farm is blossom clusters of elder, which I indeed do harvest in wild settings. My favorite haunt is a winding brook a few feet in depth where the white blooms cascade down over the water. In I go, happily cooled by the stream on a hot summer day. The fragrant blooms that quickly fill the big gathering baskets will dry to a much smaller volume in our solar drying tunnel. I'm keenly aware of elder's bank preferences as often I need to wade from a less steep entry point a goodly distance upstream.

38. Removing elder flowers that second season (and thus delaying berry production) will help develop a stronger root system in the long run.

39. Our daughter Gracie, when younger and so much more apt to believe, would sleep out on Midsummer's Night in the midst of the elder guild, this being the night the fairy realms are said to open and the Queen of the Fairies herself appear among the sacred elder. Such myths become dreams . . . and we know our little girl slept well with the nearby mints for a soothing pillow.

40. Ripe elderberries will knock off when the cluster is thumped a few times against the side of a bucket, leaving any unripe berries still attached to the umbel. What's surprising is how very few of the fine stems break off with the ripe berries. Picking out bugs that were hiding in the umbel is another matter entirely. Alternatively, berry clusters can be run over a garbling screen made of metal hardware cloth and then rinsed in a bucket of cold water, whereby the majority of unripe berries and stems floats to the surface. Sitting around the picnic table with friends and doing all this by hand is slower and far more meticulous . . . but it sure makes for healthy conversation!

41. Research from Israel has demonstrated that elderberry juice not only stimulates the immune system but also directly inhibits the influenza virus. The trials used the juice of the berries, made into a syrup. Israeli researcher Madeleine Mumcuoglu, PhD, of the Hadassah-Hebrew University Medical Center in Ein Karem, Israel, performed the initial research and discovered that elderberry constituents disarm the neuraminidase enzyme within twenty-four to forty-eight hours, halting the spread of the virus. In clinical trials, patients who took the elderberry juice syrup reported fast termination of symptoms. Twenty percent reported significant improvement within twenty-four hours, 70 percent by forty-eight hours, and 90 percent claimed a complete cure after three days. Patients receiving the placebo required six days for recovery. As proof that elder has more to it than the enzyme-neutralizing constituents, researchers found that the patients who

took it also had higher levels of antibodies against the flu virus. Please know that many more such studies can be found!

42. The constituents in the berry act to neutralize the activity of hemagglutinin (a protein) found on the surface of several viruses by disarming the neuraminidase (amino acid chain) enzyme. The first letters of those two big words might be familiar to those of you aware of flu lingo. Different strains of influenza virus are identified by the letter H and the letter N, respectively—the bird flu scare this past decade springing specifically from the H5N1 virus, for instance.

GLOSSARY

abscise. The natural separation of plant parts, as in leaves falling or fruit fully ripening.

aerated compost tea. A liquid extract of compost containing a wide diversity of microorganisms as well as food resources. Aeration and temperature are critical in achieving a more fungal brew for foliar use in the orchard.

allopathic spray options. Any spray has impact on the orchard ecosystem. Spray materials that work by toxic means to address insect and disease symptoms are considered allopathic, whether they're chemical or organically approved.

apical dominance. The ability of the growing tip of a shoot to produce auxin hormone, which prevents nearby lateral buds (found at the base of single leaves) from developing into shoots. The degree of dominance of the apical bud determines a tree's branch habit and its response to pruning.

arboreal food web. The fascinating interaction and mutual dependency among fungi, bacteria, nematodes, protozoans, arthropods, and more on the surface of plants. Holistic disease management is based on supporting competitive colonization of plant surfaces and the stimulation provided by microorganisms to tree resistance mechanisms to disease. *We have too long overlooked the arboreal food web!*

ascospore. Primary infection spores of the apple scab fungus, sexually produced in the fall on previously infected leaves and fruit, and released into the air from mature spore sacs by the tens of thousands by a spring rain.

assimilation. The taking up of nutrients directly from a mineral source or via the immobilization pathway of microorganisms. The net result of depositing inorganic ions in the soil food web and in plant matter prevents otherwise soluble nutrients from leaching away.

auxin. A growth-regulating hormone produced in shoot tips that both stimulates cambial cell division and inhibits lateral bud development.

bark inlay graft. The grafting splice most often used for successfully topworking an existing variety. Parent limbs are headed across to reveal the green cambium that rings the inner circumference of the cut. Scionwood is inserted into slits made in the bark of the parent limb, cut lengthwise on the diagonal with the edges chamfered back to maximize cambium contact. Wrapping must be used to hold multiple scion insertions snugly in place and prevent drying out of exposed surfaces.

bark slipping. The bond between cambium layers becomes juicy with sap flow when new cells are actively growing come spring. This allows the bark to be pulled away from the inner wood without ripping or tearing when bark grafting.

base saturation. The extent to which the carrying capacity of a soil is saturated with exchangeable cations like calcium, magnesium, and potassium. The ratios between base saturation percentages are one of the principal things to contemplate on soil tests.

bench cut. Inflexible shoots with narrow crotch angles can be corrected by pruning back to one bud on the underside of that shoot. That bud in turn will develop into a lateral shoot that can be trained to a more desirable crotch angle.

bench graft. A propagation technique of late winter in which scionwood is grafted to sized rootstock (being out of the ground, and thus on the "bench").

beneficial accumulators. Flowering plant species that provide adult habitat for beneficial insects and thus build populations of good bugs in the orchard ecosystem.

biochar. Unburnt charcoal from biomass is virtually pure carbon and chemically very stable. Highly fertile soils in the Amazon basin (called *terra preta*) are dark and rich in stored carbon. Long ago farmers built up these soils with charcoal. Such biochar helps prevent the leaching of nutrients out of the soil, increases available nutrients for plant growth, regulates soil moisture levels, and dramatically reduces the need for fertilizer.

biodiversity. Variation of life-forms within a given ecosystem.

biodynamics. A regenerative agriculture focused on soil health, the integration of plants and animals, and biodiversity. Individual farms are designed to be minimally dependent on external inputs by emphasizing the living dynamics of the farm itself. Biodynamics originated out of the work of Rudolf Steiner, the founder of anthroposophy.

biodynamic tree paste. A slurry of half native clay, half cow manure applied to the trunk and main branch structure of the fruit tree to maintain bark health and mitigate canker infections.

biological mowing. Even cutting the grass has influence on orchard dynamics. Timing this first shearing of the green around tree root cycles abets nutritional uptake for the tree just as fruit begins sizing.

biological reinforcement. A number of factors work against full colonization of competitive organisms on all surfaces of the fruit tree. Applying effective microbes and/or compost tea adds to species diversity and numbers, thereby making it more difficult for pathogens to sustain disease presence.

bitter pit. Calcium deficiency can lead to the formation of dark dry spots on the skin of the fruit, along with brown pitting beneath the peel, going into harvesttime and even once the fruit has been stored for later use.

blind wood. A portion of stem bare of either lateral shoots or flowers.

botanical trunk spray. An application of pure neem oil saturating bark tissues at the site where borers seek to lay eggs deters this act. Any successful grub incursions are subject to insect growth regulation (and thus their probable demise) by the azadirachtin compounds in neem. Drench the soil right at the base of the trunk at the time of spraying as well. This may be the easiest and surest approach to knocking back incessant borer numbers that organic growers have ever utilized.

branch collar. The attachment structure at the base of a branch where it joins the trunk or parent limb. This must be left intact to produce protective tissue to properly close a pruning wound.

Brix. The total measurement of soluble solids in plant tissue (which includes a combination of sugars, amino acids, and proteins) as viewed with a refractometer. Fruit grown with the intention of maintaining a higher Brix will be more nutrient-dense and of better quality. Plants with a Brix reading of 12 or more are said to be less likely to attract insect pests, have increased disease resistance, and better withstand climatic stress. Foliar nutrients are often used to successfully increase Brix levels. The term itself comes from Adolf Brix, a German mathematician who developed this particular scale for specific gravity of liquids.

budding. A propagation technique of midsummer utilizing a single vegetative bud of the desired variety inserted into a matching site on the bark of the rootstock.

bud sport. A new varietal strain arising when a mutation occurs in the initiation of a bud. The resulting shoot eventually fruits and exhibits altered traits that are deemed desirable by growers. Such sport mutations over the years took the fuzz off the peach to create the first nectarines and (*forgive us for we have sinned*) an ever-redder Red Delicious.

burr knots. Clusters of initiated roots that develop on

the exposed portion of the trunk beneath the graft union.

calcium. An essential secondary nutrient for all plants. Calcium levels on orchard soil tests may be adequate but can be poorly distributed within the tree, resulting in fruit with low calcium, showing up as bitter pit in apples and cork spot in pears.

callus. Healing growth that develops over the graft union and binds the scion tissue in place.

calyx. The dried-up sepals (base leaves) of a flower that by implication become the blossom end of the fruit itself. When the flower is in bud, the sepals enclose and protect the more delicate floral parts within.

cambium. The thin green layer of actively dividing cells found just under the bark. Vascular cambium cells grow radially in both directions: Outer cells (phloem) become bark, and inner cells (xylem) become wood.

canker. A localized diseased area on the fruit tree (found on the trunk, branch, or twig) caused by pathogenic fungi or bacteria.

catalyst spray. An application of pulsing agents that stimulates both soil and arboreal biology into full gear.

catfacing. Feeding damage caused by stink bugs to peaches and nectarines destroys part of the developing fruit. The damaged portion of the fruit stops growing, resulting in healthy tissue riding up and over the underlying scar to produce a fruit injury typically resembling the cheeks of a cat. *You will need to be imaginative about this!*

cation exchange capacity. The sum total of exchangeable cations (calcium, magnesium, potassium, sodium) that a soil can adsorb. Clay soils and soils high in organic matter have higher cation exchange capacities than sandy soil.

central leader. A style of pruning that develops one strong trunk in the center of the tree from which branches radiate at strong, wide angles that can safely bear heavy loads of fruit.

certified organic. Commercial growers that meet the national standards for organic production and *pay for the right to use the o-word* can be certified as such by the USDA through regional inspection agencies. The defining emphasis here is on using natural inputs as opposed to synthesized chemicals. Biological health is not necessarily honored in the approved protocols.

chelation. Organic acids form chelates (pronounced *KEY-lates*) with certain absorbed minerals to prevent the precipitation (and thus locking up) of that nutrient with other nutrients within plant cells. This natural process enables such nutrients to move freely from cambium to leaf to fruit. Similarly, organic substances in the soil secreted by roots and certain microorganisms will form chelates in making nutrients bioavailable for plant uptake. Natural organic chelation agents include amino acids, citric acid, fulvic acid, and some types of sugars.

chill factor. Deciduous tree fruits require chilling to break their winter rest. Buds do not come out of dormancy until a certain number of hours between 32°F and 45°F (0°C and 7°C) have accumulated in the dormant season.

chlorosis. A condition in which leaves produce insufficient chlorophyll. Because chlorophyll is responsible for the green color of leaves, chlorotic leaves on fruiting plants are pale and often yellowing. An affected plant has little or no ability to manufacture carbohydrates through photosynthesis and may die unless the nutritional cause behind such leaf symptoms can be addressed.

cider. The fermented juice of the apple. (Precisely as the word *wine* refers to the fermented juice of the grape.) The tendency to refer to this fine beverage as "hard cider" in American culture is matched only by our saying "sweet cider" when referring to freshly squeezed apple juice. Both terms are acceptable on this continent . . . but now the record has been set straight!

cocoon. A covering composed of silk spun by moth larvae to protect the pupal stage.

cold preconditioning. Winter hardiness is a function of buds going dormant first, followed by cambium in the limbs and down through the trunk zone doing the same. This gradual hardening requires cooler days and nights in fall to facilitate the ability of cells to deal with the deeper cold to come.

community orchard. Producing fruit for local markets is vital work regardless of scale. Holistic orchardists who produce more bushels than the family can use are essential to community sustainability. *We need to grow healthy food in all the places that we live!*

compatibility. The performance of scion and rootstock depends on a graft union that makes a strong physical connection and displays a physiological harmony of the two genetic systems. A number of incompatibilities in trees are induced by viruses. However, graft unions where the scion outgrows the rootstock (or vice versa) can be perfectly compatible.

conidia. Asexually produced infection spores of fungal disease organisms, released into the air from existing lesions as well as splashed by rain onto neighboring plant surfaces.

conventional. Using this term to refer to modern orchard practice comes with a caveat. Chemical proponents assume that spray choices of the last hundred years represent the norm; that not to use chemicals to grow fruit is somehow unconventional. The right words here are *nonbiological* and *biological* when we take Nature's perspective.

cordon. Espalier training where the plant extends in rope-like fashion as a vine, be it vertically, horizontally, or obliquely (at an angle).

cover crops. Broad-area crops planted specifically to contribute organic matter, shift soil life dynamics, smother weeds, and reduce erosion.

cover sprays. Traditionally, orchard spray applications were made automatically every ten days following petal fall to "cover" the entire planting. There were no exceptions for integrated understanding. Speaking of *first cover* or *second cover* and so forth still provides a general sense of timing when discussing holistic spray options through the summer months.

crop load. The amount of fruit being carried by the tree to harvest. Savvy growers who thin away excess fruitlets in a timely manner will grow bigger fruit as well as ensuring stronger bearing for the following season.

cultivar. A fruit variety that has been selected intentionally, given a name, and maintained (beyond the original seedling tree) through grafting.

cuticle. The covering of waxes and other exudates (carbon, nitrogen, extracellular polysaccharides, and so on) that serve as a protective zone between fruit and leaf surfaces and the environment.

cytokinins. Growth-regulating hormones responsible for regulating apical dominance and branching, controlling bud initiation, preventing abscission of fruit and leaves, and inhibiting root initiation.

deep organics. A regenerative agriculture that goes beyond substituting natural materials for synthetic chemicals and recognizes that ecosystem dynamics are best supported by prioritizing soil health.

degree-days. Tracking the accumulated warmth of the sun above a specified threshold temperature allows orchardists to accurately predict many orchard events like the rapidity of bud growth, scab ascospore maturity, and codling moth egg hatch.

diameter-based pruning. An exceedingly valuable pruning rule that dictates the removal of upper branches to make way for new growth: Any upper lateral branch that gets to be half the size of the trunk where it joins should be removed.

dormancy issues. Bud hardiness fluctuates with winter weather patterns. Warmer days cause buds to de-harden, thereby setting up flower cells to be zapped by deep cold following a thaw. Stone fruits like peaches, nectarines, and apricots are especially vulnerable.

dormant pruning. All large branch cuts and most thinning are done when the buds are at rest for the winter, generally after risk of a deep freeze is past in order to avoid winter injury.

dripline. The outer diameter of the canopy of a fruit tree, extrapolated to ground level.

drupelet. Raspberries and blackberries are aggregate fruits. Each berry is composed of fleshy seed capsules called drupelets, held together by almost invisible hairs. Each drupelet usually has a single seed, though a few have two.

dwarf tree. Size-reducing rootstock limits the vigor of a given variety. The smallest of these that require support (in the form of a stake or trellis) are said to be fully dwarfing.

dynamic accumulator. Taprooted plant species that bring minerals up from the subsoil into its leaves, which upon leaf decomposition are made bioavailable to fruiting plants in the orchard ecosystem.

effective microbes. A special culture of beneficial microorganisms (photosynthetic bacteria, lactic acid bacteria, and yeasts) that are used as a probiotic inoculant to promote ecosystem health in both the soil food web and the arboreal food web.

espalier. A fruit plant trained to an orderly two-dimensional form.

exchangeable nutrient. A nutrient held on soil particle surfaces but able to move into soil solution and be absorbed by the growing plant.

fatty acid knockdown. Applications of fatty acid constituents (found in pure neem oil and liquid fish) at higher concentrations can be used to shift microbe populations. This works against fungal and bacterial pathogens overwintering in bark and bud crevices, especially when followed with biological reinforcement a day later to successfully colonize the plant surfaces under contention.

feathered tree. Nursery stock that has developed three or more wide-angled laterals.

feeder root. The white absorptive roots of the tree access new nutrient zones in two distinct flushes of active growth. Nutrients for this season's fruit (as well as the initiation of next year's fruit buds) are taken up in a first growth flush around the time of fruit set. Nutrients to fuel next spring's bud growth are taken up in a second growth flush from harvest-time on into early winter.

fermented herbal tea. Certain plant constituents help other plants in turn. Nettle, horsetail, and comfrey are valuable orchard herbs in this respect. Herbal brews are deliberately fermented to make those constituents bioavailable for foliar absorption.

fire blight. A serious bacterial infection of apples and pears that can cause outright death of afflicted trees.

flagging. Plant shoot damage caused by insect feeding or bacterial disease, in which the terminal end of the shoot wilts, darkens, and often hangs. Growers can readily spot this sign of something gone awry.

floral initiation. Flower cells begin to form (in almost all fruits) the growing season before blossoms unveil their allure the following spring. This establishment of fruiting potential a year ahead plays a big part in specific pruning recommendations for each fruit.

floricane. Second-year cane of bramble fruits. Flower initiation the autumn before establishes berry prospects here. Floricanes are spent (die off) after fruiting.

foliar spray. Application of nutrients to the leaf surface to stimulate healthy growth. Slow drying conditions optimize stomata uptake into the plant's vascular system.

forest-edge ecology. Fruit trees and berries claim a niche based on fungal dominance of the soil ecosystem and access to sunlight. Organic matter in the form of falling leaves, broken branches, and woodsy stems in the understory renews the healthy underpinnings of such a forest-edge locale. Observing how Nature works in turn determines the ecosystem guidelines we would be wise to emulate in our own orchards.

frass. Larva poop, be it caterpillar or beetle. *Let this be a sign unto you of trouble!*

freestanding tree. Semi-dwarf, semi-standard, and standard (seedling) trees require far less fuss in maintaining fungal duff, procure balanced nutrition and moisture through a vaster root system, and thus are more likely to succeed with holistic approaches to disease. Supporting such trees with a stake is unnecessary . . . though admittedly support might be useful for leaning varieties in the training years.

fruit finish. The appearance of the fruit, particularly as regards coloration, lack of russeting caused by fungicides or oils, and absence of spotting attributed to disease or nutrient deficiency.

fruiting spurs. Short shoots on wood two years or older that bear fruit.

fungal duff management. A fungal-dominated soil ecosystem supports orchard health. Growers in turn are advised to manage the zone beneath fruit trees and berry plantings accordingly. Compost, ramial wood chips, raked leaves, rotting hay, and taprooted plant allies set the scene. Subtleties that keep pest and disease pressure in balance are engaged by managing the orchard understory more like the floor along the forest's edge.

garden compost. Compost made with a carbon-to-nitrogen ration of 25:1, turned often to generate heat, will be bacterially dominated. Annual vegetable plants in the garden benefit from compost made this way.

glomalin. A carbon-rich glycoprotein secreted by mycorrhizal fungi that binds soil aggregates to create favorable soil structure for plants.

gummosis. A nonspecific condition of stone fruits in which gum is exuded and deposited on the bark of trees. Gum is produced in response to any type of wound, regardless of whether it is due to insects, mechanical injury, or disease. Hardening of this gum can indicate that the wound area has sealed off, whereas consistent oozing indicates an ongoing problem.

gypsum. A soil amendment consisting of calcium sulfate, mined from the earth, that is far more water-soluble than lime and thus does not change soil pH. Calcium levels can be increased using gypsum while at the same time excess magnesium and/or potassium will be leached out.

haphazard mulching. Life thrives in a diverse environment. Try to let go of Western notions of the manicured garden, at least with your fruit trees. Use an assortment of woodsy mulch materials piled at different times to create nutrient diversity for the soil biology and thus the feeder roots. Being neat is not necessarily the goal from the tree perspective.

heading cut. The shearing of a shoot or branch along its length and thus out from the point of attachment with another branch. This type of cut induces hormonal responses that are best reserved for specific horticultural purpose.

heading height. The height at which lower scaffold branches are encouraged to develop on a nursery whip. A scaffold branch started 30 inches from the ground stays put on the trunk at that height. As the branch enlarges in diameter, it will actually appear to get slightly closer to the soil line.

holistic spray options. Any spray has impact on the orchard ecosystem. Spray materials that support arboreal health and tree immune function to achieve reasonable balance with pests and disease work on the deepest levels of biological diversity.

Hugelkultur. Creating planting mounds consisting principally of decomposing wood and other compostable roughage. This permaculture technique makes for raised beds loaded with organic material, nutrients, and air pockets for roots. The deep soil of the bed becomes incredibly rich and loaded with soil life as the years pass.

humates. Soil amendments rich in humic and fulvic acid chains that help boost the ability of the soil food web to assimilate micronutrients. Humic substances actually coat mineral surfaces with a membrane-like layer, which aids in the release of otherwise insoluble compounds by dissolving, complexing, and chelating the dissolved nutrients. Marketable products from concentrated organic matter (of long ago) can be found in leonardite, brown coal, various forms of lignite, humic shale, and carbonaceous shale.

humification. Long-term stabilization of organic matter into humus by the soil food web. The process of changing from recognizable bits and pieces of plants (or animals) to an amorphous, rotted dark mass creates long-term fertility.

humus. A fairly stable, complex group of nutrient-storing molecules created by soil life through the conversion of organic matter. Humic substances make up about 80 percent of the soil organic matter in dark soils. Humus contains the most chemically active compounds found in soils, with cation and anion exchange capacities far exceeding those of clays.

hyphae. The thread-like filaments sent out by fungi to access food resources.

immobilization. The assimilation of inorganic ions through the metabolic activity of microorganisms. The consumed nutrients in turn will be made bioavailable to plants as the next round of microbes consumes the first round of microbes.

inoculum. The living part of the pathogen, usually the spores, that initiates disease and causes its spread.

integrated pest management (IPM). Chemical orcharding done with a desire to limit spray applications to only those times when pest thresholds indicate the need. Modern understanding has come a long way from the time when "conventional growers" sprayed automatically on a calendar basis regardless of what was going on in the orchard.

interstem. Scionwood grafted between a vigorous rootstock and the fruiting cultivar to induce dwarfing or address compatibility issues.

June drop. Shedding excess fruitlets a month or so after fruit set is a natural tree response. Production of seeds within the fruit requires nutrients and hormones and good photosynthesis (sunshine) during this first month. Abscising overabundance is the tree's attempt at balance.

kairomones. *Good job. You've found the bonus word for the quiz.* These chemical cues are used by the insect world to indicate food sources, aggregate for overwintering advantage, recognize predators, and even mark a blossom cluster as claimed so the next female goes elsewhere. Pheromones drive sexual activity, while kairomones represent a whole new frontier for clever humans to shift insect perception.

king blossom. The first flower to open in the pome blossom cluster will yield the largest fruit come harvest.

latent bud. A bud, usually concealed, more than a year old, that lies dormant in the bark tissue, until such time as severe pruning or bark injury causes that bud to grow.

lateral growth. A shoot directed sideways forms the branch structure where the majority of fruiting will occur.

leaching. The removal of materials in solution from the soil. Leaching occurs as excess water drains through the soil profile.

Lepidoptera. The family grouping for those species of moths with unwavering affinity for the fruits of orchard trees.

lime. A soil amendment consisting principally of calcium carbonate (along with varying degrees of magnesium carbonate) used to furnish calcium and magnesium and thus neutralize soil acidity.

liquid fish. Liquid fish fertilizer is made from the first pressing of genuine fish parts and has not been pasteurized—and thus contains the fatty acids and enzymes so important to beneficial microbes. This nutrient-rich formulation of biological fish will sometimes be called *hydrolysate*.

macronutrients. The essential nutrients that plants need in larger amounts are nitrogen (N), phosphorus (P), potassium (K), calcium (Ca), magnesium (Mg), and sulfur (S). Plants also need carbon (C), hydrogen (H), and oxygen (O), derived from air and water. All nine are collectively referred to as *macronutrients*.

meristem. Plant tissue whose cells actively divide to form new tissues that cause the plant to grow. The originally undifferentiated cells of the meristem can produce specialized cells to form the tissues of roots, leaves, and fruit buds.

micronutrients. The essential nutrients that plants need in very small or trace amounts are boron (B), copper (Cu), iron (Fe), manganese (Mn), molybdenum (Mo), zinc (Zn), and chlorine (Cl).

mineralization. Breakdown of organic matter by microorganisms into soluble nutrients that are readily bioavailable for uptake by plants.

modified central leader. A style of pruning that allows the central leader to eventually branch off to form several tops; it's often easier to maintain than other forms of pruning, as trees naturally grow this way.

molting cycle. The growth stages by which insects progress from a larval stage through the shedding of skin to eventually become adults.

mummies. Immature fruit subject to fungal infection (primarily rots) dry up and tend to hang on the tree into the following season. Such sources of disease inoculum should be plucked from the tree and destroyed. Decomposition of mummified drops can be enhanced by chickens scratching under severely afflicted trees.

mycorrhizal accumulator. Woodsy plant species that support an undisturbed soil ecosystem abundant with mycorrhizal fungi. Herbs such as rosemary, thyme, and lavender favor many of the same species as fruit trees and berries.

mycorrhizal fungi. Soil-dwelling fungi that live in and around the roots of plants. The fungi and the plants form mutually beneficial associations in which the fungi receive carbohydrates from the plants and the plants receive nutrients and other benefits from the fungi.

node. Positions along the shoot where bud formation occurs.

non-aerated compost tea. Matured compost soaked for a day or two in a bucket, stirred on occasion, then strained, yields a helpful range of organisms to enhance leaf decomposition on the orchard floor in the fall.

npk fertilization. Nutrient balance certainly requires nitrogen (N), phosphorus (P), and potassium (K)—these being the three numbers provided on a bag of fertilizer to indicate its fertility value—yet we shouldn't stress this part of the picture over the rest. Biological growers are correct in viewing the *fertilization trinity* as subordinate to the soil food web.

nurse limb. Leaving a branch or two on a topworked tree ensures that the root system has a photosynthesis connection up above for that first season after grafting. Shoot growth of the new variety by the following spring can then take over, allowing the nurse limb to be removed if so desired.

nutrient-dense food. What we eat reflects the health of the soil on which it was raised or grown. Crops harvested with a broad spectrum of different minerals, vitamins, phytonutrients, and anti-oxidants are the end product of a highly functional biological system.

open vase. A style of pruning that allows complete sunlight penetration in the interior of the tree. Scaffold branches are trained to form an inverted umbrella without a central leader to achieve this.

orchard compost. Compost made with a carbon-to-nitrogen ration of 40:1, never turned for a year or more, will be fungally dominated. Woodsy fruiting plants in the orchard benefit from compost made this way.

orchard health. *Yeah, we're talking radical consciousness here!*

orchard probiotics. Microorganisms that help stimulate diversity in the soil food web and the arboreal food web. This term applies equally to effective microbes and aerated compost tea.

organic matter. The carbon-based portion of the soil consisting of living vegetation (root mass), decomposing vegetation, soil humus, and soil organisms.

oviposition. The act of depositing eggs by insect females, be it inserting such eggs onto the surface of the plant, behind a cut in the bark tissue, or directly into the soil or even into another insect.

paradigm. The assumptions underlying the framework upon which we humans make what seem to be rational choices. Einstein said this: *No problem can be solved from the same level of consciousness that created it.*

parasitoids. Small wasps that lay eggs in the larvae or eggs of other insect species. Such biological control of orchard pests is enhanced by attracting the adult wasps to the orchard with a diversity of nectar sources.

pathogenic fungi. Disease-causing organisms that get a foothold in fruit trees during wet periods in spring and then again in fall.

permaculture. A set of techniques and principles for designing sustainable plant communities.

perry. The fermented juice of the pear.

petal fall. A significant timing event in the orchard calendar when blossom petals fall to the ground and fruit set initiates as a result of pollination.

pH. The negative logarithm of the effective hydrogen ion concentration in terms of gram equivalents per liter, used to express acidity or alkalinity on a scale of 1–14. A value of 7 represents neutrality; less than 7 represents acidity; more than 7 represents alkalinity.

pheromones. The chemical signals used by insects to attract mates. Orchardists use chemically synthesized scents of moths (each species has its own distinctive pheromone) to draw insects to monitoring traps and to saturate the air for mating disruption purposes.

phyllosphere. Leaf surfaces and more, being the aboveground canopy area of a fruiting plant considered specifically as habitat for microorganisms.

phytoalexins. The plant chemistry underlying a tree's immune response to disease organisms. These secondary plant metabolites consist primarily of isoflavonoid and terpenoid compounds.

pinching. Nipping off the tip of a growing shoot with a fingernail.

pink. A significant timing event in the orchard calendar when fruit buds reveal first color. Properly speaking, a number of stone fruits reveal "white" at this moment.

pistil. The female parts of the fruit tree blossom. The sticky *stigma* receives the pollen, which then moves down to the seed ovary by way of the tube-like *style*.

point of runoff. Orchardists gauge full spray coverage in order to thoroughly wet leaf and fruiting surfaces alike by spray droplets just beginning to run to the ground.

pollen tube. The growth extension of the style following germination of the pollen grain. The male seed has been planted, so to speak, and now must be transported in order to reach the ovule for fruit initiation to begin.

pollinator. An agent of pollen transfer—for example, bees and other insects.

pollinizer. The plant cultivar that produces the pollen.

precocity. Coming into flowering and fruiting in the early years after planting; a relevant trait for evaluating variety and rootstock choices.

primocane. First-year cane of bramble fruits. Fall-bearing types have fruit here that same season; summer-bearing types require a year's more development.

proper crotch angle. A branch comes off the trunk at a given angle. Too steep an angle makes for included bark and a weak union. An angle on the order of 45–60 degrees from the vertical makes for strongly bonded wood that can support future crop loading.

pseudothecia. Fruiting bodies that hold the ascospores (prior to springtime release) of the scab disease organism that overwinters on the fallen leaves and fruit on the ground from the previous season. *Sometimes it's fun to know big words like this to impress your friends!*

pulsing agents. Nutritional sprays used to activate the ecosystem in early spring and right after harvest for specific purpose tied to root happenings and the resource needs of the arboreal food web. The fatty acids in liquid fish and pure neem oil are what fuel the biological engine.

pure neem oil. Unadulterated, raw, cold-pressed oil from the seeds of the neem tree used for a multitude of orchard intentions.

push and pull. Use of a repellent strategy on most trees will drive insects to a targeted trap tree. The *push away* from the treated trees can in turn be coupled with an *enhanced pull* to the unprotected tree.

ramial wood chips. The tops of deciduous trees and woodsy shrubs subsequently run through a chipper into coarse pieces are what rock the biological kasbah. The newest growth of a deciduous tree contains soluble lignins that have not yet polymerized into outright wood. These in turn are used by soil organisms to build long-lasting humus.

real cider. Unpasteurized sweet cider pressed from sound ripe apples that offer all the nutrients, enzymes, and pleasure American tradition demands.

refractometer. A light-deflecting device used to

measure plant sap from either leaves or fruit to determine levels of soluble solids. Brix readings on the high end of the scale are indicative of good plant health and nutrient density in the fruit.

rhizosphere. The zone surrounding root surfaces, being the belowground structure of a fruiting plant considered specifically as habitat for microorganisms.

ring mulching. Newly planted trees have need to grow wood for several years before coming into production. Wood chip or hay mulch (often applied over newspaper or cardboard) extending around the tree suppresses sod growth completely so that tree feeder roots can supply developing branch structure to the max.

rootstock. The rooted bottom of any grafted tree, selected principally for sizing influence, uniformity, and disease resistance.

root suckers. Shoots from the roots of the tree, which, being below the graft union, will grow into a not necessarily desirable cultivar within your tree if not cut away.

saprophytic fungi. Decomposing fungal species that work with invertebrates, bacteria, algae, and actinomycetes to consume organic matter.

scab. A fungal disease of apple and pear. Regional strains of this fungus complicate what growers experience with respect to different varieties.

scaffold. The framework layers of the bearing tree, each composed of three to five main branches, which allow better sunlight penetration and airflow than would otherwise be had in an unlayered tree.

scion. A shoot of dormant budwood, ideally first-year growth, used for grafting rootstock (or individual branches) to a desirable cultivar.

senescence. The final stage of the leaf cycle in which nutrient resources are degraded and exported, leading to abscission. The brilliant reds and yellows of the orchard landscape in fall are due to pigment changes in tree and berry leaves undergoing this aging process.

shuck split. That moment on the stone fruit calendar when the growth of the fruitlet splits the papery shuck left in place after the spent flower parts have fallen away.

soil amendments. Specific nutrients can be obtained from rock dusts, mined minerals, and animal proteins to address soil test deficiencies. Trace mineral condiments such as Azomite and kelp are often best applied through the compost pile. The goal behind supplementing soil nutrients is to provide a proper starting gate for the biology, which in turn provides a well-balanced meal for the feeder roots of our fruiting plants.

soil food web. The fascinating interactions and mutual dependency among fungi, bacteria, nematodes, protozoans, and arthropods in the soil that break down organic matter and build humus. *This microorganism web makes our life on earth possible!*

sporulating. Fungal cankers reproduce as fruiting bodies that send spores out into the ecosystem to infect anew.

spraying. Choosing to spray to sustain system health is very different from choosing to spray to kill. A sprayer is merely a tool—how we choose to use that tool is where ramifications lie. *Shift gears, please, if you're in the camp that has always regarded the "need to spray" as the ultimate reason not to grow fruit.*

stamen. The male parts of the fruit tree blossom. Pollen grains form the *anther*, which waves atop a *filament* to await the pollinator.

sticker. Certain substances can be used to hold spray materials to the leaf. Pine resin, yucca extract, and refined fish oil are organically-approved for this task.

stomata. Small openings in the epidermis of leaves, through which water vapor and gases pass. Water vapor is lost through each stomate in the process of transpiration; oxygen is taken up and absorbed in the process of respiration; and carbon dioxide is absorbed in the process of photosynthesis.

stubbing cut. A heading cut made into older wood to reduce the length of a limb and encourage replacement laterals.

summer pruning. The removal of watersprouts after terminal bud set helps light reach the interior fruit, while at same time checking vegetative regrowth. Cuts on trees-in-training are often made in early summer to lessen an overly vigorous response. Peaches and nectarines benefit from early-summer thinning of that season's shoot response to strengthen the remaining fruit buds for the following year.

suture. The longitudinal line on one side of stone fruits running from tip to base. This imprint in the skin is usually apparent as a slight depression. Sometimes the suture can be raised and one side of the fruit will appear larger than the other.

tank-mixing. Most spray materials are compatible and therefore can be applied at the same time. Mixing these in the same spray tank does not degrade any of the biological activity or nutrient contributions of the other.

terminal bud set. Late summer marks the end of growth in the growing point of the tree at the very tip of every shoot. Bud set here initiates hardening off in the rest of the tree in preparation for winter's cold.

thinning cut. The removal of an entire branch at its junction with another branch. These non-invigorating cuts are used to open up airflow and increase sunlight penetration to interior fruit buds.

third leaf. A young tree in its third growing season. Obviously, the numeral suffix can be changed to reflect the year of growth. This notion of on-site aging falls short if you account for earlier seasons in the nursery, however.

tight cluster. The blossom-cluster-to-be remains wrapped within the leaf sepals, with each bud snuggled up tight to its neighbors.

topworking. Splicing another variety to an existing tree framework can be accomplished with bark inlay grafting. The entire tree can be converted or different branches chosen to yield entirely different varieties.

triploid. An apple cultivar with fifty-one chromosomes (triple set), an odd number that affects fertility. The pollen of such varieties is virtually useless, though it will sometimes pollinate itself to a limited extent.

understory. The ecosystem found on the orchard floor consisting of the fungal duff, diverse flowering plants, and grasses.

vascular system. The circulatory system of the tree distributes water and nutrients between the roots and the leaf canopy above. The cells that produce vascular tubes are found on both sides of the cambium. The *xylem* transports water and becomes the wood (marked by annual growth rings). The *phloem* moves organic nutrients and distinguishes the innermost layer of the bark.

watercore. A physiological disorder in apple causing a buildup of sorbitol (the same sweetener used in chewing gum), resulting in a water-saturated appearance in fruit tissues. Watercore is promoted by excessive thinning, high fruit nitrogen, and low fruit calcium.

watersprout. A vertical shoot arising from the trunk or main branches of the tree, often in response to increased sunlight penetration resulting from a substantial pruning cut.

whip. Nursery stock that has yet to develop lateral growth.

whip-and-tongue union. The grafting splice used in making a bench graft. This interlocking method mechanically binds the scion to the rootstock and maximizes cambium contact.

whole plant medicine. Earth-centered herbalists work with healing remedies derived from the proper plant part (flower, leaf, root, sometimes indeed the "whole plant") rather than isolated constituents extracted with chemicals to create a patented product. The synergy of all constituents in the herb makes holistic medicine a far more effective choice.

BIBLIOGRAPHY

Albrecht, William. *Soil Fertility & Animal Health* (The Albrecht Papers, volume 2). Austin, TX: Acres USA, 1975, 2005.

Allen, Will. *The War on Bugs*. White River Junction, VT: Chelsea Green, 2008.

Altieri, Miguel, and Clara Nicholls. *Manage Insects on Your Farm*. Beltsville, MD: Sustainable Agriculture Network, 2005.

Ashton, Richard. *Plums of North America*. Tempe, AZ: Third Millennium Publishing, 2008.

Bailey, Liberty Hyde. *The Principles of Fruit Growing*. New York: MacMillan, 1897, 1926.

Baker, Harry. *Growing Fruit*. London: Mitchell Beazley, 1980, revised 1999.

Bolgiano, Chris, and Glenn Novak. *Mighty Giants: An American Chestnut Anthology*. Bennington, VT: American Chestnut Foundation, 2007.

Bowling, Barbara. *The Berry Grower's Companion*. Portland, OR: Timber Press, 2000.

Bruges, James. *The Biochar Debate*. White River Junction, VT: Chelsea Green, 2010.

Bunker, John. *Not Far from the Tree*. Palermo, ME: Fedco Trees, 2007.

Caldwell, Brian, et al. *Resource Guide for Organic Insect and Disease Management*. Geneva, NY: Cornell University, 2005.

Calhoun, Creighton Lee Jr. *Old Southern Apples*, 2nd edition. White River Junction, VT: Chelsea Green, 2011.

Chaboussou, Francis. *Healthy Crops*. Charlbury, England: Jon Carpenter Publishing, 2004.

Chapman, P. J., and S. E. Lienk. *Tortricid Fauna of Apple in New York*. Geneva, NY: Cornell University, 1971.

Coleman, David, et al. *Fundamentals of Soil Ecology*. Burlington, MA: Elsevier, 2004.

Conrad, Ross. *Natural Beekeeping*. White River Junction, VT: Chelsea Green, 2007.

Cranshaw, Whitney. *Garden Insects of North America*. Princeton, NJ: Princeton University Press, 2004.

Flint, Mary Louise, and Steve Dreistadt. *Natural Enemies Handbook*. Berkeley: University of California Press, 1998.

Grissell, Eric. *Insects and Gardens*. Portland, OR: Timber Press, 2001.

Hanson, Beth, et al. *The Best Apples to Buy and Grow*. Brooklyn, NY: Brooklyn Botanic Garden, 2005.

Hemingway, Toby. *Gaia's Garden: A Guide to Home-Scale Permaculture*. White River Junction, VT: Chelsea Green, 2001, revised 2009.

Hill, Lewis. *Fruits and Berries for the Home Garden*. Pownal, VT: Storey, 1977, revised 1992.

———. *Pruning Made Easy*. Pownal, VT: Storey, 1997.

Howitt, Angus. *Common Tree Fruit Pests*. East Lansing: Michigan State University, 1993.

Ingels, Chuck, et al. *The Home Orchard*. Berkeley: University of California Press, 2007.

Ingham, Elaine. *The Compost Tea Brewing Manual*, 4th ed. Corvallis, OR: Soil Foodweb Incorporated, 2000.

Jacke, Dave, and Eric Toensmeier. *Edible Forest Gardens*. White River Junction, VT: Chelsea Green, 2005.

Janick, Jules, and Robert Paull. *The Encyclopedia of Fruits and Nuts*. Wallingford, UK: CABI, 2008.

Jones, A. L., and Turner B. Sutton. *Diseases of Tree Fruits in the East*. East Lansing: Michigan State University, 1996.

Kinsey, Neal, and Charles Waters. *Hands-On Agronomy*. Austin, TX: Acres USA, 1993, revised 2006.

Kourik, Robert. *Roots Demystified*. Occidental, CA: Metamorphic Press, 2008.

Landis, J. N., et al. *Fruit Crop Ecology and Management*. East Lansing: Michigan State University, 2002.

Lowenfels, Jeff, and Wayne Lewis. *Teaming with Microbes*. Portland, OR: Timber Press, 2010.

Manhart, Warren. *Apples for the 21st Century*. Portland, OR: North American Tree Company, 1995.

Masumoto, David. *Epitaph for a Peach*. San Francisco: Harper, 1995.

McClure, Susan. *Fruits and Berries*. Emmaus, PA: Rodale, 1996.

Morgan, Joan, and Allison Richards. *The New Book of Apples*. London: Ebury Press, 2002.

Page, Steve, and Joe Smillie. *The Orchard Almanac*, 3rd ed. Davis, CA: agAccess, 1995.

Phillips, Michael. *The Apple Grower*. White River Junction, VT: Chelsea Green, 1998, revised 2005.

Phillips, Nancy, and Michael Phillips. *The Herbalist's Way*. White River Junction, VT: Chelsea Green, 2001, revised 2005.

Reich, Lee. *Uncommon Fruits for Every Garden*. Portland, OR: Timber Press, 2004.

Rowe, Alan. *Success with Apples and Pears to Eat and Drink*. Norfolk, England: Groundnut, 2002.

Stamets, Paul. *Mycelium Running*. Berkeley, CA: Ten Speed Press, 2005.

Torgrimson, John, and Joanne Thuente, eds. *Fruit, Berry and Nut Inventory*, 4th ed. Decorah, IA: Seed Savers Exchange, 2009.

Watson, Ben. *Cider, Hard and Sweet*. Woodstock, VT: The Countryman Press, 1999, revised 2008.

Westwood, Melvin. *Temperate-Zone Pomology*. Portland, OR: Timber Press, 1978, revised 1988.

Index

Michael Phillips is a farmer, writer, carpenter, orchard consultant, and speaker who lives with his wife, Nancy, and daughter, Grace, on Heartsong Farm in northern new Hampshire, where they grow apples and a variety of medicinal herbs. Michael authored *The Apple Grower* (Chelsea Green, 2005) and teamed up with Nancy to write *The Herbalist's Way* (Chelsea Green, 2005). His Lost Nation Orchard is part of a diversified mountain farm in northern New Hampshire, and he also leads the community orchard movement at www.GrowOrganicApples.com.

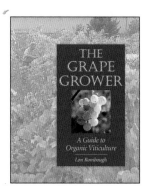